Patterns in Prehistory

Pattern

HUMANKIND'S FIRST THR

SECOND EDITION

NEW YORK OXFORD

n Prehistory

ILLION YEARS

Robert J. Wenke

XFORD UNIVERSITY PRESS   1984

Copyright © 1980, 1984 by Oxford University Press, Inc.

Library of Congress Cataloging in Publication Data

Wenke, Robert J.
Patterns in prehistory.

Includes bibliographies and index.
1. Man, Prehistoric. 2. Archaeology. I. Title.
GN740.W46   1984   573.3   83-22033
ISBN 0-19-503441-4
ISBN 0-19-503442-2 (pbk.)

This printing (last digit):   9 8 7 6 5

Printed in the United States of America

For Chris and Ann Wenke

Preface

Woody Allen once said something like "thanks to a speed-reading course I was able to read *War and Peace* in one hour. It's about Russia."

This second edition of *Patterns in Prehistory*, like the first, is an attempt to summarize three million years of cultural development in a few hundred pages, and yet present it in such a way that the reader, when finished, will know more than that it's about archaeology. I've tried to give the reader a sense of why archaeologists devote their lives to the study of the past, and what all these years of digging and sorting through the garbage of the past mean.

But one can't just write about the things archaeologists find; one must adopt a theoretical perspective on it all. To understand my perspective, I have to refer to a formative experience I had on the dry bed of the ancient lake that used to border Mexico City.

I had come to Mexico as a graduate student at the University of Michigan, and it was then that institution's wise policy to immerse its students in the literature of comparative history and the "science of culture," and then to send them out as laborers in the *gulag* of Michigan archaeological projects around the world. Thus, I came to spend some years sorting pottery in Turkey, excavating prehistoric Iranian villages near the Persian Gulf, and retrieving flint tools from the marshes of the Netherlands.

So, when I encountered the pyramids, temples, and towns of ancient Mexico, I was immediately impressed by the similarity of these relics to those of Old World civilizations. Here was a graphic demonstration of what I had read about in the works of V. G. Childe, Karl Wittfogel, Robert McC. Adams, and many others: Old and New World civilizations had apparently gone through extremely similar developmental

histories, in which hunters and gatherers gave way to village agriculturalists, who were then transmuted by time and circumstance into
denizens of great states and empires. And having dismissed the juvenilia
of cross-oceanic contacts and extraterrestrial contacts of any kind, as well
as the implausible notion that Old and New World peoples had simultaneously and coincidentally *thought* their way into these parallel histories, I could reasonably assume only that it was the material forces of
environment, technology, and demography that were responsible for
these developments. And if so, one must assume that these forces could
be identified and measured, and history, thereby, explained.

Since my Mexican adventures I've occasionally wavered on this last
point, but what has stayed with me (other than a veritable United Nations of intestinal parasites and aphasia in four languages) is the convic-
tion that the billions of bits of people, settlements, and artifacts that we
have dug up are ultimately patterned and that we can know the processes that determined these patterns.

Thus, like the first edition, this book asks the reader to consider the
evidence relevant to a simple syllogism: that there are patterns and
regularities in the millions of years of the human past, that there is hope
of understanding what these patterns are and why they exist, and that,
therefore, the study of world prehistory is of relevance to our own lives.
I throw in *gratis* the opinion that a life spent in ignorance of the ancient
world is a life hopelessly stunted.

Surveys of world prehistory do not age well. Archaeologists are accused of "physics envy" because we want but do not have general principles with which to interpret all the data of the past; without such
principles it is difficult to integrate new discoveries into our general
understanding of the past. In the five years since the first edition of this
book was written there have been many archaeological finds, and I've
tried to incorporate as much of this new material as possible. But I've
also tried to write a book that will not be made obsolete by each year's
discoveries. I could easily festoon this book with the most recent literature citations, but the most recent studies are not always the best.

I've tried to organize the data around five central topics: the origins
of culture, the development of physically "modern" people, the spread
of Pleistocene cultures, the establishment of agricultural economies,
and the rise of complex states and empires.

Compared to the first edition, I've had to reduce the coverage of some
areas substantially. I'm sorry to have slighted Europe, Southeast Asia,
Australia, and other interesting areas, but my colleagues' suggestions
that I write a book that a student could read in a year were compelling.
Moreover, the volume of archaeological literature these days is such that

no one can hope to cover even the secondary literature for the whole of the world, and the rate of discovery in archaeology is such that a comprehensive and yet still portable textbook is becoming impossible—especially if one takes time off occasionally to go out and dig things up oneself.

One of the hardest parts of writing a book like this, other than dealing with the volume of relevant material, is to present a coherent philosophy of archaeology. Archaeologists fight among themselves concerning problems of method and theory, and these are not polite academic disputes. Arguments that first divided the scholars of classical Athens are still fought afresh each year at anthropology conferences. To sort out all these philosophical issues of anthropology and archaeology is not only difficult, it is also boring on a scale imaginable only by people who have read the complete works of Hegel. Yet it is necessary to understand some of these issues to understand what modern archaeology is all about. I've tried to summarize some of these philosophical issues, but the reader is warned that all of them involve complexities that are not even alluded to here.

Another problem is the amount of archaeological detail one must wade through before these issues of method and theory make any sense. I've tried to take some of the tedium out of this by relating these data to general questions and problems, but I've yet to hit on a way to make fascinating the recitation of how many handaxes or fishbones Professor X found at Site Y.

Generally, I've tried to write a book that would be useful in a college course in world prehistory, but I would be gratified if a few civilians read it, as well.

I would like to acknowledge the many people who helped me with this edition, particularly my editors at Oxford, Susan Rabiner and Susan Meigs. Susan Meigs made many excellent suggestions about the text and orchestrated with great skill and patience the flow of manuscript and proofs between New York, Cairo, and Seattle. The text editor, Abby Levine, did her usual fine job.

Nanette M. Pyne endured her seventh complete reading and editing of *Patterns,* all while finishing her doctorate (in Medieval Persian History). Without her help I never would have finished—or started—this book.

Robert Dunnell, Dick Drennan, Jerry Eck, Robert Schacht, Tim White, and others gave me much good advice (not all of which I took) about the content of this book, and I appreciate their help. Mary Ellen Lane, Colin Davies, and Dianne and Alexander Nikas each made distinctive and important contributions.

Having finished this manuscript I am now going to return to Kom el-Hisn, in the western Egyptian Delta, where we are excavating what was an important town of the Old Kingdom. I hope we find something spectacular, something that will tell us marvelous things about the nature of the Egyptian past. But the point of this book is that this is not likely to happen. We already know much about the Egyptian—and the world's—antiquity. What we lack are the principles to understand and explain the past.

The "Fostat"
Cairo, Arab Republic of Egypt, 1984   R.J.W.

Contents

Patterns in Prehistory

1

Prehistory, History and Archaeology

History is philosophy teaching by examples.

Dionysius of Halicarnassus
(ca. 40 B.C.)

The archaeologist-heroes of films like *Raiders of the Lost Ark* never seem to have any doubts about what they are looking for or why they want it. "It" may be the Ark of the Covenant, a curse-protected pharaoh's tomb treasures, or the Golden City of the Incas, but whatever it is, our heroes seem to spend little time in the laboratory assessing their finds or writing dull books about their contribution to the study of comparative history.

How very different is the real-life practice of archaeology. In this prosaic age, it will come as no surprise to most laymen that archaeologists usually spend half of their lives gathering small bits of stone, bone, and pottery that would not arrest the attention of a museumgoer for more than fifteen seconds; or that archaeologists usually spend the other half of their lives asking themselves "What does all this stuff *mean?*"

In every country of the world, museum shelves groan with the centuries' accumulation of ceramic pots, stone tools, broken skulls, and other artifacts. Archaeologists have excavated everything from the first known human camps of 2 million years ago to the municipal dump of Tucson, Arizona. And every year, archaeologists in the thousands spread out across the globe to do research, inflicting upon their colleagues and

3

the world hundreds of thousands of books, articles, and lectures about their discoveries.

In the rest of this book, I will review hundreds of these studies, describing in the process thousands of artifacts, defining scores of terms, and testing the reader's patience with seemingly innumerable names for cultures, sites, phases, and the like.

What is the point of wading through this sea of specific facts and figures? Are there any general themes or concerns that tie all these details together?

To begin with, most archaeologists have focused their attention on the crucial *cultural transformations* of prehistory. Sometime several million years ago, our ancestors in Africa used the first tools in ways that no other life form does; millions of years later, these hominids spread out into the rest of the world and over the millennia became vastly more intelligent and physically more like ourselves; about 10,000 years ago, the first farmers and agricultural villages appeared in widely scattered places, and within a few thousand years in each instance, the descendants of these first farmers erected great states and empires.

The problem is that while archaeologists know a lot about *where* and *when* these cultural transformations occurred, they know very little about *why*. This raises more fundamental questions: What can we hope to learn about the past, and what should we do with this knowledge?

Should our objective be a detailed description of the events and cultures of the past, or can we hope to explain the past in terms of general principles? Are there patterns or regularities in prehistory and history that suggest our physical and cultural development can be accounted for in terms of laws? Does prehistory have any relevance to the world of today?

Many people spend an obligatory few years—often as college undergraduates—in earnest debate about questions concerning the nature of history and human existence, but eventually most go on to more immediate and resolvable concerns. Archaeologists, however, have developed arguments about these issues into an art form. Debates about the proper goals of archaeology and the significance of prehistory have been particularly spirited during the last two decades, and while there are still many contending views about what the goals of archaeology should be, there is at least general agreement about what most archaeologists have been doing in the past.

The traditional objectives of archaeology have been: (1) the compilation of culture histories; (2) the reconstruction of the lifeways of ancient peoples; and (3) the description and analysis of cultural processes (Binford 1968; Willey and Phillips 1958).

1.1   When Cortez and his men first landed in Mexico, they were treated as gods and were offered women and goods. The Spanish were astounded that the Aztecs had cities, great pyramids, and other wonders. Since the sixteenth century, scholars have been trying to explain why Old and New World civilizations developed in such similar patterns.

Because these specific goals form the structure of all that follows in this book, as well as the foundation of modern archaeology, it is important that we consider each in detail. As will become clear in later chapters, the physical processes of doing archaeology—the digging, sorting, and describing of artifacts—are well within the abilities of most reasonably coordinated and minimally trained people. The difficulties and complexities of archaeology are encountered mainly in trying to compile ancient culture histories, reconstruct ancient lifeways, and explain cultural processes.

COMPILING CULTURE HISTORIES

Until the nineteenth century, most Western people accepted the biblical premise that the world was about 6,000 years old and that almost from the very beginning our ancestors had lived in towns, engaged in agriculture, and organized themselves in great states and empires. Indeed, in the 1850s the eminent Dr. Lightfoot of Cambridge University, on the basis of his study of the Book of Genesis, proclaimed that the world had been created on October 23, 4004 B.C., at the civilized hour of 9:00 A.M.

However, with the archaeological demonstration that our ancestors had lived for millions of years as hunters and gatherers, interest grew in finding out when, where, and how the great transformations of prehistory had occurred. Eventually these questions coalesced into the goal of locating every prehistoric culture in time and space and arranging all of them "in a way which accurately reveals their generic affinities" (Binford 1968:8).

But how do you do this with prehistoric people who left no written records and of whom we have little more than the occasional skeleton and bags of pottery and stone?

The main method of culture history—and one that most archaeologists still use—is to make large collections of artifacts (the things people make) from each "site" (the houses, graves, or workplaces of ancient people) and then make a lot of brave inferences about the people who made these pots, stone tools, or whatever.

To take an example, I once walked the plains of southwestern Iran with several other archaeologists, collecting bags of broken pottery from the thousands of ancient villages and towns to be found there. Most of these old settlements are now just mounds (called *tells* in Arabic, *teppehs* in Persian) of decomposed mud bricks and garbage and are littered with thousands of bits of broken pottery and stone. Through dating methods (to be discussed in the next chapter), we knew the styles of pottery that were in use in most of the ancient periods in this part of the world. Thus, when we finished collecting our pottery samples, we emptied out each bag and counted up the numbers of different types of pottery styles from each site. Sites that had very similar kinds of pottery were assumed to have been occupied at about the same time and to have interacted socially or economically: those with markedly different pottery styles were assumed to have been occupied at different times. On this basis, I constructed settlement maps for several successive periods of occupation in this area (Wenke 1975–76).

This kind of culture history does not work quite so well when one has nothing but crude stone tools to go on, and archaeologists have perhaps been too quick to see massive invasions of new cultural groups when "breaks" appear in the sequence of artifact styles in a given area. But culture history "works" in the sense that through using these methods, we now know roughly what kinds of cultures inhabited most of the world during most of the past. Few archaeologists would classify themselves as culture historians these days, although most do culture history at one time or another.

Much of this book is simply a summary of what culture historians have done, even though most archaeologists recognize the nonexplanatory nature of culture histories. It is unfortunate but probably inescapable that some culture historians have shown a pronounced Western bias: since American and Western European cultures are technologically the most "advanced," the archaeological record has often been viewed in terms of the way in which modern Western man evolved from the first culture-bearing animals. Thus, cultural historical "explanations" of, for example, the appearance of agriculture and urban communities have tended to assume that these developments were the "natural" and inevitable products of prehistoric peoples who, like many Westerners, were constantly trying to improve their standard of living.

In any case, the essence of culture history is *description,* not explanation. The usual tactic of culture historians has been to arrange settlement patterns in chronological order and then to call upon war, invasion, climate changes, trade, or some other conditions or events to account for variability in the numbers, spatial arrangements, and contents of archaeological sites. Plausible stories about the past can be constructed in this fashion, but archaeologists have traditionally sought a higher level of explanation than that provided by cultural historical analysis.

RECONSTRUCTING PAST LIFEWAYS

Much of the last century of archaeology has been devoted to trying to reconstruct as completely as possible the diet, technology, residences, burial practices, seasonal movements—in short, the lifeways—of ancient peoples. Archaeologists have usually done this by excavating sites and interpreting their discoveries with the help of analogy, inference, and liberal amounts of imagination.

A classic example of cultural reconstruction is Henri de Lumley's reconstruction (1969) of life at Lazaret, a 300,000-year-old cave site in France. By measuring the location of every artifact and bit of bone that remained, de Lumley was able to show quite convincingly that ancient peoples had piled up kelp (inferred from the remains of snails that live only on kelp) and covered it over with bearskins (inferred from the position of the claws) to form a comfortable bed in a shelter in this cave. Additional analyses estimated the number of people in the cave, their diet, the months they visited the cave, and so on.

1.2   Detail of a bronze figure
from a Greek shipwreck, ca
460 B.C. Greek art reflected
Greek philosophical ideas of
wholeness, perfection, and
symmetry.

Thus, archaeologists often see themselves as ethnographers of ancient
peoples, and just as an ethnographer describes the daily life of the people he or she is studying, a cultural reconstructionist, substituting analogy and inference for direct observation, tries to describe daily life in
extinct cultures.

The last twenty years have seen remarkable advances in the methods
of cultural reconstruction. Techniques have been devised to recover
and identify minute plant and animal fragments so that ancient diets
can be precisely defined. There are even archaeologists whose specialty
it is to sort through ancient dried feces for clues to diets. Microscopic
analyses of artifacts provide new insights into ancient technologies, and
advances in soil chemistry and infrared photography have contributed
greatly to the accuracy of inferences about ancient lifeways. Elaborate
mathematical models and computers are now routinely used to analyze
archaeological data.

Attempts at cultural reconstruction have also been strengthened in
recent years by changes in the *logic* of archaeological research. Many
early expeditions were conducted with few explicit research objectives
beyond finding specimens for museums. As a result, excavation and
analytical techniques were not as productive as they might have been.
There is now a growing recognition that the archaeological record is

finite and that to use it most effectively we must specify the objectives of each project and then try to formulate precise hypotheses that can be "tested" by data gathered in the course of the fieldwork. These issues are discussed more fully below.

Despite these many improvements in the ways and means of reconstructing ancient cultures, cultural reconstructions often include a large measure of speculation, particularly when dealing with extremely ancient societies, whose artifacts and lifeways may have no historical analogs.

The possibilities for cultural reconstructions are essentially infinite: one can always excavate another site and fill in one more tiny bit of knowledge. And once the thrill of discovery has worn off, most archaeologists begin to wonder just how important it is to know whether this or that group ate more salmon than reindeer, or vice versa.

In any event, cultural reconstructions, like culture histories, are *descriptions,* not *explanations.* Should time travel ever be invented—to take a somewhat improbable illustration—these two goals of archaeology would be entirely fulfilled. Still, many archaeologists continue to do both culture history and cultural reconstruction, regarding them as indispensable steps to the third major goal of archaeology, the explanation of cultural processes.

EXPLAINING CULTURAL PROCESSES

If one reads the professional archaeological journals up to the mid-1960s, one finds an occasional nasty quarrel about the age of this or that culture, or the classification of some groups of pots or stone tools, but there are very few disputes about what archaeology is all about.

All this changed in the late 1960s, when arguments about the goals of archaeology broke out with a ferocity such that today some archaeologists do not speak to their ideological rivals, and academic jobs and research grants have often been awarded on the theoretical allegiances of applicants.

How could a discipline as musty and vague as archaeology produce such intense feelings?

It has to do mainly with the problem of explaining cultural processes.

The reader anxious to get to the blood and sex of prehistory may at this point recoil from a plunge into the philosophy of science and history, but there is simply no other way to understand what contemporary archaeologists are doing and why. The major problem in trying to explain contemporary archaeology is the diversity of philosophical positions. If, for example, one were to ask a sample of archaeologists to elaborate on the proposition that the major goal of archaeology is "to explain cultural processes," one would likely find a majority in favor of the proposition, but they would probably agree about the meaning of only one word in that proposition. The common denominator in these philosophic positions, however, is the idea that we can do more than just describe the past: we can understand it in terms of general principles, even if these general principles are not yet formulated.

A Brief Look at Explanatory Prehistory

The world's literature is littered with attempts to make sense of the past and to set forth the nature of culture, but few of these ideas have withstood the test of time.

Ancient Middle Eastern views on this subject, especially as presented in the comparatively late form of the Old Testament, envisioned a static, created world in which great changes came about through divine intercession, and where the ultimate explanation of events was God's will. And of God's will and design, we see only "as in a glass, darkly." In this view, even if we could see the divine design of history more clearly, we would see that it is predestined, beyond the realm of human initiative.

As an Oxford student named M. E. Hare once put it:

> There once was a man who said, "Damn!
> It is borne in upon me I am
>   An engine that moves
>   In predestinate grooves,
> I'm not even a bus I'm a tram."

From the perspective of modern archaeology, one of the most important ancient theories of culture originated in classical Greece in the fifth century B.C. Greeks like Thucydides and Herodotus were the first, as far as we know, to travel widely and compile extensive descriptions of the people, cultures, and places of their world. In his history of the Peloponnesian War, Thucydides tried to explain how the struggle began. He described the personalities involved, the strategies of the various warring powers, and the economic realities of the time. In short, by arranging the events and circumstances preceding the war in what he thought was a causal chain, he wrote what we now recognize as a modern history. Archaeologically based culture histories are founded precisely on this logic.

Another aspect of classical Greek thought that has profoundly influenced anthropology, archaeology, and history is the concept of the "Great Chain of Being," the *Scala Naturae* (Lovejoy 1960), which is founded on Greek ideas about the nature of God and "perfection." Greek philosophers found it inconceivable that the world they knew could have arisen by chance, because there seemed to be such a precise design in its every part. The migrations of birds, the intricate interdependences between plants and animals, the regularity of the seasons—all argued to them the existence of a Supreme Intelligence, and therefore they defined God as the perfect being who created and controls the world. The Greeks' conception of perfection, however, had a somewhat different connotation than it does for us, for they understood it to be in essence wholeness, or completeness—a concept vividly evident in classical Greek statuary and literature.

Aristotle assumed that the natural world would be rationally ordered according to what he charmingly called "powers of soul," representing different levels within the perfectly whole universe. Thus, a horse is higher than a sunflower because a horse can think, after a fashion, and a man is higher than a horse because he can reason and apprehend God. It is impossible that there should be any "missing links" in the chain, or that any parts of the chain should cease to exist. God, being perfect, could not create an imperfect, that is, incomplete, universe; nor could his sustaining powers allow a whole level of this perfection to vanish:

> Vast chain of being! which from God began,
> Natures aethereal, human, angel, man,
> Beast, bird, fish, insect, what no eye can see,
> No glass can reach; from Infinite to thee,
> From thee to nothing.—On superior pow'rs
> Were we to press, inferior might on ours;
> Or in the full creation leave a void,
> Where, one step broken, the great scale's destroy'd·
> From Nature's chain whatever link you strike,
> Tenth, or ten thousandth, breaks the chain alike.

> Alexander Pope

The idea of this Great Chain of Being pervades literature and science well into the nineteenth century and, obviously, there were grave difficulties in reconciling this concept with the evolutionary theories and the discoveries of modern archaeology. For if God had created and sustained every bacterium, every sparrow, every Neanderthal, how could it happen that thousands of species had come into existence, flourished, and vanished? How could humans possibly have evolved from lower primate species and lived for millions of years as "subhuman" races and species now long since extinct?

Yet it is easy to understand the attractiveness of the Great Chain. It placed humanity, the masterwork of the Creator, "but little lower than the angels." Furthermore, it explained why we were here and why the world seems so marvelously intricate and designed: God designed the world in every detail for his purposes.

THE ENLIGHTENMENT

"We are all Greeks," it has been said, because so much of modern Western thought is ultimately traceable to ancient Greece. But it was not until the "Enlightenment" of the eighteenth century that the intellectual foundations of modern archaeology were securely established. It was in the eighteenth and nineteenth centuries that the crucial elements of *determinism, materialism,* and *evolutionism* were combined with the *scientific method* to study the past.

There can be no absolute definition of the scientific method, for rather than a method it is a state of mind, a complex set of assumptions. The key ideas are that most, if not all, things and events can be understood in terms of identifiable physical forces, and that the best way to identify and measure these forces is to conceive ideas and then expose them to rejection through scientific experimentation.

Although this sounds to most people like nothing more than common sense, the documents of history show that it is a rather late and rare perception of the world. For most ancients and for many moderns, the world swarms with phenomena and forces that can never be understood by science.

Building on Greek ideas, seventeenth and eighteenth century scholars observed natural, social, and historical phenomena, devised hypotheses about their causes, and then *tested* these ideas by dropping balls off high towers, observing the orbits of planets, flying kites in lightning storms, and so on. What was scientifically essential was that the ideas be *operationalized,* or expressed in terms that could be measured; that they be exposed to falsification or contradiction by some sort of experimentation; and that, above all, the explanation of something be considered not absolute, eternal truth but just the best current theory, subject to correction in the light of new research.

The *materialist* and *determinist* elements in this kind of science were the assumptions that unless shown otherwise, the phenomena of this world—including historical and cultural phenomena—had some ultimate causation in (were in some way *determined* by) material factors like population growth, infections, or gravity. It was in the deterministic laws and processes governing the attributes of phenomena that one should look for explanations, not in human wishes or aspirations. The *evolutionary* component was the notion that over time there had been and would continue to be an increase in complexity in the biological, historical, and political world.

Thus, by 1800 Galileo, Newton, Kepler, Descartes, Bacon, and many others had shown that the natural world was understandable in terms of the elegant (i.e., comprehensive yet reduced to the simplest possible terms) ideas of mathematics and physics, and as a result scholars everywhere began to apply the scientific method to the understanding of human history and the problem of cultural origins. For example, the Marquis de Condorcet (1743–1794), a French philosopher, proposed a series of universal laws he thought governed the history of human social organizations, and he went so far as to use his analysis to try to predict the future of the world.

Such direct applications of the physical science model to history might seem strange to us now, but one must understand the eighteenth-century mind. "Common sense" tells us that history and culture are far too complex to explain in terms of simple mathematical laws, but common sense also tells us that we walk about on a flat earth, around which revolves the sun. The scholars of the Enlightenment had only recently been shown how treacherous was common sense and how the mysteries of the universe were being reduced to the commonplaces of science. And all around them great advances in the biological and historical sciences were being made (Grayson 1983).

In France, Georges Cuvier (1769–1832) undertook an extensive analysis of fossilized bones and concluded that hundreds of animal species had become extinct and that there seemed to be an evolutionary trajectory to the biological world. In the early 1800s, the French naturalist Jean Lamarck (1744–1829) published his reasons for believing the world to be much older than the 6,000 years described in the Bible, and he arranged the biological world in a sequence, from human beings to the smallest invertebrates, in a way similar to later evolutionary schemes.

In England in the 1830s, William "Strata" Smith and Charles Lyell,

1.3   The excavations at Pompeii in the mid-eighteenth century fired the imagination of Europeans and interested them in the classical past.

among others, attempted to show that the earth was formed through the action of slow geological processes—processes still in effect. Lyell's contributions were particularly important because the dawning realization of the earth's great age had led some scientists and clergy to a belief in a series of "catastrophes," the last of which was Noah's flood. Adherents of this position saw the fossil animal bones deep in the earth's strata as evidence that God had "destroyed" the world at various times with floods. Although contemporary scientists suspect that the geological processes forming the earth may have been more abrupt than Lyell thought, his research still stands as remarkably accurate.

In 1848 John Stuart Mill published his *Principles of Political Economy*, in which he set forth the same basic evolutionary account of prehistory and history his eighteenth-century predecessors had designed, but Mill elaborated it into a series of six stages: (1) hunting; (2) pastoralism; (3) Asiatic (by which he meant the great irrigation civilizations of China and the Near East); (4) Greco-Roman; (5) feudal; and (6) capitalist. He complemented this classification with an extensive analysis of the economic factors determining these stages.

At about the same time Mill was writing, another Englishman, Herbert Spencer, published several books that proved to be a watershed of theory for scholars in many fields. Spencer's primary contribution was that he applied the concepts of "natural selection" to human societies some years before Darwin applied them to the biological world.

Spencer was much influenced by Thomas Malthus, who in 1798 had noted that human societies—and indeed all biological species—tended to reproduce in numbers far faster than they increased the available food supply. For human groups this meant a life of struggle in which many were on the edge of starvation and more "primitive" societies lost out in the struggle for survival to the more "advanced" cultures. Spencer believed that eventually natural selection would produce a perfect society.

> Progress, therefore, is not an accident, but a necessity. Instead of civilization being artifact, it is part of nature; all of a piece with the development of the embryo or the unfolding of a flower. The modifications mankind have undergone, and are still undergoing, result from a law underlying the whole organic creation; and provided the human race continues, and the constitution of things remains the same, those modifications must end in completeness. . . . So surely must the things we call evil and immorality disappear; so surely must man become perfect. (1883: 80)

DARWINIAN EVOLUTION

On a warm Saturday afternoon in June 1860, about a thousand people gathered in Oxford, England, to witness a debate on Charles Darwin's theory of biological evolution. For years Darwin had studied the flora and fauna of South America, and he believed that his ideas about "descent with modification" were a contribution to natural historical studies. But he was reluctant to publish his views for various reasons. Only when he knew that others were about to publish evolutionary studies did he advance his opinion that the biological sciences had been in error for centuries concerning the origins and nature of biological species. Before Darwin, most people, including many influential scientists, had assumed that all varieties of plants and animals were the direct product of God's creative might; mankind itself was viewed as a special act of creation.

But Darwin's research convinced him that the natural world and its workings could be explained in more straightforward and scientific terms. He had been impressed by the great diversity of plant and animal life in the Galapagos Archipelago off the coast of Ecuador, where he found islands geologically similar and within sight of one another,

1.4   Charles Darwin (1809–1882) altered forever our conception of the nature of the universe and mankind.

but nevertheless inhabited by significantly different species of plants and animals. Why should there be such diversity in such a small area?

> It was evident (after some reflection) that such facts as these could only be explained on the supposition that species gradually became modified; and the subject haunted me. But it was equally evident that neither the action of the surrounding conditions, nor the will of the organism . . . could account for the innumerable cases in which organisms of every kind are beautifully adapted to their habits of life—for instance, a woodpecker or a tree-frog to climb trees, or a seed for dispersal by hooks or plumes. I had always been much struck by such adaptations, and until these could be explained it seemed to me almost useless to endeavor to prove by indirect evidence that species had been modified. (Darwin, quoted in A. B. Adams 1969: 334)

Darwin knew of course that for millennia farmers had used selective breeding to improve their animals in specific ways, such as sheep-tending abilities in dogs. But these changes were the result of purposeful intervention in these animals' breeding patterns. How could such *selection* come about in the natural world?

Scholars differ on whether it was Malthus's idea of population "pressure" or Adam Smith's ideas of economic competition that most influenced Darwin, but whatever the source, Darwin hit on the idea of competition: "Being well prepared to appreciate the struggle for existence which everywhere goes on from long-continued observation of the habits of animals and plants, it at once struck me that under these circumstances favorable variations would tend to be preserved and unfavorable ones to be destroyed" (quoted in A. B. Adams 1969: 335).

With these observations and simple conclusions, Darwin provided the world with answers to a whole range of perplexing questions. Why did animals and plants change over time? Because their environments had changed and those best adapted to these new environments survived to pass on their personal characteristics. Why was there such variety in the biological world? Because many different environments could be inhabited, and natural selection was constantly shaping biological populations to fit into any newly created environments.

Darwin knew nothing about the genetic mechanisms we recognize today as the agencies through which natural selection operates, and he believed that characteristics acquired by an organism in its lifetime could be passed on to its offspring. We now know this to be a misconception. We also know that Darwin was intellectually in great debt to people whom he did not acknowledge in the proper scientific fashion (Eiseley 1979). But all this does not detract from his great contribution.

Darwin never really lost his belief in Christianity, and he tried to minimize the relevance of his theories to questions of culture and religion; but he had put in motion an intellectual revolution that has continued to the present and has battered the very foundations of Western ideas about the nature of God, mankind, and history. Through logic and evidence, Darwin and his proponents showed there had been hundreds of millions of years in which the world had been dominated by reptiles, years in which there were no people. The implications were inescapable. How could God be glorified by countless generations of snakes and lizards and dinosaurs breeding, fighting, and dying in primeval swamps? Why should we consider mankind a special act of creation if man, too, developed from earlier, simpler forms, from ancestors who were no more imaginative, intelligent, creative, or religious than any other animal?

It is difficult for us today to appreciate the profound shock generated by the ideas of Darwin and his proponents. Evolutionary biology is now the only generally accepted theory of biology, and few scientists doubt its essential validity. But in that room at Oxford in 1860, Darwin and his advocate, Thomas Huxley, were reviled and ridiculed. This hostility characterized reaction to Darwinian ideas well into our own times, and it is not at all surprising that this should be so. For the

Man Found only in a Fossil State—Reappearance of Ichthyosauri

A LECTURE: "You will at once perceive," continued Professor Ichthyosaurus, "that the skull before us belonged to some of the lower order of animals; the teeth are very insignificant, the power of the jaws trifling, and altogether it seems wonderful how the creature could have procured food."

1.5   Nineteenth-century cartoonists derived a lot of amusement from evolutionary ideas.

logical extension of Darwin's ideas to the origins of humanity could be seen from the beginning to strip away comforting illusions about man's purpose and place in a world that "made sense."

> Until Darwin, what was stressed . . . was precisely the harmonious co-operative working of organic nature, how the plant kingdom supplies animals with nourishment and oxygen, and the animals supply plants with manure, ammonia, and carbonic acid. Hardly was Darwin recognized before these same people saw everywhere nothing but *struggle*. (Friedrich Engels, quoted in Meek 1953: 186)

In the poem "Dover Beach," Matthew Arnold likened the Christian faith and view of the world to a comforting tide that surrounded the world as a shining sea, but which was withdrawing under the onslaught of revolutionary ideas of the nineteenth century including Darwinism:

The Sea of Faith
Was once, too, at the full, and round earth's shore
Lay like the folds of a bright girdle furl'd.
But now I only hear
Its melancholy, long, withdrawing roar,
Retreating, to the breadth
Of the night-wind, down the vast edges drear
And naked shingles of the world.

Ah, love, let us be true
To one another! for the world, which seems
To lie before us like a land of dreams,
So various, so beautiful, so new,
Hath really neither joy, nor love, nor light,
Nor certitude, nor peace, nor help for pain;
And we are here as on a darkling plain
Swept with confused alarms of struggle and flight,
Where ignorant armies clash by night.

In a sense, Darwin completed Galileo's revolution. A critic of Galileo "proved" finally and utterly that Galileo was wrong because Galileo said there were moons orbiting Jupiter. As this critic pointed out, if these moons were too small to be seen, they were too small to affect the earth, and since God designed the earth as the focal point of the whole universe, Jupiter could, therefore, have no moons. Galileo showed that the earth was one among an inconceivably large number of celestial bodies, without apparent special claim to centrality; Darwin showed that today's human being is one of many related life forms and is always a "transitional form," constantly changing.

In this way, Darwin and other evolutionists posed the essential problems archaeologists must deal with. They showed that the institutions of man—the cities, arts, crafts, agriculture, domestic animals, religion, governments—all evolved out of earlier, simpler forms; they implied that we have no special claim to exemption from the processes of the universe. And, perhaps most important of all, Darwin's ideas made it reasonable to ask whether or not there were principles with which to understand our cultural as well as our physical evolution.

EVOLUTION AND MATERIALIST DETERMINISM

The full impact of nineteenth-century evolutionism was achieved when its ideas were blended with the materialism of Karl Marx (1818–1883) and his disciples, particularly Friedrich Engels (1820–1895). Even ar-

1.6   Karl Marx (1818–1883)
profoundly influenced anthropology and archaeology by
showing that a society's government, religion, and social
structures were in some ways
determined by economic and
technological forces.

chaeologists who consider Marxism a bankrupt political ideology are
in debt to Marxian thought in many of its elements of materialist determinism. In a way, this is what one would expect, for archaeologists
deal principally with the *material*—the houses, stone tools, storage bins,
pots, weapons, irrigation canals, and other items that constitute the
"means of production" of ancient peoples.

Certainly one of the most diverse—not to say solipsistic—associations
of all time is that group of individuals who have tried to explain what
Marx meant. People have killed each other in disputes over Marxian
interpretations, and neo-Marxist variants on the basic Marxian gospel
are so diverse as to defy summarization. The student with a sense of
humor and a German dictionary is invited to read Marx's original description of the all-important "relations of production" and then to
follow the exegesis of this term into the contemporary era (see, e.g.,
Harris 1979). Scholars with every inclination of Platonic Idealists now

claim to be Marxist materialist-determinists, all on the strength of their interpretation of "relations of production."

But what has all this got to do with archaeology? Precisely this: for some of the most influential American and European archaeologists, the only way to explain the past is with the concepts first clearly stated by Marx.

Suppose, for example, you had just spent two years traveling from archaeological site to site in Egypt, and that you had examined and made copious measurements of every ancient site from the pyramids of Giza to tiny hamlets of the early Islamic period. Most Marxist archaeologists and historians would argue that the only way to *understand*— to *explain*—this long and ancient history is to invoke the basic Marxist assumptions. These are: (1) political and social systems change through history because of changes in the technological, economic basis of these systems; (2) technological change is necessary and deterministic, and therefore social and political change is necessary and deterministic; (3) all societies through history have conformed to a general, unilinear pattern of development; and (4) the rules and patterns of historical development are natural laws of the physical universe (after Cohen 1978).

In the last several decades, there have been numerous reworkings of Marxian theory, and the most recent archaeological expressions of these ideas (e.g., Friedman and Rowlands 1977) stress the social relations that people enter into in producing and consuming goods. These, rather than just the blunt forces of climate, crops, and technology, are seen as the determinant factors of history.

We shall come back to these ideas in chapter 7. It is sufficient here to note that materialist determinism is strongly embedded in modern archaeology and that many archaeologists draw directly on the works of Marx in trying to understand and explain the past. It may also become clear why some archaeologists consider the Marxian elements of archaeology to derive more from Groucho than from Karl.

MODERN EXPLANATORY PREHISTORY AND ARCHAEOLOGY

In the previous sections, I have tried to show that the general idea of explanatory prehistory developed out of the evolutionism, materialism, and determinism of the Enlightenment and the nineteenth century. But the incorporation of these ideas into the actual practice of archaeology was not simple or automatic.

Evolutionary and materialist forms of archaeology go back at least to the eighteenth century, when Scandinavian archaeologists like J. J.

Worsae and P. F. Suhm developed the *three-age system*—the discovery that in many parts of Europe ancient people first made tools of stone, then of bronze, and finally of iron. And many European archaeologists of the nineteenth century were evolutionists mainly in the sense that they were concerned with showing how Western Europeans had reached the apex of history and were superior to all other cultures.

Reaction to misapplications of evolutionary and materialist ideas produced an emphasis in the early twentieth century on the patient accumulation of artifacts and a minimum of interpretation. This period was the "Golden Age" of cultural reconstruction and culture history. It was widely assumed that progress in explaining prehistoric cultural developments would be made only when much more archaeological evidence had been accumulated and the "facts were allowed to speak for themselves." Many archaeologists of this era also thought that the New World cultures had been heavily influenced by migrations and contacts from Old World cultures prior to the fifteenth century, and that any parallels between Old and New World cultures were either the result of these contacts or were unpatterned, independent inventions.

Even by the 1920s, however, there was a growing frustration with the idea of an archaeology limited just to an endless series of inferences about ancient houses and diets. In trying to make a more powerful science, archaeologists then did the obvious thing: they tried to imitate the procedures of sciences they considered the most scientific. Thus, in the late 1950s and the 1960s, American archaeology began a return to the evolutionary perspective, scientific objectives, and materialist approach anticipated by Spencer and Marx.

Although major shifts in theory and method are never the result of a single individual, Lewis Binford has played a particularly important role in shaping contemporary archaeology. While a student at the University of Michigan, Binford was greatly impressed with Leslie White's evolutionary, materialistic vision of anthropology (1949), and in an influential and programmatic series of papers Binford argued that archaeologists should turn their attention away from endless excavations and attempts to reconstruct ancient cultures and culture histories, and concentrate instead on the study of cultural processes and the formulation of cultural laws. Binford particularly stressed the importance of problem orientation and the testing of hypotheses. He and many like-minded contemporary archaeologists assert that archaeological research should be conducted by: (1) selecting a general problem, for example, the origins of agriculture; (2) formulating a series of testable statements, or hypotheses, about the causal relationships involved; (3) designing and executing the field research necessary to evaluate the hypotheses; (4) accepting, rejecting, or modifying the hypotheses on the basis of the fieldwork; and (5) modifying the general model of cultural process in the light of the reworked hypotheses, and formulating new testable hypotheses.

It is in this idea of hypothesis testing that we see the clearest expression of the centuries-old idea of making archaeology and the study of prehistory a scientific discipline that, like physics, would make predictions about the behavior of things, then test these hypotheses and eventually formulate laws on the basis of these experiments.

For example, a scientist confronted with a solar eclipse can *explain* this event by connecting the specific knowledge of what day and time it is and where he or she is located with a body of principles and laws involving gravity, velocity, mass, and the properties of light. Not only can our prototypical physicist *predict* the eclipse; he or she could, theoretically, *control* it (possessing a death wish and sufficient nuclear bombs to move the earth out of the sun's orbit). That is, the physicist knows all of the principles that produce an eclipse to the point that with adequate resources, he or she could alter the outcome.

So why not a science of history and archaeology, where instead of atoms and molecules and cells whirling around according to known quantifiable laws, we have handaxes or villages or ancient people in predictable (or, horrible word, *postdictable*) patterns according to laws of history and culture?

Although this idea may sound absurd at first, it has had and continues to have rational defenders. The idea of "free will," for example—that people are unlike atoms because they can exercise choice, which moves them beyond the blind forces of nature—is not necessarily the only way in which one can view humanity. Marx is just one of the people who have claimed that a person's environment and circumstances *determine* his or her actions, that free will is an illusion. To the objection that history has direction and is thus unlike the eternal unchanging forces of nature, one could note that the universe too has a time direction, with constellations coming into existence and then disappearing on an unimaginable time scale. Artifacts, too, are just congregations of matter and energy whose physical attributes can be located in time and space.

In an effort to imitate the scientific method, archaeologists in the 1960s and 1970s debated the validity of many hypotheses about many "origins" questions, such as the origins of agriculture (chapter 6). Scholars hypothesized that people first became farmers because of, variously, population pressure, climate change, technological inventions, and so forth. Archaeologists went to many parts of the world to test these ideas (showing that just before the first farming communities appeared, there was an increase in population densities, a climate change, or whatever). Eventually, it was hoped, the most important factors in agricultural origins could be measured and expressed in terms of some kind of laws. This sense of hypothesis testing and the general application of the scientific method in the context of a materialist determinism and cultural evolutionism was widely seen in both the United States and Europe as the future direction of archaeology.

Archaeology and the Scientific Method: A Reassessment

There are various problems with the idea of a "physics of culture." First, no one has ever formulated a cultural law that anyone would consider essentially like the laws of physics and that "works" as well. Of course, this does not mean that it is not possible to formulate such laws; however, at least three centuries of serious consideration have provided no laws of culture or history like those of the natural sciences.

Second, all of the laws, principles, and regularities that have been proposed by archaeologists (including the Marxists, who of all people are most strident in their claims for the validity of cultural laws) are in fact *logically different* from physical laws. The assertion that gravity is a function of mass and distance is assumed to be true by definition, and applies to all phenomena past, present, and future. Most so-called archaeological or cultural laws are *empirical generalizations:* summary statements about observations of specific phenomena through time, such as the observation that most of the earliest states and empires developed state religions that helped organize and control these societies.

Third, there are problems with the hypothesis-testing approach. Consider, for example, our crocodiles. Excavating in Egypt in 1981, we found that one site of the late fourth millennium B.C. had many crocodile bones but no crocodile heads or teeth. Our geologist convinced us that this particular site was located near the edge of the ancient Fayyum Lake, and our other finds suggested that it was probably a temporary camp, occupied in spring and fall, where people came to fish and hunt migratory birds. Fueled by one, perhaps two, Stella beers, we evolved the plausible notion that they were hunting these things for God knows what reason, and to aid in transporting their game back to camp, they gutted the animals, cut off their heads and other inedible parts, and left them to rot on the shore.

Now the point here is that in our future work in this site, we could go back and "test" this hypothesis by excavating other sites to see if the same pattern is found, or by checking the crocodile body bones carefully for cut marks, or in any number of other plausible ways. We could also generalize this specific idea and test the hypothesis that hunters and gatherers tended to transport the shortest distance those animal parts with the least meat on them. Or we could generalize still further and test the notion that people tend to avoid work as much as possible.

But in terms of developing a science of culture and history, such testing of hypotheses cannot be expected to give us laws like those of physics. One problem here is that different combinations of factors can produce the same results. In our crocodile example, it might also be that people cut off crocodile heads and used them in religious ceremonies in which all the heads were buried in some well-hidden cave—and we could just as well support that hypothesis with the available data. We could test hundreds of hypotheses and excavate hundreds of sites and test increasingly complex and specific hypotheses, but in the end all we would have is greater and greater faith in the correctness of our inferences. And, in most cases, we would be trying to make more plausible a *cultural reconstruction* rather than a generalization about culture, so our efforts in the end would still be mainly descriptive. We could convince ourselves that people really did cut the heads off these animals and leave them by the water's edge, even if the more general proposition that "the transport distance of a faunal part varies directly with its potential use" remains mainly a statistical abstraction, often violated.

None of this has much in common with the assertion that the volume of a gas is related to its temperature and pressure (Salmon 1982).

Lewis Binford considers the distinction between *functional* forms of analysis, such as in our crocodile example, and higher forms of analysis as one of the most important in archaeology:

> One of the greatest confusions to have plagued the social sciences is the confusion between regularities in the internal dynamics of cultural systems (synchronic and internal-functional) and the nature of the dynamics which conditioned changes in the organization of systems themselves and in their evolutionary diversification and change (diachronic and external-ecological). I have tried to suggest that with regard to the former problem archaeologists seek to understand the dynamic conditions which produced the statics remaining for us to observe. This may well involve us in many arguments regarding the relationships between "nonmaterial" or "nonpreserved" aspects of past systems and material derivatives of these "nonmaterial" dynamics. I have called this middle-range research, and it is obviously research which would ideally permit the accurate *description* of past conditions. When we turn to the interesting job of explaining the nature of past systems, we

move into the mode of diachronic patterning and ecological-evolutionary theory building. Functional understandings can never serve as the explanations of evolutionary changes. This fundamental distinction seems to have been overlooked and to be merged in a confusing way . . . [by archaeologists] advocating a "social archaeology." (1981: 181)

Here Binford suggests that there is value in trying to describe the conditions that produced our crocodile remains in Egypt, but that describing these conditions by testing successive hypotheses will not produce an evolutionary science of culture.

Many archaeologists still view hypothesis testing as a valid way to do archaeology and as a major advance from pre-1940s archaeology in which the excavator set forth with little more than the hope that he would find something interesting. It is just that most forms of testing hypotheses in archaeology are not set in any useful theory, are not capable of identifying precisely which combination of factors produced a particular cultural result, are usually used mainly to increase one's confidence in one's cultural reconstruction, and are usually fatally compromised by sampling problems.

Fourth, one must consider that if it *is* possible in the future to formulate powerful mathematical laws about historical processes, is this really what archaeologists want? Is an explanation of the glory that was Greece and the grandeur that was Rome ultimately to be explained by 237 pages of computer output?

For all these reasons, then, the early 1980s find archaeologists returning from the frontiers of science, like Napoleon from Moscow, somewhat depressed but in possession of a valuable lesson: imitating a tactic that was successful in one instance does not guarantee success in other applications.

Nevertheless, the search for an explanatory prehistory continues as archaeologists turn to such forms of analysis as biological evolutionary theory, systems theory, mathematical modeling, and even cognitive psychology for inspiration.

The Explanation of Cultural Processes: Conclusions and Summary

Having wandered, in this abbreviated intellectual history of archaeology, from ancient Athens to contemporary America, we come back to two fundamental questions: What can we know about the past and how should we go about knowing it? As we have seen, answers to these questions have ranged from the notion that history is God's plan and ultimately unknowable to the idea that history can be the subject of scientific methods of analysis and can ultimately be expressed in eternal, universal laws. Contemporary archaeologists include those who are working on complex computer models designed to extract historical processes, those who are trying to produce highly detailed culture histories, and those who have given up all pretense of doing anything other than finding interesting items (the "gold-bowls-and-mummies" school of archaeology).

In the chapters that follow, I shall try to illustrate some of the more promising approaches to the problem of analyzing cultural processes. None of these is so powerful at present that it is worth exploring in painful detail; most are understandable only in terms of specific examples. In all this, the reader should bear in mind three basic points: (1) most archaeologists want more powerful ways to understand cultural processes and the nature of history; (2) recent attempts to make archaeology a "science" in order to understand cultural processes have been logically flawed and not terribly impressive in their results; and (3) the diversity of theoretical approaches to archaeology suggests that as a discipline, archaeology has entered a period of loss of confidence in its theoretical structure—the kind of period, as it happens, that in other disciplines has often presaged great advances in method and theory.

2

Fundamentals of Archaeology

To be ignorant of what happened before you
were born is to be ever a child. For what is a
man's lifetime unless the memory of past events
is woven with those of earlier times?

Cicero

People are messy animals. About 2 million years ago, our ancestors began littering the African landscape with stone tools and gnawed bones,
and ever since we have been sinking deeper and deeper into our own
garbage. Strictly speaking, all this junk, from the first stone tools to today's indestructible plastic bottles, is the *archaeological record*. And the
major premise of archaeology is that we can look at selected segments
of this accumulation of debris and see reflections of the factors that
have shaped our physical and cultural evolution.

Archaeologists tend to look at the archaeological record largely in
terms of *artifacts, features,* and *sites*. Artifacts are things that owe any
of their physical characteristics or their place in space to human activity (Dunnell 1971: 201). Thus, a carefully shaped stone arrowhead is an
artifact, but so is a stone that has simply been pushed aside so a Pleistocene hunter could sleep more comfortably. Bones, pollen, and other organic remains can also be considered artifacts or *ecofacts* (Binford
1964), if they owe characteristics of form (as do domesticated plants) or
placement to human activity. Archaeologists usually analyze artifacts
not simply as objects but as constellations of *attributes* such as size,
shape, color, and material.

Hearths, ovens, wells, pits, tombs, and other nonportable clusters of
artifacts representing specific activities are usually referred to as *features*.
The concept of an archaeological *site* is less precise than the concept

28

2.1 A great part of the world's archaeological record is composed of stone, wood, and clay artifacts. The flint knife depicted here dates from about 4000 B.C., from Egypt. Its ivory handle is carved with scores of delicate animal figures. The ceramic pot and figurine are also from Egypt, from about 3100 B.C.

of an artifact, but typically it means a particularly dense concentration of artifacts and features. Thus, the ancient city of Babylon in Mesopotamia is a site, but so is DK 1 at Olduvai Gorge, where just a few score stone tools lie amid broken animal bones. Ancient villages and towns are easily identifiable since they are marked by walls and massive quantities of pottery and other debris, and it is convenient to think of the archaeological record in this case as composed of many discrete sites representing different settlements. But the areas between these sites are often littered with artifacts representing temporary labor camps and other activities, and if we concentrated only on the settlement sites, we would miss much of the archaeological record. The concept of an archaeological site is particularly imprecise when applied to the archaeological record left by the countless bands of hunters and gatherers who roamed the world for millions of years before the first settlements appeared, and whose tools and other debris are scattered in hunting camps, tool-manufacturing sites, kill sites, and base camps. In general, therefore, sites are regarded simply as high points in plots of artifact densities.

PRESERVATION

A depressing number of things can destroy archaeological remains. Floods wash them away, glacial ice sheets grind them to fragments, rodents go out of their way to burrow through them, and rivers and winds bury them under blankets of soil. The greatest destruction, however, is caused by people. Thousands of sites have been buried beneath parking lots or destroyed by other construction.

But it is not only modern civilization that is to blame; people of all ages have knowingly and unknowingly destroyed the record of the past.

In recent years the worst destruction has occurred through looting. In many countries it has become a flourishing industry; peasants rob sites and sell their finds to antiquities dealers, who ship items mainly to the Americas and Europe. Archaeologists are usually not interested in artifacts for their own sake; artifacts are most useful when they are recovered in the context in which they were used and deposited. Thus, once a looter removes artifacts from a site, the most valuable characteristics of the artifacts are forever lost. The amateur who is just trying to find a few arrowheads or nice "Indian pots" probably does not realize that he or she is destroying invaluable and irreplaceable information and objects.

Even those sites relatively untouched by environmental and human

2.2 "Tollund man," a 2,000-year-old hanging victim from the peat bogs of Denmark, illustrates the "pickling" properties of weakly acidic environments.

disturbances are greatly altered by the natural processes of decay. Stone tools are almost indestructible, but bones, hides, wood, plants, and people rot. Certain artifacts, however, do preserve well under such conditions as extreme aridity, cold, or—for some things—complete immersion in water. Entire mammoths have been retrieved from frozen pits in Siberia, and well-preserved human corpses thousands of years old have been recovered from peat bogs in Europe (Figure 2.2). Dry caves provide excellent preservation conditions, where corpses, feces, leather, and other things can be found in near-perfect condition.

LOCATING ARCHAEOLOGICAL REMAINS

Many archaeologists find that the question they are most often asked by laymen is "How do you know where to look?" It does not take a trained archaeologist to locate the pyramids of Egypt, but many other archaeological remains are less evident, such as those covered by drifting sand or alluvial soils, buried beneath contemporary settlements, or located in remote, unsurveyed areas.

Until very recently, most archaeological sites were found by accident or unsystematic exploration. The construction of a subway system in Mexico City in the 1960s, for example, turned up many previously unknown but highly important archaeological remains.

In modern archaeology, however, one no longer sets out on expeditions to remote places on the Micawberish assumption that something interesting will turn up; instead, archaeologists usually work within the context of a specific problem and design their research to locate remains directly relevant to this problem. If one were interested in the origins of maize agriculture in ancient Mexico, one would read the many reports written on this subject, define a geographical region where maize is likely to have been first cultivated, and then conduct archaeological surveys to locate relevant sites within this region.

Actually locating such sites might involve walking surveys, where five or ten archaeologists, working from maps or aerial photographs, simply line up and walk over a selected area, recording sites as they are found. Aerial photographs and other photogrammetric techniques can often be used to reveal ancient agricultural fields, roads, and other features not visible from the ground. Underwater archaeological surveys have been conducted by divers, although the cost of such surveys is high and the area covered usually very small. However they are located, archaeological sites can either be simply mapped and recorded, or they can be excavated—depending on the resources and objectives of the project.

The methods used to excavate archaeological sites depend on the kind of remains involved and the objectives of the archaeologists. Normally the first step is to make a careful map of the site so that objects and features found can be given precise three-dimensional coordinates—the *provénience*. Then the site is gridded into, say, five-by-five-meter blocks, and a sample of these blocks is selected for excavation. Actual digging is done with dental tools, paintbrushes, trowels, shovels, bulldozers, or dynamite—depending, again, on the objectives and context.

Whatever kind of site is being excavated, a great deal of time and care is required. One usually tries to excavate according to the *cultural stratigraphy* (Figure 2.3) of the site, so that the different layers of debris are removed as depositional units—as opposed to simply digging the site by arbitrary levels. Most of the sediment removed from a site

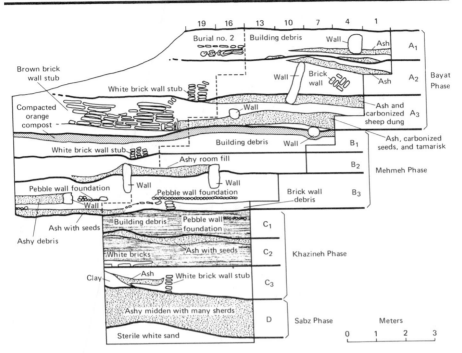

2.3   This profile drawing shows the depositional history of a community at Tepe Sabz, near Deh Luran, Iran, from about 6500 to 4000 B.C. Skill in field archaeology is largely the ability to discern such cultural layers in the confusing jumble of mud-brick, stones, ash, and other debris.

should be passed through fine mesh screens so that small bones, beads, and other remains are retrieved.

Every archaeological site is unique and nonrenewable, and once excavated, the remains can never be replaced. Thus, the greatest care must be taken to recover as much information as possible. Most contemporary archaeological research projects involve geologists, botanists, palynologists (experts on plant pollen), architects, faunal experts, and other specialists, because no one archaeologist can hope to know about the most recent research in all these fields.

In numbers, the great majority of archaeological remains are either stone tools or pottery. Huge volumes have been written on the manufacture, use, and analysis of stone tools. The mechanics of stone-tool manufacture are quite simple. A chunk of fine-grain stone is struck with something in order to send a shock wave through the stone at a certain force and angle. Classrooms all over the world are bloodied each autumn as instructors attempt to demonstrate for their classes this process. Nothing is sharper than a fragment struck from a substance like volcanic glass (obsidian), which shatters into tiny particles when not struck at the correct angle. Through experimentation, though, some archaeologists are able to produce copies of almost every stone tool type used in antiquity.

Ceramics were in use much later than the first stone tools, but they were used in such massive quantities in antiquity that for many archaeologists, life is mainly the slow sorting and analyzing of potsherds. Ceramic pots were first made by hand and dried in the sun or low-temperature kilns, but in many areas of the Old World, the invention of the potter's wheel and high-temperature kilns produced pottery that is virtually as indestructible as glass.

The other major artifacts of the past, in such materials as metals, wood, composite tools (e.g., bow and arrow), and textiles, were usually invented in several places independently.

SAMPLING IN ARCHAEOLOGY

In a famous film scene, W. C. Fields was dealing cards and was asked by a prospective player, "Is this a game of chance?" Fields—felonious eyes agleam—replied, "Not the way I play it!"

Some archaeologists do archaeology the same way: they find an area they think is likely to produce nice finds and then dig. But more and more archaeologists are using chance, in the form of probability sampling, to determine where they should excavate or collect artifacts. They use the technique of *statistical sampling*, the essentials of which are familiar to most people. American polling organizations regularly ask a few thousand people how they are going to vote in an election and use this information to make very reliable predictions about the voting behavior of the larger *population* (all individuals who actually vote). One of the reasons sampling works in elections is that pollsters *stratify* their samples: they know from previous elections that people in the North vote differently from those in the South, and that certain occupational groups are far more likely to vote than others. Thus, they break up, or stratify, their samples so that these and other subpopulations are proportionately represented. Then, by using complex procedures of statistical inference, they are often able to estimate election results quite precisely.

Archaeologists also use sampling theory and procedures. If they wish to know something relatively straightforward, such as the number and kinds of sites in a large region, they can divide the area up into sub-areas—perhaps stratifying it according to ecological zones—and then go

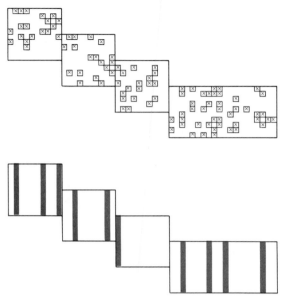

2.4   Various practical and mathematical factors must be considered by archaeologists when they construct sampling designs. Two of the simplest and most popular designs are random quadrants (*above*) and random transects (*below*). In these designs the overall area to be studied is divided into squares or rectangles of equal size and each square or transect is assigned a number. A table of random numbers is then used to select the areas (shaded in this illustration) that will be excavated or surveyed.

out and record the number of sites in perhaps 10 percent of all the *sample units*. Excellent results are usually obtained from such procedures, if the objective is simply an estimate of site numbers.

One critical sampling problem derives from the great size and complexity of the archaeological record. Suppose, for example, that you have the idea that trade in items like silver and textiles was the key element in the rise of the first states of ancient Mexico. The only way to test your idea would be to show that there was a significant increase in the amount or kinds of these products at sites occupied just prior to or during the period when the first states appeared. To do this with statistical precision, you would have to excavate at least portions of a statistically valid sample of perhaps thirty or forty sites—something just not feasible in today's archaeology.

This does not stop archaeologists from testing such hypotheses, of course. No marketing executive or even drunk riverboat gambler would bet on the odds that archaeological sampling designs usually deal with in testing such hypotheses; but archaeologists deal only in history and science, whereas gamblers deal in money.

In the face of such difficulties, archaeologists have opted for the only realistic strategy: they use statistical sampling techniques, knowing that they often don't meet the theoretical requirements for optimal statistical inference, but feeling that useful—if not perfect—results can be obtained. Fortunately, most statistical sampling techniques are very "robust" in that one can strain their assumptions badly and still get quite reasonable results.

Dating Methods in Archaeology

A large proportion of early archaeological research was devoted to estimating the dates of important "firsts," such as the domestication of the first plants and animals. But even with the recent increased interest in more general archaeological problems, it has still been important to estimate the age of archaeological finds. For example, in a later chapter we shall consider the hypothesis that wars brought on by expanding human population densities were the primary cause of the rise of state societies in ancient Peru. To evaluate this possibility it is necessary to be able to estimate changes in ancient population densities, and this must be done archaeologically by estimating the ages of hundreds of sites, so that we can determine which were occupied concurrently.

To solve these and other problems of chronology, archaeologists rely on two different kinds of dating methods. In some situations the objective is to obtain a *chronometric* date: that is, an age expressed in years, such as "that house was built 7,200 years ago." In many situations chronometric dates may be difficult to obtain or simply unnecessary for the problem at issue, and for these situations archaeologists have devised several methods of *relative seriation,* in which the objective is to arrange sites or artifacts in a sequence that reflects the order in which they were created—even though we may not know for certain the actual age of any of them.

CHRONOMETRIC DATING TECHNIQUES

Dendrochronology is an exact and reliable method of dating based on the analysis of the cross-sections of tree trunks. Most trees add a single "ring" each year to their circumference, and the width of this band is determined mainly by water availability. Thus, if we count the number of rings, the age of a tree can be precisely established. Normally the tree grows faster in wet years than in dry ones; therefore, over the centuries there is a unique series of changes in ring widths, and a record of these changes can be established by comparing cross-sections of trees that overlapped in time (Figure 2.5). By comparing beams, posts, and other artifacts to cross-sections taken from trees that live for thousands of years (like the bristlecone pine), it is often possible to deter-

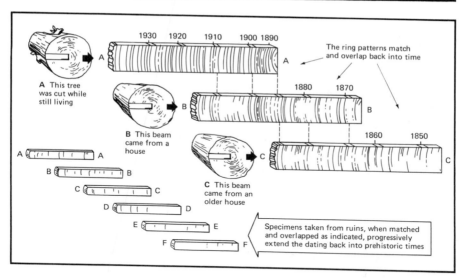

1930 1920 1910 1900 1890

A

A

The ring patterns match
and overlap back into time

A This tree
was cut while
still living

1880 1870

B

B

B This beam
came from a
house

1860 1850

C

C

C This beam
came from an
older house

A   A
B   B
C   C
D   D
E   E
F   F

Specimens taken from ruins, when matched
and overlapped as indicated, progressively
extend the dating back into prehistoric times

2.5   The most precise dates in archaeology are derived through dendrochronology.
In many important areas of the world, however, a dendrochronological sequence
has not been established, and in other areas, such as Mesopotamia, there are no
native, long-lived species of trees.

mine the exact year in which the tree used to make the artifact was cut.

Since local climates vary, dendrochronological records must be built
up for each region, and at present detailed records are available only
for the American West and a few other places.

The most widely used chronometric technique is *carbon-14 dating,*
the theory of which was first outlined in the 1940s by Willard Libby.
It is based on the fact that solar radiation striking the upper atmosphere converts a small amount of atmospheric nitrogen into the radioactive isotope C^{14}. Wind and other factors mix this C^{14} throughout the
atmosphere, and because all living organisms exchange gases with the
atmosphere, the ratio of C^{14} in their cells is equal to that in the atmosphere. When the organism dies, the C^{14} trapped in its cells begins to
revert to nitrogen. Because we know that approximately half of any
given quantity of C^{14} will disintegrate in about 5,730 years, we can estimate the time an organism has been dead by measuring the amount of
C^{14} remaining in its cells. After about 50,000 years, too little persists to
be measurable with standard laboratory methods, although some new
methods may extend the range to about 100,000 years (Browman 1981).
Radiocarbon dates are often given in years "B.P." (Before Present), and
1950 is the standard for computing dates B.P.

Carbon-14 dating works best on wood and charcoal, but paper, leather, bone, skin, peat, and many other organic materials can also be dated by this method. Grains and grasses make excellent archaeological samples when charred by fire, because they preserve well and are short-lived compared to trees. A tree trunk used as a roof beam may be re-used in several successive buildings over centuries.

The ratio of C^{14} in the atmosphere has not been entirely constant over the last 50,000 years, and thus carbon-14 dates have had to be "cor-rected" by measuring the ratio of C^{14} in tree rings dated through den-drochronology. Samples used for C^{14} dating must be collected very care-fully to ensure that they are not contaminated with younger or older carbon sources, such as ground water or petroleum deposits.

Potassium-argon dating is based on the fact that a radioactive isotope of potassium (K^{40}), present in minute quantities in rocks and volcanic ash, decays into the gas argon (Ar^{40}) at a known rate (half of a given amount of K^{40} will change into Ar^{40} in about 1.3 billion years). Be-cause Ar^{40} is a gas, it escapes when rock is molten (as in lava), but when the rock cools, the Ar^{40} is trapped inside. By using sensitive instru-ments to measure the ratio of K^{40} to Ar^{40}, it is possible to estimate the time since the rock or ash cooled and solidified.

Because of the long half-life of K^{40} (1.3 billion years), potassium-argon dating can be used to estimate dates of materials many millions of years old. Presently, techniques have been developed to date accu-rately materials as young as 50,000 years old, but potassium-argon dating works best with samples between 100,000 and 5 million years old.

Carbon-14 and potassium-argon dating remain the mainstays of chro-nometric dating, but there are now many other techniques involving chemical changes, most of which are subject to considerable error and many qualifications. Yet the search for better methods will continue, because if archaeology is to be explanatory in any real sense, it will have to examine *causes,* and the idea of causation in the archaeological record is mainly a matter of showing a correlation in time and space.

RELATIVE DATING

As a novice graduate student, I once watched two archaeologists wan-der over an ancient Mesopotamian town, occasionally stooping to pick up a potsherd and saying things like, "Obviously this area was occu-pied into the Late Uruk, whereas that part must have been abandoned by the Terminal Susa A Period."

This kind of relative dating involves the concept of *style*. Mesopo-tamian potters, like all other people, differed with the passage of time

Method (function)	Potential time range (years B.C.)

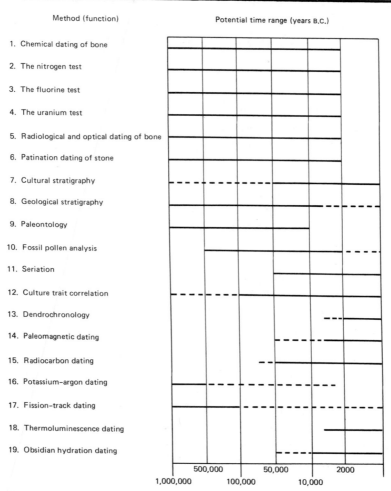

2.6   Effective time range of various archaeological dating techniques. Broken line represents less reliable range of technique.

in the styles of pottery they produced. Therefore, the pottery in each succeeding century or two can be distinguished in form, color, and decoration.

The distribution of stylistic elements through time and space tends to follow certain patterns, whether the objects involved are skirt lengths, musical forms, or stone tools. Styles originate in some small area, spread to adjacent ones, reach a peak in popularity, and then die out. To some extent, styles reflect rates of interaction and common aesthetic preferences, and these are not always exact functions of time and distance. Dress styles, for example, in midtown Manhattan may be more similar to those on Rome's Via Veneto than to those in a small town in rural New Jersey, even though this pattern of stylistic similarity "reverses" their relative distances. And often a style dies out at its point of origin long before it reaches its ultimate dispersal.

Archaeologists use relative dating for a variety of purposes. If one excavates a two-thousand-year-old town in Missouri, one can take samples of artifacts from each level as one goes down through the site, and it can be assumed that each successive layer is earlier than the one above it. But to compare the artifacts from this site with those from the scores of other sites within a twenty-five kilometer radius requires a relative seriation (Figure 2.7).

Another common application of relative seriation occurs when many *surface collections* of artifacts have been made. The only systematic way to compare the collections from site to site and infer their relative periods of occupation is with a statistical relative seriation.

One of the great cottage industries of archaeology is to devise mathematical, computerized improvements on the graphical seriation technique illustrated in Figure 2.7 (Drennan 1976; LeBlanc 1975; Marquardt 1979), and these sometimes add to the precision with which relative seriations can be employed. Useful relative seriations usually require massive quantities of data from artifacts of a highly decorated nature (like pottery) from a relatively small area, and they tend to be least precise when extended to relatively undecorated objects like early stone tools. Not all variability we think of as stylistic does in fact conform to the requirements of stylistic elements for a relative seriation, which are, chiefly, that the style be *unimodally distributed* through time and space. That is to say, any "style" that has two different peaks or "modes" of popularity (like Hula Hoops, which had peaks in the 1950s and 1970s), or is discontinuously distributed across space, is not really a "style" as far as relative seriations are concerned. Elements must be found that meet the requirements of the seriation method.

Analyzing Artifacts

A fundamental procedure of science, or any form of analysis, is classification. To understand how the world operates, we have to break it up into groups of similar things and discover the relationships between these groups. Modern chemistry or physics, for example, would be inconceivable were it not for classes such as electrons, atoms, and molecules and the laws of thermodynamics. In the same way, evolutionary

Cochuma
incised

Cochuma
black–on–white

Cochuma
white–on–red

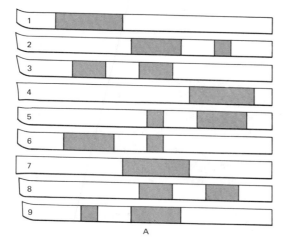

A

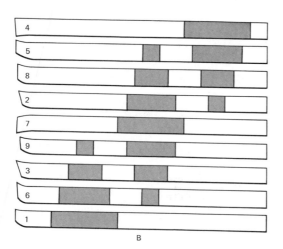

B

2.7   Relative seriation of nine archaeological sites on the basis of three pottery styles from the American Southwest. The percentage that each pottery style represents of the total pottery found at each site is represented by the width of the colored area on the strip of paper. Since most styles tend gradually to grow in popularity and then slowly die out, a seriation can be produced by arranging the paper strips in such a way that the three pottery styles have this "battleship shape" distribution through time. The inferred order of the nine sites is shown in b. Mathematical models and computer programs have been developed to sort scores of sites and pottery styles into these kinds of graphs. Such mathematical aids are often needed, because the number of posible orderings of 9 sites is 9!, or 362,880.

41

biology is possible only because of concepts of chromosomes, cells, and species and the principles of population genetics.

These notions about classification and analysis are quite straightforward and simple, but when we consider the kinds of data that archaeologists work with, we find that archaeological classifications and analyses have differed somewhat from those of other disciplines. The archaeologists' broken pottery, house foundations, and stone tools have not been organized in classifications in the same ways the atom and the cell have. A potassium atom is exactly the same thing to a Japanese chemist and an American chemist; but when a French archaeologist describes stone tools from southern France as "handaxes," the artifacts he is describing differ in many respects from North Chinese "handaxes" as described by a Chinese archaeologist.

Part of the difference between atoms and handaxes in this respect is of course a matter of perspectives: every potassium atom, like every artifact, is unique in its location in time and space, and only by the mental process of classification can we find their common structure and consider them all representatives of a single class. But as we shall see, archaeological classifications have generally been constructed with much more limited purposes in mind than have the units of the natural sciences.

One of the most common classifications in archaeology has been in terms of *functional types*. An example of this is Mary Leakey's categorization of the 1.75-million-year-old tools from Olduvai Gorge as "cleavers," "scrapers," and "handaxes." Such a classificatory system is based in part on ideas about how our earliest ancestors actually *used* these tools. Obviously, imagination plays a role in creating functional types, particularly when archaeologists are dealing with very old remains left by people very unlike known or existing cultures.

Another widely used archaeological classificatory approach employs *chronological types*. Chronological (or "historical") types are artifacts whose combination of attributes is known to be limited to particular time periods. We have already noted that stylistic elements such as pottery styles and house architecture have limited distribution in time, and by sorting artifacts into groups based on their similarity of stylistic elements we can often devise relative chronologies of archaeological remains.

While depending on chronological functional types, archaeologists continue to search for more powerful systems of arrangement. There is much to be said for the idea that there are no "real" atoms, stars, foxes, or potsherds: these are only convenient ways for us to break up the world into understandable parts, and it is theory—whether Newtonian,

Darwinian, or Marxian—that tells us how most effectively to break up the world for analysis. If archaeologists ever hope to treat cultural processes, they will need all the classificatory systems they now use as well as the classificatory units required by more powerful cultural theory.

Most current archaeological classifications and typologies are inward-looking, descriptive, and remind one of Antony trying to describe a crocodile to Lepidus in Shakespeare's *Antony and Cleopatra:*

> LEP. What manner o' thing is your crocodile?
> ANT. It is shaped, sir, like itself; and it is as broad as it hath breadth; it is just so high as it is, and moves with its own organs: it lives by that which nourisheth it; and, the elements once out of it, it transmigrates.
> LEP. What colour is it of?
> ANT. Of its own colour too.
> LEP. 'Tis a strange serpent.
> ANT. 'Tis so. And the tears of it are wet.
> CAES. Will this description satisfy him?

THE PRACTICE OF ARCHAEOLOGY

Having reviewed in this chapter the mechanics of archaeology, it is appropriate to consider in somewhat narrower focus the practice of the discipline. No amount of description can substitute for the actual experiences, but the following is an attempt to answer some of the more common questions about an archaeologist's life.

When trapped in the seat of an airplane or up against the wall at a party, archaeologists who reveal their occupation are usually confronted with the following sequence of statements and questions: "I've always been interested in archaeology," "How do you know where to dig?" "Where do you get the money to do excavations?" "It must be marvelously exciting to be an archaeologist!"

First, a few facts. Most of the archaeologists practicing in the United States have doctoral degrees, the dubious prize of an average of six years of schooling beyond the bachelor's degree. "Those who can, do; those who can't, teach" does not apply to archaeology, where almost every major professional holds a teaching position. In the early 1980s there is an acute job shortage, so the competition for university teaching jobs is ferocious.

As an example of archaeological field work, I offer the Fayyum Archaeological Project, which I co-directed in Egypt in 1981. I offer this not because of any exceptional merit, but because in some ways the fieldwork was typical of that of many archaeological projects.

The moving force behind the Fayyum Archaeological Project, which was wholly conducted in Egypt, was in fact the Iranian Revolution. I worked in Iran for some years excavating and surveying archaeological sites and was due to resume work there in 1979, on a day almost exactly between the Shah's departure from Iran and the first seizure of the American embassy. Through a series of events too baroque to recount here, I had the good fortune to be able to go instead to Egypt, where in 1980 I directed a small archaeological project.

I had long been interested in the origins of agricultural economies, and I was much impressed by some new ideas about agricultural origins in Egypt (see chapter 6). So while in Cairo, I started searching a map of Egypt for a place in which to investigate the origins of Egyptian agriculture.

Many of the most important sites in Egypt have been excavated for decades and are already within the concession of another archaeologist; one cannot just decide to excavate this or that site. I wanted an area that was currently unworked yet would have important archaeological remains. Professor Michael Hoffman of the University of South Carolina suggested we look at unsurveyed parts of the Fayyum Depression (see Figure 9.1), where years of work had shown evidence of early agriculture but which was currently not being explored.

Archaeological projects in Egypt usually have on their staffs an Egyptologist—someone who reads ancient Egyptian writing—and I was fortunate enough to recruit a recent graduate from the Sorbonne, Dr. Mary Ellen Lane, as co-director and project bon vivant. With a representative of the Egyptian Antiquities Organization, we made several trips into the deserts of the southern Fayyum without finding much except a restaurant where you could get deathly ill for only ninety piastres.

In the 1920s, the British archaeologist Gertrude Caton-Thompson had driven around the southern edge of the Fayyum Lake, noting here and there scatters of Neolithic-style stone tools. One day, driving in an area near where she had surveyed, we saw a large pile of bones. On inspection it proved to be the remains of a hippopotamus, and we were delighted to see that near it were stone projectile points ("arrowheads") of a Neolithic type. Within a few hours of survey, it was evident that we had found a dense scatter of hearths, pottery, stone tools, and animal bones, and the styles of artifacts suggested a date of about 4500 B.C.

Back in Cairo, our readings convinced us that what we had was significant, and that we should try for our first field season in the summer of 1981—a year later. We needed only three more things: $200,000, a staff of at least twenty trained archaeologists, and permission to dig from the Egyptian government.

Famed felon Willie Sutton, when asked why he robbed banks, replied, "Because that's where the money is!" Archaeologists, too, must go where the money is, and in this era it is mainly to the government. After months of writing proposals, we received $25,000 from the United States National Science Foundation and $200,000 from the United States Agency for International Development. We then recruited our staff of specialists in ancient plant remains, animal bones, and geology as well as a professor from the University of Rome, eight graduate students, and various others—all of them transported and housed in Egypt at project cost.

On June 4, 1981, we left Cairo for the four-hour drive to the Fayyum. We lived that summer and autumn in a large gray house that looked across a green palm grove and the blue of the Fayyum Lake to the white limestone cliff of the Jebel Qatrani. Our villa—a vacation home of a wealthy Cairo family—was a lovely International Style building in the midst of mud-hut villages. It had every convenience but three: water, electricity, and a sewage system.

With assistance of the local authorities, we arranged for water deliveries. The remoteness of the area meant that our diet was almost wholly composed of tuna fish, a vile processed cheese, rice, tomatoes, and several thousand chickens, who were executed on our kitchen steps and then converted into indescribable meals. "Fire-cracked veal" was an occasional holiday treat.

The morbidity rates—physical and psychological—on archaeological projects are usually high, especially when, as in our case, water for cleaning was scarce and our cook did not believe in the germ theory of disease. Laboratory tests over the season totaled up five different strains of parasitical and bacterial infections among our crew, and we lost many days to illness. There was also one emergency appendectomy (mine), performed in Cairo after a thought-provoking four-hour truck ride from the desert.

When we began our fieldwork, we geared most of our efforts to reconstructing as precisely as possible the ways of life of the people who had lived in the Fayyum in the Qarunian period (ca. 6500 B.C.), just before the appearance of domesticated plants and animals in this region, and in the succeeding Fayyum A period (ca. 5000 B.C.), when the first agriculturalists appeared here. Ultimately we hoped to reconstruct the complete pattern of human settlement in the Fayyum between 7000 B.C. and A.D. 1500, and we wished to explain the changes in these settlement patterns over this long period.

We began by making a topological map of the area we intended to work in. We then devised a sampling program and collected every artifact in the sampling units defined, that is, in the hundreds of 5 x 5 meter squares in our study area. The average temperature during much of this work was over 40°C (104°F), and by midday the stone tools were often so hot that one could not handle them for long. Afternoons were spent sorting, drawing, and photographing artifacts, drinking warm water, and drawing each other's attention to the heat. In September we began excavations, mainly of the hearths and pits that were the dominant feature of both the Qarunian and Fayyum A occupations. In most we found charred animal bones, some carbonized plant remains, and other debris.

To evaluate our "model" of how agriculture appeared in the Fayyum and why, we had to collect sufficient evidence to make statistical arguments about certain kinds of conditions and events in Fayyum prehistory. The details of these arguments are not relevant here, but it should be stressed that as in most archaeological projects, not all the information we had hoped would be there was actually found. But most of it was, and the analysis of this information will continue for at least another year. Hundreds of thousands of lines of numbers representing our measurements of artifacts, topographic elevations, animal bone types, and so on must be entered into computer files and crunched through statistical analyses.

In Cairo, after the season was over, we delivered the artifacts to the Egyptian Museum and made preparations to leave. It is traditional, after the privations of the field, to treat oneself to some rest and relaxation, and some project members agonized between such choices as the nude beach at the Club Med on the Red Sea or the twelve restaurants within 250 meters of Rome's Piazza Cavour. Most just went home and slept.

3

The Origins of Culture

Man is an exception, whatever else he is. If it is
not true that a divine being fell, then we can only
say that one of the animals went entirely off its
head.

G. K. Chesterton

One of the most memorable scenes in recent cinema occurs in *2001: A Space Odyssey,* where African ape men of several million years ago scamper frantically around a huge black monolith, which later reappears in a twenty-first-century excavation on the moon. Stanley Kubrick's film vision of Arthur Clarke's story cleverly presents the monolith as a simple black stone, allowing the viewer to see it as a symbol of the Hand of God, human destiny, extraterrestrial powers, or anything else (neither Clarke nor Kubrick was prepared to say what the monolith "meant"). Although the anthropological quest for an understanding of human origins has a lot less mythic power than *2001,* it asks the same questions: Where did we come from, and why?

We may be, as a Greek long ago suggested, the progeny of spores blown here millions of years ago through the reaches of space; we may be the result of divine intervention in biological processes; we may even be self-deluding creatures whose origins are in galactic processes of which we have not the slightest intimation. But the scientific point of view is that before we accept any of these possibilities, we must try to account for our origins in more commonplace factors.

To begin with, what are we trying to explain when we speak of the origins of culture? It is difficult to reduce mankind to this or that constellation of attributes and say that one has captured the essence of being human. For the Roman Catholic theologian, for example, the few thousand protoplasmic cells of an aborted human fetus are human in the only way that really matters, being invested with an immortal soul. But from an anthropological point of view, what distinguishes us from other life forms and constitutes the focal point for attempts to understand ourselves through the study of our past?

A traditional view is that humans are unique in their ability to manipulate symbols and that the evolution of this ability underlies all human achievements. As Leslie White (1949) argues, chimpanzees are clever animals who can be made to use plastic counters, computers, and sign languages to express simple emotions and primitive wants, but they are fundamentally different from ourselves in that they can never understand something like "holy water" or the casting of a vote. White also notes that no primates except humans pass any significant new knowledge from generation to generation.

White's ideas are widely disputed, but they have a certain plausibility. Human virtuosity in manipulating symbols seems of a wholly different order from the simple perceptual worlds of other life forms. This is most vividly illustrated, perhaps, by human aesthetic capacities. It is unlikely that even chimpanzees can listen with great emotion to a Bach cantata or feel the vibrancy of a Van Gogh landscape.

But paleontologically and archaeologically we have to concentrate on *things* to study the origins of symbolic capacities. For the early period of human evolution, this mainly means looking at changing morphology of hominid skulls and at stone tools and other objects that our ancestors used to convert energy to their own purposes. The search for these kinds of evidences is only about a century old.

Both Darwin's ideas about the biological evolution of the human species and the discovery of stone tools in association with the bones of extinct animals in extremely ancient geological strata convinced many scholars of the great antiquity of the human race. Nevertheless, as long as no bones were found that could be attributed to a human ancestor intermediate between ourselves and other primates in physical form, it was still possible for many to cling to the idea that humans were an exception: that we were an extremely old species, older than had previously been suspected, but that we had not evolved as other species had.

Those who had studied Darwin and Lyell, however, and who were aware of the archaeological evidence of early humans in Europe knew it was just a matter of time before the first fossil "missing link" was found. The great French scholar Boucher de Perthes, grown old and tired of waiting, offered a 200-franc reward to the discoverer of the first

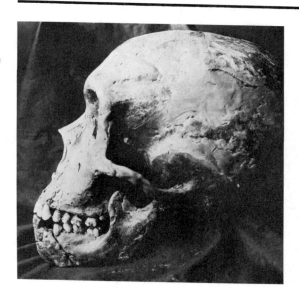

3.1 A reconstruction of a Neanderthal cranium—an early, disputed clue about our ancestry.

"antediluvian" man in France. His enterprising workers were soon "finding" human remains in many places—all put there, of course, by themselves in hopes of collecting the money.

Ironically, the first premodern hominids had already been discovered some years before, although they were not found in association with stone tools and extinct animals as de Perthes had hoped. In 1848 work at a quarry on Gibraltar had revealed a skull whose receding chin, heavy brow ridges, and thick bones indicated a being who, if not a "missing link," was certainly not a type of human still living anywhere. Eight years after this find, another discovery was made that ultimately was to corroborate the significance of the Gibraltar fossil.

This was a skullcap (Figure 3.1) and some limb bones found in 1856 in a cave in the Neander Valley near Dusseldorf, Germany, and although these remains were dismissed by the great German anatomist Rudolf Virchow as those of a deformed human, Johann Karl Fuhlrott, the discoverer of this first "Neanderthal," argued from the beginning that the remains were of an early form of human. But Virchow's opinion, and those of others who variously labeled it an ancient Celt, a victim of rickets, an idiot, or a Cossack, conspired to deny these bones their proper significance for many years. One French savant even suggested that the huge brow ridges of the Neanderthal came about because his deformed arm caused him such pain that he continually furrowed his brow, and the expression became ossified.

In 1886 two partial skeletons similar to the Neanderthal specimen were recovered in a cave in Spy, Belgium, in direct association with stone tools and the bones of rhinoceroses, mammoths, and other animal species known to have been long extinct. Although Virchow also refused to accept these as ancient men, the tide of opinion had turned and scientists everywhere were soon looking eagerly for additional specimens of early hominids.

One such individual was a young Dutch physician, Eugene Dubois, who was so convinced the ancestral homeland of our species was Southeast Asia that he arranged to have himself transferred to an army post in the Dutch East Indies so that he could search for fossils.

Dubois spent years wandering the wilds of Sumatra without finding much of interest, and only when he arranged a transfer to Java did he make his great discovery. In 1890 he unearthed a fragment of a lower jaw, and over the next few years he recovered a skullcap and a femur (thighbone). Comparative studies and measurements of cranial capacity and other criteria soon demonstrated that his finds represented an individual at an evolutionary stage somewhere between nonhuman primates and modern humans, and he eagerly accepted his find as the "missing link."

For the next thirty years, controversy raged over Dubois's find, some authorities again claiming it to be a deformed freak, others identifying it as a gigantic form of chimpanzee with no relation to human ancestry, and still others recognizing it as an early form of our genus and a direct ancestor of modern humans. Dubois's fossil had an approximate brain volume of 1,040 cc, about a third less than modern people have. This suggested to its discoverer that if this animal were in fact a human ancestor, it was an ancestor considerably different from ourselves and from "Neanderthal man" (whose cranial capacity was slightly larger than ours).

In 1906 the German anatomist Gustav Schwalbe proposed three successive stages of hominid evolution: *pithecanthropine* (represented by Dubois's fossils), *Neanderthal*, and *modern*. It was apparent, however, that if this were the correct succession of hominid forms, there would have to be many intermediate types not yet found.

The recognition of a presumed fourth and earliest stage of hominid evolution did not come until the 1920s, when Raymond Dart, a South African anatomist, discovered a nearly complete skull of a very strange-looking child encased in stone quarried from a mine some 300 kilometers from Johannesburg, at the Taung site. The skull indicated a brain volume much less than that of an individual of similar age of either pithecanthropine, Neanderthal, or modern type, and the teeth and other physical characteristics convinced Dart he had found mankind's earliest, most primitive ancestor, which he labeled *Australopithecus africanus* ("Southern ape of Africa"). Dart's conclusions were discounted by some of the most influential scientists in Europe, mainly because it is generally difficult to interpret crania from extremely young primates and also, perhaps, because Dart had little standing in the rigidly hierarchical academic communities at Oxford and Cambridge. But while Dart's claims were being challenged, another important find was made, this time in northeastern China, 60 kilometers from Peking at a mining installation called Choukoutien.

Fossilized bones from the area had been used for centuries as aphrodisiacs, but a somewhat more scientific interest was stimulated in 1921 when a single human-looking tooth was given to the English anatomist Henry Black. He recognized the tooth as belonging to an ancient form of hominid, and as a consequence excavations at Choukoutien were begun. Altogether, the remains of about forty individuals were found, including many skull fragments, and it was obvious that these individuals were similar in brain size, facial structure, and other characteristics to the hominid found by Dubois on Java. This supported Schwalbe's proposed pithecanthropine stage, and fossils of this type were accorded the name *Sinanthropus* or *Homo erectus* ("erect man").

Thus, by the 1930s four categories of early hominids had been recognized by at least some of the scientific community: *australopithecines, Homo erectus, Neanderthals,* and modern humans. Since that time the arguments have focused not on whether mankind evolved from some sort of nonhuman ancestor, but on what these various ancestral forms were, how they are related taxonomically, and what evolutionary mechanisms were at the base of this development.

The Ecological Context of Cultural Origins

> In the bleak mid-winter
>   Frosty wind made moan
> Earth stood hard as iron,
>   Water like a stone.
> Snow has fallen, snow on snow,
>   Snow on snow,
> In the bleak mid-winter
>   Long ago.
>
> Christina Rossetti

One of the central facts of human physical and cultural evolution is that the appearance and first 3 million years of our genus coincides with the *Pleistocene* ("most recent") geological period, when much of the world was, on the average, cooler than it is today. And before attempting to analyze the factors that shaped our evolution, we must have some understanding of the Pleistocene environments in which this evolution occurred.

The names that have been given to the many subdivisions of the past are often redated and redefined. The "Pleistocene' refers to the several million years before about 10,000 years ago. Average worldwide temperatures have fluctuated much more rapidly in the last 14 million years than ever before, and a world as warm as our own has been a rarity during the last 2.5 million years. There have been, however, occasional *interglacials*—periods usually of about 10,000 years when temperatures rose almost to present-day levels. Even during the main glacial periods, there were *interstadials,* short warming phases when the temperature rose but did not reach today's level. Archaeologists use the term "Holocene" to refer to the last 10,000 years, but only time will tell if our age is a short interglacial or a long term warming trend.

During the glacial periods themselves, ice sheets spread from the poles and from higher elevations to cover much of the higher latitudes. So much of the seas were locked in ice during the coldest periods that the sea level dropped up to forty meters, exposing coastal areas that are now covered with water. Land bridges formed between North America and Asia, Europe and Britain, and Southeast Asia and what are now offshore islands. This facilitated the spread of peoples throughout the world long before the last glacial period ended.

During glacial periods many areas that are now quite temperate were either under ice or in permafrost conditions. Other areas, like parts of China, were much drier than they are today. Elsewhere, as in North America, runoff from glaciers opened up a lush lake-forest environment. Unfortunately, Pleistocene ice sheets have ground to powder many critical archaeological sites, and the rising seas of the postglacial periods have covered thousands of others.

Why the ice ages began is a question for geologists, not archaeologists, but it seems to have been one or a combination of factors such as changes in the earth's orbit, fluctuations in solar radiation, mountain-building activity, or changes in the earth's atmosphere (Bowen 1978; Flint 1971).

The Evidence of the Evolution of Culture

There are several lines of evidence we can follow in tracing our ancestors' cultural and physical evolution: (1) paleontology, the study of ancient forms of animal life, including the ancestors of mankind; (2) the study of contemporary or recent hunting and gathering peoples, whom we assume to be living in environments and patterns similar to those of our Paleolithic ancestors; (3) the study of contemporary nonhuman primates, whose behavior patterns may give us clues to the behavior of our own ancestors; and (4) the analysis of the archaeological record—the stones and bones and other tools used by our ancestors.

All these lines of evidence should eventually be combined to produce "models of cultural origins"—complex hypotheses about the factors that combined to change our ancestors from unremarkable primates to human beings. We should then be able to test these models against the archaeological and paleontological record and—eventually—have something of a compelling explanation of our past.

But, in fact, we currently have only a little of the required data for constructing and testing such models, and we are only beginning to formulate the ecological and cultural principles that will form the structure of these models.

So our review here of the major lines of evidence about cultural origins is necessarily somewhat tentative and incomplete.

PALEONTOLOGY AND CULTURAL ORIGINS

Animal and plant life on this planet go back billions of years before the first humans appeared. Vertebrates—animals with internal skeletons—appeared only about 600 million years ago, marking a major evolutionary advance. Dinosaurs appeared perhaps as early as 200 million years ago and were widespread until the age of mammals, which began perhaps 100 million years ago. Since that time mammals, including ourselves, have radiated into most parts of the world (see Table 3.1).

Taken as an overall sequence, is there any trend in the evolution of animal life on this planet that would help us understand the appearance of culture and our own physical type?

One possible answer to this question is suggested by the comparison of the ratio of brain size to body size in successive animal forms during the many millions of years before the first culture-bearing animals

TABLE 3.1   Geologic Time Scale and Recent Life History of the Earth

Era	Period	Epoch	Began millions of years ago	Duration in millions of years	Some important events in life of the times
Cenozoic	Quaternary	Recent	.01	.01	Modern genera of animals with man dominant.
		Pleistocene	3(2.5–3.0)	3	Early men and many giant mammals now extinct.
	Tertiary	Pliocene	10	7	Anthropoid radiation and culmination of mammalian specialization.
		Miocene	25	15	
		Oligocene	40	15	Expansion and modernization of mammals.
		Eocene	60	20	
		Paleocene	70(±2)	10	
Mesozoic	Cretaceous		135	65	Dinosaurs dominant to end; both marsupial and placental mammals appear; first flowering plants appear and radiate rapidly.
	Jurassic		180	45	Dominance of dinosaurs; first mammals and birds; insects abundant, including social forms.
	Triassic		225	45	First dinosaurs and mammal-like reptiles with culmination of laborinthodont amphibians.

appeared. The anatomist Harry Jerison has devised an *encephalization index* by dividing the total brain volume of each animal by the two-thirds power of its body size (the exponent was used because of the geometric relationship between surface area and volume in three-dimensional objects). This simple index thus represents a scaled ratio of brain volume to overall size.

Jerison's results (Figure 3.2) give us an answer of sorts to our questions. The *increase* in human brain size—from 500 to 1,450 cc in only a few million years—has been extraordinarily rapid, but overall, we seem to be a continuation of a process that began at least 600 million years ago, a process involving long-term natural selection in some animal forms for increased brain-to-body ratios, and, presumably, mental capacity.

	Began millions of years ago	Duration in millions of years	Some important events in life of the times
	270	45	Radiating primitive reptiles displace amphibians as dominant group; glaciation widespread.
	350	80	Amphibians dominant in luxurious coal forests; first reptiles and trees.
	400	50	Dominance of fishes; first amphibians.
Silurian	440	40	Sea scorpions and primitive fish; invasion of land by plants and arthropods.
Ordovician	500	60	First vertebrates, the jawless fish; invertebrates dominate the seas.
Cambrian	600(±20)	100	All invertebrate phyla appear and algae diversify.
Not well established	Back to earth origins 4.5+ billion years ago?		First known fossils as early as 3.3 billion years ago. A few soft multicellular invertebrates in latest phases.

(left margin labels: Paleo; Pre-cambrian)

SOURCE J. B. Birdsell. 1972. Human Evolution. Chicago: Rand McNally.

In many fictional treatments of the future, people are portrayed with enormous heads and correspondingly impoverished physiques. Is this likely, given Jerison's data? Human brain size in fact seems to have decreased slightly since a high point of about 1,550 cc in the average Neanderthal living in western Europe 60,000 years ago, but 60,000 years is insignificant in the span of animal life on our planet, and encephalization ratios may well continue to increase—or decrease—during the next millions of years. We too, no doubt, are in a sense "missing links" in the ancient evolutionary experiment that is the history of animal life on this planet.

Jerison's data do not mean that we can equate simple brain volume with intelligence. Certainly a gross correlation exists between the two, but in the human species at least, increases in what we may vaguely label "intelligence" were probably achieved by internal restructuring of the brain as well as by overall size increases. Obviously, there is a biological limit to the amount of body energy that can be invested in gross amount of brain tissue while still allowing successful live birth and normal functioning in the other biological requisites of animal life.

Other paleontological evidence about our origins can be found in the general history of the primates. One of the most difficult things for the people of the nineteenth century to accept was the idea that as a species we are the progeny of nonhuman and extinct primates. Thus it is perhaps fortunate that the study of our evolution had not progressed to the point where our ultimate primate ancestor was recognized—even the educated evolutionist of the 1860s might have balked at the idea that we are the descendants of a small, pink-nosed, libidinous, insect-eating animal, whose modern form, the shrew, is on a pound-for-pound basis among the most ferociously effective predators known (Figure 3.3).

Our evolution from these tree shrews of 60 million years ago to the first tool-using, culture-bearing animal of perhaps 3 million years ago is a muddled affair in which we have too few specimens.

Paleontologists have focused on the teeth, skull shape and size, and posture of early primates to try to ascertain their relation to ourselves. The supposition is that it was a change in feeding habits or habitat

3.2   Brain size plotted against body size for some 200 species of living vertebrates that represent an evolutionary sequence through time. The points connected by lines represent the extreme variations of measurements reported for *Homo sapiens sapiens*.

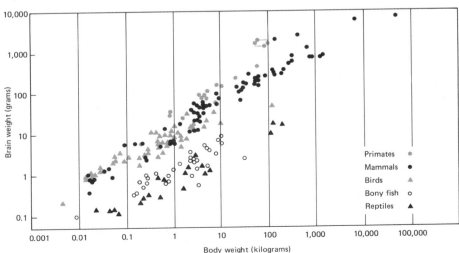

3.3 This species of Southeast Asia tree shrew resembles closely the small insectivorous ratlike animals believed to be ancestral to all primates, including ourselves.

that sparked the initial transition to mankind. To make a human out of early primates, the legs had to be lengthened greatly in relation to body size, the hip and knee joints had to be repositioned to allow bipedalism, and the spine had to develop an S-shaped curvature to cushion the brain against the shocks of bipedal locomotion. The face, jaw, and teeth had to be changed from the straight-row, prominent canines-and-incisors configuration of early primates to the curved human dental arch with reduced canines and incisors, and adapted to grinding rather than puncturing. Most of all, the brain had to be greatly expanded and probably changed dramatically in internal structure.

Bits and pieces of various animals have been placed into our family tree as far back as 20 million years ago (Figure 3.4), but the first known animal that evokes a definite sense of kinship is *Ramapithecus*, fragments of whom have been found from China to East Africa and into southern Europe in geological strata dating to about 10 to 12 million years ago. We don't know much about *Ramapithecus*, but his bones and their distribution suggest an omnivorous primate who spent a lot of time in trees and looked something like a chimpanzee.

Australopithecus and Early *Homo*

The crucial period in the evolution of culture was between 5 million years ago, when the first australopithecines appeared, and a million years ago, by which time all (or almost all) the world's hominids belonged to a single general type, *Homo erectus,* a hominid who on the basis of physical form, tool use, and patterns of social organization must be classed as our own direct ancestor.

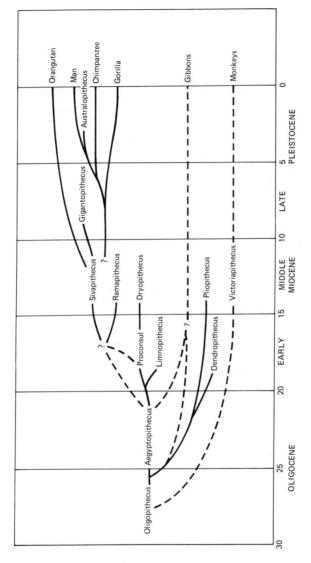

3.4 A highly simplified scheme showing the hypothetical genetic relationships of our probable ancestors.

Fragments of several hundred hominids have been found and dated to before a million years ago, and while much progress has been made in interpreting them, severe problems remain. It has been well and truly said that human paleontology shares with theology and extraterrestrial biology the peculiar trait that there are many more practitioners than objects of study (Pilbeam and Gould 1974). This situation has given rise to many conflicting hypotheses.

A book on world prehistory, such as this, is no place to try to sort out the problems of physical anthropology that attend all these early fossils, except insofar as they relate to the question of cultural origins. Thus, of the hundreds of hominid fragments that date to between 4.0 and 1.0 million years ago, I present here only a few summary points.

Much of the story of cultural origins may have been "over" by 3.7 million years ago. Mary Leakey found human footprints of this age at Laetolil, Kenya, indicating that our ancestors already walked upright—and there is a sort of destiny in bipedalism. The hands are free to manipulate tools; the field of vision gives a slice of time and distance that rewards planning; and the arrangement of the limbs and cranium seems to require only additional brain tissue to "convert" a primate into something human.

But upright posture in the absence of tools—and we have no stone tools until about a million years *after* the Laetolil footprints—means something else. It means that an animal roughly of our body shape (but about two-thirds our size) and with our approximate powers of vision, smell, locomotion, etc., could compete in a world alive with awesome predators. Without speed, claws, significant teeth, night vision, or protective coloration, these primates of 3.7 million years ago flourished, and there is some reason to suspect that they could do so because they already possessed the critical elements of cultural behavior: intelligence, protective human family structures, and tool use (perhaps like that of chimpanzees, who use sticks and unmodified stones).

If our ancestors of this era did indeed have these quasi-human capacities, then our answer to the question of why culture appeared may be in undetectable climate changes that selected for bipedalism and life in savanna environments, along with the teleological assumption that given the way the world is, placing a primate in certain kinds of environments will produce bipedalism.

If we look for hominid ancestors of those who left their tracks at Laetolil, we have only a few fragmentary candidates. David Pilbeam's discovery in 1984 of parts of a hominid who lived well before 6 million years ago may be the earliest known representative of the "basal australopithecine stock."

Other bits of early australopithecines have come from Lothagam (about 5.5 million years) and Kanapoi (about 4.0 million years) in East

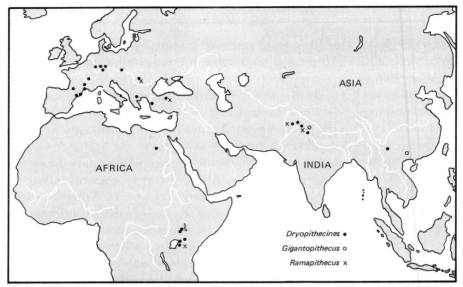

3.5 Distribution of some fossil finds of great apes of the Oligocene, Miocene, and later periods. The Dryopithecines (●) flourished for more than 25 million years and gave rise to the great ape *Gigantopithecus* (○) and to *Ramapithecus* (×), a probable hominid and human ancestor.

Africa, but it is in the Hadar region of Ethiopia that we find the most substantial early remains. This is "Lucy," the hominid subject of a popular book by Donald Johanson and Maitland Edey (1981). About 3.0 million years ago, Lucy strode upright through the river valleys of Ethiopia, as part of a group of primates who were around 1.2 to 1.5 meters tall, but who varied greatly in size and morphological characteristics. If Lucy and her kinfolk made stone tools, these implements have yet to be found.

Without tools, we cannot really know much about Lucy and her group—the "First Family" to use Johanson's label. By counting up the number of different bones, we can tell that there were at least thirteen people in Lucy's group, four of them children. A few bits of geological evidence and the absence of other animal bones near the hominids raise the possibility that the First Family was trapped in a ravine by a flash flood, but there is just no way to tell.

Even if conclusive evidence is eventually discovered that most of the important cultural behaviors were present by 3 to 4 million years ago—beyond the reach, in other words, of archaeology—there would still be many interesting aspects of the period between 1 and 3 million years ago, for it was then that the first elaborate tools were invented and the range of our ancestors was extended over much of the Old World.

The hundreds of fossils dating to this period have been sorted into many different schemes. Physical anthropologists are a naturally contentious lot, and they disagree heatedly about the interpretation and taxonomic status of almost every early hominid. Some issues in these debates relate directly to our hypotheses about the origins of culture, such as: (1) what are the phylogenetic (evolutionary) relationships of the early hominid fossils to each other and to *Homo sapiens sapiens,* and (2) which of these hominids made the tools at Olduvai Gorge, Koobi Fora, and the other very early sites? This first question arises because of the great variation in size and shape of some physical features of these early hominids. There is marked diversity among living humans, too, of course, particularly in height, cranial volume, skin color, musculature, and other features. But if we consider the hominids of between about 3 and 1 million years ago, there seems to be more relative variation in tooth size and shape, cranial volume and shape, overall height, and other factors than is present among ourselves. And, significantly, these types of variation involve physical structures that seem intimately tied to the diet and activities of these animals, indicating perhaps very real differences and changes in their basic ecological adaptations.

Some scholars think that none of the australopithecines made tools or were truly culture-bearing animals. They prefer instead to classify some of these fossils as early *Homo* and to place *Homo* on our line,

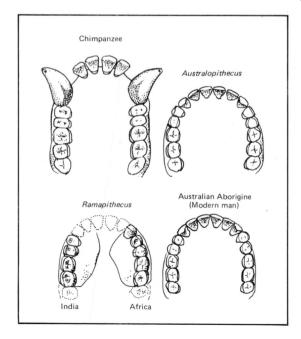

3.6   Teeth preserve best of all body parts and are useful indicators of the diet and adaptation of primates.

separate from that of the australopithecines. Others think that at least some of the australopithecines made tools and that no such animal as an early *Homo* existed before the australopithecines.

In fact, all that really seems clear at this point is that from 3 to 1 million years ago, bipedal primates of about 1.25 to 1.75 meters height roamed the grasslands and forests of Africa, the Middle East, and probably as far east as China. At least some of these animals made tools.

Many archaeologists who saw the recent film *Quest for Fire* had a good time but faulted the movie on two points: about five different genera (or at least species) of humans were depicted as living at the same time, and most of them spent their lives trying to drive each other into extinction—except for one Neanderthalish man and an almost ultramodern looking woman, whose miscegenation was fertile across species, perhaps generic, lines. The majority position in anthropology these days is that there were at most two or three different species of human beings at any one time and that, if studies of hunters and gatherers and of animal ecology (Swedlund 1974) are any guide, continuous battles to extinction between rival human species just never happened.

For one thing, the organization of people into family units and their use of tools seem to have changed their selective environments so that the rate of speciation was much less than for other animals. Thus, for over 100,000 years there has only been one genus of human being, *Homo sapiens,* despite the fact that people lived in every part of the world, in a diversity of environments that no other animal species has been able to adapt to. We must assume, then, that already by several million years ago, when people first started using stone tools, the biological diversity of hominids was beginning to be simplified toward a single species (Brace 1979).

But to know how this "simplification" was accomplished, and which variants of human beings were tool users and which (if any) were not, we will need much larger fossil samples and much more powerful theoretical models of early hominid behavior. In the meantime, Figure 3.8 illustrates some of the more popular views of the taxonomy and phylogeny of human evolution. (The reader can postpone memorizing these in the sure and certain knowledge that they will all be changed and expanded in the future.)

The Mode and Tempo of Evolution

Even if we fight through all these issues of taxonomy and eventually reach a consensus, we will be left with a more important and profound

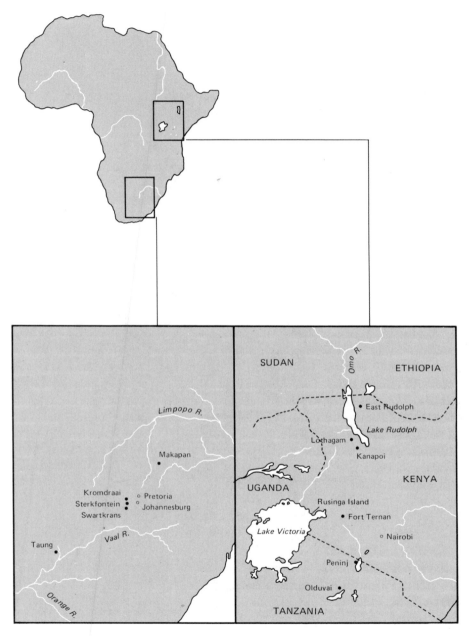

3.7   Distribution of some important early hominid sites in East and Southern
Africa.

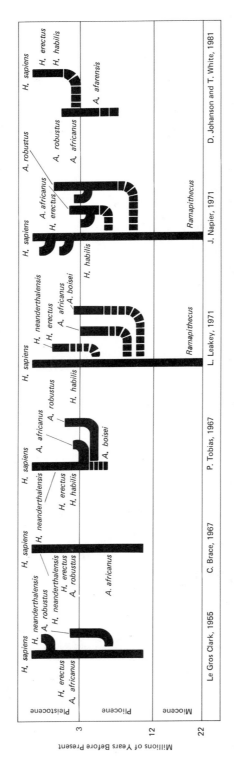

3.8 **Hypothetical ancestral relations of various human ancestors. The divisions may represent errors based on normal variability in populations for which we have small samples.**

64

question—the nature of the *mode* and *tempo of* human physical and cultural evolution. The question is this: Does evolution in such things as human cranial capacity, technological efficiency, administrative centralization, urbanization, and so forth proceed gradually, with approximately the same rate of change, or are there long periods of stability punctuated by periods of rapid change? As Robert McC. Adams phrased it in the context of early states (1966), does the simile of a "ramp" or of a series of "steps" best describe our evolutionary history?

This simple question involves some fairly murky political issues (we shall explore some of them in chapter 7). Here, in the context of early hominid studies, it is sufficient to say that some people think the Marxian concept of dialectical development means that even in such matters as the physical changes from the australopithecines to ourselves, we should look for a developmental pattern showing long periods of stability punctuated by periods in which physical characteristics changed relatively rapidly. Thus, Gould and Eldredge (1977) say that "no gradualism has been detected within any hominid taxon." But J. E. Cronin and others (1981) who have analyzed the measurements on fossil hominids from 4.0 million years ago to ourselves found no evidence of "stasis" or "punctuation," and believe that the record of human evolution is best seen as an example of gradual change with some periods of varying rates of evolution. Figure 3.9 indicates their reconstructed pattern of changes in cranial capacity and mean body weight, and they extend their analysis to include measurements of forty-four morphological traits. To have any kind of conclusive test of these competing ideas, we need at least a thousand more early hominids, at least some of which fall in the time "gaps" for which we now have no information.

CONTEMPORARY HUNTERS AND GATHERERS

Paleontological evidence offers us a framework of evidence about cultural origins, but to build up some sort of picture of *how* and *why* we came to have this evolutionary ancestry, we have to look for evolutionary mechanisms—conditions and events that produced cultural behavior. One source for such mechanisms is hunter-gatherer ethnography.

The expansion of industrialization has been such that although anthropologists do not really outnumber living hunters and gatherers, it is a certainty they soon will. People who get most of their resources from hunting and gathering undomesticated animals and plants persist only in the Arctic, Australia, South America, Africa, and a few other places, and even in these marginal areas hunters and gatherers have

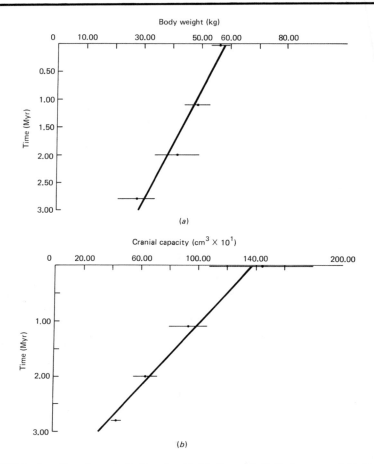

3.9   With data like these J. E. Cronin, N. T. Boaz, C. B. Stringer, and Y. Rak (1981)
have tried to show that human physical evolution was a long gradual process of
change. In (a) means of body weight estimates of human ancestors in the "gracile"
line (which usually excludes *Australopithecus robustus*) are plotted through time
(Myr = millions of years) and a regression equation derived. In (b) cranial capacity
has been similarly plotted through time. If change through time were not gradual,
it would be difficult to fit regression equations with these shapes and values to these
data. But some anthropologists dispute the data, statistics, and inferences in this
study.

been much influenced by trade, disease, and other "disruptive" contacts with more complex societies.

Nonetheless, some aspects of contemporary or recent hunting and
gathering societies may be relevant to the problem of the origins of
culture. Particularly relevant are peoples like the Kalahari Bushmen,
who until recently lived in the African savanna environments in which

the first tool users appeared, and the Australian Aborigines, who were
perhaps the least "disturbed" by modern societies when first studied.

The low level of productivity of the Bushmen's hot, arid environment, as manipulated by their simple technology (bows, arrows, digging sticks, and so forth), requires that they spend most of the year in
groups of twenty-five people or less, often on the move from one camp
to another. Most of their diet is made up of vegetable products, tortoises, and other small game, but occasionally giraffes and other large
animals are killed, usually through cooperative hunting by several
males. There is no formal "leader" among the Bushmen, but a man
may achieve some measure of prestige by being especially good at hunt-

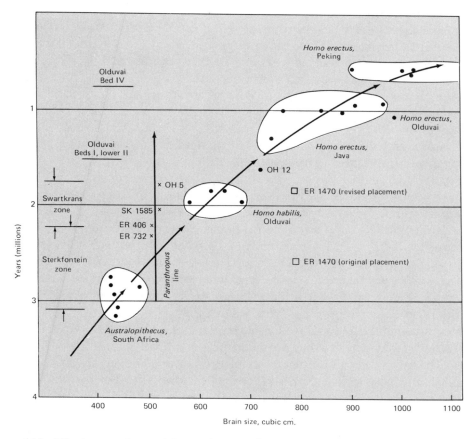

3.10   The increase in cranial capacity over time in our ancestors was enormous
and rapid by evolutionary standards, but the rate of increase has slowed in the last
100,000 years, and we may have reached the limits allowed by the mechanics of
human birth and locomotion.

ing or singing. No one, however, can claim more food or other resources simply because of his or her status.

As in most if not all hunting and gathering societies, males have greater prestige than females, although females provide the bulk of the group's food by gathering and processing plants and eggs, nestlings, turtles, and other small animals. Men do all the hunting of large animals among most known hunting-gathering societies, including the Bushmen and Aborigines. The role of women in some hunting activities may have been underestimated (Fisher 1979), but probably not by much.

Hunter-gatherer economic life is dominated by the principle of reciprocity: food and other resources are exchanged among kinsmen, balancing out the periodic shortages that may afflict any member or nuclear family in the band.

Like most hunting and gathering societies, the Bushmen are at least somewhat territorial. They move often but always within a relatively restricted region, usually twenty-five to thirty kilometers in all directions from a central water hole or home base.

Clearly, some degree of territoriality is an advantage if resources are not uniformly distributed; it is an advantage to know where reliable sources of flint, vegetables, game animals, and water are within one's territory, and the group forced out of its territory is faced with unpredictable supplies and, perhaps, the hostility of the group whose territory it is trespassing upon. Thus, any models or reconstructions we make regarding our early hominid ancestors should incorporate the assumption that they were probably at least loosely territorial.

Hunter-gather population densities are directly determined by resource availability and are maintained by what seem to us harsh methods of population control. The aboriginal population density of most of Australia, for example, can be predicted with a high degree of accuracy (0.81 correlation coefficient) simply from the amount of average rainfall in the various areas. This balance between population and resources is maintained mainly by marriage rules and female infanticide. Birdsell (1979) reports that 15 to 30 percent of all babies are killed, usually by the grandmother, who places her hand over the infant's mouth and nose as it is born so that it never draws its first breath. She acts out a group's unstated decision that keeps a mother from carrying more than one infant while she works.

In her study (1971) of hunters and gatherers in New Guinea, Patricia Townsend observed that although women produce over 90 percent of one group's food, this society is strongly patriarchal. Townsend found that the women in this group usually marry soon after puberty and have about six children. Malaria and other diseases kill off about 43 percent of the children early in life, but girls die from diseases at a much greater rate than boys, probably from malign neglect. If thought necessary, unwanted girls are killed by strangulation with a vine soon after birth.

Most hunter-gatherers keep their numbers at a level far below that which could be supported in any average year, and studies of other animals suggest that this is a common strategy. There is a selective survival advantage to keeping densities below the absolute limits of the environcent because this protects a population from the "boom or bust" cycles that eventually may put it on the edge of extinction.

Hunter-gatherer ecology offers many more ideas about the origins of culture than we can consider here, but the basic ideas seem to be that, if we try to imagine circumstances in which an early primate moves from noncultural to cultural behaviors, we should look for factors having to do directly with food and demography. The costs of various food-gathering strategies are calculated so precisely with regard to population densities that this is an obvious area to investigate.

But modern hunter-gatherers are far different from our protocultural ancestor. Where can we look for a more suitable model?

COMPARATIVE PRIMATOLOGY

Because chimpanzees, baboons, and other primates inhabit physical environments similar to those in which our first culture-bearing ancestors appeared, a study of the physical and behavioral characteristics that distinguish us from other primates may enable us to construct some testable ideas about the origins of culture.

Debates about the usefulness of chimpanzees and other primates as models for studying human origins are wide-ranging. Some think primates are almost without relevance; others see in them prototypical behavior for everything that is human (reviewed in Teleki 1981). Teleki, for example, argues that nonhuman primates do virtually everything that people do, such as hunting game, sharing food, cooperating, carrying objects, having lifelong kinship ties, practicing labor division by sex, having incest prohibitions, making tools, exhibiting linguistic capacities, possessing long-term memory, and so on (1981: 339).

Many analysts feel that the key to understanding the origins of these kinds of behavior lies mainly in the sex and violence of primate history. Consider first the simple matter of size. Human brain size, scaled according to weight, is much greater than that of other primates, and

	Fibrinopeptides A and B		Cytochrome c
R	GAGGGAGGACCCG	AGAGAGAAGCCUAG	AAUUCAUCCCUAC
S	GCGUGGGGAACCG	AGGGCAACUCCUGA	GCAGCUUACACGA
E	CAGAGAGGAACAG	AGGACAAGUACUGA	GCAGCUAACACCA
K	CAAAGAGACAACG	AGGGUAAAGAGGGA	GCAGCUAAUCCGC
M	GAGGACAGAAAAC	AGCAAGUGAAUUAG	GCAGGUUACCCGC
O	GCGGGAAACAAAC	AGCGAGAGUUUCGA	GCAGGUUACCCAC
D	AUAAGAGGAAACG	AGGAUGUAGACGGA	GCAGCUUACACGC
P	GGCAAAGGAACCG	AGGCCAAGUCAGGA	GCAGCUUACACGA
H	GUGGGAGGACCCG	UAAGAGAGGUUUAG	AAUUCAUCUCUAC
C	GCCCAGGGACCCG	AGGCCAAGUGGUGG	GCAGCUUACACGA
A	GUGGGAGGACCCG	UAAGAGAGGUUUAG	AAUUCAUCUCUAC

3.11   The sequences of nucleotides—chemical constituents of animal cells in various genera. Note that human and ape sequences are identical and similar to the sequence of monkeys but differ from other genera. (R = monkey, S = sheep, E = horse, K = kangaroo, M = mouse, O = rabbit, D = dog, P = pig, H = human, C = cow, A = ape). There is some evidence that genetic relatedness and the length of time since any two genera had a common ancestor can be derived from data like these.

our sexual dimorphisms—size and shape differences that distinguish the sexes—are at once similar to and different from those of other primates. Among some primate species, one of the most evident sexual dimorphisms is simple physical size, although a survey of numerous primate species (Napier and Napier 1967) indicates that a pronounced size difference between the sexes is relatively infrequent, being largely confined to the Old World apes. We must assume then that "marked morphological and behavioral dimorphism is not a primitive characteristic of primates but has evolved in certain genera in relation to particular patterns of living" (Crook 1972: 235).

One clue as to what patterns of living these might have been can be seen in the size differences of the sexes in living nonhuman primates. Male and female gibbons, who spend most of their lives in trees, are almost identical in size; among chimpanzees, who spend some of their time on the ground, males are usually larger than females; and among gorillas, who are almost completely terrestrial, males average almost twice the size of females. Why should the physical size of the sexes show this association with terrain?

A probable factor in the evolution of both sexual dimorphisms and the overall increase in size of *Homo sapiens sapiens* of both sexes was the need for defense against predators. Our ancestors apparently evolved in open savanna-type environments where competition and predation by large cats and other carnivores would have been significant, and thus it is not at all surprising that part of our evolution in these environments would have been in the direction of greater physical size. A human with a rifle, or even a crude spear, would have some reasonable defenses, but until tool use reached this point there would no doubt have been strong direct selection for increasing physical size. Our earliest tool-using ancestors were only about three or four feet tall, weighing perhaps sixty or seventy pounds—not too formidable compared with their competitors. Today, on the savannas of Africa, baboon populations are able to survive, despite occasional predation by leopards and lions, partly because they have retained impressive canine and incisor teeth (Figure 3.12). By ramapithecine times, however, our ancestors had probably lost these dental defenses.

In some animal species, sexual dimorphisms seem to be linked to differences in feeding strategies of males and females. While this may have been of some importance to our early primate ancestors, the kinds of food eaten by males and females probably overlapped considerably soon after tool use began and embryonic human social organizations formed (Pianka 1974). Nonetheless, early hominid males and females would probably have been under increasingly different selective pressures as soon as males began specializing in hunting and females in gathering—specializations that may have appeared only comparatively late and sporadically.

3.12 Baboons occasionally capture and eat small animals.

Crook (1972) points out one sexual dimorphism in humans that may be tied to subsistence specializations: for every 100 female children conceived, 120 males are conceived, although of these only 105 survive to birth. (Also, mortality is 25 percent higher for males in the first year of life.)

Subsistence specializations may also have changed selective pressures to produce in males somewhat greater physical strength, on the average. This extends to more than simple gross musculature: males have a stronger heart than females and have more red blood cells per unit volume of blood. Again, one interpretation of this would seem to be that through our evolutionary history there has been a greater positive selection for these characteristics in males than in females as a result of the requirements of having to defend the group against predators, of having to be effective predators themselves, and, perhaps, of competition among males for females.

One other aspect of sexual dimorphism among humans is particularly intriguing when seen in comparison with nonhuman primates: namely, the secondary sexual characteristics that differentiate human males and females. Among human females, breasts are significantly larger than among males—in fact, the size, shape, and other differences distinguishing male and female breasts are much more pronounced than in any other mammal species. This difference cannot be explained in terms of function, since breast size seems to have almost no relationship to effective functioning in human beings. Similarly, the human penis is far larger, relatively and absolutely, than that of any other primate, including the gorilla. In addition, human females have softer skin and higher voices than males and have lost more of their body hair—although compared to the other species of primates, males also have remarkably little body hair.

Another major difference betwen humans and other animals is that human females do not exhibit *estrus;* that is, women's receptivity to sexual intercourse does not seem to increase to any large extent with the rise in estrogen levels that precedes ovulation. This is a matter of degree, and it is perhaps unnecessary to point out that human females are not constantly sexually receptive; but as a statistical generalization, they are much more so than other female primates. How can we account for this?

One interesting possibility is that

in all probability the evolutionary development of hair reduction, increased skin sensitivity and tactile changes involving skin tension were [sic] all associated with increasing the tactile sensations of coital body contact, especially in the frontal presentation. Likewise the breasts of young women taken together with other features (limb contour, complexion, and the like) seem to represent the main visual sexual releasers for the male. While the latter features may have been due to straightforward intersexual selection by ancient males the former features have probably been selected in both sexes for their effect in improving sexual rewards, in inducing sexual love and in maintaining pair bonds. The same is also likely to be true for the presence of orgasm in women and the absence of the more typical mammalian estrus. The functional significance of all these correlated changes is most plausibly seen within the context of the adaptations of seed-eating and of later partially carnivorous protohominids to open country life with associated shifts in social organization. (Crook 1972: 254)

Crook's suggested link between adaptations to savanna environments and the evolution of human sexual dimorphisms bears directly on our major problem here, the determinants of the evolution of culture, and it suggests that we might be able to learn something about this by examining behavior patterns in nonhuman primates.

Baboons

Baboons inhabit a diversity of environments, but our most reliable and complete information comes from savanna-adapted populations in Central and East Africa. Savannas are relatively flat, arid expanses with scattered trees and occasional water holes, and their mixed grasses, shrubs, and other plants usually support very high densities of grazing animals such as zebras, buffalos, and other ungulates.

Unlike humans, baboons, although having complex and efficient communication systems, do not possess "language." Similarly, while baboons have been observed using sticks and stones for minor manipulations of the environment, this behavior is sporadic, largely unplanned, and does not seem to increase in range or efficiency from generation to generation, as does human tool use.

Consider also the matter of what zoologists call a *dominance hierarchy*. Within the baboon troop, the eldest males have almost unimpeded access to food and sex, and they protect their privileges with aggressive behavior. Younger males are allowed access to females only on the sufferance of more dominant males, although they are constantly testing this dominance by attempting to strike up meaningful relationships with concupiscent females. Often this will incite a dominant male to charge and make threatening gestures and rude remarks. Similarly, when desirable but limited food is available, such as fruit or a clutch of eggs, the dominant males and females take what they want first. A mother and child may share some foods, but there is no systematic food sharing between adult members of the group.

Thus, in trying to explain how culture-bearing individuals developed from our primate ancestors, we must look for factors or conditions that would tend to break down these dominance hierarchies and promote the distinctive human family structure, with its food sharing, division of labor, and pair bonding.

When baboon troops move across savanna or open environments, they typically position members according to age and sex. Adolescent males are on the periphery, adult, dominant males are in the center, adult females are behind the adult males, and dependent young are stationed near the adult females. This is of course an excellent defensive formation, offering the best protection to the young and females, upon whom the perpetuation of the group depends. There are many more adolescent males than necessary for reproduction, so although they would suffer the most losses to predators, the stability of the group would not suffer much. Significantly, when the baboon troop moves into more forested areas, the positioning becomes much more fluid and dispersed, indicating, not too surprisingly, that terrain is an important determinant of behavior for baboons, and that savanna environments seem to put a premium on group cohesiveness and dominance hierarchies.

Chimpanzees

Chimpanzees also inhabit diverse environments, and generalizations about their behavior are as dangerous as in the case of baboons. The most studied chimpanzees are those of the forests of Tanzania. The chimpanzees of this area behave very differently from the savanna-dwelling baboons. Access to food and sex is much less rigidly controlled, and the entire dominance hierarchy seems to be less in evidence. In one instance where a female was sexually receptive for a record twenty-one days, the males of the chimpanzee group, young and old alike, stood in line for her favors with only minor apparent bickering (van Lawick-Goodall 1971). Strictly speaking, chimpanzees do not have true estrus cycles, but they do have periods of greater and lesser sexual receptivity. This is not always typical behavior, and the adolescents were effectively barred from mating with some females in many cases, but in comparison with baboons, chimpanzees are absolute libertines in sexual matters.

Similarly, there is also a diminution of territoriality. Chimpanzees

3.13 Chimpanzees regularly hunt small game and share the meat in relationships based on age and sex. Some anthropologists believe that hunting and meat-sharing were important determinants in the origins of human family structures and sexual nature.

run for kilometers along trails through the forests, often alone or with one or two others, and individuals frequently leave one small group to go live with another. So relaxed are chimpanzees, in fact, about sex and territoriality, that they have aroused envious feelings in some human observers. "Chimpanzees, it seems, successfully achieve what *Homo sapiens* radicals only dream of: peaceful, non-competitive, non-coercive, non-possessive, egalitarian, jealousy-free, promiscuous, non-tyrannical communes" (Van den Berghe 1972: 772).

This may be a somewhat idealized picture. Chimpanzees have elaborate threat rituals and do menace each other according to a well-developed hierarchy. In addition, chimpanzees are the only animals besides ourselves who regularly use objects as weapons, usually wooden clubs or thrown rocks and debris (van Lawick-Goodall 1971). They fight over food and females, and sometimes over rank (van Lawick-Goodall 1968, 1971, 1973), and they are the only other primates known to practice cannibalism, having been observed on several occasions eating young chimps alive.

Books such as *African Genesis* by Robert Ardrey and *The Naked Ape* by Desmond Morris argue that much of our mentality, anatomy, and physiology is a result of millions of years of bloody, relentless hunting and killing. Indeed, if we look at chimpanzee predatory behavior, we see that in its emotional content and its implications, hunting and meat eating may not be just another way of getting food. Primatologist G. Teleki (1973) has observed the hunting behavior of chimpanzees, and he found that hunting, loss of estrus, economic reciprocity, and human family structure may be intimately interrelated. He notes that adult males often cooperate in hunting small mammals and that there is a partial suspension of the dominance hierarchy during these times, as demonstrated by the fact that a low-dominance male sometimes leads the hunt. Significantly, although females and juveniles participate in hunting only rarely, they are often given meat by the males who make the kills, and females who are sexually receptive are more likely to get and eat meat (Symons 1975: 46–47). Symons describes how this might have contributed to the evolution of hominid social structure:

> Thus, there may have been a pattern in early human evolution in which the amount of meat a female received from males was directly proportional to the length of time she was in estrus, providing strong selective pressures for continued fertility and receptivity during lactation and an increasing segment of a female's cycle. Selection might then favor males who used surplus meat to increase their reproductive success at the expense of other males. (ibid.: 47–48)

If these speculations are correct, they would at least demonstrate the accuracy of the epigram about the world's oldest profession. But we must be cautious about reading our whole evolutionary history in these few observations; a great deal more research must be done before we can assume these important links between loss of estrus, hunting, and food sharing (for a somewhat different perspective, see Martin and Voorhies 1975).

In reviewing recent studies of hunting by chimpanzees, Teleki (1981) notes the difficulty of gathering reliable data, but he makes several summary observations. He points out that cooperative behavior among chimpanzees while hunting has not been shown to produce more kills, and he suggests that difficulties in defining what is cooperative and in measuring effectiveness leave this point moot. He concludes that sexual receptivity, kinship ties, and social status all determine how meat is distributed after a kill is made. Teleki suggests that there is sexual division of labor among chimpanzees that is not dependent solely on hunting behavior. He reviews various studies which show that female chimpanzees spend a much greater proportion of their time collecting termites and other invertebrates than do males—a prelude, he argues, to the sharp division of labor in human hunting and gathering groups.

Models of Cultural Origins

We have considered many disparate bits of evidence and information, ranging from fossil hominids to the sexual behavior of chimpanzees, and we can now try to put everything together in a compelling explanation of how our ancestors made the first steps from noncultural, chimpanzeelike animals to the social, tool-using hominids of 2.0 million years ago. The following scenario draws from the ideas of various authorities, but the reader is warned that the evidence is inadequate, interpretations are suspect, and that the same data can be fashioned into several other convincing "models."

Let us begin with bipedalism. It now appears, given the ramapithecines and the Hadar fossils, that primates walked upright for millions of years before they used many or any tools. But why should a slow, diurnal, not terribly clever primate walk upright? The question is important for, as we shall see, bipedalism may be the wellspring of cultural behavior.

Owen Lovejoy has recently (1980) argued that bipedalism as an evolutionary product is essentially a matter of sex. The "problem" with bipedalism is that it is a slow method of movement and an animal expends great amounts of energy just holding itself up. Why then should it appear? Lovejoy argues that since our ancestors evolved in trees and forests, they evolved to be climbers, clingers, and jumpers rather than the quadrupedal swift animals of the savannas. All apes, he feels, are potentially semierect animals by virtue of natural selection for "handedness"—the constant use of the hand to forage for food. And if one's evolutionary niche does not reward great bursts of speed over the short run, bipedalism is quite effective for long periods of methodical hunting and gathering.

Lovejoy notes that through the later history of the primates, there has been an evolution in the reproductive strategy. The trend has been toward decreasing the number of offspring a female has but increasing the parental investment in each one so that they have a better chance to survive and in turn reproduce. (Ecologists call this a "k-strategy," as opposed to the "r-strategy" of something like the housefly, which has thousands of offspring, only a few of which survive.)

The heart of Lovejoy's argument is that bipedalism was selected over quadrupedalism in our ancestors because it was a way to increase reproductive success. It allowed our ancestors to have more offspring while maintaining a high level of parental investment in the form of food provision, protection, and training. This was accomplished by

evolving an economic adaptation and social organization that allowed
the mother to spend less of her energy getting her own food and more
of her time taking care of offspring. There was only one way to do this
in the case of our primate ancestors: the male had to be induced to
provide the female with food on a regular basis, to take part in other
tasks of raising many children, and to do it all without competing with
other males to the point that the group would break up into murderous, insanely jealous individuals. What was needed here, obviously, was
a male who could get enough food to share and carry it back easily, but
who could limit his sexual drive sufficiently so that he was attached to
one or a few females and did not rape every one he met. Enter the
Hadar primates, or the later *Homo,* a bipedal, tool-using, sociable male
who had the emotional capacity, perhaps, to feel "love"—or at least
some vague ups and downs of emotion.

If all this is true, bipedalism, which allows the male to carry back
food, probably came before tool use. Food sharing, with or without
tool use and hunting, would tend to lengthen the period during which
a female was sexually responsive, if sex served as an inducement to
food sharing. And this was an important evolutionary change in more
ways than one. Human females are fertile for only a relatively unpredictable three days a month, so intercourse at least a few times a week
would be necessary for successful fertility rates.

In an analysis of these arguments about the link between sexual behavior and other aspects of culture, Donald Symons (1979) has addressed
many rather controversial questions, such as whether or not there is a
biological basis for men's apparent tendency to be more promiscuous
than women, why sexual behavior is treated as the most private and
concealed of human activities, why women cross-culturally and historically report a lower ratio of orgasms to sexual experiences than do men,
and why in marriages female infidelity is usually treated much more
harshly than male infidelity.

Admitting the great plasticity and potential for variability of human
sexual behavior, Symons thinks that there is a strong biological, genetic basis to these apparent behavioral differences between males and
females and these cultural aspects of sexuality. For millions of years the
evolutionary advantage has been with males who have had intercourse
with as many women under the age of about forty as they could—provided that the resulting progeny could be raised to reproductive age. In
evolutionary terms, the true loser is the male who provides for another
male's offspring, giving rise to the observation that much of the social
organization of human hunting and gathering societies is designed to

allow a man to go on long hunting trips without returning and finding himself the provider for some other man's children.

But given the difficulties of measuring the effects of societal factors
on human sexuality, as well as the corresponding difficulties of understanding the genetic and physiological complexities of human behavior,
none of these questions about the role of human sexuality and the rise
of culture can be answered definitively.

In any case, sex is not everything. To convert our newly bipedal primate into australopithecines, *Homo erectus,* and finally, ourselves, we
have to consider technology, ecology, and economics.

The importance of tools to our ancestors can perhaps best be appreciated if one imagines oneself standing about 4 feet tall on the Serengeti
Plain of 2 million years ago, trying to resolve into its component parts
a small antelope one has just killed. Half-starved and already harried
by vultures and other scavengers, one tries to rip into the body with
one's teeth and nails. Even with the relatively stout dentition of *Australopithecus,* or of our more distant relative, *Ramapithecus,* it would
have been almost a hopeless task. The most nutritious parts, the liver,
brain, and other internal organs, are protected by thick layers of skin,
flesh, and bone that resist the puny tearing motions to which our ancestors would have been limited. But just a chip off one of the quartz
pebbles abundantly scattered over this area would instantly have opened
up life-saving rations for several individuals.

With cooperative hunting and stone tools then, a vast new niche
would have opened to our ancestors. Even in our zoologically impoverished era a recent survey of Albert National Park, along the Ugandan
border, revealed hippopotami, antelopes, elephants, and other large
mammals in such numbers that there are an average of 130,000 pounds
of big game per square mile (Pfeiffer 1978: 128).

As zoologists George Schaller and Gordon Lowther note:

The means by which scavenging and hunting hominids might fit into
the ecological community without competing too extensively with other
predators pose a number of questions. Their primate heritage suggests
that they were diurnal, and selection pressure from their primate and
carnivore way of life undoubtedly favored a social existence. The only
other diurnal social carnivore is the wild dog, which hunts at dawn and
dusk, and favors prey weighing 60 kilograms or less (about 130 pounds).
An ecological opening exists for a social predator hunting large animals
and scavenging during the day, an opening some early hominid may
well have filled, assuming that none of the saber-toothed cats did so.
(1969)

Some have argued that systematic predation in savanna environments would have been the major factor in this developmental sequence; specifically, that group cooperation, food sharing, language, and other cultural behavior developed out of the selective forces that would come into play as hominids adapted to savanna environments and a reliance on big-game hunting (Cachel 1975). We know climates in eastern and southern Africa were drier just prior to the periods when the first stone tools appeared, and possibly the increasing aridity forced some of our ancestors to expand their reliance on hunting. Some marginally habitable savanna environments, in particular, would have selected for increased hunting, for here meat may have been the difference between survival and starvation.

There are, however, a number of severe problems with this attractively simple scenario, particularly in the matter of big-game hunting. Early hominids, even those with crude stone tools, would have had a difficult time capturing and killing large game, even if they were alone on the savannas, simply because they were small and slow and faced ferocious competition from lions, canids, and other predators. Thus, other scholars suggest our ancestors combined scavenging and hunting small game with intensive foraging for eggs, plants, and other small resources. Even scavenging is not as easy as it might sound. Many animals die and are killed in savanna environments, but predators eat most of their kills within six or seven hours, and competition from canids and other scavengers is considerable. Washburn says that if baboons in areas of Africa where there are still many lions tried to subsist on scavenging, they would have difficulty obtaining an ounce of meat a day per baboon (1968); it is noteworthy that no other primates appear to scavenge (Poirier 1973: 108).

Even if their scavenging was quite limited, early hominids could still have significantly augmented their vegetable foods by turning, not to big-game hunting, but to the hunting of sick and newborn animals. Competition would have been severe, but using group strategy and their evolving intelligence, early hominids could have stalked these sick and young animals, causing them to "freeze," making them easy prey. Bushmen and other groups regularly engage in this sort of predation, and such kills can be supplemented by gathering eggs, invertebrates, tortoises, colonial nesting birds, and similar resources.

These forms of small-game hunting and scavenging would have rewarded group cooperation, reduced dominance hierarchies, improved communication systems, and encouraged the development of stone tools for processing meat and vegetable foods.

Marshall Sahlins (1972) summarized this intertwining of sex, food, and violence as follows:

Sexual attraction remains a determinant of human sociability. But it has become subordinated to the search for food, to economics. A most significant advance of early cultural society was the strict repression and canalization of sex, through the incest tabu, in favor of kinship, and thus mutual aid relations. Primate sexuality is utilized in human society to reinforce bonds of economic, and to a lesser extent, defensive alliance. *"All marriage schemes are largely devices to check and regulate promiscuous behavior in the interest of the human economic scheme."* (emphasis added)

The reader is reminded that all of these ideas are subject to change on the basis of new evidence and is urged to consider the context of these ideas about cultural origins. It is perhaps no coincidence, for example, that most of the models of cultural origins that stress sexual drives and hunting have been constructed by young to middle-aged men, and those stressing the female–child bond and female economic role written by women (e.g., Martin and Voorhies 1975; Tanner 1981; also see Hamilton 1984).

In any case, having constructed an "explanation" of sorts of cultural origins, we have very little archaeological evidence relevant to our explanation.

THE ARCHAEOLOGICAL RECORD AND
THE ORIGINS OF CULTURE

Archaeologists the world over have a recurrent fantasy in which it is early morning, about 2.5 million years ago, at a water hole on the East African savanna. Thousands of animals, including many of the first hominids, have come together, the hominids to scavenge, collect plant foods, and prey on the drinking animals. After hunting and killing animals and collecting other foods, the hominids make more tools, butcher the animals, eat them, and then disperse into their social units to sleep it off. Suddenly a nearby volcano becomes active, spewing out clouds of poison gas, dust, ash, and red-hot particles, killing all of the animals, including the hominids. The hominids and their tools and prey would thus be perfectly preserved under a thick blanket of protective ash, which would also facilitate radiometric dating.

Although such sites have not been found, a catastrophe of this type is not impossible. In 1902 on Martinique about 28,000 people were killed within minutes when a volcanic eruption sent a landslide of ash, lava, and debris cascading over part of the island.

In the "real" world, however, our evidence of the initial period of the evolution of culture is extremely meager, and we are limited to just a few small sites, almost all of which are in southern and eastern Africa.

Olduvai Gorge

About 5 million years ago, a large lake covered about 130 square kilometers of what today is the Serengeti Plain, in central East Africa. Countless generations of animals, including, no doubt, our hominid ancestors, lived near this lake and the streams that fed it, and today fossilized bones are thickly distributed through the black clay of the ancient shoreline and lake bed. About a half million years before the appearance of culture-bearing animals in this part of the world, the lake and the adjacent areas were the scene of dramatic geological activity. Volcanoes near the lake had been erupting for millions of years, and there was a particularly violent episode about a million and a half years ago, when a volcano to the south of the lake covered it and surrounding areas with a layer of ash and molten rock some 5 meters thick. Similar eruptions occurred in succeeding millennia, and today we can measure the intensity of each volcanic episode by gauging the thickness of each superimposed ash level. Sometime during and after these volcanic eruptions, the climate of the area began a cycle of alternating dry and wet periods. These millions of years of volcanic activity and climatic change eventually covered the original lake and adjacent lands with a 100-meter-thick deposit of sand, ash, and lake sediments, the surface of which is the present Serengeti Plain. Ancient floods cut down through this plain at several points, revealing scores of archaeological sites.

Site DK I, for example, has been radiometrically dated to about 1.75 million years ago, making it one of the oldest in Olduvai Gorge. The site is composed of a layer several meters thick of bones, worked and unworked stone, and other debris. Because of the complex stratigraphy, it is difficult to separate this accumulation into different levels with any assurance that the divisions represent discrete hominid occupations.

The most prominent archaeological feature at DK I is a semicircle of stones (Figure 3.14) lying within a concentration of stone and animal bones. Measuring approximately 3 meters in diameter and made of chunks of vesicular basalt, this feature is interpreted by many as a foundation for a windbreak or some other temporary structure. But the lack

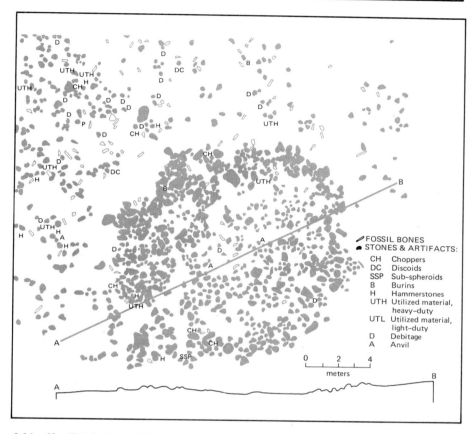

3.14 Site DK I. Plan of the stone circle and the remains on the occupation surface. Stones, including artifacts, are shown in grey. Fossil bones are shown in outline.

of control of fire and other evidence make it unlikely DK I was a home base (Binford 1981).

The tools found here are similar to the other materials from Beds I and II at Olduvai: hundreds of crudely flaked stones, some of them showing evidence of use, others simply byproducts of the manufacturing process.

Site FLK I is particularly important because several hominid bone fragments were found in its various levels, including the remains of an early hominid that Leakey named *Zinjanthropus*. This "Zinjanthropus floor" covers an area of more than 1,036 square meters and contains over 4,000 pieces of worked stone. Many stone artifacts and pieces of shattered bone are concentrated in a "working area" some 5 meters in

diameter, and a relatively clear arc-shaped area in the midst of all this
debris suggests that there may have been a temporary shelter here.

Lewis Binford has recently (1981) published an extensive analysis of
the sites in Olduvai Gorge. Binford is particularly concerned with the
relationship between the animal bones and the stone tools of the Olduvai
sites. By determining which specific bones of animals are present and in
what proportions, and by closely examining the damage to the bones,
Binford tries to separate bones deposited at Olduvai and altered by natural forces (e.g., animals drowned in floods and eaten by other animals)
from those of animals killed and butchered by people. His complex approach is highly mathematical and can only be briefly summarized here.

Binford found that the statistical patterns of animal bone damage
and loss were often more consistent with animals gnawing the bones
than with human butchering. He argues further that few or no sites at
Olduvai reflect incidents in which hominids killed large game animals,
since most of the bones that would carry the best cuts of meat occur in
low numbers.

Although Binford's conclusion has been challenged (Bunn 1981),
his critique of his critics' arguments shows that we are a long way from
understanding the complex interplay of factors that produced the
Olduvai sites, and that we do not yet understand their significance. On
the other hand, Olduvai is marked by thousands of stone tools lying
amidst thousands of animal parts, and this is not likely to be some vast
coincidence: it seems evident that by 1.8 million years ago, hominids
were making stone tools, in part for the purposes of extracting food
from animals. Whether this was meat, marrow, or organs from hunted
or scavenged animals is not clear.

There are various other sites in Africa with stone tools and animal
bones dating back to 1 to 2 million years ago, but in most instances
these are small, inadequately described, of questionable date, or in some
other way inappropriate for statistical analysis.

In short, Olduvai is the only site we now have that can tell us much
about cultural origins, and it probably is representative of a time long
after the major transitions to cultural behavior had been made.

Homo Erectus and the Invasion of Temperate Climates

Every hominid fossil and artifact dating to more than a million years
ago has been found in the warm regions of either Africa or Asia, but by
about 900,000 years ago, our hominid ancestors had spread out along the
margins of the temperate latitudes and had begun to invade Pleistocene

Table 3.2   The problem of understanding our earliest culture-bearing ancestors is in many ways a *statistical* problem in which archaeologists use mathematics and computers to sort through great masses of bones and stone tools for patterns that indicate how ancient people lived. Here, Lewis Binford (1981: Table 6.07) has analyzed the animal bones found at 24 Olduvai Gorge sites dating to about 1.7 million years ago. The statistical technique used is a form of factor analysis. The bones found at these sites fall into five different broad patterns: Factor 1—bones that have been severely damaged by people, animals, or some other agent; factor 2—bones that have been separated from animal carcasses and transported some distance; factor 3—an unspecified, unknown pattern; factors 4 and 5, which are "kill or residual faunal assemblages that have not suffered heavy attrition." The number listed for each site on each factor is called a "loading" and is a complex mathematical measure of how important that factor is in the overall assemblage of bones at that site. Sites with similar loadings may have been created by similar activities, and thus these different patterns of loadings may now indicate specialized activities of people (or the scavenging activities of different kinds of animals).

		Factors				
	Number	1	2	3	4	5
FLK 5	38	.950	0	0	0	0
FLK 4	37	.891	0	0	0	0
HWK 3–5	32	.863	0	0	0	0
FLK 3	36	.856	0	0	0	0
MNK MAIN	54	.852	0	.274	0	0
FLK ½	35	.810	0	.252	0	0
LG DEN MODEL	57	.806	.414	0	0	0
BK II	49	.803	0	.370	.306	0
SM DEN-MODEL	59	.799	.389	0	.304	0
DK I-2	47	.731	.423	.262	0	.261
NN 1	43	.726	0	0	.329	0
SM KILL MODEL	58	.701	0	0	.389	.469
DK I-3	48	.697	0	0	.284	0
HWK 1	34	.675	.484	.271	0	0
LG KILL MODEL	56	.573	0	0	.557	.517
HWK 2	33	.401	.809	0	0	0
NN 2	44	.360	.755	.428	0	0
MNK H13	55	0	.657	0	0	0
FLK 6	39	.529	.614	0	0	0
FLK 15	41	.369	0	.862	0	0
FLK 13	40	0	0	.683	0	0
NN 3	45	0	0	.643	0	.590
FC TUFF	52	0	.546	−627	0	.339
FLK 22	42	.394	.365	.325	.706	0
FC/FL	53	.418	0	0	.676	0
DK I-1	46	0	0	0	.499	0
TK UF	50	0	0	0	0	0
TK LF	51	.284	.389	.390	.366	0
	VP	10.508	3.764	3.076	2.417	1.279

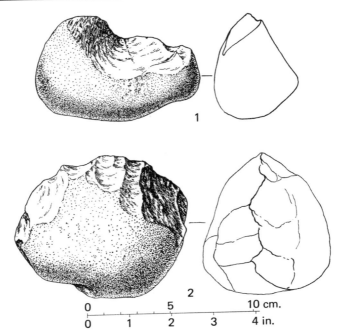

3.15   These 1.7-million-year-old tools from Olduvai Gorge are crude, but the fracture patterns mark them as unmistakably human tools.

Europe and northern Asia (Figure 3.16). The intrepid individuals who made the first forays into temperate climates were probably either a transitional form between *Australopithecus* and *Homo erectus,* or full-fledged *Homo erectus,* were a few inches short of five feet tall (about 1.3 meters), walked fully erect, and had a cranial capacity of from 700 to 900 cc (Howells 1973: 61–64; Pilbeam 1975: 826–27).

These hominids (and all hominids, including ourselves) were tropical animals who could not possibly have survived Pleistocene European winters without clothing, fire, and tools. Fire was particularly vital, not just for keeping warm, but for cooking food and, perhaps more importantly, for evicting bears and other carnivores from caves and rock shelters—the safest and warmest places to live in northern latitudes. There is also the somewhat romantic notion that fire may have been important in the evolution of the uniquely human sense of kinship and community, as for hundreds of thousands of years countless generations of hominids clustered around evening campfires, while outside storms raged and predators prowled (Pfeiffer 1978).

The problems of living in northern climates go beyond simply keeping warm. In winter most of the plants suitable for human consumption die, and many species of small game are no longer available. Under these conditions large mammals have only four ways to avoid starvation: they can hibernate, migrate, eat winter vegetation, or they can prey on animals that do one or more of these. The last was the only realistic alternative for our ancestors.

On the African savannas and in other warm environments, women supply most of the food in hunting and gathering cultures, and even pregnant women, children, and the aged can gather much of their own food all year long. But such self-reliance would not have been possible in northern latitudes, where snow covered the ground for five to six months of the year.

One of the most interesting aspects of the movement of hominids into temperate climates is that they changed significantly in physical

3.16 Distribution of *Homo erectus* sites. *Homo erectus* was the first hominid to invade temperate climates and may have been more widely distributed than is represented here. Land bridges, now submerged, facilitated *H. erectus* movements.

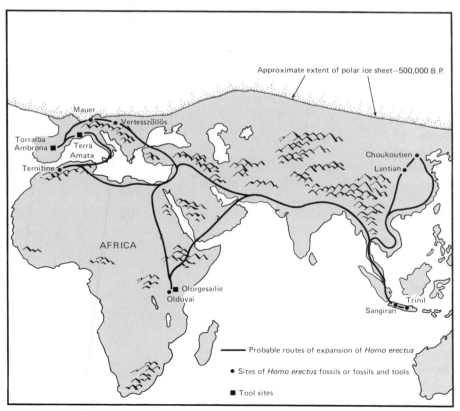

form and cultural repertoire during the period they were moving north. Between about 1 million and 350,000 years ago, from the first occupation of northern areas until most of Europe and northern Asia were inhabited by humans, the versatility and efficiency of tools increased, and people became larger, bigger-brained, and more "modern" in facial structure. The hominid associated with these changes is *Homo erectus*, whose physical form was intermediate in many characteristics between ourselves and the australopithecines, and who is almost certainly our direct ancestor. *H. erectus* is thought to have emerged between 2 and 1 million years ago and to have evolved into *Homo sapiens* by about 300,000 to 200,000 years ago; but most of our fossil evidence for *H. erectus* dates to the relatively short period between 600,000 and 250,000 years ago.

Homo erectus remains have been found in most areas of the Old World, including Java, China, the Near East, Africa, and—in very fragmentary form—central and western Europe. Variation is considerable (Grimaud 1980), but cranial volumes average between 750 and 1,200 cc, and, compared to us, these hominids had flat skulls, large brow ridges, thick cranial bones, and almost no chins. From the neck down, however, *Homo erectus* was very similar to modern human populations, although a bit shorter. Males averaged about 5'1" (1.4 meters) in height, females a few inches less.

Because the important physical and cultural changes associated with *Homo erectus* occurred at the same time these hominids were invading temperate latitudes, the possibility of a cause-and-effect relationship is raised. Only those groups that developed systematic food sharing and efficient hunting technologies and strategies would do well in these rigorous environments, and there would also probably have been some "natural selection" for larger body size (to conserve heat) and bigger brains.

If big-game hunting in northern climates was the stimulus to these varied cultural and physical developments, as some suggest, we should find this relationship reflected in the archaeological record. For example, we would expect that the first sites showing more efficient tools than the Olduwan styles would be found in northern latitudes, most likely in association with masses of bones of large animals. We would also expect to find evidence of the first systematic and widespread use of fire in sites in northern latitudes.

The rigors of this adaptation may also have selected strongly for food sharing, and out of this may have developed the complex kinship networks and social relations we know to characterize all contemporary human groups, even the most "primitive" hunters and gatherers. If so, we might expect to find in northern latitudes the first sites reflecting the coordinated activities of larger groups than are characteristic of hominids in warmer latitudes. And if the rigors of life in cold climates also selected for increased brain and body size, we might expect differences in these dimensions if we compare skeletal materials from northern and southern sites.

Except for these gross correlations, however, it is difficult to test the hypothesis that adapting to cold climates and big-game hunting was a primary evolutionary force. It is also difficult to delineate subtle patterns of cause and effect with the available fragmentary archaeological evidence. Cultural innovations, such as the use of fire and more efficient stone tools, must have spread quickly from area to area, and it is difficult to pin down their centers of origin. Most hunting and gathering societies have exogamous marriage patterns, meaning they marry outside the group they spend most of the year with, and this produces a constant mixture of genes and cultures.

Thus, it is possible that the use of fire, more efficient stone tools, and bigger brains were stimulated by the selective environments along the northern periphery of the Old World, but we would expect that these and other innovations would have soon spread to human populations all over the Old World. And, given the gross dating techniques available to archaeologists, it is very difficult to determine precisely the exact origins of these developments.

EAST AFRICA

Ironically, to consider the hypothesis that northern adaptations and big-game hunting played important roles in hominid cultural and physical evolution, we must first turn our attention to the warm regions of East Africa, where recent finds raise serious problems with this attractive hypothesis.

The critical evidence comes principally from Olduvai Gorge, where at least one hominid has been found that suggests *Homo erectus* had evolved in this area about 1 million years ago. This is Olduvai Hominid 9, from Upper Bed II, radiometrically dated to between 1 million and 900,000 years ago. The cranial fragments of this hominid have many characteristics in common with the *Homo erectus* of East Asia, including a cranial volume of about 1,000 cc. Equally important, as Glenn Isaac notes, the *Acheulian*-style (named after the French site at Acheul) stone tools associated with *Homo erectus* in Europe at a much later date (ca. 600,000 years ago at the earliest) were apparently already present in many East African sites more than a million years ago (1975: 504). Thus, Isaac concludes that the hypothesis of the importance of big-game hunting in human evolution is probably wrong and that the evidence from East Africa, in any case, "is not compatible with this view in its simplest form. The Lower Pleistocene does not emerge as a small-game hunting stage—nor is the contrast between the Lower and Middle Pleistocene that marked" (ibid.: 516). Given these various lines of evidence, Isaac contends that the original evolution of the distinctive physical and cultural characteristics of *Homo erectus* was limited to Africa and perhaps the warmer parts of Asia (ibid.: 495).

The site of Olorgesailie, located about an hour's drive outside Nairobi, Kenya, is one of the few *Homo erectus* sites in Africa with a large concentration of undisturbed artifacts. The site area comprises many small concentrations of stone tools and bones spread out along a peninsula in an extinct lake. Most of the tools are cleavers and handaxes, and some show considerable chipping and blunting wear. Associated animal bones are from several species of large mammals, including a hippopotamus and, curiously, sixty-three individuals of an extinct species of baboon (but no hominids). The distribution of stones and bones suggests a hunting and scavenging hominid. There are no hearths or burned bones, but microscopic pieces of charcoal have been found all over the site. Whether these were the result of human or natural activity remains unclear. Potassium-argon dating of the Olorgesailie formation yields an age of about 480,000 years (Isaac 1975: 504; see also Isaac 1977).

Poirier interprets this site as evidence of relatively stable bands of twenty to thirty *Homo erectus* individuals, systematically hunting and scavenging in seasonal patterns, and thinks that the diversity of tool kits and site sizes indicates relatively cohesive social groups returning regularly to the same area and perhaps remaining in essentially the same place for several months (1973: 151–52).

If Olorgesailie is really a case of hominids hunting baboons, as some suggest, it is possible we have been underestimating the linguistic and physical prowess of *Homo erectus*. It is instructive to try to imagine oneself about two-thirds size, going out at night with stones and clubs to kill sixty-three baboons.

But, as Binford (1977, 1981) has suggested, it is difficult to demonstrate conclusively that these kinds of sites are the remains of hunting as opposed to simple non-hominid scavenging. The Acheulian "handaxe" that occurs in great numbers in these sites may even have been mainly a tool for digging vegetables rather than one for dismembering animals. One archaeologist invoked aerodynamic studies to argue that Acheulian handaxes were in fact often thrown at game. Considering the difficulties of hitting a cave bear or rhino in a vulnerable spot with such an implement, one might suspect that there would be direct natural selection against the hunter who lost his "arm." No team, as one anthropologist observed, ever would have lived more by its pitching.

There are many Acheulian sites in Africa besides Olorgesailie, but for the next several hundred thousand years the evolutionary focus seems in some ways to have shifted to the margins of the range of *Homo erectus,* to the temperate latitudes of Europe and Asia.

EUROPE

The earliest well-documented archaeological site in Europe is Vallonet Cave, on the coast of southeastern France, where a small concentration of stone tools and broken animal bones has been dated to about 950,000 years ago (de Lumley 1975: 752). The tools from Vallonet look rather like the Olduwan implements; they are mainly crude choppers made from fist-sized pebbles and also include several flake tools. A number of apparently worked animal bones were also found, and the occupants of this small cave probably brought in antlers shed by deer (ibid.). The most abundant animal bones are from extinct forms of wild cow and bear, and there are also remains from antelopes, deer, boars, rhinoceroses, elephants, horses, hippopotami, seals, and a monkey. Several bones appear to have been deliberately broken and a few flakes were struck off the end of a rhinoceros leg bone, but the large number of bear bones in the cave suggests that most of these animals were probably not brought back to the cave by hominids: cave bears no doubt carried their prey back to dens in these caves, and the presence of many of these bones is probably a result of the bears' activities. Frost-cracked rocks and annual layers of ceiling-fall at Vallonet reflect at least some periods of cold, but there is no evidence of any hearths or fires. These would not have been necessary during the warmer parts of the year, of course, particularly since Vallonet is located on the coast, where the Mediterranean greatly moderates the climate. The presence in the cave of the bones of a monkey also suggests a fairly moderate climate.

Vallonet is the only well-documented site in Europe dating to about a million years ago, but there are many scatters of crude and perhaps equally old stone tools on the ancient river terraces of southern France. Most of these tools are very crude pebble-tool choppers and flakes that resemble closely the Vallonet artifacts, and in the few cases where animal bones are associated with the tools, they are the same species found at Vallonet (de Lumley 1975).

The sites of Torralba and Ambrona, located about 1.5 kilometers apart in a deep valley some 150 kilometers northeast of Madrid, provide convincing evidence that at least some groups in Middle Pleistocene Europe engaged in big-game hunting. Excavations at Torralba in the early 1960s by F. Clark Howell exposed about 300 square meters of stratified archaeological deposits, from which were collected hundreds of pollen samples, several thousand stone tools, and countless animal bones. Analysis of the pollen samples has convinced most scholars that Torralba dates to about 400,000 years ago, but some think it is only about 200,000 years old. Pollen analysis indicates the area was a cool, swampy valley when the site was inhabited (Freeman 1975: 664). No hominid remains were found at the site, but presumably the occupants were *Homo erectus.*

The remains of at least thirty elephants were found at Torralba, as well as about twenty-five deer, twenty-five horses, ten wild oxen, and several rhinoceroses. Almost all the skeletons were disarticulated, and many of the bones were smashed and split in an effort to get at the marrow. Nearly all the elephant skulls are missing, as are many of the other bones bearing the most edible cuts of meat—suggesting they were moved some distance to be butchered, and perhaps indicating the efforts of a large, cooperating work force. The distribution of ages and sexes of the animals at this site is about what one would expect from a nonselective sample from local populations: that is, there is no evidence these hunters were concentrating on younger or older animals—they simply took what animals they could.

Thousands of bits of charcoal were found mixed with the bones and stones at Torralba, raising the possibility that these animals were driven into the bog with intentionally set fires. Scattered among the charcoal and other debris were preserved bits of wood, and some have speculated that wood may have been brought to the site to cook the butchered meat. Not a single hearth, ash concentration, or depression has been found, however.

The process of driving animals into the swamps and killing and butchering them must have been quite a spectacle, with great clouds of smoke, shrieking, demented animals, and running, shouting hominids. But we don't know how they actually slaughtered the animals. Not a single stone spearpoint was found at the site, and Freeman suggests that the animals were either stoned to death with the many fragments of rock found amid the bone or dispatched with wooden spears. It is a bit difficult to envisage stoning three or four large elephants to death, but however these animals were dispatched, it must have been a fantastic

Hitchcockian nightmare played out in this Spanish valley hundreds of thousands of years ago.

The stratigraphy at Torralba is complex, and the site probably represents not one, but many different hunting episodes. Based on the distribution of tools and the number of animals killed, Freeman estimates that

> the total size of the cooperating social groups which provided the personnel responsible for the Torralba occupation residues was very large— perhaps on the order of a hundred individuals or more. Such large population aggregates might have been feasible only periodically or seasonally, but it is quite possible, given the undoubted natural wealth of the region in mid-Pleistocene times, that large human groups were a constant feature of the landscape. (1975: 682)

The site of Ambrona is similar to Torralba, and includes the remains of about forty elephants, as well as those of many other animals, mixed with numerous stone tools and clusters of carbon and ash. The only recognizable elephant cranium found had been smashed in what was almost certainly an attempt to get at the brains, and one of the elephant tusks had been whittled to a sharp point.

In 1965 a bulldozer operation in an alley named Terra Amata in Nice, on the Mediterranean coast of France, uncovered twenty-one discrete sites dating to about 300,000 B.P., when the level of the Mediterranean was twenty-five meters higher than it is today, and the climate somewhat cooler and more humid. The inhabitants of Terra Amata constructed large huts, ranging from eight to fifteen meters in length and from four to nearly six meters in width, most of them oval in shape and estimated to have sheltered ten to twenty people. Nothing remains of the huts themselves, but their pattern is clearly evident in the long lines of postholes where supporting logs were driven into the sand, as well as in the rows of stones evidently used to brace the walls. Inside each hut was a hearth, and the floors of the huts were thickly covered with ash and the residue of organic debris, except for some areas close to the fire that were relatively free of debris, perhaps indicating places where people slept. Flat limestone blocks within the huts may have been seats or convenient places to prepare food (de Lumley 1969; Pfeiffer 1978: 141). The outlines of these various huts are so exactly superimposed and separated by such thin layers of sand that there is little doubt that the same or closely related groups were coming back each year to the same spot to build their huts and exploit local resources. Analysis of fossilized human feces revealed great quantities of

94 PATTERNS IN PREHISTORY

pollen from plants that bloom in the spring and early summer, suggesting a temporary occupation each year at this time. Most of the animal bones found at the site were from stags, elephants, boars, ibex, and rhinoceroses, but there were also bones of birds, turtles, rabbits, rodents, and a few fish and shellfish.

The stone tools from the site are mainly the large bifacially worked Acheulian tools found elsewhere in Africa and Europe at this time, and there are also a few bone tools. Unfortunately, not a single human remain has been found at Terra Amata, but it is likely that *Homo erectus* occupied this site. A single footprint was uncovered during excavations, and its modern shape and length indicate a fully bipedal hominid of about 5'1" in height.

Terra Amata's occupants were probably territorial hunters and gatherers who made regular seasonal rounds to exploit a diversity of resources, and who did considerable big-game hunting.

At Vertesszölös, a rock quarry west of Budapest, Hungary, about 400,000 years ago there were hot springs, and several layers of human occupational debris have been found near what would have been the banks of these springs. Excavations in the 1960s uncovered about 3,000 stone tools, many smashed and burned animal bones, and the occipital bone from one hominid and a few teeth from another (Vertes 1965). Initial measurements indicated that the teeth almost certainly came from a *Homo erectus*, but the estimated cranial capacity was about 1,400 cc—far larger than the *H. erectus* average. Since the animals associated with these human fossils date the hominid bones to about 400,000 to 350,000 years ago, such a large-brained individual would be very surprising. In fact, based on the estimated cranial capacity, many anthropologists concluded that the Vertesszölös hominid was a very early form of *Homo sapiens*, living at the same time as *H. erectus*. However, Milford Wolpoff has argued that the occipital bone almost certainly should be classified as *H. erectus*, because its physical characteristics are much more similar to known *H. erectus* fossils than to *H. sapiens* and because the initial estimates of cranial capacity were based on arguable reconstructions of certain morphological characteristics (1971: 209–16). In form and type proportions, the tools most closely resemble the Choukoutien and "evolved" Olduwan assemblages (discussed below), lending some tentative support to the idea that it was *H. erectus* whose activity we see reflected here. No hearths have been found at the site, but there are burned bones, indicating the use of fire.

A few fragments of teeth and bones found at Prezletice near Prague, Czechoslovakia, in 1960 may be the oldest human remains yet found in Europe. The animal remains from the site are of a species thought to have lived in glacial periods many thousands of years earlier than those found at Vertesszölös (Poirier 1973: 144). About fifty crude stone tools were found at the site, as well as an apparently worked deer bone.

THE NEAR EAST

To date, few well-documented *H. erectus* fossils have been found in the Near East. An occipital bone and part of a frontal bone were found at Kibbutz Hazorea in Israel, in association with numerous Acheulian handaxes and heavy flakes (Anati and Haas 1967; Birdsell 1972: 279). However, analysis of this site is incomplete, and the disturbed context of the find makes it difficult to date with any precision.

The site of 'Ubeidiya, three kilometers south of the Sea of Galilee in Israel, is somewhat better documented: About fourteen distinct archaeological assemblages have been uncovered at this site, all of them dating to no later than 640,000 years ago, and perhaps much earlier (Bar-Yosef 1975). The tools found here seem very similar to those from Middle and Upper Bed II at Olduvai Gorge, being mainly choppers, spheroids (rounded stones), handaxes, and used flakes. The faunal remains include large mammals, mollusks, and fish, but the remains have not been fully analyzed.

Many other Middle Pleistocene sites have been found in Palestine, most of them, unfortunately, small surface scatters very difficult to date and analyze. The majority are near springs or on lake shores, but others occur in mountain passes, plateaus, and the edges of mountain valleys (Bar-Yosef 1975). There are a few cave sites, but none has substantial depth.

EAST ASIA

One of the most important *H. erectus* sites is Choukoutien (literally "Dragon Bone Hill"), a cave site located forty-three kilometers southwest of Peking in a range of limestone hills. Excavations in collapsed cave debris at the site between 1927 and 1937, and briefly in the late 1950s, revealed the remains of more than forty hominids, as well as over 100,000 stone tools, countless animal bones, and many hearths and ash layers, all well stratified in a deposit that is an astonishing fifty meters deep. Not all this was cultural debris—cave bears and other animals alternated with hominids in occupying the cave and they probably brought in many of the animals. But Choukoutien has more superimposed occupational layers than any other known *Homo erectus* site. Analysis of the fauna and hominids and potassium argon dating suggest a date of between 400,000 and 360,000 years ago for most of the cultural debris, although the basal layers may be somewhat older (Poirier 1973: 140).

The 14 skullcaps, 6 skull bones, 10 jaw fragments, 147 teeth, and assorted arm, leg, and hand bones found at Choukoutien all appear to have come from *Homo erectus*. Brain volumes average about 1,040 cc—somewhat larger than the *H. erectus* from Java—and teeth sizes fall between ourselves and australopithecines (actually, they are only slightly larger than contemporary native Australian populations). Based on the few leg-bone fragments recovered, it is estimated that the Choukoutien hominids averaged about 5'1" in height—which may seem short, but it is significantly larger than australopithecines and only an inch or two less than the average height of most people of just a few hundred years ago.

The refuse at Choukoutien provides evidence for many insights into how these hominids lived. The winters of 360,000 years ago probably would have made fire a necessity, simply to avoid death from exposure, but the many cracked and burned animal bones indicate the inhabitants of these caves also cooked some of their food. Most of the meat was roasted venison (70 percent of the animal bones were from deer), but the hominids also ate elephants, rhinoceroses, beavers, bison, boars, and horses. Some hackberry seeds from Choukoutien are the oldest known vegetable remains from an archaeological site, and they are probably found at Choukoutien only because the inhabitants of the site used fire, which chars and thus preserves organic material. This underscores the bias in the early hominid archaeological record toward animal bones, because all hominids ate considerable amounts of vegetable foods, but only when fire was used are these remains found.

Recent reanalysis of Choukoutien stratigraphy indicates that the winters during hominid occupations may have been more moderate than previously thought, but during the winters big-game hunting was probably still a necessary part of food gathering—as indicated by the massive concentrations of butchered animals. And here, too, we might wonder how these animals were killed, since not a single spear point or arrowhead was found among the more than 100,000 tools from this site. Traps and drives may have been used, but the diversity of species killed and the consistency with which they were dispatched suggest that much of the time people were hunting single animals without resorting to trapping them in bogs or driving them over cliffs. Possibly, sharpened

3.17   Excavating at Choukoutien. The rope enclosures mark areas where hominid skulls were found.

wooden weapons were used, and if so the hunting prowess of *Homo erectus* was indeed remarkable.

The resemblance of the Choukoutien tools to the earliest European industries has often been noted, but most archaeologists place these tools within the "chopper–chopping tool tradition" that apparently developed independently in Southeast Asia and China, and they exclude the possibility of any significant contacts with European or African populations (Shapiro 1974: 82).

One other aspect of Choukoutien deserving comment is the possibility of cannibalism. Not a single skull from this site had an attached face, and the base of each skull was broken (Poirier 1973: 140). The evidence for cannibalism at Choukoutien, however, has been questioned by Binford (1981), who argues that the mixture of bones brought in by nonhuman predators with bones of cultural origins, as well as other factors, makes suspect any conclusions about cannibalism here.

Arens (1979) rejects the notion that cannibalism was a common practice for very long in any culture, ancient or recent. He may well be right, because ecologically (Garn and Block 1970), systematic cannibalism is a poor food-procurement strategy. Compared to almost any other animals, people are hard to catch in relation to the food they supply, and one risks depleting the stock extremely quickly if cannibalism is at all frequent.

The best evidence of ancient cannibalism should be in the archaeological record, and on that basis I have my suspicions about *Homo erectus*. Even the brightest of his ilk probably spent little time discussing the mind-body problem or the caloric return of cannibalism.

All the Choukoutien hominid remains disappeared while being transferred from Peking to an American ship during the Japanese invasion of China prior to the Second World War. Recently, a woman in New York City, describing herself as the widow of one of the marines involved in this transfer, arranged a meeting with an American businessman who had been trying to locate these bones for some time. At the meeting, which at the woman's insistence took place on the observation deck of the Empire State Building, she showed him a photograph of some bones but mysteriously fled when some tourists with cameras appeared. A copy of the photograph of the bones was eventually obtained from the still unidentified woman, and one skull looks very much like a true *H. erectus*—at least to Harry Shapiro, Philip Tobias, and William Howells, all experts on the Choukoutien fossils (Shapiro 1974). To date, no progress has been made in locating any of the fossils, but fortunately, at the time of their discovery the great German anatomist Franz Widenreich made excellent plaster casts of them all and described them in superlative detail. It would be interesting to have the original bones, of course, but their metrical characteristics are already well established.

Hominid fossils found at various places on Java by Dubois (p. 50) and others seem to range between 1.9 million years and 500,000 years ago in age, but they appear to have changed remarkably little over this span—much less so than the European and African varieties of *Homo erectus,* perhaps (Thorne and Wolpoff 1981).

Our summary of the artifacts and fossils of the Middle Pleistocene must conclude with that most familiar of all archaeological laments, "More research is needed." Nonetheless, given the evidence from East

Africa, as well as the possibly early development of *Homo erectus* in Southeast Asia, it would appear that the movement into northern latitudes and subsequent big-game hunting were not, by themselves, the major factors in the evolution of *Homo erectus* or his cultural repertoire. Generally, we have little positive evidence about exactly what factors were most powerful in producing the rapid increases in brain size and significantly more effective technologies of the Middle Pleistocene. Once the step to toolmaking and use and essentially human forms of social organization and communication had been made, subsequent cultural changes seem to have been shaped by strong competitive pressures, so that some innovations in material culture or behavior were strongly and directly "selected for." The circularity of this assessment can only be eliminated through evidence and analyses we do not yet possess.

In fact, discoveries yet to come will probably greatly alter even our basic idea of what *Homo erectus* was. In 1984 Richard Leakey reported finding in Kenya the almost complete skeleton of a twelve-year-old *Homo erectus* male that dated to more than a million years ago. Based on leg measurements, Leakey estimates that as an adult this individual would have been almost 2 meters tall—far taller than most anthropologists estimate most humans were until modern times.

4

The Emergence
of *Homo sapiens sapiens*

Man is the missing link between anthropoid apes
and human beings.

Anonymous

By about 400,000 years ago, our *Homo erectus* ancestors had become
skilled hunters and gatherers, exploiting environments from the temperate zones of Pleistocene Europe to the tropics of Africa and Java.
And if the evidence from Torralba-Ambrona has been interpreted correctly (chapter 3), at least some of them were living in complex webs of
social relationships involving many individuals (Sigmon and Cybulski,
eds. 1981).

In his way of life, then, *Homo erectus* appears to have been very similar to modern hunters and gatherers; yet there is something alien about
the creature. We look for artifacts expressing ritual or complex symbol-
ism, but not a single figurine, wall painting, or rock carving can be securely attributed to *Homo erectus*. In some Upper Paleolithic sites (ca.
30,000 to 10,000 years ago), there are hundreds of beautifully crafted
stone tools, some so delicately worked that even moderate use would
ruin them—tools that must have been made in large part simply for the
pleasure of creating something beautiful. But the tools of *Homo erectus* are, with few exceptions, undeviatingly simple, efficient, utilitarian
objects.

Perhaps even more revealing, there are no known *Homo erectus*
burials or ritual dispositions of corpses. Over the last 100,000 years,
death has almost everywhere been an occasion for the outpouring of
human emotion, and even the simplest hunters and gatherers during

this span usually disposed of their dead by digging a hole and placing a few stone tools or bits of shell in with the body; but not a single *Homo erectus* anywhere in the world appears to have been even intentionally buried, let alone sent off to the next world with a few provisions and expressions of goodwill.

These various absences of stylistic behavior among *Homo erectus* can be interpreted in several different ways. *Homo erectus,* with his brain about two-thirds the size of our own, may simply have lacked the mental equipment to generalize and symbolize his experiences as we do. On the other hand, if the archaeological record is to be believed, many later, more "advanced" *Homo sapiens* cultures also neglected to bury their dead and to make figurines, wall paintings, and other aesthetic expressions. Some therefore suggest that *Homo erectus* had the potential for almost the same stylistic, religious, and social impulses that modern people feel, but lived in circumstances that did not elicit such expressions.

It is difficult to overstate the importance of the evolution of aesthetic, ritual, and social feelings, for as we shall see, it was precisely these kinds of mental characteristics that made possible the rise of great civilizations. Thus, we are particularly concerned in this chapter with the conditions under which these feelings first appeared (as reflected in the archaeological record) and with their concurrent important cultural developments.

The differences between *Homo erectus* and *Homo sapiens,* and the time period from 250,000 to 30,000 years ago in which they occur, are generally referred to as the "Middle/Upper Paleolithic transition" and involve the following elements: (1) an increase of average human brain size from about 1,100 to about 1,450 cc (although local variability was high at various times early in the Middle Paleolithic); (2) changes in human facial architecture and increases in body size; (3) increased human population numbers and densities—again with considerable local variation; (4) many technological innovations, including the bow and arrow, atlatl (throwing stick), bone and wood tools of diverse types, and techniques for extracting a relatively great amount of cutting edge from a given amount of stone; (5) figurines, usually of bone or stone, beautiful wall paintings and rock carvings, and burials and arrangements of bones and tools that clearly reflect a developed aesthetic consciousness; (6) a shift from generalized hunting patterns to concentrations in some areas on gregarious herd mammals like deer and horses; and (7) the appearance of artifact styles and trade in exotic items that bespeak the first manifestation of some sort of regional "ethnic" identity that exceeds by a wide margin the local band society.

What we have, then, is the "total restructuring" of social relationships during the Middle/Upper Paleolithic transition (White 1982) and
some dramatic physical anthropological change as well.

The obvious question is, How were our ancestors changed by time
and circumstance in these highly significant ways in the relatively short
period between *Homo erectus* and ourselves?

Successors to *Homo erectus*

Despite considerable local variation, *Homo erectus* remains and artifacts look quite similar, all the way from Java to France. But the evidence is poor. We have only a few remains for the crucial period from
325,000 to 100,000 years ago. Our earliest well-documented evidence
for the initial stages of the evolution of *Homo erectus* into *Homo sapiens* comes from Swanscombe, England, along the Thames River, not
far from London. In 1935 workers in a cement plant uncovered a cranial bone from a gravel bank, and a year later another cranial bone
fragment was found nearby that articulated perfectly with the first
bone. Later, during excavations connected with preparations for the
Allied invasion of France in 1944, another bone from the same skull
was found just twenty-five meters from the site of the first find. It is
very possible, incidentally, that more hominid bones were included in
the gravel used to make concrete for floating docks during the D-Day
operation (Pfeiffer 1978: 173).

In the same gravel layers whence these bones came, excavators recovered the bones of extinct forms of elephants, deer, rhinoceroses, and
pigs which, together with subsequent chemical analysis and geological
evidence, dated the Swanscombe fossils to an interglacial period about
225,000 years ago, when the abundance of horses, elephants, rhinoceroses, and other big-game species would have made England an ideal
place for generalized hunting and gathering groups. Nor is there any
problem explaining how these hominids would have gotten there, since
Britain and Ireland were physically joined to Europe by a land bridge
at various times during the early and middle Pleistocene.

The Swanscombe cranial remains are probably those of a woman of
twenty to twenty-five years of age, with a cranial capacity of about 1,275
to 1,325 cc (Poirier 1973: 158)—well within the range of modern humans. Handaxes roughly similar to those of the Acheulian assemblages of France and Africa are among the most frequent tools in the
level where the skull was found, but lower levels contain only flakes
and choppers. Similar flakes and choppers have been found elsewhere

in England and are commonly referred to as the *Clactonian* assemblage (Roe 1981). A wooden spear fragment found at Clacton is the earliest wooden artifact recovered anywhere, dating to 400,000 to 200,000 years ago. Stone projectile points are not found at Swanscombe, Choukoutien, or any other site prior to about 150,000 years ago, and thus the wooden spear fragment from Swanscombe may be a clue to how these Middle Pleistocene peoples managed to kill big game without sharp stone-tipped spears. If animals were trapped in bogs, they could have been killed by multiple stab wounds with wooden spears—although it could not have been pleasant work.

Another possible technique is that used by Native American hunters in northern Canada to kill Kodiak bears. The hunter braces against his foot a long, pointed spear held at a 45° angle to the ground and then induces the bear to charge. There are some "ties" but few second rounds in such contests. However Pleistocene colleagues of the Swanscombe woman dispatched their prey, it was probably with a "grace under pressure" that would make the protagonists of Hemingway's novels seem a bit effeminate.

A nearly complete skull found in 1933 at Steinheim, Germany has helped to clarify the taxonomic position of the Swanscombe and Clactonian material. This cranium, dated to about 250,000 years ago, probably belonged to a young woman whose brain size and facial features place her between *H. erectus* and ourselves. The cranial volume is between 1,150 and 1,175 cc—within the range of *H. erectus*—but the teeth and other parts of the masticatory apparatus are very different from those of most other *H. erectus* and quite similar to our own. All of the molars, for example, are smaller than the corresponding averages for modern Australian Aborigines. Because the brain size falls within the low end of the range of variation of modern European peoples and the facial architecture seems smaller and more "modern" than that of most *Homo erectus* and Neanderthal individuals, some classify the Steinheim woman as a subspecies of our own species, that is, *H. sapiens steinheimensis*. The important thing here is that we should interpret these fossils in terms of the *range* of variability we might expect from any given population, and in this context it is significant that both the Swanscombe and Steinheim fossils are well within the range of modern humans. Anatole France, one of the most creative minds of his generation, had a cranial capacity of little more than 900 cc, and similar variability exists in contemporary populations.

Unfortunately, no artifacts were found with the Steinheim skull, so we cannot compare the site with the material from southern England. Nonetheless, the physical differences between this individual and *Homo*

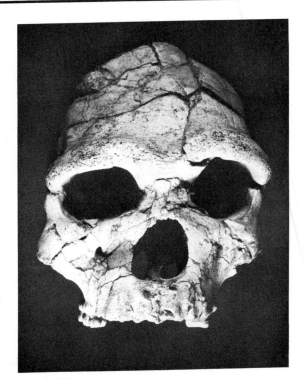

4.1 The Arago skull, from
France. This approximately
twenty-year-old man had more
robust facial features than
many Neanderthals and is
probably intermediate be-
tween *Homo erectus* and
Homo sapiens.

erectus indicate that the transition from *H. erectus* to *H. sapiens* was
well underway by 300,000 to 250,000 years ago and was taking place in
more than one part of western Europe.

Recent excavations in a cave site in the French Pyrenees unearthed
a skull (the Arago skull) and two mandibles (Figure 4.1) dated to about
200,000 years ago that seemed to fill the gap between the Javanese
Homo erectus and the European Neanderthals (M.-A. de Lumley 1975).
The skull possesses some morphological characteristics of *Homo erectus* in the Far East but lacks the incipient sagittal crest usually found
in these populations. The large size of the teeth and mandible and the
structure of the chin seem to foreshadow the features of the "classic"
(western European) Neanderthal.

Late *Homo erectus* remains have also been found at Bilzingsleben in
the German Democratic Republic, along with a somewhat atypical assemblage of very small tools with much larger implements, all quite different from the typical Acheulian assemblage.

Few human fossils dating from 400,000 to 100,000 years ago have
been found in Asia or Africa, and until they are, we cannot determine
whether the emergence of *Homo sapiens* from *H. erectus* was happen-

ing worldwide or was a more localized phenomenon, perhaps centered in Europe. Analysis of the artifacts associated with the European fossils has been hampered by small samples and the disturbed contexts in which they are usually found, but generally the Middle Pleistocene does not seem a period of substantial change in basic adaptation. Tool technology, diet, site locations, and average group size in Europe about 200,000 years ago do not seem much different from those of several hundred thousand years earlier, as represented at Choukoutien and Torralba-Ambrona. Clearly, however, population densities were increasing, and as people moved into more diverse niches there was an increasing variety in the stone tools associated with them.

In searching for causes of the increasing brain size and other changes between 400,000 and 100,000 years ago, we might note that rates of evolutionary change frequently seem to be higher along the margins of a species' range. This may have been the case with *Homo erectus,* as bands of these hominids probed far into England, northern Europe, and perhaps northern Eurasia, and began to specialize in big-game hunting. Seen in this light, the Swanscombe and Steinheim individuals, with their nearly modern brain size, may be reflections of these developments along the northern periphery. Gene flow in most hunting and gathering societies is sufficiently high that these changes in brain size and facial architecture would probably have been quickly disseminated over a wide area.

Stephen Gabow (1977) has proposed a complex explanation for the rapid rate of increase in cranial capacity that is based on a population-genetics model. Noting that there were probably great internal changes in human brain tissue as well as an absolute increase in the amount, he sought a cause for the overall developmental pattern in the "subdivision" of Pleistocene human populations into many small groups of people adapted to somewhat different environments. For mathematical reasons too involved to be considered here, it seems likely that the optimum situation for producing the kinds of massive physical changes associated with Pleistocene cranial capacity increases was one in which people adapted to local environments and interbred within large groups for long periods and then (because of the colonization of new environments, migrations, and so on) interbred with different groups. This condition of "oscillating gene flow" was probably common during the Pleistocene, as people developed the technology to cope with many different environments ranging from the littorals of Southeast Asia to northern Eurasia.

It is difficult to determine what factors made increased brain size an advantage, particularly since brain tissue has a relatively high "cost": it consumes great amounts of energy and oxygen. Also, the birth of large-brained offspring requires pelvic bone structure that reduces maternal mobility. Since *Homo erectus* was obviously an efficient hunter, forager, and toolmaker, perhaps the increased brain size was related to increasing emotional capacities rather than big-game hunting skills or improved rationality. Great advantages would accrue to a Pleistocene hunting and gathering group that could organize itself as part of a social network involving many different bands and hundreds of individuals, and perhaps the increasing brain size had to do with the selective advantage of being able to generalize emotions to scores of "kinsmen." Nevertheless, the great variability of cranial capacity among "normal" humans and the fact that human brain size seems generally to have increased quite uniformly up to about 100,000 years ago should warn against simplistic explanations of this phenomenon.

Not every characteristic of our ancestors can be seen as the direct result of natural selection, however, because selection operates on the whole organism. Thus, some characteristics or features may be selected for simply because they are biologically associated with another feature that is the real focus of selection (for examples of the fallacy of "hyperselectionism," see Gould 1980).

The Neanderthals

Between about 100,000 and 35,000 years ago, Europe, the Near East, and perhaps parts of Africa and Asia were occupied by *Homo sapiens neanderthalensis* ("Neanderthal man"). Fossils classed as Neanderthals or "Neanderthaloids" have come from scores of sites, from China to Germany. The characteristics most frequently used to define them are: (1) a receding or virtually absent chin; (2) large cheekbones and prominent brow ridges curving over the eye orbits and connecting across the bridge of the nose; (3) prognathism (protruding lower face); (4) a strong masticatory apparatus, including larger front teeth than are found in most modern human populations; (5) short (average of perhaps five feet) but powerful stature, with thick and slightly curved long bones; and (6) a cranial capacity some 50 to 100 cc greater than that of modern European populations. The "classic" or western European Neanderthals are sometimes seen as cold-adapted physical types, who may have been reproductively isolated to some degree from other populations. Thus, some do not think it useful to extend the term *Neanderthal* to populations of Africa and Asia (Howells 1975: 405).

As any winter resident of the North knows, movement into northern

4.2 This artist's reconstruction of a Neanderthal band on the move depicts these individuals as somewhat more brutish in appearance than they probably were.

climates means getting whiter and fatter. Up to 80 percent of the energy value of food goes simply to maintain body temperatures, and it is an inescapable fact of physics that spheres lose heat more slowly than an elongated rectangle of equal volume. Even with the pervasive movements of people during the last century, the relationship between body shape and mean temperature—as epitomized by the Watusi and the Eskimo—is strong (Roberts 1953).

The white skins of northern peoples have to do most directly with the fact that people are dependent on Vitamin D, which is present in some foods but can also be synthesized in humans by the action of sunlight on skin. Whiter shades of skin are more susceptible to cancer, acne, and psoriasis than darker tones, so the selection for whiter skins as people moved farther north was not an unmixed blessing. It is also probable that these later invasions of cold climates gave rise to subtle genetic changes in mankind. Even such apparently minor matters as

blood types may have been developing at this time in response to factors we cannot isolate. Blood type "O," for example, seems to be more
resistant to diabetes, heart attacks, anemia, and even certain kinds of
bone fractures (Jorgensen 1977), but we don't know how or when the
different blood types evolved.

NEANDERTHAL SUBSISTENCE AND SOCIAL ADAPTATION

The fossil that gave this stage of human evolution its name was found
in the Neander Valley in southwestern Germany in 1856, and because
it belonged to the first premodern human identified, the Neanderthals
received much of the initial hostility to the concept of human evolution. From the beginning anthropologists, clergy, and others held that
the Neanderthals were an aberrant stage in human development, not
directly related to our own, presumably superior, ancestors.

   C. Loring Brace (1964) has argued that the initial classification of
Neanderthals as off the main line of our own evolution was rooted in
the errors of nineteenth-century French paleontology. The chief vil-
lain in Brace's history of Neanderthal studies is French paleontologist
Marcellin Boule, who between 1911 and 1913 published studies that depicted the Neanderthals as bow-legged, slouching, simian-looking individuals who were neither very intelligent nor agile. He did not actually state that Neanderthals couldn't walk and chew gum at the same
time, or that they drooled incessantly, but Boule used the words *ape-
like, primitive,* and *inferior* so frequently that neither he nor later
scholars were anxious to claim Neanderthals as ancestors. And for many
years Neanderthals were widely thought to be inferior side branches on
the human evolutionary tree.

   Before and after Boule's publications, however, some scholars concluded that the Neanderthals were the connecting link between *Homo
erectus* and at least some populations of *Homo sapiens sapiens.* Once
fossils with Neanderthal characteristics were found in western and central Europe and the Near East, it was difficult to see them as a small isolated minority that had developed in its own peculiar and unrewarding
direction. In 1957 a conference on the Neanderthal produced evidence
that Neanderthal brain size on the average was *larger* than that of most
human groups and that there were no grounds for concluding that
their brains were structurally inferior or that they did not walk fully
erect. In fact, it was suggested that "if he could be reincarnated and
placed in a New York subway—provided that he were bathed, shaved,
and dressed in modern clothing—it is doubtful he would attract any

more attention than some of its other denizens" (Straus and Cave 1957).

With the rehabilitation of the Neanderthals as physical specimens came an increased interest in their subsistence and social adaptations. The Neanderthals are identified with the *Mousterian* stone-tool industry (named after the site of Le Moustier in southern France), which includes several distinctive stylistic and functional elements.

There are scores of Mousterian sites in the Dordogne region of southwestern France, including cave sites, rock shelters, and "open-air" locations. The Dordogne is one of the most beautiful regions of France, where glaciers and rivers have gouged the land surface into hundreds of small valleys and plateaus, all heavily forested and abundantly watered by rivers and streams. The region is a massive limestone formation with caves and rock overhangs, and during the Pleistocene these formations provided warm and dry shelters for countless generations of people.

One of the largest and most complex Mousterian sites in this area is a cave in the Combe Grenal Valley, twenty-two kilometers from the village of Les Eyzies, near the Dordogne River. François Bordes uncovered sixty-four superimposed occupational levels in this cave, spanning the period from about 150,000 to 40,000 years ago, with few long periods of abandonment. The lowest levels contained tools resembling the Acheulian tools found at Swanscombe, but all later levels had the classic Mousterian tools usually associated with Neanderthals. More than 19,000 Mousterian implements were collected and analyzed from this site, and the tools from different levels contrast sharply. Some levels contained many small flakelike pieces of stone, while others had concentrations of scores of "toothed" or "denticulated" tools. Moreover, analysis of the different levels revealed that certain types of tools tended to be spatially associated with a number of other types. That is, levels containing a relatively high number of projectile points would usually contain relatively large numbers of scrapers and flakes—but few denticulates.

What is the significance of this diversity? No scholars have spent as much time trying to answer this question as Denise and François Bordes. Through years of excavation and analysis, they built up a classification of Mousterian stone tools that has been the framework for much of the work done on this period. They (e.g., F. Bordes 1961a) classified all Mousterian tools into four categories, based on the relative frequencies of certain types. François Bordes observed that these four different assemblages seem to occur in different levels of the same sites, as well as at sites in very different areas, and he originally thought this was because the different assemblages reflected different activities car-

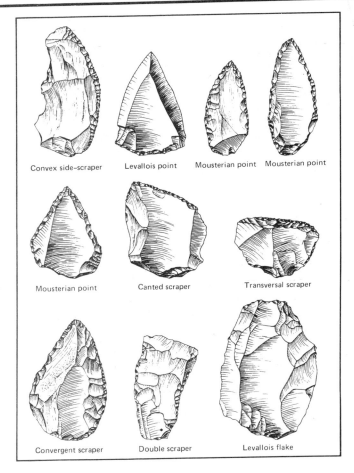

Convex side–scraper   Levallois point   Mousterian point   Mousterian point

Mousterian point   Canted scraper   Transversal scraper

Convergent scraper   Double scraper   Levallois flake

4.3 Some of the typical tool types of the Mousterian period.

ried out during different times of the year. But he soon rejected this possibility because analysis of bones and botanical evidence showed that each of the four assemblages could be found in deposits representing each season. His second supposition was that different tool assemblages represented activities engaged in during different climatic periods, some having been used during colder millennia of the Pleistocene and then replaced by others during warmer, interglacial periods. Excavations revealed, however, that all assemblages could be found in areas as different climatologically as the Near East, Africa, and western Europe.

Bordes considered the possibility that these differences represent change through time, but his final hypothesis was that the four dif-

ferent clusters of tools are the remains of four distinct cultural traditions, or "tribes," which developed certain kinds of tool manufacture
and retained these distinctive expressions over the 30,000 years of the
Mousterian period.

> All the history of Europe shows . . . that man exchanges his genes
> more readily than his customs. Moreover, in primitive societies, con-
> servatism is usually very strong, and if one supposes that a Mousterian
> of Acheulian Tradition married a Quina woman, she might well have
> gone on using the thick scrapers to which she was accustomed, but we
> doubt that her daughters would have done the same. It is, however,
> possible that the sporadic occurrence of tools which are characteristic of
> a given type of Mousterian, among the tool kit of another type, may be
> a trace of such a contact. (Bordes and Bordes 1970: 65)

Bordes's vision of the Mousterian, then, was one in which different
tribes of Neanderthals wandered much of the Old World for generation
after generation, through tens of thousands of years, each group maintaining its unique styles of tool manufacture and meeting the others in-
frequently and usually with hostility.

Bordes's analysis of Mousterian variability was questioned by American archaeologists Lewis and Sally Binford, who raise some theoretical
issues whose importance transcends the empirical question of the significance of Mousterian tool variability. They argue that studies

> in many parts of the world have shown that formal variation in mate-
> rial items that is inexplicable in terms of function of raw materials can
> be termed *stylistic* variation . . . ; these stylistic variations tend to clus-
> ter spatially in direct relationship to the amount of social distance
> maintained between societies. Spatial clusterings of the Mousterian as-
> semblages are not demonstrable; in fact, in the Dordogne region of
> France the four types of Mousterian assemblages occur interdigitated at
> several localities.
>
> In view of the demonstrated alternation of industries, one must envi-
> sion a perpetual movement of culturally distinct peoples, never reacting
> to or coping with their neighbors. Nor do they exhibit the typically hu-
> man characteristics of mutual influence and borrowing. *Such a situation
> is totally foreign in terms of our knowledge of sapiens behavior.* (1966:
> 240; emphasis added)

Thus, in contrast to Bordes, the Binfords assume that (1) such things
as tool variability are best analyzed in terms of how these different tools
enabled individuals to adapt to their environment; and (2) that cultural traditions in close proximity do not become and remain distinct

for tens of thousands of years for no reason other than an unexplainable human capacity for this type of behavior. In short, the Binfords' position is that if we cannot connect the Neanderthals with ourselves in terms of fundamental cultural processes common to both, then the archaeology of the Mousterian and earlier periods can be nothing more than speculative descriptions of these extinct cultures. They assume that Mousterian tool variability was largely a reflection of the different tasks Neanderthals had to perform to meet successfully the demands of their environment. They do not dispute that the Neanderthals expressed themselves stylistically; they simply believe that Neanderthal stylistic expressions would follow patterns similar to those of all other humans.

They tested these ideas through a statistical analysis of Mousterian tools from three widely separated Neanderthal sites: the Jabrud Rock Shelter (near Damascus, Syria); Mugharet es-Shubbabiq Cave, in Israel; and an "open-air" station near Houpeville, France. Each site contained several different levels, representing different occupations, the total number of which for the three sites was sixteen. Lithics from each site were classified in terms of Bordes's system and statistically analyzed to search for evidence that these groups of tools were used for different economic activities, rather than simply representing stylistic traditions. The statistical method used, *factor analysis,* is a procedure for analyzing correlation or covariation matrices and was employed in this case to determine which of the tool types were usually found in close proximity to one another in the various levels of the different sites. If representatives of two or more tool types were frequently found close to one another, the inference was made that they were a tool kit, that is, were used for the same activities.

The Binfords' factor analysis revealed that the sixteen different Mousterian occupations from the three sites could be reduced to five main specialized tool kits (1966: 249–58).

1.   Tool Kit I: twelve tool types including borers, end-scrapers, and knives. These may have been used to work bone and wood into shafts or hafts and to work skins for cordage. These tools are associated with toolmaking and maintenance activities.
2.   Tool Kit II: twelve tool types, including three kinds of points, scrapers, and burins. The inferred function is hunting and butchering.
3.   Tool Kit III: seven tool types, most of them flakes and knives. The inferred function is fine butchering.
4.   Tool Kit IV: four tool types, including used flakes and scrapers. The suggested function is preparing wood and plant foods and possibly the scraping of bones.

5. Tool Kit V: six tool types, including a projectile-point type, discs, scrapers, and blades. This kit appears to be a blend of hunting and butchering and perhaps other kinds of tools.

The distribution of the different tool kits at these three sites seems in line with the Binfords' inferences about their uses. The cave site in Israel, for example, is a large well-lighted area that would probably make an excellent base camp for Neanderthal hunters, and the preponderance of tool kits I, II, and III here would seem to support this inference. Tool kit I, supposedly a maintenance and toolmaking assemblage, was particularly frequent at this site, as one would expect if this were a base camp. And several hearths found near the entrance of the cave were surrounded by a high proportion of tool kit III knives and flakes—tools thought to be used for delicate cutting and food preparation and other activities associated with a base camp.

The Syrian rock shelter is much smaller than the Israeli cave and apparently was a temporary work camp used by hunters during forays away from their base camp. Tool kits II and V—both associated with killing and butchering activities—predominated.

The Binfords' study stimulated interest in statistical analysis of archaeological data and solidified the Neanderthals' position in the evolution of modern humans. The interpretation of stone-tool variability as evidence of different functions may seem an obvious point, but the Binfords' assumptions about culture as an adaptive mechanism and the dynamics of human cultural expression differed from the ideas of many archaeologists at the time. Since then, various people have criticized the specifics of their statistical analyses, but their basic approach has been widely imitated.

Also, recent evidence (M.-A. de Lumley 1975) suggests that the Bordian typology applies only to a small percentage of the total number of Mousterian sites in western Europe; many others exhibit variability that the typology cannot adequately capture.

NEANDERTHAL CULTURES AND SOCIETY

As if the slurs cast on Neanderthal intelligence and posture by early archaeologists were not enough, some anthropologists have recently questioned whether or not Neanderthals were able to produce the range of sounds necessary for normal human speech. P. Lieberman and E. Crelin (1971) reconstructed the vocal apparatus of Neanderthals using a computer simulation based on the measurement of a classic Neanderthal and, using the vocal tracts of chimpanzees and human infants for comparison, they concluded that western European Neanderthals would not have been able to make some vowels, such as /e/, and, perhaps, some labial and dental consonants, such as /b/ and /d/. Others doubt that the Neanderthals could speak at all. However, since parrots have been taught to make most of the sounds of many languages, it is difficult to see much significance in differences between Neanderthal and modern vocal anatomy; and there is no conclusive evidence that osteological dimensions and topography are certain indicators of speech abilities (Carlisle and Siegel 1974).

Whatever their fluency, the many Neanderthal burials indicate that they invested their life and death with considerable ritual. Excavations at La Chapelle-aux-Saints revealed a corpse laid out in a shallow trench, with a bison leg placed on his chest, and the trench filled in with bones, tools, and other debris—perhaps representing offerings of animal flesh and implements. At La Ferrassie, a Neanderthal "cemetery" was found, where a man, a woman, two children, and two infants had been carefully buried. A flat stone slab had been placed on the man's chest, the woman was in a flexed position, and, toward the back of the cave, the skull and skeleton of one of the children were buried in separate holes, about one meter apart. The skull was covered by a triangular piece of limestone whose underside appears to have been engraved with cup-shaped markings. At Monte Cicero, in Italy, a Neanderthal skull—with a hole cut into the base—was placed in the middle of a circle of stones. At Teshik-Tash, in Siberia, a Neanderthal child was buried in a grave surrounded by six goat skulls whose horns had been jabbed into the ground. At Shanidar Cave in Iraq, the soil near a Neanderthal burial contained massive quantities of flower pollen. Ralph Solecki, the excavator, and the palynologist, Arlette Leroi-Gourhan, concluded that the skeleton had been buried with garlands of flowers. The evidence is somewhat equivocal, however (Brace 1975: 86).

Besides these mortuary evidences of solicitude, there is evidence that Neanderthals were not insensitive to the plight of their physically disadvantaged comrades. Some Neanderthals evidently suffered terribly from arthritis or had lost limbs and so could not have contributed much to the group's food supply. Yet, they must have been supported by the rest of their society. Despite these rather touching displays of societal concern, there is considerable evidence that Neanderthals killed, butchered, and perhaps ate one another.

S. Garn and W. Block (1970) have pointed out that the edible muscle mass of a 110-pound-man would only be about 10 pounds, and thus eating humans does not make much ecological sense under normal conditions. Still, at Krapina in Yugoslavia, excavations revealed twenty Neanderthals, men, women, and children, whose skulls had been smashed to bits and their long bones split lengthwise, perhaps so that the marrow could be extracted. Many of the bones were charred. Other fossils from Java, Gibraltar, Germany, and France suggest that cannibalism in the Mousterian period was not unique to any specific regional cuisine.

All Neanderthals were apparently hunters and gatherers, but they must have varied considerably throughout their range in the kinds of resources they exploited. The archaeological record is no doubt biased, because most Neanderthal sites found and excavated are those made evident by masses of animal bones associated with stone tools; the remains of plant foods and wooden tools, of course, do not preserve nearly so well and are not as easily found.

Neanderthals were probably very like recent human hunters and gatherers in habits and abilities. Population densities appear to have been low, and it is likely that most Neanderthals lived with the same group of twenty-five or fifty people their whole lives long, from time to time meeting other bands for mate exchanges. They were skilled big-game hunters, locked into seasonal migrations with the animals they hunted, but in most habitats they probably foraged widely for eggs, birds, plants, and other small resources. They competed quite successfully with other predators for game but must have occasionally lost out to the zoological carnival of horrors whose ranges they shared. Giant cave bears, saber-toothed cats, and wolves occasionally "selected out" an unfortunate Neanderthal: "Some days you eat the bear, some days the bear eats you" was probably no empty cliché in the Mousterian period.

Homo sapiens Neanderthalensis AND *Homo sapiens sapiens*

Few aspects of Neanderthal existence have aroused such interest as has their demise, primarily because it was originally thought that the Neanderthals "disappeared" as a physical type rather abruptly after about 35,000 years ago. No Neanderthal bones have been found postdating this time, and in some sites tool types widely believed to be associated with Neanderthals are overlain with levels containing tools different in style.

Some think the Neanderthals may have evolved directly into modern European peoples. Few if any reliable hominid fossils from the period between 45,000 and 25,000 years ago in western Europe have been found, so we do not know much about what was happening to the physical form of these populations during this interval. C. L. Brace (1967) has suggested that the improved efficiency of Mousterian tools greatly relaxed the selective pressures for a heavy masticatory apparatus, which is the primary difference between Neanderthal and modern skeletal material (Smith and Ranyard 1981). Most Neanderthal dentition shows evidence of extreme wear on the front teeth, so the process may have been only beginning in the early Mousterian period. Others have argued that the Neanderthals were killed off by people very similar to contemporary Europeans. This theme is skillfully used by William Golding in his novel *The Inheritors,* where peaceful, egalitarian, vegetarian Neanderthals face oblivion at the hands of villainous, meat-eating, beer-drinking *Homo sapiens sapiens.*

But there are many problems with this idea from an anthropological point of view. Extended, high-casualty warfare has never been observed among peoples living at this stage of cultural evolution, and it is difficult to imagine Neanderthals diverging so radically and pointlessly in this direction. If *Homo sapiens neanderthalensis* and *Homo sapiens sapiens* did live at the same time, there was probably a significant amount of genetic exchange between them rather than warfare. Throughout the ages humans have expressed a fine democratic spirit in sexual affairs, and wherever different "races" have coexisted, they have interbred.

Some anthropologists have suggested that the extinction of the western Neanderthals may have resulted from the expansion of *Homo sapiens sapiens* possessing superior linguistic and technological skills. B. Campbell speculates that even if these more modern peoples did not directly kill off the Neanderthals, "natural selection would have worked at maximum efficiency to weed out the slow talkers and foster better speaking skills" (1976: 375). But as noted previously, we really have no solid evidence that the Neanderthals were any less fluent than other people, and it is not at all clear that superior language skills beyond a certain level would be that much of a selective advantage to small groups of hunters and gatherers.

The Upper Paleolithic

To understand the disappearance of the Neanderthals, we must consider the period of from about 40,000 to 10,000 years ago, the *Upper Paleolithic.* The term *Upper Paleolithic* has been used to refer both to the period of the late Pleistocene and to the evolution of more efficient stone tools—a development that occurred at different times in different areas. For present purposes we are concerned mainly with the period between about 40,000 and 10,000 years ago, during which the last several major glaciations took place.

The major developments of this period, aside from the demise of the Neanderthals and the appearance of anatomically modern people, include: (1) the expansion of humans into most of the world's habitable areas, including the New World and Australia; (2) the relatively sudden and widespread appearance of figurines and other artifacts reflecting heightened interest in art and ritual; and (3) a wide range of technological innovations, including more efficient methods of stone-tool manufacture, the bow and arrow, bolas, harpoons, and many kinds of fishing equipment. In addition, there is some evidence that the Upper Paleolithic was a time of considerable social reorganization. Upper Paleolithic groups in some areas may have been much larger than their predecessors, and some of them appear to have traveled less frequently and shorter distances. There is some evidence that toward the end of the Upper Paleolithic, there were changes in the kinds of foods people were exploiting and the ways they were exploiting them; this led in some areas to domestication and agriculture. Finally, some anthropologists think the "racial" characteristics of some contemporary human populations emerged during the Upper Paleolithic—a biologically incidental, but for our age, at least, socially important development.

The "classical" model (Bricker 1976) of the Upper Paleolithic had its origins when, in 1868, five very ancient-appearing human skeletons were found in a rock shelter during a road-widening project near Les Eyzies in southern France. The first Neanderthals had been discovered a few years before, and uneasy feelings about our descent from such barbaric-looking creatures had already begun to surface. But the bones from near Les Eyzies—named *Cro-Magnon man* after the rock shelter where they had been found—proved to be from individuals very much like modern Europeans in physical form. Here was an extremely ancient man, but of a race with which nineteenth-century Europeans could feel a strong sense of kinship and even pride. The discovery of these respectable ancestors stimulated great interest in prehistory, and amateur archaeologists soon began to pillage sites all over Europe.

French archaeologists initially defined the Upper Paleolithic into periods based on specific types of tools, such as "end-scrapers," "burins," and long bladelike tools, and various kinds of bone, antler, and ivory artifacts; and because these tools were not known in many areas, including Southeast Asia and sub-Saharan Africa, they concluded that these areas did not "have" an Upper Paleolithic, even suggesting that some of these areas were culturally "retarded."

Another aspect of this "classical" model of the Upper Paleolithic was the belief that the Upper Paleolithic archaeological materials were the work of anatomically modern humans and the Mousterian assemblages were the products of Neanderthals or other premodern humans. A direct equation between anatomy and technology was made, and it was thought that one could determine the physical form of the people who inhabited a particular site simply by looking at the artifacts at that site.

A third key element in the classical model of the Upper Paleolithic is the idea that the humans and the technological developments associated with the Upper Paleolithic had come into western Europe from the Near East, Asia, or some other place. Adherents of the classical model usually envisioned a single place of origin, from which modern humans had diffused to the rest of the world.

The evidence usually adduced to demonstrate that modern humans swept into Europe and annihilated the Neanderthals is a number of sites where levels containing Mousterian tools are directly overlain by levels containing punch-blades, bone tools, and other artifacts thought to have been made by anatomically modern humans. But this conception is questionable on a number of points. First, it is significant that the earliest industry usually associated with the Upper Paleolithic, the Chatelperronian (ca. 35,000 to 32,000 B.C.), has never been found in unmistakable association with human skeletal material, and, as Bricker notes, the "anatomy of the Chatelperronian artificer must be considered unknown" (1976: 140). Of even greater significance is the now almost certain proof that Mousterian styles of tools were being made by people physically indistinguishable from contemporary Europeans. Most of this evidence comes from outside western Europe (specifically Afghanistan, Israel, and central Europe), but at least one site in Spain, La Cueva de la Cariguela, may show this Mousterian tools–*Homo sapiens sapiens* association.

Although no site has been found in Europe with Neanderthal skeletal remains in direct association with Upper Paleolithic tools, there are almost no human skeletal remains *of any kind* reliably associated with the precise transitional period when the Neanderthals disappeared. Further, it is now apparent that some of the tool types most strongly associated with the Upper Paleolithic, such as the punch-blade technique, were in common use during the period when the classic Neanderthals were thought to be occupying Europe.

In any case, the superpositioning of Upper Paleolithic tools over levels containing Mousterian tool styles simply cannot be interpreted as the "abrupt" displacement of one group by the other. Caves and rock shelters were occupied on a periodic basis throughout the Pleistocene, and even if the classic western Neanderthals evolved directly into Cro-Magnon populations, we would still expect to find many sites where Mousterian tools were overlain by Upper Paleolithic tools, with no evidence of transitional forms separating them. There are many sites and fossils dating to the Middle and Upper Paleolithic periods, but only a few of them have evidence directly relevant to the problem of explaining the replacement of *Homo sapiens neanderthalensis* by *Homo sapiens sapiens*. Sites such as Krapina in Yugoslavia and Petralona in Greece have produced skeletal parts that seem to show a mixture of Neanderthal and modern characteristics, but the best examples of this possible blending come from six caves in Palestine: Zuttiya, Tabun, Skhul, Jebel Qafzeh, Shukba, and Amud.

The fossil finds at Skhul and Tabun were responsible for major revisions in our understanding of hominid evolution. The Tabun Cave contained a large mandible and a well-preserved female skeleton, both dated by the C^{14} method to about 41,000 years ago, showing mainly Neanderthal features. The cranial capacity of the female, 1,270 cc, is well within the lower limits of Neanderthal averages, and the low skull profile, arched brows, and other characteristics are indistinguishable from those of western European Neanderthals. In a few physical characteristics, however, she appears to be somewhat closer to modern populations.

Ten nearly complete hominid skeletons were found at Skhul, dating to approximately 5,000 to 10,000 years later than those from Tabun. The most striking thing about these individuals is their morphological diversity. Some of the skulls are almost indistinguishable from modern *Homo sapiens sapiens*, while others show clear affinities with Neanderthals. Some have argued that the Skhul individuals represent the descendants of intermarriage between Neanderthals and modern individuals, although it is not clear where the modern people were living at this time since there are no confirmed fossils of this type in levels contemporary with the classic Neanderthals.

A recent study of the Tabun Cave stone tools by Arthur Jelinek (1982) raises some interesting possibilities. From the present floor of the cave to a depth of over twenty-five meters (comparable to the height of an eight-story building) are hundreds of superimposed layers of human garbage, tools, and other debris. Near the top were found Neanderthal remains in association with stone tools that look very much like those found in the nearby Skhul Rock Shelter. But at Skhul these tools were found in association with "modern" non-Neanderthal *Homo sapiens* (the Skhul remains are, nonetheless, more robust than modern humans). To make matters more complicated, the remains of modern

Homo sapiens sapiens were found at Qafzeh, near Nazareth, in levels containing tools that also look much like those of Skhul and Tabun.

There are at least two possibilities here, given the many problems of classifying bones and stones and the complexities of geological strata. The Neanderthals of Tabun could be relative latecomers to the Levant. They could have come from western Europe, where Neanderthals may have developed after fully modern humans were present in the Levant (represented, perhaps, by the Qafzeh remains). This argument is based on faunal evidence concerning the presence and absence of an archaic form of rodent at the various Levant sites.

Jelinek's argument is quite different. He interprets the paleontological and palynological evidence in the context of the changes in stone-tool styles through the twenty-five meters of deposit at Tabun to suggest that there was "an orderly and continuous progression of industries in the southern Levant, paralleled by a morphological progression from Neanderthal to modern man" (1982: 216). The centerpiece of his argument is the increasing variability in certain kinds of stone tools over time at Tabun. An example of this is presented in Figure 4.4 where the variance of the ratio of width to thickness of stone flakes at Tabun is graphed against time. "Variance" here is a statistical concept referring to the variability within a sample. In this case, the higher the variance, the more variable the tools are with respect to the ratio of their maximum lengths and widths.

Interpreting this graph, Jelinek concludes

This continuous change in flake shape through time is one of the most remarkable findings to emerge from the analysis of the Tabun collections. A question of great importance is whether this trend represents a purely local phenomenon, related to such factors as the exploitation of the flint sources near the Wadi Mughara, or a fundamental underlying pattern of increasing manual dexterity and control arising from the conceptual development of the hominids that were responsible for the succession of lithic industries. If the latter is the case, then it may be possible to temporally correlate isolated collections from the Levantine region by calculating the width-to-thickness ratios of samples of complete flakes. At the very least this progression provides further strong evidence for the continuity of cultural development at Tabun.

Taken altogether, the evidence from Tabun and other Levantine sites strongly supports a continuous sequence of cultural development from the Late Acheulian of Tabun unit XIV to the latest Levantine Mousterian. (1982: 1374)

Some of the physical characteristics associated with the Neanderthals are found as far east as China, at sites like Ma-pa. But there is also evi-

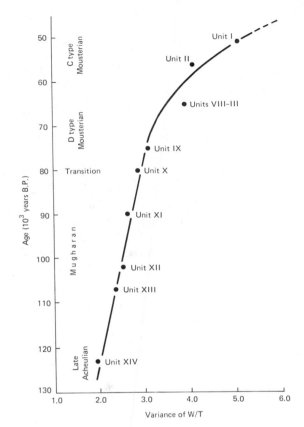

4.4 The gradual change in the variance of the width to thickness ratio of stone flake tools at the Tabun site may indicate that the Neanderthals slowly changed in physical form and culture into "modern" *Homo sapiens sapiens.*

dence, such as the apparently modern *Homo sapiens sapiens* from Border Cave in South Africa (which may be as old as 105,000 years), that in some areas the Neanderthals had either been replaced or had evolved into a modern form.

In partial contrast to Jelinek's argument, there seems to be a revival, especially in European circles (Protsch 1982), of the notion that the Neanderthals were essentially side branches of human evolution, having died out without significant genetic contribution to modern man. Some scholars have concluded that the skeleton of the Neanderthals, especially the limbs and hip bones, is so different in size and morphology from that of moderns that there would have been insufficient time for direct evolution from them to the modern skeleton. The torsional strength of Neanderthal leg bones, for example, is about *twice* that of moderns (Lovejoy and Trinkhaus 1980). Tools, they argue, may have had a role in changing the selective pressures on the teeth, but how could tools or any other factor have altered the skeletal parts? Thus some scholars have concluded that *Homo sapiens* evolved through Steinheim and Swanscombe stock, or perhaps through African or Near Eastern *Homo erectus,* without much genetic contribution from the classic Neanderthals. Doubtless this issue will employ physical anthropologists for many years to come.

Late Pleistocene Adaptations

With the appearance of modern humans after about 35,000 years ago, hunting and gathering societies began to appear in almost every part of the Old World, and in Australia and the Americas as well.

In Europe, hundreds of sites and over 200 human skeletons have been found that can be reliably dated to the period between 40,000 and 10,000 years ago. One of the most densely occupied areas during this period seems to have been near the confluence of the Dordogne and Vezere rivers in the south of France. As noted earlier, the Dordogne is a well-watered, heavily forested, limestone formation, honeycombed with caves and rock shelters offering excellent places to live. Mammoths, horses, and many other animals were hunted by these Upper Paleolithic peoples, but the reindeer was the staff of life: at many sites 99 percent of all the animal bones found belonged to reindeer; reindeer hides provided clothing and coverings for shelters; reindeer antlers were the hammers, or the "batons," used to produce the long elegant blades for which these people are justly famous; and reindeer bone was the raw material for fish gorges, needles, awls, and other important tools.

Reindeer travel long distances each year as they follow the grazing lands from one climatic zone to another. Thus, Upper Paleolithic peoples of southern France could exploit through the reindeer herds land they had never seen: the reindeer would browse their way to the far north each year and then return to southern France for the winter, at which time they could be harvested.

Average group size may have been relatively large during the Upper Paleolithic in Europe, the Near East, and other areas because of the requirements of hunting large gregarious mammals such as reindeer, horses, and wild cattle. The Neanderthals apparently specialized in mammoths, rhinoceroses, and other animals whose movements are not easily manipulated by people and whose habits are, in some cases, more solitary than those of reindeer, horses, and wild cattle. With these latter species, an efficient hunting technique is the *drive,* where many people work together to stampede a herd over a cliff or into a bog. Such mass slaughter also requires many people to process the carcasses, else the great majority of the animals would be wasted. Further, a larger group size would have been advantageous in these circumstances as a means of defending particularly favorable places along migration routes.

In addition to increased group size, there apparently was an overall population increase in some parts of Europe—and probably much of Eurasia—during the late Upper Paleolithic. Several factors were probably important in this population growth. The stone-tool technology of this period, with its indirect percussion and punch-blade techniques, was vastly more efficient than previous industries. Spear throwers, or atlatls, were also in common use—a very significant innovation, considering the heavy reliance on big game. It is estimated that an atlatl increases the range of a short spear from about 60 meters, if thrown by hand, to about 150 meters. The bow and arrow would have added significantly to hunting effectiveness, but it is unclear exactly when the first bows were used. Some of the earliest evidence comes from the Stellmoor site, near Hamburg, Germany, where about a hundred wooden arrows dating to approximately 10,000 years ago were recovered.

By about 14,000 years ago, the people of western Europe had developed fish traps in order to harvest the countless salmon that migrate up the rivers there each year. This relatively late exploitation of fish in Europe has a striking parallel in prehistoric southeastern North America, where Indians lived for thousands of years subsisting primarily on deer, mussels, and a variety of plant foods, almost totally ignoring the myriad fish in nearby lakes and streams. If salmon were present in great numbers in European rivers during the Mousterian and early Upper Paleolithic, their exploitation may have been blocked by the terms of human adaptation to reindeer and other animals. Reindeer and other game would have been a more dependable resource in the sense that at least some of these animals would have been available year round, while the salmon would have been sharply seasonal. Salmon runs, in fact, might have conflicted with the scheduling of reindeer hunting, and as a consequence these peoples may have been far from the river, exploiting different resources, at the time the salmon were most available. Perhaps even more important, the successful exploitation of salmon would have required technological readaptation on a major scale. Catching salmon one by one would not have been especially productive; their real utility probably came only after nets, fish weirs, drying racks, smoking racks, and other largely nonportable technology came into common use.

The slow growth of worldwide human population density through

4.5   This reconstruction of a 27,000-year-old settlement at Dolni Vestonice
(Czechoslovakia) illustrates how people used shelters to colonize the frigid plains
of eastern Europe.

most of the Pleistocene would seem to suggest that Upper Paleolithic
populations were not in any sense "driven" by growing population size
to exploit new resources, such as reindeer and salmon. Rather, it seems
more likely that the late Upper Paleolithic social reorganization into
larger groups and the development of fishing technologies were the
bases on which subsequent human population growth took place.

One of the most amply documented Upper Paleolithic cultures in
eastern Europe is the Kostenki-Bershevo culture centered in the Don
River Valley, about 470 kilometers southeast of Moscow. About 25,000
to 11,000 years ago, the Kostenki-Bershevo area was an open grassland
environment, with no rock shelters, caves, or other natural habitations,
and with very little wood available for fires. People here left a variety
of archaeological sites, including base camps, where pit houses were
constructed by digging a pit a meter or so deep, ringing the excavation
with mammoth bones or tusks, and then draping hides over these supports. The savage winters of Pleistocene Russia must have required
constantly burning fires, and the great quantities of bone ash found at

these sites indicate that these fires were often fed with mammoth bones in lieu of very scarce wood. Some excavated pit houses were relatively large, with many hearths, suggesting that several families may have passed the winter together. The people of Kostenki subsisted primarily through big-game hunting, mainly of mammoths or horses, with an occasional wild cow or reindeer. Numerous wolf and fox bones at these sites probably reflect the hunting of these animals for their fur for clothing. Like their Upper Paleolithic counterparts elsewhere, the Kostenki culture people manufactured a variety of decorative items, including "Venus" figurines (representations of women, usually with exaggerated sexual characteristics).

Throughout much of central and eastern Europe, big-game hunting was the main subsistence basis for thousands of hunting and gathering bands, much as it had been for tens of thousands of years. But the mammoth hunters of central and eastern Europe probably did not aggregate into relatively large groups, as the people in western Europe and the Near East at this time are thought to have done. Mammoths probably were not as gregarious as reindeer, horses, or wild cattle, and their hunting would not have rewarded any major changes in social organization.

In Africa, archaeologists initially found little evidence that African cultures of the late Pleistocene paralleled European developments in tool-manufacturing techniques and subsistence and social changes. In recent years, punch-blades, bone implements, and other artifacts similar to some of those of late Pleistocene Europe have been found in Africa, but the general pattern of artifacts and sites in Africa contrasts significantly with those of Europe. Generally, in most parts of Africa, hunters and gatherers of the late Pleistocene appear to have been exploiting a diversity of environments and producing technological and cultural innovations parallel in many ways to those occurring in Eurasia.

Until recently, few Upper Paleolithic sites were known in East Asia. Excavations at Choukoutien revealed levels dating to about 10,000 years ago containing approximately seven individuals—all of whom had been killed, but apparently not eaten. One individual had clearly died from an arrow or small spear wound to the skull, and another had been beaten about the head with a large stone. Elsewhere, two skulls have been retrieved from Wadjah, in central Java, but dating these has proved difficult.

Recent research in India has indicated at least a few "blade and burin" Upper Paleolithic industries. Sites in the Pushkar Basin in northwestern India appear to have been "factory sites" for the production of tools in many ways like the late Upper Paleolithic tools of Europe, and similar types of tools have also been found in eastern India

(Bricker 1976: 136). Clearly, more research is needed before we can realistically hope to understand late Pleistocene developments here.

No late Pleistocene human skeletal remains have been found in Japan, but hundreds of sites have been reported. Dating these sites is difficult, but the classic European Upper Paleolithic blade and burin industries are well represented in Japan, particularly in the northern areas across from Siberia.

One of the more curious aspects of late Pleistocene cultures in Asia is the movement of people into Australia and New Guinea (which were connected by a land bridge). Between 30,000 and 50,000 years ago, the ancestors of the Australian Aborigines somehow managed to cross at least eighty to one hundred kilometers of ocean to reach Australia.

It's perhaps not so unlikely that an occasional boat of fisherfolk was shipwrecked on the New Guinea–Australia coast, but computer simulations that take into account normal fertility rates and genetic diversity of modern populations make it unlikely that just a few boatloads of people were the founding population for that continent's present inhabitants (White and O'Connell 1979). By 50,000 years ago, people in East Asia may already have been experienced coastal sailors—a notion difficult for most prehistorians to accept.

How people got to Australia is just one of the archaeological puzzles of that unusual continent. Two distinct subspecies of ancient people have been found there, one bigger and more robust than modern Australian Aborigines, the other smaller and more gracile (Thorne 1980). Of the various possible reasons for this morphological divergence, the most likely one now seems to be colonization by two different groups, the more robust type by 50,000 years ago, the more gracile people before 20,000 years ago.

Once we understand how people got to Australia, and in how many subspecies, we can then face the question of how they lived. Like their contemporaries in America, the late Pleistocene peoples in Australia lived at a time when many large and small animal species were becoming extinct, and their possible role in this extinction pattern remains a matter of controversy.

Late Pleistocene peoples of the Americas are considered in the next chapter.

LIFE, ART, AND RITUAL IN THE UPPER PALEOLITHIC

In 1868, near the Spanish port of Santander, a hunter's dog fell into a crevice in some boulders, and in rescuing the animal the hunter moved some rocks, revealing the opening of a cave. The owner of the land on which the cave (known as "Altamira") was located, a Spanish nobleman and amateur archaeologist, eventually began to excavate the cave floor. He found some stone artifacts, but, according to the story, was unaware of the paintings in the cave until his twelve-year-old daughter visited the site and happened to glance at the ceiling. In the glow of her lantern she saw beautiful paintings of animals. Upon closer inspection it was discovered that the central painting was a group of about twenty-five animals, mainly bison, with a few horses, deer, wolves, and boars. Roughly life size, these paintings were done in rich browns, yellows, reds, and blacks, and the natural configuration of the cave ceiling had been used to emphasize the shape of the animals. The rounded haunch of a bison, for example, was painted over a natural bulge in the stone ceiling, creating a three-dimensional, realistic effect (Prideaux 1973: 93–94).

Scholarly reception to the Altamira discoveries was almost uniformly negative. Some respected prehistorians even hinted that Don Marcelino, their discoverer, had hired an art student to fake these paintings, while another scholar dismissed them as simply the expression "of a mediocre student of the modern school." So abused by critics was the Don that eventually he padlocked the cave, and he died in 1888 without having seen his discoveries accepted as true Paleolithic art. Years later, when many more paintings and other art works had been discovered, the antiquity of Altamira was finally acknowledged, and most of these paintings are now given dates between about 34,000 and 12,000 years ago. Analysis shows that the colors were produced by mixing natural mineral pigments, such as ocher and manganese dioxide, with a binder (blood, urine, vegetable juice, or something similar), and that they were either brushed on with an implement made of animal hair or applied by making a kind of crayon from the pigments and lubricant. Some painting may also have been done by using a pipe to blow the powdered pigments on a surface prepared with animal fat.

During World War II paintings on a scale comparable to those of Altamira were discovered at Lascaux Cave, in France. Researchers have agreed upon a date for the cave paintings of from about 34,000 to 12,000 years ago, the consensus being that they were made on many different occasions within this span. Many different animals are depicted here, including some one hopes were imaginary. The animals are often painted as if they are in motion, and the general effect is very impressive (Figure 4.6). One of the many curious things about these and other Upper Paleolithic cave paintings is that while the animals are depicted in very real, very representational terms, the figures of humans are either simple stick drawings or else weird half-humans, half-animals.

4.6   Lascaux Cave paintings may have been rituals designed to increase the chances of successful hunting, but they are superb art whatever their purpose.

The more than seventy cave paintings in France, as well as those in Spain, have often been treated as "Rorschach tests," in the sense that modern-day observers have tried to read into them the mind and spirit of primitive man, but they perhaps have learned more about their own psyches than about the primitive. We shall never know exactly why these paintings were made, but their technique and other characteristics offer some clues. Many of the paintings are in small, hidden passages, where working conditions were very cramped, suggesting that these pictures were not created for the pleasure of the general viewing public. Then again, many of the paintings are superimposed on one, two, or even more older ones, indicating perhaps that these efforts were ritual in nature, not simply artistic. The conventional wisdom about most of the cave paintings is that they represent forms of sympathetic magic where, by picturing animals with spears stuck in them or as caught in traps, Upper Paleolithic people may have thought they increased their chances of killing and trapping these animals. In fact, the most common themes of these Upper Paleolithic artists were food and sex, with food receiving most of the attention.

The disemboweled bulls, prancing deer, and other hunting scenes, plus the popularity of the penis and vulva motifs, suggest to some that these earliest of Spanish and French impressionists were men (Figure 4.7). But recently Elizabeth Fisher (1979) has argued that students of cave art have concealed the high frequency of female sex organs represented and thus the implication that many of the artists were probably women. Line markings that some archaeologists have considered calendrical devices she thinks may be records of menstrual periods.

It would not be surprising, however, if the many incisings and markings that one finds on Upper Paleolithic artifacts and in caves are in fact calendrical or astronomical in nature (Marshack 1976). A Pleistocene hunting and gathering group surprised by the onset of winter or the seasonal unavailability of plants and animals would not only have been invincibly stupid, it would have been in deep trouble.

More than one archaeologist working on the Upper Paleolithic has expressed the opinion that if reincarnation "works," one could do worse than to come back as an Upper Paleolithic hunter and gatherer. Most such fantasies are set in the ruggedly beautiful mountains of southern France and are based on visions of the simple, healthy life of a continual round of reindeer feasts, cave painting, and fertility ceremonies.

The archaeological evidence, however, suggests that life in the Up-

[handwritten margin note: Come on! Women can't see their own parts to draw them — why would they want to?]

4.7 Many cave paintings include realistic depictions of sexual organs, and some scholars interpret some abstract cave paintings as stylized sexual representations. Leroi-Gourhan here illustrates three groups of symbols for each sex in normal, simplified, and derived form.

	Oval	Rectangle	Key shape		Hook	Barb	Dot
Normal							
Simplified							
Derived							

4.8   Cast of Venus figurine
from Willendorf, Austria.

per Paleolithic was somewhat more severe than is often imagined. From
a sample of seventy-six Upper Paleolithic skeletons drawn from sites in
Europe and Asia, Vallois (1961) found that less than half these individuals had reached the age of twenty-one, that only 12 percent were over
forty years of age, and that not a single female had reached the age of
thirty. In fact, the distribution of ages and sexes represented by these
skeletons was not significantly different from what one might expect
from a comparable sample of Neanderthals (Vallois 1961). But even
worse, many skeletons evidenced rickets, malnutrition, and other diseases and deformities. Not content with nature's provisions for recy-
cling, people of the Upper Paleolithic were also given to slaughtering
each other. At the site of Sandalja II (12,000 years ago), near Pula, Yugoslavia, the skeletal remains of twenty-nine people were found in a
smashed and splintered condition. Elsewhere, there is unmistakable evidence of wounds from arrows and spears.

RECENT APPROACHES TO PALEOLITHIC ARCHAEOLOGY

Part of the problem in explaining Middle Pleistocene developments is [*This will always be a problem.*] the way research has been carried out in the past. There has been little formal theory or even a body of explicit assumptions from which to deduce hypotheses that can be tested archaeologically in any systematic fashion.

In an attempt to improve on this situation, a number of archaeologists have recently turned to a research strategy known as *simulation modeling*. Simulations are most familiar from fields like forestry, economics, astrophysics, and engineering. Rumors abound in computer circles about top-secret government computer-simulation models that regularly fight World War III out on paper. Complex simulation models are possible only with the help of high-speed computers, since the possible variable interactions in complex situations are almost limitless.

The essence of constructing a simulation model is to construct a picture of some aspect of the world and then use this picture to predict the future—or in the case of archaeology, to describe the past. Obviously, simulation models are *simplifications:* the point is to reduce the complexity to what the researcher feels are the most important factors in a given process, and then to try to determine how these factors interact over time.

One of the most influential simulation models in archaeology was developed recently by H. Martin Wobst (1974a), some aspects of whose work are discussed here, both as an important contribution to Paleolithic archaeology and because his approach exemplifies what may become an important archaeological research method.

Wobst's model was based on several conclusions and assumptions derived from studies of recent hunting and gathering societies and on archaeological data. He assumed that all Paleolithic societies were composed of small bands of perhaps twenty-five related individuals and that some of these bands occasionally aggregated to exchange marriageable females, share food, and to perform other social activities. Wobst called the larger social unit the *maximum band,* and it is an observed fact that all recent human hunting and gathering societies belong to such maximum bands and that they usually spend most of the year in groups of about twenty-five. Wobst also assumed that Pleistocene hunters and gatherers were territorial, to the extent that while they no doubt roamed far from their home bases, they nonetheless spent all or most of their lives in areas of perhaps 100 kilometers' diameter. Because these groups had no beasts of burden or wheeled vehicles, everything they accumulated had to be carried, placing restrictions on the distance covered and ease of movement.

Wobst's third assumption was that Pleistocene hunters and gatherers inhabited roughly hexagonal territories. The basis for this assumption is both empirical and theoretical. Surveys of existing hunting and gathering bands from all over the world show that most of them feel surrounded by approximately six neighboring bands. Laid out on a map, these territories do not look at all like equilateral hexagons, but, as a statistical approximation, it is legitimate to conceive of the territories of hunters and gatherers as hexagonal in shape. There are also theoretical reasons why the territories of hunters and gatherers should be hexagonal (Wobst 1974a: 153).

Based on these and other assumptions, Wobst then created a world in which there were sixty-one bands, with twenty-five members each, dispersed over an idealized landscape in perfect hexagonal territories. Each individual in the population was identified by name, age, sex, place of residence, marital status, and relatives (1974a: 158). Then, employing what is known as the *Monte Carlo technique,* Wobst simulated life in these bands over 400-year periods. He used studies of contemporary hunters and gatherers to estimate the chance each individual had of dying in any particular year, the chance of a married woman giving birth during any particular year, and the chance of any particular birth being a girl or boy. Wobst's simulation program also allowed him to vary social conditions, so that the simulated society could be monogamous, polygamous, endogamous, exogamous, patrilocal, incestuous, or various combinations of these.

The actual simulation procedure was done with a computerized program. The first step was to age each individual by one year. Next, those individuals widowed or of marriageable age entered the "mating loop," where an appropriate mate was found. Each couple was then "moved" to the appropriate band according to the marriage rules and residence patterns then in force. Following mating, each female entered the "procreation loop," where random numbers and probability tables were used to decide whether the child's sex would be male or female. Other components of the program determined when a group had reached sufficient size to split and move into different territories.

Wobst found that the model had to be simulated for at least 400 years to provide reliable results—a procedure requiring only a few minutes execution time on the computer. He also found that a band of about twenty-five would be close to the optimum size for maintaining the marriage networks and group spatial arrangements usually found in hunting and gathering societies. His calculations suggested that incest would not be advantageous to these groups because it would make mate selection much less predictable.

These and other implications of Wobst's model and of similar attempts to model Pleistocene societies await additional research, and their implications have not yet been fully analyzed. But they would seem to offer improved methods for planning archaeological surveys and excavations and for reconstructing Paleolithic societies.

5

The First Americans

At break of day the shore was thronged with people all young . . . all of good stature, fine looking. . . .

I was anxious to learn whether they had any
gold, as I noticed that some of the natives had
rings hanging from holes in their noses. . . . I
tried to get them to go for some, but they could
not understand they were to go.

Christopher Columbus
13 October 1492

Most of the first European "discoverers" of the New World were not
surprised to find "Indians" there, because they thought they had landed
in India or even Japan. But when they finally realized they were not in
the Orient and became aware of the diversity of New World cultures,
they began to struggle with the problem of the origin of the Native
Americans. The Bible, final authority for most Europeans of this era,
seemed strangely silent on the very existence of this "second-earth," so
Europeans began speculating on how the Indians could have reached
the New World from the Garden of Eden, where they were assumed to
have originated. It was widely believed that the Indians were the descendants of Ham, one of Noah's sons, who was also thought to have
been the father of the Egyptians. Early explorers were greatly impressed
by such similarities between Egyptian and aboriginal American cultures as pyramids and certain forms of artistic representation (Stewart
1973: 60).

Another popular idea was that the American Indians were descen-

5.1   An early photograph of a
Native American.

dants of the "lost tribes of Israel," Jews who had been evicted from Palestine by the Romans and Babylonians (movie fans will remember this
idea in *Cat Ballou*). The "lost tribes" idea eventually was incorporated
into the doctrines of the Church of the Latter-Day Saints, whose Book
of Mormon explains how the Indians were remnants of tribes of Israel
that had come to the New World by ship sometime around A.D. 421.
Equally intriguing are the Atlantis and Mu theories, which hold that
Native Americans are descendants of people who fled islands in the Atlantic Ocean that were destroyed thousands of years ago by volcanic
eruptions.

   The currently accepted and well-documented ideas about the matter
were known as early as the sixteenth century. In 1590 a Spanish Jesuit,
José de Acosta, proposed that in the extreme northern part of America
there was a land bridge over which many animals had come into the
New World, and by 1781 Thomas Jefferson could describe the peopling
of the New World in terms we know today to be largely accurate.

Late discoveries of Captain Cook, coasting from Kamschatka to California, have proved that if the two continents of Asia and America be
separated at all, it is only by a narrow straight. So that from this side
also, inhabitants may have passed into America; and the resemblance
between the Indians of America and the eastern inhabitants of Asia,
would induce us to conjecture, that the former are the descendants of
the latter, or the latter of the former: excepting indeed the Eskimaux,
who, from the same circumstances of resemblance, and from identity of
language, must be derived from the Groenlanders, and these probably
from some of the northern parts of the old continent. (Quoted in Stewart 1973: 70)

In their search for clues to the origins of Native Americans, Jefferson
and others of his age were struck by the fact that in physical form the
American Indians closely resemble Asian races in having dark brown
eyes, black, coarse, straight hair, and, relative to Europeans, widely
spaced cheekbones. But differences were also apparent: except for the
Eskimos and Aleuts, the aboriginal Americans did not have the fleshy
eyelid (epicanthic) folds that distinguish East Asian populations, and
many Native Americans had relatively prominent noses.

It was soon noted that the New World included an impressive diversity of languages and cultures, that none of the languages of Native
Americans bore much resemblance to Old World languages, and that
many American languages were unrelated and mutually unintelligible
to their speakers. Thus, it seemed certain that although the aboriginal
Americans were probably descendants of Asian peoples, they must have
lived in America for a long time for such physical and linguistic divergence to have occurred.

Today the view that the first Americans came from East Asia via a
land route is generally accepted, but considerable controversy remains
about when the first migrations occurred. Some archaeologists maintain
they took place only about 14,000 to 10,000 years ago, while others
think it was about 35,000 years ago or earlier. Some clue as to the date
of original colonization is suggested by the fact that intensive research
has failed to turn up any New World human skeletons that cannot be
comfortably fitted within the class *Homo sapiens sapiens*. Because the
first *Homo sapiens sapiens* appear in the Near East and Europe about
35,000 years ago, we might assume that the aboriginal Americans must
have come over since then, but we really don't know when the first
Homo sapiens sapiens appeared in the East Asian areas from which the
first Americans apparently came. Anatomically modern populations
may have appeared there long before they did in the Near East or
Europe. The alternative view, that there are undiscovered Neanderthal

or earlier hominid remains in the New World, has a certain lay popularity, but no informed archaeologist regards this as at all likely.

Although it is uncertain when East Asian populations developed epicanthic folds, small noses, and relatively flat facial profiles, in view of the prominent noses of most Native Americans and their non-Mongolian eye shapes, it is apparent that either the Americans are only distantly related to these populations, or that they emigrated before the Asian populations developed their distinctive features. We have very little evidence on which to estimate rates of evolutionary change in these superficial physical characteristics, but the overall similarity of New World populations suggests that the natural selective pressures that produce variation in these characteristics have not had very long to operate. It is also possible that the physical characteristics of New World peoples were largely determined by "accident" (genetic drift) and isolation. Even in the most temperate periods, the northern Arctic would have supported few people, and perhaps only a dozen or so bands of hunters and gatherers and their direct descendants had crossed the land bridge before the rising sea levels isolated them from the Old World populations. Therefore, all Native Americans (except for later migrants, mainly the Eskimo) could have descended from relatively few people, and the "accidental" characteristics of this gene pool would determine the dominant physical characteristics of subsequent Native Americans.

THE BERING LAND BRIDGE

Today, Eskimos using skin boats easily cross the 90 kilometers of open sea separating Siberia and America, but such a sea crossing would not have been necessary during much of the Pleistocene. During periods of glacial advance within the last million years, enormous quantities of water were converted to ice, lowering the sea level sufficiently to expose a 1,500- to 3,000-kilometer-wide expanse of the floor of the Bering Sea. This land bridge—usually referred to as *Beringia* (Figure 5.2)—was probably available at least four times in the last 60,000 years.

One might think the ice and cold in Siberia and Beringia would have formed an impassable barrier to hunting and gathering groups, but Pleistocene sediments here reveal that this was not the case. Low precipitation, the flat terrain, and warm ocean currents created an ice-free, tundra-covered connection from eastern Siberia across the land bridge and into central Alaska. These conditions are reflected in the many non-Arctic adapted animal species that crossed from Asia to America during the Pleistocene. Prior to 10,000 years ago, species of

Ice cap

Glaciers

Formerly exposed land areas

Present-day shorelines

5.2   Formation of a land bridge across the Bering Sea and the extension of shore-lines during the second major Wisconsin glaciation. Glaciation may not have been as extensive as shown here.

deer, bison, camels, bears, foxes, mammoths, moose, caribou, and even rodents crossed from Siberia into the New World. Going the other way—from America to Asia—were foxes, woodchucks, and, during the early Pleistocene, the ancestors of modern forms of horses, camels, and wolves (Haag 1962: 269). Nonetheless, there is no palynological evidence that the land bridge was a thick grassland—there is even the possibility of dust storms, so dry and barren was most of it (Cwyner and Ritchie 1980).

THE ROUTE SOUTH

How could the first Americans have survived the ice and snow of inland Pleistocene Alaska and Canada and reached the lower latitudes of North and South America?

An influential early hypothesis was that these southward migrations could have occurred only a few times, because it was thought that for most of the Pleistocene the way would have been blocked by coalescing ice sheets. Even if these ice sheets did not completely bar the way south, most authorities thought that a narrow open corridor between them would have had too little food to support groups of hunters and gatherers—who require large territories to support even low population densities.

Some archaeologists continue to believe that humans entered the lower reaches of the New World only after the last glacial retreat, but this interpretation has a number of problems. Ten thousand years would not seem sufficient time to account for the tremendous linguistic and cultural diversity evident in the New World cultures, and more important, except possibly for a period of a few thousand years, the corridor southward appears to have been open for almost all of the Pleistocene (Reeves 1971). Also, as we shall see, there is some possible archaeological evidence of human occupation prior to 12,000 years ago.

The exact path the first Americans took is not known, but the most likely would be along the coast of the land bridge, then into Alaska north of the Brooks range, up the Yukon River Valley, then into the Mackenzie River Valley, and from there southward, along the eastern slopes of the Rockies and on into the Dakotas and then further southward. Along the coast of the land bridge were probably abundant resources in the form of fish, birds, eggs, invertebrates, and many plant foods. If groups did come this way, it is unlikely that we shall ever be able to document their journey archaeologically, for the rising seas of the post-Pleistocene era have submerged the ancient shoreline.

We might expect that if the immigrants crossed the land bridge primarily along the coast, then the groups migrating south would have retained some elements of the generalized hunting, fishing, and foraging economies required in the intertidal zone. If, on the other hand, they came across the middle of the land bridge, a greater reliance on big-game hunting would have been essential.

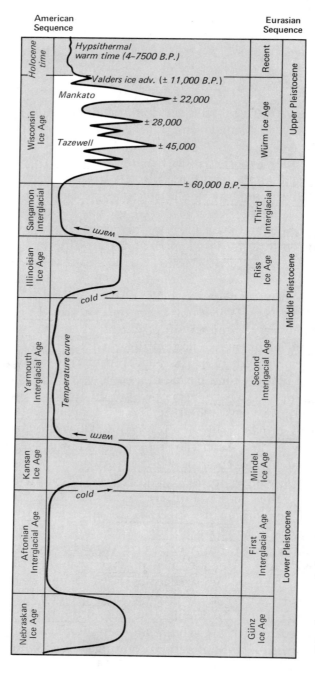

5.3 Some periods and events of the Late Pleistocene in North America.

...laptation, the migrants were almost certainly not
...ve southward; no doubt these population move-
...by *budding-off*, as groups grew to certain numbers,
...moved some distance from the parent group. This
...one in cases when new species move into empty
...thousands of years may have passed between the time
...foot on the land bridge and the year the first groups
...ental United States.

...owing off the kilometer-high glacial ice sheets made the climate or much of Pleistocene North America much different from today's. Much of Nevada and Utah was covered by Lake Bonneville, of which only a shrinking remnant (Great Salt Lake) remains. Wyoming, Iowa, and other parts of the Great Plains were vast pine, spruce, and tamarack forests and lush open grasslands. To the south, the area between the Mississippi River and the Rockies was a verdant mosaic of grasslands, lakes, and birch and alder forests. In eastern North America huge expanses of coniferous forests stretched from the edge of the glacial ice sheets to the lower Ohio River Valley.

The animals inhabiting this wilderness of 14,000 to 12,000 years ago closely approximate a modern hunter's vision of paradise. Giant moose, three meters and more in height, could be found in many of the wetter areas, along with *Castoroides,* a type of beaver as large as a modern bear. Along the woodland edges of the southeastern United States were large populations of giant ground sloths, ungainly creatures fully as tall as modern giraffes. In more open country were vast herds of straight-horned bison, caribou, musk-oxen, and mammoths—some species of which stood four meters high at the shoulders. In the more forested areas of the East and South were the mammoth's cousin, the mastodon, a more solitary animal than the mammoth and apparently a browser rather than a grassland grazer. Amid all these large creatures were rabbits, armadillos, birds, camels, peccaries, and other animals. And the carnivores that such a movable feast attracted were equally impressive. Packs of dire wolves roamed most of the New World, as did panthers as large as modern lions and two species of saber-toothed cat, one about the size of a lion (Martin and Wright 1967: 32–33). Thus, the first Americans were hardly entering an "empty niche," as these ferocious predators no doubt provided stiff competition for people trying to specialize in hunting.

Central and South America were also rich game preserves during and just after the Pleistocene, but in the rainforests of the Amazon Basin, the great coniferous forests of the North American South and East, and a few other locations, so much energy was in the form of inedible and

5.4   Some large mammals of Pleistocene America. The scale preserves relative size.

unnutritious vegetation (cellulose) that there would have been few resources for primitive hunters and gatherers.

The First Americans: The Archaeological Record

Given the probable southward migration routes, we might expect to
find a long trail of archaeological sites stretching from northeastern Siberia along the sea floor of the now submerged land bridge into central
Alaska, and then southward, between the ice caps. If these early immigrants were big-game hunters, we would expect many of the sites to be
concentrations of animal bones, hearths, and flint tools appropriate for
killing and preparing these animals.

Alas, the gap between the real and ideal—so persistent in all archaeological research—is particularly great in this case. Some sites do fit this pattern, but the evidence is far from conclusive. First of all, adequate surveys of northeastern Siberia have never been completed. Aside from the rigors of the Arctic climate, the politics of doing surveys amid ICBM missile silos and radar stations have deterred most Western scholars. Soviet scholars, however, have been working in these areas, and we may soon have more data (Dikov 1977).

Present evidence suggests that before about 30,000 years ago, Siberia had extremely low population densities or was unsettled altogether. The great frigid interior swamps and forests of Siberia may have barred human colonization, at least until huts had been developed. In any case, the earliest known sites in northeastern Siberia date to about 23,000 years ago and reflect a life focused on the hunting of mammoths and other large animals. Projectile points, scrapers, and burins—tool types associated with big-game hunters all over the Old World—are the most frequent implements at Mal-ta, Afontova gora II, and other sites of this period. To the east, on the Aldan River, Diuktai Cave has yielded crude pebble tools, including scrapers and points, some of which apparently resemble early American artifacts, but it has not yet been possible to date this site with any confidence.

Some archaeologists see similarities between these pebble and flake tools of Siberia and the earliest artifacts in the Americas, but others dispute this. As we shall see, the earliest American sites may contain crude pebble tools, not projectile points or finely worked blades or scrapers. Thus it is difficult to tie them to these big-game hunting cultures of late Pleistocene Siberia.

The evidence is also somewhat sketchy on the American side of the land bridge. The Alaskan and northern Canadian climates make surveys very difficult, and farther south the constant waxing and waning of the glacial ice sheets and the vast riverine systems that drained them have thoroughly chewed up much of the land along the Canadian corridor. No doubt many sites in these areas have long since been scoured away by ice or water.

Some crude bone tools from the Old Crow site in the Yukon have been radiocarbon-dated to between 28,000 and 23,000 years ago, but the bones may have been deposited many thousands of years before they were made into tools. Occasionally, other Alaskan and northern Canadian sites are reported in the 20,000 years and older time range, but so far none has been conclusively demonstrated to be of this age.

The earliest well-dated Arctic sites are Dry Creek, Trail Creek Cave, and similar occupations, most of which date to between 11,000 and

8,000 years ago. These sites seem to be hunting camps in unglaciated areas and are marked by bifacial knives, tiny blades, and the bones of horses, bison, hares, ducks, and other animals. By this time, these Arctic hunters may have been pursuing a dying way of life, as the glaciers and the rich animal life they supported were slowly withdrawing (Hopkins et al., eds., 1982).

Although there are presently no well-dated sites in the "corridor" through Canada, where glacial and water activity was most destructive, human skeletal fragments from southern Californian sites have been dated by the amino-acid racemization method (which involves measuring changes in bone proteins) to more than 50,000 years ago (Bada and Helfman 1975). But the disturbed contexts of these finds and lingering questions about the accuracy of the dating method have engendered debate. Other sites have also been dated to before 30,000 years ago, such as American Falls, Idaho, and Calico Hills, California, but in every case the evidence is ambiguous.

The reader wishing to follow a typical debate among professional archaeologists about early Americans is advised to consult the 1981 issues of the *Quarterly Review of Archaeology*. The subject is Meadowcroft Rock Shelter, near Avella, Pennsylvania, where many layers of alluvial sediments were deposited by a tributary of the Ohio River. Interspersed in these alluvial sediments are many clear indications of human occupation, including prismatic flint blades, basketry, and hearths.

The question is, how far back does its earliest occupation date? The site was excellently excavated, and there is no question about the provenience of the artifacts. A bit of charred basketry from near the bottom was radiocarbon-dated to $19,650 \pm 2,400$ and $19,150 \pm 800$ years B.P. Charcoal from a level beneath the basketry dates to as old as 37,000 years ago, but there were no artifacts. Unfortunately, there is some suggestion that the samples may have been contaminated by groundwater and that the site's stratigraphy has been misunderstood (Dincauze 1981; cf. Adovasio et al. 1981).

But if the dates for Meadowcroft are accepted, it means that people were in the continental United States *before* the last glacial advance, which implies that the ice sheets were in fact no barrier and that the scarcity of sites found is a matter of inadequate searching, low population densities, and the postdepositional destruction of sites.

The oldest widely accepted dates for a New World site come from Pikimachay Cave in Peru, where archaeologist Richard MacNeish excavated crude stone tools and animal bones that have been radiocarbon-dated as early as 22,000 years ago (MacNeish 1978: 203). The association between these stone tools and some forms of extinct animals is unmistakable in 12,000-year-old levels of the site, but some archaeologists doubt that its earliest levels represent human occupation, and all early Peruvian dates seem at least somewhat equivocal (e.g., Vescelius 1981). Whatever the specific earliest date for Pikimachay, we would obviously expect to find earlier sites north of Peru, but for this the evidence is not overwhelming.

Several sites dated to about 11,000 B.C. have been found in Mexico, most of them composed of the debris from killing and butchering mammoths. The consistency with which mammoths are found in these sites may seem to reflect an economy specialized in hunting large animals, but most of the people of Mexico at this time were probably generalized hunters and gatherers and only because of the great size and preservation of the mammoth bones do we find so many of these sites. As MacNeish noted, these early hunters probably killed one mammoth in a lifetime—and never stopped talking about it.

Some of the other sites thought to date between 30,000 and 20,000 years ago are shown in Figure 5.5 and although none of them are unequivocal, as a group they suggest that people may have entered the New World no later than 30,000 to 25,000 years ago.

The artifacts found at the earliest sites differ greatly, but most sites lack the projectile points that in later periods are among the most frequent types of tools. This has led to the characterization of the earliest New World cultures as the *Pre-projectile Point Stage* (Krieger 1964). The absence of projectile points and the simplicity of these early artifacts probably mean that the earliest immigrants were not highly specialized big-game hunters, which suggests that they came over during the warmer periods of the Pleistocene as generalized hunters and gatherers. We cannot be certain, of course, because successful big-game hunters (like *Homo erectus*) used crude stone tools; but these early American tool complexes do not look as if they were specialized killing or butchering implements. Nor have they been found with butchered animal bones or in environmental circumstances suggesting specialized hunting.

If people entered the New World 30,000 or more years ago, it might seem surprising that more archaeological sites have not been found dating to this period; after all, hundreds of Old World sites date to this age. But population densities in Europe and other parts of the Old World had been slowly building for hundreds of thousands of years before people entered the New World. In addition, most European sites of this age are found in caves and rock shelters, and there are relatively few of these along the probable route into the New World. Alternatively, the first Americans may have worked out adaptations to cold

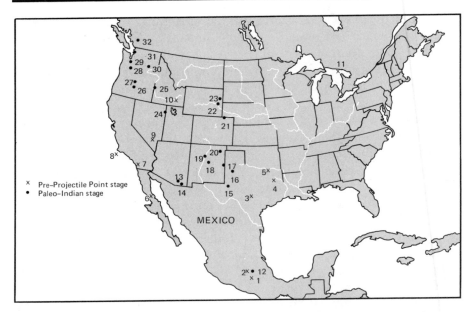

5.5   Location of some possible early American occupations. Some are of questionable date or are not demonstrated to be of human origin. The "Pre-Projectile Point
stage" is widely considered to be the earliest. North American sites and complexes:
(1) Valsequillo, (2) Tequixquiac, (3) Friesenhahn Cave, (4) Malakoff, (5) Lewisville,
(6) Lake Chapala Basin, (7) Scripps Campus, (8) Santa Rosa Island, (9) Tule Springs,
(10) American Falls, (11) Sheguiandah, (12) Iztapan, (13) Lehner, (14) Naco, (15)
Scharbauer, (16) Lubbock, (17) Blackwater Draw, 18) Lucy, (19) Sandia Cave,
(20) Folsom, (21) Lindenmeier, (22) Hell Gap, (23) Brewster, (24) Danger Cave,
(25) Crane Creek, (26) Fort Rock Cave, (27) Cougar Mountain Cave, (28) Five-Mile
Rapids, (29) Indian Well, (30) Ash Cave, (31) Olcott, (32) Yale.

climates that did not require caves. Their ancestors must have done
this, because there are no caves along the Siberian-Beringia-Alaska
route.

Another problem in locating early sites in eastern North America is
that in much of the lower Mississippi area, alluviation has been so great
that many such sites would be buried under tens of meters of soil. And
in the rest of the South and East, because the glacial ice sheets never
reached these areas, the present land surface is millions of years old.
Thus, soft-drink bottles and ancient artifacts can be found in virtually
the same soil, because accumulation of soil over these areas has been so
slow for millions of years. Additionally, bones and other datable materials do not preserve well under these humid, exposed conditions.

In conclusion, people certainly had entered the New World by at
least 14,000 to 12,000 years ago, and they were probably here long be-

fore that. It is thought that they reached interior Alaska and Canada by 40,000 or more years ago, most likely as generalized hunters and gatherers with simple pebble and flake tool kits. For many thousands of years after people reached mid-continental and southern latitudes in the New World, population densities were probably extremely light, and most bands no doubt stayed in the same general mixed forest and grassland environments their ancestors had adapted to in more northern areas. By about 12,000 years ago, however, they began to display greater diversity in subsistence strategies as they evolved adaptations to a greater range of environments.

EARLY AMERICAN ADAPTATIONS

In 1926 a cowboy was riding along the edge of a gully in New Mexico, near the town of Folsom, when he discovered some "arrowheads" and animal bones protruding from a layer of soil about six meters beneath the surface of the plain. Eventually, his find came to the attention of J. D. Figgins, director of the Colorado Museum of Natural History, who began a long series of excavations at this site. The bones associated with the artifacts turned out to be those of a species of bison that had been extinct for about 10,000 years, and so skeptical were most archaeologists and other people of the idea that humans had been in the New World that long that Figgins insisted on excavating the site with a committee of archaeologists there to watch his every move, so that no one could claim the evidence had been faked.

In 1932 another important find was made, this time near the town of Clovis, New Mexico, and here too large blade tools were associated with extinct animals. But at this site artifacts somewhat different from those at Folsom (Figure 5.6) were found in a layer *beneath* some "Folsom points." Analysis suggested a date of about 12,000 years ago for the earliest Clovis-style artifacts, and within a few years artifacts similar in size, shape, and style to the Clovis points were discovered at many different places in North America. Since then, stone points resembling Clovis artifacts have been found in every state of the Union, as well as far north into the Arctic and deep into South America.

It is difficult to reconstruct the subsistence systems of the people who made these points. The easiest archaeological sites to find are those with large stone tools and the bones of large animals, and most of the sites in the grasslands of North America are of this type: dozens of stone tools intermixed with mammoth, bison, and other bones, often near streams or bogs where hunters ambushed these animals. But there may

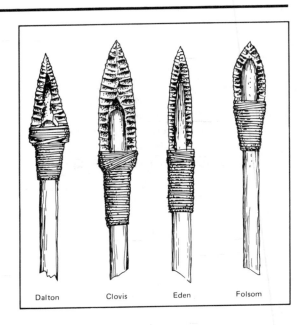

5.6   Some types of early
American projectile points.

Dalton   Clovis   Eden   Folsom

be many less obvious sites—sites not yet found because they are not marked by masses of animal bones.

Many archaeologists question the presumption that even the Clovis and Folsom peoples were mainly big-game hunters. Shortly after 8000 B.C., however, at least some groups in the American West were undoubtedly specializing in hunting big game. They often practiced "jump hunting," in which many people cooperate to stampede bison herds or other animals over a precipice, killing them by the score. Where there were no convenient precipices, animals were driven into natural cul-de-sacs, where they could be easily killed. In sites reflecting these practices, archaeologists find the bones of hundreds of bison, many showing clear butchering marks. By drying the meat, these hunters could accumulate large food reserves, and the skin, hide, and bones of the bison had many uses.

It used to be widely believed that the first wave of immigrants to the New World stayed mainly on the western side of North America, colonizing the area east of the Mississippi River only about 10,000 years ago, but recent archaeological evidence suggests that the East may be a much earlier cultural center. Of particular interest are the so-called "pebble-tool" complexes that have been found in Tennessee, Alabama, the Ohio Valley, and elsewhere. These crude tools have been found in both open-air sites and rock shelters, and occasionally in levels containing the Clovis-type points dated to about 12,000 years ago in the Great

Plains. Some archaeologists think these pebble tools were used by people entering the North American East 20,000 or more years ago (Dragoo 1976). We have noted that the land surfaces of much of the East are millions of years old and that preservation is generally poor, so it is not surprising that we do not have good carbon-14 dates for these early cultures. The ancient date given to these tools is based on their simplicity and extreme patination in comparison to other artifacts, and also on their resemblance to crude pebble tools and other implements found in Peru and dated to between 19,600 and 14,150 B.C.

The earliest distinctive and widely distributed tool complex found in the North American East is distinguished by the presence of large stone projectile points. Most such points are between twelve and thirty centimeters long and occasionally have been "fluted" by detaching flakes along the long axis of the core. Formerly, many archaeologists thought these eastern points were imitations of the Folsom and Clovis points, but it is now evident that these larger points occur as early—and probably earlier—in the eastern woodlands as on the Plains and are more numerous in the East: Alabama alone has yielded more points than the entire western half of North America (Dragoo 1976).

A particularly interesting eastern site containing Clovis-type artifacts is St. Albans, in West Virginia, where stratified occupations to a depth of eleven meters have been found. Radiocarbon dates ranging around 7900 B.C. have been derived from deposits at depths of about nine meters, and further excavations may help clarify many details of early eastern occupations.

By about 5000 B.C., the glaciers had retreated to the point that the flora and fauna of the eastern United States were very similar to what they are today—except where changed by human activity—and there was a broad cultural readaptation to the changing environments. In the Ohio, Cumberland, and Tennessee river valleys, for example, there are huge middens containing the refuse of centuries of shellfishing. At Koster in lower Illinois, excavations revealed that Middle and Late Archaic people (the Archaic period is about 7000 to 5000 B.C.) here subsisted principally on fishing, deer hunting, and gathering wild plants. To the north in the "Lake Forest" areas of Michigan, Wisconsin, and Ontario, hunting was still the major protein source, with deer, elk, moose, and bear getting most of the attention. Farther to the north, in the Canadian Shield area, subsistence was based even more on the hunting of large herd mammals as people followed the retreating glaciers and tundra-adapted game northward.

Along the coasts of eastern North America a variety of specialized adaptations evolved, based on the exploitation of seals, sea birds, and, along the southern coast, fish and shellfish. In all these "specialized" adaptations, however, the people were actually exploiting a great diversity of plant and animal foods.

In the "Desert West," the areas between the Rockies and the Cascades, there is at least 12,000 years of human history. People over the millennia worked out adaptations to the deserts, lakes, and mountains of this region. Its many sites offer the archaeologist an excellent opportunity to study the mechanics of human adaptation in what can be a rather extreme environment. Radiocarbon dates from the earliest levels of cave hearths in Nevada and Oregon cluster around 9000 to 8000 B.C., and evidence has slowly accumulated for the existence of cultures using the Clovis-style fluted points all over the Desert West.

From about 11,000 to 8,000 years ago, many of the Desert West peoples apparently organized their economies around the resources of lakes and marshes, while groups in more arid areas probably adopted a more generalized hunting and gathering strategy. Remains of pole-and-thatch huts have been found in some areas, but the size, location, and contents of most sites of this period suggest that for most of the year Desert West peoples lived in small bands and followed complex seasonal rounds, exploiting different resources as they became available.

Analysis of the animal and plant remains from sites dated between 9,000 and 2,500 years ago reveals an extremely diverse diet. Rabbits, rats, and squirrels were trapped—probably with twined nets—and bison, antelopes, and mountain sheep were also occasionally taken. At sites near bodies of water, grebes, pelicans, herons, ducks, swans, geese, and even hawks and ravens appear to have been eaten (Jennings 1974: 143). The number of grinding stones and digging sticks found in Desert West sites suggests that, as with most hunters and gatherers, much of the diet was supplied by plant foods. At Hogup Cave in Utah, for example, human feces contain masses of pickleweed seeds, and the archaeological deposits are stained yellow by pickleweed chaff (Aikens 1978). Quids, the fossilized expectorated fibers of succulent plants, have also been found in great numbers in Desert West sites, and their numbers suggest they may have been a source of both food and water.

In many areas of the West, there seems to have been a shift after 6000 B.C. to an increased reliance on seed gathering. As we shall see in the next chapter, this kind of shift elsewhere in the world led to agricultural economies and the village—as opposed to mobile—way of life. These western cultures thus may help us understand why people move away from certain kinds of resources to others, and why in some instances this results in agricultural economies while in others it results

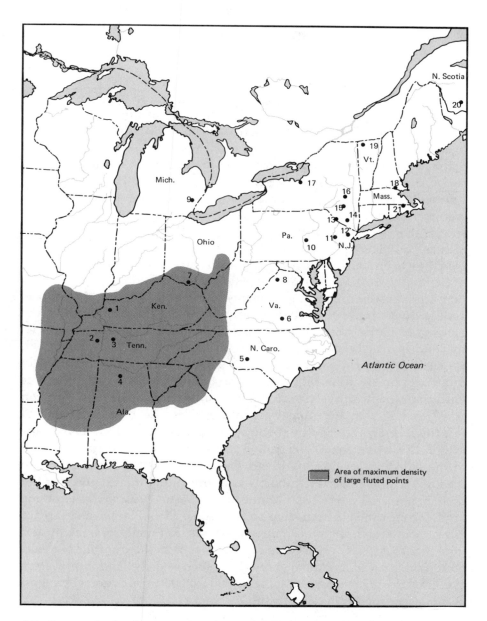

5.7   Some early sites in eastern North America. (1) Parrish, (2) Nuckolls, (3) Wells
Creek, (4) Quad, (5) Hardaway, (6) Williamson, (7) Adams Co., (8) Flint Run,
(9) Holcombe Beach, (10) Shoop, (11) Plenge, (12) Port Mobile, (13) Ziert, (14)
Dutchess Quarry, (15) West Athens Hill, (16) Kings Road, (17) Potts, (18) Bull
Brook, (19) Reagen, (20) Debert, (21) Wapanucket.

mainly in a change in diet and a bit less seasonal movement (Aikens 1978).

<h2 style="text-align:center">PLEISTOCENE EXTINCTIONS</h2>

The spread of human hunting and gathering societies over the New World after the last glacial period coincides with the extinction of many animal species, and by about 8,000 years ago, all or most of the mammoths, mastodons, long-horned bison, tapirs, horses, giant ground sloths, dire wolves, camels, and many other creatures had disappeared. Extinction is, of course, a natural evolutionary development and can be accounted for by known biological processes. But the number of animal species that became extinct in the New World and their apparent rate of extinction has led some to conclude that human hunters forced many New World animals into extinction shortly after the Pleistocene.

Generally, however, the evidence does not seem to support the view that humans were important elements in the extinction of New World species. In a sample of thirty-five early sites in North America, the animal bones found were mainly those of mammoths and bison—species that did in fact become extinct; but many of the other large animals which became extinct during this period are either not found at all in these sites or are found in very limited numbers. Perhaps even more significant, game species were not the only ones to die out. Grayson (1977) has shown that numerous bird species also became extinct at this time, and it is difficult to believe that people could have played any role in this. Also, some "big-game" species such as the mastodon lived in the North American South and East while humans were there and are known to have perished shortly after the end of the Pleistocene, but their bones have never been found in association with artifacts of any kind. Thus, it would seem that at least some of the larger animals became extinct without much human assistance. Finally, we might also note that there is no archaeological evidence that the hunting practices most likely to lead to animal extinctions, such as drives and jumps, were ever used during the period, some 10,000 to 8,000 years ago, when most of the larger species became extinct.

If we rule out human hunting as the most important factor in these extinctions, what alternative explanation can we give? Many have been suggested, but none is really very satisfactory. Clearly, the immediate post-Pleistocene period was one of radical climate change, and no doubt this was of some importance. Of thirty-one genera of mammals that became extinct, however, only seven had entered the New World during the last 70,000 years, and thus all the others had managed to adapt to

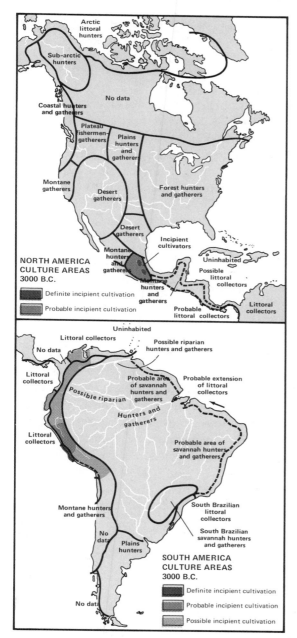

North America Culture Areas 3000 B.C.

Arctic littoral hunters

Sub-arctic hunters

No data

Coastal hunters and gatherers

Plateau fishermen-gatherers

Plains hunters and gatherers

Montane gatherers

Desert gatherers

Forest hunters and gatherers

Desert gatherers

Incipient cultivators

Montane hunters and gatherers

Uninhabited

Possible littoral collectors

NORTH AMERICA CULTURE AREAS 3000 B.C.

Montane hunters and gatherers

Littoral collectors

Probable littoral collectors

Definite incipient cultivation

Probable incipient cultivation

South America Culture Areas 3000 B.C.

Uninhabited

Littoral collectors

No data

Possible riparian hunters and gatherers

Littoral collectors

Probable area of savannah hunters and gatherers

Probable extension of littoral collectors

Possible riparian

Hunters and gatherers

Littoral collectors

Probable area of savannah hunters and gatherers

Montane hunters and gatherers

South Brazilian littoral collectors

No data

Plains hunters

South Brazilian savannah hunters and gatherers

SOUTH AMERICA CULTURE AREAS 3000 B.C.

Definite incipient cultivation

Probable incipient cultivation

Possible incipient cultivation

No data

5.8 Some varieties of American adaptations at about 3000 B.C.

the climatic changes of previous interglacial periods, which were fully as dramatic as those after the last glacial retreat. Why did they become extinct after the last glacial period?

Some have suggested that New World animals might have been decimated by diseases introduced from the Old World during one of the later intervals when the Bering land bridge route was open—a situation reminiscent of the frightful casualties inflicted on aboriginal Americans by smallpox, measles, and other diseases introduced by the Europeans. Such epidemics, however, usually do not cause species to become extinct: they decimate local populations over a large area but generally leave small pockets of resistant individuals who eventually reestablish the species.

OTHER EARLY AMERICAN CULTURES

Although the cultures of the Desert West, Great Plains, and eastern North America are the best known examples of the late Pleistocene-early Holocene in the New World, there were many other specialized hunters and gatherers during this period. Generally, the early Holocene in the Americas was a time of cultural specialization, as technologies, social systems, and subsistence systems were evolved to meet diverse and changing environments. Human population densities rose in many parts of the New World, and, as we shall see in chapter 15, by 7,000 years ago some hunting and gathering societies were already in the process of domesticating plants and beginning the transition to the agricultural, complex cultures of late prehistoric America.

6

The Origins of Domestication,
Agriculture,
and Sedentary Communities

> The greatest events come to pass without any design; chance makes blunders good. . . . The important events of the world are not deliberately brought about: they occur.
>
> George C. Lichtenberg

The several million years separating the first tool users from the hunters and gatherers of the late Pleistocene was a time of tremendous change. Human brain size trebled, stone-tool technologies became more complex, and people colonized most of the Old and New Worlds. But in one important respect all Pleistocene societies were alike: they made their living through hunting and gathering, that is, through *nonagricultural* subsistence systems. Every Pleistocene society hunted and gathered its own food, made its own tools, and generally replicated almost all the economic activities of every other society.

I have already commented on the impressive durability of hunting and gathering as a way of life. Hunters and gatherers managed to adapt to a wide variety of environments and still persist despite great pressures from more complex societies. But about 10,000 years ago, the first domesticated plants and animals appeared in Southwest Asia, and not much later they appeared in Mesoamerica, China, and Peru. Over the next ten millennia, these domesticates were incorporated into agricultural economies that in many environments were able to produce much greater amounts of food than hunting and gathering could. Although hunters and gatherers occupied much of the world as recently as three centuries ago, today they exist only in the Kalahari Desert, the Arctic, and the few other places where hunting and gathering is still more productive than agriculture.

One of the most significant aspects of the origins of agriculture is that the correspondence between agriculture and the towns, cities, and other cultural elaborations we call *civilization* is absolute. All civilizations have been based on the cultivation of one or more of just six plant species: wheat, barley, millet, rice, maize, and potatoes. The critical advantage of modern industrial peoples over hunters and gatherers is not so much in energy conversions through water power, fossil fuels, or atomic power as it is in *food production:* if, for some reason, the world's present population were required to resume our ancestors' reliance on undomesticated plants and animals, most of us would surely starve, despite our automobiles, nuclear energy, and hydroelectric plants.

For millions of years our ancestors subsisted solely on the proceeds of hunting and gathering, yet within just a few thousand years, between about 10,000 and 3,500 years ago, domesticated plants and agricultural economies independently appeared in several different parts of the Old and New Worlds. What conditions elicited these parallel cultural responses, and why did these conditions exist only within this relatively short period of time? Is the coincidence of domestication and agriculture in both the Old and New Worlds explainable as a result of contacts between peoples in these different places, or does it have to do with local, ecological, or cultural circumstances?

Domestication, Agriculture, and Sedentary Communities

We have been using the terms *domestication, agriculture,* and *sedentary communities* very generally, but careful distinctions should now be made. Most definitions of *domestication* appeal to the active interference by people in the life cycles of plant and animal species such that subsequent generations of these organisms are in more intimate association with, and of more use to, people. Domestication is thus often measured in terms of the *loss of fitness* of domesticated species relative to their wild relatives. Domesticated maize, for example, no longer has an effective natural mechanism for seed dispersal, because the seeds are all clustered on a cob that, without human intervention, usually remains tightly attached to the plant. Similarly, a variety of sheep in Southwest Asia has been selectively bred over the last several thousand years so that its tail is a five-to-eight-pound mass of fat, making it necessary, it is said, for people to help these animals mate.

Archaeological evidence indicates that the physical changes associated with domestication in many plants developed, initially at least, not out of the desire or intention of making these plants more useful to people, but rather out of relatively simple changes in exploitation patterns, brought on by changing ecological and cultural conditions. Any plant or animal regularly eaten or used by people will reflect this relationship in its genetic characteristics, and thus all through the Pleistocene hunters and gatherers had some effect on the genetic makeup of various plant and animal species. But the low Pleistocene population densities and mobile way of life prevented people from exploiting plant and animal populations with sufficient intensity to perpetuate the kinds of mutations represented by maize and fat-tailed sheep. Domestication, then, is not an event, but a process in which the physical characteristics of plant and animal species change as these species' relationships to their human consumers change.

Agriculture is a particular kind of subsistence system in which efforts are made to modify the environments of plants so as to increase their productivity and usefulness to people. Here too people modify the environments of plants and animals simply by collecting and eating them; but agriculture is the systematic modification of environments in order to increase productivity. This definition of agriculture, like that of domestication, is a relative one. At the one extreme are the simple efforts a group might make to suppress weeds near a stand of wild wheat; at the other extreme are contemporary agribusinesses where crops are grown on precisely leveled fields and treated with pesticides and fertilizers, and where chickens live out their lives in computer-regulated environments. One of the most important consequences of agriculture is that it concentrates food resources and makes them somewhat predictable, allowing large population densities.

Sedentary communities are composed of people who are domiciled in the same place for all or most of every year. Such communities probably first appeared in Southwest Asia as much as 1,000 years before agriculture or domesticated wheat or barley, while in Mesoamerica at least five plant species were in the process of domestication several thousand years before the first sedentary or agricultural communities appeared. Sedentary life usually involves the construction of permanent structures.

For a million years and more before agriculture, people built crude shelters and lived in caves, but in almost every case they moved to other camps for part of the year. When our ancestors began living year-round in the same villages, a complex set of relationships between people, plants, and animals was established that had never existed before. Village life imposes a certain kind of psychological reality on people that hunters and gatherers do not have: it alters fertility rates, increases the chances of epidemic diseases, and encourages family-unit economic production.

There is a tremendous "inertia" in village agriculture, once it is established. In only a few environments can people move easily from agricultural to other kinds of economies, for the essence of agriculture is that one concentrates one's energies on a very limited number of species that are very reliable. In most agricultural economies, activities that conflict at all with agricultural production are soon abandoned. In Denmark, for example, analysis of human bone composition shows that in one area along the ocean shore, people before 4000 B.C. lived mainly on marine resources, but after that time they lived almost entirely on agricultural products, even though their villages were within 200 meters of the rich fish and other resources of the shore (Tauber 1981).

Grahame Clark's recent survey of agricultural origins (1980) emphasizes the crucial role of the preadaptation to agricultural economies that can be seen in the Pleistocene, such as the efficient exploitation of plants and expanding regional social networks. He sees agricultural origins as a rather continuous pattern of cultural origins without any real "jumps" in which evolutionary change was rapid. Let us look first, then, at the predecessors of the first agriculturalists.

Early Domestication and Agriculture: The Background

All cultures involve the interaction of countless social and environmental variables, and to understand a particular development we must often know something about the system at a point long before the first appearance of the phenomenon to be explained. Thus, to understand the appearance of the first domesticated plants and animals and the first agricultural communities, we must look at developments during the several thousands of years preceding these events.

This period, between 15,000 and 8,000 years ago, was a time of major cultural and climatic change. In western Europe population densities shifted as the herds of reindeer and horses that once supported many hunting bands moved northward with the retreating glaciers. Some people moved with them, but others worked out subsistence strategies stressing plants, smaller game, and fish. Salmon became especially important in Europe as traps, drying racks, and other tools were developed to make salmon exploitation a reliable way to make a living. In Southwest Asia, parts of Africa, and parts of the Americas, some late

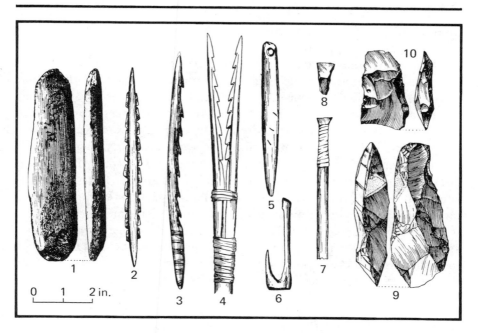

6.1   Mesolithic fishing and hunting equipment: (1) limpet hammer, (2) bone fish-spear with microlith barbs, southern Sweden, (3) barbed point in red deer antler, ca. 7500 B.C., Star Carr, Yorkshire, (4) leister prongs of Eskimo fishermen (shows how the barbed point may have been used), (5) net-making needle (?), and (6) bone fish hook, Denmark; (7), (8) microliths or transverse arrowheads, one found in peat hafted in wood with sinew binding, Denmark; (9) core-axe with transversely sharpened edge, Sussex; (10) flake-axe, Denmark.

Pleistocene and early post-Pleistocene human groups increased markedly their consumption of smaller game, fish, waterfowl, invertebrates, and plants, although in many areas the earlier big-game hunting specializations persisted. In North America, for example, the Folsom hunters centered their lives around vast bison herds.

Where a shift to smaller, more varied resources was made, technologies also changed. The bow and arrow and throwing stick replaced the stabbing spears, and new tools were developed to dig plants, trap wildfowl, and prepare a more diverse range of foods. Small, simple geometric stone tools predominated in many areas of the world (Figure 6.1). The world of about 8,000 years ago, then, was probably more culturally diverse than in the Pleistocene, with more and different subsistence adaptations, as some groups remained big-game hunters while others took up fishing, intensive foraging, and other pursuits. Thus, a great diversity of plants and animals was being exploited with varying intensities and technologies in a wide range of climates. It is out of this vast

mixture of peoples, plants, animals, and places that the first domesticates and farmers appeared.

We will consider in detail only one case of plant domestication here,
but it is worth noting Kent Flannery's observation that all the major
seed crops on which current economies are based, such as wheat, barley,
millet, and rice, appear to have derived from wild ancestors that were
third-choice foods: plants that were usually more difficult to gather and
process than other wild plants and thus were probably first eaten in
quantity because the people had to, not because they wanted to (1973:
307). On the other hand, all of these wild plant species have characteristics that help explain why these particular species were domesticated:
most are annuals, yield a high return, tolerate a wide variety of habitats,
store easily, and are genetically plastic. The disadvantages of these foods
are mainly that they require more work to gather and process than other
food sources, and they also tend to produce unstable ecosystems because
they replace complex, varied ecosystems with simplified ecosystems dominated by just a few species.

The Origins of Domestication, Agriculture, and Sedentary Communities in Southwest Asia

THE ECOLOGICAL SETTING

The development of domestication, agriculture, and sedentary communities in Southwest Asia involved complex regional processes that crys-
tallized over a large area of the "Fertile Crescent" (Figure 6.2). The
physical characteristics of this zone were formed millions of years ago
when movements of the earth's crust forced the Arabian Peninsula toward the stable Iranian Plateau, compressing the land in between so
that it is pleated like the folds of an accordion.

At the end of the Pleistocene, the uplands of the Fertile Crescent
supported large herds of wild sheep, goats, cattle, and pigs and, in many
areas, dense stands of wild wheat and barley. In lower elevations and
wetter regions were lakes and streams with abundant supplies of waterfowl, fish, and other resources.

The cold and the reduced ocean levels of the late Pleistocene meant
that many parts of Southwest Asia that had been forests became dry
steppe country. In these climates the "Mediterranean" vegetation that
includes grasses ancestral to modern cereals would have been greatly
restricted, mainly to upland areas where there was winter rainfall sufficient to support the open-woodlands habitats where these grasses are

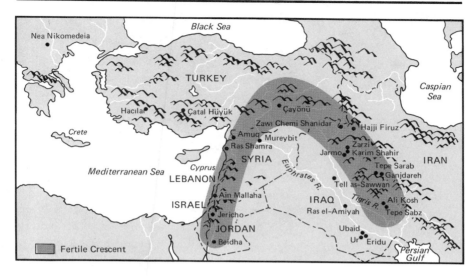

6.2   The "Fertile Crescent" and some important early preagricultural and agricultural sites.

found. But with the end of the Pleistocene 10,000 years ago, the warmer, wetter weather patterns would have extended these cereals' ranges into the areas of Southwest Asia where the first domesticated plants and agricultural communities later appeared (H. E. Wright 1976). Also, the rising sea levels would have submerged from ten to twenty kilometers of coastal plains around much of Southwest Asia, perhaps forcing people into new areas.

Since there were many previous glacial fluctuations that did not produce agriculture, these climatic variations are obviously not a complete explanation of agricultural origins; but it is not without significance for the timing and location of agricultural origins that they coincided with these environmental changes.

CEREAL DOMESTICATION

The domestication of wheat and barley—economically the most important plants in Southwest Asia—involved a complex series of changes in at least four native wild grasses, including wild barley (*Hordeum spontaneum*), wild einkorn (*Triticum boeoticum*), and wild emmer wheat (*Triticum dicoccoides*), each with different habitats and characteristics.

1	Wheat (8000 B.C.) Tell Mureybit, Syria	8	Llama (3500 B.C.) Andean Highlands, Peru
2	Barley (7000 B.C.) Jericho, Jordan	9	Ass (3000 B.C.) Nile Valley, Egypt
3	Lentil (7000 B.C.) Hacilar, Turkey	10	Bactrian Camel (3000 B.C.) Southern U.S.S.R.
4	Rice (4000 B.C.) Non Nok Tha, Thailand	11	Dromedary (3000 B.C.) Saudi Arabia
5	Millet (3500 B.C.) Yang-shao, China	12	Horse (3000 B.C.) Ukraine, U.S.S.R.
6	Maize (5000 B.C.) Tehuacán, Mexico	13	Honeybee (3000 B.C.) Nile Valley, Egypt
7	Common bean (5600 B.C.) Guitarrero Cave, Peru	14	Banteng (3000 B.C.) Non Nok Tha, Thailand
8	Potato (400 B.C.?) Chiripia, Bolivia	15	Water buffalo (2500 B.C.) Indus Valley, Pakistan
1	Sheep (8500 B.C.) Zawi Chemi Shanidar, Iraq	16	Duck (2500 B.C.) Near East
2	Dog (12,000 B.C.) Palegawra, Iran	17	Yak (2500 B.C.) Tibet
3	Goat (7500 B.C.) Ganj-Dareh, Iran	18	Domestic fowl (2000 B.C.) Indus Valley, Pakistan
4	Pig (7000 B.C.) Çayönü, Turkey	19	Cat (1600 B.C.) Nile Valley, Egypt
5	Cattle (6500 B.C.) Thessaly, Greece; Anatolia, Turkey	20	Goose (1500 B.C.) Germany
6	Guinea Pig (6000 B.C.) Ayacucho Basin, Peru	21	Alpaca (1500 B.C.) Andean Highlands, Peru
7	Silk moth (3500 B.C.) Hsi-yin-t'sun, China	22	Reindeer (1000 B.C.) Pazyryk Valley, Siberia, U.S.S.R.

6.3   Early archaeological occurrences of some important Old World and New World domesticates. Domestication is a process, not an event, and these specific sites represent only some early occurrences of species domesticated over wide areas.

Domestication of these plants, as elsewhere, was a long process in which certain kinds of mutations were perpetuated through changing patterns of exploitation.

In most of these wild grasses, the *rachis,* the segment of the stalk to which the kernels are attached, becomes extremely brittle as the plants ripen. This brittleness is essential to the successful propagation of these plants because it allows the seeds to be separated from the plant and dispersed by the merest touch of an animal or simply the force of the wind. The head of the plant becomes brittle gradually, from top to bottom, and the seed dispersal is spread over one to two weeks. Al-though this is advantageous for the plant because it prevents the seeds from sprouting in a dense mass of competing seedlings, it poses prob-lems for the human collector. If the grain is gathered when quite ripe, the slightest contact will cause the rachis to fall off, so harvesting with a sickle is difficult—although holding the stalk over a basket and tap-ping it with a stick works. If, on the other hand, the grain is harvested

6.4   Domestication of wheat, one of the world's most important crops, involved both human manipulation and natural hybridization between related genera. Human intervention appears to have been aimed at producing free-threshing, non-shattering varieties. The simplest wheats are "diploid," meaning that they have two sets of seven chromosomes. Hybridization with related species produced tetraploid wheats, with four sets of chromosomes. Hybridization eventually pro-duced hexaploid wheats, with six sets of chromosomes, which occur only in cul-tivated species of wheat. By mixing genetic material from various species, early farmers produced forms of wheat that could adapt to diverse habitats.

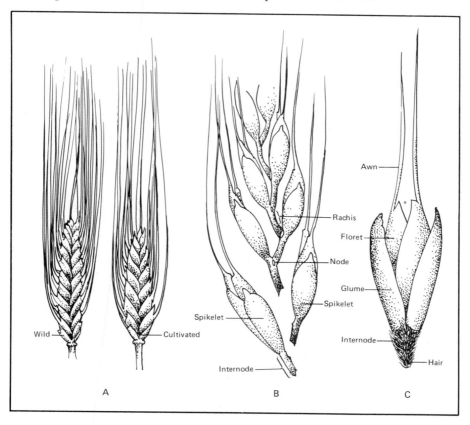

before it is fully mature, excess moisture in the unripe kernels will cause them to rot in storage. A plant with a tougher rachis and on which the kernels ripen at about the same time would clearly be more useful to people.

A second problem with some wild cereals as a food source is that the kernels are enclosed in very tough protective husks, called *glumes*. These protect the seeds from frost and dehydration, but primitive threshing often will not separate the seeds from the glumes, and the human digestive tract cannot break down their tough fibers. Thus a cereal with less tough and less developed glumes would be more digestible.

A third problem is that each stalk of wild grain has only two rows of kernels. Domesticated varieties have six rows, rendering them much more productive as a food resource, and wild species had to change in this direction before it was profitable to invest energy in sowing, cultivating, and harvesting wheat and barley in many areas—particularly in those areas where natural conditions were not optimal for wild cereals.

One other difficulty with wild wheat and barley as foods is that their distribution is sharply limited by temperature, soil, and moisture. As a result, stands of these grains can be widely scattered and therefore difficult to harvest. Much greater efficiency could be attained if these plants could be adapted to a greater variety of temperature, soil, and moisture ranges—especially the hot conditions of the flat lowlands.

In addition to these botanical limitations, wild wheat and barley posed a number of technological and social problems for the peoples who subsisted on them. Tools for cutting and transporting the grain, for example, would have been of great use. Some people in Southwest Asia still harvest wild grains by stripping the seeds from the plants by hand, but this is laborious and inefficient. Also, a sedentary lifestyle would have been advantageous, because of the cost of moving large quantities of grain and because successful harvesting requires that collectors be near stands at very precise times. In contrast to many plants, wild grain can be collected only during the few days when the plants are ripening, and even then there is considerable competition from birds and other predators. Another consideration is that women and children in collection societies could contribute a great deal to the food supply, whereas in societies specializing in hunting, women and children have less direct economic return.

We shall review the archaeological evidence concerning how and when these wild cereals were domesticated, but first it is important that we examine some aspects of animal domestication in Southwest Asia, for these were parallel and complementary processes.

TABLE 6.1   Important Cereals of Southwestern Asia

Species	Characteristics
Hordeum spontaneum (wild barley)	Most tolerant and widespread of wild cereals in Southwest Asia. Primary range in uplands of much of the Fertile Crescent. Tolerates disturbed habitats very well and follows seasonal stream beds from the mountains out onto hot steppes and arid plains.
Triticum boeoticum (wild einkorn wheat)	Tolerates cold better than wild barley. Found in extremely dense stands between 1500 and 2000 meters in the Taurus and Zagros mountains of Turkey, Iraq and Iran.
Triticum dicoccoides (wild emmer wheat)	Most sensitive of common wild cereals in Southwest Asia. Does not tolerate cold or aridity well. Its range is split into two distinct segments, a robust, large-seeded race occurring in dense stands in Palestine, and a smaller-seeded variant occurring in the lower oak woodlands of the Zagros and Taurus ranges. The Palestinian race forms fertile hybrids with cultivated emmer wheat (*Triticum dicoccum*), suggesting that it may be the ancestor of today's domestic emmer wheats, and focussing attention on the Israel-Lebanon area as a center of early emmer domestication and cultivation.
Aegilops squarrosa (goat-face grass)	A wild grass growing principally near the Irano-Turkmenistan border, near the Caspian, and flourishing in disturbed habitats. This species may have hybridized with emmer wheat to produce "bread-wheats." Most forms of early wild and domestic wheat were unsuitable for making bread and were used mainly in porridge.

SOURCE   After Flannery 1973.

ANIMAL DOMESTICATION

Animal domestication may well have preceded grain domestication in Southwest Asia. In some areas, such as the southern Mesopotamian Alluvium, permanent settlement was not possible until domesticated animals were available to supply the fats and proteins that were not readily obtainable from any other source. Domesticated animals also provided a way of converting highland grasses, weeds, shrubs, surplus grain stubble, and other plants into storable, portable, high-quality foods and other usable products. Later, some animals, such as cattle, horses, and donkeys, provided draught and transport power.

Sheep, goats, cattle, and pigs all were domesticated in Southwest Asia between about 9000 B.C. and 6000 B.C. Domesticating these—and other—animals involved breeding controls through selective slaughter, castration, and directed matings, such that the genetic composition of an animal population was altered.

Detecting the process of animal domestication on the basis of archaeological data is a complex problem usually entailing three classes of evidence (Perkins and Daly 1968): (1) the presence of an animal species outside its natural range, such as the presence of highland species of sheep in lowland environments; (2) morphological changes in the bones and other preserved parts of the animal, such as the loss of horns in female domestic sheep (morphological changes can also occur at the microscopic level); and (3) abrupt increases in the number of some species relative to others that cannot be accounted for by natural causes (for example, at many sites in Southwest Asia at about 8000 B.C. the proportion of sheep and goat bones increased dramatically).

The dog (*Canis familiaris*) is no doubt the oldest animal domesticate in Southwest Asia, probably having been fully domesticated between 22,000 and 10,000 B.C. Hunters and gatherers the world over are known to have remarkably unsentimental ideas about pets, and we should probably see the early domestication of dogs as a result of a symbiotic, utilitarian relationship. Dogs probably served as watchdogs, assisted in the hunt, and were eaten as a starvation food.

In economic terms the most important domesticated animals in Southwest Asia are sheep (*Ovis*) and goats (*Capra*). From about 9000 B.C. to the present, most meat, milk, and hide products used in Southwest Asia have come from these animals.

Horn size and shape in wild populations is a major determinant of reproductive success, since the larger males fight with their horns to establish breeding rights. As humans domesticated these animals, however, they relaxed selective pressures for large, strong horns (Figure 6.5).

The first evidence of *Ovis* domestication may be the presence of sheep bones in Neolithic (ca. 9000 to 6000 B.C.) settlements in the Jordan Valley. These bones reflect no morphological changes in the direction of domestication, but sheep and goats are not native to this area, and their presence here probably reflects intentional introduction.

Ethnographic studies of modern pastoralists suggest that they typically sell or eat 50 percent or more of the animals born each year, principally the males, since the females can be kept for reproduction and only a few males are required to service the breeding population. Once a male has reached two years of age, any further investment of food or time in him yields little additional return.

Evidence from two sites near Zawi Chemi Shanidar in Iraq indicates that this selective slaughtering may have been underway as early as 9000 B.C. Prior to 12,000 B.C., only about 20 percent of the animals

Type of Horn Core

Phase	Site	Zone	Cross section quadrilateral	Cross section lozenge-shaped	Medially flat, but untwisted	Medially concave, helical twist	Too young or too broken to diagnose
Bayat	TS	A₁				1	
Bayat	TS	A₂				1	
Mehmeh	TS	A₃			1	3	1
Mehmeh	TS	B₁			1		
Mehmeh	TS	B₂				1	1
Mehmeh	TS	B₃					1
Khazineh	TS	C₁					1
Khazineh	TS	C₂					
Khazineh	TS	C₃					3
Sabz	TS	D			2	1	6
Mohammad Jaffar	AK	A₁	4	1		1	7
Mohammad Jaffar	AK	A₂					8
Ali Kosh	AK	B₁		1	2		3
Ali Kosh	AK	B₂	11	7	8		27
Bus Mordeh	AK	C₁	2?	2			
Bus Mordeh	AK	C₂		2			7

Ca. 3700 B.C. (top) — Ca. 7500 B.C. (bottom)

6.5 The essence of archaeological interpretation is to discern patterns of change in the archaeological record over time. Here, the goat horn cores found at some sites in western Iran indicate that the shape of these horns was changing rapidly between 7500 B.C. and 3700 B.C. One explanation is that in the process of domestication the selective forces that kept these horns quadrilateral—and therefore relatively strong—were being relaxed, probably as a result of the domestication process. Farmers kept goats in herds and selectively bred them, and the strength of the horns apparently was no longer an important determinant of the reproductive success of these goats.

167

killed and eaten at one of the sites were immature, but by 8650 B.C., 44 to 58 percent of the sheep and 25 to 43 percent of the goats eaten were immature when butchered. And at the other site (dated to about 8900 B.C.), the percentage was approximately the same (G. Wright 1971: 463 (see also Solecki 1981).

By 6000 B.C. there is evidence of domestic sheep and goats at sites all over Southwest Asia and even into Greece and southern Europe, and it appears that once domestication was well advanced, the spread of sheep and goat raising was very rapid. In every agricultural community there are hedgerows, thorny plants, clippings, and stubble that are perfectly acceptable to the rather undiscriminating sheep and goats, and these animals, with their heavy fleece, are well protected against the sun and heat of the Middle East.

Members of archaeological projects spending their first season in the Middle East are often surprised to find that they eat chicken almost every day but almost never get lamb, even though the villages swarm with sheep. It is mainly because lamb is extremely expensive (an unwary archaeologist in Egypt paid about $30 in 1981 for "totaling" a lamb with a Land Rover). Even before the distortions introduced by modern urban markets, the economic importance of sheep and goats was mainly in the milk, cheese, yoghurt, and wool obtained from these animals. A well-kept animal can supply many times its own weight in nutritious, storable foods each year for several years, so only young males are regularly slaughtered.

Domestic cattle were herded on the Anatolian Plateau (central Turkey) by about 5800 B.C. and were probably present in the Balkans by 6500 B.C. As with sheep and goats, cattle domestication seems to have been a widespread phenomenon, probably beginning sometime after 9000 B.C. and occurring in many areas from China to western Europe. Domestication of cattle focused on reduced size, increased docility and milk production, and increased tolerance of climatic conditions.

Cattle were probably especially important to the first settlers on the southern Mesopotamian Alluvium. During the dry, hot summers in this region, few reliable protein sources are available to primitive agriculturalists, and cow meat and milk apparently provided a crucial nutritional component. Oxen (castrated bulls) may have been used to pull plows and carts. In many areas of Southwest Asia where rainfall is sufficient for cereal cultivation, plowing is essential because natural vegetation is thick. Later, the horse, donkey, and mule were also used as draft animals.

Another important domesticated animal was the pig. The bones of this animal have been recovered from sites all over Southwest Asia. By

6000 B.C. and even as late as 2700 B.C., pig bones represented 20 to 30 percent of all mammal remains at many large sites. Curiously, however, sometime after about 2400 B.C., pork apparently was religiously proscribed in most Mesopotamian cities, as well as in Egypt and elsewhere in Southwest Asia.

Food Taboos and Agricultural Ecology

Eventually Islam, Judaism, and some Hindu religions instituted complete bans on pork to the extent that even today, riots flare in some parts of the world if pigs invade religious areas.

Pigs are one of the most efficient converters of garbage, animal wastes, and other materials discarded by farmers—better in many respects than goats, sheep, or cows. In preindustrial economies and today in Europe, America, and China, the pig is used to convert grains that are not made into food or whiskey into portable, storable food.

Why should the sturdy farmers of the Middle East reject such a good food source after millennia in which the pig was a staple part of the diet?

This question has sparked one of the longest debates in modern anthropology, and it is worth a short digression here. It has set into conflict people who believe that all such religious prohibitions, *and almost every other aspect of cultural behavior,* can be understood directly in terms of technological, ecological, and demographic variables, and those who think it is impossible to explain adequately such things as religious food prohibitions and religious and social behavior generally in terms of the conditions of technology, ecology, and demography.

Speaking for the former is Marvin Harris. Harris (1974) dismisses the notion that this prohibition had anything to do with the common infection of pigs with trichinae, parasites that can kill people. Recent studies have shown that pigs raised in hot climates seldom transmit this disease; moreover, Southwest Asian farmers ate cattle, sheep, and goats, which carry anthrax, brucellosis, and other diseases as dangerous or more so than anything pigs can transmit.

Instead, Harris explains prohibitions of pork in terms of the cost-benefit ratio of the animal in early subsistence agricultural systems. Pigs, unlike sheep, goats, and cattle, cannot subsist on husks, stalks, or other high-cellulose foods; their natural diet is tubers, roots, nuts, and fruits, and they completely lose their advantages over cattle as a converter of plant foods if forced to subsist on high-cellulose diets. Also, pigs are native to woodlands and swamps and do not tolerate direct sun and open country well. Thus, the clearing of land and felling of forests coincident with the spread of agriculture in Southwest Asia greatly reduced the habitat and natural foods available to pigs and, increasingly, pigs had to be fed on grain, which brought them into competition with people; they also had to be provided with artificial shade and considerable water. Moreover, in contrast to other domesticates, as Harris points out, pigs cannot be milked, sheared, ridden, or used to pull a plow. In short, they lost their cost effectiveness relative to sheep, goats, and cattle, and their eventual proscription made excellent economic "sense."

And, as in all instances, it is not important that people ever recognize their motives in cases of such prohibitions: natural selection "fixes," or perpetuates, economically sound behaviors, regardless of what people think their motives are. Harris extends his argument to many other animals, in particular the sacred cow of India and the animals listed in the Old Testament. In every case he tries to show that when one considers the economic conditions in which these prohibitions arose, one can see that there was at least some minor overall advantage to be gained. Thus, he notes that the Old Testament forbids eating any insects other than locusts, which just happen to be the only ones that have much caloric value in relation to the cost of capturing them (and they are crop pests as well).

Against Harris and his supporters are many people who believe that Harris is propagating a bastardized version of a misconception of Marxian theory (e.g., Friedman 1974; Sahlins 1976). Sahlins, for example, points to the United States, where millions of cattle are slaughtered every year but where virtually every horse lives out its full life in relative luxury and, usually, enjoying considerable affection. Why, Sahlins asks, do Americans arbitrarily proscribe horsemeat and accept beef? Sahlins answers his own question, arguing that it is because every culture creates its own belief systems from its unique blend of economy, society, and ideology. The essential point, Sahlins says (1978), "is that material rationality exists for men not as a fact of nature but as a construct of culture. . . . The natural conditions of viability (selective forces) comprise merely negative constraints, limits of functional possibilities, which remain indeterminate with respect to the generation of particular cultural forms." Moreover, he says, one can never read directly from material circumstances to cultural order as from cause to effect. "It is not that these techno-environmental variables have no effect, rather that everything depends on the way these properties are culturally mediated—given meaningful organization by a mode of cultural organization" (1978).

All this is rather far from the poor abandoned pigs of Southwest Asia, but the point is an important one. For if archaeologists must seek the causes of changes in the archaeological record (like the succession of pig bones by sheep and goat bones in the levels of a site) in the cultural mediation of "the mode of cultural organization," they will have to apply techniques of archaeological analysis presently not known or, possibly, not within the capacities of any other than a Divine Intellect.

Harris argues that one can show by the relative susceptibility to disease, dietary requirements, and other economic and historical factors that it makes economic "sense" to eat cattle and not horses in contemporary America. He does not insist all human behavior has such a delicate economic tuning or that there can be no whimsical aspects of culture. He says only that in the long run, if one is trying to understand something like these different uses of animals, one should look first at the economics of the situation.

The Archaeological Record of Plant and Animal Domestication in Southwest Asia

Archaeological sites throughout Southwest Asia during the late Upper Pleistocene, from about 20,000 to 16,000 B.C., are monotonously alike in their concentrations of stone tools, ash, and the bones of large, hoofed mammals. Almost all the meat eaten by people came from just a few species of *ungulates* (hoofed mammals), mainly gazelles and wild cows. Based on the tools and other artifacts from Southwest Asian sites of this period, it appears that the basic social unit was a band of about fifteen or twenty people, comprising several families, who season after season moved through this area hunting animals and gathering plants. Sometime after about 16,000 B.C. in Southwest Asia there was a subtle but fundamental shift in subsistence strategies that is termed the *broad-spectrum revolution*.

In some areas there are significant indications of increasing exploitation of grasses and cereals. For example, the locations of Kebaran sites in the Levant, and the stone tools found in them, suggest that already by about 15,000 B.C., wild cereals were being exploited with some intensity (Wendorf and Marks eds., 1975).

Accompanying the broader diet of the late Pleistocene was the appearance of a more diverse technology. Barbed spears and arrows, bows, knives made by setting obsidian and flint flakes into bone or wood, and other tools bespeak a broadening range of subsistence activities. Some animal species were exploited systematically for the first time, and the grinding stones, "sickles," and other new tools indicate that vegetable

6.6 An early Natufian house, situated on virgin soil at Tell as-Sultan, Jericho. The round shallow pits in the floor were probably storage pits, and the stone querns to the left were probably used for grinding cereals.

foods, including wild cereal grasses, may have been important parts of the diet. Minor local trade in obsidian and sea shells was carried on, and substantial huts appeared in some areas. Apparently, population densities were slowly increasing in some areas—although the achaeological evidence for this is not at all clear (Solecki and Solecki, 1980).

Shortly after 10,000 B.C. there were still no agricultural economies in Southwest Asia, but sedentary communities appeared for the first time, such as those of the *Natufian* culture, represented by scores of sites located in a wide strip of land running from southern Turkey to the edge of the Nile delta. At about 10,000 B.C. intensive collectors and hunters in this area subsisted largely on gazelle hunting, fishing, and the collection of wild cereals. The importance of cereals in these communities is reflected in large numbers of sickle blades, many of which have a glossy sheen from continued contact with the rough stems of cereal plants.

Some Natufian peoples retained a mobile way of life, but others established sedentary communities, such as at Ain Mallaha, near Lake Huleh, Israel, which between 9000 and 8000 B.C. comprised about fifty huts, most of them circular, semisubterranean, and rock-lined and from 2.5 to 9 meters in diameter. Mortars and pestles litter the site and occur in most huts, and storage pits were found both in individual huts and in the interior of the compound.

This same basic housing pattern, compounds of circular huts, has a wide distribution in Southwest Asia. Kent Flannery (1972) has noted that many contemporary African peoples also live in compounds of circular huts and that most such societies share several characteristics: only one or two people are usually housed in each hut; many of the huts are not residential, but are used for storage, kitchens, stables, and the like; huts are often placed in a circle around a cleared space; food storage is usually open and shared by all occupants; and, perhaps most important, the social organization of the typical compound, like that of hunting and gathering groups, usually consists of six to eight males, each associated with from one to three women and their respective children, and there is a strong sexual division of labor.

Flannery argues that settlements of adjacent rectangular buildings— which he calls *villages*—have advantages over settlements of circular buildings—which he calls *compounds*. The former are more expandable because rooms can simply be added on, whereas increasing the number of circular residences rapidly increases the diameter of the settlement to an unwieldy size. Villages are also more defensible than compounds for a number of reasons. But the primary difference is in their respective capacities for intensification of production. In compounds, storage facilities are open and shared, and the basic economic unit is the group; but in villages the basic unit is the family, which maintains its own storage of supplies and thus has greater incentives for intensification of production (Flannery 1972: 48).

If Flannery is correct, the transition which occurred between 9000 B.C. and 7000 B.C. from compounds of circular structures to villages of rectangular rooms is a reflection of changes in the social organization of the Greater Mesopotamian peoples, with the nuclear family gradually replacing the hunting and gathering group as the unit of economic production. And although the circular-building tradition continued for several thousand years in parts of Southwest Asia, it was eventually entirely supplanted by rectangular-unit villages.

To return to the archaeological evidence for early domestication, it is evident that Natufian culture contrasted in many ways with its predecessors. Sickles, querns (hand mills), mortars, pestles, pounders, and other ground stone tools occur in abundance at Natufian sites, and many such tools show signs of long, intensive use. Fish hooks and

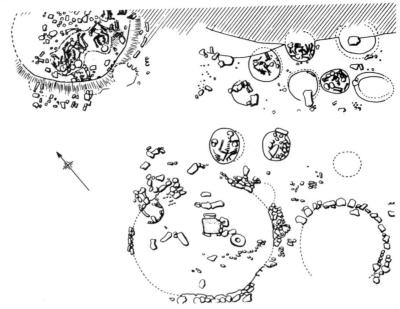

6.7   Simplified plan of an early settlement at Ain Mallaha (Israel). Compounds of circular huts such as those at Ain Mallaha were widespread in Southwest Asia after about 8000 B.C., but by 6000 B.C. had been superseded largely by villages of rectangular units.

gorges and net sinkers attest to the growing importance of fish in the diet in some areas. Stone vessels indicate an increased need for containers, but there is no evidence of Natufian clay working or pottery.

Compared to the Pleistocene cultures of the Levant, there appears to have been considerable social change in the Natufian. Cleverly carved figurines of animals, women, and other subjects occur in many sites, and Natufian period cave paintings have been found in Anatolia, Syria, and Iran. Trade in shell, obsidian, and other commodities seems to have been on the rise, and we suspect that exchange of perishables, such as skins, foodstuffs, and salt, was also increasing. With the increased importance of wild cereals in the diet, salt probably became for the first time a near necessity, perhaps for food preservation and to compensate for the lowered salt content of the diet.

More than 200 Natufian burials have been found, most of them simple graves set in house floors. Grave goods are infrequent, but some burials indicate concern with the philosophical implications of death; at Ain Mallaha skeletons were buried with their heads wedged between two stones and their joints covered with large stones "to ensure perhaps that the deceased would not rise from his grave" (Mellaart 1975: 50).

Some of the earliest evidence for domesticated grain cultivation in the Levant comes from lower levels of Jericho (ca. 8350 to 7350 B.C.), next to the springs in the center of this oasis. At some time during this period domestic forms of wheat and barley were cultivated in quantity here. Neither wild wheat nor barley appears to have been native to the arid wastelands that surround the site, so these grains were probably brought down from the uplands of the Jordan Valley and grown at Jericho, perhaps as wild species initially. No domestic animals were used in this period, but wild gazelles, goats, cattle, and boars were intensively hunted. Two thousand or more people probably lived at Jericho at any time between 8350 and 7350 B.C., and although the earlier communities were apparently unwalled, around 7350 B.C. the inhabitants built a massive stone wall, 3 meters thick, 4 meters high, and perhaps 700 meters in circumference. Asphalt, sulphur, salt, and a little obsidian seem to have been traded, but in moderate quantities. The apparent destruction of the settlement without obvious violence at about 7350 B.C. is unexplained.

While the Natufian and early agricultural cultures were developing in Palestine, groups in and around the flanks of the Zagros and Taurus mountains were also making the transition to sedentary communities based on intensive plant collection. One of the earliest such communities was at Tell Mureybit, on the Euphrates River east of Aleppo, Syria. There, at about 8200 to 8000 B.C., people built circular stone huts, similar in almost every respect to the circular huts at Ain Mallaha. Charred wild einkorn seeds have been recovered from Tell Mureybit, as well as the remains of wild barley, lentils, bitter vetch, pistachios, toad rush, and possibly peas. Most of these plants can be found locally, but the wild einkorn and barley are not native to this area and in fact can be found in natural stands no nearer than the Anatolian hills some 100 to 150 kilometers to the northwest (Mellaart 1975: 46). The impracticality of moving large amounts of grain this distance suggests that Tell Mureybit may be one of the earliest agricultural settlements in Southwest Asia, that here and in adjacent areas intensive collectors first tried to plant, cultivate, and harvest their own fields of grain. Tell Mureybit is a deep site, and its many levels of construction, first of circular compounds of crude huts, then larger rectangular villages, suggest the success of this experiment.

Soon after 8000 B.C., sedentary communities and domestic plants and animals had appeared at several places along the flanks of the Zagros. At Ali Kosh, situated on the arid steppe of western Iran, at about 7500 B.C. people hunted gazelles, onagers (wild asses), and pigs, fished in the Mehmeh River, collected shellfish, and snared wild fowl.

6.8   Common implements for grinding and preparing grain in Iraq, between 7000 and 4000 B.C. The ceramic husking tray above was used to strip grain from chaff; the heavy stone quern and round pestle below were used to grind grain to flour.

They also collected vetch and other plants, and between 8000 and 6500 B.C. they began growing domestic, two-rowed, hulled barley and emmer wheat. These early farmers lived in crude clay huts furnished with reed mats, and they had stone bowls and a few other small household goods, but this settlement was neither rich nor impressive. Possibly the people came here only in the winter, since summers are unearthly hot and the cooler mountains would have provided many plant and animal products. Wild wheat is not native to the Ali Kosh area, but wild barley is available within a few kilometers (Hole 1971: 473), and the people here may have been growing grains that had been domesticated elsewhere.

By 6000 B.C. there were agricultural villages over much of Southwest Asia, most of them comprising just a few score mud huts, a few hundred people, and the same essential economic functions. From Greece to Afghanistan, these villages look very much alike. Taken on the basis of their archaeological remains, they are not impressive in their material wealth. Even sites like Jericho and Çatal Hüyük (see chapter 8), which were larger than most and had relatively impressive art and architecture, were self-sufficient communities without many economic, political, or social ties outside their region. The vast majority of these villagers were simple farmers without great aesthetic, religious, or social diversions.

But in these villages, we can see the products of one of the greatest transitions in human history. Although unremarkable by our standards, these people were the first to focus their lives on agricultural products and to evolve the sedentary communities that even today are the basic component of Middle Eastern settlement patterns. And as early as 6000 B.C., the processes that were to transmute these villages into states and empires were already underway.

Other Examples of Domestication and Agricultural Origins

OLD WORLD

The domesticates and allied agricultural economies developed in Southwest Asia proved both successful and adaptable to the extent that within centuries of their appearance they had spread far outside the Fertile Crescent. By 7000 B.C. farmers at Argissa-Maghula in Greek Thessaly were subsisting on cultivated emmer wheat and barley as well as domestic cattle and pigs. Recent recalibration of carbon-14 dates for scores of early European sites reveals that the basic wheat-barley/cattle-pigs-sheep complex diffused at a rate of about a mile a year, reaching Bulgaria about 5500 B.C., southern Italy about 5000 B.C., and Britain and Scandinavia between 4000 and 3000 B.C. (Figure 6.9) (Ammerman and Cavalli-Sforza 1972). To the east, domestic wheat and barley reached the Indus Valley by at least 3000 B.C. (and probably much earlier), and by the late first millennium B.C., domestic wheat was in cultivation in northeastern China.

The processes by which these domesticates and their associated agricultural techniques replaced hunting and gathering economies in much of the Old World are not well known but appear to have involved both the replacement of hunters and gatherers by agriculturalists and the conversion of hunters and gatherers to agricultural ways of life.

The grasslands and forests of temperate Europe and Eurasia contrast sharply with the steppes and arid plains of the Fertile Crescent, and the

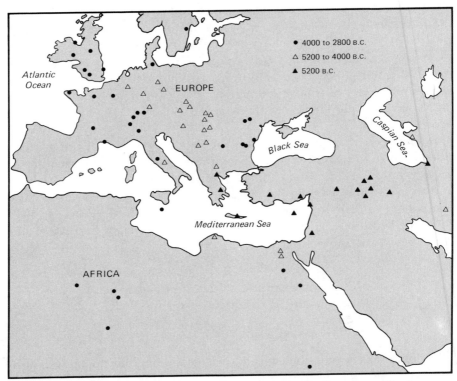

6.9   The spread of agricultural economies from the Fertile Crescent to Northern Europe was in part dependent on the development of technologies to clear the dense forests of these temperate zones. Recent recalibration of these radiocarbon dates suggests that the ages of these sites are 500–1,000 years older than is indicated here.

spread of agriculture northward and eastward required new strains of plants and animals and different social and technological adaptations. Methods had to be developed to clear the dense northern forests; and in some areas the rich hunting, gathering, and fishing resources formed such a productive food base that there was considerable "resistance" to the introduction of agriculture, with its unpredictability and heavy labor expenses.

   To the east, many herbs, fruits, and other plants were domesticated in India and Southeast Asia, but it was rice and millet that provided the majority of the food energy for the great Asian civilizations. Imprints from rice-grain husks have been found in potsherds from the site of Non Nok Tha in central Thailand in levels dating to between 6800 and 4000 B.C., but it is difficult to determine whether these represent domesticated rice. The use of the husks as tempering in ceramic manu-

facture may suggest domestication, but they may have been from collected wild species of rice. Other than this, the earliest known domesticated rice is from a site near Shanghai in levels dating to about 3000
B.C. Rice cultivation may go back much earlier than this in other parts
of Southeast Asia, but to date we lack any solid evidence on this point.

We do know, however, that by about 8700 B.C. some groups in
Southeast Asia were intensive plant collectors. Excavations at Spirit
Cave in northwestern Thailand revealed the remains of five different
kings of nuts, a bean (*Vigna* or *Phaseolus*), bottle gourds, water chestnuts, black pepper, and cucumber. None of these plants showed any
convincing signs of domestication (Flannery 1973).

One form of agriculture, *vegeculture,* may have developed very early
in Southeast Asia—perhaps far earlier than rice domestication. In vegeculture plants are propagated not from seeds, but from cuttings taken
from leaves, stems, or tubers of plants like manioc, yams, potatoes, and
taro. As Flannery has pointed out, vegeculture often produces complex
ecosystems because many different species of plants are frequently
grown in the same fields, and although these crops are often less productive than seed crops, they are more stable ecologically because they
more closely resemble the natural vegetation in warm, moist environments (1973: 273). They also require relatively little work once the
plantings have been made.

One of the world's most important cereals, millet, was apparently domesticated and first cultivated on the great Yellow River flood plain in
North China (see Figure 6.3). The alluvial soils in this area are extremely fertile and are sufficiently arid that there was little vegetation
to clear for agriculture in many areas. By about 4000 B.C. there were
scores of villages in North China, most of them subsisting on millet and
a few other domesticates and considerable hunted and gathered food.
These villages usually contained about two or three hundred inhabitants housed in wattle-and-daub houses that looked very much like the
circular houses and compounds that marked the evolution of agricultural communities in Southwest Asia some 3,000 years earlier.

Another crop of considerable importance in North China was soybeans, several wild varieties of which are native to this area. The little
evidence available suggests soybeans were in cultivation by at least 1600
B.C. Soybeans are a remarkably versatile crop with high food value. In
addition, they are good "green manure," enriching the soils on which
they grow through nitrogen fixation. The substitution of soybeans for
milk and meat in early Chinese diets may have to do with the fact that
many oriental populations never evolved the enzymes necessary to di-
gest milk products, causing them to suffer intestinal upsets if they eat

these foods. Similar intolerances are found in Africa, South America, and elsewhere.

New World

In the New World, many think the most important domesticate was cacao, from which chocolate is derived, but maize, beans, squash, and domestic fowl produced most of the calories for New World civilizations. For reasons not clearly understood, New World peoples did not domesticate any large draft animals or meat-milk-skin producers like cattle or sheep. This may have to do with the absence of suitable native species (although the Rocky Mountain sheep has possibilities). They did extremely well with cocoa, mushrooms, and various other "recreational" plants, however.

The background of New World domestication, like that of the Old World, is many millennia of hunting and gathering by people who

6.10 Some areas of early American domestication and agriculture. Other areas may be buried under coastal waters or undiscovered in dense coastal vegetation zones.

were in equilibrium with their environment. Kent Flannery (1968) has shown, for example, that the foods the aboriginal foragers of Mexico relied on, such as maguey cactus, prickly pear, and rabbit, were species that could withstand intensive human consumption for many millennia without changing much in their physical characteristics as genera, and that because of the nature of their seasonal movements, these people rarely exerted great pressure on these resources for any length of time. (For example, cactus-fruit collecting had to be done during a two-to-three-week period, and during this period rabbits would not be hunted.) This seasonal concentration on resources kept groups small and dispersed for most of the year, and one wonders why the Spanish found Mesoamerica (roughly from northern Mexico to southern Guatemala) a world of cities and farms instead of still the domain for hunters and gatherers.

Despite effective mechanisms that maintained the hunting and gathering way of life for so long in Mesoamerica, sometime after 8000 B.C. these people—probably unintentionally—began to domesticate maize, beans, squash, peppers, and other plant species. Domesticated maize was the most important food through much of later Mesoamerican prehistory, and at present it is the only domesticated plant from this area whose evolutionary history we know in any detail. A few fragments of early forms of beans, squash, and peppers have been found, but not enough to reconstruct recent changes in their morphological characteristics.

Until about 1970 the most widely accepted view of maize domestication was that advanced by a geneticist, Paul Mangelsdorf, who argued that domesticated maize evolved from a "wild maize," now extinct, with small cobs topped by small tassels. This would have been a "pod-corn"—that is, the individual kernels would have been enclosed in chaff rather than the cuplike fruit case of domesticated varieties. Mangelsdorf (1974) explains the extinction of this wild maize as a result of overgrazing by European-introduced cattle and as a result of its having been genetically "swamped" by continual hybridization with emerging species of domesticated maize.

In the early 1960s, Richard MacNeish excavated several sites near Tehuacán, Mexico, and his findings seemed to confirm Mangelsdorf's hypothesis: the earliest corn cobs found (dating to about 5000 B.C.) were very small, and the tassels did indeed emerge from the tops of the fruits. And the discovery shortly thereafter of "maize" pollen in sample cores from 60,000-year-old levels of the lake in the Valley of Mexico seemed to be conclusive evidence of the validity of Mangelsdorf's hypothesis. But the early maize found by MacNeish seemed to have many

6.11   The evolution of maize cob size at Tehuacán. Smallest cob (*left*) dates to about 5000 B.C. Dates, successively (*left to right*), are 4000 B.C., 3000 B.C., 1000 B.C., and (*far right*) an entirely modern variety dating to about B.C./A.D.

morphological similarities to another wild perennial grass common in the semiarid, subtemperate regions of Mesoamerica, a grass called *teosinte* (*Zea Mexicana*), and some botanists felt somewhat uneasy about the whole reconstruction proposed by Mangelsdorf, partially because the placement of kernels on a cob such as wild and domesticated maize were supposed to have had would seem a very inefficient mechanism for seed dispersal.

In 1972 plant geneticist George Beadle reasserted his argument of some decades previous: that there had never been a "wild maize," that domesticated corn, instead, was a descendant of teosinte (Beadle 1972, 1980). Teosinte is a tall (up to two meters) annual grass found throughout the semiarid and subtropical zones of Mexico and Guatemala, where it thrives in disturbed areas and rapidly invades open areas such as abandoned cornfields. Teosinte can be found growing in fields that also include wild beans and squash, with the beans twining around the teosinte stalk. Thus, the three staffs of life for Mesoamerica—maize, beans, and squash—are a "natural" association.

Chemical analyses of teosinte and maize, and studies of their genetic characteristics (Galinat 1971) have recently seemed to support Beadle's view of teosinte as the major ancestor of maize—although Mangelsdorf mounted a spirited counterattack (1983). Beadle's supporters claim that the 60,000-year-old pollen from the Basin of Mexico has been shown to be indistinguishable from teosinte pollen (Galinat 1971), and that the "wild maize" cobs from Tehuacán can just as easily be viewed as representatives of an early stage in the transformation of teosinte to maize.

If we accept teosinte as the ancestor of domesticated maize, the primary changes in the domestication process were: (1) the development of a less brittle rachis, followed by the evolution of the cob; (2) the development of a soft fruit case, so that the kernels could be shelled free of the cob; and (3) the evolution of larger cobs and more rows of kernels. A single gene—the so-called *tunicate allele*—controls to some extent the brittleness of the rachis and the toughness of the fruit case, and thus these features could easily have been produced by direct selection of mutants with these characteristics. The third change, increased cob size, was very gradual and probably differed sharply from area to area. The cobs from Tehuacán dating to about 5000 B.C. averaged a little less than 2 centimeters in length and were remarkably uniform. Cobs dated to between 3400 and 2300 B.C. averaged 4.3 centimeters, and by A.D. 700 the average size was still less than 4.4 centimeters. Between A.D. 700 and 1536, however, the maize cobs from Tehuacán reached an average of about 13 centimeters in length.

While maize is an excellent food source, it is deficient in a number of important proteins and vitamins, and the evolution of agricultural economies in Mesoamerica derived considerable impetus from the domestication of other species, the most important of which were beans and squash. Three species of beans (common beans, runner beans, and tepary beans) have wild ancestors in Mesoamerica, and changes in their morphological characteristics began to appear at about the same time as those of maize. Wild bean remains recovered in caves in Tamaulipas date to 7000 to 5500 B.C., and in Oaxaca from 8700 to 6700 B.C., but the earliest known domesticated beans did not make their appearance in these areas until between 4000 and 3000 B.C.

The domestication of beans seems to have involved: (1) increased seed permeability, so that the beans need not be soaked so long in water before being processed; (2) a change from a corkscrew-shaped, brittle pod that shatters easily to a straight, limp, nonshattering pod; and (3) in some cases, a shift from perennial to annual growth patterns (Flannery 1973: 300). The primary importance of beans is that they are rich in lysine, which maize is deficient in; thus the two are nutritionally complementary.

The domestication of squash and pumpkins, members of the genus *Cucurbita*, seems to have been aimed at improving the seeds (rather than the flesh) since wild *Cucurbita* have flesh so bitter or thin that they have little food value. The earliest cucurbit seeds are found in cave deposits in Oaxaca and Tamaulipas dating to 8000 to 7000 B.C., but since only seeds and a few stems are preserved, we know relatively little about recent morphological changes in this genus. Even less is known about the various peppers and other plants domesticated in Mesoamerica during this period.

Some scholars think that maize, beans, squash, and perhaps other plants were domesticated over a wide area of highland, and perhaps lowland, Mesoamerica, but that the stimulus for the adoption of the agricultural and village way of life came from coastal areas. There, rich resources in the littoral terrestial interface may have provided sufficient food for nonagricultural but sedentary communities (Flannery and Coe 1968; Stark and Voorhies eds., 1978). In time, these sedentary communities could have incorporated the new domesticated plants into their "preadapted" economies and social organizations, forming the first agricultural communities. From that point on, the superior productivity of village-based agriculture would have ensured its rapid spread over all the areas where these crops could be grown successfully. Presently, there are not sufficient data to evaluate this reconstruction rigorously, but recent evidence indicates that it may be correct. Large mounds of shellfish remains and cracked rock and stone tools have been found on both the Gulf and Pacific coasts of Mesoamerica, but few have been excavated or firmly dated. Radiocarbon dates as early as 2000 B.C. have come from shell middens at Sanja and Puerto Marquez, along the coast of Guerrero, but the humid climate probably has destroyed much evidence of earlier occupations.

Some interesting evidence has come from Ecuador, however, where several sites, both along the coast and further inland, may be the remains of sedentary communities where maize and other crops were grown by 3000 B.C. or even earlier. These settlements were part of the *Valdivia* and *Early Cerro Narrio* cultures, both of which have been securely radiocarbon-dated to between 4000 B.C. and 2000 B.C. Many sites appear to have been located in order to exploit both coastal and floodplain environments, but some are in the highlands. At sites in lower elevations, large middens often contain shellfish remains, fish bones, and other refuse, and at several sites near the coast, investigators have found what they believe to be the impressions of corn kernels in the surfaces of ceramics. Other ceramics appear to have been decorated with applied clay effigies of maize cobs. Significantly, these kernel and cob decorations appear on ceramics quite securely dated to about 2900 B.C., and the type of maize apparently reflected is an eight-rowed, large-kernel variety that, if dated correctly, would have been far more "advanced" than the maize of one thousand years later at Tehuacán. Roasted snail shells, which may have been used as lime to prepare corn, were also found at these sites, as were many large storage pits and tools that may have been used to grind corn. The humid conditions make it difficult to recover botanical remains, but at least one corn cob has been tentatively identified.

In view of these various lines of evidence, the investigators of these occupations suggested that

> maize was first brought to a high level of productivity in some place in the moist tropics of northern South America. But our data shed no light on the zone in which maize was first domesticated. We believe the precocious occurrences of efficient maize cultivation in the coast and highlands of Ecuador had marked effects on population growth rates and the development of more complex societies. We further suspect that the demographic imbalances triggered by the efficient level of agriculture in early Ecuador impinged on both Mesoamerica and Peru. (Zevallos et al. 1977: 389)

The domestication histories of cotton, chili peppers, squash, potatoes, and other crops in South America are poorly known. Flannery concludes that domestication and agriculture in Peru began too early to have been stimulated initially by a diffusion from Mesoamerica and that from the very beginning the Amazonian slopes must have played an important role, despite our lack of archaeological evidence from that region (1973: 303).

The role of animal domestication in early Peru is unclear, but llamas and guinea pigs were certainly domesticated in central Peru by 3500 B.C. As in Mexico, however, hunting continued to play an important role in many areas until quite late.

The relationship of plants and animals, agriculture, and sedentary communities in northwestern South America in general suggests that domestication and sedentary communities may have preceded specialized agricultural economies in some areas by many centuries, particularly on the coast, where small sedentary communities of fishers, foragers, and part-time bean and squash cultivators were established before maize cultivation was of any importance.

Eventually, domesticated plants and animals and agriculture became the bases for human settlement in most of the prehistoric New World as maize, beans, squash, and other plants were adapted to environments as far north as Canada and as far south as the tip of South America.

Hypotheses about the Origins of Domestication, Agriculture, and Sedentary Communities

We have described the botanical and cultural changes involved in the domestication of several plants and animals, noting in the process some of the relevant archaeological evidence. At this point let us consider some ideas about how and why domestication, agriculture, and sedentary communities appeared.

To begin with we can dismiss the idea that people domesticated plants and animals because someone came from outer space and taught them how to do it, or because someone in ancient Syria had a brilliant idea and it spread around the world, or because people simply got sick of chasing animals and wanted an easier way to live.

The roughly contemporary appearance of a vast variety of domesticates, from palm trees to potatoes, across the same approximate latitudes around the world, and the several millennia it took to domesticate most species, pretty well rule out the first two of these possibilities, and ethnographic studies cast grave doubt on the third. Although there is great variability, hunters and gatherers tend to have more leisure time than do primitive agriculturalists (Just 1980), and hunters and gatherers rarely spend this time designing cathedrals or in general "improving their lot"; they spend it either talking or sleeping—skills, as Sharp notes, they have already thoroughly perfected (quoted in Just 1980).

So we need a less psychological explanation.

THE OASIS HYPOTHESIS

Among the first hypotheses about agricultural origins was the so-called *oasis hypothesis*, also known as the *propinquity hypothesis*, which was an attempt to explain the origins of agriculture in terms of the climate changes associated with the end of the Pleistocene some 10,000 years ago.

With the gradual shrinking in dimensions of habitable areas and the disappearance of herds of wild animals, man, concentrating on the oases

and forced to conquer new means of support, began to utilize the native plants; and from among these he learned to use seeds or different
grasses growing on the dry land and in marshes at the mouths of larger
streams on the desert. With the increase of population and its necessi-
ties, he learned to plant the seeds, thus making, by conscious or uncon-
scious selection, the first step in the evolution of the whole series of
cereals. (Pumpelly 1908: 65–66)

In 1904 the geologist R. Pumpelly led an expedition to Turkestan in
central Asia to test his ideas, and at two mounds in an oasis named
Anau he found the remains of a sedentary argicultural community
whose date he estimated as about 5000 B.C. He felt this supported his
hypothesis because at that time it was the earliest known agricultural
settlement, and since he found no walls or weapons at this site, he concluded that these people had had no need for defense and had developed in virtual isolation from the rest of the world.

The oasis hypothesis was accepted in whole or in part for many years,
but a number of empirical and logical problems were obvious from the
first. By 1926, for example, it had been demonstrated that the wild ancestors of wheat and barley did not grow in the areas of the central
Asian oases, but rather were native to the uplands of Southwest Asia.
In addition, excavations by G. Caton-Thompson in 1934 suggested that
settled agricultural communities had existed in Egypt by 5000 B.C.,
making it doubtful that the oases of central Asia were the first to evolve
agriculture; and by the 1950s there was also evidence that there had not
been a major climate change in Southwest and central Asia at the time
domestication began—a blow to the oasis hypothesis.

Recent work in Egypt (e.g., Hassan 1980) suggests that a change in
rainfall patterns may have forced people out of oases and into the Nile
Valley, thereby stimulating the later stages of the agricultural revolution there, but generally, the oasis hypothesis seems fatally flawed.

THE NATURAL HABITAT HYPOTHESIS

Harold Peake and Herbert Fleure suggested in 1926 that the first domesticates and agriculturalists would have appeared in the upper valley of the Euphrates River, because they knew that this is the "natural
habitat" of wild species of wheat and barley. Accordingly, in the early
1950s Robert Braidwood of the University of Chicago organized a series
of excavations to evaluate post-Pleistocene climatic changes and to look
for early farming communities in northern Mesopotamia. His expeditions were among the first to include specialists in botany, geology, and

zoology as well as archaeology, and this "multidisciplinary" approach has proven to be a highly successful research strategy.

Braidwood's excavations (1960) at *Jarmo* in the hill country of northern Iraq revealed an agricultural settlement dating to about 6500 B.C.— much earlier than had been found either at Anau or in Egypt. About 6500 B.C. Jarmo was a settlement of a few dozen mud-walled huts inhabited by about 150 people who relied partly on wild plants and animals, such as snails, pistachios, and acorns, but who also seem to have been herding domesticated goats and, perhaps, sheep. But Braidwood also found at Jarmo the remains of partially domesticated wheat in association with grinding stones, sickle blades, and storage pits.

Braidwood conducted excavations at a number of other sites within the natural habitat zone of wild wheat and barley and eventually became convinced this was indeed the home of some of the first agriculturalists. As an explanation of why domestication, agriculture, and sedentary villages first appeared in this area, Braidwood wrote:

> In my opinion there is no reason to complicate the story with extraneous "causes." The food-producing revolution seems to have occurred as the culmination of an ever increasing cultural differentiation and specialization of human communities. Around 8000 B.C. the inhabitants of the fertile crescent had come to know their habitat so well that they were beginning to domesticate the plants and animals they had been collecting and hunting. At slightly later times human cultures reached the corresponding level in Central America and perhaps in the Andes, in southeastern Asia, and in China. From these "nuclear zones" cultural diffusion spread the new way of life to the rest of the world. (1960: 134)

Braidwood's research into agricultural origins was one of the few systematic investigations into this problem at the time, and his work has had substantial and positive influences on subsequent investigations in this area, but as L. Binford pointed out (1968), Braidwood's account of the factors responsible for the appearance of domestication and agriculture was not complete. Why, for example, didn't agriculture develop during previous interglacial periods?

There were also empirical problems with Braidwood's hypothesis. Frank Hole, Kent Flannery, and James Neeley (1969) conducted excavations at several sites on the Deh Luran Plain in southwestern Iran and found evidence that by 6700 B.C. domestication and agriculture were already evolving in this area, which is just outside the natural habitat of wheat and barley (wild barley grows quite close by, but very sparsely) (Hole 1971).

Also damaging to the basic premise of the natural habitat hypoth-

esis was a series of experiments performed by J. Harlan in eastern Anatolia in 1966, in which, using a crude sickle made with flint blades set
in a wooden handle, he was able to harvest wild emmer wheat at the
rate of about 6.25 pounds per hour (Harlan and Zohary 1966). A family
of four or five could probably have collected a year's supply of grain
with only a few weeks' labor, and this would seem to suggest that the
people who lived in the natural habitat of wheat and barley had perhaps the *least* incentive to farm it, because they could collect more than
enough from wild stands.

Because of these and other problems with the natural habitat hypothesis, archaeologists began to try to formulate a more comprehensive
and defendable hypothesis about the origins of domestication and agriculture in Southwest Asia, and they also attempted to explain how and
why sedentary communities could have appeared so long *before* domestication or agriculture occurred.

It is ironic, however, that as most of these alternative schemes have
been shown to be inadequate, Braidwood's notion—that agriculture appeared when it did because of the accumulation of people and exper-
tise—seems at least as compelling as do many contemporary explanations.

THE EDGE-ZONE HYPOTHESIS

Lewis Binford's approach to the problem of the origins of domestication and agriculture was based on his idea of culture as an adaptive
device. "If we seek understanding of the origins of agriculture or 'of the
spread of the village-farming community,' we must analyze these cultural means as adaptive adjustments in the variety of ecosystems within
which human groups were participants" (1972: 431). Thus, Binford attempted to describe the selective environments that would favor domestication and cultivation. He assumed that prior to the first agriculture,
hunting and gathering bands were in equilibrium with their natural
environment, using wild plants and animals but not altering them in
ways we recognize as domestication.

What could have upset this ancient equilibrium? Binford argues that
this was essentially a case where changes in the demographic structure
of one region resulted in the impingement of one group on the territory of another, upsetting the equilibrium and increasing the population density in some areas to the point that manipulation of the natural
environment in new ways in order to increase productivity would be
favored. He notes that Southwest Asia is an ecological mosaic, with close

juxtapositioning of very different climates and plant and animal communities, and suggests that late Pleistocene hunters and gatherers in such an area would fall into one of two categories: (1) *closed systems,* groups whose population size was regulated by their mobile way of life, infanticide, abortion, marriage rules, and other practices, with very little emigration or immigration; or (2) *open systems,* groups that used budding-off as the primary mechanism for population-size control. This phenomenon, noted in many parts of the world, involves a group slowly increasing its size up to a certain number, at which point, because of squabbling or insufficient resources, the group splits, with half the people emigrating to another, usually adjacent, territory.

Budding-off can also become the primary population-control mechanism if a new resource or subsistence technique—such as domestication and agriculture—opens a new niche. Binford notes that budding-off usually happens before any substantial overcrowding or major food shortages occur and that

> the shift to the exploitation of highly seasonal resources such as anadromous fish and migratory fowl did not occur until the close of the Pleistocene. This shift . . . established for the first time conditions leading to marked heterogeneity in rates of population growth and the structure of the ecological niche of immediately adjacent sociocultural systems. (1968: 334)

Given these varying population growth rates, Binford maintains that budding-off would have certain consequences that could have led to domestication and agriculture.

> From the standpoint of the populations already in the recipient zone, the intrusion of immigrant groups would disturb the existing density equilibrium system and might raise the population density to the level at which we would expect diminishing food resources. This situation would serve to increase markedly for the recipient groups the pressures favoring means for increased productivity. The intrusive group, on the other hand, would be forced to make adaptive adjustments to their new environment. . . . There would be strong selective pressures favoring the development of more efficient subsistence techniques by both groups. (1968: 331)

Thus, Binford is particularly concerned with describing situations that would select for, or *reward,* a cultural innovation like domestication or agriculture. He assumes that for at least the last several hundred thousand years, people had the mental and physical abilities to interact with and domesticate plants and animals and that domesticable plants and animals have always been available. But domestication did not occur in these earlier periods because situations that would reward these innovations did not exist. Once the population-to-resources balance was disturbed, however, there was a premium on every resource, and domestication might have come about in a number of ways. Perhaps the immigrant groups, in an attempt to regain the resources of their former habitats, would have tried to introduce wild wheat and barley into these marginal, "edge" zones. This would have exposed these plants to different selective environments, and domestication might have occurred as people manipulated these plant communities in these new environments.

Binford's *edge-zone hypothesis* provoked much discussion and research relating to the origins of Southwest Asian domestication and agriculture, but the hypothesis has some weaknesses. For one, as Flannery notes (1973), it makes climate changes and population growth into "prime movers," and it has not been demonstrated how these forces would produce agriculture or that they even existed. Most of the earliest agricultural communities in Southwest Asia, for example, have been found in areas like the Negev Desert, where it is difficult to imagine any form of "population pressure."

If we grant that there were significant changes in climates and regional population densities in Southwest Asia in the late Pleistocene and early Holocene—and at least some change in these variables is undeniable—then our problem becomes one of connecting these factors in a more direct way with domestication and agriculture.

Despite Flannery's questioning of the force of population growth in agricultural origins, recent studies have shown possible ways in which population growth may have been tied to the agricultural way of life. Studies of hunters and gatherers show that fertility rates are suppressed significantly simply by maternal mobility: a pregnant woman's chances of spontaneous abortion go up considerably if she walks a lot and works heavily. Thus, with the late Pleistocene shift to a broader spectrum of resources and the establishment of long-term camps near salmon runs and wild cereal patches, we might expect a rise in fertility rates.

Also, there is a direct correlation between the amount of carbohydrates in the diet and fertility rates. Studies (Frisch and McArthur 1974) have shown that it is almost impossible for a woman to become pregnant until she has about 27,000 calories, or 20–25 percent of her body weight, stored as fat (the author assumes no liability for the accuracy of this statistic). Nursing a child requires about 1,000 calories a day. In many hunter-gatherer societies, the rigors of mobility and the high-protein diet can mean that nursing itself prevents sufficient fat buildup for a successful pregnancy for about three years. But with the change to a high-carbohydrate, cereal-based diet and the restricted mobility of sedentary life, fertility rates may well have risen rapidly (Harris 1977). All of which brings us to harvester ants.

Rindos notes that harvester ants do essentially everything to plants that people do.

> Cultivator ants prepare special beds, generally of plant debris, cut-up leaves, flowers, and excrement, in special chambers in the ant nest. The ants are meticulous about growth conditions within the chamber; numerous ventilation passages are dug, and these are opened or closed to regulate both temperature and humidity. To construct the beds, the ants chew the substrate material to make a pulpy mass and deposit it in layers in the chamber. The bed is then planted with propagules from previously maintained beds. Constant care is given the beds. The ants remove alien fungi and add anal and salivary secretions which apparently have a positive effect on the growth of the fungi. These cultivation activities encourage the production, by the fungus, of small whitish round bodies, the so-called kohlrabi structures. These structures are the principal food of the ant colony. (1980: 754)

Rindos does not note the presence of tiny scarecrows or silos among these ants, but his point is well taken: in terms of their ecological relationship with the sustaining species, ants do not differ significantly from us. And if this is true, the import of his observation is obvious: what we consider the uniquely human activities of domestication and agriculture are in fact somewhat common ecological relationships that can be "fixed" by natural selection without regard to the intelligence of the organism involved. Thus, Rindos asserts that some of our debates about agricultural origins are clouded by assumptions about intention and illogical typological thinking: we may label as "hoarding" a squirrel's burying acorns, but as far as the propagation of oak trees is concerned, this distinction between planting and hoarding is meaningless (1980: 757).

Rindos's argument is complex and ultimately mathematical in nature, as it depends on expressions of resource instability, population density, and rates of domesticatory changes. Given the widespread human desire to believe that we choose our adaptation while other species have theirs thrust upon them by nature (Rindos 1980: 769), it is not surprising that Rindos's explanation of agricultural origins was not immediately hailed as a solution to the problems posed at the beginning of this chapter. Specifically, Rindos's model does not answer the question of why human domestication of plants occurred when it did and where it did.

One of the more plausible attempts to combine evolutionary and historical explanations for agricultural origins is Brian Hayden's *resource-stress model* (1981). Like the Binford-Flannery construction, Hayden's account is mainly an involved *functional explanation* in which certain relationships and events in the process of agricultural origins are arranged in a historical sequence and causal links are posited.

In Hayden's view, ancient hunters and gatherers were, like most people, trying to increase their *resource reliability*. From the precultural herbivorous hominids to Pleistocene *Homo sapiens,* our ancestors diversified their "income" by eating a wide range of plant and animal species and developing digging sticks, handaxes, nets, and all the other implements of preagricultural peoples. They also became in many areas sophisticated predators of large gregarious herbivores like deer.

Rather than a constant drive from population growth or "pressure" which forced these innovations and broadening of diets, Hayden envisions great stability in the population-to-resources balance. Unlike Cohen (1977), he expects that if we had complete human skeletal evidence from the Pleistocene, we would see no more evidence of dietary stress in the late Pleistocene than in the early Pleistocene.

But by the end of the Pleistocene 10,000 years ago, all the larger, more obvious animal species had been exploited, and people faced with the same kinds of cyclical food shortages that always had been man's lot could only turn to grasses, seeds, fish, and mice—in other words, the smaller, in some ways less desirable species. Hayden uses here a division of the animal world according to reproductive "strategy": "k"-selected species, like deer, are long-lived, tend to have long maturation periods, have only one or a few offspring each reproductive cycle, and are susceptible to overexploitation; "r"-selected species, on the other hand, like grasses, which reproduce in incalculably large numbers, are genetically plastic, live only a year, are extremely resistant to overexploitation, and quickly re-establish themselves after floods, fires, and droughts.

Switching to a diet of mainly "r"-selected species, Hayden argues, would have encouraged a sedentary way of life, stimulated the development of ground-stone tools, wooden implements, and other agricultural devices, stabilized the food supply, and lessened the need for group cooperation and common food storage.

In Hayden's view, then, the rise of agriculture is just a "natural and logical extension of the trends" that led to the late Pleistocene refocusing of exploitation strategies from big-game animals to smaller animals and plants.

As for the *timing* and *location* of the first agricultural economies:

> It cannot be coincidental that the first domesticates began appearing almost contemporaneously with the first appearance of the Mesolithic and Archaic. Moreover, this is precisely what the present model leads us to expect.
>
> It is especially notable that domestication did not first occur where the environments were rich enough to support sedentary, hunting-gathering-based ranked societies, with wealth competition and primitive valuables, such as those found in California, the Northwest Coast, Florida, and Palestine. According to my model, even though these areas had the highest population densities, their resource bases would have been much more stable and they would have experienced resource stress relatively infrequently. Because sedentism, wealth competition, and ranking in rich environments did *not* result in domestication in these areas, it is reasonable to conclude that such developments were not sufficient, or perhaps even necessary, conditions for domestication. Instead, domestication can be more usefully linked to the same Paleolithic processes which gave rise to the Mesolithic and Archaic: the effort to increase resource reliability in areas of frequent stress. (Hayden 1981: 530)

OPTIMAL FORAGING THEORY

Another recent approach to the problem of agricultural origins is based on the concept of *optimal foraging strategies*. This concept is an outgrowth of evolutionary ecology studies in which mathematical analyses are made of the feeding strategies of various species. Implicit in most of these analyses is the assumption that natural selection and competition are inevitable conditions resulting from the nature of biological reproduction in finite environments (Pianka 1978: 12; Winterhalder and Smith, eds. 1981: 14–15).

The "optimal" part of the concept of optimal foraging strategies refers to the assumption that natural selection over time tends to promote "efficiency" in the strategies that species evolve in their choice of foods, the amount of time they spend pursuing their prey, and the size of the group in which they pursue it.

Optimal foraging theory is used to predict on the basis of environmental variables what kinds of feeding strategies will evolve. As ap-

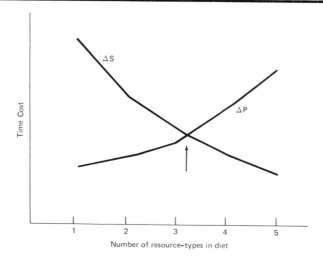

6.12   The McArthur and Pianka Optimal Diet Breadth Model. The S curve plots decreasing costs in time spent searching for food, and the P curve plots increasing average expenditures of energy as an increasing number of resources are added to the diet. The resources are ranked in terms of their value to the forager in terms of the cost-benefit measure adopted.

plied to people, optimal foraging strategies are complicated by the existence of technology for, obviously, technology will be a major consideration in how a group decides to exploit its resources.

Arthur Keene (1981) has used optimal foraging theory to construct a computerized mathematical model of the hunting and gathering practices of people in southeastern Michigan between 4000 and 1000 B.C. He estimated the costs and benefits of almost every resource in this area—from bears to berries—and then combined this information with demographic and technological estimates of these ancient peoples in order to "predict" where archaeological sites would be found and the kinds of technological and plant and animal remains that would be found in these sites. Keene notes that models like his have various uses in archaeology, such as in designing surveys and testing hypotheses about ancient economies.

Optimal foraging theory underscores an important point about human adaptations: although people choose this or that blend of resources for reasons that are forever beyond the reach of archaeology, natural selection does not "care" what the people thought about their world. Natural selection fixes foraging strategies strictly on the basis of the costs and benefits of these strategies, regardless of the hopes, fears, ideologies, and preferences of the people involved.

Domestication, Agriculture, and Sedentary
Communities: Conclusions

Some scholars have suggested that the very different sequences in which domestication, agriculture, and sedentary communities appeared in Mesoamerica and Southwest Asia resulted from the gross differences between these areas in the amount of available animal protein. Marvin Harris (1977), for example, shows that in both Mesoamerica and Southwest Asia, the end of the Pleistocene was accompanied by a great reduction in the large herd animals that had previously been the basis for subsistence in both areas, but that in Southwest Asia there were wild sheep, goats, cattle, and pigs that could be domesticated and combined with cereals to replace and extend the Pleistocene food base. In Mesoamerica, in contrast, according to Harris, there were few or no large, domesticable animal species, and sedentary life based on agriculture was delayed until a complex cropping strategy and coordinated interregional exchange achieved sufficient economic productivity to support village life.

The reduced availability of animal protein in Mesoamerica may in fact explain to a great extent why sedentary agricultural communities were established in Mesoamerica so long after initial domestication, but considerable additional research will be required to test this hypothesis.

We seem to be left with two major variables as potentially important factors in the origins of agriculture: climate change and increasing population densities. Despite the limitations on these factors as explanatory devices, it remains true that the environmental changes and climatic changes of the late Pleistocene and early post-Pleistocene periods are not well documented for all areas of independent agricultural origins, and thus we cannot be certain of their effects. Still, on a general scale it also seems true that the only unique aspect of the period when domestication and agriculture appeared is that there were more people and higher population densities than in previous interglacials.

Generally, we have no evidence that people of the immediate post-Pleistocene era experienced recurrent periods of starvation, or that they "invented" domesticates and agriculture as a way of addressing their immediate food supply problems. Instead, the situation may well have been one in which, as population densities slowly rose, people gravitated into various niches where exploitation of wild wheat and barley, teosinte, and other third-choice plants was marginally increased. Even if they were not forced into these areas by expanding population densities and were not under the dire threat of imminent starvation so that they radically increased their consumption of these third-choice foods, the plasticity of some of these species was such that minimal changes in selective pressures might have quickly and directly rewarded this increased exploitation.

In this sort of reconstruction it does not seem likely that the timing of wheat and barley domestication, for example, was the result mainly of "lucky" mutations, or that the distribution of the ancestors of these plants was vastly different before the last glacial period. All over the post-Pleistocene world so many diverse animal and plant species were domesticated that explaining them in terms of "lucky" mutations would require coincidences of a highly unlikely nature. Nor was this a technological revolution: the first intensive cereal collectors required only minimal tools—implements certainly no more complex or imaginative than the fish traps, bows, and arrows of the late Pleistocene.

Finally, for the individual with too few things to worry about, we might note that almost all of the world's population now depends for most of its subsistence on only about twenty genera of plants. And as hybrid strains are planted in more and more areas, the genetic "pool" of these plants decreases in variability. As a result, a newly mutated crop disease that attacks one or two of these genera could have catastrophic effects on a scale never before experienced.

The transition to economies based on domesticated plants and animals thus is a process still in operation and one whose future direction is unclear.

7

The Origins of Complex Societies

I should like to see, and this will be the last and
most ardent of my desires, I should like to see the
last king strangled with the guts of the last priest.

J. Messelier (clause in a will, Paris, 1733)

Although many people have echoed Messelier's sentiments, the appearance of priests, kings, and other elites seems to mark one of the most
profound cultural transformations of all time. Several thousand years
ago in Southwest Asia, Egypt, the Indus Valley, China, Peru, and Mesoamerica, the economic and social structure of some communities became sufficiently complicated that no person, or small group of people,
could perform all the activities required to keep these communities in
operation. In hunting and gathering societies, virtually any family can
and does perform all the activities of every other family, but in these
first complex societies this independence was forever lost. Once this economic and social differentiation and interdependence appeared, these
communities inevitably seem to have evolved social and economic elites,
relatively high population densities, the elaboration of arts, crafts, and
architecture, and many other characteristics we associate with "civilization." Moreover, although such societies have existed for only the last
five or six millennia, they have almost completely replaced the simpler
cultural forms in which our ancestors had lived for a million years or
more. Today, in the Arctic, the Kalahari Desert, and a few other places,
hunting and gathering bands still follow the ancient ways, but soon
they will be extinct and the "victory" of complex societies complete.

Scholars disagree on the definitions of complex and simple societies:

hierarchical elites, urbanism, intensity of agricultural and craft production, writing systems, and many other criteria have been used to measure cultural complexity, and different authorities attach primary significance to different criteria. But no matter how they are defined, the origins and development of complex societies involve some of the most fascinating and significant problems of anthropology and archaeology. For, as in the case of early agricultural communities, complex societies evolved independently in the Old and New Worlds, and once formed, they followed similar developmental patterns. Why, after millions of years, did the successful and resilient band form of human social organization give way so decisively and in so many places to more complex societal forms?

In this chapter we shall consider these and related questions by examining several explanatory models, which in later chapters we shall test with archaeological data. Because of the nature of archaeological data, we shall have to limit ourselves primarily to the artifacts of these extinct civilizations, the bones and stones and houses that have survived them. But we might note in passing the tremendous impact that the evolution of cultural complexity has had on the way people view themselves and the world.

Immanuel Kant said that the essence of immorality is to treat other people as objects, and in a way this is the "original sin" of cultural complexity. If recent band societies resemble Pleistocene band societies, most Pleistocene people were deeply embedded in social and family relationships and had a clear role in society. But in complex societies, from ancient times to the present, people often have felt themselves to be replaceable and minor elements in a machine that operates mainly for the benefit of others. Even some of the earliest writings of the first complex societies, those in Mesopotamia in the fourth and third millennia B.C., contain complaints about poverty, taxes, oppressive rulers, governmental harassment, and other ills of cultural complexity. Today there are still many who want to go back to a simpler place and time, when political, religious, and economic hierarchies did not exist, when all people were considered of equal worth, where all had an equal share, and where no one had power over any one else.

This theme of the loss of the "purity" that was ours in simpler societies and the idea of alienation because of the nature of cultural complexity are the wellsprings for many major philosophical movements. As Marshall Sahlins (1968) expresses it, our hunting and gathering ancestors took the "Zen road to affluence": people living in complex sedentary communities seem to live in the eternal economic dilemma of unlimited wants and limited means, but simpler societies have adjusted to their limited means by having few wants. Hunters and gatherers can't accumulate many goods because they are frequently moving, and they live in such small and scattered groups that social hierarchies are of little use. Thus, for millions of years our ancestors probably lived with comparatively little of the crime, class consciousness, alienation, anxiety, and other ills of modern societies. It would seem difficult, therefore, to support the argument that complex societies evolved because people saw that they represented an obviously superior way of life. Indeed, we might suspect that the transition to social complexity was made in spite of its effect on the quality of life, and that its causes are not to be found in the choices of individuals or groups about how they want to live, but in the material factors of ecology, economics, and technology.

Social and Cultural Taxonomies

In order to analyze the origins of cultural complexity, it is useful to classify societies according to their relative complexity. Recent approaches to cultural and social taxonomies have been heavily influenced by anthropologists Morton Fried (1967) and Elman Service (1962), and although their schemes were formulated principally to classify the diversity of extant and recent cultures, their ideas have been widely applied by archaeologists to prehistoric societies. The use of ethnographic data to categorize ancient societies that exist only as rubble and discarded artifacts can, of course, be misleading, particularly since most of the ethnographic record was collected during the last two centuries, when most "primitive" societies had already long since been influenced by more complex ones. Nonetheless, the ethnographic taxonomies of Fried, Service, and others are explicit or implicit in so much of recent archaeology that we must consider them briefly here.

Fried and Service differ on important aspects of these classifications, and their terms are not strictly equivalent; further, both have recently questioned the archaeological utility of some of their distinctions. Nonetheless, archaeologists still frequently use these concepts when discussing the archaeological record, and the following categories represent a blending of Fried's and Service's ideas.

BANDS

The Copper Eskimo, Kalahari Bushmen, Australian Aborigines, and other contemporary hunting and gathering societies are examples of this type of social organization. Based on archaeological evidence discussed below, it appears that prior to the appearance of agriculture, all people lived in bands, which are very simply organized. There are minor differences among members of the group in terms of prestige, but no one has any greater claims to material resources than anyone else. In most of these societies, older males who are good providers gain the most respect, but they have no political power. Band members spend most of their lives in groups of fifteen to forty people, moving often as they exploit wild plants and animals. Territoriality, ceremonialism, and descent reckoning are usually very weakly developed. Division of labor is along basic age and sex lines, and the economic structure is a sort of practical communism: money is not used, and exchange usually takes place between people who consider themselves friends or relatives. This gift giving is usually done very casually, and relationships are frequently cemented by offers of reciprocal hospitality.

TRIBES

Tribes are seen as differing from bands in several respects, the most obvious of which is size. People living in tribes are often subsistence farmers, such as the Pueblo Indians of the American Southwest or the New Guinea highlanders. Tribes often have a nominal leader who acts to redistribute food and perform a few minor ceremonial activities but, as in band societies, he has no privileged access to wealth or power. He can lead only by example and serves at the pleasure of the tribe. Exchange in such societies is still usually accomplished through reciprocal trading within a kinship structure. Typically, tribal societies are larger, more territorial, have more elaborate ceremonialism and kinship systems, and make more distinctions in terms of prestige than band societies (Flannery 1972). Service now asserts that for archaeological purposes at least, a distinction should no longer be made between tribes and bands (1975), and it may be that recent tribal societies are direct outgrowths of the influences of state societies.

CHIEFDOMS

While in many cases tribes seem little more than large bands, chiefdoms represent a quantum change in social organization. Chiefdoms are based on the concept of *hereditary inequality:* differential status is ascribed at birth, and members of the society are classed as "chiefly" or "common" regardless of their individual abilities (Flannery 1972). These differences in prestige usually correlate with preferential access to material resources, so that chiefs and their families can claim the best farmlands or fishing places as well as more food and more exotic and expensive items than "commoners." They are often regarded as divine and typically marry within noble families. The economies of these societies typically show a greater degree of specialization and diversification than those of tribes or bands. Craftsmen exist, but they are usually also farmers, and there is no permanent class of artisans as there is in states. Chiefdoms are much larger than tribes, often involving thousands of people. Examples of chiefdoms include the precontact Nootka of British Columbia and early Hawaiian societies.

STATES

States typically have centralized governments composed of political and religious elites who exercise economic and political control. In addition to being larger in population and territory than other societal forms, states are characterized by having full-time craftsmen and other specialists, and residence within a settlement is often determined more by occupational specialization than by kinship ties. The state codifies and enforces laws, drafts soldiers, levies taxes, and exacts tribute. States have powerful economic structures, often centered upon market systems, and they have a diversity of settlement sizes, such as villages, towns, and sometimes cities.

Early states formed essentially independently in at least six areas of the ancient world: Mesopotamia, Egypt, the Indus Valley, China, Mesoamerica, and Peru.

EMPIRES

A still more complex societal division is the empire, which has more people, controls more territory, exploits more environments, and has more levels of social, economic, and political stratification than early states (Eisenstadt 1963). Many of the early states seem to have been involved in competitive relationships with adjacent states, and for long periods this factor apparently limited their size and power. Eventually, however, in all the early centers of state formation these competitive relationships broke down and one state was able to increase its size and influence drastically—usually so rapidly that it had few competitors. In fact, its ultimate size seems to have been limited only by the level of its communications technology and its administrative efficiency.

Empires of this type first appeared in Mesopotamia toward the end of the second millennium B.C. and within a thousand years thereafter in Egypt, the Indus Valley, and China. The Inca state of Peru and the Aztec state of Mexico also seem to have achieved imperial dimensions just before the arrival of the Europeans, in the sixteenth century A.D.

CULTURAL COMPLEXITY AND CULTURAL RELATIVISM

One of the oldest and commonest human errors has been to confuse cultural complexity and cultural worth. Already by 2500 B.C., a haughty citizen of a city state in Iraq disparagingly described his nomadic neighbors as "[barbarians], who know no house or town, the boor of the mountains . . . who does not bend his knees [to cultivate the land] . . . who is not buried after his death" (Roux 1964: 161). Even in our own age, it is difficult to avoid the notions that civilizations have emerged because of the special gifts and vitality of their populaces, that simpler societies are incompletely developed, and that all the world's cultures are at various points along a gradient whose apex is the modern Western industrial community.

The above classification of societies in terms of their social stratification, size, and the complexity of information, matter, and energy exchanges is a research tactic that has as its goal the elucidation of the processes that produce these forms of complexity; we should not consider these measures as ultimate criteria. If we categorized human societies in terms of piety, social cohesiveness, "justice," or other abstract but important concepts, an ordering of societies very different from that having to do with "cultural complexity" would result.

The Archaeology of Complex Societies

Archaeologists regularly talk about the band societies of the Middle Pleistocene and the early chiefdoms of prehistoric Mesopotamia, but we do not have these societies trapped in amber; we have only the bones and stones and other artifacts, and we use the words *bands,* *tribes,* and *states* to describe them only with some license. To deal with this problem, archaeologists typically equate these terms with specific categories of physical evidence, such as the appearance and frequency of certain types of houses, irrigation canals, monumental buildings, and mortuary complexes and the various spatial relationships of ancient settlements.

At the heart of most conceptions of cultural complexity is the idea of changing forms and levels of matter, energy, and information exchange. Each person and each society exists because it is able to divert energy from the natural world, through food sources and technology, and some of these changes are selective advantages. The greater the amount of energy a culture can capture and efficiently utilize, the better its competitive chances. And we can measure this in part by measuring such variables as the population density supported and agricultural and commodity productivity.

Leslie White's (1949) equation of cultural evolution with the amount of energy captured per person per year has been widely criticized, but it remains popular among archaeologists. A certain unimaginativeness among archaeologists, many of whom work in the Third World, often makes them blind to the psychological richness and ethnic charm of mudhut villages; also, the fundamental data of archaeology are usually the stones and pots and other implements with which people converted energy to their purposes—the very appliances of energy use, in other words, that White stressed.

The particular artifacts that one considers most significant for studying cultural evolution depend entirely on one's theoretical perspective: those who believe in the impetus of population pressure organize their research to find evidence of this type, while the Marxian theorists may look for the extravagant tombs and houses that bespeak social classes.

ARCHITECTURAL EVIDENCE OF CULTURAL COMPLEXITY

Perhaps the most obvious differences between the archaeological record of the Pleistocene and that of the last five or six millennia is the presence in the latter period of massive amounts of residential and public architecture. Pleistocene hunters and gatherers occasionally built huts and shelters, but only with the increasing population densities and altered subsistence strategies of the post-Pleistocene period did some intensive collectors and hunters and agriculturalists alike take up life in sedentary communities comprised of permanent buildings.

The appearance of residential and other buildings, then, is mainly a reflection of economic productivity: if a group produces or gathers sufficient resources within a small enough area, it can become sedentary, and in most climates shelter is worth the cost and effort required to build houses.

Soon after permanent communities appeared in both the Old and New Worlds, the architecture of these settlements began to reflect changing levels of cultural and social complexity. Whereas the first houses in all communities were built very much alike and had the same contents, later communities were composed of residences that varied considerably in expense of construction and furnishing. Ethnographic evidence leaves little doubt that this architectural variability reflects economic, social, and political differentiation within the community, but the essential point is that, relative to earlier societies, there was a change in patterns of investment of societal energy and resources. Similarly, once residential architectural variability appeared in many of these early communities, "monumental" architecture also appeared. Pyramids, earthen or brick platforms, "temples," "palaces," and other constructions protrude from the ruins of ancient settlements from North China to the high mountain valleys of Peru, and here, too, the important thing is that the ability and incentive to make these investments are radically different from the capacities of Pleistocene bands.

MORTUARY EVIDENCE

For much of its history archaeology has been almost synonymous with grave-robbing. Its early practitioners were primarily concerned with finding ancient burials in order to loot the beautiful and curious goods that people so often have lavished on their departed. The importance of mortuary evidence to archaeologists is still considerable, partly because the preservation of items carefully enclosed in burials is usually much better than those in houses or toolmaking sites. Also, death for our earliest ancestors, as for ourselves, was invested with more ritual than any other cultural aspect, and in many burials we have, so to speak, the crystallization of complex religious and social forces, as well as reflections of social status. Corpses can be buried, burned, ritually exposed, or entombed; they can be laid out flat, on their sides, flexed, or oriented to the cardinal points of the compass; and placed in earth, in caves, in crypts, in trees, or on refuse heaps. Burial contents can range from nothing to enormous quantities of jewelry and furnishings and scores of sacrificed human attendants and animals.

It is a fundamental archaeological assumption that a correlation exists between the level of social complexity of a people and the way they treat their dead. In a test of this relationship, Lewis Binford (1971) examined the burial customs of forty "primitive" societies, including hunters and gatherers, nomads, pastoralists, shifting agriculturalists, and sedentary agriculturalists. There was considerable variation within this group, but as a general rule, the correlation between subsistence strategy, social organization, and mortuary practices was very direct: bands and tribes differed comparatively little in mortuary practices, while sedentary agriculturalists varied their practices according to a wide range of age, sex, and status distinctions.

The presence of juveniles buried with rich grave goods has been given considerable importance in defining the cultural complexity of ancient societies, because such burials are considered indications of ascribed status: it is assumed that young individuals could not have earned these goods on their own. Similarly, some ancient cemeteries have three or four distinct classes of burials. Some types are well constructed of stone, have rich grave goods, and are centrally located, while others are simple graves with little in them except the corpse. And it is a reasonable inference that these divisions correspond to different economic and social classes (O'Shea 1984).

EVIDENCE OF FUNCTIONAL DIFFERENTIATION
AND INTERDEPENDENCE

A particularly important part of cultural and social complexity is occupational specialization, the division of a community into functionally interdependent entities of such complexity that no small group of people can maintain all that community's activities. To translate this into archaeological terms, we must look for concentrations and distributions of artifacts indicating a certain level of activity specialization. In early agricultural villages, each house and each group of houses had approximately the same contents in terms of numbers and types of ceramics, stone tools, figurines, and garbage. But in later societies we find concentrations of artifacts that clearly represent such things as pottery workshops and stone tool–manufacturing workshops, indicating that people specialized in these activities. Again, we infer that they were specialized, but the significant point archaeologically is that certain classes of artifacts are found in places, volumes, and diversities far different from that which would be produced by, say, a hunting and gathering group. Certain differences will also be evident if we compare the contents of settlements. Some settlements might specialize in saltmaking, or barley agriculture, or pottery manufacture. This variability in the artifacts found within discrete but contemporary sites is a key element in our definition of cultural complexity.

SETTLEMENT PATTERN EVIDENCE

In addition to looking at things excavated at specific sites to measure cultural complexity, we can also look at *settlement patterns*. First, we can look at variability in settlement size and configuration. Early agricultural villages in Southwest Asia were almost all of approximately the same size, but settlements in the region several thousand years later were of many different sizes, ranging from a few hundred square meters in area to several square kilometers. Similarly, the basic shape of the settlements changed; some were apparently fortified rectangular compounds, while others were amorphous collections of small huts. Thus, any archaeological analysis of cultural complexity will involve measuring the variability in site size and shape in a large sample of contemporary sites.

Second, we can look at the placement of settlements relative to the environment and to each other. A major part of the cost of exploiting any resource is the distance it must be transported. This applies equally to the deer hunted by Paleolithic bands and the irrigated rice of ancient China. It also applies to the cost of making decisions about resource production, movement, and storage. With primitive communications systems, for example, an official in one settlement cannot make many timely decisions about the agriculture or craft production of thirty or forty other settlements many kilometers away, because the cost of gathering the relevant information and accurately and rapidly acting on it is too high.

As a consequence, some arrangements of settlements are more common than others under certain conditions, and we can tell something about the relationships between settlements by analyzing their respective locations. On a relatively broad agricultural plain, settlements, under some economic conditions, tend to be placed so as to form a pattern of interlocking hexagons (Figure 7.1) because this arrangement is especially efficient if there is a high level of movement of goods and people among the various settlements (Berry 1967). We will see several instances in our discussion of the archaeological record relevant to the origins of cultural complexity where ancient settlements in fact fit neatly into a lattice of hexagons or some other pattern. Here too it is relatively unimportant whether or not the distribution of ancient settlements corresponds exactly to the patterns observed among present ones. What is important is that we know there has been a major change in settlement patterning over time. Paleolithic hunters and gatherers

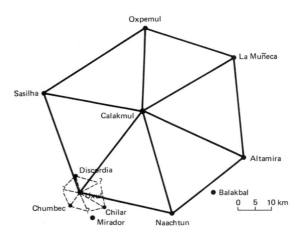

7.1   Archaeologists often do "site surveys," locating all the major sites in an area, and then try to interpret the spatial distribution of the settlements using mathematical geographical models. The *Central Place* model suggests that on a flat plain where all resources are uniformly distributed, the settlements will be arranged in different patterns, depending on the strength of marketing, transport, administrative, and other factors. No perfectly uniformly endowed plains exist, of course, but actual maps of archaeological settlements can be matched against the theoretical ideal and similarities noted to these ideal models. The hexagonal areas surrounding the settlements in the above models are produced by assuming that on a featureless plain each settlement would have a circular area around it, the inhabitants of which would go to the center for goods and services. But since a plain packed with such circular "demand zones" would leave some areas outside these circles, the theoretical model assumes that the circles are slightly overlapped and that the overlapping areas are bisected. The resulting figures are hexagons. Modern settlement maps as well as archaeological site maps for a given area often roughly approximate the variations of hexagonal distributions illustrated above. Thus if in a large area of, for example, Mesopotamia, one finds that settlements of 4000 B.C. age are randomly distributed spatially, but those of 3000 B.C. begin to approximate this form of hexagonal distribution, one might consider the inference that important economic developments had occurred.

and early agriculturalists lived in locations determined largely by the availability of material resources. But later in some areas of the ancient world, settlements began to be located with less regard for natural resources and more concern for trade routes, political frontiers, and administrative networks. Again, these changes occurred in settlements that were also building monumental structures, achieving denser population concentrations, and evolving some or all of the other elements of cultural complexity.

To summarize archaeological approaches to complex cultures, we have several specific lines of evidence: we can look for changes in architecture, technology, settlement size and location, and mortuary complexes, and we can attempt to link these changes to different levels and forms of energy and information usage and overall thermodynamic capture.

Most of the rest of this book is a summary of how different cultures in various parts of the world made the transition to complexity, and this summary is based on these forms of evidence of evolving complexity. But before considering these specifics, let us look first at the general problem of *explaining* these evolutionary patterns. As in the case of the origins of cultural behavior itself, and the appearance of agricultural economies, we would like some kind of theoretical constructs that will help tie all these separate early states together as members of a class and then will account for the time and location of their appearance.

Explaining the Origins of Cultural Complexity: The Search for Causes

The earliest scholars believed the rise of cities and states and other elements of evolving cultural complexity required no explanation, because they assumed these developments to be mainly or entirely the work of the gods. Even the Greeks, as we noted in chapter 1, tended to explain the diversity of sociocultural forms in terms of the preferences and habits of the people who lived in them. The scholars of the Enlightenment and subsequent centuries usually explained the origins of cultural complexity in evolutionary terms. Drawing a parallel with the biological world, they felt that competition between human societies was inevitable.

Darwin thought that "civilized nations are everywhere supplanting barbarous nations, excepting where the climate opposes a deadly barrier; and they succeed mainly, though not exclusively, through their arts, which are the products of the intellect. It is, therefore, highly probable that with mankind the intellectual facilities have been gradually perfected through natural selection" (1871: 154).

And because these evolutionary ideas placed western European civilization at the apex of human development, the cultural evolution of the whole world was viewed to some extent as an offshoot of Western traditions. The ancient states of China, India, and even the Americas were thought to have been prodded to higher achievements by contacts with the European/Near Eastern core areas. Thor Heyerdahl's *Kon-Tiki* and *Ra* expeditions perpetuate this notion that all civilizations are derived from a Near Eastern or, at least, Old World source.

Within the last half century, students of the origins of cultural com-

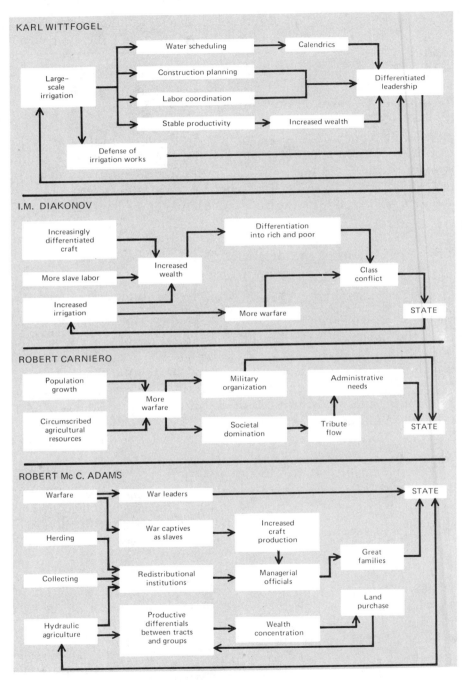

KARL WITTFOGEL

Large-scale irrigation → Water scheduling → Calendrics
Large-scale irrigation → Construction planning → Differentiated leadership
Large-scale irrigation → Labor coordination → Differentiated leadership
Large-scale irrigation → Stable productivity → Increased wealth → Differentiated leadership
Large-scale irrigation → Defense of irrigation works → Differentiated leadership

I.M. DIAKONOV

Increasingly differentiated craft → Increased wealth
Increasingly differentiated craft → Differentiation into rich and poor
More slave labor → Increased wealth
Increased irrigation → Increased wealth
Increased irrigation → More warfare
Differentiation into rich and poor → Class conflict
More warfare → Class conflict
Class conflict → STATE

ROBERT CARNIERO

Population growth → More warfare
Circumscribed agricultural resources → More warfare
More warfare → Military organization
More warfare → Societal domination
Military organization → STATE
Administrative needs → STATE
Societal domination → Tribute flow → Administrative needs

ROBERT Mc C. ADAMS

Warfare → War leaders → STATE
Herding → War captives as slaves → Increased craft production
Collecting → Redistributional institutions → Managerial officials
Increased craft production → Managerial officials
Managerial officials → Great families → STATE
Hydraulic agriculture → Productive differentials between tracts and groups → Wealth concentration → Land purchase → Great families

7.2 Several models of the evolution of cultural complexity. (Source: Wright 1977.)

plexity have been much influenced by archaeological evidence indi-cating that all the earliest complex societies developed in similar physi-cal environments, followed similar developmental trajectories, and yet had negligible contact with each other. To some this has suggested that the explanation of the appearance of complex cultures. must be quite simple, perhaps consisting of one or two key factors operating in each of these early cases.

The coincidence of the village farming way of life with the rise of cultural complexity represented to some a sufficient explanation of the evolution of cultural complexity. People then finally had enough lei-sure time and sedentary habits, it was argued, to develop architecture, art, writing, cities, and the rest of "civilization." The problems with this explanation are apparent upon even a superficial examination. Many agricultural groups apparently never developed into "states," while at least one early complex culture may have developed without a primarily agricultural economy. In any case, many hunters and gath-erers have more leisure time than primitive agriculturalists. Although agriculture is the foundation of almost all early complex cultures, it is not a sufficient explanation in and of itself, and within the last several decades, attempts have been made to combine agriculture with other factors in order to explain the general process of the evolution of cul-tural complexity.

RESOURCE VARIABILITY AND CULTURAL COMPLEXITY

Anthropologist J. Athens (1977) contends that while we may not be able to explain the rise of complex cultures as the direct and inevitable result of agriculture, there is an immediate causal relationship. Agri-culture, he notes, is an effort to maintain an artificial ecosystem, and in some climates, such as arid or temperate environments, the plowing, ir-rigating, and other efforts needed to maintain agricultural ecosystems are so great that it is doubtful that "the more intense forms of agricul-tural production would be developed or become adopted unless there was a compelling reason to do so" (1977: 375). Athens maintains (as does Ester Boserup [1965]) that the only reason sufficient to account for the enormous efforts required to maintain agricultural systems would be an imbalance between the population and available food supply.

In arid and temperate environments, annual agricultural production can vary greatly because of crop disease, weather, and other factors, and there is some incentive to try to stabilize production in these areas by augmenting the irrigation system, intensive weeding, land leveling, and other tasks that require a lot of work. In arid, semiarid, and temperate regions, the growing season is often sharply restricted by the weather, and thus "cultivation . . . does not permit cycling of plantings in such a way as to equalize the labor requirement throughout the year" (Athens 1977: 366). Each spring, for example, many different activities might have to be performed in order to avoid poor harvests, and under these conditions, according to Athens, there is a strong selection for certain kinds of cultural complexity. Increasing the territorial size of the cultural system would help meet crises brought on by a flood or some other disaster striking a single village; individuals and villages might also become specialized in trades and crafts to make production more efficient; and perhaps most important, it would be advantageous to have a hierarchical administrative organization, so that work and production could be closely and efficiently administered.

Athens argues that any comprehensive explanation of cultural complexity will require a detailed examination not just of the productivity of ancient agricultural systems, but also of the precise details of planting schedules, water requirements, disease patterns, and hundreds of other variables.

IRRIGATION AS A PRIMARY CAUSE OF THE
EVOLUTION OF SOCIAL COMPLEXITY

Perhaps the most obvious common denominator of ancient complex societies was extensive irrigation systems. Even today aerial photographs of Mesopotamia, Peru, and most other areas of early state formation clearly show the massive remnants of these ancient structures, and similar constructions were built by early "chiefdoms" in such places as Hawaii and southwestern North America. This led some scholars to conclude that it was the construction and operation of complex irrigation systems that was at the heart of the origins of complex societies. A particularly influential proponent of this view is Karl Wittfogel, whose *Oriental Despotism* (1957) is a detailed excursion into comparative history and sociological analysis.

Wittfogel places considerable emphasis on the special characteristics of water. He notes that the limiting factors on agriculture are soil conditions, temperature, and the availability of water. Of these, water is the most easily manipulated, but its weight and physical characteristics impose limitations on this manipulation. To divert water to agricultural fields requires canal systems, dams, and drainage constructions that can only be built efficiently with organized mass labor; and once built, irrigation systems require enormous investments of labor and re-sources annually to clean and maintain them. In addition, these systems necessitate complex administration and communication, because crucial decisions have to be made about construction and repairs, water alloca-tion, and crop harvesting and storage. Thus, a complex irrigation sys-tem under ancient conditions required cooperation and centralized hierarchical decision-making institutions.

Irrigation systems also have the intrinsic capacity to create another element in the process of the evolution of complex societies: wealth and status differentials. Fields closer to main rivers are better drained, more easily irrigated, and possess a higher natural fertility, and thus control of such lands would create immediate wealth differentials. Cor-respondingly, wealth and status would most likely accrue to the elites of the decision-making hierarchies. Wittfogel concludes that irrigation-based agriculture has many other effects on a society. It encourages the development of writing and calendrical systems, so that records can be kept of periods of annual flooding, agricultural production statistics, the amounts of products in storage, and the allocation of water. Con-struction of roads, palaces, and temples would also be encouraged, be-cause the mobilization of labor for the canal works could be general-ized to these other endeavors very easily, and roads would contribute to the movement of agricultural produce and to the communication re-quired for efficient operation of the systems. The construction of tem-ples and palaces would also serve to reinforce the position of the hier-archy. The creation of standing armies and defensive works would also likely follow, because irrigation systems are extremely valuable but not very portable, and they are easily damaged by neglect or intentional destruction.

The actual steps by which social complexity increases in this scheme are approximately as follows (Figure 7.2): (1) a large number of *sepa-rate* community irrigation systems emerge in a particular region; (2) a *hydraulic region* develops, irrigated by a single integrated system and dominated by a community; and (3) the hydraulic region establishes control over other areas that include societies that either don't irrigate at all or irrigate only a small proportion of their land. This last stage Wittfogel terms as *empire.*

The deciding factor in moving societies from (1) to (2) and (3) is the amount of irrigated land and the amount of rainfall. Wittfogel con-siders Peru a classic case of "oriental despotism" because civilization there arose initially in the desertic plains of the alluvial coast; on the other hand, he sees Mesoamerican civilization as a "loose hydraulic" society because, although the key to success there was still the irrigation systems of the Valley of Mexico, only part of the area was actually artificially irrigated.

While Wittfogel's hydraulic hypothesis still has some currency (e.g., Sanders and Price 1968; Harris 1977), there are a number of logical and empirical problems with his ideas as a *general* model of the origins of cultural complexity. There is no a priori reason, for example, why community irrigation systems could not have evolved without the simultaneous appearance of despotic religious and social systems. In fact, low-level chiefdoms in several parts of the world have recently been observed operating extensive irrigation works with no perceptible despotic administrative systems or rapid increases in social complexity (Woodbury 1961). More damaging to Wittfogel's hypothesis is the scarcity of archaeological evidence of complex irrigation systems dating to before, or to the same time as, the appearance of monumental architecture, urbanism, and other reflections of increasing cultural complexity in Southwest Asia and perhaps other areas where complex societies appeared independently and early. Nonetheless, irrigation systems were important in the *later* stages of cultural evolution in some areas, and we shall consider these cases in subsequent chapters.

HUMAN POPULATION GROWTH

Another persistent candidate for the prime mover in the evolution of cultural complexity is human population growth.

What causes human population growth? When I framed that question in a graduate school paper, the instructor's marginal comment was brief, rude, and unprintable. The question, rather, is what causes variations in human fertility rates and densities, and how are these related to the notion of cultural complexity?

George Cowgill remarked that many analysts of cultural evolution have assumed

> that a pervasive and powerful factor in human history has been the strong tendency of human populations to increase up to the point where serious shortages of important resources are in the offing; and that experience or anticipation of such shortages has been a major factor, or even the dominant factor, in stimulating intensification of agricultural production and other technical and social innovations. In extreme versions, the entire history of complex societies and civilizations is seen as hardly more than the outcome of measures that began as ways of coping with problems posed by relentless human fertility—what might be called the "strictly from hunger" point of view of developmental processes. (Cowgill 1975: 505).

It is easy to see the attractiveness of these ideas, for if one examines history, a strong positive statistical correlation between population growth and cultural complexity is evident. The relationship between human population growth and cultural complexity may not be one of direct cause and effect, however, for correlation does not necessarily demonstrate causation. Moreover, even if the relationship is in some sense causal, it may be that the evolution of cultural complexity leads to rising population densities, rather than the reverse. Empirically, too, there seem to be some problems with the idea that human population growth somehow caused the evolution of cultural complexity. All societies have evolved mechanisms like abortion, infanticide, marriage rules, and contraceptive techniques in order to control population growth, and thus we might expect people faced with stresses because of overpopulation to impose population controls, rather than "invent" cultural complexity.

It is worth stressing that the greatest recent falls in fertility rates came not as the result of food shortages or technical advances in contraception, but from increasing educational levels, greater social mobility, increasing urbanization, and the expanding role of women in the work force.

The actual causal mechanisms by which these factors are translated into reduced fertility are unknown, however (it has never been shown, for example, that such things as cities or the employment of women have reduced the frequency of sexual intercourse to the point that fertility rates would be affected). In any case, there is no evidence human populations have ever increased at anything approaching the biologically feasible rate. If the world's population 5,570 years ago were only one thousand people and their annual rate of increase since then were four per thousand people—a relatively moderate growth rate—the world's present population would be between 7 and 8 *trillion*. Obviously, human populations in the past have been under fairly stringent natural and cultural controls, and if we are to link population growth to increasing cultural complexity, we must specify additional factors or principles whereby this relationship operated.

POPULATION GROWTH, WARFARE, AND ENVIRONMENTAL FACTORS IN THE EVOLUTION OF CULTURAL COMPLEXITY

"War is the father of all things" said Heraclitus, and given its frequency in human affairs, we should not be surprised that many scholars see warfare as a natural adjunct of population growth in effecting cultural evolution.

Anthropologist Robert Carneiro argues that warfare was the primary mechanism for the evolution of social complexity in ancient Peru, Mesopotamia, Egypt, Rome, northern Europe, central Africa, Polynesia, Mesoamerica, Colombia, and elsewhere. He believes, however, that warfare

> cannot be the only factor. After all, wars have been fought in many parts of the world where the state never emerged. Thus while warfare may be a necessary condition for the rise of the state, it is not a sufficient one. Or, to put it another way, while we can identify war as the mechanism of state formation, we need also to specify the conditions under which it gave rise to the state. (1970: 734)

Carneiro sees two such conditions as essential to the formation of complex societies in concert with warfare: *population growth* and *environmental circumscription*. He notes that human population densities have been increasing in many areas for millennia, but that only in certain *environmental zones* can population growth join with warfare to produce highly complex early civilizations. These environmental zones are exceptionally fertile areas "circumscribed," or surrounded, by areas of lesser productivity such as deserts, mountains, or oceans. As an example, Carneiro points to the coast of Peru where approximately seventy-eight rivers run from the Andes to the ocean through an eighty-kilometer stretch of some of the driest deserts on earth. Here, he says, are fertile, easily irrigated strips of land along the rivers, but in any direction one soon encounters desert, mountains, or the ocean. Similar conditions, he asserts, prevailed in Mesopotamia, Egypt, and the other centers of early civilizations.

How does warfare combine with population growth and environmental circumscription to produce social complexity? Again using Peru as an example, Carneiro suggests that shortly after the accomplishment of domestication and the adoption of the village farming way of life, these fertile riverine areas were thinly occupied by small autonomous villages. For reasons not specified, he concludes that village populations grew and, as these populations increased, villages tended to divide because of internal conflicts and pressure on agricultural lands. Some of the inhabitants would then establish a new community some distance away. Such movements were easily accomplished in this early period because there was no shortage of land and there was little investment in terracing or irrigation systems. As a consequence, the number of villages increased faster than village size, and all communities remained essentially the same in political and social organization.

Eventually, however, given this constant population growth and the proliferation of villages, all the land that could be irrigated and exploited easily became occupied, and the expanding population rapidly began to outrun the available food supplies. Since they could not move into the sea or deserts or easily colonize the mountains, early Peruvian farmers chose agricultural intensification. They built terraces and irrigation canals and tried to keep pace with their population growth rates, but they were caught in the Malthusian dilemma: food supplies can be increased, but not nearly as quickly as population increases. At this point, Carneiro concludes, they turned to warfare as the only alternative to starvation. The village under the most stress would attack the weakest adjacent village, and the victor would expropriate the land and harvests of the loser. The conquered people not killed in the fighting could not simply move away and reestablish their villages, and they could not emigrate to the highlands because their whole culture was based on the village farming way of life. They were either taken back to the victors' village, where they became slaves or artisans, or else they were left as serfs who were taxed so heavily that they had to reduce their own consumption and intensify their production still further.

These developments encouraged the formation of an institutionalized bureaucracy to administer the taxes and slaves, and the establishment of the bureaucracy in turn intensified wealth and status differentials, as the most successful military men were given the administrative posts. In addition, the defeated peoples came to constitute a lower class, and thus the stratification of society increased as the level of warfare rose. Carneiro believes that warfare continued in Peru until all of each river valley was under the control of one integrated center, a development he terms a *state*. Subsequently, again because of the never-ending pressure of population, these states contended with each other until a whole series of river valleys was controlled by a single dominant center.

While Carneiro uses ancient Peru as an example of this developmental pattern, he argues that it applies almost point-for-point to the other major centers of early development.

Carneiro's ideas are diagrammed in Figure 7.2, where it can be seen that the whole structure rests on two "causal" factors: (1) the assumption that constant population growth among early village agriculturalists would inexorably demand increases in food production; and (2) the assumption that warfare is the most likely response to these conditions.

Since many primitive societies had remarkably precise control of their population-to-resources balance, population growth cannot be regarded as automatic. There is no demonstrated and inevitable reason why these populations could not have maintained their size below the stress level rather than resorting to agricultural intensification or warfare. Thus, to strengthen Carneiro's hypotheses we must stipulate other factors that encouraged or allowed these presumed growth rates.

In a recent reconsideration of Carneiro's model, David Webster (1975) maintains that warfare's principal importance in the evolution of the first states was the role it played in breaking down the kinship ties that organized early chiefdoms. He notes that chiefdoms apparently are kept from evolving into states partially because the chief's power and prestige are tied to his role as a redistributive head, and if he begins to hoard wealth or exploit people, the chief begins to lose the support of his kinsmen and deputy rulers. Webster proposes that warfare produces a potent environment for evolutionary change to state-level societies by rendering ineffective many of the internal constraints that keep chiefdoms in a stable sociopolitical status. Continued warfare between chiefdoms would place great adaptive value on a stable military leadership, thereby dampening the constant petty squabbles between rival rulers. A chief who is successful in warfare can also claim more wealth in the form of booty than he could on the basis of his redistribution of his own society's production.

It is difficult to test archaeologically Webster's and Carneiro's ideas about the interrelationship of population growth, warfare, and cultural change, because we must find evidence of conflict and demonstrate that it is linked to pressures exerted on resources by increasing population densities. If Carneiro is correct, we should find that the first complex societies appeared only after a long period of population growth in circumscribed environments, and that monumental architecture, irrigation systems, urbanism, land terracing, and other aspects of "civilization" emerged only at population density peaks and are associated in time and space with defensive constructions, mass burials, burned settlements, concentrations of weapons, and other evidences of conflict.

To the extent that it is possible to test these associations, it appears that population densities in sedentary agricultural communities do tend to increase under many circumstances; and the use of social complexity in many early areas of development probably did involve some population growth. But warfare and relatively high population densities seem to have emerged *after* the development of complex societies in most cases.

CLASS CONFLICT AND THE ORIGINS OF SOCIAL COMPLEXITY: RECENT MARXIAN APPROACHES

For many of today's social scientists, there is really no doubt about the answer to the problem of the evolution of social complexity. Friedrich

Engels' remarks at Karl Marx's grave expressed this certainty: "As Darwin discovered the law of evolution in organic nature so Marx discovered the law of evolution in human history" (quoted in Harris 1968: 217).

The critical part of this law is the Marxian dictum that the social, legal, religious, and ideological spheres of societies are determined by their economic, environmental, and technological foundations (cf. Legros 1977). Despite attempts by many to discard Marx's ideas on this point as simplistic and wrong, and despite the interweaving of Marx's economic analysis with dubious political polemic, there is no denying the tremendous influence Marx's contributions have had on the analysis of social systems.

Marx himself, however, had very little to say specifically about the origins of complex societies. His primary attention was given to detailing the problems of capitalism and the dynamics of the transition from feudalism to capitalist societies. Much more attention was paid to the problem by later followers of Marx, particularly Engels and Lenin, and, recently, V. V. Streuve and I. Diakonov.

Until the origins of agriculture, these scholars suggest, all societies were classless, all goods were shared, no one really owned anything, and all were treated equally. But gradually, after the achievement of domestication and the agricultural way of life, some people managed to control more than their fair share of the land, which is of course the basic source of wealth in an agricultural community. By controlling land these elites were able to enslave others and to force these people to work the land for them. In time the ruling classes developed the state, laws, and the church to justify, protect, and perpetuate their economic and political privileges. The state then is seen as an exploitative mechanism created by the elites to control and oppress the workers.

According to Marxian theory, every economic system based on the division of society into socioeconomic classes and on exploitation carries within itself the seeds of its own destruction, because generally the means of producing wealth constantly improve, technologically and otherwise, and at a certain stage outgrow the social system constructed on them. Thus, slave societies would eventually give way to feudal societies, and eventually, Communist societies will replace capitalist societies.

Diakonov's model (1969) of early Mesopotamian state formation (Figure 7.2) rests on the assumption that if wealth differentials can arise, they will, and that once these differentials exist, antagonism between socioeconomic classes will follow and eventually the state will form to promote and protect the vested interests of the ruling class.

These various assumptions are unproven. We do know, however, that once sedentary communities were established, social and economic stratification and conflict everywhere replaced cooperative egalitarian ways of living. Evidence from early Mesopotamian and Egyptian societies does support some aspects of the Marxian reconstruction: wealth differentials developed early and were impressive, and slavery existed, as did communal labor pools, warfare, irrigation systems, trade networks, and other elements integral to the Marxian scheme. But that is not to say that this scheme is correct or complete. Much of it was constructed on the basis of evidence from early documents, and there is considerable evidence that the Mesopotamian states, at least, evolved several hundred years prior to any significant writing systems; thus the textual evidence might be of only limited relevance to the origins of social complexity. More important, it is very difficult to test the Marxian reconstruction with archaeological data. We cannot demonstrate class conflict or slavery in the absence of written records, and nowhere in early states do we find documentary or archaeological evidence that force was used to maintain the position of the elites over the masses (Service 1975: 285).

The rather simplistic rendering here of the Marxian approach to problems of cultural change should not, however, obscure the fact that there may yet be important advances made in archaeological analyses through the implementation of Marxian ideas. Marx and his interpreters' contributions to historical analyses have not always been properly interpreted by American anthropologists because their conceptions of mode of production, social formation, and other Marxian ideas have been wrong (Legros 1977).

A recent and detailed attempt to understand the origins of complex societies from a perspective at once Marxian and archaeological is that of Friedman and Rowlands (1977).

This study defies easy translation and summary, but it contains at least the following elements.

1. Friedman and Rowlands assert that White (1949), Steward (1949), and Harris (1980)—all of whom argue that the social structures, politics, and ideology of societies are determined by their technological, environmental, and economic bases—exemplify materialist approaches that are wrong or greatly limited because they are "unconcerned to determine the specific kinds of relations that link production to the other institutions of society."

2. To rectify this, Friedman and Rowlands argue, it is necessary to "reconstruct the structures of reproduction of particular social forms,"

which they define as the "social structures that dominate the process of production and circulation and which therefore constitute the socially determined form by which populations reproduce themselves as economic entities."

3. As an illustration, Friedman and Rowlands use Figure 7.3, which they interpret as follows:

Each of the levels of the social formation is structurally autonomous in such a way that the properties of one level cannot be derived from those of another level. While structurally independent, the levels are inextricably linked in the material process of reproduction by two kinds of intersystemic relation. From ecosystem up is a hierarchy of constraints which determine the limits of functional compatibility between levels— hence of their internal variation. This is essentially a negative determination since it only determines what cannot occur. Positive determination would only exist where we could find necessary and sufficient conditions for the occurrence of a given structure, i.e., where only one set of productive relations could dominate the process of reproduction. This would appear never to be the case. Working in the reverse direction, relations of production, as we have defined them above, organise and dominate the entire process of social reproduction and determine its course of development within the limits of functional compatibility between levels. When these limits are reached breakdown in the system is immanent. The limits are themselves determined by the internal properties (as a function of time) of the subsystems which make up the larger reproductive totality. It is absolutely necessary in this model to distinguish between institutional structures and the material structure of reproduction which they form in combination with one another. Thus, a kinship structure can be infrastructural if it distributes the labour input and output of society. Similarly, money may be merely superstructural if it is only used in children's games. This does not deny the fact that the internal structure of an institution determines the way it will behave in whatever functional position it occupies in material production.

As the properties of reproduction can only be defined with respect to time the model is necessarily a dynamic one. Dominant relations of production determine a given developmental pathway and functional incompatibilities in the larger totality generate divergent transformations over time. Change in cultural form as well as place in material production occur simultaneously in the process of reproduction so that evolutionary "stages" are always generated from previous stages in such a way that we might speak of epigenesis; structural transformation over time in which the nature of the trajectories is determined by the properties of an arbitrarily chosen initial state in given conditions of reproduction. (1977: 203-4).

Friedman and Rowlands qualify all this by noting, among other things, that cultural systems are dynamic, that relationships of these kinds change with the passage of time, and that the nature of any one society must always be understood in relation to other societies. Nonetheless, they attempt to explain the origins of the "asiatic state" in North China, Mesopotamia, Mesoamerica, and Peru in terms of a single, generalized model.

Although Friedman and Rowlands' complex approach deserves careful consideration, it presents the following difficulties. First, in matching their ideas to the stones, bones, and buildings of the archaeological record, they encounter the same problems discussed in terms of the crocodiles in chapter 2. That is to say, it is difficult to sort out the various causes of cultural phenomena. For example, the causes of the appearance of "high-status" burials, palaces, and other reflections of evolving cultural complexity have not been shown by Friedman and Rowlands to be more in agreement with their scheme than with many other competing ideas. These same developments could have resulted from other causes. This does not show Friedman and Rowlands to be wrong, of course, but only insufficiently demonstrated to be right.

Second, important aspects of relations of production and other of their concepts cannot be recovered archaeologically. Here, too, this does not prove them wrong; it may be that a satisfactory explanation of the origins of cultural complexity will ultimately be untestable archaeologically (although it seems unlikely).

Perhaps most damaging, however, are ambiguities in the matter of *causation*. As has often been repeated in this book, without some hope of explaining historical phenomena in terms of real-world measurable causes, archaeology becomes simply a matter of collecting things and making up stories about them. In Friedman and Rowlands's approach, as in so many Marxist-Structuralist endeavors, causation is expressed in terms of *dominances* and *constraints* (Figure 7.3). Friedman and Rowlands say that the physical environment, technology, and general economic forces impose a system of constraints that make certain kinds of things unlikely to evolve (like a drive-through bank set up and frequented by hunter-gatherers); but working in the opposite direction, the relations of production dominate the entire functioning of the system, determining its characteristics and developmental pattern. To find "relations of production" archaeologically, however, and then to demonstrate how they were the causes of other cultural phenomena is difficult. In Friedman and Rowlands' approach, something like an organized system of ancestor worship can in a given society and instance be

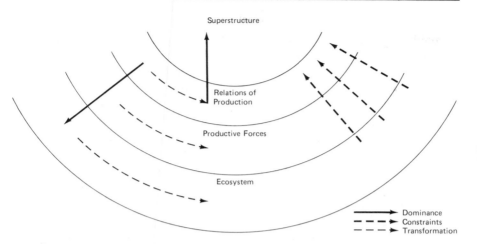

7.3   Friedman and Rowlands' view of cultural evolution is a modified Marxian model in which the four levels of social formation depicted above have structurally autonomous properties that cannot be derived from those of another level. That is, one can never be certain about the properties of one level, just because one knows that the society involved is a hunting-gathering one, or that they have a national religious cult. But some levels can impose "constraints" on other levels (rice farmers cannot be truly nomadic). The "relations of production" do, however, organize and dominate the whole process of social development. An appreciation of what relations of production are and how these levels of social formation inevitably become incompatible—and the cultural system then breaks down—requires intensive reading in the works of Marx and his successors.

the *result* of a complex of economic factors, and in another society and time organized ancestor worship can be a *cause* of economic behavior.

This leaves the poor archaeologist sitting amidst his or her pile of bones, stones, and pots, without much hope of ever understanding much about the *causes* of more than the most obvious cultural attributes of the societies whose remains he or she is studying.

It may well be that the kinds of cultural causality that Friedman and Rowlands are concerned with are not now and will never be accessible through archaeology. It may also be that Friedman and Rowlands are wrong in their ideas about the nature of cultural causality.

SYSTEMS THEORY AND CULTURAL COMPLEXITY

Kent Flannery (1972) has proposed an analysis of the problem of the origins of cultural complexity based on general *systems theory*. The fundamental premise of general systems theory is that there are processes so basic to all living systems that all such systems can be compared on criteria having to do with these processes.

Two such processes are *centralization* and *segregation* (Flannery 1972). Centralization is the degree of linkage between the various subsystems and the highest order of controls in society, while segregation is the amount of internal differentiation and specialization of the subssytems of a general system—whether it be a mold culture or an ancient state. To illustrate this hypothesis, let us consider a typical community of simple agriculturalists living on the northern Mesopotamian plains at about 6000 B.C. These villagers grew wheat and barley, herded sheep and goats and perhaps a few cattle, did some hunting, and gathered several kinds of wild plants. Each of these *economic subsystems* would have required control and administration. Someone had to make decisions about when to plant, when and where to hunt, as well as what products to trade, and so forth. These decisions were made by comparing results with goals: the amount of wheat harvested, for example, was compared with the needs and expectations of the community members, and if there was too little wheat, additional planting would be done the next year; if there was a surplus, it might have been invested as feed for sheep and goats—an ideal storage mechanism under these conditions, because sheep and goats are portable and turn the grain into highgrade protein.

The point is that this society was—and all societies are—composed of economic, religious, political, and social subsystems, and that all of these constantly require monitoring and control.

In a hunting and gathering society, this monitoring and controlling can be done by a single headman or a few older adults, for they are able to acquire the knowledge to make correct decisions about the relatively simple operation of the group. They are essential to the society's survival, and they are "cheap" because they process information without taking any "overhead" in the form of larger portions of food or the palaces, thrones, jewels, and other items which are often the trappings of power in more complex societies.

But if we consider the early agricultural villages, it is apparent that the subsystems and the monitoring and control apparatus needed by such communities are more numerous and complexly related than in the hunting and gathering groups. A hunting and gathering headman may be able to make decisions and control a group of at most about seventy-five people, but an early agricultural village probably required a hundred or more people just for existence, because its economy was more complex. Animals had to be cared for at the same time as grain had to be harvested, storage facilities had to be built and administered, irrigation systems required constant repair, decisions had to be made about water allocation, and pottery manufacture required planning and organization. No one could make all the decisions or acquire and store all the knowledge needed to make the best decisions about all sectors of community life. The person who spent his time herding sheep and goats was in the best position to make decisions about when and where to pasture them and which to slaughter, but he was not in the best position to make decisions about irrigation or cultivation.

Under these conditions a society would profit by investing more of its resources in administrators and control systems. One person might be charged with the administration of cultivation, another with the administration of the animals, a third with the religious sector, and so forth. To make the system operate efficiently, a single individual would have to be placed over these lower-level administrators, so that the activities of the various sectors of the community would be integrated. It would be vital, for example, to make decisions about how many animals to keep in the context of how much grain would be available for feed.

To translate this example into Flannery's terminology and the concepts of centralization and segregation, we can see that, compared with hunters and gatherers, village agriculturalists were more *segregated:* their economy involved more subsystems than did that of the hunters and gatherers. The concept of *centralization,* the degree of linkage between the various subsystems and the highest order controls in a society, is more relevant to people living in states and empires than to the hunters, gatherers, and primitive agriculturalists of our example. Thus, we can measure every society in terms of its centralization and its segregation, and to some extent this can be seen as a measure of evolutionary level.

Now for the crucial question: how does a society become more segregated and centralized? Flannery has proposed two evolutionary mechanisms and suggests that there are others. The two he considers are *promotion* and *linearization.*

> In promotion . . . an institution may rise from its place in the control hierarchy to assume a position in a higher level. . . . Alternatively a new institution may arise out of what was simply one role of a previously existing institution, as the office of chieftainship presumably rose out of the leadership role of the informal headman in a simpler society.
> . . . In linearization . . . lower order controls are repeatedly or per-

manently bypassed by higher order controls, usually after the former have failed to maintain relevant variables in range for some critical length of time. (1972: 413)

In explaining *promotion,* Flannery uses as an example some economic and social developments in an agricultural village in Oaxaca, Mexico. During the late nineteenth century, there was little concentration of power or wealth in this community because of two regulatory mechanisms: the *cargo* system, in which the village governmental offices were rotated among the more important members of the community; and the *mayordomía,* an arrangement whereby the cost—and prestige—of sponsoring the annual religious festivals was rotated among the richer families.

In the late 1880s an enterprising villager named Marcial Lopez managed to subvert this nicely balanced system. With the help of some friends in the clergy, he forced the council of elders to appoint the sponsor of the festivals without regard to ability to meet the heavy expenses of these affairs. Social and religious pressures were such that few could turn down an offer to sponsor the fiestas, and Lopez astutely began offering loans to such individuals—providing they put up their land as collateral. Debts in this culture pass from father to son, and by 1915 the Lopezes and a few other families owned about 92 percent of the village's arable land. And because they staunchly backed the clergy, their privileged position was soon institutionalized and religiously "validated."

In systems theory terminology, the rise of the Lopez family is a case in which a special-purpose institution, the church, was *promoted* to a general-purpose system, in that it took over the function of appointing the *mayordomía*—which had formerly been accomplished by another general-purpose system (the town government).

In the end, the concentration of wealth and privilege in the hands of a few great families produced such stresses, and the *mayordomía* and *cargo* systems were so ineffective in maintaining the equilibrium of the society, that these systems were bypassed by a higher-order control system—in this case the Mexican Revolution with its policy of land reform and the abolition of the power of the clergy.

The use of systems theory concepts has proliferated in American archaeology in the 1970s and early 1980s (e.g., Hill 1977), and elaborate and—in some cases—persuasive analyses of cultural changes have been done in this idiom. Systems theory applications are flexible in that they can admit the interactions of many different variables that influence each other in complex ways; unlike the Marxist-Structuralists perspective, they do not require that everything be explained by reference to mechanical economic factors; and they hold out the hope that there *are* general principles that we can apply to all systems.

From the point of view of explaining the origins of cultural complexity, however, the use of systems theory poses some difficulties. Even if those who feel that there are only trivial similarities across all systems are wrong (e.g., Berlinski 1976), the form of most systems theory applications to archaeological problems is that of a "functionalist argument."

Functional arguments attempt to explain the origins of something (e.g., the human heart) in terms of the functions it performs (e.g., blood circulation). To the question, why do people have hearts, the answer that some device is needed to circulate blood is an explanation of sorts, but it does not explain why some other kind of life support system did not evolve, nor does it explain the evolutionary history of the heart or the selective pressures that shaped this history.

But functionalist arguments have their uses, and in archaeology they have the strong heuristic value of suggesting hypotheses about a specific development and indicating crucial variable relationships (Figure 7.4).

The problem of matching functionalist systems theory ideas with the question of the origins of cultural complexity (Wenke 1981) thus has many aspects. Nevertheless, the general idea of explaining the archaeological record in the form (if not always the vocabulary) of systems theory remains strong.

NEOEVOLUTIONARY EXPLANATIONS OF
THE ORIGINS OF CULTURAL COMPLEXITY

In part because of the limitations of functionalist explanations, in part because of the great power of modern evolutionary theory, there has been a revival of interest in applying the principles of biological evolution to cultural phenomena (R. N. Adams 1981; Alexander 1975, 1979; R. Cohen 1981; Dunnell 1978; Dunnell and Wenke 1980). Many scholars argue that the modern theory of evolution has never really been applied to archaeological data. A key difficulty has always been that the objects of the archaeological record do not reproduce as people do, and thus the rules of genetics cannot be applied; also, whereas change in the biological world is through the relatively slow processes of genetic mutation, drift, selection, and so on, cultural changes can be conveyed quickly and pervasively from one group to another (as in the spread of agriculture).

So how might we apply evolutionary principles to archaeological

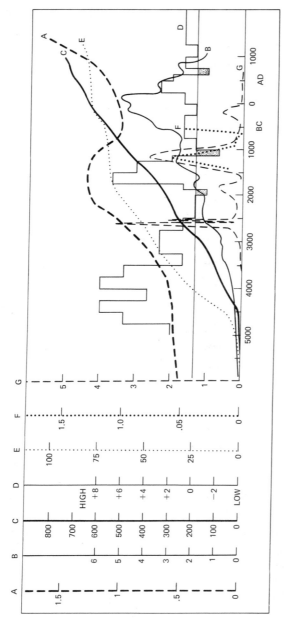

7.4 A major theoretical problem in modern archaeology is how to study the causes and effects of cultural changes on the basis of archaeological data. In this chart, a sample of variables from ancient Egypt have been plotted on comparative scales. One might look for intervals where many important variables changed significantly (such as between 3000 and 2500 B.C. here) to try to explain the origins of complex societies in Egypt. But the archaeological data are meager, correlation does not prove a causal connection, and the shape of these plots will depend on how the data are statistically transformed. The variables are (A) coefficient of rank-size distribution of settlement size, (B) population in millions, (C) population density per square kilometer, (D) increased lake volumes and stream discharge in east Africa, (E) percentage of domesticated animals in total faunal assemblage (estimated from reports on excavated materials), (F) price of farmland per unit (in silver), (G) monumental architecture in cubic meters of worked stone. Many other variables could be plotted (e.g., average transport distance of craft items).

problems? The answer is not at all clear, but there are a few interesting ideas. As Dunnell (1980) has said, what matters in evolutionary theory is not so much how a characteristic is transmitted—whether by genes or culture—as it is the mechanisms by which traits are perpetuated in an individual. Thus, whether a person gets eye color through genetic inheritance or religious beliefs through parental instruction is irrelevant in the sense that both traits have been transmitted. In short, we don't have to concern ourselves overmuch with the fact that the behaviors at the base of cultural complexity are not transmitted genetically.

In this spirit, Cavalli-Sforza and Feldman (1981) have tried to derive mathematical models that describe the propagation of whole sets of cultural behavior (like agriculture) through space and time, based on their relative costs and benefits.

There is also the matter of *group selection*. In the biological universe, the transmission of traits takes place at the level of the individual. It is the individual genes of the plant or animal that do or do not get perpetuated, not the species or group of plants and animals. Therefore, the most productive point at which to analyze a given evolutionary problem is the transmission of traits from individual to individual. But in cultural situations, many individual traits, specifically behavioral ones, are the products of instruction by the complete community of parents, teachers, and friends. And people act in corporate groups in ways that make these the functional units of the society. For example, in the next chapter we shall see that religions appeared early in all great civilizations and that these formed effective ways to get people to act in concert for the corporate good, such as in fighting wars, clearing irrigation canals, and building pyramids. To summarize, in the production and transmission of cultural characteristics, cultural selection can act on groups as well as individuals.

Figure 7.4, a largely imaginary conception of change in selected variables in Egypt during its period of state-formation, is an attempt to illustrate some of these questions. The purpose of the graph is to show that had we enough data, we could try to find a point in time where there were intersecting patterns of rapid change, which would suggest that in seeking the explanation of this cultural history we might concentrate our attention on that period. The graph also illustrates that not all variables—once adjusted for increasing population size—are significant in cultural evolution.

Even if we had the data to establish very accurately this sort of graphical cultural history, however, we would not have *explained* this history. These graphs serve only to draw our interest to the time, place, and variables that may be most important in the developmental pattern we are trying to explain.

There are numerous other recent theoretical departures in the study of cultural evolution, ranging from cognitive psychology (Lumsden and Wilson 1981) to hierarchy theory (Johnson 1980, 1982), and we shall consider some applications of these in subsequent chapters. Most of these approaches, however, are functionalist explanations: they try to show that given certain conditions of economy and society, certain cultural developments are beneficial and thus likely to appear.

In all of this, archaeologists must come to terms with a fundamental problem: most of the origins and development of ancient societies cannot be explained on the basis of the archaeologically retrievable facts of climate, technology, economy, and demography. Cultural evolution instead must be analyzed at some level above these basic conditions—at the higher level of the social, economic, and political relationships of peoples and social entities. But how do we get at these higher-level interactions through the data and methods of archaeology?

The approaches we shall review in subsequent chapters are not solutions to this problem, but they may be steps in the right direction.

8

The Evolution of Complex Societies in Southwest Asia

---

19. And Babylon, the glory of kingdoms, the beauty of the Chaldees' excellency, shall be as when God overthrew Sodom and Gomorrah.

20. It shall never be inhabited, neither shall it be dwelt in from generation to generation: neither shall the Arabian pitch tent there; neither shall the shepherds make their fold there.

21. But wild beasts of the desert shall lie there; and their houses shall be full of doleful creatures; and owls shall dwell there, and satyrs shall dance there.

22. And the wild beasts of the islands cry in their desolate houses, and dragons in their pleasant places: and her time is near to come, and her days shall not be prolonged.

Isaiah 13

Isaiah was right. Today the city of Babylon—one of the brightest stars in a galaxy of brilliant ancient cities—is a great rubbish heap, picked over by such "doleful creatures" as archaeologists and the infrequent tourist.

The story of the world's first complex societies takes place in the several millennia preceding and including Babylon's time, and in the areas around that ancient city. By the late fourth millennium B.C., at a time when most of the world's people were dirt-poor illiterate farmers or hunters and gatherers, and when the peoples of the New World were still 2,000 years from village life, the area around Babylon was a cosmopolitan world of cities, libraries, schools, shops, international commerce, roads, taxes, temples, and many of the other elements we identify with the "civilized" way of life. Indeed, it is no exaggeration to say that most of us today are still living in patterns laid out in these Southwest Asian cities over 5,000 years ago.

Southwest Asian civilization has been studied for well over a century, and we know in great detail how these people constructed their buildings, what they ate, with whom they traded, what things they made, and what they wrote about life, death, war, love, and taxes. What we don't know is exactly why and how these societies developed as they did, why this part of the world was the first to produce complex cultures, and why the basic pattern of cultural development in ancient Southwest Asia was repeated in most of its essentials in Egypt, the Indus Valley, China, Mesoamerica, Peru, and perhaps elsewhere. We have, however, a few clues about these developments.

The Ecological Setting

The world's first complex societies developed in a relatively small area of southern Iraq and Iran, but the factors that produced them involved a much larger area, "Greater Mesopotamia," which can be divided into several ecological zones.

The Judean, Taurus, and Zagros mountains extend in a great arc, whose lower elevations were the natural habitats of wild wheat, barley, sheep, and goats. In ancient times this area was covered with great grasslands and oak and pistachio forests, and even as late as the nineteenth century, sheep grazing these verdant uplands were brought to lowland markets with their wool stained scarlet by wild flowers in their range. But today the forests are almost entirely gone, and the whole area is severely overgrazed.

The first complex societies arose on the alluvial lowlands, but early on they used the gold, silver, copper, stone, and animal and plant resources of the mountain areas. Today there is still no more efficient way to bring these areas into the regional agricultural economy than by using sheep and goats to convert mountain vegetation into milk, meat, and hides, which can then be exchanged for lowland products.

The Piedmont, comprising the foothills and rolling plains adjacent to the Taurus and Zagros mountains, was the location of some of the earliest agricultural villages. Annual rainfall is adequate for reliable dry farming and good grazing conditions part of the year, and oak and pistachio trees thrive in the higher elevations of this zone.

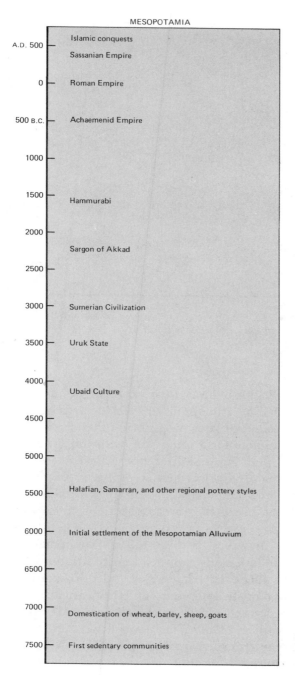

MESOPOTAMIA

A.D. 500 — Islamic conquests

Sassanian Empire

0 — Roman Empire

500 B.C. — Achaemenid Empire

1000 —

1500 — Hammurabi

2000 —

2500 — Sargon of Akkad

3000 — Sumerian Civilization

3500 — Uruk State

4000 — Ubaid Culture

4500 —

5000 —

5500 — Halafian, Samarran, and other regional pottery styles

6000 — Initial settlement of the Mesopotamian Alluvium

6500 —

7000 — Domestication of wheat, barley, sheep, goats

7500 — First sedentary communities

8.1   Chronology of early
agriculture and complex
societies in Mesopotamia.

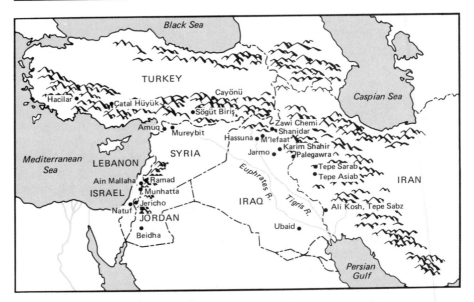

8.2 Southwest Asia. The world's first complex societies evolved in the alluvial plains of the Tigris and Euphrates rivers and their tributaries.

North and northwest of Baghdad lie the dry, undulating northern Mesopotamian Plains. Rainfall here is insufficient for unirrigated agriculture, except in a few areas. Since later prehistoric times these zones have been thick grasslands suitable for grazing and, with the invention of the plow, for agriculture. The Tigris and Euphrates have cut deeply into the land surface, so that irrigation here requires sophisticated damming and canalization. But with irrigation, the high productivity of this area made the northern plains the "breadbasket" of some of the greatest empires of antiquity.

The most important area, however, is the southern Mesopotamian Alluvium. The historian Arnold Toynbee argued that civilizations first evolved in physical circumstances that challenged the inhabitants to overcome severe problems of climate and resources. His ideas have been largely abandoned, but the modern visitor to the southern Mesopotamian Alluvium, the lower courses of the Tigris and Euphrates, might come to have considerable sympathy for Toynbee's point of view.

Nothing in this region appears to account for its pivotal role in human history. It is an unprepossessing few thousand square kilometers of flat, hot plains, with essentially no usable stone, metal, or lumber, and with a climate whose extremes of heat and humidity have been a main topic of conversation for generations of archaeologists.

The Tigris and Euphrates rivers created the Alluvium with annual deposits of flood-borne fertile silt and clay, and they provide the irrigation water that makes agriculture possible here. The swamps and wetlands formed by the rivers support a variety of usable wild plants, such as flax for textiles and rushes for basketry, but in addition to irrigation water the major gift of the rivers is fish. The scrub forests along the rivers cannot support many game animals, and thus fish—and later domestic cattle—furnished the protein indispensable to survival on the Alluvium. Vegetarianism was not an option for ancient agriculturalists here, because the blend of vegetable proteins necessary to substitute for animal protein was not always available. Fish fill this lack admirably, however, and there are many clues to its importance for the early inhabitants: "altars" in buildings dating to the fifth millennium B.C. have been found covered with layer upon layer of fish bones.

Another major resource of the Alluvium is the climate. From May to October, the average daily high temperature is over 40°C (104°F), and hot winds dry the soil to over a meter and darken the sky with choking clouds of dust. Veterans of Mesopotamian summers find it unsurprising that several Middle Eastern religions have envisoned an afterlife where heaven consists of sitting by streams in cool palm groves, eating fruit while attended by servants. But with adequate irrigation, the Mesopotamian Alluvium is ideally suited to plant growth, and throughout history this region has been celebrated for its wheat, barley, dates, olives, lentils, oranges, onions, and other crops.

The Archaeology of Early Southwest Asian Complex Cultures (8000 to 250 B.C.)

Southwest Asian peoples have lived in agricultural communities for almost ten millennia, and there is hardly a square meter of large parts of central Mesopotamia that does not contain a few sherds, stone tools, bones, or old irrigation canal banks. Nevertheless, the most common unit of analysis in Southwest Asian archaeology is still the "site," which usually takes the form of a mound, referred to as a *tell* or *tapeh*. These tells are a result of the construction and continual reconstruction of buildings on the same spot. For thousands of years, people here have used clay (adobe) as their basic building material, and their settlements have taken the form of closely packed small rectangular structures (Fig-

8.3   Excavating a typical mound site, at Chogha Sefid, Iran. Note outlines of mud-bricks.

ure 8.3). Although ideally suited to the climate and resources of the area, such buildings become so dilapidated after fifty or a hundred years that it is easier to rebuild than to repair them, and because there are incentives to rebuild on the same spot (less land is lost to cultivation and higher elevation gives better drainage and protection against floods and attack), settlements become mound-shaped as they are constantly reconstructed on the debris of the previous ones.

Hundreds of thousands of such mounds dot the landscape of Southwest Asia, some of them rising fifty meters or more above plain level, while others—occupied for only a few decades or so—are only imperceptibly higher than the surrounding plains. The mounds are littered with stone tools, bones, broken pottery, broken clay bricks, collapsed walls, eroding ovens and pottery kilns, and corroding metal. Burrowing animals, well and terrace construction, and erosion often mix the layers of these mounds so that usually one finds the remnants of every phase of a site's occupation on its surface. This allows archaeologists to estimate a site's periods of occupation simply by inspecting the surface artifacts.

Besides mounds, the most obvious archaeological features of Southwest Asia are irrigation canals. Seven millennia of irrigation agriculture have resulted in a landscape criss-crossed with canals, and it is not unusual to find abandoned irrigation canals several thousand years old with banks still two or three meters high. Aerial photographs are particularly useful in charting these ancient waterworks.

This richness of the Southwest Asian archaeological record is at once a problem and a blessing. Because of the time and expense of archaeological excavation and the destruction of sites, far fewer than 5 percent of all sites dating from 8000 to 2350 B.C., for example, have been, or will ever be, properly excavated, and thus our analyses must be tempered with some tentativeness. On the other hand, the rich archaeological remains provide an opportunity to use sampling procedures and to test hypotheses; and by using aerial reconnaissance and surface surveys, archaeologists can fit many unexcavated sites into their approximate periods of occupation. This is done through archaeological surveys and regional analysis. In the case of Mesopotamia, a generation of archaeologists has followed Robert McC. Adams (1965, 1981; Adams and Nissen 1972) in performing regional surveys.

As a graduate student, I studied Iranian Mesopotamia, concentrating on the period between 600 B.C. and A.D. 640. As I visited the various mounds evident on my aerial photographs, I found on top of every mound a small pile of about twenty to thirty pottery sherds. These proved to have been left there ten years previously by Robert McC. Adams and represented part of his evidence for assessing the periods of occupation of each site. Although my samples were somewhat larger and were much more brutalized by computerized statistical analysis (Wenke 1975–76, 1981), Adams's summary culture history was remarkably in agreement with my own.

In the best of all possible worlds, both Adams and I should have made a detailed topographic map of each site, collected artifacts in a stratified random sampling design of hundreds of 2×2 meter squares, then test-excavated each site in order to confirm its occupational periods.

In the real world, each of us spent many months just making sketch maps of the sites, picking up informal samples, and inferring the site's cultural history from these evidences. Time and resources are usually so limited that it is on this kind of research that we must construct our culture history of Mesopotamia.

THE BACKGROUND TO MESOPOTAMIAN
CULTURAL COMPLEXITY (8000 TO 6000 B.C.)

When we left the first farmers of Southwest Asia in chapter 6, they were living in most areas with sufficient rainfall to support wheat and barley without extensive irrigation. They were seemingly unware of the potential for greed, ambition, rank, privilege, warfare, and urbanization that their new-found economic system could support. Now, as noted in chapter 7, we must look at their archaeological record and that of their predecessors and determine when and where we see the first monumental buildings, the first graves with riches greater than others, the first luxurious houses, and—more fundamentally perhaps, the first spatial arrangements of settlements that reflect sustained exchanges of goods, information, and political control.

By 7000 B.C. most of the villagers of the Middle East were living in mud huts and showed no signs of cultural complexity whatsoever. But in a few areas, there were signs of change.

The Levant

At Jericho, even though the populace was still hunting and gathering wild resources to complement their primitive agriculture, soon after 7000 B.C. they had built a stone wall some 1.5 meters thick and more than 3.5 meters high around a complex of stone houses (Figure 8.4). If an essential element in cultural complexity is activity specialization to the point that large populations are socially and economically interdependent, Jericho was not a complex community; but the construction of the wall indicates that its people were beginning to direct their energies in a way quite different from that of most hunters and gatherers.

But most sites in the Levant dating between 8000 and 6000 B.C. were small simple farming communities with little to distinguish them from each other; each was composed of tiny single-room mud or stone houses with mud-plastered walls and perhaps a few woven mats on the floor. In and around the houses were numerous hearths, storage pits, ovens, grinding and threshing floors, and garbage pits, and at most settlements the only "public architecture" was a retaining wall or a modest stone platform. At Munhata, north of Jericho in the Jordan Valley, the people built a large plaza, at the center of which was a platform of large basalt blocks carved with water channels (Mellaart 1975: 58), and a small room at Jericho included a niche in which was placed a stand-

8.4   Millennia of rebuilding at Jericho formed many superimposed layers containing stone walls.

ing stone, suggesting, perhaps, a cult room. But nowhere are there palaces, pyramids, or the like.

The disposal of the dead, usually an excellent reflection of changing cultural complexity, suggests that people at Jericho and perhaps elsewhere were not much different socially from their predecessors. Forty headless adult bodies were found buried beneath one room at Jericho, and further excavations revealed a cache of skulls that had been reconstructed with plaster, painted, and then decorated with "eyes" made from seashells. Whether these represent ancestor worship, war trophies, or some other ritual is unclear.

As an archaeologist I have often wished that the bulldozer had never been invented, but I have to admit that we would know a lot less about the past if it had not. An excellent demonstration of this occurred in the late 1970s, when a bulldozer cutting a road through a hill in northern Amman, Jordan, exposed long, thin lines of compact, reddish sediments that mean one thing to Middle Eastern archaeologists: house floors. Such floors are created by the normal activities of families living in mud-brick houses without artificial floors. People pack down the mud, then paint, plaster, or sand it, tread garbage into it, and build in hearths and storage pits. The result is that these floors are usually quite obvious in archaeological excavations.

In 1982 archaeologists began excavating these floors near Amman and discovered they were part of what is now called Ain Ghazal, the largest known Neolithic site in the Middle East. Gary Rollefson of the American Centre for Oriental Research in Amman and Albert Leonard, Jr., of the University of Missouri found at least four periods of occupation, some of which were Pre-Pottery Neolithic B (7400–6000 B.C.) (Leonard, personal communication). Covering approximately thirty acres, Ain Ghazal is about three times larger than Jericho. It probably had at one time at least 1,000 inhabitants, who ate wheat, barley, lentils, sheep, and goats, made cattle figures, erected a fifteen-meter, interior-divided "public building," and buried their dead in the floors of their houses.

If one were able to stroll up to a village like Ain Ghazal at the time it was occupied, it probably would not be very different from the typical Middle Eastern village of today. And unless one counts as an entrancing habit the slow conversion of the kitchen floor into a cemetery, these ancient villagers seemed to do little that was different or more interesting than what their modern counterparts do. Once one has watched the women carrying water in pots on their heads, heard the men complain about too much or too little rain, and eaten a meal of bread, boiled mutton, and greasy greens, one probably has exhausted the social resources of the village.

But, as we shall see, the people of villages like Ain Ghazal were on the verge of a cultural revolution.

Anatolia

"It may be said without undue exaggeration that Anatolia, long regarded as the barbarous fringe to the fertile crescent, has now been established as the most advanced center of neolithic culture in the Near East. The neolithic civilization revealed at Catal Hüyük shines like a supernova among the rather dim galaxies of contemporary peasant culture" (Mellaart 1965: 77).

There is some question, as we shall discuss, whether or not Çatal Hüyük (pronounced rather like "Chatel Huooyook") merits all the superlatives its excavators have showered on it, but it is undoubtedly one of the most interesting sites in all of Southwest Asia. Located in south central Anatolia and first occupied at about 6250 B.C., Çatal Hüyük was probably inhabited continuously until its abandonment at about 5400 B.C., and during some of this time it may have extended over thirteen hectares and had a population of about 4,000 to 6,000—several times larger than any other known site in this period (Mellaart 1975).

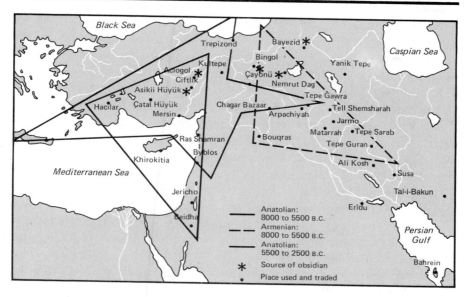

8.5 The circulation of obsidian throughout Southwest Asia was an important economic process that may have contributed to the evolution of political and economic institutions.

Nestled against the first ranges of the Taurus Mountains, Çatal Hüyük controls access to a critical resource: the obsidian sources at the Hasan Dag volcano. Each obsidian source is chemically distinctive, and thus we know that after 7000 B.C. great quantities of obsidian from the Çatal Hüyük area were distributed throughout Anatolia, the Levant, and Cyprus (Figure 8.5). Beautiful obsidian artifacts were found in Çatal Hüyük itself, but so far no obsidian storage or workshop areas have been found in the less than one hectare of the site that has been excavated.

Most of the 158 structures uncovered at Çatal Hüyük are little different from their contemporaries elsewhere in Southwest Asia: each is built of shaped mud and composed of rectangular rooms with plastered walls and floors, and most houses are one or two stories high and abut one another, except where occasionally separated by an open courtyard. Inside most rooms are two raised platforms, probably for sleeping, and an occasional rectangular bench. Two aspects of these buildings distinguish them from their contemporaries at most other sites: access to the rooms is only by ladder through the roof—there are no front doors—and there are about forty structures that are larger and more richly furnished and decorated than the others. The roof access may reflect a need for defense, for once the inhabitants had pulled up the ladders on the outside walls, the settlement would have been difficult to attack successfully. Other Southwest Asian sites had walls at this time, but most settlements were small unfortified hamlets.

In terming Çatal Hüyük a city, Mellaart placed considerable emphasis on the more than forty *shrines*, to use his term, found at this site. These buildings have essentially the same floor plan as the others, but their walls are more richly decorated with paintings, reliefs, and engravings expressing many naturalistic themes, most concentrating on the two staples of Paleolithic and Neolithic art—fertility and death. Vultures are portrayed ripping apart headless human corpses, women give birth to bulls and ride leopards, and other symbols such as breasts, navels, deer, vultures, bulls, and rams abound. Some of the rooms have intricate arrangements of cattle skulls and horns (Figure 8.6) that no doubt served a ritual function.

But are these buildings quantitatively and qualitatively different from those at contemporary sites? With so few excavations it is not possible to answer definitively. They do not seem to have required the expenditure of vast amounts of labor and resources for essentially noneconomic purposes, as did the monumental construction of later periods. Nor do they enclose radically different amounts of expensive goods, indicating great wealth disparities. Little about them, in fact, conflicts with the interpretation that they were kinship-cult centers in a simple ranked society.

Such a conclusion would be strengthened if we found only minor variability in mortuary practices, and indeed this seems to be the case. Many corpses appear to have been taken outside the settlement and exposed to the vultures and the elements until the flesh was gone, after which the bones were interred in the house floors. Men, women, and children were buried in much the same way, either in baskets or simply in holes. Most of the graves contained no goods, but some women and children were accompanied by shell and stone necklaces, armlets and anklets, and, occasionally, obsidian mirrors and bone cosmetic implements. Some men were buried with mace heads, flint daggers, obsidian projectile points, clay seals, and other items.

In one complex of rooms, the so-called *Vulture Shrine,* six individuals were buried in the floor with significantly richer grave goods than were found in the residential burials (Mellaart 1975: 101–05). However, we do not find any infants at Çatal Hüyük buried with disproportionately rich or numerous grave goods, nor do we find any significant variation in construction expense of the graves themselves; there are no stone coffins, tombs, or the like.

8.6   These reconstructions of "cult-centers" at Çatal Hüyük show the importance of the cattle motif.

The people of Çatal Hüyük subsisted on the typical late Neolithic combination of agriculture, hunting, and gathering. Emmer, einkorn, a bread wheat, barley, pea vetch, and other crops were grown in quantity, but with simple techniques. Domestic cattle supplied meat, hides, milk, and perhaps traction. There was considerable trade but mainly in small quantities of exotic items. Shells from the Mediterranean (160 kilometers distant) and Syrian flint were found here, perhaps taken in trade for obsidian artifacts (Figure 8.5). But there is no evidence of voluminous trade in agricultural products, or even in large amounts of obsidian, and there are no obvious workshops for goods, no stores of obsidian, no complex technologies.

Thus, Mellaart's conception of Çatal Hüyük as a "supernova" among the contemporary dim, drab peasant communities elsewhere in Southwest Asia must be viewed with some skepticism—at least until more excavations are conducted.

Settlements dating to between 7500 and 6000 B.C. have also been found at Asikli, Çayönü, Hacilar, Suberde, Can Hasan, and elsewhere, but all of these are very simple, undifferentiated farming communities with little discernible public architecture, intense occupational specialization, or elaborate mortuary practices.

The Zagros Mountains

Jarmo, in Iraqi Kurdestan, is an excellent example of the drab peasant culture that Mellaart invidiously compared to Çatal Hüyük. Jarmo was first settled sometime before 6750 B.C. and was occupied intermittently to 5000 B.C., and thus it overlaps with Çatal Hüyük for perhaps as much as 1,000 years. But unlike Çatal Hüyük, Jarmo was probably home to no more than 200 people, and for most of its existence it consisted of only twenty to twenty-five small, rectangular mud houses.

Burials at Jarmo are quite uniform, as are the contents of the houses. There is not nearly the diversity of aesthetic expression found at Çatal Hüyük, nor wall paintings, masses of finely worked obsidian, or the like; there are just a few clay figurines of pregnant women and some animals. There are no fortified walls or large, nonresidential buildings, and the technology seems to have been mainly devoted to the processing of plant foods. Perhaps the most significant difference between the two sites is that Çatal Hüyük controlled a localized and important resource (obsidian), whereas Jarmo didn't. Until additional excavations are conducted at Çatal Hüyük, however, it will be difficult to determine how significant its obsidian trade was.

Elsewhere in the Zagros, northern Mesopotamia, and the Iranian Plateau, communities established between 8000 and 6000 B.C. were undeviatingly simple, undifferentiated farming villages, with little public architecture, elaborate mortuary cults, or occupational specialization.

With these various sites in the Levant, Anatolia, and the Zagros as examples of late Neolithic farming settlements, we have some reasonable idea of what kinds of communities were first transmuted into cities, states, and empires. To understand this transformation, however, we need clear evidence of changes in population densities, settlement architecture, mortuary patterns, and many other variables. In a rightly ordered world, combined international archaeology faculties and their students would arrange themselves in a long line just north of Lake Van in Turkey and then work their way southeast to the Persian Gulf, stopping to map and excavate each site encountered.

For now, however, our evidence consists only of fewer than a hundred well-excavated settlements and perhaps twenty or thirty regional site surveys.

THE FIRST ARCHAEOLOGICAL EVIDENCE OF COMPLEXITY

An early indication of social change in Southwest Asia is evident in the distribution of pottery styles. As with agriculture, the invention of pottery seems to have occurred independently in many areas of Southwest Asia, where clay had previously been used for figurines and storage pits for centuries. The multiple origins and rapid spread of pottery after about 6500 B.C. no doubt reflect the increasing importance of containers in these agricultural economies—initially probably largely for water transport and food storage and preparation.

Soon after ceramic vessels came into general use in Southwest Asia, the first sophisticated uniform pottery styles appeared, and by about 5500 B.C., two distinctive styles, the *Samarran,* and somewhat later, the *Halafian,* had achieved wide distribution (Figure 8.7). Halafian and

8.7 Distribution of Samarran and Halafian pottery. One of the first steps in the evolution of complex societies seems to be a rapid expansion of an art-style over a large area.

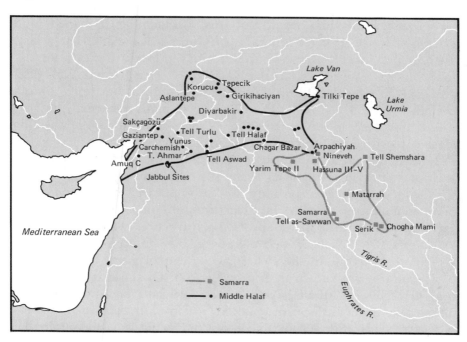

Samarran ceramics differ from earlier artifact distributions in that they are found at most settlements within a large area, occur in massive quantities, and are quite uniform stylistically within the area of their distribution.

The artistry of these richly painted ceramics suggests at least some occupational specialization—perhaps at a higher level than among earlier communities. On the other hand, despite the wide geographical distribution of these design elements, there is little evidence that ceramic production was centrally organized and administered.

The distribution of Halafian and Samarran ceramics coincides with the extension of cultivation to the arid lowlands and the consequent accelerating pace of cultural evolution. A significant site of this period is Tell as-Sawwan (Abu es-Soof 1968; Yasin 1970), located in north central Iraq at the juncture of the northern arid steppe country and the alluvial plains. This is the "last frontier," so to speak, before moving out onto the Alluvium itself.

Preliminary excavations indicate that from 6000 to 5000 B.C., Tell as-Sawwan was home to a few hundred people, most of whom were engaged in simple irrigation farming of wheat, barley, and linseed. They also kept domestic goats, sheep, and cattle, hunted onagers, antelopes, and other animals, and gathered fish and mussels from the Tigris, which ran close to the site.

In most ways, this settlement resembled other early agricultural villages; granaries, kilns, ovens, and small rectangular T-shaped mud-brick houses are arranged around open courtyards. In addition, a large ditch or moat was constructed around the site by cutting into the natural conglomerate rock strata on which the site was located. This ditch averaged 2.5 meters wide and 3 meters deep and was buttressed, in one period, by a thick clay wall. The discovery of many hardened clay balls ("sling missiles") in the ditch led its excavators to suppose it was a defensive structure, reminiscent of the fortifications at Jericho.

The residential architecture of Tell as-Sawwan contrasts somewhat with that of other settlements of the period, consisting mainly of huts with stone foundations (possibly used as granaries) in addition to the more common rectangular clay structures, although there is still little variability in building size or apparent construction cost.

At least 128 burials at Tell as-Sawwan date to approximately 5500 B.C., and they contain the richest assortment of grave goods for this period of any site known in Southwest Asia. Of the classifiable skeletons, fifty-five were infants, sixteen were adolescents, and thirteen adults. The graves differ little in orientation, location, or construction. Most bodies were placed in a contracted position, facing west, in simple shallow oval pits dug into house floors. Although most rooms had many burials (one had up to twenty-three), one room contained only an adult male's burial, whose relatively rich grave goods may reflect emerging status ascription.

Almost all graves had at least one craft item, mainly carved alabaster, beads in exotic stones, or pottery. There is a significant difference in the distribution of these goods, with burials of adults and juveniles having, on the average, more numerous and varied goods than infants. The range of variability is great, however. If we require great diversity in the construction of graves and the interment of infants with rich grave goods as indications of social stratification, it is clear that the inhabitants of Tell as-Sawwan do not provide this evidence. Nonetheless, these graves are very rich, compared to those of contemporary sites, and the disparity among graves may indicate emergent ranking and status ascription.

Shortly after the appearance of Halafian, Samarran, and other pottery styles, the developmental focus shifts to the southern Mesopotamian Alluvium.

INITIAL SETTLEMENT OF THE MESOPOTAMIAN ALLUVIUM (6000 TO 3500 B.C.)

As far as we know, there were few or no permanent settlements in lowland Mesopotamia much before 5800 B.C. The first sites found here all cluster near the estuary of the Persian Gulf, and there is some evidence (Larsen and Evans 1978) that with the end of the Pleistocene, the Gulf shoreline moved inland as much as 180 kilometers. Thus, the key settlements in the transition to life on the Alluvium—and the origins of cultural complexity here—may be under one hundred meters of seawater.

The few sites on the Alluvium that may antedate 5800 B.C. are poorly known—in part because they are covered by much larger sites, in part because the thick blanket of alluvial samples makes it difficult to obtain a representative sample.

As we have noted, developments here may initially have been limited by the lack of game animals and edible wild plants, but eventually fishing, cattle raising, and irrigation agriculture provided a nutritious—if uninspired—cuisine. Subsistence in most parts of the Alluvium is more complex than in the highlands, requiring many timely decisions in which floods must be anticipated and controlled, land irrigated and drained, and cattle pastured, tended, and milked. Fishing adds to this

8.8 This "Susa A" style jar, from early fourth millennium B.C. Iran, exemplifies the hand-painted, highly decorated pottery styles that were widely distributed in Southwest Asia just before initial cultural complexity.

complexity because it is seasonal to some extent and requires coordination to be maximally effective. Even getting sufficient stone for simple agricultural implements necessitates considerable organization in the lowlands, for such stone often had to be obtained in the mountains, far from lowland settlements.

If the evidence from Ali Kosh in eastern Mesopotamia (Hole, Flannery, and Neely 1969) is typical, the movement onto the Alluvium required a very generalized diet, in which many small plant seeds eventually were discarded in favor of the wheat-barley-lentil group, augmented by sheep-goat-cattle proteins. There is some evidence that the cuisine centered on a variant of the one-pot approach, a stone or clay vessel filled with as many edible plants as one could find and bits of whatever animals were about. Like the meals of ancient Sparta (described as consisting of two courses, the first a kind of porridge, and the second, which was a kind of porridge), the diets of these Mesopotamian villagers probably relied on blending as many plant and animal nutrients as possible without the luxury of much choice. What breakfast must have been like does not bear thinking about.

In the Sumerian account of the creation of the Universe, the city of Eridu was the first to have emerged from the primeval sea that covered the world before the creation of man. Eridu is in fact one of the earliest known settlements on the southern Mesopotamian Alluvium, having been established at about 5400 B.C. Virtually no other contemporary sites have been found here, but the lowest levels of many large ancient mounds have not be excavated.

At Eridu, the earliest known structure is thought to have been a temple. Archaeologists have been accused of bestowing this term on virtually any structure large enough to stand upright in, but the earliest building at Eridu is very similar to others known through texts and other evidence to have been temples. A single small room (3.5 by 4.5 meters) with an "altar" faces the entrance, and there is a pedestal in the center; in these specifics the building is nearly identical to the temples of later periods. The ceramics found here resemble those of Halaf and Samarra, but there were few other artifacts. This "temple" may reflect a low level of social complexity, perhaps including an institutionalized religion and the capacity for construction of minor public architecture. But we can say little on the basis of this single occupation.

At sites dating to just after 4500 B.C., however, we finally find solid evidence of evolving cultural complexity. "Overnight," relatively speaking, the southern Mesopotamian Alluvium—and only a little later the northern Plains—is dotted with full-fledged towns, public buildings, and all of the other characteristics we associate with early complex societies. The name usually associated with this period of transformation is the *Ubaid* (c. 5300–3600 B.C.), a term used to refer both to a period and to artifact forms. By 4350 B.C. the Ubaid culture was remarkably uniform over most of the Alluvium: all the settlements seem to have been located on reliable water courses and almost all were less than ten hectares in size (most of them only one or two).

The spread of the Ubaid culture is remarkable for many reasons,

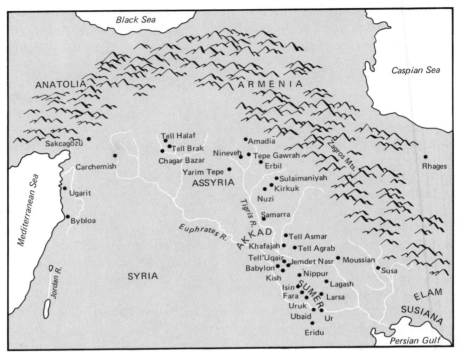

8.9   Distribution of some early sites on the Mesopotamian alluvium.

particularly its apparent extent. Ubaid-style ceramics are found far into
central Turkey, to the southwest in the Arabian Plateau, and in highland Iran—an area much greater than that encompassed within the
Halafian and Samarran stylistic zones.

Virtually every Ubaid settlement had a large nonresidential building, probably a temple, built of mud-brick on platforms of clay or imported stone. Access typically was by a flight of stairs, to a room about
ten meters in length, with a broad platform at one end and a table or
small "altar" at the other. Smaller rooms were built on both sides of
the main room, and ladders in these would sometimes give access to a
second story. The exteriors of the buildings were often decorated with
projections and recesses, with which light and shadows created pleasing
effects. In later periods, mosaics of colored ceramic cones and bitumen
were used as decorations. At Eridu, seventeen such "temples" were
found superimposed, giving the later ones considerable elevation. Such
structures are found all over Greater Mesopotamia soon after their appearance on the southern Alluvium.

The temple architecture of the Ubaid period raises an important point. As we shall see in surveying other early complex cultures around the world, one of the most consistent signs of evolving cultural complexity is the diversion of enormous amounts of energy and materials into pyramids, ziggurats (stepped pyramids), palaces, platforms, and other essentially nonutilitarian constructions. Why would people who could just as easily and certainly more profitably build irrigation canals, terrace slopes, weave wool, or do other productive tasks instead "waste" their labors on these mammoth construction projects?

On first reflection one might think that it is a human instinct to build monuments like this. As Shakespeare said, "If a man does not erect in this age his own tomb ere he dies, he shall live no longer in monument than the bell rings, and the widow weeps." But we know that not all people in all times and places have built huge mortuary complexes—so why do some build them and others not?

The answer to this question may lie precisely in the fact that these constructions are, in a limited sense, "wasteful." They may, for example, have prevented high and unstable rates of population growth, perhaps by deflecting investments in food production. "It would appear that the ruling class was frequently confronted with the problems of over-production and the threat of technological unemployment or a surplus of population among the lower classes. Their great public works programs, the wholesale disposition of wealth in mortuary customs, etc., enabled them to solve both these problems with one stroke" (White 1949: 383).

Just as important, monumental construction programs could reinforce social and political hierarchies. Frankfort (1956: 56–58) speculates that

> the huge building, raised to establish a bond with the power on which the city depended, proclaimed not only the ineffable majesty of the gods but also the might of the community which had been capable of such an effort. The great temples were witnesses to piety, but also objects of civic pride. Built to ensure divine protection for the city, they also enhanced the significance of citizenship. Outlasting the generation of their builders, they were true monuments of the cities' greatness.

Until about 5000 B.C., settlements seem to have been located primarily with regard to the availability of resources and the agricultural potential of the land, not on the basis of political and economic relationships. People tend to organize their territories in patterns reflecting changing social and economic conditions, and thus, when the movement of people and goods between settlements becomes important, and the area is agricultural and relatively flat, these settlements often are

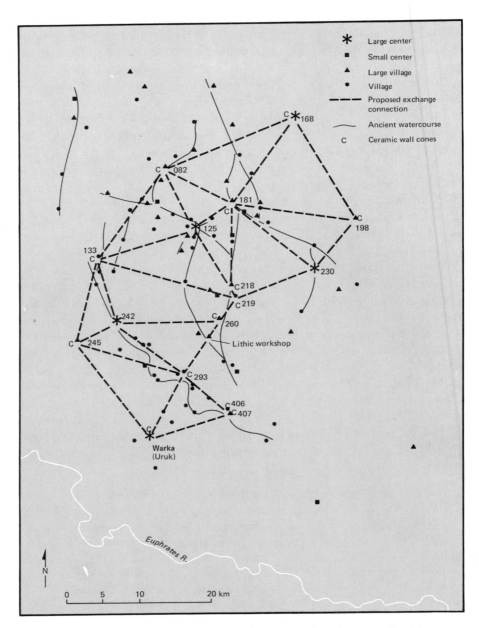

8.10 In simple societies the location of settlements with respect to each other is dictated mainly by ecological factors like water availability. But as societies become more complex, political and economic relationships begin to influence where settlements are located and how large they become. In this reconstruction of exchange networks among late Uruk Period (ca. 3200 B.C.) settlements in southern Iraq, the spatial arrangement of the settlements with respect to one another is quite regular (the wall-cones were used to decorate administrative centers, and their distribution may indicate lines of political authority).

quite regularly spaced, as is evident in both the Warka area and the Susiana Plain (Figure 8.10).

By 4000 B.C., the number of small settlements had increased dramatically in many areas, and there was increasing variability in their arrangement and composition. At Uruk, for example, population may have reached 10,000 as early as 3800 B.C. (Adams 1972), and for some distance around the town there were many smaller villages and towns, whose sizes and distribution suggest they may not have been tightly integrated into Uruk's political and economic systems. Then, at about 3000 B.C., the city of Uruk apparently grew rapidly and had about 50,000 people living behind substantial defensive walls. There is also evidence of widespread simultaneous abandonment of almost all the rural settlements surrounding Uruk—leaving little doubt, Adams suggests (1972: 739), that the growth of the city was a result of the immigration or forcible transference of the population from the hinterlands into the city.

The urbanization of this period is difficult to explain. Toward the end of the Ubaid period, almost all major settlements were fortified, and documents written ca. 2600 B.C. speak at length of conflict between the people of Ur, Uruk, Umma, and the other city-states. In subsequent chapters, we shall see that urbanization in other parts of the world also seems to be related to defensive needs. Egypt, which was protected from hostile outside forces by the deserts and the sea, developed urban societies only comparatively late, while in the Indus Valley, much more of a crossroads for nomadic and other groups, urbanism was present almost from the very first. In this context, Adams argues that early Mesopotamian urbanization may have been imposed on a rural populace by a small, politically conscious superstratum that was motivated principally by military and economic interests (1972: 743).

Because of defensive considerations and the cost of transporting labor and products, agricultural land nearest the urban areas would have been most intensively exploited, and this may have stimulated the construction of large irrigation systems. Another important possible effect of urbanism is that it might have created—and to some extent have been created by—the large nomadic populations thought to have been present in Southwest Asia as early as 6000 B.C. Most of these people were probably similar to the present-day Bakhtiari of western Iran, who herd sheep and goats in the uplands during much of the year but come down to the lowlands in the winter to sell their animals' wool, meat, and milk products and to buy craft items, food, and other products. The relationships between these upland nomadic and lowland sedentary groups are varied and complex. Historically, when central governments have weakened in Southwest Asia, some marginal cultivators, in times of war or poor harvests, revert to nomadic pastoralism, while some pastoralists become laborers or marginal farmers if they lose too many sheep. One of the effects of urbanism suggested by the archaeological record—the depopulation of the countryside—may have given nomads and semisedentary populations a new niche. By working the mountain areas and highlands for most of the year, the nomads could have come down and exploited the marginal areas between urban centers—peacefully most of the time, but other times with hostility—and then traded with the townsmen.

THE RISE OF CITY-STATES (3500 TO 2350 B.C.)

The ancient settlement of Uruk (known as *Warka* in Arabic and *Erech* in the Bible), located in the heart of the southern Alluvium, is one of the oldest cities in the world and may have been the center of one of the earliest states.

Initially settled before 4000 B.C., by the late fourth millennium B.C. Uruk was already an impressive settlement of perhaps 10,000 people and several large temples. Between about 3200 and 3100 B.C., the "White Temple" at Uruk was built on a ziggurat some twelve meters above ground level. Made of whitewashed mud-brick and decorated with elaborate recesses, columns, and buttresses, it must have been an impressive sight—especially to peasants coming into the city on market days. Inside the temple were tables and altars, all arranged according to the same ritual plan evident at Eridu some 2,500 years previously.

The residential architecture of Uruk indicates a diversity of occupational, economic, and social classes. All the buildings were mud-brick, but some were larger, better-built, and more elaborately decorated. Many of the people lived in small rectangular buildings built along narrow winding streets through which ran both above- and below-ground drainage canals. Apparently, houses were one story high for the poor and two stories for the wealthier, but both types were essentially very similar. Built of mud-brick and whitewashed, they represent an ideal architectural adaptation to the climate. Similar houses today are comfortable and attractive, their whitewashed walls contrasting effectively with beautiful dyed rugs and textiles.

By the middle of the fourth millennium B.C., the population of Uruk included specialists in scores of arts and crafts. Potters, using molds and mass-production techniques, turned out enormous quantities of pottery, mainly in crude utilitarian forms. In earlier periods great numbers of beautifully painted vessels were made at most larger settlements, but by the middle and late fourth millennium, pottery manufacture had become a centralized, administered activity at Uruk and many other settlements. Millions of crude pottery bowls, for example, were made in regularly graduated sizes—possibly reflecting standard amounts of food (perhaps grain or yogurt) being rationed out from centralized warehouses. Other specialists apparently included stonecutters, metalsmiths, bricklayers, farmers, fishermen, shepherds, and sailors. Writing did not come into general use in Mesopotamia until about 3000 B.C., but at Uruk and other sites in levels dating from the fifth millennium onward, archaeologists frequently find stamp and cylinder seals, which were used to impress clay sealings for containers, bales of commodities, and documents. Some of these seals convey in picture form the economic specialization of the community. Boats, domestic animals, grain, deities, and many other motifs are portrayed; and these seals may have functioned as administrative devices, certifying the contents of the containers. Even without written documents, it is obvious that the highly specialized and integrated economy of a city like Uruk in the mid-fourth millennium could not have functioned without scores of administrative specialists to oversee social, religious, economic, and political affairs.

The immediate predecessors of written languages may have been the clay tokens that are found in about ten geometric shapes at many early Mesopotamian sites. Denise Schmandt-Besserat (1981) argues that these tokens, which were usually enclosed in clay envelopes, represented such commodities as pots of grain, numbers of animals, and areas of land.

Sumerian Civilization

To the modern urbanite, it may seem inappropriate to label as a "state" a collection of twelve or fourteen cities with a combined population of perhaps 100,000 and an area of only a few thousand square kilometers, but as someone once observed, it is the small states, like Sumer, Athens, Florence, and Elizabethan England, that have put posterity most in their debt.

Approximately thirteen city-states made up the Sumerian "civilization" between about 3000 and 2350 B.C. Through most of their history, these city-states were politically autonomous, but they belonged to the same cultural tradition and by 3000 B.C. had collectively developed many of the classical elements of Southwest Asian civilization, including ziggurats, brick platforms, the potter's wheel, wheeled carts, metalworking, sailboats, and writing.

8.11   A cuneiform text on a
clay brick.

The fact that the Sumerian language was essentially unlike those of
the contemporary but less-developed "Semitic" cultures that surrounded
the Sumerians has led some to place Sumerian origins in Turkey, Bah-
rain, or even outer space. The Sumerians, of course, thought of themselves as a distinct and superior culture, and their myths speak of origins in some distant land; but we shall probably never determine the
ethnic origins of the Sumerians, and in a sense this is an unimportant
problem. The achievements of cultures cannot be explained in terms of
the special characteristics and mental gifts of the people of these cultures: people are constants in the equations of cultural evolution, and
it is their circumstances and position in place and time that determine
their cultural "achievements."

SUMERIAN WRITING   We have a remarkably detailed picture of life in
these Sumerian city-states because shortly before 3000 B.C. they began
to develop a written language. What we know about the Sumerian language is derived from the thousands of clay tablets on which they wrote
(Figure 8.11). Their script is known as *cuneiform,* from the Latin for
wedge-shaped, a reference to the fact that Sumerian was written by im-

pressing wet clay with the end of a reed, leaving wedge-shaped marks.
When baked, these clay tablets are extremely durable and can survive
thousands of years.

If we have to point to the first known written documents, the best
candidates may be clay tablets and sealings from levels V–IV at Uruk
(ca. 3400 B.C.). There are signs for *carpenter, donkey, boat, copper,* and
many other things, totaling fifteen hundred symbols in all (Figure 8.12).
Some signs seem to mean *to buy,* others refer to *en,* the title of a lord,
and to *unken,* which may have been a people's assembly (Oates 1980).
These faint suggestions of a commercial, class-structured society are reflected in the growing diversity of settlement patterns.

The ability of this cumbersome writing to convey abstract concepts

8.12　The evolution of Sumerian writing. Fourth millennium B.C. tablets were
inscribed vertically with pictographs, but in the early third millennium, the direction of the writing and the pictographs was rotated to the horizontal. In succeeding
millennia the symbols were stylized and given phonetic meanings.

EARLIEST PICTOGRAPHS (3000 B.C.)	DENOTATION OF PICTOGRAPHS	PICTOGRAPHS IN ROTATED POSITION	CUNEIFORM SIGNS CA. 1900 B.C.	BASIC LOGOGRAPHIC VALUES		ADDITIONAL LOGOGRAPHIC VALUES		SYLLABARY (PHONETIC VALUES)
				READING	MEANING	READING	MEANING	
	HEAD AND BODY OF A MAN			LÚ	MAN			
	HEAD WITH MOUTH INDICATED			KA	MOUTH	KIRI₃ ZÚ GÙ DUG₄ INIM	NOSE TEETH VOICE TO SPEAK WORD	KA ZÚ
	BOWL OF FOOD			NINDA	FOOD, BREAD	NÍG GAR	THING TO PLACE	
	MOUTH + FOOD			KÚ	TO EAT	ŠAGAR	HUNGER	
	STREAM OF WATER			A	WATER	DURU₅	MOIST	A
	MOUTH + WATER			NAG	TO DRINK	EMMEN	THIRST	
	FISH			KUA	FISH			KU₆ HA
	BIRD			MUŠEN	BIRD			HU PAG
	HEAD OF AN ASS			ANŠE	ASS			
	EAR OF BARLEY			ŠE	BARLEY			ŠE

or the spoken language was quite limited, but in the centuries after 2900 B.C. the Sumerians devised ways to generalize and improve the information-carrying capacity of their script. *Phoneticization,* by which some signs came to represent distinct words and syllables of the spoken language, was most important. Thus, the sign of an arrow came to mean both *arrow* and the Sumerian word for *life,* the connecting link being that the spoken word for both was *ti* (Diringer 1962). Eventually much of spoken Sumerian was represented by written symbols, and the pictographic elements slowly lost their representational character as the scribes stylized them to make writing more rapid. Unique signs were developed for most Sumerian vowels and syllables, but the language was never reduced to an *alphabetic* system where every distinct sound in the language is represented by a unique sign. Instead, it remained a welter of signs that represented pictographs of concrete objects, signs that represented syllables of speech, and signs that represented ideas. This made reading the script a complicated process, requiring the memorization of hundreds of different characters. One sign, for example, which ultimately derived from a pictograph representing a mountain, acquired a total of ten possible phonetic values and four ideographic values as well (ibid.: 40). At first the reader had to infer the exact meaning of the word by considering its context, but eventually the Sumerians devised a system of *determinatives*—signs placed before or after a word to indicate the general category to which the word belonged, such as birds, male proper nouns, or deities.

Over the centuries the Sumerians' successors managed to reduce the complexity of the written language still further, but even as late as about 1900 B.C., the written language had between six and seven hundred unique elements. At this stage it was similar to Chinese and a few other modern languages, which faithfully represent the spoken language and are adequate for most purposes, but which, compared to alphabetic systems, are very cumbersome. It is difficult to construct typewriters or computers for languages with hundreds of unique elements, and even minimal literacy in such languages is the product of long and arduous training. (To become literate in modern Chinese, for example, one must memorize several thousand characters.) Most Semitic languages were—and still are—written without the short vowels, but this is no barrier to effective communication if one is accstmd t rdng th scrpt nd spkng th lngg.

The first truly alphabetic written languages appear to have developed toward the end of the second millennium B.C. among Semitic-speaking peoples in Palestine and northern Syria. In the tenth or ninth centuries B.C., the Greeks adapted the Syrian or Phoenician variant of these early alphabets to their own language, reducing the number of signs to fewer than twenty-five and making several major refinements in the process. The Greek alphabet was thus the basis for all modern European writing systems, including the Cyrillic alphabet of eastern Europe.

The role of writing in early Mesopotamian societies seems largely economic. Simple pictographs and the spoken language are adequate to communicate, process, and store information in a hunting and gathering society or a community of farmers, but they cannot efficiently meet the requirements of a society that has surpluses to be stored and redistributed, water to be allocated, land rights to be assigned and adjudicated, ritual prayers to be said, and all the other tasks we find in complex cultures. In fact, only the Inca of Peru managed to develop states and empires without developing a written language, but they had a fairly efficient substitute in the form of a vast bureaucracy and the *quipu,* a system of knotted strings in which the length of strings and placement of knots was used as a device to assist the memory of the record keeper.

The way of life described by the Sumerian texts, and by texts of other Southwest Asian cultures of the third millennium B.C., is still recognizable to anyone who has traveled in these areas. Sheep, goats, and cattle are tabulated, taxed, and exchanged; children are shepherded to school—as always, much against their will; a council of elders meets to consider grievances against the inhabitants of an adjoining city-state; and Sumerian proverbs express ideas recognizable in many societies:

> Upon my escaping from the wild ox,
> The wild cow confronted me.

> When a poor man dies do not try to revive him.

> (Hamblin 1973: 104–05)

But when they turn to mythological and eschatological themes, the ancient Mesopotamians are less accessible—perhaps even a bit bizarre— by our standards, as in this section of the myth of the revival of the goddess Inanna:

> Go to the underworld.
> Enter the door like flies.
> Ereshkigal, the Queen of the Underworld, is moaning
> With the cries of a woman about to give birth.
> No linen is spread over her body.
> Her breasts are uncovered.
> Her hair swirls about her head like leeks.

When she cries, "Oh! Oh! My inside!"
Cry also, "Oh! Oh! Your inside!"
When she cries, "Oh! Oh! My outside!"
Cry also, "Oh! Oh! Your outside!"
The queen will be pleased.
She will offer you a gift.
Ask her only for the corpse that hangs from the hook on
    the wall.
One of you will sprinkle the food of life on it.
The other will sprinkle the water of life.
Inanna will arise.

(Wolkstein and Kramer 1983)

Our own, Western, philosophy is deeply influenced by the philosophies first propounded in ancient Greece, philosophies very different from those of ancient Sumer. Thus, we see the world in terms of beginnings and ends, causes and effects, and the importance and "will" of the individual. We cannot completely reconstruct Sumerian philosophy on the basis of fragmentary texts, but it seems evident that the Sumerians saw a much more static and magical world than we do. Although their technology and complex organizations demonstrate that they were shrewd, rational people, there seems to have been little emphasis or analysis of human motivation or the physical world. They saw the earth as a flat disk under a vaulted heaven and believed that a pantheon of anthropomorphic gods guided history according to well-laid-out plans and that the world continues without end and with little change. Each god was in charge of something—the movements of the planets, irrigation, or brickmaking, for example—and each was immortal and inflexible. As with humans, the deities were hierarchically arranged in power and authority and were given to power struggles and many vices.

SUMERIAN ECONOMY   The economy of Sumerian city-states was based on intensive agriculture. Wheat, barley, vegetables, and dates were the major crops, while cattle raising and fishing were of almost equal importance. Cattle were raised for draft power, hides, and milk and meat. Fish was a staple, as were pigs.

Out of each measure of wheat or barley, the Mesopotamian farmer probably fed about 16 percent to his animals, reserved about 10 percent for the next year's sowing, and lost about 25 percent in storage. If ethnographic studies are to be believed, in the absence of modern transport people did not cultivate fields much more than four kilometers from their houses. At any given time, much of the land around a village in ancient times would have been fallow, while other land would be unirrigable or of marginal productivity. All in all, Adams (1981: 87) estimates that each person would need for subsistence about one hectare of barley and wheat fields, along with additional land for pastures, orchards, and other ground.

One of the less desirable "firsts" of Sumerian civilization was probably in the field of epidemic diseases. Just as there are certain disastrous things a hunter and gatherer can do (e.g., presume on too slight evidence that a cave bear is not at home), one of the worst things a villager can do is mix drinking water with sewage, and this is hard to avoid in a primitive town. Typhoid, cholera, and many other diseases require certain levels of population density to evolve, to maintain a reservoir of infected individuals, and to perpetuate themselves. These levels were probably reached for the first time in Sumer. Once people started digging wells and irrigation canals in areas with many people and animals, disease and epidemics quickly followed.

Few economies in history or prehistory have been as organized as the Sumerian. Tablet after tablet records endless lists of commodities produced, stored, and allotted. Ration lists, work forces, guild members— all are recorded in numbing detail. Even the city's snakecharmers were organized.

The question of who owned the farms, shops, and general wealth of Sumer may seem mainly of interest to specialists, but this question goes right to the heart of our interpretations of Mesopotamian cultural evolution. In the Marxian scheme of things (e.g., Diakonoff 1969), it is important to see the gradual emergence of capitalistic elements like great wealth differentials and the resulting potential for conflicts. Thus Gelb's (1969) contention that much of the land and property of ancient Sumer was privately bought and sold is of interest. Gelb argues the emergence of a three-tiered economy through much of Mesopotamian history, with the state, religious community, and ordinary populace all holding, trading, and using resources in complex interrelationships.

Although this society was still structured through kinship, people also belonged to and acted through occupational and social classes. In the event of war, for example, members of different "guilds," such as silversmiths or potters, would be under the command of their "guild president." One of the major trends in the evolution of complex societies generally was the change from a kinship-based society to one based on divisions along occupational, social, and economic class lines, and by 3000 B.C. there is evidence that this trend was developing in Mesopotamian societies. Even so, throughout the history of Southwest Asia kinship ties have been powerful social forces.

8.13   Temple precincts in Sumerian cities often included a large mud-brick "ziggurat," or stepped pyramid. The extant remains (rebuilt) of the ziggurat at Ur are shown here.

At the pinnacle of Sumerian society was a god-king, assumed to be a descendant of and in contact with the gods. Beneath him was a leisured class of nobles. We know from the records that there was also a class of wealthy businessmen who lived in the larger, better houses of the city; beneath them were the many artisans and farmers, including smiths, leatherworkers, fishermen, bricklayers, weavers, and potters. Scribes apparently held fairly important positions, and literacy was an admired accomplishment. At the bottom of society were the slaves, often war captives or dispossessed farmers.

Money, as we know it, did not exist in ancient Sumer; most exchange was "in kind," the trading of products for other products. Local and long-distance trade was voluminous, however, and ships sailed up the rivers from the gulf carrying shell, carnelian, lapis lazuli, silver, gold, onyx, alabaster, textiles, and food and other produce.

One of the most spectacular differences between Sumerian societies after 3000 B.C. and their predecessors is in mortuary practices. At the end of the Ubaid period (3800 B.C.), graves varied little, even at the largest settlements; but after 3000 B.C. there was a radical shift. The famous death pit at Ur is an impressive display of wealth and pomp. Excavating here in 1927–1928, Sir Leonard Woolley (1965) came upon five bodies lying side by side, each with a copper dagger and a few other items. Beneath them was a layer of matting on which the bodies of ten women were encountered, lying in two rows, each individual richly ornamented with gold, lapis lazuli, and carnelian jewelry.

Lying nearby was a gold- and jewel-encrusted harp, across which were the bones of the gold-crowned harpist. At this point it was evident that the bodies were lying on a ramp, and as the excavators continued down this they encountered a heavily jeweled chariot, complete with oxen and grooms. Then the investigators began unearthing masses of gold, silver, stone, and copper vessels, as well as additional human bodies, weapons, and other items. Nearby another set of six male skeletons equipped with copper knives and helmets was found, as well as the remains of two four-wheeled wooden wagons—also decorated with harnesses of gold and silver and accompanied by the skeletons of grooms and drivers. Other arrangements of human skeletons, harps, wagons, and model boats appeared as the excavations continued. Finally, at the end of the tomb was a wooden bier containing the remains of the queen. The entire upper part of her body was hidden by a mass of beads of gold, silver, lapis lazuli, carnelian, agate, and chalcedony. Her headdress and other furnishings were lavishly ornamented with gold, silver, and precious jewels. Liberally strewn about the chamber were human bodies, jewelry, vessels of precious metals, silver figurines, silver tables, cosmetics, seashell ornaments, and a number of other treasures.

All together some sixteen "royal" burials were found at Ur, all of them distinguished from the myriad common graves by the fact that each was not merely a coffin but a structure of stone, or stone and mudbrick, and by the inclusion of human sacrifices—up to eighty in one case. In fact, at least three distinct categories in burials seem evident, ranging from the sixteen royal graves to less elaborate but still richly furnished graves to the simple graves in which presumably the common people were placed.

Like their predecessors in Mesopotamia, the Sumerians built huge mud-brick temples, most of them decorated with colored clays, paints, and stone sculpture.

The Biblical Flood?

When Woolley was excavating Ur of the Chaldees, he found three meters of clean sand separating the Ubaid and Uruk levels and dating, therefore, to about 3500 B.C. Woolley thought these deposits might date to the great flood recorded in Sumerian legend and later expressed in the Old Testament, and there are stories that members of his expedition sold vials of sand labeled "Samples from the Great Flood."

The absence of sand strata at many other nearby sites, however, and the evidence of life as usual all over Mesopotamia at this time, rule out fairly conclusively any scientific evidence for the biblical flood, except

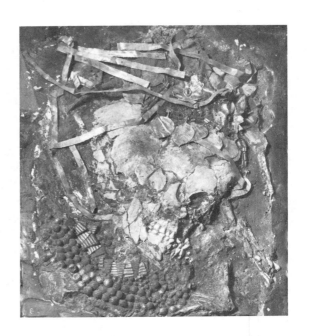

8.14 Crushed skull of a female attendant in the death pit at Ur. Note the gold jewelry and precious stones. This Sumerian model of a goat and a tree is made of wood, lapis, and gold, and is about 51 cm high. It was found at Ur and dates to about 2600 B.C.

in the opinion of the people who keep climbing Mount Ararat looking for pieces of the ark. Popular press reports of a Russian pilot who saw the outline of a boat far above the tree line on this mountain have fueled several expeditions to recover the ark, but so far only a few questionable bits of wood have been found. Only the drearily unimaginative archaeologist would be impressed by the fact that all the samples of wood were radiocarbon-dated to about 3,500 years ago (Taylor and Berger 1980)—a time for which there is no evidence that people in the rest of the world were threatened by floods.

SOUTHWEST ASIA AFTER 2350 B.C.

For centuries after 3000 B.C., the Sumerian city-states engaged in almost constant warfare, with first one and then another gaining temporary ascendancy. With the rise to power of Sargon of Akkad at about 2350 B.C., however, the political fabric of ancient Southwest Asia was forever changed. Sargon and his several immediate successors used the city of Akkad as a military base from which they mounted spectacularly successful attacks in all directions. Akkadian historical documents re-

8.15   Gypsum statuettes of an aged couple, residents at about 2500 B.C. of Nippur, one of the largest cities in southern Mesopotamia during this period.

count thirty-four battles fought by Sargon against the southern city-states, during which he moved down the Alluvium, capturing many kings, smashing city walls, and, finally, "cleansing his weapons in the sea." Sargon appointed Akkadians to administrative posts in the conquered city-states and then began expanding his other frontiers, invading Syria, Lebanon, and western Iran.

After 2200 B.C. quarrels arose among rival claimants to the Akkadian throne, and the "empire" fragmented under the onslaught of peoples moving in from the highlands on the margins of the empire. We know little about this "dark age" until about 2100 B.C., when one or more Sumerian kings were able to evict the invaders and reestablish political control over much of the southern Alluvium under what has come to be known as the *Neo-Sumerian* or *Ur III dynasty*. One ruler, Ur-Nammu, established a political center at the ancient city of Ur and from there aggressively extended his influence into much of the area formerly encompassed by the Akkadians. Great volumes of obsidian, lapis lazuli, and copper are thought to have passed into central Mesopotamia from as far away as India and the Aegean. Legal texts of the late third millennium describe in detail problems of land use, irrigation rights, compensation for bodily injury, penalties for adultery, and many other elements of daily life.

Despite its apparent stability, the Ur III political system of the late third millennium was constantly under pressure from internal political rivalries, as well as from the incursions of nomads and rival groups along the empire's frontiers. The coup de grace was administered at about 2004 B.C., with the invasion from western Iran of the Elamites, who led the king of Ur away in captivity.

From about 2000 to 1800 B.C., Greater Mesopotamia was politically fragmented as kings at Isin, Larsa, Susa, and elsewhere established contending petty states. Eventually the ancient city of Babylon became the most powerful political entity and by 1792 B.C. Hammurabi established the Babylonian Empire, based mainly on the southern Alluvium. The many documents of his reign reflect a skillful politician who was equally adept at bureaucratic and military means of gaining and using political power, and his famous law code, although not particularly enlightened by modern standards, was a model of efficient administration. Both Hammurabi and his successors encountered opposition from southern city-states and from a rival state in Assyria, to the north. As always, the nomads and other peoples on the empire's periphery, in this case the Kassites and Hurrians, made inroads as soon as the central government weakened, and eventually they overran much of the Babylonian Empire.

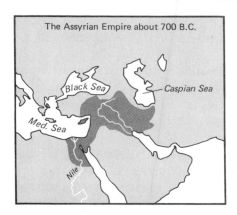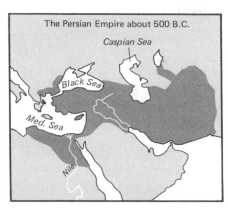

8.16   The extent of the Assyrian and Persian (Achaemenid) empires.

After about 1600 B.C., the political history of Southwest Asia becomes extremely complicated, with frequent political realignments and, overall, the gradual extension of imperial power (Figure 8.16). Assyrians, Elamites, Achaemenids, and other cultural groups established empires, and eventually the political and military scale became distinctly international as empires centered in Egypt, Anatolia, and Iran met and, more often than not, came into conflict.

The Origins of Cultural Complexity in Southwest Asia: Summary and Conclusions

It is possible that some archaeologist will one day be sweating over a Mesopotamian mud-brick building foundation and suddenly discover a library of cuneiform tablets on which are recorded in great detail a history of the origins of the Mesopotamian state. In this fantasy, populations of cities, war casualties, changes in the weather, average fertility rates, and a demographic analysis of the whole critical two millennia of state origins will be precisely set down.

While waiting for this discovery, however, archaeologists interested in understanding Mesopotamian state origins must deal with the available, entirely unsatisfactory data. For those archaeologists disconcerted by the occasional air strike and tank attack, there are few places in the Middle East where one can presently do archaeological surveys on the problem of evolving cultural complexity, so most of our analyses are based on data already collected.

Let us consider then in sequence some of the factors that may have produced the early complex cultures of Mesopotamia.

AGRICULTURE, IRRIGATION, WARFARE, AND POPULATION

To begin with, a complex society—at least as we have defined it here—requires many people living in a relatively small area (compared to that of hunters and gatherers and primitive agriculturalists), and many people living in a small area have one absolute requirement: they all have to eat.

For several thousand years, villagers farmed the uplands of Mesopotamia with no apparent increases in cultural complexity. Only after settlement was established on the Alluvium was there clear evidence of change. So it seems unlikely that in agriculture itself we will find a complete explanation of cultural evolution; we must look instead to the nature of agriculture on the Mesopotamian Alluvium. We must look for factors other than simple farming that, given certain circumstances, can produce complex societies.

To begin with, given proper irrigation and farming, the Alluvium has the potential to produce tremendous quantities of food, more than is required in most years to meet the requirements of millions of people and their domestic animals. Such surpluses do not necessarily *create* great differences in wealth, but they certainly *allow* the formation of rich and poor social classes, and it seems to be a pattern that wherever one finds economic systems that produce great surpluses, one also finds elaborate social hierarchies of administrators to organize, store, distribute, and exploit these surpluses.

What factors, then, stimulate the production of surpluses and thus create the conditions for the establishment of social classes and administrative hierarchies?

A frequent nominee for the crucial link between agricultural economies and cultural complexity is complex irrigation systems, but our review of the evidence from Southwest Asia suggests that at least as conceived by Wittfogel, irrigation cannot be said to be the "primary cause" of early Southwest Asian cultural complexity. Activity specialization, monumental architecture, changes in settlement spacing and size hierarchies, architectural variability, mortuary stratification—in short, the whole range of physical evidence of cultural complexity—appears *before* evidence of significant extension of irrigation systems. This is true for both the heartland of Sumer and for the Susiana Plain in southwestern Iran—the two areas for which we have the best archaeological data.

In much of Southwest Asia, in fact, increased investments in irrigation systems appear to be the result of urbanism (Adams 1972). Population agglomeration (urbanism) requires that the surrounding areas be particularly productive, because it is not feasible for the city dwellers either to farm or to defend areas more than several kilometers from the city. Irrigation was absolutely necessary for any sedentary existence on the Alluvium, but if the spread, integration, and construction of irrigation systems were the mechanisms whereby complex societies first evolved and developed, we would expect to see a direct and positive correlation between the size and complexity of irrigation systems and the complexity of cultures based on them.

Instead, we find that Ubaid, Uruk, and early dynastic settlements subsisted on the produce of fields irrigated by relatively simple, *autonomous* canal works. Only many centuries after the appearance of the first complex societies were there complex, integrated irrigation systems.

Many scholars have tried to explain the origins of cultural complexity in Southwest Asia and elsewhere as mainly the result of human population growth. The persistence of this view must be seen in large part as a result of the fact that if one graphs the approximate population of Greater Mesopotamia from about 8000 B.C. to about 3000 B.C. against evidence of activity specialization, monumental architecture, agricultural productivity, and the other evidences of cultural complexity, then an impressively close correlation is apparent. In the *long run* there *is* an obvious statistical relationship between these variables. One can't have an empire with 250 people. Furthermore, it makes a sort of intuitive sense that as you get more people, communities need more and more complex structures to feed and organize them.

But how can population growth be *directly* related to the evolution of cultural complexity?

Eventually, though there were important local variations in the pattern, the inhabitants of Greater Mesopotamia began to reach the limits of colonization as a solution to the population problem given existing subsistence systems. At this point a trend toward intensification on all levels appeared, including improvements in the irrigation system and a shortened fallow period. In time and in certain circumstances the amount of land available for cultivation actually began to decline. Conflict became more common. Both factors accelerated the need for intensification. When and where the pressures were the greatest urbanism appeared on the scene as a means of organizing and controlling the increased population, and the labor force which made that intensification possible. In time there followed royal kings and empires. (Young 1972: 838–39)

So perhaps we can fashion a convincing explanation of Mesopotamian cultural evolution by linking warfare—or at least conflict—with population growth and certain environmental conditions.

It is difficult to sort through the Mesopotamian archaeological record and not be impressed by the evidence for warfare as a potent factor in cultural evolution. Great walls of mud-brick ring cities and villages alike in some periods, and there are caches of weapons, chariots, documents, and representational art to tell us that warfare formed the very weft and warp of Mesopotamian history. Nor is this sustained level of warfare merely a historical curiosity: if some adult male citizen of ancient Mesopotamia of almost any century were transported through time to our own age, the thing he would find most familiar, perhaps, is the battle raging through the early 1980s between Iran and Iraq. Armies have met here in this same general area in almost every century for more than 5,000 years.

If we apply the principles of evolutionary biology, warfare is simply an expression of *competition,* which is common to all life forms. To give it a name, however, is not to explain it. In any case, the data from Mesopotamia are inconclusive about the notion of warfare in concert with population growth as *primary* stimuli to cultural complexity.

Given the ambiguities of the archaeological record and the difficulty in demonstrating the existence of warfare from archaeological data, perhaps the most significant thing we can point to is the presence or absence of substantial city walls. One might expect that with the cheapness of clay construction there would be many more walled settlements in the early civilizations, if warfare were a frequent curse. The walling of towns does occur very soon after the emergence of urbanism, and warfare may have played a significant role in the major increases of cultural complexity that *followed* the earliest "states," but extensive circumvallation of sites is common on the southern Alluvium mainly after about 2900 B.C.—some centuries after the appearance of other evidence of cultural complexity. After 2900 B.C. the historical records leave no doubt that warfare was almost continuous throughout Southwest Asia.

Consider Wright and Johnson's settlement statistics for the Susiana Plain (Table 8.1), truly a circumscribed area, where some of the earliest Near Eastern complex societies occurred.

The available data show that there was a period of population decline prior to state formation. States emerged perhaps during a period of unsettled conditions as population climbed back toward its former level. As Carneiro suggested, warfare may have a role in state formation, but in this case, increasing population in a circumscribed area cannot be the sole or direct cause of such warfare. If the hypothesis that population increase was the primary cause of state formation were correct, the state should have emerged in Susiana times [before 4000 B.C.] because population in that period seems to have been as high as in early Uruk times [3700 B.C.]. (1975: 276)

The Susiana Plain, however, is an area where rainfall agriculture is possible, and there are some questions about the reliability of Wright and Johnson's population estimates (Weiss 1977). What about the southern Mesopotamian Alluvium, the Sumerian heartland? Robert Adams concludes that

possibly the attainment of some minimal population level was necessary to set the process [of urbanization] into motion. But such evidence as there is suggests that appreciable population increases generally followed, rather than preceded, the core processes of the Urban Revolution. Particularly in Mesopotamia, where the sedentary village pattern seems to have been stabilized for several millennia between the establishment of effective food production and the "take-off" into urbanism, it may be noted that there is simply no evidence for gradual population increases that might have helped to precipitate the Urban Revolution. (1966: 44–45)

Adams here is principally concerned with the phenomenon of urbanism rather than complex societies in general, but his "Urban Revolution" includes many of the essential transitions we have defined as the basis for the evolution of complex societies.

TABLE 8.1 Environment and Settlement Characteristics of Three Lowland Plains in Southwestern Iran*

	Deh Luran	Susiana	Ram Hormuz
Area in Square Kilometers	940	2280	445
Hectares Site/100 km² Level Land			
Susiana d (c. 5000 B.C.)	6.4	6.2	4.0
Susa A	2.7	3.9	1.0
Terminal Susa A	.5	2.2	.3
Early Uruk	3.0	6.5	.5
Middle Uruk	3.2	8.5	1.0
Late Uruk (c. 3200 B.C.)	1.0	3.5	.5

* The first states, as defined by Wright and Johnson, appeared in the early Uruk period.

Source H. T. Wright and G. A. Johnson. 1975. "Population, Exchange, and Early State Formation in Southwestern Iran," *American Anthropologist*. 77: 276.

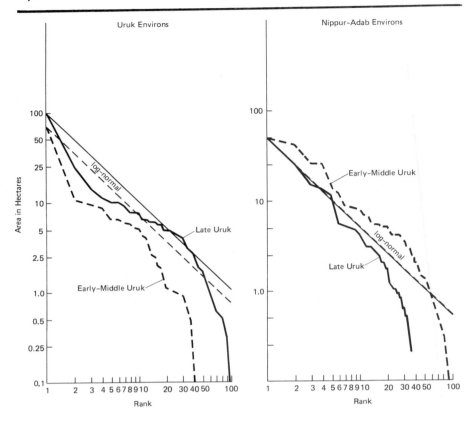

8.17   Settlement rank-size plots for two areas of Mesopotamia during the Early
Middle Uruk period (ca. 3400 B.C.) and the Late Uruk period (ca. 3200 B.C.), the
periods when the first "states" were appearing in this part of Mesopotamia. Rank-
size plots like these are formed by ranking the settlements from largest to smallest
and then plotting a settlement's rank against its size on a log-log scale. Geographers
have found that different shapes of such plots correlate with certain kinds of economic and political situations. The "flat-top" plot of the Early Uruk in the Nippur-
Adab region (b) often is associated with very loose economic integration, whereas a
log-normal distribution (the dotted lines in the graphs) is associated with considerable political and economic integration. The fact that both the plots for the
Late Uruk period—when the first developed complex societies here were in operation—changed over time in the same direction from markedly different original
plots, may reflect the growing economic and political interdependence of settlements
in the late Uruk "state."

What about agricultural intensification? In Carneiro's scheme this is
a direct result of population pressure; thus we should find evidence of
increasingly intensive irrigation and of farming of marginal lands just
before, and along with, the evolution of cultural complexity. Insufficient research has been done here to decide the issue absolutely, but

major investments in irrigation and land reclamation seem to have occurred *after* the emergence of urbanism and other evidences of cultural complexity and, as Adams notes, urbanization seems to have involved the widespread *abandonment* of large areas of formerly intensively farmed lands. Furthermore, there is no evidence that any of the areas of early state formation ever approached their agricultural limits: that is, with only minor investments in additional irrigation systems, they could have enormously increased the numbers of people who could be supported; yet the population size remained quite stable. In short, agricultural intensification seems to have been more a result than a cause of the emergence of complex societies.

SOCIAL HIERARCHIES

What about the possibilities of a Marxian analysis of Mesopotamian state origins? As noted in chapter 7, the Marxian view of state origins can be a complex, multilevel one, not just a dubious assertion that by and large, economic and technological factors are important determinants of sociopolitical arrangements. But despite elaborate attempts to link the "things" of the archaeological record with the notions of modes of production, historical dialectics, class structures, and the like (Friedman and Rowlands 1977: 201–76), the links inferred are tenuous and the available data are simply not adequate to the task of testing these ideas in any meaningful manner.

Wright and Johnson (1975) have introduced a rather novel model of the evolution of Southwest Asian cultures. First, instead of trying to formulate a model for the change from simple agriculturalists to fully developed complex societies, they have been principally concerned with the origins of the "state," which they define as a society with at least three levels of hierarchically arranged, specialized administrators. For example, in a simple agricultural village, there are many decisions to be made about what crops to plant, how much of the harvest is to be stored, who gets what share of the land, who marries whom, and so forth. Many of these decisions are made by individuals, but some of those which directly affect the whole community are made by a village headman. We might say, then, that this village headman represents the first level of the decision-making hierarchy—he directs the activities of others who do the work. A second level of administrative hierarchy would exist if there were people charged with coordinating the activities of these village headmen and correcting or approving their decisions—perhaps government agents charged with taxing and administering local affairs. Such agents would be under a third administrative level, and additional levels may exist above this.

Wright and Johnson suggest that: (1) the ancient state can be defined as a society with at least three such levels of specialized administrators; (2) the effectiveness of such societies and their dominance over other societal forms is tied to their ability to store and process information and make correct decisions at specific points along the control hierarchy; and (3) it is possible to demonstrate archaeologically the initial changes from societies with one or two levels of decision-making institutions to those with three or more.

In a series of extensive archaeological survey programs, Wright and Johnson have examined some of the areas where the first Mesopotamian states developed, trying to locate specific evidence for this change. One type of evidence was the actual administrative "documents" themselves. In most of Mesopotamia at this time, the administration of people and goods was facilitated by using pieces of inscribed stone to impress clay with signs of authorization. These stones were usually either in the form of "stamps," used like the rubber stamps of today, or cylinders that were rolled across the clay to make an impression, and they varied in size and in the complexity of the symbols incised on them. Fortunately, the clay impressed with these seals and the seals themselves are often preserved in archaeological sites, and they can be used to infer the levels of administration in these extinct societies. The impressed clay can be divided into two classes. *Commodity sealings* were used to certify the contents of a container such as a vessel, basket, bale, or storeroom. They were made by placing a lump of clay over a knot which had to be untied to gain access to the container, so that unauthorized entry could be detected. Discarded commodity sealings indicate the receipt of stored or redistributed goods. Other seals are termed *message sealings* and convey or store facts about goods or people. Some of these are plain counters whose shape indicates a numerical unit, others (*bullae*) are small spheroidal jackets which were once wrapped around sets of counters, and still others are flat rectangular "tablets" stamped with numerical symbols (Wright and Johnson 1975: 271). Writing, as we know it, did not exist until after the state, as defined by Wright and Johnson, emerged, but these stamps and seals obviously conveyed a great deal of information.

In one study focusing on the Susiana Plain, Wright and Johnson used the number of commodity or message sealings found at specific sites to reconstruct some aspects of the production, transport, and administration of goods. They concluded that they could determine when the change was made from one- and two-level decision-making institutions to the three levels which define the state.

Wright and Johnson also analyzed the locational arrangement of the settlements in southwestern Iran and found that after about 3600 B.C. there were trends toward more regular spacing of settlements and the emergence of distinctive site size groupings—both of which are consistent with the change from a two-level to a three-level control hierarchy. They concluded:

> This pattern of developing settlement arrangements correlated with changes in the technology of administration is apparently not unique to southwestern Iran. The transition seems to occur in several adjacent regions in Iraq between [3700 B.C. and 3250 B.C.] around the ancient centers of Nippur, Nineveh, and Uruk. . . . Thus rather than one case of state emergence, there was a series of emergences of individual states in a network of politics. (1975: 273–74)

In trying to explain why this shift came about, Wright and Johnson propose several factors. Decisions involving problems posed by drought, overpopulation, conflict, or some other single factor could probably be handled by a two-level hierarchy—something on the order of a chiefdom, perhaps—but a combination of problems would require additional decision-making capacity. They suspect that one important factor in early Southwest Asian state formation may have been the economic interactions between nomadic pastoralists and lowland farmers, probably in the form of the exchange of cheese, rugs, meat, minerals, and other highland resources for pottery, grain, and other lowland commodities. Economic models suggest that fluctuating demand for certain craft products in relatively simple economies often stimulates the centralization of workshops and economic administration, and Wright and Johnson believe that in prehistoric Mesopotamia the economic demands of nomads on lowland economies may have fluctuated sufficiently to produce a similar effect, with the eventual emergence of a three-level hierarchy.

In subsequent analyses of the Susiana data, Johnson (1977, 1982, in press) has applied various concepts from what is known as "hierarchy theory" (Pattee 1973) and the so-called rank-size rule (Johnson 1982).

Hierarchy theory is essentially a search for explanations of how everything, from molecular structures to world governments, seems to involve hierarchical orderings. The assumption here is that there are principles common to all these forms of hierarchies and that the processes by which hierarchies change and appear can be mathematically analyzed.

The rank-size rule, in contrast, is simply an empirical observation that many settlement patterns have a common form in terms of the relative sizes of their component settlements. Thus, in any region, state, or country, one can expect that the distribution of people will be somewhere between the extreme distributions of everyone in one settlement and everyone in a number of settlements of equal population. And if one ranks each settlement in terms of its population, assigning the number one to the largest, two to the second largest, and so on, and then graphs the actual population of each settlement against the rank of that settlement, one can produce the *rank-size plot* of that distribution. (For statistical reasons these plots are done on a logarithmic scale.) Geographers have noted that for many developing countries, such as Egypt, the rank-size plot will be a *primate* one. For example, Cairo is much larger than any other settlement and forms such a large proportion of the total Egyptian population that a rank-size plot of Egypt is sharply concave, relative to a distribution in which settlement in the hierarchy is precisely proportional to its rank.

Without pursuing the arithmetical subtleties of this approach, it is sufficient to note that major shifts in the political and economic organization of an area are usually reflected in its rank-size plot. To use Egypt as an example again, the great growth of Cairo to over 12 million people during the last fifteen years has correlated with the growing power of the national government and the rapidly industrializing economy. Prior to 1965, a much greater percentage of Egyptians lived in smaller towns and villages than do now.

The archaeological applications of this are obvious. If we know when a site was occupied and how big it was, we can then estimate population sizes, construct rank-size plots, and perhaps detect when great political and economic changes were taking place. The application of this idea to various areas of Mesopotamia yields mixed results. Clearly there were different rank-size patterns at different times, which might signal the origins of state-level societies (Crumley 1979).

There are two main problems, however, in the use of rank-size plots. First, it is difficult to estimate the populations of sites in different time periods with precision. Second, no one really knows what the different kinds of rank-size plots mean. They are essentially empirical generalizations without any theory to explain them.

Nonetheless, the fundamental problem of archaeology is to define patterns in the distribution of artifacts through space and time, and these rank-size plots at least have the virtue of showing us some possible patterns.

The most recent synthetic treatment of the origins of the Mesopotamian city and state is Robert McC. Adams's *Heartland of Cities* (1981), the product of over twenty years of research in which he personally surveyed thousands of archaeological sites in Iran and Iraq. Adams does not reduce his comprehensive treatment of the subject to a flow-chart or series of propositions. He prefers instead to arrange the archaeological evidence of Mesopotamia within its ecological and historical context and to defer until more information is available any general explanation of the whole.

Much of Adams's analysis centers on how the various successive political entities of Mesopotamia accommodated themselves to their economic and demographic environment, but in his search for causes, he notes that the same landscape that produced these cities ultimately witnessed their destruction. Thus, we can conclude that this pattern of urbanization and economic development "was not generated by any unique propensities of the landscape, and that we must look instead to the human forces that were harnessed in the building of the cities themselves" (1981: 252).

Yet Adams sees environmental factors as important. While rejecting Wittfogel's major premise that irrigation is the primary *cause* of cultural complexity, he nonetheless states:

> In the largest sense, Mesopotamian cities can be viewed as an adaptation to [the] perennial problem of periodic, unpredictable shortages. They provided concentration points for the storage of surpluses, necessarily soon walled to assure their defensibility. The initial distribution of smaller communities around them suggests primarily localized exploitation of land, with much of the producing population being persuaded or compelled to take up residence within individual walled centers rather than remaining in villages closer to their fields. Tending to contradict a narrowly determinist view of urban genesis as merely the formation of walled storage depots, the drawing together of significantly larger settlements than had existed previously not only created an essentially new basis for cultural and organizational growth but could hardly have been brought about without the development of powerful new means for unifying what originally were socially and culturally heterogeneous groups. (1981: 244)

Adams counts irrigation management as just one major stimulus to Mesopotamian developments. He notes that generalized risk-reduction strategies were essential, since so many factors (like crop disease,

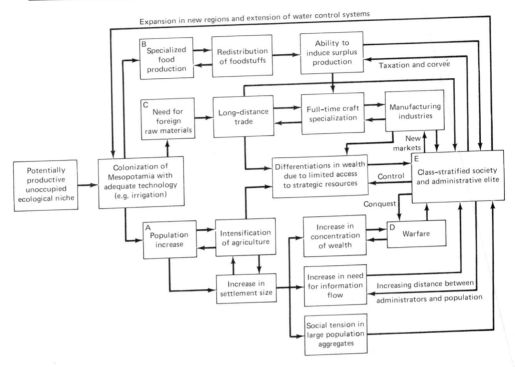

8.18   A "flow-chart" illustrating hypothetical cause and effect relationships among variables that led to the formation of class-structured "states" in Mesopotamia.

droughts, floods, locusts, salinization, and armed attack) were unpredictable and uncontrollable through existing technology.

Somewhat in contrast to Wright and Johnson's stress on information flow and decision making, Adams argues that the evidence suggests "that the primary basis for [political-economic] organization was . . . religious allegiance to deities or cults identified with particular localities, political superordination resting ultimately on the possibility of military coercion, or a fluid mixture of both" (1981: 78).

Taken as a whole, Adams's hundreds of graphs, maps, charts, and pages of discussion provide more of a compendium of evidence to be explained than an explanation of the evidence. But he has greatly facilitated such explanations by showing just how variable and complicated cultural evolution in Mesopotamia was and how many plausible "functional" accounts can be made for the same phenomena.

Another elaborate and plausible functionalist account of Mesopotamian state origins is that of Charles Redman (1978) (Figure 8.18). Redman connects several crucial environmental variables with sociological conditions to explain the origins of state political organizations, national religious cults, and other complex sociocultural phenomena.

Redman, Adams, and others have described with considerable insight the kinds of environments and historical conditions that might have produced—or at least, elicited—the first complex societies of Mesopotamia. But we are still far from a complete knowledge of why these societies appeared when, where, and in the form that they did.

9

The Origins of
Cultural Complexity in Egypt

Concerning Egypt I shall extend my remarks to
a great length, because there is no country that
possesses so many wonders, nor any that has such
a number of works which defy description.

Herodotus, ca. 440 B.C.

Ancient Egyptian civilization came into full flower centuries later than
Mesopotamian cultures and may have been influenced by them, but the
cultural evolution of Egypt was largely an independent process so distinctive and brilliant that ancient Egypt remains the most widely renowned of all ancient civilizations.

For the archaeologist long trained in seeing the functional, the economic, in art, artifacts, and architecture, there is little problem in defining the common denominators that link Egypt and other early civilizations. In Egypt, too, people took centuries to turn from hunting and foraging to agriculture, then built huge monuments, sent armies against each other first and then against their neighbors, and eventually lived as citizens of great empires at a time when most of the world knew nothing but illiterate bands and tribes.

But because we can see the similarities between Egypt and, for example, Mesopotamia, we should not be blind to the unique genius of either.

Egypt was a distinctive civilization, of an excellence in arts, letters, and science that can only be dimly glimpsed in its artifacts that lie in museum cases all over the world.

The Ecological Setting

Until the dams in southern Egypt were constructed in the 1960s, the torrential spring rains of central Africa sent silt-choked floods pulsing down the Nile Valley, depositing along the way innumerable tons of rich soil, and emptying finally into the Mediterranean in late autumn. Along the river's course this natural alluviation has produced one of the world's richest agricultural niches, which with even the simplest tools supports as many as 450 people per square kilometer.

Although highly productive, the Nile Valley is only an extremely elongated oasis (Figure 9.1) where agricultural lands are sharply circumscribed in most regions by rocky deserts. From the Sudanese border to Cairo, the cultivable strip along both banks of the river is only three kilometers wide in most places, and so sharp is the demarcation that one may literally stand with one foot on the red desert sands and the other foot on the black, irrigated croplands. North of Cairo, the Nile breaks up into many small streams, creating a delta area, about 250 by 160 kilometers, of flat, well-watered, fertile land.

Temperatures along the Nile regularly exceed 100°F, and rainfall is sparse: irrigation is required everywhere for agriculture. The heat can often be oppressive, but the climate is perfect for plant growth, allowing the harvesting of three crops a year and the cultivation of a wide range of plants. From antiquity, the staples have been spelt (a kind of cereal), barley, legumes, onions, cucumbers, melons, and figs, and the pastures and gardens of the alluvium have long sustained sheep, goats, pigs, cattle, and fowl. Even without agriculture, the Nile itself is generous, supporting myriad fish, ducks, geese, turtles, crocodiles, hippopotami, and other game animals, dense stands of rushes and reeds for basketry, flax for linen and canvas, and papyrus for cordage and paper.

The deserts that parallel the Nile are dotted with a few oases, but elsewhere they provide barely enough to support a few nomads. They are, however, rich in building stone. Copper can be found in the Sinai Desert, while immense gold and silver reserves used to be available in the Eastern Desert.

The bleak and inhospitable deserts and the lack of any natural harbors in the Delta protected Egypt from foreign influences and invasions until well after the first Egyptian states had formed, and such characteristics as very late and weakly developed urbanism in Egypt may have derived mainly from this isolation (Butzer 1976: 226).

Another important environmental factor was the communications and transport route provided by the Nile, which allowed the ancient

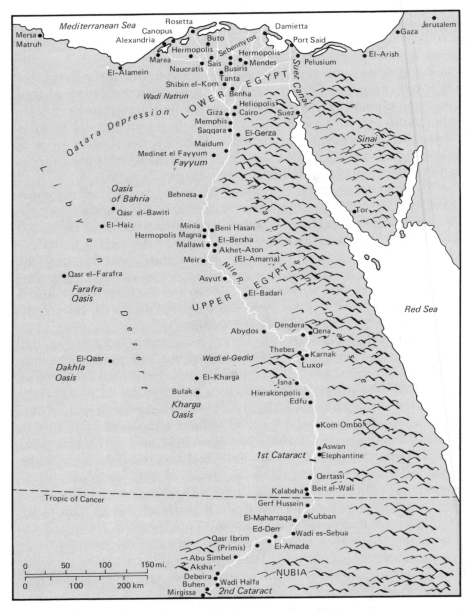

Mediterranean Sea

Rosetta
Mersa
Matruh
Canopus
Alexandria
Buto
Damietta
Gaza
Jerusalem
Port Said
Hermopolis
Marea
Sebennytos
Hermopolis
Pelusium
El-Arish
El-Alamein
Sais
Mendes
Naucratis
Busiris
Shibin el-Kom
Tanta
Wadi Natrun
Benha
Heliopolis
Suez
Suez Canal
LOWER EGYPT
Giza
Cairo
Memphis
Saqqara
El-Gerza
Sinai
Maidum
Medinet el Fayyum
Fayyum
Oasis
of Bahria
Behnesa
Tor
Qasr el-Bawiti
El-Haiz
Minia
Beni Hasan
Hermopolis Magna
El-Bersha
Mallawi
Akhet-Aton
Meir
(El-Amarna)
Qasr el-Farafra
Asyut
Nile R.
UPPER EGYPT
El-Badari
Farafra
Oasis
Red Sea
Abydos
Dendera
Qena
El-Qasr
Wadi el-Gedid
Thebes
Karnak
Dakhla
Oasis
El-Kharga
Luxor
Isna
Bulak
Hierakonpolis
Kharga
Edfu
Oasis
Kom Ombo
Aswan
1st Cataract
Elephantine
Qertassi
Kalabsha
Beit el-Wali
Tropic of Cancer
Gerf Hussein
El-Maharraqa
Kubban
Ed-Derr
Wadi es-Sebua
Qasr Ibrim
(Primis)
El-Amada
Abu Simbel
Aksha
Debeira
NUBIA
Buhen
Wadi Halfa
Mirgissa
2nd Cataract

Libyan Desert

0   50   100   150 mi.
0   100   200 km

9.1   Some major Egyptian sites. Egypt's desert and mountain frontiers protected it for many centuries against outside influences, but already by 3000 B.C. its trade and military contacts extended into Palestine, Nubia, and the Mediterranean world.

Egyptians to traverse the length of their country in just a few days of pleasant sailing. This was undoubtedly a key factor in the centralized states that developed in later Egyptian antiquity, and it is not surprising that in the southern reaches of the Nile, where five cataracts (steep rapids) constitute impassable barriers to navigation, the power of the Egyptian states weakened.

Although there have been major fluctuations in the annual volume of the Nile—for example, catastrophically low water levels in some of the years between 2250 and 1950 B.C.—the Nile floodplain has existed in essentially its present form since about 3800 B.C. (Butzer 1976: 28).

Early Egyptian Agriculture and the Predynastic Period
(ca. 9500 to 3100 B.C.)

Egypt beyond the green and vibrant Nile Valley is a starkly beautiful land, where clear blue sky and rocky reddish-yellow desert comprise a simplified and, to all appearances, lifeless world. But at many times during past millennia, these deserts bloomed under seasonal rains that supported vast grasslands and cattle, gazelle, hares, antelopes, turtles, birds, and other animals.

If one walks out into the desert along the great erosional gulleys (called *wadis*) that lead into the river valley, one finds scatters of stone tools and bleached bones—all that remains of Paleolithic Egyptians and the animals they hunted. They probably lived here as early as 250,000 years ago, perhaps earlier, and as the rain patterns shifted and made these areas deserts again, they probably moved back into the Nile Valley and its rich riverine resources.

Archaeological excavations by Fred Wendorf and Romauld Schild (Wendorf and Schild 1980) at Wadi Kubbaniya, in southwestern Egypt, appeared to produce some evidence that by 15,000 B.C. the hunters and gatherers of this area already had domesticated barley and were living in small camps that changed location with the seasons. Wendorf and Schild found no evidence that these communities had grown substantially in size, number, or complexity over several millennia, during which barley may have been cultivated. Such stability over time would have been radically at variance with the pattern in most other areas of the Middle East, since a growing dependence on domesticates and farming in these other areas was almost always followed by rapidly rising population densities, evidence of social stratification, and the establishment of villages and towns.

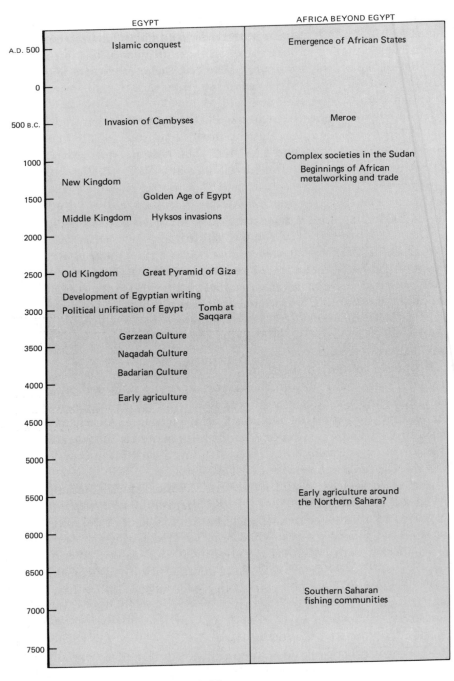

EGYPT | AFRICA BEYOND EGYPT

A.D. 500 — Islamic conquest

Emergence of African States

0 —

500 B.C. — Invasion of Cambyses

Meroe

1000 —

Complex societies in the Sudan

Beginnings of African
metalworking and trade

New Kingdom

1500 —

Golden Age of Egypt

Middle Kingdom — Hyksos invasions

2000 —

2500 — Old Kingdom — Great Pyramid of Giza

Development of Egyptian writing

3000 — Political unification of Egypt — Tomb at Saqqara

Gerzean Culture

3500 — Naqadah Culture

Badarian Culture

4000 — Early agriculture

4500 —

5000 —

5500 — Early agriculture around the Northern Sahara?

6000 —

6500 —

Southern Saharan fishing communities

7000 —

7500 —

9.2   Some important events in Egypt's history.

In excavations in 1984, Wendorf and Schild meticulously excavated additional areas of Wadi Kubbaniya, and they also conducted additional analyses of plant remains from previous excavations. They now believe that the hunters and gatherers of Wadi Kubbaniya were simply gathering plants rather than farming them, and that barley was not grown at the site until the modern era.

Despite having rejected an interesting hypothesis about early agriculture, Wendorf and Schild have given us one of the few detailed archaeological analyses of the way of life of hunters and gatherers in the critical period of the late Pleistocene, the five thousand years just before the appearance of the first domesticates. Their work suggests—for the peoples of Wadi Kubbaniya, at least—a highly diversified food base, with seasonal concentration on different foods and animals, strict control over population densities, and substantial movement of groups within large territories.

In an earlier study (Wendorf 1968), Wendorf also produced interesting information that suggests that the "noble savages" of the Pleistocene were in some ways more savage than noble. At Jebel Sahaba (southern Egypt), Wendorf found a cemetery with the skeletons of fifty-eight people who had died in the years between about 12,000 and 10,000 B.C., many of them children under the age of three years. As Wendorf describes the burials:

> one of the unusual features of the burials was the direct association of 110 artifacts, almost all in positions which indicate they had penetrated the body either as points or barbs on projectiles or spears. They were not grave offerings. Many of the artifacts were found along the vertebral column, but other favored target areas were the chest cavity, lower abdomen, arms, and the skull. Several pieces were found inside the skull, and two of these were still imbedded in the sphenoid bones in positions which indicate that the pieces entered from under the lower jaw. (1968: 959)

One must be a bit wary of cemetery data, for they may give us a biased view of death. For all we know, 99 percent of the people contemporary with those in the Jebel Sahaba cemetery died in peace, full of years and in the bosom of their families. But the Jebel Sahaba corpses are not reassuring.

With the end of the last ice age at about 8000 B.C., the Nile Valley and its adjacent deserts took on much the form and climate that they have today. The way of life in the period just after 8000 B.C., at least as we know it from excavations in the Fayyum, at el-Kab near the Red Sea, and at many sites in southern Egypt, was apparently a slow seasonal round of hunting the desert margins for wild cattle, gazelle, birds, and many other animals, and exploiting the Nile for fish, fowl, and other animals and plants.

But this way of life was on the wane. By about 6000 B.C., people in the Fayyum and perhaps elsewhere in Lower Egypt were probably exploiting a few species of plants and animals with a systematic intensity that was tending toward "domestication." Sometime between 6000 and 5000 B.C., domesticated wheat, barley, sheep, goats, and cattle were introduced from outside Egypt to become the staple food sources in the Fayyum and parts of the Delta. Whether these domesticates were introduced for the first time in this millennium or were just *successfully* introduced for the first time is unknown, as are their ultimate origins. Some of these plants and animals may have come from Southwest Asia, where they had already been in agricultural use for 2,000 years, but some may have come from oases in the Libyan Desert, where there is some evidence of very early domestication and use (Butzer 1976; Hoffman 1980).

Although some of the earliest Egyptian domesticates known date to 5000 B.C. (from Merimde in the western Delta), our most systematic evidence about these earliest agriculturalists is from the Fayyum. The intrepid British archaeologist Gertrude Caton-Thompson did excellent excavations along the lake's north shore in the 1930s, and Fred Wendorf's work there in the 1970s greatly augmented Caton-Thompson's findings. In 1981 I and a large staff spent six months excavating and surface-collecting in the deserts on the southern side of the lake, and when our evidence is combined with that of our predecessors, we are left with a great deal of information about these early farmers but also with two important and unresolved problems. The first is, where are all the Neolithic peoples of the Fayyum? In excavations that now span sixty years, almost every artifact the Fayyumis used has been recovered, but they coyly put their corpses someplace where we have not looked, or where they were not preserved. Not one of their bodies has been recovered.

A second and more important problem is that while the ancient Fayyumis used grinding stones and sickle blades, and manifestly had domesticated wheat, barley, sheep, and cattle, not a single one of their residences has ever been found. The high proportion of fish and wild animals in the Fayyum diet raises the possibility that rather than being full-fledged farmers, they were still mainly hunters-collectors, and thus did not reside in permanent villages. But competition for ripe cereals by birds and rodents is great, and the investments needed to make silos, grinding stones, and sickles is such that it is more likely that Fayyumis lived in villages made of reed huts that did not leave many traces.

By 4000 B.C. agriculture had spread over much of Egypt, including the southern areas that had taken a few tentative steps toward agriculture in the late Pleistocene. Local variations on the agricultural theme probably embraced different mixes of domesticates and wild resources— some people still depending on fish and wild plants for much of their food, others pretty well locked into the wheat-barley, sheep-goat combination that underlies so much of Middle Eastern cultural evolution.

If one were to ask archaeologists working in Egypt what was the most impressive and puzzling thing about the archaeological record of that country, many would ignore the pyramids and tomb paintings to single out the rapidity and comprehensiveness with which these hundreds of unconnected and functionally similar villages were transmuted into an organized social, economic, and political unity—the first Egyptian state. This transmutation began at about 4000 B.C. in the south and rapidly spread to the north, encompassing most of the delta by 3100 B.C.

It is convenient to talk about the rise of the Egyptian state in the late Predynastic as if we have the documents attesting to its political makeup, but what we mean when we say *state* here is really a bold inference based on several classes of insufficient evidence. These are: (1) the spread over much of Egypt of pottery and architectural styles that suggest close, continuing contacts among people over large areas of the country; (2) the "waste" of massive amounts of resources in tombs and monumental buildings in such a way as to suggest an unequal distribution of wealth, power, and prestige; and (3) some equivocal signs, like the Narmer Palette (Figure 9.3), which seems to indicate a potentate in the process of exercising kingly authority.

By far the largest and most complex cluster of Predynastic settlements in Egypt are those at Hierakonpolis, where excavations have spanned almost a century (they are currently under the direction of Michael Hoffman [1980, 1982]).

Hierakonpolis is so diverse that it is dangerous to draw a stereotype of its way of life at any one time in the Predynastic. But for much of its occupation, people seemed to have lived in rectangular, semisubterranean houses of mud-brick and thatch; worshipped in small, perhaps wooden shrines; made and distributed regionally several kinds of pottery, some of it very beautiful; hunted, herded, fished, and farmed the by now traditional array of Egyptian plants and animals; and buried their dead in rock and mud-brick tombs of a size and content to reflect the social power and prestige of the individual.

9.3   The Palette of Narmer,
an engraved thin sheet of
stone that was possibly a symbol of the political unification
of Egypt. From Hierakonp-
olis.

The Archaic, Old Kingdom, and First Intermediate
Periods (ca. 3100 to 2040 B.C.)

The *Archaic* and *Old Kingdom periods* were the great formative era of
Egyptian civilization, the time when Upper and Lower Egypt were first
united politically and Egyptian forms of writing, architecture, administration, and ideology emerged.

Traditional sources suggest that Menes (also known as Narmer), a
minor official from Upper Egypt, rose to power and conquered Lower
Egypt at about 3100 B.C., and that he and his successors established a
theocratic political system over the entire navigable length of the Nile.
Menes is recorded as having built a capital at Memphis, diverting the
stream of the Nile to create a strategic position at the junction of Upper and Lower Egypt. His next several successors were also powerful
kings, but there is some evidence of internal dissension at about 2900

B.C. Later, peace appears to have been restored, and major construction projects were undertaken in the centuries before 2700 B.C.

The archaeological evidence from these early centuries is limited to some badly looted tombs, monuments, and a few excavated sites. From these have been recovered beautiful artifacts of diorite and other varieties of hard stone as well as skillfully fashioned copper implements and a few items of gold. Such distinctive Egyptian materials as faience (a glassy substance made from molded and fired crushed quartz) and papyrus paper were in use at this time, and contemporary documents written on this paper show that the Egyptians were already skilled in astronomy, geometry, accounting, surgery, and architecture.

It appears that by 2700 B.C., the economic sphere was already quite complex, involving long-distance trade to Syria and beyond and considerable local exchange of craft goods and foodstuffs; but most Egyptians of the Old Kingdom period continued to live in unwalled, largely self-sufficient villages. Apart from Memphis there were few towns or cities, a situation that may have contributed to the political integration of the country, since there were no urban power centers to resist incorporation (Service 1975: 228). Large areas of the Middle Nile Valley were only sparsely settled, and population growth was quite slow, with little competition for agricultural land or irrigation water (although many new settlements appear to have been founded in the Delta). Apparently, the slow population growth during the Old Kingdom period (Butzer estimates an annual rate of 0.8 per 1,000) eventually did begin to exert some pressure on available resources toward the end of the period, since large game almost disappeared from the Alluvium and contemporary documents describe a shift away from pastoralism to a greater reliance on grain agriculture (Butzer 1976).

The middle of the third millennium B.C. was for Egypt a marvelous age in which many of the greatest pyramids and palaces were built, an integrated royal bureaucracy formed, and arts and crafts brilliantly executed. Because of the relatively comprehensive documents from this period, we know many of its political and social details (Trigger 1982).

Djoser, the second king of the Old Kingdom period, was able to organize the people and economy of Egypt to the extent that he, or his grand vizier, Imhotep, could arrange construction of the great step pyramid at Saqqarah as his tomb. The actual crypt was built inside the pyramid, whose six levels rose over 60 meters and were surrounded by large buildings and a stone wall more than 9 meters wide with a perimeter of more than 1.6 kilometers. The pyramid complex at Saqqarah was the world's first large-scale stone building and one of the most beautiful,

9.4 The pyramids at Giza are surrounded by temples, tombs, and other monuments of many different periods.

and in terms of the effort and materials required for its construction, it dwarfs the monumental architecture of all other early complex societies. It truly must have been an impressive sight, forty-five centuries ago, with its crisp white limestone facing contrasting with the cobalt blue sky, green palm groves, and desert sands.

Djoser's successors, particularly those of the Fourth Dynasty (ca. 2613 to 2494 B.C.), also built massive pyramids and experimented with designs and constructions until the "perfect" pyramid form was achieved by King Khufu—as exemplified by the pyramids at Giza (Figure 9.4). It is not just the massive size of this and other pyramids of the era that is so impressive, but also the complex engineering, the deft execution of stone sculpture, and the precise planning such projects would have required.

The Great Pyramid of Giza required the quarrying, transport, preparation, and laying of 2,300,000 stone blocks, each with an average weight of 2.5 tons, and it is estimated to have required a labor force equivalent to about 84,000 people employed for eighty days a year for twenty years. It is not known how these people were mobilized and administered, but many think the construction was done by the peasantry during seasons when little agricultural activity was required. What appear to be barracks, with a capacity for at least 4,000 people, have been found near one of the pyramids, and the administration, feeding, direction, and planning required to control such a work force, which included many highly trained craftsmen as well as laborers, would obviously argue a high degree of political and bureaucratic centralization. The king was apparently able to call on all the resources of the country, and direct them and the people to virtually any end, and at times the entire national economy was probably focused on these projects. The absolute control of the monarch is directly reflected in the texts and in the mortuary complexes of the various levels of high-ranking administrators who served him, many of whose tombs are laid out around the king's own tomb, perpetuating the king's control over them even into eternity.

Shortly after 2495 B.C. there was a change in dynasties as well as in the religious and political texture of the Old Kingdom. The worship of the sun god, Re, emerged as the dominant religion, and the devolution of kingly power seems to have been matched by increasing power among the nobility and provincial authorities.

The breakup of central control came in the *First Intermediate period* (ca. 2160 to ca. 2040 B.C.), a time of political and religious upheaval. The increasing prominence of the god Osiris cut away at the foundation of the old state religion of Re in which the king was central and absolute, and at the same time there was a rapid succession of weak kings and consequent insurrections.

As a whole, the political and economic structures of the Old Kingdom are those of a highly complex civilization, but some characteristics distinguish it from Mesopotamian and other early complex societies. For example, there seem to have been no standing armies during most of the Old Kingdom and no economically significant slavery. In some ways the economic system—although highly administered—was a simple redistributive, almost chiefdom-like system, quite different, perhaps, from that of early Mesopotamian states.

Economic exchange was apparently controlled almost entirely through the king; there were no "merchants," in the capitalistic sense at least, until 1,000 years after the end of the Old Kingdom. Craftsmen, scribes, peasants, and everyone else were required to perform some services in the name of the king and were liable for military and civil conscription, but there is a clear contrast here with the partially capitalistic, multi-tiered, highly differentiated economic system characteristic of the later Mesopotamian states.

The political breakdown of Egypt toward the end of the Old Kingdom may have been in part a result of dramatic climatic changes. Rainfall decreased in much of Egypt after about 2900 B.C., and Butzer notes that decreasing rainfall would have reduced the resources and numbers of desert nomads as well as eliminating much of the seasonal pastoral movements into the deserts of valley folk. It may even have interrupted travel between the Nile and the Red Sea and the Libyan oases (Butzer 1976: 26–27).

The Middle Kingdom (2040 to 1570 B.C.)

The history of the *Middle Kingdom* contains the same cycles of expansion and collapse that can be seen in all the great ancient empires. Periods of well-regulated trade, an expanding economy, and brilliant advances in art, architecture, and literature were punctuated by periods of revolution, poverty, and political fragmentation. The Middle Kingdom originated in the great civil unrest of the twenty-first century B.C., when according to a contemporary account,

> Corn has perished everywhere. . . . People are stripped of clothing, perfume, and oil. . . . Everyone says, "There is no more." . . . Strangers have come into Egypt everywhere . . . Men do not sail to Byblos today: What shall we do for fine wood? Princes and pious men everywhere as far as the land of Crete are embalmed with the resins of Lebanon, but now we have no supplies. . . . The dead are thrown in the river. . . . Laughter has perished. Grief walks the land. (Aldred 1961: 102)

Conditions began to improve radically after 2040 B.C., when Mentuhotep II, the first king of the Middle Kingdom, brought Upper and Lower Egypt once again under the rule of a single royal house. Mentuhotep and his next several successors reorganized the country with considerable energy, undertaking expeditions into Nubia, Libya, and Syria, reopening trade routes to the Red Sea, and commencing again the construction of monumental buildings.

In about 1999 B.C., Amenemhet came to power, and he and his successors inaugurated one of the most glorious epochs of Egyptian civilization. The capital was reestablished near Memphis, from which both Upper and Lower Egypt could be ruled effectively, trade routes were extended, fortresses were built along the country's frontiers, territories were annexed, and various administrative innovations were made, including the tradition of co-regency, in which sons were made co-rulers toward the end of their fathers' reigns, thereby eliminating some of the bloody battles for succession that had plagued previous dynasties.

There were also advances in Egyptian art and architecture during this period, many literary classics were composed, and the cult of Osiris completed its replacement of the colder, sterner religion of Re and gave the common people some hope of the afterlife that in the past had been restricted to royalty.

From about 1786 to about 1720 B.C., various kings managed to remain in general control of most of Egypt, but gradually the power of Asiatic peoples in the eastern Delta increased as they took advantage of the weakening monarchy. The origins of these foreigners, collectively referred to as the *Hyksos,* are uncertain, as is the manner in which they took over Egypt and the extent of their domination. But at about 1674 B.C. they captured Memphis, and the Hyksos king adopted the trappings of Egyptian royalty. Artifacts made in the manner of the Hyksos have been found all along the Nile Valley and as far south as Karnak, but it is not clear how directly they were able to control most of the population.

The New Kingdom and Late Periods (1570 to 330 B.C.)

King Ahmose, a native of Thebes, began at about 1570 B.C. to expel the Hyksos from the Delta, and after several battles he managed to drive them beyond the eastern frontier. He even captured the city of Sharuhen, in Palestine, and the rich spoils from this city were the basis for the creation of an influential social class, as military officers were made administrators of the conquered territories. Ahmose and his successors reformed the bureaucracy, modeling it after that of the Middle Kingdom.

Perhaps the greatest ruler of this period was Thutmose III, who established Egypt's Asiatic empire with his conquest of much of the eastern Mediterranean coastal areas. Even powerful Assyria paid material tribute to the Egyptian Empire, as did the Babylonians and the Hittites.

Thutmose III was a master military strategist, and his surprise attack on Megiddo and his amphibious operation against the Mitanni, a powerful kingdom in Southwest Asia, established Egypt as a world power. By about 1450 B.C. Egypt had commercial contacts on a large scale, exchanging products with Phoenecia, Crete, the Aegean Islands, and its traditional African trading partners. Military pacification programs were extended far into Nubia, and vast quantities of Nubian gold and building stone were shipped to the Nile Valley.

One of the most famous monarchs of the *New Kingdom* was Akhnaton, who altered the basic religious structure of Egypt by introducing a semimonotheistic religion and trying to eradicate vestiges of older polytheistic elements. He built many marvelous temples to Aton, the new god, and constructed a new capital at Tell el-Amarna in central Egypt, complete with magnificent religious and administrative buildings. Akhnaton's influence on art and architecture was substantial, but soon after his death the old religions were reestablished by Smenkhkare and the famous Tutankhamen. Another famous pharaoh of the late New Kingdom was Ramses II, the oppressive king who held the Israelites in bondage. It may have been his successor, Merneptah, who refused to let the Israelites leave and gave Charlton Heston such a difficult time.

Egypt's society and religion remained quite stable throughout the second millennium B.C., although its internal cohesion and ability to exert itself internationally fluctuated considerably. At about 1000 B.C., Egypt lost military control of Nubia, and the breakup of its Asiatic empire brought it into confrontation with the Israel of David and Soloman. The Egyptians captured a city on the border of Israel and agreed to peace upon the marriage of the pharaoh's daughter to Solomon. But five years after Solomon's death Seshonk I invaded Israel, plundered Jerusalem, and reestablished Egypt's control.

During the first millennium B.C., Egypt had various periods of resurgence when particularly strong kings were able to reassert Egyptian influence in Palestine and Africa, but increasingly Egypt slipped under foreign domination, and it never really recovered its autonomy. At about 525 B.C., Cambyses, a Persian king, conquered Egypt and reduced it to a vassal kingdom, proclaiming himself pharaoh. In 332 B.C., Alexander the Great marched into Egypt, evicted the Persians, and built the city of Alexandria. Later, the Romans, Arabs, and British would complete the conquest of Egypt, submerging almost entirely this distinctive civilization that was for so many years the light of the ancient world. Not until 1952 was Egypt again ruled by Egyptians.

Ancient Egyptian Art and Thought

The rich Egyptian tombs and literature irresistibly seem to elicit theories about Egyptian "character," even though not all Egyptians thought alike and the Egyptian world view and life view were not static. Nonetheless, there are some persistent, deeply embedded themes in Egyptian culture. For one thing, Egyptians seem to have been a God-intoxicated people, "half in love with easeful death." Herodotus noted that they were the most "religious" people he had encountered and that they were given to incessant and elaborate religious rituals and supported an enormous priestly bureaucracy. Their concern with death, and the vast energies and richness they invested in preparing for it, are manifestly evident, but they are also a testament to a people so passionately alive that they tried everything to perpetuate life into death. To our own, essentially Greek, minds, the Egyptians were perhaps unable to distinguish between things and their substances. J. Wilson argues (1946: 72) that the Egyptians saw no difference between supplying a dead king with real loaves of bread, wooden models of bread, or loaves painted on the walls; it was not the actual thing that mattered, it was the idea. The physical man needed physical bread, but in the spirit world, "spiritual" bread was appropriate (ibid.).

Egyptian deities were conceived of as very human in their behavior, even to the extent that they could be intimidated. Egyptians recited prayers in which they ticked off the services rendered a god, demanding payment in the form of the prayer answered.

For the Westerner, the physical world is a rather neutral place, where a lightning bolt or virus may strike one down, but on the basis of chance, without malevolence. Rocks are rocks, the dark is peopled only by morbid human projections, and death is inevitable, final, complete. For the ancient Egyptian, however, the world swarmed with unseen but animate, conscious forces; malignant spirits were everywhere, as were forces for good; and, with sufficient effort, some of the inconveniences of being dead could be mitigated.

They seem to have been *monophysitic,* in that everything in the universe was thought to have been derived from one substance and was an expression of that substance. The god Amon, for example, might reside in a stone statue but also in a well-formed ram or a duck or in all three at the same time. Nor were these considered just different representations; rather, "the image was the god *for all working purposes"* (Wilson 1946: 73).

The symbolic, mythical element seemed to pervade even quite practical areas, such as medicine. One remedy for schistosomiasis (a disease characterized by bloody urine) was to shape some cake dough like a penis, then wrap it in meat, recite an incantation, and feed it to a cat (Farooq 1973: 2).

In all of this supernatural and symbolic content, we should not lose sight of the practical, canny Egyptian. These were not people paralyzed by the Infinite: they built houses, boats, and beautiful buildings, and they enjoyed themselves in a world of color, play, and physical pleasures that still seems attractive and alive, even when viewed only in fragmentary 4,000-year-old paintings on tomb walls.

For much of its history, Egyptian society seems to have been highly hierarchical, but well ordered and even "fair." Central to the culture was the concept of *ma'at*, which is usually translated as "justice," "truth," or "right-dealing." It is interesting that English really has no word equivalent to the sense of *ma'at*, or to the somewhat similar Greek concept of *virtue*. For the Egyptian, *ma'at* was recognizing the order of the world and universe and the necessity of doing the right thing, which usually meant following religious and civil laws and customs. Justice tempered with mercy, giving to the widow and the orphan but encouraging self-reliance and planning, doing one's share—all these and more were part of *ma'at*. One could demand justice and respect as a moral right, based on *ma'at*.

In word-association tests, the word *Egypt* would probably be followed in most people's minds by the words *mummies, pyramids,* or *hieroglyphs.* A few words, then, about each.

MUMMIFICATION

Mummification was an attempt to preserve the body for use in the afterlife, when it would be revived and rehabilitated. "Reserve" heads of painted stone are often found, for example, in tombs, so that when the individual's head fell off through decay, he or she could strap on the reserve head and sally forth to meet eternity.

Burial in the arid desert sands must have been the first form of mummification, but chemical methods were already developed by the Old Kingdom period. The process, as described in New Kingdom accounts, was elaborate. After death, the corpse was placed on a board and washed. The brain was removed by a hooked wire passed through the nose, an incision was made in the abdomen, and all the internal organs except the kidneys and heart were removed. A Greek of the third cen-

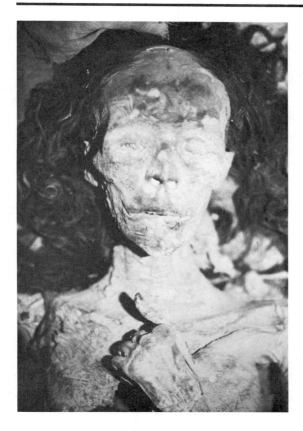

9.5 Mummy of Queen Tiye (d. about 1350 B.C.). The position of the left hand on the chest is typical of pharaohs.

tury A.D. reported that at that time the intestines were placed in a box and offered to the sun god, with the incantation "If I have sinned in eating or drinking what was unlawful, the fault was not mine, but of this" (showing the box in which was the stomach). There is no report of whether or not other organs were offered in absolution for other kinds of sins.

The heart was left in—if the tomb paintings are realistic—so that on the final day it could be weighed against a feather, to see if its sins would tip the balance against eternal life. After the internal organs had been removed, the abdomen and chest cavity were washed in palm wine, and the viscera were placed in a container of natron (hydrated sodium carbonate) for forty days. They were then placed separately in four *canopic* jars, the liver, lungs, stomach, and intestines to be guarded over by four different deities. The body was then stuffed with sand or straw and covered with natron to dessicate it for another forty days. Then it was washed once more and rubbed with wine, spices, and oils. The cheeks were restored to lifelike dimensions with rag stuffings, the incision was sewn up, and the hair and complexion were touched up with paint. The entire body was then protected with a coating of resin, placed in a coffin or tomb, and carried across to the west bank of the Nile for interment. At the close of ceremonies, the priest would incant: "You live again, you revive always, you have become young again, you are young again, and forever."

We have only Boris Karlov in *The Mummy* as evidence that these spells worked, but it must have been a great comfort to the ancient Egyptians to hear these words and see the care of the dead.

THE PYRAMIDS

As for pyramids, so much has been said and imagined, yet we can hope to know so little. The minds that designed them and invested them with meaning are these many centuries gone to dust. Even the techniques of their construction are known only in outline.

Cairo sprawls out and around the pyramids today in such clamorous ubiquity that the only way to *see* the pyramids in a manner anything like that of the ancient Egyptian is to come in from the west, in the early morning, in the absolute quiet of the desert.

The pyramids were all located on the west bank of the Nile, an equation no doubt with death and the setting sun. They are all within a short distance of a major ancient city, such as Memphis, and they are situated on the closest suitable stone outcrop on the river's edge. This evidently was to facilitate transfer of millions of blocks of limestone and alabaster, some of which had to be shipped down the Nile and then transported up the bank to the construction area.

Exactly how the blocks were quarried and transported remains unknown, but we have some clues. Quarrying probably involved a combination of hammering with hard stones, chopping with copper adzes, and fracturing by heating the rock with fires and then splashing cold water on it. The transport and erection into pyramids of the blocks is the subject of an excellent treatise by Lehner (in press), where the various possible combinations of ramps, rollers, and so on are checked against the physical requirements of the process.

Limited as they were by the lack of electronic survey equipment and precisely engineered tools, we cannot expect Egyptian craftsmen to have been up to modern construction standards. The north corner of the Great Pyramid, for example, is almost an inch higher than the south corner.

With the construction techniques available, a pyramid-shaped struc-

9.6 Members of the Chicago Cubs baseball team play a road game.

ture is the only form that could support its own weight, but we also have to account for the dimensions and angles used. Edwards (1961) makes the interesting suggestion that the upward angle of the pyramids parallels that of the slant of light on winter afternoons in Egypt, and he says the texts hint that the pharaohs ascended into heaven by walking up the rays of light. The pyramids thus would be a first step to the union with the sun god and eternity.

On hot summer nights, tourists continue experiments to determine if the pyramids retard aging, heighten sexual potency, cure diseases, or in other ways give off powerful emanations. The answer, it seems, is still in doubt.

HIEROGLYPHS

One of the many mysteries of Egypt is the origin of its written language, or *hieroglyphs* ("sacred carvings") (Figure 9.7). These were used from shortly before 3100 B.C. until about A.D. 40 (and still today by the crafty forgers in modern Cairo's tourist traps), and they went through a period of aesthetic and linguistic development. But hieroglyphic writing first appeared in such a developed form that we cannot see the full transition from what must be assumed to be a pictographic writing that may have been first expressed on papyrus. The notion that the idea of writing was introduced from Mesopotamia has little to recommend it, given the great differences in the characters and materials used.

To a much greater degree than in modern English, hieroglyphs were written in a manner that expressed both contemporary aesthetic styles and the subject matter. Thus, we get simple, grave characters in early religious writings and more overblown, showy texts in later military texts.

The Origins of Complex Societies in Egypt: Conclusions

Many simplistic notions about the origins of cultural complexity have foundered on the evidence from Egypt. Population growth, for example, may have produced fairly dense concentrations of people in favorable agricultural areas, but the long-term pattern of population growth was probably one of very slow increase through most of antiquity. Karl Wittfogel's (1957) notion of large-scale irrigation as a powerful impetus to empire may have some mild application to Egypt, for irrigation no doubt was important early on, and some of the first Egyptian stone en-

EGYPTIAN SCRIPTS (Alphabet)

Hieroglyphic sign	Meaning	Transcription	Sound value	New Kingdom Hieratic	Demotic	Coptic
	vulture	ꜣ	glottal stop			omitted or єι
	flowering reed	ỉ	I			єι or є
	forearm & hand	ꜥ	ayin			omitted
	quail chick	w	W			oγ
	foot	b	B			π or β
	stool	p	P			π or β
	horned viper	f	F			ϥ
	owl	m	M			м
	water	n	N			N
	mouth	r	R			ρ or λ [ε]
	reed shelter	h	H			8
	twisted flax	ḥ	slightly guttural			8 or omitted
	placenta (?)	ḫ	H as in "loch"			8 or ϭ
	animal's belly	ḫ	slightly softer than ḥ			8
	door bolt	s, z	S			c
	folded cloth	s, ś	S			c
	pool	š	SH			ϣ
	hill	ḳ	Q			κ, ϭ
	basket w. handle	k	K			κ, ϭ
	jar stand	g	G			ϭ
	loaf	t	T			τ, θ
	tethering rope	ṯ	TJ		(ⲡϩ)	х, т
	hand	d	D		(ⲁ_ᴅ)	т
	snake	ḏ	DJ			ϫ

EGYPTIAN ROYAL TITULARY

Horus Name (srḫ)	Nebty Name (nbty)	Golden Horus Name (Ḥr nbw)	Prenomen (ny-sw bit)	Nomen (s3 Rꜥ)

9.7 As Egyptian writing evolved, the original hieroglyphics were assigned phonetic values, and the characters became highly stylized to facilitate writing.

gravings apparently show royalty in the process of opening irrigation canals (Hoffman 1980: 315). But irrigation in ancient Egypt was primarily through the passive blessings of the Nile flood, and such irrigation works as were constructed seem to have been small, local installations that did not require a lot of people or "paperwork" to run them. Similarly, the Egyptians were fond of murals showing their kings de-

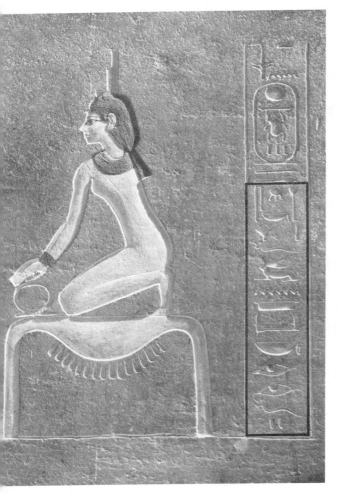

Hook signs and long-handled mace, phonograms for *s* and *hd,* spell the word for illumine, *shd*. The sun is a determinative, the basket a masculine suffix for "you." Literally, "May you illumine."

Face ideogram has value of *hr* and also means *face*. Vertical rod signals "here symbol means what it depicts."

Horned viper is masculine suffix -*f* and signifies "he," "him," or "his."

Desert hare stands for the sound *wm*—the word for "open"—reinforced by the wavy water symbol *n*. Two determinatives follow: Door on its side indicates "open," forearm holding stick adds the idea of "force" or "effort."

Basket: masculine suffix for "you." Coupled with preceding group, it makes the five signs read: "May you open."

One eye is an ideogram that can stand for "see." But two indicate the "eyes" themselves.

Horned viper: "his."

9.8   Hieroglyphic writing usually was a combination of ideograms (signs of things or ideas), phonograms (signs representing the sounds of the spoken language), and determinatives (signs added to clarify meanings). The inscription to the right of the kneeling figure, from the sarcophagus of Amunhotep II, reads "Illumine his face, open his eyes."

feating hordes of foreigners, and people in the competing areas of pre-state Egypt may well have been given to bloody civil wars. But the disposition of settlements, the lack of walled towns and forts, and the art and literature do not support the notion that Menes or someone else strapped on his sword, massed his troops, and marched to the Mediterranean, leaving a unified political state in his wake.

Nor is there much solace for the orthodox Marxian searching for the power of class conflict to produce states. Many scholars can and do see Egypt as a good example of the validity of Marxian theory, but Egyptian literature and iconography seem to exhibit more mutually supportive bonds of kinship and religion than naked class struggle. Recent Marxian analyses of Egypt (e.g., Friedman and Rowlands 1977) have focused on the changing "mode of production," but that, like beauty, is very much in the eye of the beholder.

The pressure of nomads and others on the Egyptian periphery seems to have been a factor occasionally, but there is not much of a parallel here with the situation in ancient China, where nomad-farmer relationships were a central theme in imperial developments.

9.9 By the late second millennium B.C., Egyptian sculpture had become a vibrantly representational art, as in this limestone figure of a nobleman's wife.

A comparison of Mesopotamian and Egyptian settlement patterns underscores the fact that urbanization is just one strategy, not an indispensable condition of cultural complexity. Whereas the people of Mesopotamia early and dramatically aggregated into fortified towns and cities, from which they conducted agricultural, industrial, religious, and administrative operations, the Egyptians did not even have a permanent capital until late in the second millennium, when Thebes emerged as a center—although recent excavations reveal a greater degree of urbanization than was previously thought to have existed. The comparatively slow development of Egyptian urbanism probably had many causes, including: (1) the absence of any powerful foreign peoples on Egyptian borders; (2) the uniformity of the environment all along the Nile, so that there was little to be gained from large-volume, interregional exchange of food or craft products; and (3) the pronounced political centralization, which inhibited development of secular, economic differentiation.

When the largest pyramids and other structures were built, population growth rates were slow, there was apparently little pressure on the country's resources, and there were large areas of uninhabited but fertile land. If we view these pyramids as mechanisms to mobilize and train a large work force, we must ask why such a work force would be an advantage, because when the first pyramids were built there were few large irrigation works and little demand for a standing army. If we view the vast expenditures of wealth in the funerary complexes as a means of "balancing" the economy by taking out of circulation inordinate amounts of gold, silver, or craft items, there is some difficulty in explaining why this would have been necessary in a society whose economic system and long-distance trade were strictly controlled by the monarchy and where there were few large markets and almost no free enterprise or capitalism of any kind.

In conclusion, it has proven remarkably difficult to prise apart the many causes and effects that make up Egyptian cultural history, but we are beginning to understand at least some aspects of this history. And, like other early civilizations, there is much about Egypt that is interesting and rewarding at a level beyond that of the mechanics of its history.

10

The Rise of Civilization
in the Indus Valley

As a civilization [the Harappan] had not been
very remarkable, its techniques being imported
and never improved, its buildings utilitarian and
its artifacts unattractive, and the completeness of
its destruction its only claim to fame.

C. McEvedy (1967)

Traditionally listed among the six "pristine" civilizations is the *Harappan* culture of the Indus flood plain. It is considered here only briefly, in large part because the most critical phases of its archaeological record lie more than ten meters under the Indus floodplain, far beneath the water table.

Along with the pleasures of sloshing through mud against a background whine of pumps, the archaeologist working on early complex societies in the Indus must be prepared for the collapse of huge walls of debris as he or she cuts down through the Alluvium to the earliest levels. For those and other reasons, the pace of archaeological research here has been slow.

Since the discovery of its archaeological remains in the 1920s, the Harappan "civilization" that flourished in the Indus Valley late in the third millennium B.C. has been considered a sort of poor relation to the civilizations that graced the Mesopotamian Alluvium and the Nile Valley. Not only did the Indus Valley cultures mature thousands of years later than those in Egypt and Southwest Asia, but they also neglected to leave much in the way of the pyramids, tombs, and palaces prized by the archaeological fraternity. Nor was the Harappan a particularly long-lived civilization, having appeared, matured, and "died" all within the space of five centuries.

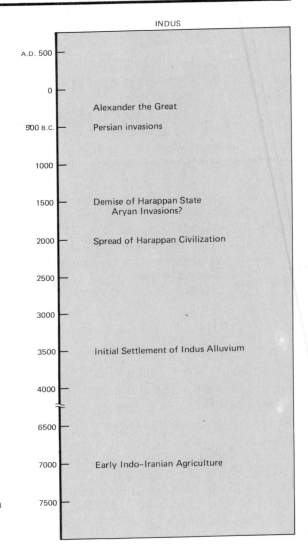

10.1   A chronology of South
Asian prehistory and early
history.

Thus, it is hardly surprising that until quite recently, most archaeologists believed that Indus Valley developments were directly stimulated by the great civilizations of ancient Mesopotamia. But it has now
become evident that the development of cultural complexity in the
Indus Valley was a largely independent phenomenon that drew on the
resources and cultures of a wide area but was little influenced by any
other complex culture. It is also clear that the Indus Valley cultures are
of great interest for the study of the origins of cultural complexity:
(1) they developed a writing system that has never been adequately de-

ciphered; (2) they constructed massive cities laid out on very "modern"-looking grid systems, with broad avenues, carefully planned residential areas, and perhaps the ancient world's most advanced municipal water and sewage system; (3) their area of cultural and political influence and control extended over almost 1,300,000 square kilometers—considerably more territory than any other Old World civilization of this period; and (4) the distribution of wealth appears to have been much more equitable in the Indus cities than in other early Old World civilizations.

The Ecological Setting

Fifty million years ago, movements of the earth's crust forced the Indian subcontinent against the main Eurasian land mass with such pressure that the land in between was squeezed upward, creating the dramatic Himalayan Mountains. Every spring melting snow in these highlands sends floods down the mountains and across the lowlands to the sea.

So little rain falls on most of this plain during the average year that large-scale, reliable agriculture is possible only through irrigation from the river, but—unlike the Nile—the Indus is very unpredictable. From year to year there can be great fluctuations in its volume and course. Much of the silt carried by the river is deposited in its own bed, raising the river above the level of adjacent plains so that it frequently breaks through its banks, flowing across the countryside in devastating floods. Countless centuries of this have left the Indus flood plain a maze of old river channels and great deposits of silt, all smoothed down by the action of wind and water. The great fertility of these soils is complemented by the arid, hot climate, which, like that of Egypt and Mesopotamia, supports several crops a year and a great diversity of plant species—as long as there is sufficient water.

Because the Indus is navigable over much of its length, it no doubt contributed to the political integration and economic success of ancient Indus Valley cultures.

While the Indus Valley was the focus of the first complex communities in the subcontinent, adjacent areas also played an important role. To the west, the foothills and mountains of Pakistan, Afghanistan, and Iran sharply limit the extension of agriculture, but they provide valuable minerals, metals, animal products, and other goods, and they are also the homelands of pastoral and nomadic peoples who exerted great influence on lowland civilizations. The diffusion of new ideas, objects,

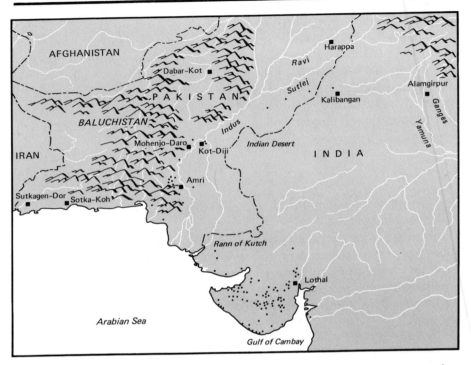

10.2   The central focus of Harappan civilization was the Indus Valley, an area of
almost 300,000 square kilometers. Almost all archaeological work has been concentrated on the large Harappan cities (*black squares*), but there were also numerous
smaller communities (*small black dots*).

and peoples into the Indus Valley was mainly along routes through
these western borderlands, or along the thin coastal strip on the Arabian
Sea, since the Himalayas to the north were a formidable barrier to
influences coming from that direction. The Great Indian Desert to the
east of the Indus Valley reduced contacts with the rest of the subcontinent.

Thus, the Indus Valley was, like Egypt, an area of rich agricultural
lands sharply bounded by highlands and desert.

Neolithic South Asia

As in the case of the Tigris and Euphrates, the arid lands along the Indus River appear to have been largely uninhabited for many centuries
after agricultural villages appeared in adjacent highland areas. Domes-

ticated wheat and the remains of domesticated sheep and goats have been found in levels dating to about 7000 B.C. in several sites in Afghanistan and Baluchistan, and the evidence suggests that thereafter the agricultural and pastoral ways of life spread gradually, from west to east, throughout highland areas where rainfall and perennial streams provided enough water for dry farming of wheat and barley.

Many settlements in the highlands west of the Indus at about 3500 B.C. were probably based on simple wheat farming supplemented by sheep and goat raising and some hunting and gathering. These farmers made pottery and used a few copper tools, but some of the villages are so insubstantial that they suggest a relatively mobile population and perhaps only seasonal occupation (F. R. Allchin 1974: 337).

Recent research in South Asia (reviewed by Jacobson 1979) reveals that we may have to make major revisions of our understanding of this area and its place in the evolution of cultural complexity. A radiocarbon date of about 4500 B.C. for a Neolithic settlement at Koldihawaa, on the Ganges Plain, makes the domesticated rice grain impressions in pottery there the oldest evidence we have for domesticated rice. And all over South Asia in the period of 9,000 to 7,000 years ago, there is evidence of intensive use of many cereals, most of which never became domesticated (Vishnu-Mittre 1977).

The abruptness with which the Harappan civilization appeared is somewhat less impressive when one considers the density and sophistication of farming communities that were already densely distributed over areas in Baluchistan, in central Pakistan, by 6000 B.C.

Between 3000 and 2400 B.C., settlements appeared at Kot Diji, Harappa, Kalibangan, and elsewhere, perhaps founded by people moving in from the western highlands. The few excavated settlements of this period reveal a very simple agricultural way of life, with the people residing in mud-brick houses in small villages scattered in areas where no extensive irrigation would have been necessary. Some villages were walled, though there was certainly no shortage of land or pressure on other resources at this time. At Kalibangan ancient plow marks indicate that fields were plowed in a manner similar to that of the recent past, but there are also many stone projectile points and other evidences of considerable hunting and gathering.

These various lowland settlements prior to 2400 B.C. show some stylistic uniformity and a great deal of economic and architectural similarity, but they appear to have been economically and politically independent and self-sufficient, and they reflect none of the rigid planning typical of later settlements here.

The Indus Civilization

Harappan artifacts in Mesopotamian sites show that by 2500 B.C., Harappan culture was already a regional force. And within a few centuries after 2400 B.C., the simple, scattered agricultural societies of the Indus Valley were transformed into a large, complex, urban-based sociopolitical system that we might legitimately call a state society. Once again the archaeological evidence is so meager that we can only speculate on how this transition was effected. Population densities began increasing in the southern delta area in the middle of the third millennium B.C., after which settlements appeared all along the Indus, but there is no evidence of intensive competitive pressure on resources. At Kot Diji and Amri, thick layers of ash suggest the transformation was not a peaceful one, but this is not at all clear. It may be significant that the emergence of Indus Valley urban cultures occurred at the same time that the first Near Eastern empires were forming, since there appears to have been increased trade and other contacts between these two areas at this time, but there is no evidence that these Mesopotamian contacts somehow induced the Indus Valley peoples to form states or aggregate in cities. More frequent incursions from highland peoples occurred during this period, raising the possibility that urbanization in the Indus Valley, as it seems to have been in China, Mesopotamia, and elsewhere, was in part a defensive response to these external pressures.

HARAPPAN URBANISM

The appearance of large planned cities shortly after 2300 B.C. and the associated spread of a distinctive constellation of artifact and architectural styles over much of the Indus Valley marked the emergence of Harappan civilization, a political system that survived only about 500 years but which managed to weld much of Pakistan into a political and cultural unit.

More than 200 Harappan sites are known, but almost all research has been devoted to the largest settlements, especially Mohenjo-daro, Harappa, Chanhu-daro, Pathiani Kot, Judeirjo-daro, Kalibangan, and Lothal. At least two cities about as large as Mohenjo-daro have been located but not yet excavated (Pfeiffer 1977: 205), and doubtless many Harappan settlements are buried beneath silt or have been washed away by floods.

The spatial extent of Harappan civilization has been defined on the

10.3   General view of the Citadel at Mohenjo-daro. A stupa (Buddhist shrine) was built on the Citadel many centuries after the site was abandoned.

basis of the location of the precisely planned cities and the rigid stylistic uniformity of its settlements, and these evidences tell us that at its maximum, the Harappan culture area reached from the Arabian Sea to the foothills of the Himalayas, and from the eastern Iranian frontier to the Ganges River Valley—an extent far larger than any other Old World political system at this time.

The largest Harappan settlement, Mohenjo-daro (Figure 10.3) covers at least 2.5 square kilometers. Recent studies of this and other Harappan settlements (e.g., Shaffer 1982) show that these communities were probably not so regularly constructed as archaeologists once thought, but, compared to the jumbled anarchy of most Mesopotamian city plans, Mohenjo-daro was quite orderly. The city was bisected by a north–south running street some 9 meters wide that was flanked by drainage ditches. Public toilets and sewers connected houses with the main sewage lines. Most residences were made of fired brick, comprising several rooms arranged around an open courtyard, and the majority appear to have had private showers and toilets drained by municipal sewage systems. Some houses were two stories high and larger and more elaborate than others, but the overall impression is one of uniformity. If gross differences in wealth divided the inhabitants, these are not reflected in residential architecture, at least not to the extent that they were in Mesopotamia.

At Mohenjo-daro and the other two largest Harappan sites, Harappa and Kalibangan, the carefully arranged residential areas were flanked on the west by a great fortified "citadel" mound. Mohenjo-daro's citadel is about 150 meters to the northwest of the main settlement, separated from the residences by land that seems to have been devoid of any settlement and perhaps was regularly flooded by a branch of the river. It has even been suggested that this flooding may have been deliberate, to create a pool of water for bathing, fishing, or some other activity. The northwest complex at Mohenjo-daro is dominated by a brick platform some 12 meters high, which was perhaps built as a refuge from floods (F. R. Allchin 1974: 340).

One of the most interesting structures at the northwest complex is the "Great Bath," a swimming-pool–like structure about 12 by 7 meters and 2.5 meters in depth, constructed of baked brick and lined with bitumen. Flanking the pool are what appear to have been dressing rooms. They were carefully staggered to give maximum privacy, and some were equipped with toilets (Fairservis 1975: 246–47). The Great Bath probably figured in some religious activities, although it contained no obvious icons or other religious elements, and it may have been mainly just a public bathing facility.

Adjacent to the bath was a cluster of platforms and rooms, variously interpreted as granaries, assembly halls, and garrisons. Overall, the complex was about 450 meters long and 90 meters wide at its maximum extent—representing a major investment of labor and materials. Thus, while there is nothing at Mohenjo-daro or any other Indus city to compare with the Egyptian pyramids or the White Temple at Uruk, the Indus city dwellers nonetheless were also diverting considerable energy and resources to building projects. The major difference seems to have been that, in contrast to the largely ceremonial public architecture in Mesopotamia and Egypt, the Indus Valley constructions provided some return in the way of administrative buildings, better defenses, and more storage space. There is at least a possibility that Harappan civilization was "cut off" in the midst of its development by invasion, flood, interrupted trade routes, or some other factor, and that more "wasteful" monumental architecture might eventually have appeared at the Indus cities had they been allowed to develop for a longer period. The absence of easily accessible building stone may also account for the comparatively utilitarian and drab Harappan monumental architecture.

About 35,000 to 40,000 people probably lived at Mohenjo-daro, and the populace included farmers, herdsmen, goldsmiths, potters, weavers, brickmasons, architects, and many other specialists; streets were lined with stores and shops. Wheat and barley were the basis of the economy, supplemented by dates, melons, sesame, peas, mustard, and other crops. Cattle, sheep, goats, pigs, and domestic fowl were the major animal foods, and buffalos, camels, asses, dogs, and cats were also kept. A few elephant bones have been found. The horse was apparently rarely used until the very end of the Harappan period.

Most of the larger Harappan settlements were similar to Mohenjo-daro in architecture and economy, but the site of Lothal, although only about 300 by 250 meters in size, shows an impressive complexity for such a tiny settlement (Possehl n.d.). A large tank, which Rao (1973) and others have interpreted as a dock, is probably not (Possehl n.d.), but its function is unclear. There was a factory for making beads from carnelian, crystal, jasper, and other stones, and facilities for making ornaments out of bronze, elephant tusks, and many other commodities. Possehl (n.d.) sees in Lothal's precise layout and concentrations of exotic commodities an entrepôt, a frontier settlement of entrepreneurs who were processing raw materials from the hinterlands and sending products on to the great Harappan cities.

We know little about the smaller Harappan settlements. The few that have been examined seem to have brick walls around a district within the site, perhaps in imitation of the citadels at the larger cities, and the basic arts and crafts and subsistence practices also appear to have been patterned after those of the cities.

Harappan settlements, with their precisely administered character, would seem to be excellent subjects for the systematic analysis of settlement patterns to try to discern the economic and political forces that dictated where people lived, but generally archaeologists have not competed with each other for a chance to survey systematically the intensely hot, heavily populated Indus Plain. What we do know of Indus settlement patterns suggests at least four different size categories, with about six large centers, twenty smaller centers, and about two hundred large and small villages. Doubtless there are many more settlements to be discovered, but from this sample it is clear that Harappan settlement patterns are comparable to, for example, those of Mesopotamia in the third millennium B.C., and if we consider three or more administrative levels to be evidence of state-level political organization, then the Harappan civilization was certainly a state. In fact, the Harappan population at the beginning of the second millennium B.C. was probably at least 200,000, and the tightly organized fabric of their lives suggest an empire-like political system.

The great similarity of cities, towns, and villages of the Harappan

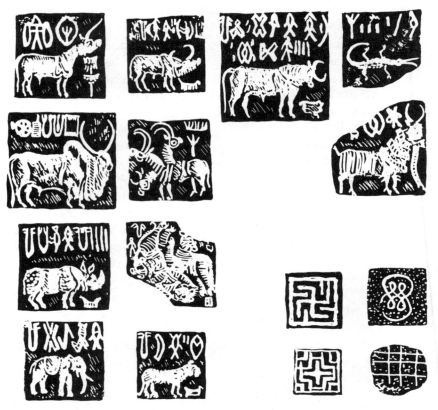

10.4   The repetition and complex arrangements of symbols on Harappan seals probably mean that they were at least a primitive written language, but no one has ever deciphered the script.

civilization bespeaks a high degree of centralization and contact among communities, but it is difficult to demonstrate this archaeologically. Clay and metal models of wheeled carts and river boats may reflect transport of goods along the Indus. Pottery, some kinds of flint tools, and other artifacts were mass produced at a few locations and distributed from place to place. The considerable degree of occupational specialization evident in these artifacts suggests intensive local trade, but there is a strong possibility that this was a kind of administered, noncapitalistic redistribution, rather than a free-enterprise or peasant marketing system. One possible key to the Harappan economic system is the hundreds of Harappan stamps and seals (Figure 10.4), which may have been used to denote ownership or make records of transactions. The apparently ritual scenes depicted in so many of these might argue against this interpretation, but the question will remain unresolved as long as Harappan script is undeciphered.

Almost all Harappan writing is in the form of inscriptions on these seals. The estimated number of unique symbols is between 350 and 425, which would seem to rule out the possibility that the writing is alphabetic. The writing system was complemented by a standardized system of weights and measures. Small, precisely cut pieces of chert in both binary and decimal arrangements were used as counterweights in balances, and several measuring sticks marked off in units of about 33.5 centimeters have been found; apparently this unit was the common measure of length, much like the English "foot," for many of the buildings are precisely constructed to this scale (F. R. Allchin 1974: 343).

Harappan art and religious architecture cannot compare with that of the same period in Mesopotamia, but they have a certain affecting quality. The most popular art was in the form of terra-cotta figurines,

10.5 This figure (11.4 cm high) of a dancing girl is one of the few bronzes discovered at Mohenjo-daro.

the majority of which were standing females, heavily adorned with jewelry.

The Decline of Harappan Civilization

Much of the interest in Harappan civilization concerns the possibility that it was suddenly destroyed by flood, drought, invasion, or some other calamity. The principal archaeological evidences relating to the demise of Harappan civilization are (1) the increasing heterogeneity of pottery and other artifact styles within the same area that in earlier centuries had been so uniform stylistically; (2) the "degradation" of art and architecture toward the end of the Harappan period—which has led some imaginative scholars to suppose that the Harappans had lost their sense of cultural unity and purpose; and (3) the discovery of about a score of human skeletons "sprawled" in the streets of Mohenjo-daro (Figure 10.6), supposedly in the aftermath of an invasion.

Hydrologist Robert Raikes suggests that Harappan civilization was

10.6   These skeletons lying in public areas of Mohenjo-daro have been interpreted as evidence of a great invasion, but there is little proof of this.

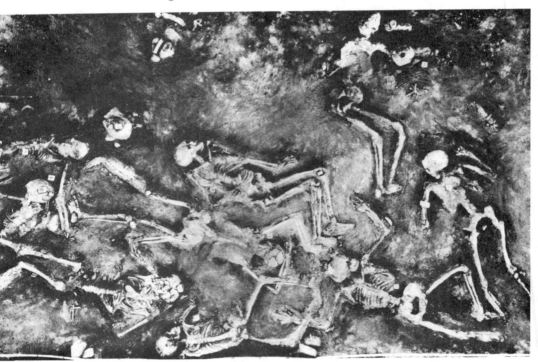

terminated by destruction of their fields and settlements through floods brought on by major shifts of the earth's crust near the mouth of the Indus River (1965). Raikes notes the lack of settlements in the area near the mouth of the river and also that the fossil beaches are many miles inland from the present coast. This is what one would expect if the river's route to the sea were blocked by an uplift of land near the mouth, since water would have been backed up into a large lake that eventually could have inundated the Harappan area. He believes that the late Harappan building projects for increasing the height of some of their larger structures may have been an effort to compensate for rising water levels.

Alternatively, Possehl (1980) notes that several strains of domesticated African millets were introduced to South Asia at about the time of the Harappan decline, and he suggests that these domesticates were better suited to this area than was the wheat-barley combination on which Harappan civilization was built. Thus, after the Harappan period, settlements shifted to areas most suitable to millet cultivation.

A more romantic suggestion is that the Harappan civilization was destroyed by repeated invasions of seminomadic peoples coming out of central Asia and Iran. The *Rig Veda,* the oldest surviving Vedic Sanskritic literature, describes the conquest of the dark-skinned natives of the Indus Plain by lighter-skinned Aryan invaders, and the Harappans have traditionally been associated with the former. The translation of Sanskritic literature, first accomplished in the sixteenth century, revealed major similarities between Sanskrit, Greek, and European and central Asian language families. These similarities were eventually traced to origins in the Caucasus Mountains of southern Russia and adjacent areas and associated with tall, long-headed, fierce peoples collectively referred to as *Aryans* or *Indo-Europeans,* who shortly after 1900 B.C. apparently invaded and influenced the cultures of India, central Asia, western Asia, and Europe. How they were able to do this is one of the great unresolved problems of history.

Bronze weapons and other artifacts traditionally associated with the Indo-Europeans have been found in the upper levels of some Harappan sites, and some scholars have identified these with the invaders referred to in the *Rig Veda.* It is difficult to substantiate these invasions, and many now believe that such invasions would have been at most only a minor part of the Harappan collapse.

The "invasion" of largely pastoral peoples into agricultural areas in the Harappan case and in similar circumstances elsewhere probably was more a gradual infiltration than a brutal massive invasion of the sort so often led by Yul Brynner and his colleagues in cinematographic histories. Overall, there may have been a gradual shift of power away from the Harappan heartland to peripheral groups in the South and East, where the "evolutionary potential" may have been higher because of the emergence there of rice agriculture, which is an extraordinarily productive crop. Political and cultural influence may well have gravitated to those areas outside the primarily wheat-growing regions of the Harappan sphere of influence (Fairservis 1975: 311).

Generally, the most productive way to look at the termination of Harappan civilization may be as the product of multiple causes. Continued pressure from peripheral groups, altering courses of the Indus River, droughts, floods, earthquakes—all may have contributed to the gradual abandonment of Harappan centers, and the final collapse probably resulted from the coincidence of several of these factors.

THE DEVELOPMENT OF INDIAN CIVILIZATION AFTER 1500 B.C.

After the Harappan downfall, many diverse cultures appeared throughout India and Pakistan, ranging from hunters and gatherers to highly sophisticated urban-based civilizations. The centers of power and influence gradually shifted from the Indus Valley to the great Ganges River Valley where, after about 1100 B.C., large cities were built and state-level political systems were formed. Many Harappan elements accompanied this transfer of power, including aspects of metallurgy, architecture, pottery styles, and agriculture.

The Indus Valley Civilization: Conclusions

There is far too little archaeological evidence from the Indus area to support an elaborate analysis of the evolution of cultural complexity there, but a few tentative summary points can be made.

The rigid planning and execution of Harappan settlements bespeaks a powerful centralized authority, perhaps rivaling that of ancient Egypt, but there is no evidence of the great tombs, palaces, and pyramids that accompanied theocratic states in Egypt and elsewhere. Some have suggested that the familiar Indian caste system was already in effect during the Harappan period and that this would have conferred the social control evident in the architecture (Service 1975: 246).

Because of its brevity, lack of great architecture, and absence of obvious wealth differential and militarism, some people have argued that the Harappan civilization was not a true state, merely a chiefdom (Service 1975).

But as Jacobson (1979) notes, recent discoveries cast doubt on this interpretation. Settlement pattern studies show at least a four-level site size hierarchy, consistent with Johnson's (1973) definition of a state as a society in which there are at least three levels in the administrative hierarchy. There was a form of writing which, even if not developed, conveyed a great deal of administrative and economic information, and recent excavations show a degree of military fortification and economic stratification not previously suspected.

In a reexamination of the Harappan data, Shaffer (1982) concludes that in some ways the analytical models applied to Mesopotamia and other early states are not really applicable to Harappa. He notes, for example, that compared to Mesopotamia, the Harappan culture did not seem to exhibit the same degree of cyclical rise and fall of state governments, and that metal objects were made in great numbers and distributed widely throughout the populace, in contrast to the use of such objects in Mesopotamia mainly as ritual and status objects. The significance of this difference in distribution of metal objects, Shaffer suggests, when combined with the other evidence, may be that

> in the Indus Valley, a technologically advanced, urban, literate culture was achieved without the usually associated social organzation based on hereditary elites, centralized political government (states, empires) and warfare (1982: 49)

Long-distance trade, particularly the flow of goods from the Indus Valley to Mesopotamia, has frequently been suggested as a key factor in the development—and decline—of Harappan civilization. Harappan seals and seal impressions have been found in limited quantities in Mesopotamia and along the Persian Gulf, and there clearly was some commerce between these areas, perhaps by way of ships sailing along the coast and caravans transversing the Iranian Plateau. Exactly which commodities would have been shipped from the Indus Valley westward is unknown, although steatite and a few other minerals and semiprecious stones would have been likely trade items. Commerce appears to have been very one-sided, however, with little going from Southwest Asia to the Indus area, and this has suggested to some that Harappan civilization may have been established and maintained mainly by Mesopotamian or Iranian states. Indeed, there are some Mesopotamian elements in the Indus cultures, such as carved stone boxes, dice, faience, wheeled vehicles, shaft-hole axes, religious art motifs, and the "ram-style" sculptural motif. But taken as a whole, long-distance trade seems to have had little importance in the evolution of cultural complexity in the Indus Valley. The volume of product exchange was very low and mainly in luxury items, and the movement of goods appears to have been accomplished through intermediaries in the Iranian Plateau, rather than through deliberate and directly administered trade between Harappans and Mesopotamians (Fairservis 1975: 297–98).

As in the case of Egypt and Mesopotamia, rates of population growth in the Indus Valley appear to have been slow, and there is no evidence of pressure on the agricultural systems until long after the Harappan civilization had collapsed.

It may be that advances in Harappan archaeology will be slow until the appearance of an archaeologist who also has a degree in hydraulic engineering and is rich, fluent in Urdu, and willing to spend his or her life on the problems of excavating beneath the Indus floodplain. It would also be a great help if someone discovered a bilingual inscription in which the Indus Valley script and some known language are used—something like the Rosetta Stone, in other words.

11

From Tribe to Empire
in North China

"Let the past serve the present."

Mao Tse-tung

At about 1800 B.C., just a century or so after Hammurabi had established a great empire in Southwest Asia, the people of North China began a period of development that was to take them from simple agricultural tribes to one of the most brilliant and complex civilizations of antiquity. Because scientific archaeology in China is only a few decades old and has been interrupted by wars and revolution, we still know only the outlines of these developments. Nonetheless, in terms of basic processes, the evolution of Chinese civilization appears to be yet another variation on the development theme we have noted in Mesopotamia, Egypt, and the Indus Valley.

The Ecological Setting

The modern political boundaries of China incorporate vastly different environments, ranging from the Himalayas to the Pacific shore, and people from many of these areas came to play some role in shaping Chinese civilization. But the initial transition from simple farming communities to complex societies had two centers: a primary focus in the middle Wei and Hsiang-ho river valleys and a secondary focus in the middle Yangtze Valley. Developments in these areas eventually overlapped, and both areas were affected to some extent by the tens of thousands of nomads who throughout early Chinese history interacted with the peoples along the margins of the agricultural zones.

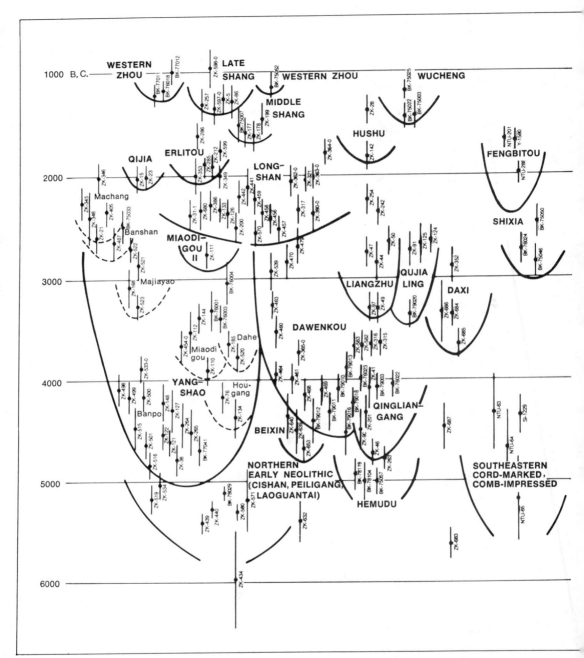

11.1 Arranging ancient China's cultural and spatial diversity is a complex matter
in which recent radiocarbon dates have been valuable clues. The length of the line
through each date represents the range of probable date, in that the actual date is
likely to fall somewhere within that range.

North China's developmental leadership was closely tied to its agricultural potential. Pleistocene winds blowing off the Gobi Desert covered parts of North China with a layer of loess that reached a depth of several hundred meters. The Hwang Ho (or "Yellow River"—from the color given it by the loess it carries) cuts through these loess plains, frequently changing its course, and through flooding and draining it has created a rich agricultural zone of lakes, marshes, and alluvial fields. Loess is the agricultural soil par excellence: it is organically rich, requires little plowing, and by capillary action manages to retain near the surface much of the sparse rain that falls on North China. Moreover, it can yield large crops with little fertilization, even under intensive cultivation.

Millet may have been domesticated elsewhere, but by about 3500 B.C., it was grown widely on the North China plains (K. C. Chang 1963: 94–95). Nutritionally as rich as wheat, millet is also quick-maturing and drought-resistant—making it admirably suited to the cold, arid plains of North China—and its stems can be used for food, fuel, and fodder. Sorghum and a few other crops were also cultivated in the early agricultural period, but it was millet, and later, rice and wheat, that provided the energy basis for the evolution of Chinese civilization.

11.2   The distribution of some of the major Neolithic cultures of China. Culture areas are defined on the basis of similarities in pottery, radiocarbon dates, and other data.

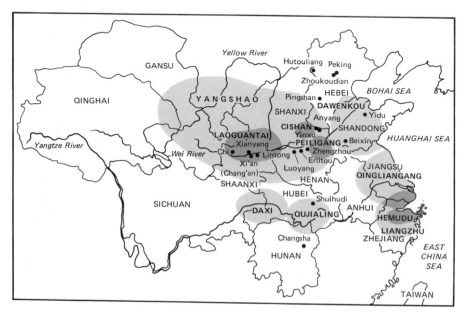

The many stone axes and adzes found in the earliest agricultural settlements in North China are a reflection no doubt of land-clearing operations to extend agriculture into the aboriginal grasslands and forests. Fire probably was also used for this purpose (Triestman 1972).

The first farmers here also depended for much of their food on hunting, gathering wild plants, and fishing—as evidenced by the hundreds of hooks, fish gorges, and net weights found. Pigs, domestic fowl, and later, cattle, sheep, and goats were eaten, but until very late in prehistoric times, hunting and gathering remained important sources of food.

THE YANG-SHAO CULTURE (CA. 5000 TO 2000 B.C.)

In a real sense, the first ancestors of the civilization we know imprecisely as "China" were the sturdy peasants of Yang-shao period villages like Pan-p'o-ts'un. Wearing rough clothes made of hemp, bunkered down in partially subterranean houses (Figure 11.3) to shield themselves from winter snows and summer heat, the people of Pan-p'o-ts'un followed the familiar agricultural cycle of China. Millet was the staple, pigs recycled wastes into what was even then perhaps a world-class cuisine, and cattle, sheep, and goats contributed their all in the form of milk, draft power, leather, and wool.

11.3   Reconstruction of a round house at Pan-p'o-ts'un. Digging the floor of the house a meter or more into the earth protected the inhabitants from cold winter winds.

The few hundred people at Pan-p'o-ts'un, like most of their neighbors, were probably self-sufficient in everything that really mattered except marriageable women.

Already in the pottery, jade-carvings, and other artifacts of these Yang-shao villages, we see the Oriental aesthetic sense for line and color. Stylized fish and animals grace some of the burnished pottery, and pottery marks suggest that the characters that eventually formed the written language were being developed.

Around the houses were many deep pits, presumably for storing millet and other commodities. No doubt most villagers were full-time agriculturalists, but some people engaged in silkworm cultivation, pottery manufacture, jade carving, and leather and textile production.

Pan-p'o-ts'un has been converted into a truly amazing museum. Most of the site has been enclosed in a building, with some of the most important houses and artifacts left in place to show how the community lived. More than 200 of the original inhabitants of this community are still there, their skeletons protruding from house floors, pits, and the periphery of the village.

Another example of China in the Yang-shao era is in the south, at Hemudu, in northern Zhejiang province. Excavations here in 1973–78 revealed a 7,000-year-old village of wooden houses built on piles along the shore of a small lake (K. C. Chang 1981: 152–53). The preservation of objects at this site is spectacular. Excavators found bone hoes, wooden shuttles for weaving, ivory carvings, and many plant and animal remains, including rice, bottle gourds, water chestnuts, domesticated water buffalo, pigs, dogs, and wild animals like tigers, elephants, and rhinoceroses.

Two aspects of Yang-shao life are of particular interest to students of cultural evolution. In the middle of Pan-p'o-ts'un was a distinctive building, much larger than the typical house and of different construction. To the Chinese excavators, this building seems most likely to have been a communal meeting hall; but one might also suspect that a bit of capitalistic inequality had infected the Yang-shao culture, and that this was the house of a "big man" or chief (Watson 1974). However, there are no evident signs of varying status in other artifacts at the site.

To get people to function together in states and empires, it is necessary to connect them with the larger social unit—even if it is simply by taxing everyone. As the owners of Wedgwood tea services know, use of the same pottery style does not necessarily mean political or social cohesion. But the extension of pottery styles over much of North China during the Yang-shao period may be our first clue that people were developing a corporate membership, on which the later Chinese states were constructed.

LUNGSHAN AND LUNGSHANOID CULTURES (?2300 TO 1850 B.C.)

The sentimentalist who believes in a distant and peaceful past, in a world of rustic simplicity and peace that was contaminated and destroyed by the emergence of the nation-state and its ills, can point to the prehistory of China as a possible case in point. In the early third millennium B.C., the people of North and central China—at least on the basis of our limited archaeological evidence—seem the very picture of egalitarian, peaceful villagers; but by the beginning of the second millennium B.C., everywhere there are signs of social rank and violence.

The transformation of the simple farming communities of third millennium B.C. China into more complex social and political forms began shortly after 2400 B.C., with the emergence of the *Lungshan* culture (variants of which are called *Lungshanoid*) in North and central China. Lungshan cultures, like the Yang-shao, are defined on the basis of similar styles of artifacts. Lungshan settlements are distinguished by highly burnished, wheel-made, thin-walled black pottery in many different vessel forms which is found, with minor stylistic variations, from the southeastern coast of China to the northern provinces. Very early Lungshan pottery and other diagnostic artifacts are found over most of the old Yang-shao heartland.

Anyone interested in the agonizing problems of cultural period subdivisions and establishing cultural relationships should read K. C. Chang's extended attempts (1977) to correlate radiocarbon dates with archaeological evidence in the matter of the Yang-shao and Lungshan cultures. Scores of difficult Chinese place names had to be integrated with almost as many phase subdivisions.

The central questions here are, what is the relationship between the Yang-shao and Lungshan cultures and what does the artificial diversity among the Lungshan cultures mean? The answer to both questions is that on the basis of the sketchy archaeological evidence, we cannot possibly know. It *seems*, however, that Yang-shao cultures in some places gave rise directly to Lungshan cultures, and that there were at least three different centers of Lungshan culture (K. C. Chang 1977: 155).

As with the Yang-shao, the Lungshan peoples lived mainly in villages made up of pit houses arranged around a central "long house," and virtually every Lungshan adult male was probably still a millet farmer who supplemented the family fortunes with hunting, collecting, and part-time craft production of pottery, jade, and a few other commodities. But Lungshan villages were, on the average, significantly larger than those of the Yang-shao period, and were likely occupied for longer periods of time. Lungshan agriculture, although still based on millet and a few domestic animals, seems to have been more intensive than that of the Yang-shao. The slash-and-burn, shifting agricultural system of Yang-shao times probably gave way to a permanent field system in the Lungshan period. Domestic poultry, sheep, and cattle became more important, and there is evidence of the increasing significance of rice agriculture in some southern areas.

There are also signs of change in social organization. Compared with Yang-shao graves, Lungshan burials exhibit significantly more variation in richness of grave goods, and there is greater specialization reflected in jade carving, pottery manufacture, and other crafts. Lungshan pottery and jade ornaments are so sophisticated and beautiful that they suggest at least some semispecialized craftsmen. In addition, Lungshan people sought knowledge through scapulimancy, the art of writing signs on bones, applying heat to the bone to crack it, and then interpreting the pattern of cracking to foretell the future. Archaeologist K. C. Chang interprets the appearance of this art in Lungshan times as a reflection of the rise of at least a semiprofessional class of shamans, an interpretation made credible by the fact that the character meaning *book* already appears on these bones and may signify the existence of specialized scribes.

At least one other significant development in Lungshan communities is the appearance of large walls of pounded earth around many settlements. Arrowheads, spears, daggers, and clubs appear frequently in Lungshan sites. Collectively, this evidence would seem to suggest at least some conflict.

Paul Wheatley concludes that the Lungshan cultures were a "stratified society in Service's sense of the term" (1971: 89), but that in economic and technological terms, the Lungshanoid communities were probably still largely self-sufficient and independent. Settlement patterns of this period are poorly known, but there is little evidence of population aggregation or regular spacing of settlements according to economic or administrative principles. Nonetheless, the transition to life in permanent villages and established agricultural fields was made over much of North China in the Lungshan period, from the western highlands into the northern Manchurian highlands and well into southern China.

Early Bronze Age China: The Shang Dynasty
(1850 B.C. to 1112 B.C.)

Much of what we know about *Shang* China comes from approximately thirty sites near the present city of Changchou where excavations have revealed deposits extending from the Lungshan period to late Shang times. During the Shang dynasty, China really became "China," in the sense that this period marked the first widespread use of the distinctively Chinese forms of writing, architecture, art, and ideology. Also during this period all the correlates of cultural complexity, such as monumental architecture, large population concentrations, occupational specialization, written records, gross differences in wealth, power, and prestige, and large public-works projects, appeared in full measure. The Shang dynasty has been divided into three phases: the Erh-li-t'ou, the Erh-li-kang, and the Yin.

ERH-LI-T'OU (CA. 1850 TO CA. 1650 B.C.)

The transition from the Lungshanoid cultures in North China to Shang civilization has often been perceived as a "sudden" development, but there are now several known sites where the transition has been documented as having been a very gradual process.

At the site of *Erh-li-t'ou*, for example, in levels dating to shortly after 1800 B.C., the persistence of the Lungshan level of cultural complexity is clearly evident: there were no monumental buildings, no written documents, no elaborate tombs, and the people still lived in wattle-and-daub pit houses arranged around a larger, more elaborately constructed long-house. As in the late Lungshan period, there is some evidence of walls around settlements, and there was also sophisticated and beautiful craftsmanship in pottery, carved jade, and turquoise. Some burials have richer collections of grave goods than others, but these differences are not significantly more pronounced than in Lungshan settlements. Some human skeletons show signs of mutilation and, in at least one case, an individual's hands were tied at the time of death or interment (Triestman 1972: 59).

Some Erh-li-t'ou phase settlements contained fish hooks, bells, pins, and projectile points made from bronze; and for the rest of the Shang period, bronzeworking was to become one of the most highly developed crafts, and bronze items were consistently used to denote status and wealth differentials.

In Western societies especially, there is a tendency to think of cultural changes as often being caused by technological change. The invention of the locomotive, for example, seems to have radically altered nineteenth-century Western society. When we look at ancient China, there is a temptation to see a culture shaped and formed by the invention of bronzeworking and ironworking. Bronzeworking seems to have been an indigenous development in Shang civilization, probably made possible by the high-temperature kilns first used to fire pottery. The requisite copper and tin could be found within several hundred kilometers of the Shang homeland, and various processes using clay models and the lost-wax process were known. The first great diffusion of Shang artifacts, which probably marked both the rise of national consciousness and ramifying political and economic networks that underlay the emergence of Shang civilization, was also marked by the spread of bronze artifacts.

But the use of bronze seems to have been mainly a stylistic phenomenon rather than a great technological advance. Though lovely to look at, the myriad bronze Shang vessels offer few culinary advantages over ceramics, and there is no evidence that bronze weapons revolutionized Shang-period warfare. And for clearing forests—which was an important part of the Shang expansion—stone axes and hoes would probably have worked at least as well as bronze tools which were, in any case, a luxury item.

Much has been made in the popular press of the very early bronze technology of Southeast Asia. Here, by 4500 B.C., people at sites like Ban Chiang, in Thailand, were already using cast-bronze spearheads and ornaments (Bayard 1979). The practice of archaeology in the heavily vegetated and humid expanses of Southeast Asia is difficult, especially when these expanses are exploding with bombs and gilded with "yellow rain." Thus, we know relatively little about these early bronze-using cultures. But it seems likely that their precocious use of bronze was a result of the proximity of copper and tin deposits, and that their evolution to cultural complexity followed that of the north in all essential elements, and occurred much later.

ERH-LI-KANG PHASE (CA. 1650 TO 1400 B.C.)

With the *Erh-li-kang phase* we move into the historical period in ancient China, and from the end of this period on there are some written documents to supplement the archaeological record.

The Erh-li-kang phase is best documented archaeologically at the cluster of settlements near Chengchou. The central area of Erh-li-kang phase settlement was a roughly rectangular arrangement of buildings extending about 3.4 square kilometers, much of which was enclosed by a pounded-earth wall some 36 meters wide at the base and 9.1 meters in height—as estimated from the segments still remaining (K. C. Chang 1976). The central area of the site is thought to have been the residence and ceremonial center of the ruling elite, and around it were thousands of pit houses, animal pens, shops, storage pits, and other features that make it clear that life in Shang China differed considerably from that of Neolithic times. Based on the number and quality of the artifacts found, there must have been hundreds of skilled, full-time craftsmen at Chengchou. In one area thousands of pieces of animal and human bone were recovered, much of it already fashioned into fish hooks, awls, axes, and hairpins. In another area were more than a dozen pottery kilns, each surrounded by masses of broken and overfired pottery. No jade, leather, or textile workshops have been found, but the circulation of these products at this time is well documented.

But the Chengchou craftsmen really displayed their skill in working bronze. Large areas were given over to workshops for casting fish hooks, axes, projectile points, and various ornaments. A kind of "mass production" was achieved by using multiple molds, made by impressing a clay slab with the forms of six arrowheads, each impression connected by a thin furrow to a central channel. A second clay mold was placed over the first, the two bound together, and then molten bronze was poured in. After cooling, the individual points could be sawn off from the central stem.

There may also be some indication in the mortuary practices that social organization was becoming more complex. Several tombs and graves have been excavated and have been reported to include human sacrifices and masses of luxury items.

Both archaeological evidence and ancient documents written after the Shang period indicate that society during the Erh-li-kang phase was headed by a king, who ruled through a hierarchically arranged nobility. Commoners were conscripted for public works and military service; there were highly organized and incessant military campaigns; and many settlements were apparently integrated into an organized inter-village system of commerce (Wheatley 1971). It has not been determined if there were large-scale irrigation systems, but at Chengchou at least a canal system was in use, perhaps to carry water to the settlement, or else to carry drainage water or sewage out of the complex (ibid.).

The great mass of Shang people, however, lived much as they did before, in villages of pit houses located along river systems, subsisting on the same kinds of crops and agricultural technology as had people of previous millennia. As K. C. Chang observes: "The transition from neolithic Lungshan culture . . . to the Shang civilization is a quantum jump of the highest order in the quality of life for the elite, yet there is no discernible corresponding change in the technology of food production" (1976: 10).

YIN PHASE (CA. 1400 TO 1112 B.C.)

The last and most brilliant phase of Shang civilization, the *Yin phase,* seems to have begun about 1384 B.C., when the Shang king, P'an-keng, is reported to have moved his capital to the city of An-yang, in Honan province.

Excavations at An-yang and contemporary sites in this area have been conducted intermittently since the 1920s, but the publication of this research is far from complete. Scores of sites within an area of about twenty-four square kilometers have been tested, and the evidence suggests that the complex at An-yang include a large ceremonial and administrative center surrounded by smaller dependent hamlets and craft centers (Wheatley 1971: 93). True to tradition, most peasants still lived in small pit houses a few meters in diameter—not very different from those of 2,000 years earlier. Scattered throughout the settlement were granaries, pottery kilns, storage pits, bone and bronze workshops, animal pens, ditches, and familiar features of ancient Chinese life.

No city wall has been found at An-yang, but apparently for the first time in Chinese history monumental buildings appear. The largest of these was about sixty meters long, rectangular in form, with large stone and bronze column bases, and founded on a large platform of compacted earth. There were at least fifty-three structures of this type (though somewhat smaller) in one group at An-yang, arranged in three main clusters. Although not lavish in construction, these buildings are surrounded by scores of human and animal sacrificial burials as well as many pits containing royal records written on oracle bones and numerous small structures thought to be for service personnel (K. C. Chang 1976: 48). Near the cluster of buildings is a cemetery with eleven large graves, replete with lavish, expensive burial goods and many human sacrificial burials—the whole complex surrounded by 1,200 smaller, much less lavish burials. Elsewhere, a complex of ceremonial buildings at Hsiao-T'un was dedicated with the sacrifice of 852 people, 15 horses,

10 oxen, 18 sheep, 35 dogs, and 5 fully equipped chariots and charioteers (Wheatley 1971). Generally, there are many burials certain to arouse the suspicions of a coroner.

The Shang ceremonial and administrative structures are perhaps not as impressive in size or cost as the ziggurats and temples of Mesopotamia, but the level of occupational specialization, the immense wealth of the burials, and the intensity of organization of the agricultural and economic systems reminds one of the Mesopotamian city-states of the late fourth millennium B.C.

Little urbanism and only a thin distribution of bronzeworking and a few other Shang cultural traits appear in most of non-Shang China at this time, and most of these non-Shang cultures were probably still at a predominantly Neolithic level of development.

Late in the Yin phase of the Shang dynasty (about 1200 B.C.), the written language had evolved to the point that texts from this period give us a detailed portrait of Shang life. Over 3,000 phonetic, ideographic, and pictographic characters were in use, of which about 12,000 have been identified, and more than 160,000 inscribed shells (of which only some have been translated) and numerous inscriptions in bronze or stone date to this period.

According to the texts, the late Shang rulers held sway over a territory extending from the Pacific shore to Shensi province in the West, and from the Yangtze River in the South to southern Hupeh in the North. At the apex of Shang society was the king, who ruled directly on many affairs of state and who was assisted by a complex hierarchy of nobles possessing considerable local autonomy in their respective territories. These lords were charged with defending the homeland, supplying men for armies and public-works projects, and with collecting and contributing state taxes. Toward the end of the Shang period, many nobles apparently achieved almost feudal status and were virtually independent in their own domains. But the king was still considered to have superior supernatural powers and to be the pivot of all ritual procedures. The kingdom was ringed with "barbarians," and Shang kings often granted them almost complete autonomy in exchange for peaceful relationships (Wheatley 1971: 63).

On occasion, royal armies of up to about 30,000 men were conscripted and led by the nobles against insurgent "barbarians" and neighboring principalities. The basis of the army was the horse-drawn chariot, supported by infantrymen equipped with bronze-tipped arrows and laminated bows, and royal records indicate that military campaigns often incurred and inflicted frightful casualties. Staggering quantities of

11.4   Royal Shang tomb at Hou Chia Chuang, Honan province. Note multiple human sacrifices.

plunder were often taken, along with thousands of prisoners, most of whom were apparently sacrificed or enslaved (Wheatley 1971).

The agricultural system seems to have been essentially the same as previously, with millet, wheat, rice, and vegetables the major crops, and cattle, sheep, pigs, and poultry, the only "new" domestic animal being the water buffalo. The proportions of these crops and animals may have been shifted somewhat, with wheat and rice expanding their range at the expense of millet, but the evidence for this is questionable. There is little evidence of large irrigation systems anywhere in the Shang domain, and hunting and gathering still supplied a large part of the diet. The mammalian faunal remains from An-yang include massive quantities of boar, deer, bear, and other hunted animals, including a few elephants, rhinoceroses, leopards, and even part of a whale (K. C. Chang 1977: 138–39). Apparently intravillage trade in foodstuffs was voluminous.

Local occupational specialization was considerable. Many villages lacked one or more of the more important handicraft workshops, suggesting that products were exchanged among these settlements (Wheatley 1971: 76). The discovery of large caches of agricultural implements (3,500 stone sickles, new and used, in a single pit at one site, for example) may indicate a degree of centralized management of both agriculture and craft production (ibid.). The Shang even had a form of money, in the form of strings of cowrie shells.

Toward the end of the Shang period, there were many walled towns and villages in North and central China, and, compared to earlier periods, a much greater proportion of the populace lived in these semiurban settings. But if we compare the settlement size distribution of late Shang China—or rather what we estimate it to have been—with those of Mesopotamia or Mesoamerica at a comparable level of development, it is clear that Shang China was a much less urbanized society. There were no settlements the size of Ur or Teotihuacán.

We cannot know the mind of the Shang Chinese in any detailed sense, but their artifacts give us clues as to what they thought of the world. Of all ancient peoples, they seem to have been the most concerned with symmetry. All temples and tombs were oblong or square and oriented to the four cardinal directions. Bronzes were always symmetrical, and even the messages inscribed on turtle shells for divinations were repeated on the right and left sides. The world was conceived of as square, the wind as blowing from four quarters, and four groups of foreigners were thought to live on China's borders. Throughout their art, architecture, and literature, elements appear two by two, four by four, and in other intricate but symmetrical arrangements.

The texts and inscriptions tell us that the Shang nobles felt in constant and clear communication with their ancestors, whom they consulted through oracles about the best actions to take in multitudes of situations.

A recent bumper sticker declared "If I can't take it with me, I ain't going"—a sentiment probably very agreeable to Shang rulers. Tomb after tomb is stocked with everything from chariots to rice. And they also employed that most efficient of all incentives to a devoted domestic staff: at the ruler's own death, all his domestic retainers were apparently killed and buried with him. Unlike feudal European nobility, few Shang nobles feared poisoning by members of their households.

Ancient Imperial China (1100 B.C. to A.D. 220)

Had we the means to see it in all its splendor, ancient imperial China may well have appeared to us as the most complex and colorful civilization of all antiquity. By about 1100 B.C., the *Chou empire* was already established (Figure 11.5) (K. C. Chang 1981: 156), and it and its

11.5   China under the Chou and Han dynasties.

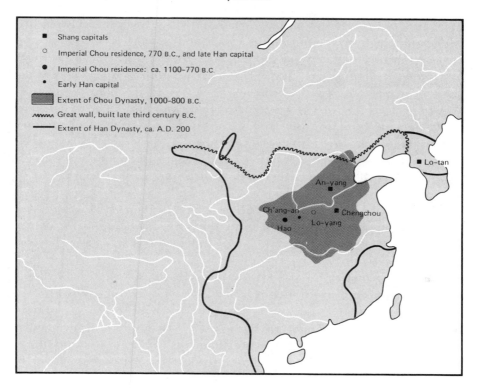

11.6   The burial clothes of a princess of the late second century B.C. The suit was
made of over 2,000 jade tiles tied together with gold wire.

successors arranged much of China in a feudal system that led to the
growth of cities, great cycles of peace followed by warfare, and baroque
administrative hierarchies. Families of nobles or commoners would rise
to power, make war on their neighbors, extend their kingdoms, and
then collapse under the onslaught of competing warlords. Through it
all, exquisite bronzes, porcelains, pots, and jewelry were made and
lavished on the rich; untold thousands of people were sacrificed to be
buried with their rulers; and millions lived and died in the eternal
agricultural cycle of rural China.

By 500 B.C. ironworking became widespread, and iron agricultural
tools were in common use. Iron weapons, mass burials, and military
annals tell of a savage form of warfare, not at all like the depersonalized
modern combat of tanks, missiles, and automatic weapons. Men in
armor fought at close quarters with swords and knives on battlefields
swarming with chariots, cavalry, and bowmen.

At about the time iron was introduced, Confucius (551–479 B.C.)
lived and taught and, together with the spread of Buddhism in the
third century A.D., moved much of Chinese thought forever beyond
the reach of the foreigner.

Amid the panoply of arts, crafts, and religion, the prosaic elements
of agriculture were also changing. After 500 B.C. great irrigation works
were brought into use, allowing the intensive cultivation of wet-rice
species as well as many other crops. This in turn supported the tremendous population densities of China. Along with the introduction of the
ox-drawn plough and the evolution of precise crop-rotation practices,

Chinese agriculture underwrote the impressive cultural elaborations we associate with the *Ch'in* (221–202 B.C.) and *Han* (202 B.C.–A.D. 120).

The world's first known imperial census in A.D. 1–2 listed 57,700,000 people, at least 10 percent of whom lived in rectangular wooden towns with populations of up to 250,000. Coins circulated, schools flourished, and a rich store of literature was created.

Through it all, along the northern and western frontiers, the nomadic horsemen and herders of Asia pressed on the periphery of successive empires. The Great Wall, built about 100 B.C., was meant to keep the nomad out and the farmer in, but it was probably not too successful. Throughout Chinese history there was a constant interchange between sedentary and nomadic cultures.

We tend to think of China as a static civilization with ancient and fixed forms. But from the long-term perspective, it has been a varied, ineffably complex cultural pageant.

The Origins of Cultural Complexity in North China: Summary and Conclusions

By Mesopotamian standards, at least, early Chinese society was less urban and less given to monumental architecture than were the Uruk and Sumerian peoples, although in later Chinese history the country became heavily urbanized.

The literature on the causes and consequences of urbanism is enormous, and many hypotheses have been suggested to account for why people aggregate in settlements of different sizes under different conditions. Unfortunately, the archaeological evidence from China during the critical periods is not sufficiently complete to evaluate the several possibilities. Some have suggested that warfare was important in determining the settlement size distribution in ancient China, and in fact warfare did have a profound influence on Chinese developments. But warfare, too, seems to be simply another—and somewhat variable—expression of more fundamental changes going on within societies as their complexity and differentiation increase.

One factor of continual importance in all Chinese developments was the great spread of nomadic and seminomadic peoples who lived on the borders of the agricultural heartland. Some of the earliest documents attesting to the rise of the Chinese state (K. C. Chang 1981), for example, imply that the Chou Empire was initiated by the movement of the warlord Tai Wang to the central Shaanxi province under pressure from his nomadic neighbors. And Owen Lattimore's comprehensive history

(1951) of relationships between nomad and farmer in China argues persuasively for the crucial role of this relationship in the formation of all later Chinese empires.

Turning to the major similarities between ancient Chinese developments and those elsewhere, in China too one of the first steps was an increasingly intensive and productive agricultural system, coupled with sedentary village communities. As elsewhere, this stage was followed by the rapid extension of pottery styles over a large region and a concurrent increased variability in residential architecture and mortuary complexes. And while monumental architecture may have been somewhat minimized and belated in ancient China, the great wall around Chengchou and other features are examples of at least some investment in "wasteful" monumental projects.

Ultimately, China fell into the same cyclical pattern of expansion and collapse we documented in the other ancient civilizations (Lattimore 1951). It is as if some internal limiting factors exist that restrain growth past a certain point, at least until certain evolutionary conditions are present.

12

Secondary States and Empires of the Old World

Agricola gave . . . official assistance to the building of temples, public squares, and . . . man-
sions. . . . He trained the sons of the chiefs in
the liberal arts. . . . And so the Britons were
gradually led on to the amenities that make vice
agreeable—arcades, baths, sumptuous banquets.
They spoke of such novelties as "civilization,"
when really they were only a feature of enslave-
ment.

Tacitus

To refer to the ancient glories of Greece, Germany, Thailand, and
other cultural centers as "secondary" states, as compared to the "primary" states of Mesopotamia, Egypt, the Indus Valley, Mesoamerica,
Peru, and China, is to imply, perhaps, more of a difference than existed.
In many ways these secondary states were independent developments—
creations of their own environments, peoples, and unique histories. But
if we look strictly at relative ages, internal functional diversity and integration, and population densities, these secondary states were less
complex than the primary states and were to some extent influenced
by them.

It is far beyond the scope of this book—and the author's competence—
to review these later, less complex political systems in any detail, and
they are mentioned here mainly to underscore the point that from
about 6000 B.C. on, none of the evolving political systems of the world
developed in isolation. World history from that date to the present is a
dizzyingly complex tapestry in which to separate individual strands and

even patterns is to do some degree of violence to the whole. The reader may also wish to consider anew the biblical prophecy that "the last shall be first," a sentiment repeatedly demonstrated in Old World culture history, where "peripheral" political systems often rose to imperial power.

Europe and the Mediterranean

Until the sixth millennium B.C., "Barbarian Europe"—the great forests and grasslands beyond the Aegean Sea and extending north into Great Britain and Russia—was a wilderness inhabited only by hunters and foragers whose major cultural achievements were probably a phenomenal skill at hunting deer and a theology based on the worship of oak trees.

But by 6000 B.C., a Mediterranean complement of domestic grains, cows, and sheep—and the technology to exploit them—had moved up the Danube into central Europe. People lived in small clusters of wooden huts, often with their animals, and farmed narrow plots near rivers and streams. Some of the spread of this form of agricultural settlement in Europe is marked after 5000 B.C. by pottery decorated with incised, linear patterns—the *Bandkeramik* style. Unlike that of the semiarid plains of the Middle East and the Mediterranean littoral, however, the agricultural way of life in Europe proper required clearing thick forests and grasslands, at first by cutting down the trees, later by plowing.

By 3000 B.C. agricultural villages were to be found from Great Britain far into eastern Russia. There were hundreds of local resource specializations, but most of these settlements subsisted mainly on domesticated cereals and cattle. Copper axes and ornaments were widely distributed, especially in central Europe and the Balkans.

The first great evolutionary center in Europe and extreme western Asia was along the Mediterranean shore, especially in Greece, Palestine, Anatolia, Crete, and Italy (Figure 12.1). By 2000 B.C. there were large trading cities in Anatolia, Palestine, and at Knossos and elsewhere on Crete. The Minoan civilization based on Crete and the later Mycenaean cultures centered on the Greek mainland were highly complex, class-stratified, aggressive states.

To the north, temperate Europe did not match the Aegean world in cultural complexity in the centuries before the rise of Greece and Rome, even with the spread of copper and iron technology and the de-

12.1 Between 2000 and 1000 B.C. the Aegean became a thriving center of international commerce. Highly skilled potters, metal-smiths, and other craftsmen imported raw materials from the Near East and Egypt and turned them into luxury goods for local consumption and export.

mands of the Mediterranean markets for European raw materials. Although the peoples of France and Great Britain built huge stone monuments like Stonehenge and may have enjoyed one of the world's most diverting mythologies and moral codes (as in the *Nibelungenleid* or *The Wicker Man*), the evidence suggests thousands of years of low-level cultural complexity built around tribal chiefdoms whose wealth and powers derived from trade and conquest.

Population densities were heaviest in the central European areas where rivers supplied broad alluvial fields, but after 3000 B.C. villages appeared in light to heavy densities over almost every area where the environment permitted stock raising and cereal agriculture. The areas where this kind of subsistence was possible were greatly expanded by the introduction (perhaps from the Near East) of the animal-drawn plow. In the absence of an arid climate or alluvial soils, it is difficult for the agriculturalist to compete with wild vegetation and to renew the fertility of the soil. But the plow gave these early European farmers a way to expose the soil for seeding, and it contributed to weed control

12.2   Europe in the early first millennium B.C. was occupied mainly by farmers, with few towns except along major trade routes originating in the Mediterranean world. But as this map shows, there was a rapid spread of Celtic-speaking cultures toward the end of the first millennium B.C., and there was also a gradual replacement of bronze tools by iron implements.

and soil fertility by plowing under vegetation (although the deep plowing of modern times was a later invention).

The Hallstatt and La Tene cultures of first millennium B.C. Europe flourished in a period of rapid population expansion, migrations of various ethnic groups, reformation of trade routes along lines dictated by Mediterranean cultures, and other major social changes.

With the expansion of Roman power between 200 B.C. and well into the first millennium A.D., the character of Europe was forever changed. It became a hybrid mix of Greek, Middle Eastern, and native elements.

Africa

Africa is so rich in gold, silver, iron, jewels, ivory, palm oil, and other resources that it is difficult to appreciate its formidable ecological barriers to the origins and spread of domestication, agriculture, and complex cultural organization. The enormous Sahara Desert, expanding and contracting with Pleistocene and post-Pleistocene climatic changes, has almost always isolated most of Africa from the critical mass of Near Eastern and Mediterranean cultures. And even in the more humid sub-Saharan regions the dense vegetation, poor soils, and unpredictable rainfall make large-scale intensive agriculture unproductive for the primitive cultivator. Nor do the great rivers, like the Niger, have the regular regimes, large semiarid alluvial plains, or latitude that make the Nile, Tigris and Euphrates, and Yellow river valleys so productive. To make matters worse, Africa has a veritable horror show of diseases, including a tsetse-fly–borne cattle illness that barred pastoralists from many areas, and malaria, which recurrently wiped out human populations in the more tropical areas.

Given these and other ecological problems, the surprising thing about African cultural evolution is not that complex societies failed to develop there as independently and early as they did elsewhere; it is that early African societies managed to produce the sophisticated arts, crafts, and religious and political systems that they did. Indeed, post-Pleistocene Africa's cultural history is an object lesson in human inventiveness and adaptability in the face of an extreme environment.

Sub-Saharan Africa of the last few millennia B.C. was probably a rich blend of hunting, foraging, fishing, and agricultural societies, with extensive trade networks in gold, salt, and foodstuffs.

The character of all these cultures was changed radically, however, by the introduction (beginning about 500 B.C.) of an ironworking technology, perhaps from Nok, in West Africa, or from Katuruka in East Africa.

The first five centuries A.D. saw the rapid spread over much of Africa of agriculturalists using iron tools and weapons and subsisting in part on indigenous domesticates like sorghum and squash, and on domestic cattle and other animals. Only in a few arid wastes like the Kalahari were these agriculturalists unsuccessful in displacing the stone age hunters who were the heirs of the millions-of-years-old tradition of African hunting-foraging.

In contrast to the earlier-held view that the first African states were "contact-states," created by the economic and political "touch" of the

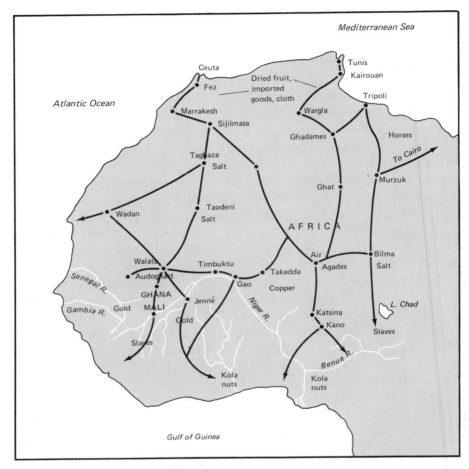

12.3   Trade routes and commodities in the west African states of Mali, Ghana, and Songhai in the early first millennium A.D.

established North African and Egyptian states, it now seems more reasonable to see sub-Saharan indigenous states as products of their own cultural matrix. The rapid population growth associated with the introduction of agriculture to these areas, the rising spiral of trade in gold, copper, salt, and slaves, and the sporadic influences of distant Mediterranean and Asian empires probably all combined to produce the rich chiefdoms and states known in Africa in the second millennium A.D.

Archaeologists are just beginning to unravel the history of these complex cultures, and it is beyond the scope of this book to review them in detail. Most seem to have been marked by some public buildings and to have been composed of a ruler and an upper class who organized and taxed a complex economic system composed of farmers, herders, miners, ironworkers, traders, and religious leaders. Cemeteries often show great variations of wealth and, presumably, social status.

By the sixteenth century, much of West Africa was divided among several states, all of them locked into trade networks that ultimately fed hundreds of products to the old civilizations of the Mediterranean or Asia.

After the sixteenth century, Africa fell increasingly under the control of non-Africans, and only in the last fifty years have most Africans retrieved their autonomy. They were held in thrall for so long by outsiders because of their inferior economic position, but also because European-introduced diseases killed many people and because of slavery: the African slave trade was organized and profited from by Africans well before the sixteenth century; some have estimated that nearly as many African slaves were shipped north into the Near Eastern and Mediterranean areas as were eventually carried to the New World.

Asia

Outside of Eurasia, nomadic pastoralists ranged from the eastern shores of the Black Sea to the Gobi Desert and eventually came to represent a major force in European and Asian developments. Domestic horses and camels were in use by the mid-second millennium B.C. in much of this area, and with the addition of two-wheeled carts, the development of a diet based on milk products rather than meat, and the emergence of an aggressive chiefdomlike command structure, Eurasian nomads terrorized Europe and sacked China time and time again.

In Southeast Asia, not only do we not know many of the most crucial links in the culture history (in part because of poor climatic conditions for archaeological preservation), but what we do know flagrantly contradicts our most comforting archaeological expectations. As Bronson notes, recent Southeast Asian culture history

> contains such disconcerting paradoxes as cannibals and collecting groups with alphabets of their own (the Batak of Sumatra and the Tagbanwa of Palawan), hunter-gatherers with the ability to make excellent steel (some Punan groups in Borneo), and even (as in nineteenth century northern Vietnam) complex and populous states without settlements that can readily be called cities. (1980: 262)

At least some of these developments, however, are the direct result of outside contacts and, generally, only northern Vietnam can be said to have the usual hallmarks of cultural complexity before about 100 B.C. The great monuments of Thailand, Cambodia, and Vietnam are all products of the late first and second millennia A.D. and are intertwined with Chinese history.

Japan's rich history was influenced by China at various critical points, but it has always been so distinctive and self-contained that on some levels it can only be understood in its own terms. But in Japan, too, the familiar developmental stages of ancient cultural complexity were followed. The initial spread of pottery styles, followed by monumental architecture and vast wealth differentials, culminated in the development of the most rigid and complex social hierarchies the world has ever seen.

To those familiar with its culture, Japan—like ancient Athens and many other early civilizations—is an object lesson in that the blunt analytical tools of archaeology, with their fixation on economy, environment, and architecture, can reveal very little of the most fascinating aspects of these societies.

Other Areas

The cultures on the extreme fringes of the Old World, from northern Scandinavia to Hawaii, repeat the common fact that most aspects of cultural complexity are the partial products of technology and agricultural productivity. Reindeer herders in Lapland and the yam farmers and pig herders of Oceania represent gradients of cultural complexity, but nowhere in these marginal areas do we find the towns, the libraries, the many-leveled hierarchical arrangements of functional interdependence, or the regional political powers that mark states and empires.

In the case of Hawaii and the many other islands of the green and coral archipelagos of the Pacific, at least, and in many other lush areas of the ancient world, it is unlikely that the absence of developed cultural complexity should be considered entirely a liability.

13

The Origins of
Complex Cultures in Mesoamerica

"The Near East," Sir Mortimer Wheeler once remarked, "is the land of archaeological sin." Such
a statement could have been made only by a man
who had never worked in Mesoamerica.

Kent V. Flannery

In Easter week of 1519, Hernán Cortez landed on the coast of Veracruz, Mexico, and began a military campaign that would end in the
crushing defeat of Aztec civilization. For perhaps 30,000 years before
Cortez's arrival, the peoples of the Old and New Worlds had had so
little contact that they were physically different and spoke entirely different languages. But here is the curious thing: when Cortez traveled
the road from Veracruz to the Aztec capital near Mexico City, he
passed through cities, towns, villages, markets, and irrigated fields; he
saw slavery, poverty, potentates, farmers, judges, churches, massive pyramids, roads, boats, pottery and textiles; in short, he encountered a
world whose almost every aspect he could understand in terms of his
own experience as an urban Spaniard of the sixteenth century.

There were of course many dissimilarities between the Spanish and
Aztec peoples. Neither the Aztecs nor their predecessors had horses,
ocean-going ships, or alphabetic writing systems. And the psychological
differences between the Aztecs and their European conquerers were
probably particularly profound. The Spanish, despite their imperialism
and murderous ferocity in warfare, viewed the Aztecs' preoccupations
with death and human sacrifice with abhorrence, and the Aztecs found
many aspects of Christianity both evil and incomprehensible.

Yet despite profound differences in their respective morals and ideas,
the Spanish and the Aztecs were fundamentally culturally alike: they

lived in hierarchically organized, class-structured, complex, expansion-
istic empires, with state churches, intensive agricultural and industrial
systems, and many other features in common.

The parallel appearance of complex societies in Mesoamerica (the
area from northern Mexico to southern Guatemala), Mesopotamia, and
elsewhere suggests that similar processes and factors were operating in
these different areas.

The Ecological Setting

In Pre-Columbian Mesoamerica (Figure 13.2), four areas seem to have
been developmental centers: the South Gulf Coast, the Valley of Mexico, the Valley of Oaxaca, and the Mayan lowlands. The evolution of
complex Mesoamerican cultures was much influenced by three general
ecological conditions: (1) the millions of years of mountain-building
volcanic activity, which left Mesoamerica a still trembling land of tow-
ering mountains and circumscribed valleys, and which in many areas
compressed extremely different flora, fauna, and climates into close
proximity, making transport and communication difficult; (2) the absence of any domesticable animal suitable for providing milk, transport, or draft power; and (3) the virtual absence of large river systems
that could be used year-round to irrigate crops—although in some
areas intensive well- and flood-irrigation was practiced.

As in all early civilizations, in Mesoamerica a few plant and animal
species were in effect the power base of cultural evolution. Given the
technology of these early civilizations, it must also be remembered that
not just any domesticated plants and animals would do: there had to
be a reliable, voluminous carbohydrate source and sufficient plant and
animal proteins—with the whole comprising enough vitamins on a
daily basis that sound nutrition resulted. In Mesoamerica most people
lived on maize, beans, squash, and peppers, augmented mainly by cactus and other fruits and protein from such mainstays as rabbits, deer,
and dogs.

The Archaeological Record of Early Complex Mesoamerican
Societies (ca. 1600 B.C. to A.D. 1524)

Although the domestication of maize, beans, squash, peppers, and other
Mesoamerican plants was well under way by 4000 B.C., the first docu-
mented sedentary agricultural communities date to only about 1600
B.C. Among the interesting aspects of these first villages is that they ap-

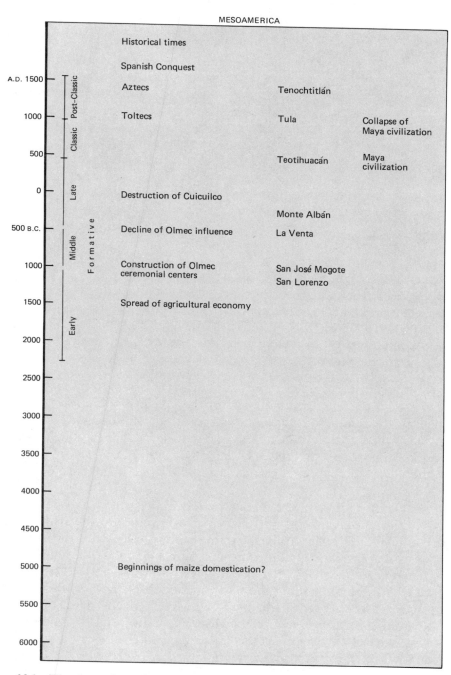

MESOAMERICA

	Historical times		
	Spanish Conquest		
A.D. 1500	Aztecs	Tenochtitlán	
1000	Toltecs	Tula	Collapse of Maya civilization
500		Teotihuacán	Maya civilization
0	Destruction of Cuicuilco		
		Monte Albán	
500 B.C.	Decline of Olmec influence	La Venta	
1000	Construction of Olmec ceremonial centers	San José Mogote San Lorenzo	
1500	Spread of agricultural economy		
2000			
2500			
3000			
3500			
4000			
4500			
5000	Beginnings of maize domestication?		
5500			
6000			

Post-Classic · Classic · Late — Formative (Middle) · Early

13.1 The chronology of Mesoamerica.

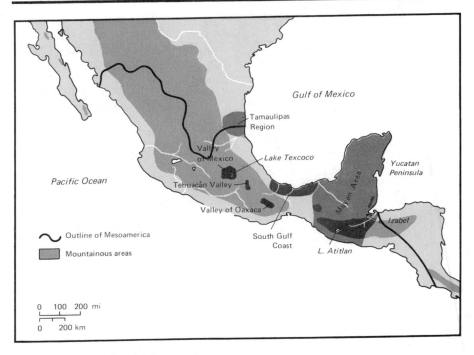

13.2   The geography of Mesoamerica.

peared at about the same time in many different areas, from the lowland coasts to the highland valleys, and they seemed to appear quite
suddenly. We cannot distinguish the ages of these early settlements
with sufficient precision to be able to see short-term changes, but there
are no known villages at 1700 B.C. in Mesoamerica, and yet by 1300
B.C. there were probably thousands—a rapid change by archaeological
standards.

A second intriguing aspect of this period is the similarity of these
early villages. From the hot, wet Guatemalan lowlands to the arid Tehuacán Valley, the earliest villages were made in essentially the same
way, were of approximately the same size, and their inhabitants apparently led very similar lives (Flannery 1976a: 13–15). Almost all houses
(Figure 13.3) were built using the wattle-and-daub method—walls were
constructed of woven reed sheets, plastered with mud, and dried by the
hot Mexican sun. Roofs were of thatched materials. Houses were seldom larger than four by six meters, with a tamped clay floor on which
fine sand was scattered; walls were whitewashed or plastered with limed
clay.

About 90 percent of all known *Early Formative* (1600 to 1100 B.C.)

sites were two hectares or less and contained ten to twelve houses inhabited by a total of about fifty to sixty people, but some settlements
were larger, such as San Lorenzo at about fifty-three hectares and
Chimalhuacán at about forty-five hectares.

Every extensively excavated Early Formative household has yielded
all of the following items: fragments of grinding stones; storage pits;
pieces of large ceramic storage jars; bones of cottontail rabbits; carbonized maize fragments; and broken pieces of ceramic charcoal braizers
(Flannery and Winter 1976: 36). In addition, ovens, middens, and
graves are very common. While the proportion of plant and animal
foods varied somewhat, all villages probably grew maize, beans, squash,
peppers, and some other crops and hunted deer and rabbits. Each village, or each extended family, may have had a specialist who did pressure flaking of stone, leatherworking, or a similar craft, and individual
villages may have concentrated on specialities like salt production,
feather weaving, shellworking, grinding stone manufacture, and the
like.

13.3 Mexico's first agriculturalists probably lived in wattle-and-daub houses
thatched with straw, much like these in a village of Nahuatl-speakers in Morelos,
Mexico.

As in Mesopotamia, China, and elsewhere, then, the background to the origins of complex society in Mesoamerica was a great scatter of relatively simple agricultural villages, where the mechanics of producing a reliable, expandable food supply had been mastered. So uniform and simple were these early Mesoamerican villages that one might suspect that their inhabitants invented complex society just to have something to break up the monotony of daily life. But the matter seems somewhat more complicated than that. Many areas of Mesoamerica contributed to the overall rise of the first Mesoamerican states, but four areas appear to have been particularly important: the South Gulf Coast, the Valley of Mexico, the Valley of Oaxaca, and the Mayan Lowlands.

THE EVOLUTION OF COMPLEX SOCIETIES ON THE SOUTH GULF COAST (CA. 1500 B.C. TO 400 B.C.)

The earliest and most radical break with the simple village farming tradition of Mesoamerica apparently occurred in the sweltering lowlands of the South Gulf Coast. Here, shortly after 1350 B.C., people built massive pyramids and other nonresidential structures, aggregated in relatively large settlements, engaged in a variety of specialized arts and crafts, and invested considerable energy and resources in drainage channels and terraces in order to intensify agricultural production. These people are known to us as the *Olmec*, a name derived from an Indian word meaning *rubber*—doubtless a reference to the rubber trees that grow in this area.

The Olmec worked jade and stone and made pottery in styles that were copied in Oaxaca, Puebla, the Valley of Mexico, and elsewhere, and although it is uncertain whether the peoples of the South Gulf Coast actually invented these styles, they do seem to have reached an expressive climax there. Some scholars have argued that the Olmec culture was the *cultura madre* (mother culture) of all later complex societies in Mesoamerica, and that they were directly responsible for transforming their neighbors by military, political, religious, or economic means into complex societies. Others have argued that the Olmec represent only one of several largely independent cases of the evolution of social complexity in Mesoamerica, and that their connection with their neighbors was mainly through limited economic exchange networks.

The Ecological Setting

The *Olmec Heartland* or *Climax Area,* as it is sometimes called, is a coastal strip approximately 350 kilometers in length, extending inland

13.4   Some Mesoamerican Formative sites of the first millennium B.C.

about 100 kilometers. It was created by the alluviation of several rivers that run to the sea from the highlands. Except for the Tuxtla Mountains in the center of the heartland or where vegetation has been cleared for grazing, the region is thickly forested. Rainfall is extremely heavy but regionally variable and quite sharply seasonal, falling almost entirely during the summer, an essential condition for swidden or slash-and-burn agriculture, the predominant agricultural system here prehistorically and currently. Swidden agriculture involves cutting down all the vegetation in a particular area and then waiting for the dry season so that the cut vegetation can be burned off; it is therefore restricted to areas where there is a sufficiently long dry season to allow this. The burning of the vegetation is essential because it returns nutrients to the soil—an important contribution when artificial fertilizers were not available. After burning the land is sown, and the crops germinate and come to maturity in the rainy season. After one or two years of exploitation, however, the land must be left fallow for variable lengths of time, sometimes for twenty years or more. If the cycle is speeded up, productivity falls rapidly, and most villagers avoid this by keeping to a complex fallowing system. In the flat lowlands of the Olmec Heartland as much as 70 to 90 percent of the land is fallow at any one time, and it is estimated that population densities of about twenty people per square kilometer can be supported on such a system (Pelzer 1945). Maize, beans, and squash were probably agricultural staples in Early Formative times, supplemented by hunting and fishing and by collecting wild plant foods. In coastal areas mussels and other rich resources of the marine interface could also be collected. Some river levees near the coast are annually inundated with water-borne silt of such fertility that two crops a year are possible using swidden techniques. Indeed, it is probable that the precocity of the Olmec in developing the first complex Mesoamerican culture was tied directly to the great agricultural potential and rich floral and faunal resources of these riverine environments.

The Archaeological Record

The Early Formative cultures of the South Gulf Coast have been the subject of research since the 1870s, but only a few studies have directly addressed the problem of the origins of complex societies. Substantial archaeological excavations have been conducted at some of the larger sites, and a few surveys have been made in rural areas (Sisson 1970), but we do not have the two essentials for studying culture change: systematic settlement surveys of large areas and extensive excavations of a diversity of settlement types and sizes (but see Coe and Diehl 1980).

OLMEC CEREMONIAL CENTERS   At San Lorenzo, in southern Veracruz, the Olmec carried thousands of tons of clay, sand, and rock in baskets to make a large platform and ceremonial complex. Excavations have not been substantial enough to date precisely much of the construction at San Lorenzo, but Michael D. Coe suspects that at least one stepped platform of sand and clay and some of the cruder stone reliefs might date to before 1200 B.C. (1968: 46, 64).

San Lorenzo actually refers to a group of sites within a diameter of about five kilometers including, besides San Lorenzo, the sites of Tenochtitlán and Potrero Nuevo. The architectural sequence at San Lorenzo is somewhat confusing, and we really don't know how much was accomplished in the critical period between 1200 and 400 B.C., but the most impressive artifacts there, the sculpted heads and monuments, almost certainly date to this period (Coe 1984). These artifacts include free-standing figures of kneeling men and carved stelae and "altars," all carefully executed from massive basalt blocks. On them are myriad engraved figures, often fantastic mythical creatures representing hybrids of snakes, jaguars, and humans.

The remains of houses and other occupational debris have been found in the area of San Lorenzo, and Coe estimates that at about 950 B.C. the population of the site of San Lorenzo was approximately 1,000. Another 1,000 lived at Tenochtitlán, and perhaps 250 at Potrero Nuevo (Coe 1968: 57). Only a few test excavations of these residential areas have been conducted, and despite a recent synthesis (Coe and Diehl 1980), we have little information about periods and densities of occupation. As a whole, the evidence is probably most suggestive of a pattern in which individual settlements rose in population and prominence and then began to contract, in part because of competition from other settlements, but just as likely from disease, crop failure, internal revolt, and other intrinsic factors.

The Olmec agricultural system was probably swidden-based maize, beans, and squash. Analysis of plant remains in hearths indicates that the area was covered by a thick tropical forest. The twenty or more artificial ponds and lagunas built at San Lorenzo before 900 B.C. were apparently drained by an elaborate system of deeply buried basalt troughs covered with slabs. Several possible uses have been suggested for these ponds, ranging from water storage to intensive hydraulic agriculture (Sanders and Price 1968: 57). Strangely, the remains of thousands of toads (*Bufo marinus*) were found at this site, and it may be significant that eating parts of these animals produces hallucinations. These toads are restricted to the very moist environments of coastal areas, and the discovery of their remains in Oaxaca—a very dry area several hundred kilometers distant—suggests that they may have been a trade item in the Early Formative.

At La Venta, on a small island in a coastal swamp near the Tonalá River, the Olmec constructed a series of mounds, platforms, courts, and pyramids covering more than five square kilometers. Much of this has been destroyed by looters and an oil well/processing installation, but excavations in the 1940s revealed a large portion of this site's plan. Dominating the area is a pyramid of clay, 128 by 73 meters at the base and 33.5 meters high. Two long, low mounds extend out to the north from the pyramid, with a circular mound between them. All these mounds are oriented 8° west of true north.

The most impressive artworks at La Venta are the famous "Olmec heads," of which four were found at La Venta. These heads are as large as 3 meters in height and invariably depict a human head with a serious, not to say sneering, facial expression, and they usually are shown wearing a "football helmet" (Figure 13.5). The basalt from which they were made was transported to the site from a source at least 130 kilometers to the west, probably by floating it down the river on rafts. Since the Olmec had no metal tools, we assume they worked with grinding

13.5   Scores of these huge
stone heads were produced
by the Olmec and transported
many miles to ritual positions
near ceremonial centers.

and pecking stone implements, and it is difficult to believe that these
sculptures were made by anyone other than skilled specialists.

Other works in stone are almost as impressive as the heads. Massive
basalt slabs were engraved with human and animal forms and erected
at various points around La Venta and other Olmec sites, and the
highly stylized designs on these monoliths may represent the first steps
toward a writing system.

Among the spectacular discoveries at La Venta were three superimposed "pavements," each composed of about 485 serpentine blocks
(about the size of small construction bricks), laid out in a traditional
Olmec design, a jaguar mask.

Unfortunately, the acidic, damp soils here do not preserve bones
well, and the only burial information we have from La Venta comes
from a tomb in a large mound near the central pyramid. The tomb was
elaborately constructed of basalt slabs, and on its limestone floor two
juveniles were laid out in fabric bundles heavily coated with red paint.
Buried with the bodies were jade figurines, beads, a shell ornament, a
stingray spine, and a few other items.

Other types of evidence relating to social complexity, such as residential architecture and settlement patterns, are not well represented at
La Venta. There is little residential debris there except for pottery and

a few clay figurines. Apparently, most of the people who built La Venta did not live there permanently.

Other Olmec ceremonial centers have been found at Laguna de los Cerros, and similar sites in the Papaloapan River Basin have been reported, but we have little archaeological evidence about them.

By 900 B.C. Olmec culture had reached its peak on the south Gulf Coast. There was considerable trade in jade, iron ore, obsidian, bitumen, magnetite mirrors, shark teeth, stingray spines, and perhaps cocoa and pottery, with goods circulating in complex patterns between the Olmec Heartland and highland Mexico and as far south as Guatemala.

On the basis of their art style, it seems the Olmec may have believed that at some distant time in the past a woman mated with a jaguar and gave issue to a line of half-human, half-feline monsters, or "were-jaguars." These are portrayed in pottery, stone, and other media in a highly stylized way, usually as fat infants of no discernible sexuality. Their snarling mouths, toothless gums, and cleft heads give them a strikingly bizarre quality that some have explained as an imitation of a birth defect of the neural tubes (Murdy 1981), or as the deformities one would expect of a mating between a human and a jaguar.

"Olmec" ceramic and sculptural designs have been found far outside the borders of the South Gulf Coast. Some bas-relief rock carvings at Las Victorias in highland El Salvador strongly resemble those at La Venta, and similar sculptures have been discovered in the highlands of Guerrero and Morelos in western Mexico. At Chalcatzingo, in Morelos, cliff sculptures include a standard Olmec motif of a man seated in what may have been meant as the mouth of a cave. Also in Morelos, at the burial sites of San Pablo Pantheon and La Juana, David Grove has found hollow ceramic "baby" figurines and other ceramics that closely resemble those from San Lorenzo. Olmec styles of pottery, worked stone, jade, and other artifacts have also been found at several sites in the Valley of Oaxaca, at Tlatilco and Tlapacoya near Mexico City, in Guatemala, and elsewhere in Mesoamerica.

There is little evidence that the Olmec had a fully differentiated and hierarchically arranged social, political, and religious organization. Their settlement patterns are not well known, but there is no indication of the hierarchical arrangement of villages, towns, and cities that we saw in the case of state societies elsewhere (Sisson 1970). Neither residential architecture nor mortuary complexes are sufficiently documented that we can infer several levels of socially and economically differentiated classes, and even the degree of occupational specialization is questionable, except, perhaps, as represented by rock-carving specialists and officials to plan and coordinate construction projects. Sanders and

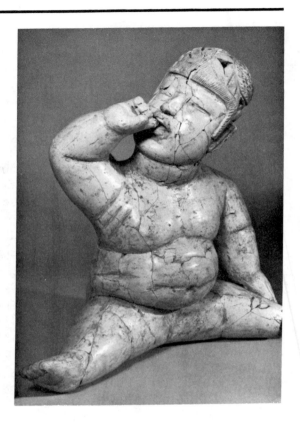

13.6   Olmec "baby" figurine.

Price, in fact, conclude that nothing about the Olmec is inconsistent with a "chiefdom" level of organization, by which they mean that there was probably no class stratification or elaborate control hierarchy (1968: 127; cf. Coe 1984).

Between 900 and 400 B.C. the Olmec civilization seems to have come to an end as a distinctive entity in Mesoamerica. The appearance at San Lorenzo at about 700 B.C. of new pottery wares, figurines, and art styles, and the apparent intentional destruction of the Olmec monuments has been interpreted to mean that the settlement was overrun by non-Olmec invaders. Or, the Olmec themselves, recognizing the collapse of their religious and economic systems, may have intentionally defaced these monuments—which may explain why some of the heads were carefully buried after having been mutilated (Drennan 1976: 362–63; Weaver 1972: 52).

Olmec culture continued for hundreds of years after 700 B.C. at Tres Zapotes, La Venta, and other sites, suggesting that all the ceremonial centers were not part of a unified system. But by 400 B.C. the Olmec Heartland was a cultural backwater. It has so remained.

Most people's lives involve sufficient continuity that it is difficult to appreciate the transitory nature of social systems. We live in an age where the very complexity of our political system and its accumulated diversity make it unlikely that—barring cosmic calamities—our essential social and cultural fabric will disintegrate. But if the archaeological record is any guide, early complex societies were rather more evanescent. These early Olmec chiefdoms may have matured and then died out more from an unlucky conjunction of disease, drought, and internal revolt than from interregional battles. Some have argued (e.g., Earle 1976) that for at least part of the time, these different Olmec centers were competing, with first one then another becoming dominant; but, alternatively, a case of sequential development centers developed and died out without much conflict among them. And they remind us of an obvious but neglected truth: that just because many settlements share styles of artifacts, and do so for long periods of time, as did the Olmec, this does not mean that they were politically integrated.

THE DEVELOPMENT OF CULTURAL COMPLEXITY IN THE VALLEY OF MEXICO (1500 B.C. TO A.D. 700)

The Ecological Setting

The Valley of Mexico is a large basin with no external drainage and rimmed on three sides by high mountain walls cut by only a few passes; even in the north where there are no mountains, the valley is delimited by a series of low hills. The valley has often been considered a "natural" analytical unit, bounded as it is by such impressive natural barriers, but archaeological research has revealed that almost from their arrival here the people of this area interacted with cultures far beyond the valley itself (Sanders, Parsons, and Santley 1979).

Of the roughly 7,500 square kilometers area of the Valley of Mexico, 3,000 square kilometers are high rugged terrain, much of it beyond the temperature limits of maize agriculture. Until the last 400 years, a large lake covered the low central portion of the valley, and much of the adjacent areas were covered by marshes, providing rich lacustrine/swamp resources such as fish, fowl, turtles, algae, and reeds.

There is not a single navigable stream or river in the whole Valley of Mexico today, and most natural channels contain water only during part of the year. There were probably many permanent streams in the prehispanic period, prior to deforestation and slope erosion, but such streams would have been relatively small, although useful for irrigating agricultural areas (Nichols 1982). Water availability for irrigation was an important element in the cultural evolution of the Valley of Mexico, because rainfall is limited and sharply seasonal and varies considerably from north to south.

The upper slopes of the Valley of Mexico, the areas above 2,500 meters in elevation, are today thinly settled. Rainfall maize agriculture can be done in a few areas, but failure rates are high. The forests and meadows here provide today, as they did in the past, many wood products, and in earlier times they supported large deer herds that were an important part of the prehistoric and early historic diet.

Formative Settlements in the Valley of Mexico
(1100 B.C. to 200 B.C.)

Between 1100 and 800 B.C., when the Olmec were rapidly developing relatively high population densities, monumental architecture, and spectacular art, there were still relatively few settlements in the Valley of Mexico, and most of these were small villages and hamlets. Only a few sites, such as Tlatilco and Cuicuilco, were larger, the latter estimated at approximately twenty-five hectares (with a population of perhaps 500) (Parsons 1974: 91).

Cuicuilco was covered with lava by a volcanic eruption around 150 B.C., and therefore little is known about it. Tlatilco has been largely destroyed by looters and the activities connected with a modern brick factory built on the site. How much of the occupation there dates to the period between 1100 and 800 B.C. will probably never be known, but apparently it was somewhat larger than that of the few other settlements in the valley at this time.

Thus, little in the settlement patterns of this period indicates social complexity. The two-tiered site size hierarchy is consistent with a simple, perhaps tribal, organization, and the distribution of settlements does not point to any political or social spacing. Settlements seemed to be located principally around the edge of the great lake, although there were a few small villages in the highlands in areas where the soil is particularly rich and deep. Differences in settlement size seem to be a result of local variations in agricultural potential.

Nor is there much evidence of complex architecture at these settlements. A few small mounds and platforms may date to before 800 B.C., but none is on the scale of the pyramids, platforms, and other struc-

13.7 Three bodies were buried with many ceramic vessels and other goods in this grave at Fabrica San José, Oaxaca (ca. 100 B.C. to A.D. 100). Note that two of the skulls were separated from their bodies and placed on the stone ledge.

tures found on the South Gulf Coast. No evidence of elaborate residential structures or monumental sculptures has been found.

The cemetery at Tlatilco provides little evidence that the occupants of the Valley of Mexico were living in complex cultures. Burial goods include pottery, shell ornaments, obsidian tools, figurines, bone tools, and jade and serpentine objects, and there is some evidence that a number of women were buried with more numerous and more expensive objects than other people in the cemetery, perhaps even with sacrificed men and children. But there are no lavish mortuary cults.

The presence of Olmec design elements on some of the ceramics found in graves at Tlatilco, along with other evidence, has led some to argue that settlements in the Valley of Mexico were becoming more complex as a result of contact with the Olmec. The "Olmecness" of the artifacts in the Tlatilco graves is somewhat dubious, however, and the vast majority do not look anything at all like Olmec material (Porter 1953).

From about 800 B.C. to about 500 B.C., the population density of the Valley of Mexico increased considerably. At least ten sites were larger than fifty hectares (each inhabited by about 1,000 people), and one, Cuicuilco, probably had a population of about 2,500, but the lava obscures the site to the point that it is impossible to make reasonable estimates. All of the larger sites are located along the lake margin, while scattered small hamlets are found in the highlands. The economic basis of these lakeside settlements appears to be similar to that of the preceding period, with a focus on agricultural, lacustrine, and marsh resources. There is some evidence (Nichols 1982) of *Middle Formative* (ca. 1100–500 B.C.) irrigation systems that may have given settlements near erosional gullies an agricultural advantage.

The pattern of these settlements may suggest some degree of political, religious, or economic interrelationship, as they are fairly evenly spaced at eight to ten kilometer intervals along the lake shore. We also infer considerable contact among these people because the degree of similarity in their pottery and other stylistic expressions is high. Site placement here, however, seems to be largely determined by food resource concentrations, not by political or economic boundaries.

For the period between about 500 and 200 B.C., however, there is persuasive evidence of changing cultural complexity in the Valley of Mexico. Population density rose considerably, and people were now living in larger settlements. Cuicuilco may have had as many as 7,500 people at this time—an unmanageable size without considerable social organization and control. Many other settlements of eighty to a hundred hectares existed, and intermediate and small settlements also increased in number. In addition, there is evidence of substantial public architecture toward the end of this period. Small "temple" platforms of stone and clay, some three to four meters high, appeared in several areas, and there were substantial stone structures at Cuicuilco and other sites.

THE EVOLUTION OF CULTURAL COMPLEXITY
IN ANCIENT OAXACA (CA. 1600 TO 200 B.C.)

The Ecological Setting

The Valley of Oaxaca, like Mexico's other mountain valleys, includes a diversity of ecological zones. On the valley floor are large fertile alluvial areas of flat land that have a sufficiently high water table for irrigation to be easily accomplished. Grading up into the mountains, the piedmont areas are less fertile than the alluvium, but they can be productively farmed by diverting water from the perennial streams that run toward the valley floor. The higher mountains are cooler and wetter than the other zones and are still covered with pine and oak trees.

Frost is not nearly the limiting factor on agriculture it is in the Valley of Mexico, although it can be a significant determinant of productivity. Since Formative times irrigation by means of canals and wells has been an important aspect of agriculture in Oaxaca.

The bedrock underlying parts of the valley is travertine, a smooth, hard stone that can be fashioned into ornaments, and this material was traded at least as far away as the Valley of Mexico and the South Gulf Coast. Also, some of the streams in the valley have extremely high salt content and were used for salt production until about 1910; presumably this production (and trade) would have been possible in the Formative period as well.

Some of the most important resources of Oaxaca were the native iron ores, including magnetite, ilmenite, and hematite. Small pieces of these materials were polished and used as mirrors and ornaments, which were then traded widely over Mesoamerica and used as marks of status.

The Archaeological Record

Shortly after 1400 B.C., the most productive areas of the piedmont and the alluvium in the Valley of Oaxaca were occupied by small villages composed of perhaps fifty people living in tiny wattle-and-daub structures. The first significant deviation from this pattern of egalitarian farmers occurred sometime between 1350 and 1150 B.C., when the inhabitants of at least one site (San José Mogote) built several "public buildings" which together covered about 300 square meters. Although these structures average only 5.4 x 4.4 meters each, they are interpreted as public buildings because the floors were carefully covered with a distinctive white lime plaster and swept clean, in contrast to the average house of this period, whose floors were usually stamped clay and sand and covered with household debris.

Other evidence suggests that these buildings at San José Mogote may have been intended for special functions: they are oriented 8° west of true north, about the same as the major monumental constructions at La Venta, in the Olmec Heartland; they were repaired and reused over longer periods of time than the obviously residential structures; and at least one of them had an "altar" or step against one wall.

Most of the other Formative villages in Oaxaca lack such public structures, although one, Tomaltepec, was found to have a large prepared mud-brick platform (Whalen 1976). In the floor of this structure was a storage pit, considerably larger than any of the others at the site, containing relatively large quantities of obsidian, ornamental seashell, and deer and rabbit bones (Whalen 1981).

Between 1400 and 1000 B.C., overlapping in time with the construction of this platform, a large cemetery was created at Tomaltepec. Eighty burials containing a total of about 100 individuals were found, and most of these burials had almost the same goods, mainly ceramics and a few other small items. In four of the burials, however, small quantities of obsidian, magnetite, and jade were found, but these differences in grave goods seem fairly small in view of the overall similarity. And, interestingly, no juveniles or infants were buried here; all were adults, suggesting that this society had not yet achieved significant social stratification.

Analysis of trade items in the valley betwen 1400 to 1000 B.C. also reinforces this impression of low-level community organization. A few items, such as obsidian, were traded, but in small amounts, and the trade was probably organized through individual households (Winter 1976). But archaeological evidence after 1000 B.C. suggests major changes in the cultural organizations of Oaxacan society. The largest site of this period. San José Mogote, had several successive public buildings of earth and adobe construction (Flannery 1976d: 335).

More crafts were apparently performed at San José Mogote than at other settlements in the valley at this time. Debris from working obsidian, jade, magnetite, shell, and other substances is found here in concentrations proportionately greater than at other sites. There was a major increase in the volume of "exotic" traded materials in Oaxaca at this time also, perhaps in response to increasing social stratification: these materials seem to have been used most frequently to make ornaments that reflect differences in social rank. There are clear resemblances between Olmec figurines and ones of comparable age from Oaxaca, particularly the baby-face style. In addition, some pottery with

Olmec motifs is found in Oaxaca. Certainly, magnetite and obsidian were moved in substantial volumes between Oaxaca and the South Gulf Coast between 1100 and 850 B.C.

Burial evidence during the period from 1100 B.C. to 850 B.C. implies some low-level ranking (Pyne 1976). Winter (1972) reports that of fifty Formative burials in the valley, decorated "Olmec" pottery definitely occurs with adult male burials, but rarely or never with female burials.

After about 850 B.C., variation in settlement size was greater than it had been earlier. By 550 B.C., San José Mogote, for example, grew to fifteen times the size of the next largest occupation. Many of the settlements excavated have public architecture, and their distribution seems to mirror the growing importance of social and political factors in determining site location. Between about 600 and 200 B.C., Oaxaca produced what some would classify as Mesoamerica's first state—a development discussed in more detail below.

In summary, the Valley of Mexico, the South Gulf Coast, and the Valley of Oaxaca all show similar patterns during these early developmental periods. In areas of naturally good agricultural productivity, or where production could be easily intensified, settlements grew large and the first expressions of monumental architecture, differential consumption of goods, and a more intricate flow of commodities and aesthetic styles can be detected.

Despite some evidence to the contrary (Coe 1965b), it seems unlikely that cultural evolution in either Oaxaca or the Valley of Mexico was directly instigated by the Olmec through military imposition, economic exploitation, or slavish imitation. The wide distribution of Olmec styles of ceramics, figurines, and sculpture and the construction in Oaxaca and elsewhere of public buildings with astronomical orientations similar to those of the Olmec buildings seem to reflect interregional trade networks and perhaps the circulation of important people, but the archaeological evidence does not support the idea of strong political or economic ties between these three regions (Blanton, Kowalewski, Feinman, and Appel 1981: 180–83; Flannery 1968; Grennes-Ravitz and Coleman 1976; Flannery, Marcus and Kowalewski 1981).

Some scholars (Grennes-Ravits and Coleman 1976: 204–05) hypothesize that many of the cultural features thought to have originated in the early Olmec occupation in the Gulf Coast region instead come from some third, and as yet unknown, area. In fact, they suggest that the great complexes at La Venta and San Lorenzo can be best understood as probably nonmilitary religious complexes, serving a large region of Mesoamerica as great market/pilgrimage centers. This would account for the wide distribution of Olmec and Olmecoid artifacts, because pilgrims and traders going to these market shrines would likely circulate figurines and ceramics.

Kent Flannery has suggested that while the Olmec may have originated various stylistic elements, these styles and other cultural elements were only diffused to Oaxaca, the highlands, and other areas where complex cultures were already developing in response to mainly local conditions. Flannery stresses the importance of trade in shell, magnetite, and other commodities among the South Gulf Coast, Oaxaca, and other areas, and concludes that the "spread of [Olmec] style was not a primary *cause* of Formative Mesoamerica's unity, but one reflection of the fact that it already was united, in an economic sense" (1968: 108).

The Rise of Mesoamerican States (ca. 600 B.C. to A.D. 900)

THE VALLEY OF OAXACA

Whereas the South Gulf Coast seems to have been the leader in the initial stages of Mesoamerican cultural evolution, it is perhaps the Valley of Oaxaca that produced the first "state"—at least as defined by multilevel settlement size hierarchies, the complex intertwining of economic specializations to the extent that many settlements were no longer self-sustaining entities, and the florescence of public art and architecture in the context of religious and political elites.

In the *Monte Albán period* (Early I) (ca. 500–350 B.C.), what some have termed a regional "capital" was established at Monte Albán in Oaxaca (Figure 13.8) (Blanton, Kowalewski, Feinman, and Appel 1981: 67). Richard Blanton (1980) has argued that the capital at Monte Albán was founded in an unpopulated area between various important settlements as an expression of a new confederation between people who previously may have been linked by rather low-level social and economic ties.

In one of the Main Plaza buildings at Monte Albán is a gallery of carved stone reliefs whose main theme seems to be the commemoration of the torture and killing of enemies. Scores of bodies are depicted with open mouths, closed eyes, and blood streaming from them in flowery patterns. The depiction of genital organs on these figures seems to have been an added insult, as nudity was regarded as scandalous in most of Mesoamerica at this time (Coe 1962: 95–96).

In their review of Oaxacan cultural developments, Blanton, Kowalewski, Feinman, and Appel (1981) estimate that Monte Albán grew

13.8   Monumental architecture at Monte Albán.

from an unoccupied, waterless wasteland to a great religious and political complex of 5,000 people in fewer than 200 years. To sustain this
rate of increase, they suggest, people would have had to move in from
other areas and have intensified agriculture in the valley and piedmont
to support the town.

By 200 B.C. the population of Monte Albán reached about 17,000—
a great city, by ancient standards. Agriculture was intensified around
Monte Albán as well, and rural population densities soared. Craft specialization in pottery and other commodities was sharpened, and the
location and products of kilns indicate some degree of regional administrative control (Blanton, Kowalewski, Feinman, and Appel 1981).

In succeeding centuries population densities and settlement patterns
varied considerably, but the investments in monumental architecture,
the hierarchical arrangements of towns in terms of the distribution of
goods and services, and other markers of cultural complexity persisted
and became more elaborate. Thus, by 200 B.C. or shortly thereafter, the
first Mexican state, by almost any definition, may have been operating
in Oaxaca.

It may be overstating the case to say that by 200 B.C. we have also
moved from prehistory to history in Mesoamerica, but the engraved

signs and symbols at Oaxaca and elsewhere in Mexico seem to be well on the way to the development of a true writing system.

TEOTIHUACÁN

Before 200 B.C. the *Teotihuacán* area of the Valley of Mexico had been relatively unimportant culturally, but it has large areas suitable for irrigated agriculture and large natural springs capable of supplying small irrigation systems. Obsidian is also available nearby, and the area is thought to have supported large stands of edible maguey cactus and nopal, a plant species which is home to an insect that can be rendered into a red dye that was highly prized in prehispanic Mexico. Moreover, Teotihuacán stands along a natural trade route to eastern Mesoamerica—an important advantage given the difficult terrain of this region.

Between about 500 and 150 B.C., Teotihuacán supported a few small villages with a combined population of at most 3,000, but between 150 and 1 B.C. the growth rate exceeded that of any other period, and a city extending some six to eight square kilometers formed and reached about one third its eventual maximum size (G. Cowgill 1974). Between about A.D. 1 and 150 the growth rate was still high but perceptibly slower; the average population during this period was probably between 60,000 and 80,000 (ibid.). At this same time work was completed on the massive pyramids of the Sun and the Moon (Figure 13.9) and on at least twenty other important temple complexes (Millon 1974: 42).

Already by about A.D. 100 there were hundreds of workshops specializing in items of obsidian, pottery, stone, and many other commodities; massive public constructions were underway; considerable variability existed in mortuary complexes and residential architecture; and the settlement patterns in the surrounding areas were heavily influenced by the city.

Teotihuacán's population rose from perhaps 80,000 at A.D. 100 to between 100,000 and 200,000 at A.D. 500. By A.D. 100 both the Pyramid of the Sun and the Pyramid of the Moon were probably approaching their final heights. The Pyramid of the Sun is over 200 meters long on each side of its base—as large as the great pyramid of Khufu in Egypt—and it rises 60 meters (half the height of the Khufu pyramid). The interior is filled with approximately 1 million cubic meters of sun-dried bricks and rubble. In volume, this probably equaled 2 million cubic meters of uncompressed fill, which would have required the excavation, transport, and shaping of the soil in an area 1.4 kilometers

13.9　The Pyramids of the Sun (*upper left*) and the Moon were the ceremonial heart of Teotihuacán. Hundreds of buildings and plazas lined the Street of the Dead, the main avenue leading to the Pyramid of the Moon. At the city's peak the population probably numbered far in excess of 100,000, and there were thousands of workshops, residential units, and public buildings.

square to a depth of 1 meter—a considerable effort by any standards. The Pyramid of the Moon is somewhat smaller (150 meters at the base, 45 meters high), but of greater architectural sophistication, with a series of inset trapezoidal platforms. Pottery fragments in the fill of these pyramids indicate that the pyramids were constructed by using material from earlier occupations near the city. Considering the size of these structures, it is little wonder that the Aztecs believed that the pyramids had been constructed by giants and that some of the gods were buried beneath them.

The rest of the city is perhaps even more significant in terms of its evidence of cultural complexity. It was laid out in quadrants, formed by the Street of the Dead intersected by streets running east to west.

Some of the quadrants were more densely occupied than others, and very different architectural styles and artifacts are found in various zones of the city. Along the main north-south street are elaborate residences, presumably for societal elites, as well as large and small temple complexes. Many of the more impressive buildings are built on platforms and often face inward on patios and courtyards. Most buildings are one story high. In some temple complexes the walls are decorated with beautiful murals depicting religious themes, warfare, imaginary animals, and scenes from daily life.

The hundreds of workshops found at Teotihuacán suggest that perhaps as much as 25 percent of its population consisted of craft specialists, turning out a variety of products in obsidian, ceramics, precious stones, slate, basalt, seashells, feathers, basketry, leather, and other materials.

The basic residential unit of Teotihuacán appears to have been the large, walled, windowless compound, made of adobe bricks and broken-up volcanic rock and faced with a fine plastered clay. Many such compounds measured 50 meters or more on a side and internally were divided into many rooms, porticoes, patios, and passageways. In some, open patios let in sun and air and drained the compounds through underground stone troughs. Many walls were decorated with frescoes of jaguars, coyotes, trees, gods, and people in naturalistic settings.

Curiously, some residential complexes at Teotihuacán were found to have concentrations of artifacts characteristic of distant areas of Mesoamerica. The *Oaxaca Barrio,* for example, included ceramics, funeral urns, burials, and other elements indistinguishable from the artifacts used in Oaxaca—over 400 kilometers to the south—and very much in contrast to the distinctive artifacts of the Teotihuacán natives. These foreign "barrios" appear to have remained culturally distinct and intact for at least several centuries and may have been trade entrepôts or ethnic "ghettos," but no persuasive explanation of these features has been made.

The city's people apparently ate large quantities of nopal and other kinds of cactus, as well as maize, beans, squash, and a variety of other domesticated and nondomesticated plants and animals. Even at Teotihuacán's peak, however, there was considerable hunting, as evidenced by about 80 percent of the animal remains found being deer bones. The discovery of many burned and cracked human bones in settlements near Teotihuacán and the depiction of human sacrifice in Teotihuacán murals suggest that the diet may have been augmented occasionally with human flesh.

By the time Teotihuacán reached its maximum size, it had apparently depopulated much of the rest of the Valley of Mexico: only one other major settlement appears in the valley at about A.D. 500, and it is but a small fraction of the size of Teotihuacán. In fact, the abandonment of rural sites correlates so closely with Teotihuacán's growth that it appears likely that populations were either drawn or coerced directly into the city; overall population growth in the Valley of Mexico at this time (A.D. 100 to 600) was probably very minor and absorbed by Teotihuacán. Also, sometime in the first or second century B.C., the city of Cuicuilco was buried under five meters of lava and the surrounding agricultural areas rendered worthless by layers of volcanic ash, an event which may have contributed to the rapid growth of Teotihuacán by removing its only large competitor (Parsons 1974).

By A.D. 500 the influence of the civilization at Teotihuacán had spread over most of Mesoamerica. Elegant vases made at Teotihuacán are found in the richly furnished burials of apparently high-status individuals on the Gulf Coast, in Oaxaca, and elsewhere.

Although it dominated the Valley of Mexico, Teotihuacán was not the only complex culture in Mesoamerica at this time. It seems unlikely that the few hundred thousand people at Teotihuacán were able to extend military control over the millions of people living in the rest of Mesoamerica: fighting a military campaign in the rough terrain of these distant areas would have been suicidal. More likely, the Teotihuacános were tied to the many other areas through trade networks. The city has no major defensive fortifications, but it does have what appear to be large market areas, and the ecological diversity of Mesoamerica would have put a high premium on large-volume trade in basic agricultural and technological commodities. By circulating these many products, people would have had a much higher standard of living and much greater protection against food shortages.

Sometime before A.D. 600, Teotihuacán's size and influence began to decline. As the city shrank in population, new centers and settlements appeared throughout the Valley of Mexico, particularly on its edges. Coe suggests that the city met its end through deliberate destruction and burning by outside invaders (1962: 116) shortly after A.D. 600, but we cannot be certain of this. Significantly, after A.D. 600 Teotihuacán styles in pottery, architecture, and other artifacts come to an abrupt end in the rest of Mesoamerica. It is as if a complicated exchange network had been beheaded, and local cultures began developing their own distinctive traditions.

Archaeologist George Cowgill has persuasively argued that Teotihuacán stopped growing in size and power after A.D. 600 because it had reached the limits of productivity of its sustaining area: there are only a few thousand hectares of land near Teotihuacán suitable for canal irrigation, and once populations at the city reached about 100,000, much of the food would have had to have come from riskier, less productive forms of agriculture and from collecting and hunting wild plants and animals (1974). At present, however, we cannot estimate with accuracy what foods were imported into Teotihuacán and in what quantities.

Teotihuacán may have been outcompeted by other political systems based on more productive agricultural and economic resources: there is some evidence that at least part of its sphere of influence was encroached upon by emerging states in the Mayan areas. Even closer to home, political systems centered at Tula, Xochicalco, and elsewhere in the Valley of Mexico may have begun to block Teotihuacán's access to needed raw materials and foodstuffs.

Thanks to William Sanders (Sanders, Parsons, and Santley 1979), Jeffrey Parsons (1971, 1974), Richard Blanton (1972), and their students, who—despite rattlesnakes and the epidemiological horrors of the Playa Azul North Bar—have done systematic archaeological surveys of the Valley of Mexico, we can now reconstruct over four thousand years of settlement history in this area.

In most of these archaeological surveys the procedure was to collect a sample of pottery from each site and then to estimate the site size, periods of occupation, and distinctive architectural features.

The limitations of such data have been intensively reviewed by Tolstoy (1981) and others, but this information is by far the most useful and systematic archaeological evidence in Mesoamerica. As such, it has been used for the application of several kinds of quantitative analyses.

Elizabeth Brumfiel (1976), for example, attempted to test the hypothesis that "population pressure" was an important factor in cultural evolution in the Valley of Mexico between 500 B.C. and A.D. 1—the important interval just before the florescence of Teotihuacán. She did this by estimating the agricultural productivity and the potential for intensification of each settlement known for this period. Defining a territory within five kilometers radius of each Formative community, she graded the agricultural potential of the land on the basis of its contemporary productivity. She then used a statistical technique called *regression* to investigate the correlation between site size, changes over time in site size, and agricultural productivity. Her argument is complex and mathematical, but one of her conclusions is quite simple: an important factor in the growth of smaller towns and villages was the imposition of tribute by elites in the largest communities. She found little convincing evidence of "population pressure" at the critical period.

Although Tolstoy (1981) criticizes Brumfiel's study, it represents an admirable attempt to discern patterns and processes in an archaeological record that is rapidly disappearing. To gather data that would meet the objections of Brumfiel's critics in terms of surface collections and so forth is in many ways beyond the resources of modern archaeology, even if these settlements were intact.

Several other analyses of these Valley of Mexico settlement patterns have been set in mathematical-locational geographical terms (e.g., Alden 1979), and the results have stimulated a great deal of discussion about Mesoamerican culture history and applicability of these kinds of analytical techniques.

THE MAYA

At about the same time the civilization of Teotihuacán was developing in the Valley of Mexico (200 B.C. to A.D. 600), another major civilization, the *Maya*, was emerging in southern Mexico, Guatemala, Belize, and Honduras.

Early Mayan civilization was influenced to some degree by Teotihuacán, but it was also an independent and unique state. The Maya devised a complex writing system, their temples and palaces are spectacularly beautiful monumental constructions, and they are thought to have organized vast areas and many peoples under a centralized government. It was formerly believed that the Maya never developed large population concentrations, but at the great Mayan site of Tikal 3,000 structures have been located within an area of 16 square kilometers, and only 10 percent of these appear to have been nonresidential, major ceremonial buildings. Estimates of Tikal's population range as high as 5,000, and other centers like Dzibilchaltún seem to have had a population of many thousands at various times (Sjoberg 1965). But these settlements never had the hundreds of thousands of people of Teotihuacán, and they had less diversity in residential architecture and perhaps less occupational specialization than existed in Teotihuacán or Oaxaca at a comparable time.

About every five years a major archaeological conference is held on the Maya (e.g., Ashmore, ed. 1981), and the conclusions each time seem to be about the same: we don't know much about them because there are no adequate regional site surveys; the Maya were essentially an independent, local evolutionary phenomenon; and there is no conclusive evidence to determine whether the Maya were a set of feudal and feuding chiefdoms, a coherent national state, or a loose confederation of tribes with a penchant for monumental architecture.

13.10   The Mayan ceremonial center at Tikal. The Maya constructed hundreds of
temples, plazas, and public buildings.

The Ecological Setting

Most of the Mayan homeland is a hot, semitropical forest, but large
areas are highlands created by a string of volcanoes that rise over 4,000
meters and extend from southeastern Chiapas toward lower Central
America. In the highlands volcanic ash and millennia of wind and water
erosion have created a rich thick layer of soil spread over a convoluted
landscape of deep ravines, ridges, and a few gentler valleys. Rainfall is
substantial but sharply seasonal.

 The tropical lowlands that form the heartland of the Mayan civilization cover the Petén and the Yucatán Peninsula, a massive limestone
shelf built up out of the seas over millions of years. The land is rugged

toward the southern part of the Petén, but most of the peninsula is flatter. There are few rivers or lakes because the porous limestone quickly drains away surface water.

The lowland climate is hot and humid for most of the year, but drought can be a severe problem because the rainfall is seasonal and localized. Recent research has revealed large irrigation systems in some areas, and during at least some periods, permanent field agriculture with annual cropping was probably very important economically in the lowlands. In much of the Mayan area, the fields used for maize, beans, squash, tomato, and pepper cultivation must be fallowed for four to eight years after about three years of production. Even then, the Mayan homeland is sufficiently productive that some estimates of the land's carrying capacity on the basis of traditional swidden agriculture are up to 60 to 80 people per square kilometer (U. Cowgill 1962). Also, exploitation of the nuts of the ramón tree (*Brosimum alicastrum*) may have been a major part of the Mayan agricultural strategy. Ramón nuts are highly nutritious and widely available in the Mayan area, and their harvests are not severely affected by even prolonged droughts. Their productivity in combination with maize is high (Dickson 1981). Underground chambers (*chultún*) may have been used to store these nuts for up to eighteen months (Puleston and Puleston 1971), and surveys indicate that in some areas, the correlation of Mayan house mounds and ramón tree groves is very high.

Most peasant cultivators use animals, whether wild or domestic, to convert brush and hedgerow vegetation into usable form, and the small Yucatec deer apparently filled this role in the Mayan lowlands.

Culture History of the Maya

At Izapa, near the Mexico-Guatemala border on the Pacific coast, there may have been some mounds and plazas as early as 1500 B.C. Population growth over much of the highland Mayan areas seems to have been slow but steady after about 200 B.C., and at about this same time the first elements of the Mayan civilization appeared. At Izapa over eighty temple mounds were built, many of them faced with cut stone, and some of the core elements of Mayan art appeared: the carvings of various designs on stone stelae, the depiction of certain deities, and the use of a two-dimensional art style emphasizing historical and mythical themes with great attention to costumes and decoration (Coe 1966: 61).

Another highland center was Kaminaljuyú, now ravaged by the expansion of Guatemala City. Kaminaljuyú was apparently a large settlement by about 800 B.C., and between 100 B.C. and A.D. 200 it reached its zenith. Beautiful sculpture in the style of that at Izapa was executed, some bearing glyphs, or signs, that are assumed to convey historical and calendrical information. Most of these glyphs were intentionally destroyed in antiquity and none have been translated, although it is thought they might be direct antecedents of the Mayan scripts developed elsewhere between A.D. 1 and A.D. 600. Kaminaljuyú also contained many temple mounds and rich burials, suggesting that it was a ceremonial center for many small dependent hamlets in the surrounding countryside.

One of the most important early Mayan sites was Chiapa de Corzo, located in Chiapas. Already occupied at 1400 B.C., Chiapa de Corzo appears to have been almost continuously occupied for about 3,300 years (R. E. Adams 1977). By 550 B.C. small pyramids and other civic buildings were under construction at the site, and by 150 B.C. there is clear evidence of gross wealth and status differences in residential architecture and mortuary complexes. Pottery and other artifacts indicate that very early on the people at Chiapa de Corzo were in contact with their neighbors at Kaminaljuyú and in the Valley of Oaxaca, and a piece of Izapa-style inscribed stele from Chiapa de Corzo seems to bear the date 36 B.C. in the Mayan calendar.

Settlements in the Petén, the Yucatán Peninsula, and other lowland areas may have been inhibited by the thick vegetative cover of this area and by other environmental factors. Xe (pronounced *shay*) on the Pasion River and a few other sites have evidence of occupation as early as 1000 B.C., but they have no monumental buildings or advanced artistic traditions.

Between 550 and 300 B.C., population densities increased markedly in the lowlands, and villages with some ceremonial architecture appeared at Dzibilchaltún, Becan, Tikal, and elsewhere. The ceramics found in the lowlands at this time are quite similar, suggesting that the people were participating in at least some generalized exchange systems, but there is little evidence of political federation or voluminous economic exchange. As we have seen in the case of the Harappan (Indus Valley) and Halafian (Mesopotamian) ceramics, however, the spread of a distinctive, uniform ceramic style over large areas often precedes rapid and fundamental cultural change. By about A.D. 1, a distinctively styled pottery was in use over the entire 250,000 square kilometers of the Mayan lowlands, and pyramids, platforms, and other large public buildings were being constructed at Yaxuná, Dzibilchaltún, Uaxactún, and elsewhere.

In the several succeeding centuries, population growth continued, as did the construction of many large ceremonial buildings, and the essentials of the Mayan calendrical and writing systems appeared. Some of these developments may have been stimulated by population and cultural intrusions from Central America and the Mayan highlands.

Between A.D. 300 and 900, Mayan civilization reached its climax as hundreds of beautiful pyramids, temples, and other buildings were completed, and painting and sculpture flourished.

The first part of this period corresponds to the florescence of Teotihuacán, and some see the Maya as developing principally under Teotihuacán's stimulus (Sanders and Price 1968). We know that the Teotihuacán civilization had a tremendous influence at this time and that trade between the Mayan area and Teotihuacán may have been considerable, but much of Mayan development was autonomous and distinctive. After A.D. 600, when Teotihuacán apparently began rapidly to lose influence and population, the Maya began a 300-year period of intense development. Hundreds of temple complexes were constructed and beautiful stone sculptures executed—many of them dated and inscribed.

But despite these material indications of their brilliant achievements, the Mayan peoples themselves seem to have lived much as their ancestors had. They still had not aggregated in cities, and although thousands of people must have cooperated to construct these great projects, most still lived in small undifferentiated rural hamlets. These dispersed agricultural hamlets were grouped around small ceremonial centers that included a small temple pyramid and a few other stone constructions. Several districts of small ceremonial centers were congregated around the major ceremonial centers of Tikal, Uaxactún, Palenque, Uxmal, and other sites. Figure 13.10 shows the complexity of construction at one of the major sites, and all over southern Mesoamerica at this time there were beautiful, gleaming white limestone pyramids and temples surrounded by marvelously executed stone sculpture and decorated with wall paintings. Most centers also had ball courts made of stucco-faced rock where, apparently, people played a game in which a rubber ball was meant to be thrown or batted through a stone ring protruding from one of the inclined walls of the court.

Tikal contains an extremely large pyramid-temple complex (seventy meters tall), many inscribed stelae, and several rich tombs. One of the greatest of all known Mayan frescoes is at Bonampak. Here, in several rooms of murals, the paintings tell a story of warfare, the torturing of prisoners of war, and a celebration. The carefully drawn mutilated bodies, richly dressed figures, and men with weapons convey an extraordinarily vivid sense of militarism, royalty, and religion.

Themes of military triumph, the torture of captives, and the power of the ruling classes were also commonly depicted in bas-relief sculpture throughout the *Classic* period—even in the Valley of Oaxaca and the peripheral areas of the Mayan sphere of influence. Individuals of presumably higher status were juxtaposed in stone carvings with persons of lower status, and differences of dress, bearing, and position sharpened the contrast. In some cases, representations of prisoners and commoners were carved into the facings of stone steps, so that they were trod on by the nobility—a not too subtle visual pun (Marcus 1974: 92).

Robert Fry and Scott Cox (1974) used mathematical studies to show that some product exchange (particularly in ceramics) was accomplished through major ceremonial centers. They suggest that most of the utilitarian pottery used by the people living within about twenty-two kilometers of Tikal was made and sold at trade fairs at that city, and that the many people living within this area focused most of their economic activities on Tikal and had little contact with other large ceremonial centers. Computer simulations have been used to suggest that as many as 77,000 people may have lived in Tikal's immediate environs at its peak (Dickson 1981).

Although we do not yet fully understand why and how Mayan civilization declined, we do know when it happened. Each new monumental building of the Maya was usually accompanied by a stone stele engraved with the date of its construction, and thus we know that while many buildings were completed during the eighth and ninth centuries A.D., by A.D. 889 only three sites were under construction, and by about A.D. 900, construction seems to have ended for good. On the basis of ceramics and other information, we know that depopulation of the countryside and centers apparently followed quickly.

Shortly after A.D. 900 there was an invasion of sorts by the Toltecs, a people whose culture was centered at Tula in the Valley of Mexico and who apparently established feudal control over some areas of the lowlands—an event setting off many years of internal dissension and local revolt. During this time various centers were built and some major population concentrations developed; but in population density, construction projects, art styles, inscribed stelae, settlement patterns, and mortuary complexes, the developmental period of Mayan culture was at an end.

The Mayan area remained isolated and relatively independent for centuries, and revolutions against the central Mexican government occurred as late as 1847 and 1860.

Many diverse factors have been suggested as causes of the development, and also the collapse, of Mayan civilization, and new interpretations sporadically appear. Not surprisingly, many involve the ecology of the Mayan homeland, which seems at first glance to be a major barrier to cultural evolution.

William Rathje argues that the Maya, at least those in the central lowlands, could have prospered only if they were able to import several basic commodities, including obsidian, stone, and salt (1973). He contends that if these essential commodities were to reach each household, a complex administrative structure had to be developed to coordinate this trade and get people involved in transport and redistribution activities. The pyramid-temple complexes and their resident elite hierarchies would then develop out of these administrative requirements.

Others have argued that there probably was no need to trade for these commodities in most of the Mayan area. The region is in fact littered with flint that could be substituted for most uses of obsidian, and only in a few areas was there a shortage of stone suitable for manufacturing grinding implements. Salt, too, is thought to have been readily available from the Yucatán coast. Overall, it appears that trade for some commodities may have been an important part of evolving cultural complexity in the Mayan areas, but trade certainly does not represent a complete explanation (Fry, ed. 1980).

Ray Matheny's (1976) discoveries of large-scale irrigation have altered our ideas about Mayan agriculture. Working from aerial photographs, he surveyed parts of Campeche and found canals, reservoirs, and moats radiating out from the ceremonial center at Edzna; he estimates that the collective effort required for these constructions was greater than that represented by the great pyramids at Teotihuacán. Some canals are about 1.6 kilometers in length, 30 meters in width, and 3 meters deep. We do not know how many such irrigation systems exist out in the tropical forests of the Mayan lowlands, and thus we cannot estimate how important they may have been in the evolution of Mayan cultural complexity, or even what the water carried by the canals was used for. Matheny proposes drinking water, irrigation water for small garden plots, and a source of mud for renewing soil fertility as possible uses, and Marvin Harris suggests that irrigation to grow two crops a year may have also been part of the motivation for these projects (Harris 1977: 91; Hunt and Hunt 1976; see also Flannery 1982).

Given the Mayan environment, under what conditions would it have been advantageous to organize into larger political and social units? Perhaps the answer lies in the necessity of local exchange to meet the threat of drought, disease, or disturbance. Rainfall is quite variable within the Mayan area, and many other things can adversely affect each community's agricultural system. Because the communities were all so similar in the crops they grew and their techniques for growing them, a major

drought, such as happens in this area every eight to ten years, could result in the starvation of many people in hundreds of hamlets. But this
could be in large part mitigated if many villages established exchange
networks that spread the risks. Each year earthquakes, droughts, disease, floods, warfare, and all the other calamities might wipe out some
sectors of the subsistence system, but if a village belonged to an organization that included many hamlets, it could get help or give help depending on its fortunes. Because of the inability to intensify drastically
agricultural production in any one area, cities were, of course, out of
the question. Similarly, population-control regulators were very important, hence the monumental construction projects in this most unlikely
of places.

Whatever is at the root of the Mayan cultural evolution, the collapse
of this culture poses equally interesting questions. Warfare seems to
have increased toward the end of the Mayan period, and we might ask
why it became more prevalent then and why the Maya were unable to
fight off its effects at this time, after so many centuries of successful deal-
ings among themselves and with their neighbors. No appreciable land
shortages or overpopulation seem to have occurred, nor is there much
evidence of foreign military pressures on these people.

We have argued that the evolution of Mayan society could probably
be tied to the necessity of spreading the "risk" of life in this area by
integrating many different settlements under a centralized authority.
But by the same token, such an integrated system might eventually have
encountered a series of catastrophes and internal problems spaced so
closely together and in such a sequence that their effects could not be
successfully fought off. Earthquakes, disease, warfare, drought, crop disease—all these have certain unavoidable periodicities, and unfavorable
conjunctions must necessarily arise if the system is sufficiently long-
lived. Also, it is important to recognize that the Maya were not the only
powerful political system in Mesoamerica at this time. George Cowgill,
in fact, has suggested an explanation of the Mayan decline based on
their competitive posture in relation to these other systems.

> I suggest that in Late Classic times there was a general economic de-
> velopment of a number of regional [Mayan] centers, perhaps at least
> in part because of the *weakening* of highland states such as Teotihua-
> cán and Monte Albán.
>   . . . Eventually the major Maya centers may have begun to compete
> for effective mastery of the whole southern lowlands. This postulated
> "heating up" of military conflict, for which there is support in Late
> Classic art and inscriptions . . . , seems to me the spur . . . which
> might have driven the Maya to encourage population growth and in-

tensify production beyond prudent limits. If so, the outcome of the competition was not an eventual winner . . . but disaster for all. (1976)

A variant of the internal-conflict hypothesis of the Mayan demise is the notion that Mayan civilization collapsed in bloody civil wars fought out as class conflicts. As Lowe (1982) points out, coups d'état by the disadvantaged are not unknown in Central America, and there have been some fairly interesting mathematical analyses of the rate and direction of the Mayan collapse that are not at variance with the idea of a proletarian revolution (e.g., Bove 1981).

But the rather weak data we have from the Mayan areas can be made to fit many different hypotheses about the source and kind of cultural changes involved.

The Mayan Achievement

Given the social and economic benefits that accrue from public-works projects, it is not at all surprising that the Maya should have built temples, pyramids, and platforms. They apparently had no metal, winches, hoists, or wheeled carts, and they never developed the barrel-vault or arch constructions that allowed Old World civilizations to build multistoried temples and palaces. Thus, the only things they could build to any height were the basic geometric forms: the coincidence of pyramids in many ancient civilizations seems largely accountable in terms of these basic facts of construction capabilities—especially for the Maya, whose homeland rested on a gigantic layer of limestone, which when wet could easily be cut with flint tools.

Based on the work of a sixteenth-century Spanish bishop, Brother

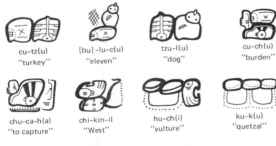

cu-tz(u)
"turkey"

[bu]-lu-c(u)
"eleven"

tzu-l(u)
"dog"

cu-ch(u)
"burden"

chu-ca-h(a)
"to capture"

chi-kin-il
"West"

hu-ch(i)
"vulture"

ku-k(u)
"quetzal"

mu-t(i)
"omen"

mu-an-il
"Muan" (month)

m(o)-o-o
"macaw"

13.11 Some standard Mayan glyphs and the phonetic values assigned to them by Y. V. Knorosov. The Mayan writing system has not yet been completely deciphered.

Landa, Mayan writing (Figure 13.11) was at first thought to be alphabetic. But scholars quickly realized that Mayan writing was to be read in double columns, from left to right and from top to bottom, and by the turn of the last century Mayan glyphs had been identified for the "zero" and "twenty" signs, the cardinal points of the compass, the basic colors, Venus, the months of the year, and the "Long Count," the system of reckoning by which the Maya figured how many years had elapsed since the beginning of their time.

Although years of research on Mayan glyphs have failed to demonstrate that they form a complete version of the spoken language, this writing system was apparently a powerful way of conveying information. Inscriptions include verbs, nouns, adjectives, and prepositions in readable patterns, but the system remains a blend of phonetic, pictographic, and ideographic elements (Marcus 1976b).

The writing system seems to have begun sometime between 600 and 400 B.C. in southern Mexico and to have evolved into four different types: the Zapotec and Mayan versions, which began as hieroglyphic stone inscriptions, and the Mixtec and Aztec systems, which were written mainly on paper or hides (Marcus 1976b: 36).

In the Middle East the first writings are almost unrelievedly economic, but in Mesoamerica the subject matter is primarily calendrical, historical, and dynastic. Mesoamericans were at pains to record when a temple was begun, when a king defeated a rival, and what lands were under the control of the state. About the daily movement of maize, hides, ornaments, and the like, they seemed much less concerned.

Unfortunately, only three Mayan "books" survive; the Dresden, Madrid, and Paris codices. These are long strips of bark paper which were covered with a layer of plaster and folded like screens. There are also of course many stone inscriptions in the same writing system.

The Maya had two calendars. One was the familiar solar calendar in which a year equaled 365 days, but whereas we intercalate an extra day every four years to compensate for the year being actually 364.25 days long, the Maya blithely ignored this and let the seasons creep around the calendar. And in contrast with our system of twelve months of from 28 to 31 days, the Maya had eighteen named months of 20 days each, with 5 days, which were considered highly unlucky, added to the end.

The second calendar involved a 260-day year, composed of the intermeshing of the sequence of numbers from one to thirteen with 20 named days (Figure 13.12). These two calendars ran parallel, and thus every particular day in the 260-day calendar also had a position in the solar calendar. The calendars' permutations are such that each named

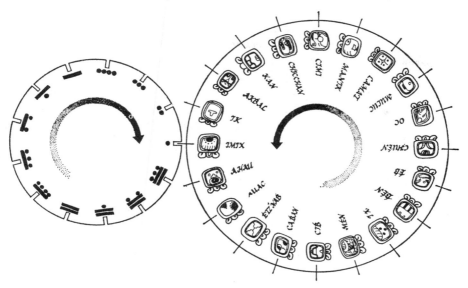

13.12 One of the Mayan calendars involved the meshing of the numbers from one to thirteen and 20 named days.

day would not reappear in the same position for 18,980 days, or fifty-two of our solar years.

Every day on the Mayan calendar had its omens, and activities were rigorously scheduled by their astrological significance. In fact, with the possible exception of some southern Californians, few people have been as obsessed with astrology as the Maya.

In some of the later adaptations of the Mayan calendar (Marcus 1976b), it appears that people were named after the day on which they were born and could not marry if they shared a numerical coefficient (e.g., Mr. "8 deer" could not marry Ms. "8 flower"). Crops were planted and harvested only on calendrically favorable days. For instructors in Mesoamerican prehistory, each term usually brings at least one request for the conversion of a person's birthdate into its corresponding Mayan calendrical date, and there are now several computer programs that do this (e.g., Doty 1979).

For reasons not entirely clear but having to do with the accomplishment of a certain number of calendrical cycles, the Maya believed that the world would end on December 24, A.D. 2011.

Post–Classic Mesoamerica (ca. A.D. 900 to 1524)

At about A.D. 900, when Mayan political power in the lowlands was beginning to wane, much of highland Puebla, Mexico, and Hildago was apportioned among several competing power centers. One of these, Cholula, in Puebla, stands along a route connecting the Valley of Mexico with the lowlands to the east, and the city's importance may have derived from defensive and commerical functions attendant on this route. After A.D. 900 a massive pyramid, covering sixteen hectares and rising to a height of fifty-five meters, was constructed at Cholula, along with many other buildings, most of which are still completely unexcavated. For a period after A.D. 900 Cholula seemed able to influence

13.13   Estimated population changes in a large part of the Valley of Mexico. Note the rapid increase in density after the collapse of Tula.

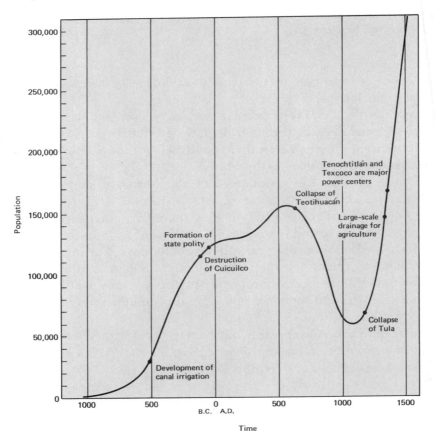

events in the Valley of Mexico. After A.D. 950 population densities in large areas of the Valley of Mexico declined, possibly as a result of conflict between Cholula and the city of Tula, located at the extreme northern end of the Valley of Mexico (Parsons 1974: 107).

At about A.D. 968 Tula apparently became the capital of the *Toltecs,* who established a military empire centered at Tula, Tollanzinco, Tenanco, and other towns north and west of the Valley of Mexico, and may soon have come into conflict with the power centers at Cholula and elsewhere in the Valleys of Mexico and Puebla. Eventually, through military and other means the Toltecs were able to dominate for a few centuries most of these rivals.

Excavations at Tula revealed the remains of an impressive city with an estimated population of 40,000 to 50,000, large temples and pyramids, magnificent sculpture and murals, and evidence of extensive craft specialization. The Toltecs established trade and military outposts in many areas of northern and western Mexico and exported metal, gemstones, and other commodities as far north as Arizona and New Mexico. To the south, the Toltecs established administrative control over Chichen Itza and perhaps other towns in the Mayan lowlands where the collapse of the Mayan civilization was delayed for a century or two.

Oral histories and art styles mark the Toltecs as an extremely militaristic people, who flourished on an intensive irrigation agricultural economy exploited by a well-structured taxation system. Eventually, however, Toltec power weakened, and, under the onslaught of invading Chichimec, a group from the North, the Toltecs broke up into many smaller, competitive groups. Tula itself was almost entirely destroyed by invaders at about A.D. 1156. Succeeding centuries saw the rise of various other cultural traditions in central Mexico, such as the Tarascan state (Pollard 1980).

THE AZTECS

One of the last tribes to invade central Mexico from the North and West was the *Aztecs,* who formed the last and greatest aboriginal Mesoamerican state. Aztec histories and legends, as recorded by the Spanish, tell of their arrival in the Valley of Mexico as rag-tag foragers and primitive agriculturalists who at first were forced by the established residents of the valley to live in the swamps around the lake, subsisting on flies, snakes, and vermin. According to legend, rival political groups in the valley enlisted the Aztecs in their campaigns but avoided other contacts with them because of the Aztecs' predilections for human sacri-

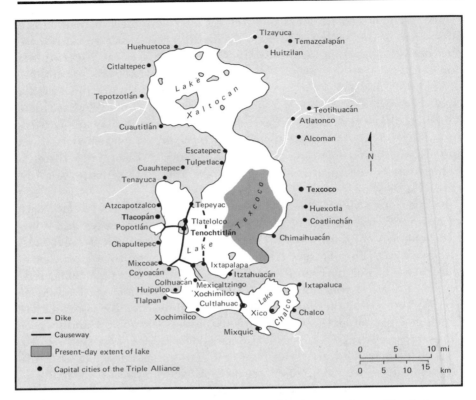

13.14   The lake was a central commercial artery for the great Aztec cities that surrounded it in the Valley of Mexico.

fice and other barbarisms. At war with various groups, the Aztecs were forced to take refuge on islands in the lake where, according to legend, they built their first city, Tenochtitlán. In time Tenochtitlán grew to become a massive complex of pyramids, courts, and other buildings, now largely buried beneath the streets of Mexico City.

As allies of the Tepanec kingdom of Atzcapotzalco, the Aztecs conquered many of the surrounding cities, and at about A.D. 1427 they turned on their erstwhile allies and through savage warfare brought most of central Mexico under their control. Military expeditions conquered peoples all the way to the Guatemalan border, and garrison towns were established from the Pacific coast to the Gulf of Mexico.

Although the Aztecs are usually associated with militarism, they also created an impressive civil and commercial administration. Between about A.D. 1300 and 1520 they drained large areas of the Valley of Mexico, transforming them into productive agricultural plots.

Michael Smith (1979) has argued on the basis of central place theory that much of the settlement pattern of the Valley of Mexico during Aztec times can be understood in terms of a hierarchically arranged marketing system of products with intense local specialization in goods and services. Many commodities, including salt, reeds, fish, stone, cloth, various crops, ceramics, gold, and wood were exchanged among hundreds of communities. In fact, the improbable location of Tenochtitlán—on an island in the middle of the lake—is probably best understood in terms of its central role in these redistributive networks (Parsons 1974: 107). In 1519 Tenochtitlán is estimated to have had about 200,000 to 300,000 inhabitants, five times the population of London at that time (Coe 1962: 161), and there were many other large cities within the Aztec domain. Many cities had broad avenues, causeways, temples, pyramids, and other large buildings, often interspersed with gardens, courtyards, and large markets.

It is estimated that between 1 and 2 million people (Parsons 1974) lived in the Valley of Mexico in late Aztec times. In the southern areas of the valley's lake system, maize, beans, squash, tomatoes, and other crops were grown on *chinampas,* long rectangular plots of ground created out of the lake bed by piling up layers of aquatic weeds, mud, human feces, garbage, and other materials. If crops were transplanted and carefully tended, as many as seven per year could be grown, and ten to eighteen people could be supported on a single hectare of *chinampa* (R. E. Adams 1977: 28). The lake also provided many fish, waterfowl, and salamanders, all of which were eaten in great quantities.

The Aztecs were organized into a highly stratified class system headed by a god-king. Beneath the king were the nobles, the *pilli,* all of whom belonged to the royal house, while the great mass of the populace were commoners, *macehuales,* and were organized in large clans, called *calpulli.* The *calpulli* were the basic units of Aztec society. Each was composed of several lineages, totaling several hundred people, one of whom was designated the *calpule,* or leader. Members of a *calpulli* usually lived in the same village or ward, fought together as a unit if drafted for war, held and worked land in common, paid taxes as a unit, and worshipped at the shrine maintained by the *calpulli.* The leaders of the *calpulli* were the direct link between the imperial government and the people.

The *calpulli* differed from one another in social rank. There was some social mobility for individuals—usually by virtue of extraordinary service to the state in warfare, trade, or religion. At the bottom of the social scale were slaves, who worked the fields, performed other menial tasks, and were sacrificed in enormous numbers to various gods.

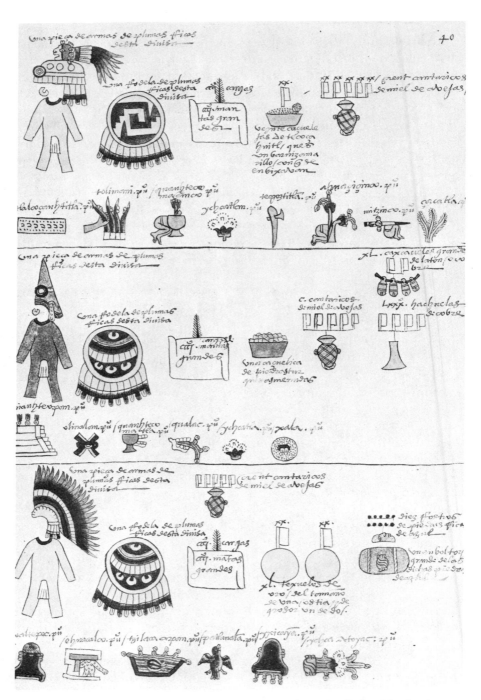

13.15 A Mexican tribute list for towns in Guerrero (from the Codex Mendoza) Each year the people paid tribute in mantles, uniforms, shields, gourds, sage, amaranth, and jade.

The Aztecs believed that the present world was just one in a succession of creations by the gods and that constant effort was required to forestall the extinction of the sun and the utter disappearance of humanity. Human blood was an essential part of the ritual (Figure 13.16) whereby the end of the world was postponed, and each time a human heart was ripped from a sacrificed person, another small step was taken toward prolonging the daily rebirth of the sun (Soustelle 1961: 97). At

13.16 Aztec ritual. The priest was dressed (A) in the skin of a sacrificed person. Another person (B) was given a shield, mirror, and other ritual paraphernalia and played the part of the god Tezcatlipoca. In (C) and (D) the victim is sacrificed and eaten. From the Codex Florentino.

times long lines of sacrificial victims snaked down the steps of the major pyramid mounds, on the top of which priests were kept busy cutting out each person's heart. After the heart and blood had been offered to the gods, the body was thrown down the steps of the pyramid and subsequently flayed and then, perhaps, eaten. Other victims were pitted in gladiatorial contests, or beheaded, drowned, or cast into fires. The Spanish conquistadores may have exaggerated the numbers of people sacrificed, but it seems inescapable that the Aztecs annually killed many tens of thousands and perhaps hundreds of thousands of people. This slaughter was not only accepted by the common people, but it seems to have been widely supported. All war captives knew their fate, and it was an act of honor to accept a sacrificial death. Young men were selected each year to lead a life of luxury surrounded by complaisant young women and feasting on the best of food, realizing full well that at the end of the year they would be sacrificed. And throughout the land parents turned over infants and children to government officials for use in annual sacrificial rites.

Many of the sacrificial victims, as well as soldiers who died in battle, people struck by lightning, mothers who died in childbirth, and other special people, were thought to spend eternity in various paradises, cosseted with the pleasures of this world.

With its emphasis on death, blood, and cosmic cataclysm, it is little wonder that Aztec theology struck the Spanish as somewhat heterodox. Even anthropologists, renowned for their cultural relativism, are impressed with the violence of Aztec religion. But human sacrifice is an old and recurrent theme in the evolution of complex cultures; in Mesopotamia, China, North America, and most other places, warfare and slaughter can be found which equaled that of the Aztecs in forms, if not in intensity.

Why did so many ancient people consider it necessary to kill each other, and why did the Aztecs outstrip most previous cultures in this regard? Michael Harner (1977) has argued that the key to Aztec sacrifice is the contribution the cannibalism of sacrificial victims made to the Aztec diet. Mesoamerica lacks any large domesticated animals that could have been effectively integrated with Aztec agricultural strategies, and this animal protein and fat deficiency may have been compensated for by cannibalism. There is little doubt that the Aztecs engaged in cannibalism, since several sixteenth-century Europeans described it as it happened, but we have insufficient evidence with which to evaluate Harner's thesis.

Despite their death cults, the Aztecs in everyday life were a colorful and in some ways engaging people. The Spanish remarked on their love of flowers and natural beauty, and their poetry contains many references to the joys of the natural world. The Spanish were amazed to find that Aztecs bathed their entire bodies most days—an obsession with personal cleanliness that would have struck even most eighteenth- and nineteenth-century Europeans as bizarre.

Dress for men and women was often a loincloth and a woven cloak, and brightly colored cotton fabrics were used for ornamentation. In the countryside women often went about naked to the waist, but middle- and upper-class urban women wore decorated blouses (Soustelle 1961: 135).

The diet of the Aztecs centered upon maize, beans, squash, and tomatoes, although the wealthier people could eat various fruits, nuts, meats, and other exotic foods. The relatively unvaried diet was sometimes alleviated with peyote and other natural hallucinogens, and by tobacco and *pulque*, a cactus-derived alcoholic drink possessing near-miraculous powers to revive and nourish the weary peasant or archaeologist.

THE SPANISH CONQUEST

The melancholy history of the conquest of Mesoamerica by Spanish adventurers in the early sixteenth century was recorded in detail by the Spanish themselves. In 1519 Hernán Cortez left Cuba with a sizable force of ships, men, armaments, and horses, and sailed to the coast of Veracruz. With the advantage of horses, cannons, war dogs, and an extraordinary esprit de corps, Cortez and his men were able to march directly into the Aztec capital at Tenochtitlán, where they were at first welcomed by the Aztec king, Moctezuma, who was under the delusion that the Spanish were gods returning to their ancestral homeland. He could hardly have been more wrong. Within a short time, the Spanish had kidnapped and jailed him and were forming alliances with local non-Aztec peoples, who were only too happy to help the Spanish displace the Aztecs. Moctezuma and many of his people were eventually killed in a fierce battle at Tenochtitlán, after which Aztec resistance stiffened; but within a few years the Spanish had captured most of the Aztec heartland and Tenochtitlán. In 1524 they hanged the last Aztec king, and thereafter Spanish domination of Mexico was rapid.

14

Aboriginal States and Empires of Andean South America

Even though the Mexicans and Peruvians are the most intelligent and orderly nations to be found in the Indies, the first considered human flesh to be a delicacy and the second ones ate a thousand different kinds of repulsive vermin, including their own body lice. So much for their main dishes.

Father Cobo (1580–1657)

The pattern of cultural evolution in Andean South America (Figure 14.1), which is referred to here as "Peru," was similar to that in Mesoamerica. In both areas between 2000 B.C. and the arrival of Europeans in the sixteenth century A.D., people developed intensive farming systems, built massive pyramids and temples, aggregated into towns, established powerful armies, and organized themselves in complex hierarchical patterns of wealth, power, and prestige.

But there were also some significant differences that make the evolution of cultural complexity in Peru a unique and interesting case. In Mesoamerica the first large sedentary communities appeared in most areas only after maize and many other domesticated plants were incorporated into agricultural economies; but some archaeologists believe that quite large and perhaps complex Peruvian communities were established in coastal areas of western South America many centuries before domesticated plants or agriculture were of much importance. Even after most South Americans came to rely on agriculture, in many areas they lived in dispersed towns and villages, in contrast to the vast urban centers of Mesoamerica such as Teotihuacán and Tenochtitlán. And while the Peruvians never developed a writing system of any sort, they

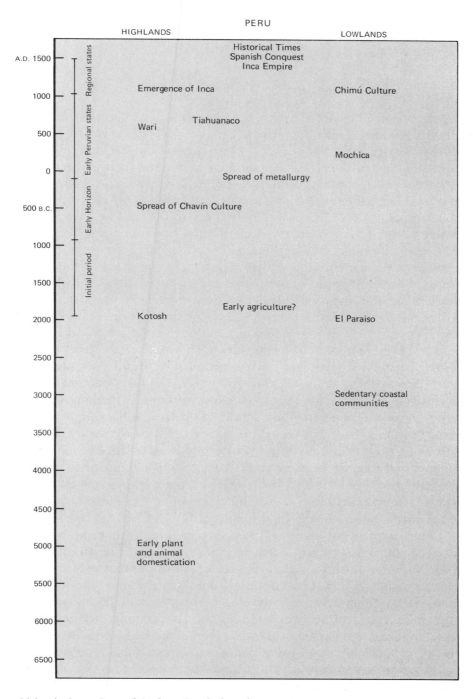

14.1 A chronology of Andean South America.

were able to establish a political system of a size, complexity, and coherence unmatched by anything in Mesoamerica or elsewhere in the New World.

The Ecological Setting

Like all the other areas where complex societies developed independently, Andean South America is a mosaic of highly varied physical environments. The Andes rise so sharply from the Pacific that only a thin strip of land, less than about sixty kilometers at its widest point, separates the mountains from the sea. And because the Andes shield the coast from the rain-bearing air currents crossing the continent from the Atlantic, most of this coastal strip is one of the world's driest deserts, where rain falls only once or twice every five years. In a few places winter fogs along the coast keep skies overcast and, in most years, provide enough moisture through condensation to support vegetation zones (called *lomas*). But most of the coastal strip is utterly dry, and when the wind blows, dunes can quickly cover houses and choke irrigation canals.

This desert is habitable only because of the fifty or so small rivers that flow down from the mountains, transverse the plain, and empty into the sea. Some contain water during only part of the year, but the larger, permanent ones support forests and shrubs and their attendant wildlife, and there are areas where the rivers keep the water table sufficiently high that cultivation is possible without irrigation. In some valleys, rivers have created broad alluvial plains that have high agricultural potential. Near the mouths of the rivers, fish, freshwater shrimp, and other resources can be particularly rich. Human life along the coast is tied directly to these rivers and streams because they provide the only drinking water. At many places along the coast are extraordinarily rich concentrations of fish, birds, birds' eggs, sea mammals, mollusks, crustaceans, kelp and other plant foods.

These rich marine resources are produced by a fascinating interplay of wind and ocean currents, where winds drive water north along the coast while the earth's rotation from east to west pushes the water westward, creating an upwelling of water from the ocean floor. Carried with these deep waters are tremendous concentrations of phosphates and other nutrients that support countless billions of microscopic plants, and these form the basis of a complex food chain comprising anchovies and other small fish that eat the plants; larger fish, birds, and sea mammals that eat the anchovies; and, ultimately, people, who exploit many links in the chain.

Occasionally, shifts in wind and water change water temperatures

14.2 Two views of Peru: sheep grazing on the puna at an elevation of about 4,000 meters and an intermontane valley near Huarascán.

14.3   The geography of Andean South America begins with coastal deserts and grades up into the valleys and slopes of the Andes. As societies became more complex and populations more dense, slopes were terraced and potatoes and other crops intensively cultivated.

and the plants die, cutting off the base of the food chain, and when this happens rotting plant and animal life fills the air with clouds of hydrogen sulfide that can blacken ships and houses (Idyll 1973). Several years may pass before the fertility of the sea is restored. The frequency in prehistory of *el niño,* as this disturbance is called, is unknown, but it has occurred with moderate impact five times since 1925; and, assuming approximately the same conditions in ancient times, *el niño* may have been a limiting factor on human population densities in coastal Peru.

In the mountains (Figure 14.3), human occupation has focused on small valleys, large basins, and high grassy plateaus (called *punas*). Hunters and gatherers here were succeeded after 1800 B.C. by agriculturalists who subsisted on potatoes, maize, quinoa, and other crops. For much of Peruvian prehistory, these *punas* were inhabited to 4,500 meters and higher by hunters and gatherers, who were later replaced by llama and alpaca herders.

The eastern slopes of the Andes, the *montaña,* are wet and heavily forested, and the combination of steep slopes and intense rain apparently limited exploitation by prehistoric peoples. East of the Andes is the Amazon Basin, a tropical rainforest whose rubber, feathers, and other products were occasionally brought into early Peruvian economic systems, but which was never significantly colonized or controlled by either highland or coastal societies.

The Archaeological Record

EARLY HUNTERS AND GATHERERS (? TO 2500 B.C.)

A few Peruvian sites have been dated to 15,000 to 20,000 years ago, but the earliest cultures for which we have substantial archaeological evidence appeared about 7500 B.C. Most sites of this age are in highland caves and rock shelters, and the abundance of projectile points, scrapers, knife blades, and animal bones at these sites reflects an intensive exploitation of deer and guanaco (an animal related to the camel) (Rick 1980). Many groups probably followed a *transhumant* way of life, moving up and down the mountains to exploit various resources as they came in season. Alpacas and llamas require constant tending and frequent moves to new pasturages. The "thin" air, intense cold, blizzards, and thick fogs of the highlands make movement difficult, and over millennia of adapting to these conditions the Peruvians developed cardiovascular systems that permit them to follow annual rounds that would kill most non-Peruvians.

The plant remains from Guitarrero Cave in the northern Peruvian highlands indicate that by 7500 B.C., tubers, beans, fruits, peppers, and guanacos and llamas were already the primary foods in this area (Lynch, ed. 1980). Maize became an important part of the diet by about 5700 B.C. and together with these other foods provided the basis for Peruvian civilizations.

Except for an occasional small hunting camp, there is limited evidence of humans in the coastal areas before about 3200 B.C. (sea-level changes may have been considerable here), but shortly after this some groups worked out a subsistence system based on the seasonal exploitation of the *lomas*, supplemented by coastal resources. The fish, invertebrates, birds, and plant foods of the littoral were probably the major food sources for the earliest coastal populations.

EARLY SEDENTARY COMMUNITIES (2500 TO 1800 B.C.)

By about 2500 B.C. many small sedentary communities had appeared along the Peruvian coast, most of them concentrating on littoral and riverine resources, but perhaps also subsisting on squash, beans, and other cultivated crops.

There are few published detailed analyses of food remains from these early coastal settlements and the possibilities of sampling error make it difficult to reconstruct with any accuracy human subsistence strategies during this period. The diet seems to have been based mainly on marine resources, with wild or domestic plants of only secondary importance (M. Parsons 1970: 297), but there was great variability from site to site.

At Chilca, the primary meat source appears to have been sea lions, but mussels, other invertebrates, and a variety of collected plants were also important. At other sites the remains of sharks, rays, cormorants, gulls, pelicans, and other animals attest to the importance of the resources of the coastal shallows, as does the presence of fish hooks, nets, and lines. No boats have been found at any of these sites, but the kinds of fish and invertebrates usually eaten along the coast are easily taken with simple nets.

By about 2000 B.C., at least a hundred communities dotted the Peruvian coastline, many of them on river deltas, bays, or right on the ocean beach. Most of these seem to have been quite simple foraging-based communities, and few of them had more than several hundred inhabitants. At Chilca the burials of thirty adults and twenty-two children and adolescents were excavated, and only minor differences in grave goods or positioning of the corpses were found. Some people were interned with spindles and spindlewhorls, others with fish hooks and lines, still others with cotton and weaving tools or a pointed stick and spatula kit that may have been used in shellfish gathering.

Shortly after 2000 B.C., at least some communities began building monumental architecture, the most impressive of which is at El Paraiso (also known as Chuquitanta), on the banks of the Rio Chillon, about 2 kilometers inland from the sea (Figure 14.4). This site is dominated by a large "temple" complex consisting of a central large structure flanked by two protruding wings, the whole complex enclosing a large patio. There are eight or nine distinct structural units at the site. The two largest complexes are built on artificial mounds more than 250 meters in length and 50 meters in width, rising to a height of over 5 meters. It has been estimated that there are over 50 hectares of such constructions at this site (Engl and Engl 1969). One complex of rooms, over 450 meters long, is among the largest buildings ever constructed in ancient Peru (Lanning 1967: 71).

The significance of El Paraiso is difficult to assess. Most of the occupational refuse at the site has been destroyed by centuries of plowing.

14.4   El Paraiso, on the Peruvian coast, was one of the earliest massive buildings in the New World.

The paucity of residential remains at the site suggests it may have been mainly a ceremonial center (Moseley [1975] estimates its population at 1,500 to 3,000 people), but it is difficult to determine how much of the site was occupied at a single time or how long it took to build the whole complex.

Moseley has argued at some length (1975) that early Peruvian complex societies, as represented by El Paraiso and similar sites, were initially based on an essentially nonagricultural economy. If so, this would be interesting but would not alter our basic understanding of cultural complexity, for it is clear that what is important in cultural evolution at this stage is overall productivity of an environment rather than the specific ways in which it is productive.

David Wilson has recently (1981) challenged Moseley's assertion that most of the calories that powered Peru's first complex societies were from maritime foraging linked with inland hunting and gathering. On the basis of archaeological data and a complicated statistical estimate of resources availability, Wilson argues that the largest Formative period Peruvian sites, like El Paraiso and Huaca Prieta, are neither large enough nor internally complex enough to be considered representative of state-level societies. He concludes that even if we consider these large settlements to be the centers of chiefdoms, the evidence suggests they were based on maize agriculture (see also Scott 1981).

Very little is known about developments in the Peruvian highlands between 2500 and 1800 B.C., when El Paraiso and other communities were flourishing along the coasts. We do know, however, that between about 5500 and 4000 B.C., people at Ayacucho and elsewhere in the highlands may have been subsisting on several species of domestic plants and animals, including llamas, guinea pigs, gourds, squash, quinoa, amaranths, and chili peppers (Flannery 1973; Kaplan, Lynch, and Smith 1973). Domestic maize is found on the coast by about 2000 B.C. and, if this plant were brought into Peru from Mesoamerica by way of the Peruvian highlands, we would expect future research to locate maize remains in the Peruvian highlands in contexts dating to long before 2000 B.C. Even in areas too high for maize cultivation, squash, gourds, peppers, amaranths, and other plants were being domesticated and perhaps grown by 5000 B.C., and additional food was provided by hunting, llamas, domestic guinea pigs, and dogs.

THE INITIAL PERIOD (1800 TO 900 B.C.)

Between 1800 and 900 B.C., Peruvian systems of settlement and subsistence changed drastically. Maize—possibly indigenous, but more likely an import from the north via the Peruvian highlands—was brought into intensive cultivation along the coast. In the highlands, where maize does not do well, tubers, quinoa, and other crops were the primary foods. Excavations at sites dating to shortly after 1800 B.C. show that along the coast people were probably eating fewer fish, shellfish, and other littoral, foraged foods, and increasing their consumption of maize, manioc, sweet potatoes, beans, peanuts, and other crops. The domestication of the llama around 1800 B.C. provided meat and wool as well as important transport power—something totally absent in Mesoamerica. The increased importance of containers in agricultural societies is reflected in the first wide-scale distribution of pottery in Peru shortly after 1800 B.C., and there seems little need to explain early Peruvian ceramics—as some have—in terms of contacts with Japanese fishermen or other sources.

These various subsistence and technological changes were paralleled by changes in the distribution of settlements, as many of the fishing communities along the coast were slowly abandoned, and people moved inland to take up agriculture. The distribution of settlements in the inland valleys and the botanical remains found at these sites suggest that simple irrigation canals were being constructed from about 1800 to 1200 B.C. to grow maize, squash, legumes, beans, sweet and white potatoes, and peanuts (Moseley 1975: 105).

The transition to inland settlement and an agricultural economy required major social and technological changes. Littoral resources could be exploited by many small independent groups with a very simple technology, and their availability in time and space was not subject to human manipulation (Moseley 1975: 106). Inland agricultural systems, however, required a technology for irrigation, ground preparation, harvesting, and storage, as well as organized, coordinated labor groups.

Pyramids were still being built close to the shore, but the largest constructions were now inland. At Cerro Sechin, for example, sometime before about 1000 B.C. a platform mound was built that stands over 30 meters high and is 550 by 400 meters at the base, making it one of the largest buildings of its type anywhere in Peru (ibid.: 107).

Developments in the Peruvian highlands during this *Initial period* (1800 to 900 B.C.) are not nearly as well known as those in coastal areas. At Kotosh, a site at about the 1,800-meter-level on the eastern slopes of the Andes, a large temple complex may have been begun before 1800 B.C. The earliest structure was built on a stone-faced platform some 8 meters high, but little of the actual building has been excavated.

Little is known about the people who built these edifices, but the earliest of these "temples" may even have been erected by nonagriculturalists (Lumbreras 1974: 47). Most of the later constructions appear to have been the work of maize farmers who relied heavily on domesticated animals, but the paucity of habitation refuse near these massive stone constructions has led some to suspect that they may have been largely ceremonial, perhaps acting as focal points of trade and social exchange between widely spaced agricultural groups.

THE EARLY HORIZON (900 TO 200 B.C.)

After about 900 B.C. people living at Chavín de Huantar (Figure 14.5) and other sites in the highlands of northern Peru began to use many of the same stylistic elements in their pottery, architecture, and other artifacts, and over succeeding centuries tens of thousands of people, from Ica in the south to Ecuador in the north, were participating in the *Chavín Horizon,* as this complex of stylistic elements was called. Chavín art is dominated by depictions of hybrid combinations of people, jaguars, and snakes (Figure 14.6).

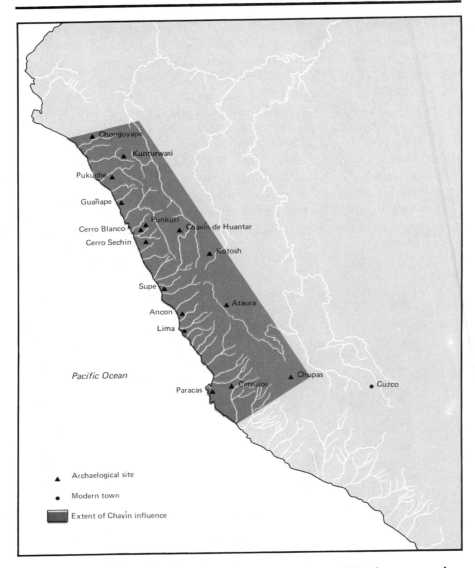

14.5   Chavín-style artifacts have been found at many places within the area noted here.

Some have argued that the spread of the Chavín art style reflects the religious—and perhaps even social and economic—organization of a large area of northern Peru, but this appears unlikely. The spread of these styles occurs at about the same time in some areas as apparent increases in product exchange, activity specialization, population densities, and investments in monumental buildings, but the general tenor of the Chavín diffusion is reminiscent of the initial spread of Olmec art in Mesoamerica—a relatively simple extension of aesthetic and perhaps religious traditions, in the absence of elaborate political hierarchies or economic elites.

Chavín de Huantar, the site after which the art style is named, boasts a ceremonial complex composed of two low platform mounds, a massive terraced platform (called the *Castillo*), and a sunken court, forty-eight meters on a side and paved with stone. Interior support for the Castillo is provided by skillfully combined adobe walls and cut stone beams, and many interior rooms appear to have been decorated with painted designs. Some of the rooms apparently served as repositories for offerings, since hundreds of finely crafted ceramic pots were found there, as well as masses of llama, guinea pig, and fish bones and sea-

14.6   Stone relief of the feline god, a standard Chavín motif.

shells that had been imported over long distances (Lumbreras 1974: 62).

Goldsmithing was developed into a high art in the Chavín era, as craftsmen cut, embossed, annealed, cast, and welded gold into ear spools, nose ornaments, plaques, crowns, and face coverings for corpses. Copper and silver were also extensively used for making ornaments, and weaving became a fine art.

The central religious symbols of Chavín, the anthropomorphic feline, the cayman (relative of the crocodile), and bird motifs, were widely distributed over the northern highlands and the northern and central coasts, as were the ceramic and architectural styles associated with this cultural horizon.

In some important ways, the Chavín phenomenon is reminiscent of the initial stages of cultural evolution in other areas. Religious traditions offer a superbly effective way to get people to act in coordinated ways, because the expenses of large buildings and the "furs and feathers" of office are cheap, compared to their power in directing the population toward specific economic and political goals. Llama herders from the mountains, maize farmers from the valleys, fishermen, artisans, and other specialists may have derived from the Chavín cult the kinds of administration and political support and integration that set the stage for the evolution of state societies.

There is some evidence in the form of fortresses (Greider 1978), for example, that the Chavín period may have been more violent than originally thought: redistribution centers and a unified religious iconography do not necessarily mean an era of ecumenism and peace.

EARLY PERUVIAN STATES (200 B.C. TO A.D. 1000)

In the first millennium A.D., Peruvian societies were transformed from relatively simple agricultural communities, perhaps organized along tribal lines, to highly stratified, populous, militaristic cultures that we can legitimately term *states*. Within this period the population of Peru rose from a few hundred thousand to approximately 4 or 5 million (Lanning 1967: 114–15), large cities appeared in scores of places, armies conquered thousands of square kilometers, irrigation systems were greatly extended, and the ceramic, architectural, metallurgical, and textile arts (Figure 14.7) reached such heights that archaeologists have traditionally referred to this period as the *Classic*.

The story of this transformation begins with the widespread disappearance of Chavín artistic styles at about 200 B.C., followed quickly

14.7   Textile from the Paracas culture. First millennium B.C.

by the emergence of as many as fifteen different areas of Peru as centers of regional development. Ceremonial centers can be found in many places in the southern Peruvian highlands at this time, as well as in the Nazca Valley and other coastal regions. Less work has been done on the residential areas of these centers than on the monumental architecture, but it now appears that some of these were sizable towns, such as Tambo Viejo in the Acarí Valley (Nazca area), which contains hundreds of rectangular rooms, most of which seem to have been residences. Also numerous along the northern coast were great fortresses, comprising terraced adobe platforms with room complexes and defensive peripheral walls.

The complexity of Classic period agriculture is well illustrated by the irrigation system of the Mochica state, where mud canals were built high in the hills, diverting water through kilometers of canals that snaked along the mountainside, down to the valleys. Because the Mochica worked only with mud, the construction of these canal systems had to be done with great precision; for if the water flowed too slowly, silt would accumulate so rapidly as to make the canal a vast waste of effort, or, if it flowed too fast, the whole system could be eroded. Cleaning the wind-blown sand from these systems probably required the annual orchestration of thousands of laborers.

We know much about life in Peru during this period (200 B.C. to

14.8   By turning over patinated stones, the Nazca used color contrasts to form enormous designs on the floor of the Nazca Valley (ca. A.D. 500). Despite suggestions about the use of these markings as signs to visitors from outer space, these were probably caldendrical or religious symbols.

A.D. 1000) because the people recorded their activities in great detail in ceramics, sculpture, paintings, and tapestries. Pottery vessels depict people hunting deer with spears and clubs, fishermen putting to sea in small canoes, blowgun hunters taking aim at birds, weavers working under the direction of a foreman, and many people engaging in war, human sacrifice, and violence. People are also shown being carried on sedan chairs, seated on thrones, receiving tribute, and presiding at executions.

But most famous of all the aesthetic expressions of this period are the frank depictions—usually in pottery—of sexual practices. While every conceivable sexual variation is amply illustrated, the vast majority involve acts currently widely considered somewhat daring (although most of these are executed with great style and wit). Pots representing sexual themes in the most explicit terms may have been used in ordinary daily life, and to drink from many of them is to perform, symbolically at least, acts still widely banned.

If the sexual practices depicted in pottery are in any way a reflection of the proclivities of the people—and reports of the Spanish and the Inca suggest this was the case (but see Donnan 1976)—then the Mochica may have devised a very efficient system of birth control. For although there are few depictions of homosexuality (most involving lesbian relationships), procreative acts of sexual intercourse are much less celebrated than nonprocreative acts in this pottery.

Another central element of life in these early Peruvian states was warfare. Every well-surveyed coastal valley has been found to have fortresses and fortified settlements dating to this period, and weapons are common in these sites, particularly along the southern coast. Artistic representations focus on warriors, battle scenes, and mutilations, and trophy heads and mummified corpses showing signs of violence are frequently found in cemeteries (Lanning 1967: 121).

Between A.D. 600 and 800, the many rival "states" of Classic Peru gave way to several larger competing political systems, one centered at Wari in the Manteco Basin, another at Tiahuanaco, at the southern end of Lake Titicaca, and a third in the Moche-Chimú area. In these and perhaps other areas, wars of conquest brought large territories under centralized, hierarchically organized governments and lessened regional isolation (Lanning 1967: 127).

Wari existed as a political system for only a century or two, but at its high point it carried out political and economic activities over most of the coast and highlands between Cajamarca in the north and Sicuani in the south. The evidence for the Wari "empire" comes mainly from the distribution of specific art styles and religious symbols over a wide area of the central highlands. Significantly, these motifs show up most frequently in the burials of individuals whose associated mortuary goods appear to reflect particularly high status. Also, while these styles were spreading, there may have been some reorganization of settlement patterns. Within a century, the entire population of the valley, most of whom had formerly lived in small towns and villages, was concentrated around the city of Wari, which had expanded to the impressive size of roughly ten square kilometers, making it one of the largest residential sites in the ancient New World.

If Wari were an expansionist state, it is probably significant that some of ancient Peru's major roadways may have been constructed during this period (Lumbreras 1974: 162), for such roads would have been very important in facilitating the exchange of goods and services over an area as large as that apparently administered from Wari.

REGIONAL STATES (A.D. 1000 TO 1476)

With the collapse of the Wari and Tiahuanaco political systems between A.D. 800 and A.D. 1000, at least seven different "kingdoms" became power centers in Peru, the best known and most developed of
which was the *Chimú* state centered in the Moche Valley on the northern coast. A capital of the Chimú political system was the beautiful city
of Chan-chan (Figure 14.9), a planned settlement covering nearly eight
square kilometers—one of the largest pre-Columbian cities in the New
World. It was divided into ten rectangular sectors, each containing
houses, terraces, reservoirs, parks, roads, and public buildings.

Goldworking and silverworking, ceramics, weaving, and sculpture
were all highly developed crafts. Chimú society seems to have been
rigidly stratified according to wealth and prestige, and extension of

14.9   The fabled city of Chan-chan, composed of burial platforms, public buildings,
shops, and residential quarters.

political and economic control appears to have been based on a highly efficient army (Keatinge 1974: 79).

Perhaps the most significant development in Peru during this period (A.D. 1000–1476) was the multiplication of urban centers. Much of southern Peru remained largely rural, but in the northern half of the country some of the greatest cities of the preconquest period were built, including Chan-chan, Pacatnamú, Farfán, and Apurlé (Moseley and Day, eds. 1982).

THE IMPERIAL TRANSFORMATION (A.D. 1476 TO 1525)

The largest and most highly integrated ancient political system ever to appear in the New World evolved in Peru within the space of only eighty-seven years. Centered in the Cuzco Valley, the *Inca Empire* (more properly known as the *Empire of Tawantinsuyu*) eventually stretched from Colombia to central Chile and from the Pacific to the eastern jungles, tying together under the administration of a single royal lineage many diverse regional economic and political systems. At its height, as many as 6 million people may have been living under Inca rule in one of the most intricately ordered societies of all time (Collier, Rosaldo, and Wirth, eds. 1982).

Native and Spanish accounts say that the Inca began their rise to power out of the dissolution of the many small competing Peruvian states of the thirteenth and fourteenth centuries A.D. The people of Cuzco were attacked by a rival state at about A.D. 1435 (Lumbreras 1974: 217) and managed to prevail. Succeeding monarchs at Cuzco added new provinces to the empire by conquest, treaty, and simple annexation. The oral histories of the Inca—recorded by the Spanish—speak of military campaigns in which Inca kings smashed the rival power of Chan-chan in the 1460s, put down large-scale revolts in the 1470s, and extended the empire to its limits in the 1480s (Lanning 1967: 159–60).

The economic basis of the Inca Empire (Figure 14.10) was a highly integrated system of fishing, herding, and farming. Rivers were channeled through stone-lined canals, and lowland irrigation systems, which had existed for thousands of years, were greatly extended and brought under a centralized authority. Llamas and alpacas were raised for wool, while dogs, muscovy ducks, and guinea pigs provided most of the meat. But the staple foods were maize, beans, potatoes, quinoa, oca, and peppers.

The food storage methods used by the Inca were very important in

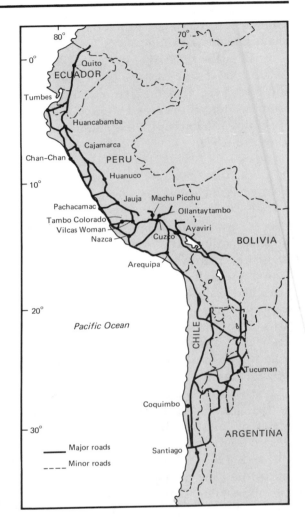

14.10 The Inca (Tawantin-suyu) Empire, showing some of the principal roads and towns. Almost every settlement was connected to the two major north–south roads.

establishing imperial food reserves. Potatoes were alternately dried and frozen to produce a black, pulpy product called *chuño,* meat was turned into jerky, and grain was brewed into *chica,* a nutritious beer.

The people of the empire were complexly organized according to a decimal system in which there were administrators for every unit of taxpayer from 10 to 10,000. Most people were members of large kin groups, called *ayllu;* marriages were between members of the same *ayllu.* The *ayllu* were usually economically self-sufficient units, and were bound together by complex patterns of reciprocal obligations, such as requiring members to work each other's lands when one was absent and to support widows and the infirm (Bushnell 1963: 131).

Farmers worked a certain amount of time on state-owned plots, while craftsmen and specialists, such as runners, weavers, and goldsmiths, contributed according to their particular talents.

Records of taxes, transactions, and census figures were kept with the aid of the *quipu*, a set of strings tied into knots at different levels (Figure 14.11) according to a decimal notation system that could be used by a special hereditary class of accountants to memorize the information (Lanning 1967: 166–67). A writing system of the type used in early Mesopotamia would no doubt have conveyed more religious and philosophical information, but looked at in terms of simple information storage and retrieval, the *quipu* appears to have been an adequate substitute for writing, particularly in view of the enormous Inca bureaucracy (Ascher and Ascher 1982).

Trade in foodstuffs appears to have been largely local (Lanning 1967: 167), but gold, fabrics, and other luxury goods were collected from over the empire for distribution among the elites. Women, too, were treated as commodities. Government agents visited each village periodically

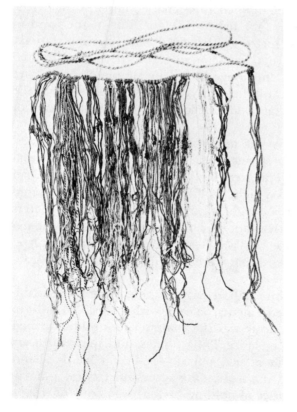

14.11   A *quipu,* a set of knotted strings used for keeping accounts.

and took the most beautiful girls of about age ten back to provincial capitals where they were taught spinning, weaving, and cooking and were apportioned out as wives for the emperor and the nobles.

The Inca Empire was possible only because it developed a system of roads and transport of extraordinary efficiency. Most villages were largely self-sufficient, but the flow of goods and information and, most importantly, the armies required to create the empire were dependent on the road system, comprising an overall network of about 16,000 kilometers of paved roads (von Hagen 1952). Road beds were excavated through hillsides, swamps were crossed by drained causeways, walls were built to protect the roadway in the windy uplands, and wide rivers and ravines were crossed by suspension bridges made of woven vines hung from stone towers. All along the road were storehouses and administrative outposts, and runners stationed about a kilometer apart were reputed to carry messages over distances as great as 2,400 kilometers in just five days.

Although they were master builders, the Inca stressed the rural, village way of life. Typical Inca residential units were rectangular walled houses of stone or adobe, subdivided into smaller units. Most of the public constructions were not for urban dwellers, but in the form of palaces, temples, granaries, fortresses, barracks, and highway stations. The skill used in these constructions is amazing, considering the limited technology. They cut stones into huge blocks by simple chipping and abrading with harder stones and then fitted them together (without the use of mortar) so precisely that, as the cliché goes, a knifeblade cannot be inserted between them.

The capital city of Cuzco was an orderly arrangement of houses, monumental buildings, and streets, well provided with a municipal water and drainage system. The great temple of Qori Kancha here had exterior walls measuring sixty-eight by fifty-nine meters, and a semicircular annex that rose to a height of more than thirty-four meters (Lumbreras 1974). A gold frieze about a meter wide ran along the exterior wall, and the entrance way was heavily sheathed in gold plate. Many other structures at the capital were lavishly decorated with gold and silver.

The comparatively great internal security of the empire made it unnecessary to defend most settlements, except with occasional hilltop forts. The heart of the Inca army was the common foot soldier armed with club, mace, battle axe, or lance. Slings, bolas, and spear throwers were used prior to the main attack, but it was brutal hand-to-hand combat that usually decided the issue. One successful tactical innovation of the Inca was the practice of holding back a large body of troops who were thrown in at a critical juncture—a simple tactic similar in a way to Napoleon's successful use of reserves.

THE EUROPEAN CONQUEST

The history of the Spanish conquest of Peru is yet another installment in the all-too-familiar story of colonial exploitation and violence. After sporadic, occasionally hostile contacts between 1527 and 1541, the Spanish under Francisco Pizzaro set out toward the provincial capital at Cajamarca, the residence of the Atahualpa, the Inca king. Their trek took them through the heart of Inca military strength, and why they were never intercepted and massacred remains a mystery. Internecine warfare between rival claimants to the Inca throne at this time was probably a factor. In any case, the Peruvians soon had cause to regret their diffidence. Pizzaro and his men entered the city on 15 November 1532, and found it to be a massive, fortified center, but surprisingly, nearly deserted. After establishing himself in a fortress with a couple of cannons and his few score soldiers, Pizzaro elected to wait until the Inca king made an effort to visit him. Eventually the emperor came, borne on a litter and preceded by thousands of soldiers, attendants, and subjects. The first Spaniard to approach the king was the chaplain who, as part of Pizzaro's contract with the king of Spain and the pope, was charged with spreading the Christian faith. Throughout the trip to Cajamarca the chaplain and the Spanish had talked to the natives about Christianity—without too much success in converting them, apparently— yet the chaplain immediately began to harangue the king, through an interpreter, about the creation of the world, the fall of Adam and Eve, the Virgin Birth, the establishment of the papacy, and other dogma of the Christian faith, culminating with the announcement that the pope had given Peru to the Spanish through King Charles of Spain.

Not surprisingly, the Inca king took exception to parts of the chaplain's speech, particularly the legality of Peru being ceded to the Spanish; he wanted to know how the pope could give away something that was not his, and how it had happened that the god of the Christians had died, since the Inca deity, the Sun, was immortal (Engl and Engl 1969: 119).

When the Atahualpa asked how the chaplain knew all these things, he was handed a breviary. The king, unable to open the clasp at first, finally broke it, looked briefly and no doubt uncomprehendingly inside, and then threw it away. At this point the Spanish attacked, and then the inexplicable happened: instead of killing the Spanish, the

Inca fled, dropping their weapons and killing themselves in their panicked flight, and the Spanish were able to dispatch hundreds and capture the king with little trouble. They remained fortressed in Cajamarca for some months, detaining the king, who tried to win his release by offering to fill a room (supposed to have been 6.5 by 4.5 meters) with gold. The Spanish meanwhile took masses of gold and silver in raids, most of it in the form of exquisitely wrought figures, which in most cases they melted into ingots.

Rumors of insurrections in the countryside convinced the Spanish to execute the Inca king, and they did so, considering themselves enlightened for giving him the option of being garroted rather than being burned at the stake—a reward to the king for allowing himself to be baptized. With the Atahualpa's death and the ensuing factionalism among rival claimants to the throne, as well as the devastation brought on by introduced diseases and the horror wrought on the populace through warfare and the destruction of the irrigation system, the population of Peru is thought to have dropped from over 6 million to fewer than 2 million within a few decades of the conquest.

The Origins of Complex Cultures in Peru: Conclusions

Not surprisingly, the evolution of cultural complexity in Peru is not explainable in terms of any single factor. As in other early complex societies, agriculture was the basis for later stages of evolutionary development, but some elements of cultural complexity may have been well developed before agriculture became a primary part of the subsistence strategy. Here too, then, the potential for food production was more important than whether the basis of food production was agriculture or intensive foraging.

Nor does large-scale irrigation seem to be the key. Such systems probably appeared in Peru—as in most other early complex societies—long after the appearance of the major elements of cultural complexity.

Population pressure and warfare also seem to be, at the very best, incomplete explanations. Carneiro (1970) argues that Peruvian cultural evolution resulted from human population growth within environmentally circumscribed valleys along the Peruvian coast. With their agricultural and marine resources, he suggests, these populations grew rapidly; but because these valleys are boxed in by the sea, the oceans, and adjoining deserts, the inhabitants had no way of coping with population growth except by intensification of agricultural productivity, and, later, when maximum productivity had been reached, by warfare. State-level societies then evolved because administrators were needed to tax and manage conquered territories, and a class society would presumably emerge as prisoners became slaves and war leaders became an elite class.

We have already reviewed extensively the idea that human population growth causes cultural evolution, and it was suggested that human population growth is usually the *result,* not the cause of these developments. In addition, warfare is somewhat suspect as a force in early Peruvian developments because there is no evidence of sustained warfare until well after the appearance of such things as monumental buildings, the coordination of regional economies, craft specialization, and the rise of great religious traditions. How, then, are we to account for Peruvian complex societies?

Obviously, the rich maritime and agricultural resources were essential ingredients in this development. In only a few areas of the world is it possible to produce and gather enough food to run complex cultures on the basis of primitive technologies, and Peru is one of these.

An important "negative" element in the evolution of Peruvian cultures appears to have been the fact that, unlike ancient China, Mesopotamia, or the Indus Valley, Peru was geographically isolated from other highly complex political systems. Evolving Old World civilizations soon came into contact with one another, and their political, economic, and social interchanges appear to have transformed each of them to some degree. But, except for Mesoamerica—which was very distant and cut off by ocean and jungle—Peru evolved alone.

The absence of a domesticable draught animal also was a limit on Peruvian development. Llamas compensated for this to a degree, but they cannot compare with the transport abilities of horses, mules, or oxen. It is difficult to judge the effects the presence of a domesticable draught animal in Peru would have had, but it may be significant that almost all agricultural areas of Peru today are plowed.

Nor is it easy to weigh the effect on Peruvian developments of the lack of accessible iron ore and the tardy development of bronze metallurgy. In the Old World ironworking seems to have been intimately associated with the expansion of great empires, and, had it been available, it might also have changed the character of later Peruvian developments. We still do not know the sources of Peruvian copper ores used in the production of bronze, but the spread of bronze weapons and implements throughout Peru and adjacent areas during the Inca period may have been as much of a stimulus to trade and agricultural technology as it was in the Old World.

Thus, in summary of Peruvian prehistory we see that cultural devel-

opments there paralleled those in other centers of independent complex society formation in most important details, including the initial
spread of a religious cult, the importance of a highly productive economy, the widespread occurrence of monumental architecture, and the
gradual emergence of highly stratified, integrated state and imperial
political systems.

15

Patterns of Cultural Change in Prehistoric North America

> You must explain to the natives of [North Amer-
> ica] that there is only one God in heaven, and
> the emperor on earth to rule and govern it, whose
> subjects they must all become and whom they
> must serve.
>
> Instructions of the Viceroy
to Fray Marcos De Ninza, 1538.

As Europeans invaded the interior of North America in the sixteenth and seventeeth centuries, they encountered what they assumed were the relics of ancient civilizations: thousands of large earthen mounds, some nearly as large as the Egyptian pyramids, dotted every major river valley of the East, and in the Southwest the colonists stumbled upon large, neatly planned adobe towns that had obviously once been inhabited by thousands.

With an ethnocentrism characteristic of the age, the Europeans assumed that these impressive works had been constructed by the Celts, the Romans, or perhaps the Vikings; they simply could not accept the possibility that the builders had been ancestors of the poor and "degenerate" Native Americans they saw about them. Some of the colonists even blamed the Indians for massacring what the Europeans believed to be an ancient "superior" American race—the ultimate in adding insult to injury, given the Indians' eventual fate.

The truth, of course, is that these mounds and abandoned settlements had indeed been built by Native Americans many centuries before the Europeans arrived, and we now know that these ancient Americans had begun to travel much the same road to cultural complexity as had the people of Mesoamerica, Peru, and the Old World.

Prehistoric North American cultures were influenced by contact with the complex cultures of ancient Mesoamerica, and it is also true that according to some criteria, aboriginal American cultures never reached the level of complexity attained in Mesoamerica, Mesopotamia, or in the other "independent" and ancient centers of cultural evolution. But the native North Americans did develop some aspects of cultural complexity, and they did so largely independently. Moreover, the ecological and cultural reasons North American cultures did not exactly parallel those of Mexico or Peru provide some insights into the general evolution of culture.

Intensive archaeological research in North America has been in progress for many decades, and we should know more about developments there than virtually anywhere else in the world, given the high ratio of archaeologists per square kilometer. But, unfortunately, American archaeologists too have yielded to the temptation of giving most of their time and effort to rich tombs and large towns. And with the curious prevalent mentality that placidly accepts the conversion of ancient Native American cultural resources into parking lots and hamburger stands, the archaeological record of North America is disappearing at such a rapid rate that we shall never know many things about the prehistory of the continent.

The old, sometimes perjorative myths about Indians are now giving way in some circles to new ones stressing the social harmony, ecological purity, and superior metaphysics of ancient Native Americans. As with all cultures, there is much to admire about ancient North Americans, but the evidence suggests that most of the Indians of the last 1,500 years were very much like people in other evolving societies—harried, small-time farmers, worrying about this year's drought and next year's deluge, shifting their crops from year to year as they exhausted the soil and timber of one place after another, and as enmeshed in slavery, exploitation, and warfare as any ancient Chinese, Egyptian, or European.

The Ecological Setting

By about 5000 B.C., the huge glacial ice sheets that once covered much of eastern North America had retreated into Canada, and the distribution of plant and animal species in this region was roughly similar to that of the recent past. Most of eastern North America is much farther from the equator than all the other areas where early complex societies developed independently, with the exception of North China; this is significant because northern latitudes have less solar radiation and

15.1 Archaeological culture areas of North America.

fewer frost-free days and thus lower absolute agricultural potential than
tropical environments, *assuming a primitive agricultural technology.*
Also, nowhere in eastern North America are there extensive, well-
watered plains where vegetative cover was sufficiently thin that large-
scale agriculture was possible without extensive land clearing, plowing,
and weeding.

Archaic Cultures of Eastern North America
(8000 B.C. to 2000 B.C.)

With the gradual establishment of essentially modern distributions of plant and animal species after 8000 B.C., North American cultures assumed many different forms, as local environments evoked varying adaptations. Many groups lived a highly mobile life, following carefully scheduled seasonal rounds and exploiting hundreds of plant and animal species as each became available with the changing seasons. *Archaic* hunters and gatherers in the lower Ohio Valley, for example, established fall camps in the uplands to harvest hickory nuts, and then moved back to the river bottoms in later fall and winter to hunt deer and migratory fowl. In spring they fished the backwater sloughs and ponds, then collected mussels and snails during the summer when they also harvested sunflower seeds, pigweed, marsh elder, grapes, strawberries, and other plant foods (Fowler 1971: 393). And as with all hunters and gatherers, population densities were low and quite stable, although the size of social groups fluctuated with the seasons, with larger groups coming together when food was plentiful but dispersing into microbands of several families during the leaner seasons. Procurement areas were large, and cultural complexity quite low.

Some groups living in coastal zones did not make these seasonal treks, because their resources were concentrated for them by the juxtaposition of the littoral and terrestrial environments, and it was probably in these areas that the first sedentary communities appeared.

Beginning about 4000 B.C., however, population densities were apparently on the rise, and several important ecological changes were underway. Nut collecting and hunting remained important food sources, but people were broadening their diets to include increasing quantities of fruits, the seeds of various annual plants (e.g., goosefoot and sunflowers), fish, and other plant and animal species.

ARCHAIC ADAPTATIONS AND PLANT DOMESTICATION

The richness of the eastern woodlands, with their large game, abundant rivers and streams, nuts, fruits, and other foods, and the intricate and skillful exploitation strategies of Native Americans in these areas combined to produce a balanced, flexible way of life of such "efficiency," to use Joseph Caldwell's (1971) term, that this way of life was not quickly

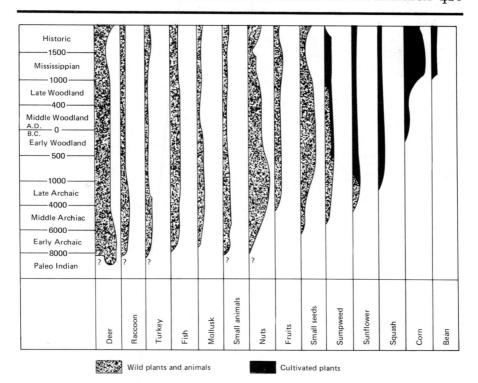

15.2 Estimated subsistence changes in the prehistoric Middle West. The stippled areas represent wild plants and animals, and the solid areas represent domesticates. The thickness of the areas reflects the relative importance of a resource.

altered by the introduction of maize, beans, and other Mesoamerican domesticates.

Archaic settlement and subsistence systems included both *specialized* subsistence strategies, such as maize agriculture or caribou hunting, in which primary reliance is placed on just a few plant and animal species, and *generalized* subsistence systems, in which a much more diverse range of plant and animal species is utilized. Specialized systems tend to be more unstable because marked reductions in the one or two species on which these societies depend have severe consequences, whereas generalized systems can withstand the loss, say, of this year's nut crop or a poor wildfowl hunting season because they have many alternative food sources. Specialized systems, especially specialized agricultural systems, often are associated with relatively high population densities (Dunnell 1967).

Cross-cutting this distinction is another, the difference between *nu-*

cleated and *dispersed* settlement systems. In nucleated settlements all or nearly all of the economic activities of a group are carried out by people who live in the same domestic unit, whether that be a village or a hunting and gathering band, whereas in dispersed settlements the full range of economic activities supporting a given population is carried out by people who live in separate places.

After the long relative stasis of the Early and Middle Archaic, the overall trend was toward increasing numbers of sedentary communities that specialized first in hunting and intensive plant collecting and later in maize and bean agriculture. Archaic patterns of subsistence and settlement persisted in many areas, however, even up to the arrival of Europeans.

Ceramic vessels, often associated with the agricultural way of life, appeared at several places in the American Southeast after 2500 B.C. (Bullen 1971), but there is no necessary connection between their use and agriculture. Some have speculated that the techniques for making ceramic vessels were introduced into North America from Mexico, but it is more likely that pottery was independently invented in eastern North America at least once, and probably several times, as containers became increasingly important in plant collection and preparation.

Because plant remains preserve poorly in the North American East, we do not know in great detail how and when domesticated plants and agriculture were incorporated into cultural systems here. Domestication is typically a byproduct of systematic collection, and thus many native plants were probably being domesticated as, century after century, hunters and gatherers made their seasonal rounds. The sunflower (*Helianthus*), perhaps the most important North American domesticate, in its wild form was a much smaller plant with smaller seeds than are characteristic of modern varieties, but by 300 B.C. average seed size was increasing—presumably as part of the domestication process. Goosefoot (*Chenopodium*), marsh elder (*Iva*), sumpweed (*Aster*), and canary grass (*Phalaris*) may also have been domesticated at the same time (Yarnell 1965).

Patty Jo Watson's excavations at Kentucky's Mammoth Cave (1974) have turned up large amounts of human feces reflecting the diet of hunters and foragers in this area during the first millennium B.C. Sunflower seeds, sumpweed, hickory nuts, and other plant foods, combined with more digestible foods, appear to have been part of these people's diet.

The collection and domestication of these various plant species seem always and everywhere to have been much less important than hunting, fishing, and nut gathering, and there is little evidence that agriculture was being practiced at this time. That is, little energy was invested in modifying the environments of sunflowers and these other plants through hoeing, watering, or weeding. Melvin Fowler (1971) notes that most of the native plants apparently domesticated in the East are species that prefer open, disturbed areas, such as would have been provided by the refuse piles that must have become increasingly available as hunters and gatherers cluttered the landscape with snail and clam shells, fish bones, and other debris.

The earliest domesticates found in the North American woodlands are gourds and squash, which appear in Missouri, Tennessee, and Kentucky by 2500 B.C. These plants probably were introduced from northeastern Mexico and used as containers and for seeds rather than eaten directly.

Between 5000 B.C. and about 1500 B.C., while the domestication of sunflowers and a few other plants was in progress, there were other important cultural changes. At the Poverty Point site in Louisiana, vast earthworks were constructed sometime between 1300 and 200 B.C. by people who seem to have been living in large, planned villages. The Poverty Point people buried some of their dead under elaborate conical burial mounds, and they also engaged in a range of arts and crafts that bespeak some degree of occupational specialization. Skilled stoneworkers made vessels out of steatite and sandstone, tubular pipes out of clay and stone, and axes, adzes, saws, weights, and other implements of hard stones. The economic basis of the Poverty Point cultures may have included some limited agriculture, but no substantial evidence of this exists; perhaps the larger Poverty Point centers were redistribution centers for surrounding communities of people still following the Archaic foraging-collecting way of life.

What may be termed base camps with "permanent shelters" (Brown 1977: 167) occur at the Koster site in Illinois by 4000 B.C., and it seems clear generally that Archaic economies in certain locales allowed stable subsistence and even substantial surpluses.

The second and first millennia B.C. were a time of significant change in many areas of North America. Burial cults, comprising large earthen mounds, intentionally broken ornaments and tools buried with infants, and significant variations in mortuary wealth are found at Archaic sites from Newfoundland (Tuck 1971) to the lower Ohio Valley (Rothschild 1979).

Much remains to be learned about Archaic developments in general, but the appearance of increased population densities, sedentary communities, mortuary ceremonialism, public architecture, and improved technologies indicates that some aspects of increasing cultural complexity were already present long before the appearance of agricultural economies.

Agriculture and the Woodland Period (800 B.C. to A.D. 800)

Between about 800 B.C. and A.D. 800, population densities in many parts of eastern North America increased sharply, maize agriculture became the basic subsistence strategy, gigantic earthworks were constructed, interregional trade expanded, and large nucleated settlements appeared. This era of change, usually referred to as the *Early Woodland period,* is associated with two major cultural traditions: the *Adena,* centered in the Ohio River Valley, and the *Hopewell,* centered in southern Ohio (Figure 15.3). These cultures were roughly contemporary, although the Hopewell was considerably larger and more elaborate; both are defined on the basis of certain styles of pottery, engraved stone tablets, textiles, and worked bone and copper.

Our picture of Adena and Hopewell life is somewhat distorted because research has focused on larger settlements and rich tombs, and although there is much to be learned from these sources, they tell us comparatively little about general subsistence and settlement.

The construction of Hopewell and Adena ceremonial mounds began with the clearing of a large area and the deposition of a thick layer of clean sand; then a large open or enclosed wood structure was erected; individual burials were made within the structure and the graves covered over with small mounds of earth; and finally, the wooden enclosure was burned to the ground, and the resulting ash layer covered over with layers of earth and stone.

Grave goods are not particularly profuse in Adena mounds, but Hopewell tombs often contain finely worked copper, pipestone, mica, obsidian, meteoric iron, shell, tortoise shell, shark and alligator teeth, bear teeth, ceramics, and other commodities; there is also evidence of the ultimate grave good—sacrificed humans. Adena and Hopewell settlements and mounds increased in size and number in the centuries before about A.D. 400, and major earthworks were often built near the burial mounds.

These burials appear to have been excellent reflectors of the dead person's rank and status within the community. Joseph Tainter (1975) carried out a statistical analysis of more than 500 Hopewell burials and concluded that there were six discrete levels of status within the Hopewell community, corresponding to six different forms of burial, ranging from simple holes in the ground to massive mounds in which the

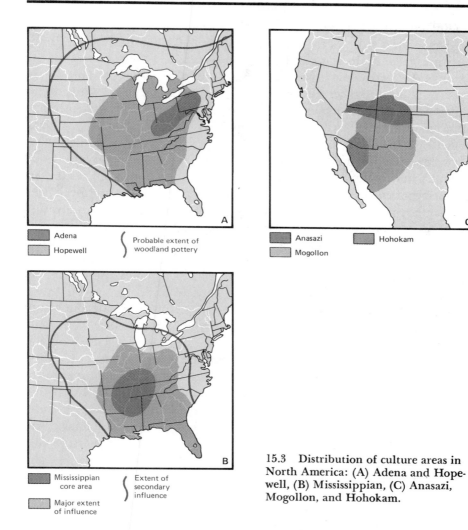

15.3   Distribution of culture areas in North America: (A) Adena and Hopewell, (B) Mississippian, (C) Anasazi, Mogollon, and Hohokam.

corpse was accompanied by the finest goods. In some Adena and Hopewell mounds, infants and juveniles were found buried with great ceremony and rich goods, indicating no doubt the inheritance of rank and prestige and the control of the society's resources by a limited number of its people.

A centralized administration seems to be evident in the later Hopewell buildings and earthworks, many of which were precisely planned and relatively expensive to construct. One of the many puzzling things about these mound complexes is that in many areas they do not seem to have any associated residential zones. Some archaeologists assumed that any society capable of building such impressive works must certainly have been composed of sedentary agriculturalists, but early Adena and Hopewell peoples for the most part probably hunted and gathered essentially the same plant and animal species as did their ancestors, with deer, ducks, small mammals, fish, snails, mussels, pigweed, lambsquarter, sunflowers, and nuts providing much of their nutrition. Outside the Adena and Hopewell spheres of influence, the Archaic subsistence and settlement systems appear to have remained essentially unchanged (Dragoo 1976: 18–19).

Although domesticated maize was found at very few Hopewell and Adena sites, many later developments of this period, such as the increased mortuary complexity and the increasing size and number of settlements and mounds, may have been directly tied to the incorporation of maize agriculture into subsistence systems. Settlements were largely confined to broad alluvial valleys having the minimum 120 frost-free days a year necessary for maize to mature. Maize agriculture, conducted on a swidden system, probably was begun in these zones late in the first millennium B.C. (Farnsworth 1973).

The earliest widespread occurrence of maize in the North American East was shortly after 500 B.C., but it remained a minor part of the subsistence base until centuries later. Maize is very sensitive to frost and length of daylight, and a substantial amount of time and cultivation was probably required to produce varieties that could mature in the shorter days of northern areas. So adaptable is the plant, however, that it was a staple as far north as Ontario, Canada, by the time the Europeans arrived in the sixteenth century. Primitive strains of maize had such small cobs when first introduced from Mexico that considerable selective breeding was required before it was worthwhile to do all the work of clearing land, weeding, and harvesting necessary for successful maize agriculture here. Nor was the Adena-Hopewell heartland so impoverished that hunters and gatherers were desperately trying to improve their subsistence base. Estimates of resources around the Hopewell settlement at Scoville, in the lower Illinois Valley, indicate that "within a half-hour's walk . . . there would annually be from 182,000 to 426,000 bushels of nuts and 48,000 to 484,000 bushels of acorns, 100 to 840 deer, 10,000 to 20,000 squirrels, and 200 turkeys. Not computed were seeds, fruits, smaller animals, fish, mussels, and migratory birds (6 million mallards were estimated to be in the Illinois River Valley in 1955)" (Jennings 1974: 232). Given these abundant environments, it is not surprising that maize agriculture apparently appeared first in poorer, more marginal environments and displaced hunting and gathering in the lushest environments only much later.

The importation and circulation of obsidian from Montana, silver

15.4   Great Serpent Mound, an Adena construction near Cincinnati.

from Ontario, copper from northern Michigan, shell from the Gulf Coast, and other exotic commodities suggest considerable contact between many of the settlements in this Hopewell interaction sphere. Within this sphere artifact styles and subsistence systems were very similar, but there is no evidence of state-level political centralization (Brose and Greber, eds. 1979). Most of the Hopewell and Adena communities were small sedentary groups of hunters and gatherers who built the burial mounds and ceremonial complexes for reasons that perhaps had to do with redistribution and population control. Whereas Archaic hunters and gatherers met their needs by following seasonal rounds and exploiting a diversity of resources, Hopewell communities accomplished the same thing by exchanging products among themselves.

Comparatively little is known about daily life for the mass of the Hopewell or Adena peoples. The few houses excavated seem to be rectangular or ovoid constructions supported on posts and covered with bark or mats (Jennings 1974: 232). Most people apparently lived in small hamlets composed of a few such houses and associated pits and refuse piles. Some craft specialization is evident in the finely knapped flint and stone and in other sophisticated artifacts, and most of these communities were probably organized around a "big-man" and his favored lineage.

Shortly after A.D. 400, burial mounds and earthworks appear to have lost their importance in Hopewell and Adena communities, and the extensive trade networks that formerly had kept in circulation large quantities of exotic items seem to have broken down. Small burial mounds were built over the next several centuries, but the general trend was toward a "reordering of priorities" (Dragoo 1976: 22).

With Hopewell as with the Olmec, the Harappan cities, and many other "collapses" of ancient societies, archaeologists have often viewed these developments as the result of climate changes, warfare, disease, or a combination of these and other factors. It may also be that the Hopewellian "decline" was an expression of the declining importance of the population control and redistribution functions of these ceremonial centers subsequent to the widespread adoption of maize agriculture, with its greater productivity.

Whatever the reasons behind these changes, the agricultural way of life *was* appearing over much of the North American East after A.D. 400, and as it spread, population densities increased and communities everywhere became stable and sedentary. Without plows or an advanced technology, the most productive agricultural strategy was to burn off the vegetation on rich, well-drained alluvial plains, plant maize and a few other crops, do some minor weeding and cultivation during the growing season, and then harvest and store the maize. After one or two seasons a given plot of land became unproductive, and the areas of cultivation—and perhaps the whole village—would have to be shifted elsewhere.

Perhaps because of competition for land, there seems to have been a marked increase in interregional hostilities shortly after A.D. 700, and by about A.D. 800 many settlements were surrounded by defensive stockades.

Mississippian Cultures (A.D. 800 to 1650)

From about A.D. 600 to about 1650, the agricultural way of life spread over much of eastern North America, accompanied by a marked increase in the level of cultural complexity. Many societies of this period are collectively referred to as the *Mississippian* culture, whose most common artifacts are types of shell-tempered pottery, tiny triangular arrowheads, and truncated pyramid mounds. Collectively, Mississippian communities represent the high point of cultural evolution in aboriginal North America, particularly in terms of geographical extent of influence, ceremonialism, public works, technology, population density, and social stratification.

Artifacts and mounds of the Mississippian type first appeared in the lower Mississippi Valley, but they soon spread into the Tennessee River drainage and by A.D. 800 to 900 occurred over much of the Ohio and Missouri river valleys. Between A.D. 900 and A.D. 1600, large towns with impressive ceremonial centers were built from Florida to northern Illinois, and from Ohio to eastern Oklahoma, but the heartland of this culture was in the central Mississippi Valley.

The largest Mississippian complex is Cahokia, in East St. Louis, Illinois, where the central pyramid is over 30 meters high, 200 by 330 meters at the base, and covers an area of more than 6.5 hectares (Fowler 1969). The 30,000 to 40,000 people estimated to have lived in the environs of Cahokia at about A.D. 1200 were distributed in four large towns, five smaller towns, and about forty-three villages (Pfeiffer 1977: 425), and no doubt people living within a large area around the settlement had some contact with Cahokia (Porter 1969). Some elite groups were permanent residents of Cahokia and other ceremonial centers, but the vast majority of the people apparently still lived in hamlets some distance from the centers, practiced maize agriculture supplemented by other crops, and did considerable hunting and gathering (Hines 1977).

Cahokia is an impressive site, but it was probably not the urban-state center some have considered it. The extensive rebuilding of residential areas and the incremental nature of the mound construction, together with Cahokia's estimated trade and market functions, are consistent with a developed chiefdom.

Mississippian village residences were usually rectangular or ovoid wattle-and-daub structures, supported by internal wooden beams, with floors of packed earth (Jennings 1974: 256). The highest Mississippian population densities were in the rich river bottoms where it was possible to combine maize and bean farming with waterfowl exploitation (Smith 1974). In some areas the river annually renewed the fertility of the soil through alluviation, and permanent field agriculture was possible.

Our view of Mississippian life comes from both archaeological and ethnological sources, as Mississippian communities were still extant when the Europeans arrived in the sixteenth century. These colonists described intensely stratified societies where the elites were able to draw almost without limit on the resources of the communities. At Cahokia, for example, one adult male was buried with 20,000 shell beads, 800 arrowheads, sheets of mica and copper, and more than 50 young women who had been ritually strangled and arranged in neat rows (Pfeiffer 1977: 429). There are many other mortuary indications of social stratification, and a fairly complex administrative hierarchy must have existed to organize the monumental construction projects and the circulation of copper, chert, mica, shell, obsidian, and agricultural commodities. Warfare among competing Mississippian chiefdoms may have been frequent and brutal (Dickson 1981).

Ethnographic accounts of Mississippian communities as they existed in the sixteenth and seventeenth centuries—long after the culmination of Mississippian culture—describe an intensely class-conscious society in which nobles and warriors alternately exploited and abused the *stink-ards*, or commoners and slaves who made up most of the societies. The upper classes were slavishly obeyed and respected. They frequently married the lower classes, but the aristocrat could divorce or kill the lower-ranking spouse, given even minor cause.

Many late Mississippian and later period mounds and burials contain ornaments, pottery, and other artifacts decorated with motifs almost identical to some Mesoamerican motifs, including plumed serpents, eagles, jaguars, and warriors carrying trophy heads, as well as the fifty-two-year calendar round. These motifs are found most frequently at the larger settlements and appear to have crossed regional cultural boundaries. Collectively, they are taken as evidence of a southern (Mesoamerican) religious cult. Opinions differ on their significance in terms of contacts with Mesoamerica, some considering them evidence of quite direct and sustained contacts, others seeing them as minor borrowings with little more than an accidental connection to Mesoamerican cultures. The southern cult, as well as the Adena and Hopewell mortuary ceremonialism, likely achieved importance in North America only after cultural complexity in the North had reached a stage where these elements "made sense" in terms of northern societies.

THE MISSISSIPPIAN COLLAPSE

After A.D. 1000 Mississippian "colonists" began to emigrate from the cultural heartland, and some groups may have founded quasi-military enclaves in Alabama, Missouri, and elsewhere. Conceivably, these daughter communities were sent with the express purpose of extending Mississippian influence over other cultural groups, but an essentially archaic way of life persisted in many outlying areas for centuries after European contact.

In contrast to most other ancient cultures, there is little question about the immediate cause of the decline of Mississippian culture. The Indians had no natural immunities to measles, smallpox, and cholera, and the densely settled Mississippian areas provided an ideal medium for the rapid spread of these highly contagious diseases (Stewart 1973). Le Page du Pratz, who lived with the Natchez from 1718 to 1734, found that even "minor" diseases were devastating:

> Two distempers, that are not very fatal in other parts of the world, make dreadful ravages among them; I mean small-pox and a cold, which baffle all the arts of their physicians, who in other respects are very skillful. When a nation is attacked by the small-pox, it quickly makes great havock; for as a whole family is crowded into a small hut, which has no communications with the external air, but a door about two feet wide and four feet high, the distemper, if it seizes one, is quickly communicated to all. The aged die in consequence of their advanced years, and the bad quality of their food; and the young, if they are not strictly watched, destroy themselves, from an abhorrence of the blotches on their skin. . . .
>
> Colds, which are very common in winter, likewise destroy great numbers of the natives. In that season they keep fires in their huts day and night; and as there is no other opening but the door, the air within the hut is kept excessively warm without any free circulation; so that when they have occasion to go out, the cold seizes them, and the consequences of it are almost always fatal.

Within a few decades of European contact in the sixteenth century, the once highly integrated and proud Mississippian people, and other cultures as well, were a much reduced and poverty-stricken group, living amid thousands of abandoned settlements and eroding mounds attesting to their former greatness.

In summary of cultural developments in the North American East, we see that, point for point, peoples in this area followed the familiar script of cultural evolution. From a hunting and gathering base, specialized hunting and minor plant exploitation gradually gave way to an intricate "broad-spectrum" hunting-foraging economy, in which fishing, nut collecting, shellfishing, and other activities were added to the subsistence repertoire according to what was probably a largely uncognized but very precise "cost-benefit" analysis; then, after centuries of manipulation and selection, maize-based agriculture displaced less-productive economies in many areas, with consequent increasing population densities and the establishment of large sedentary communities. Once food production reached certain levels, the familiar harbingers of increasing cultural complexity, such as the spread of religious and stylistic traditions, monumental architecture, mortuary cults, and increasingly diverse and interdependent arts and crafts, also appeared. Social and religious hierarchies emerged as "efficient" ways to make the decisions necessary for the perpetuation of these increasingly complex economies, and the institutionalization of prestige and privilege may have arisen as an effective way of reducing competition between these populations and of maximizing administrative efficiency.

In these essentials, then, there is little to differentiate the sequence of cultural evolution in North America from that in Mesoamerica, except that, given the available domesticates and technology, most of eastern North America had less agricultural potential than Mesoamerica, causing these northern cultures to stabilize at a much lower level of complexity. Had the Europeans not invaded and introduced their diseases, true state-level societies might well have evolved from the remnants of the Mississippian climax, but only if food production could have been increased drastically through technological, agricultural, or administrative innovations.

Prehistoric Agriculturalists in Southwestern North America

In our survey of early complex societies, the peoples of southwestern North America must serve in a sense as negative examples, for although they adopted maize-based agriculture, aggregated into large towns, and evolved some occupational and administrative specialization, they never produced class-structured, hierarchically organized, economically differentiated societies. The reasons for this relatively slow rate of cultural evolution are probably mainly ecological. The dramatic mountains, crystal skies, and primary colors of the Southwest make it an attractive place to live—if one has access to a municipal water system and a modern market and transport system. But from the perspective of a hunter and gatherer or subsistence farmer, the majority of the Southwest is not a lush environment; the region has few rivers or streams and an extreme climate of searing summers and bitterly cold winters.

Analysis of tree rings and other botanical evidence suggests that over most of the last 10,000 years the Southwest has usually been at least as hot and dry as it is today, but that there were short periods of extreme drought that might have reduced population densities and driven people from traditional farming areas.

Domesticated maize may have appeared in the Southwest by about 3500 B.C. but, if so it had little economic importance at first; it was apparently not cultivated until about 3,000 years later, when three distinctive and largely contemporary cultural traditions evolved: the *Ho-*

15.5   A sixteenth-century painting by Jacques le Moyne of the burial of a Florida Indian chief. Arrows have been driven into the ground around the grave, and the chief's houses (*left rear*) are being ceremonially burned.

hokam, which was restricted to a relatively small area; the more extensive *Anasazi* Pueblo; and the *Mogollon,* or western Pueblo (Jennings 1974: 283) (see Figure 15.3). An excellent culture history can be found in Ortiz (1979).

THE HOHOKAM

The Hohokam peoples, who flourished in the Salt and Gila river valleys (Arizona) between about 300 B.C. and A.D. 1200, apparently represent the confluence of Archaic hunting and gathering traditions and direct stimulation from Mesoamerican cultures. Some archaeologists (Haury 1976) have concluded that late Hohokam house construction, ceramics, turquoise mosaic ornaments, and other artifacts are so similar to Mesoamerican examples that they can only be the result of an immigration of Mexican people who transplanted their way of life directly to the Hohokam area, where previously there had been only hunters and gatherers.

15.6   A typical adobe village in the southwestern United States. The photograph was taken in the 1930s, but the construction methods and village type illustrated go back many centuries.

One of the most interesting aspects of the Hohokam is their agricultural system. Their homeland is set in some of the driest deserts of North America, where summer temperatures have impressed even archaeological veterans of the Near East. Beginning at about 300 B.C., the Hohokam cut channels off the Salt and Gila rivers to run water to their garden plots of maize and other crops. Modern buildings have erased much of the Hohokam irrigation system, but two canals near Phoenix were over 16 kilometers long, several meters wide, and about 60 centimeters deep when first constructed. Tightly woven grass mats were probably used as gates to open and close canal segments, and earthen dams on the rivers in some places diverted water through canals for more than fifty kilometers across the desert floor, with many small branches serving individual fields.

In the recent past, southwestern Indian irrigation systems, as well as comparable agricultural systems elsewhere in the world, have been operated by a few thousand people in relatively simple tribal organizations in which no coercion, permanent authorities, or police agencies were necessary, and this might well have been the case among the Hohokam.

Although the largest irrigation systems were apparently built sometime after A.D. 800, by about A.D. 300 there were already indications of minor increases in the complexity of Hohokam cultures. Some low platform mounds, about 29 meters long, 23 meters wide, and 3 meters high, were built at about this time at the Snaketown site, and in subsequent centuries the people of Snaketown and several nearby communities built large sunken ball courts like those found in many areas of Mesoamerica. The Hohokam ball courts were east-west oriented oval depressions about 60 meters long, with 4.5- to 6-meter-high sloping earth embankments on a side. Early Spanish observers of the ball game in Mesoamerica report that the objective was to try to knock a rubber ball (two of which have been found in the Southwest) through a goal using knees, elbows, or torso, and that losing players were sometimes executed. The southwestern ball courts were probably not stops on the northern road trips of the Mexican major leagues, but they do indicate very close southern affinities, as do the platform mounds. And between A.D. 900 and 1200, many other Mesoamerican elements were imported, including cotton textiles, certain ceramic motifs, pyrite mirrors, effigy vessels, cast copper bells, ear plugs, etched shell ornaments, and even parrots and macaws—probably imported from the South and kept and prized for their feathers.

Generally, however, there is little evidence in either subsistence practices, settlements, or mortuary ceremonies of evolving rank and wealth differences. Most of the Hohokam lived in small square pit houses roofed with clay and grass domes supported by a wooden pole framework. Early dwellings appear large enough for several families, but single-family residences became more popular in later periods.

Hohokam settlement patterns are not well known. There are few indications of a master plan in village layouts or of economic specialization of villages. Nor is there any suggestion that the villages were situated on the basis of defensive considerations (Willey 1966: 220–23). Every village probably repeated all the economic activities of every other village, except that some favored locations allowed a greater reliance on maize, beans, squash, and other crops. Nonetheless, many atlatl dart points and arrowheads have been found at each Hohokam site, and botanical remains indicate that almost every community supplemented its diet with wild mustard, amaranths, chenopods, cactus fruits, mesquite, screwbeans, and other wild products (Washburn 1975: 124). Many Hohokam elements still survive in contemporary Papago Indian cultures.

THE ANASAZI

Like the Mogollon and Hohokam, the Anasazi developed out of desert foraging cultures, and their earliest prepottery representatives are widely known as the *Basketmaker* cultures. By the last century B.C., they were living in many sedentary settlements located on old river terraces and mesa tops or in river valleys in the high plateau country of the central Southwest. The earliest houses were circular structures of wattle-and-daub set on log bases, or semisubterranean houses whose walls were founded on cobblestone (Washburn 1975: 110). These early Anasazi did not use pottery, and although they ate maize, beans, and squash, they invested little labor in cultivating these crops, relying instead on wild foods, such as roots, bulbs, grass seeds, nuts, acorns, berries, cactus fruits, sunflowers, deer, rabbits, antelopes, and wild sheep.

After about A.D. 400, the Anasazi adopted the use of pottery and began building large pit houses, most of which were circular or rectangular, from 3 to 7.5 meters in diameter, and were covered by log and mud roofs supported on center posts. Interior walls were plastered with mud or faced with stone, access was through a descending passageway, and fireplaces and benches were standard furnishings. At some sites large ceremonial pit houses, or *kivas,* were built. After about A.D. 700, above-ground masonry houses were erected in some Anasazi communities, but the pit house and kiva combination continued to be the basic village type until the end of the thirteenth century A.D.

Defensive considerations, greater exploitation of more productive strains of maize (Dickson 1975), and climatic changes beginning about A.D. 700 may have spurred the Anasazi into constructing the "cliff cities" for which they are famous. Pollen and geological studies suggest that summer rainfall, in the form of torrential storms, increased after A.D. 700, while winter rainfall decreased, and the resulting changes in water tables and stream flows may have forced the Anasazi to congregate around larger, permanently flowing rivers (Washburn 1975: 114, but see Rice 1975). Hillsides were terraced to control erosion, and diversion canals and dams were constructed to control and store as much of the vital summer rainwater as possible. On Chapin Mesa, in the Mesa Verde area, for example, the older agricultural fields were extended by an elaborate checkdam system that added 8 or 12 hectares of cultivable land.

In some areas erosion forced frequent settlement relocations, and some communities met the changing agricultural conditions by scattering into small family groups; but the prevailing response was to aggregate into large towns along the major rivers. By about 1100 A.D., prosperous enclaves were established at Mesa Verde, Chaco Canyon, Canyon de Chelly, and elsewhere, and in some ways these communities represent the high point of southwestern culture. There were twelve large

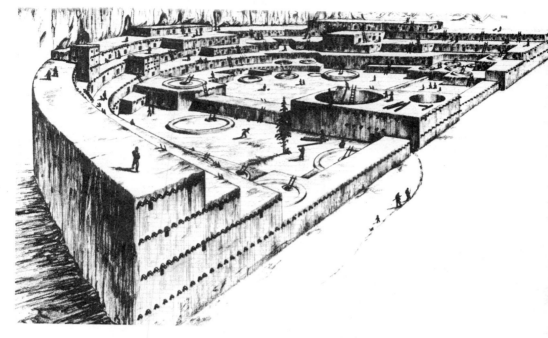

15.7   Reconstruction of Pueblo Bonito, as it may have appeared at about A.D. 1050.

towns along Chaco Canyon, of which Pueblo Bonito was the largest, with over 800 rooms and perhaps 1,200 people (Figure 15.7).

By about A.D. 1150, most of the known cliff cities (Figure 15.8) in the Four Corners area had been established, all of very similar construction. Settlements grew by simple accretion; more rooms were added as needed. The remote location of the cliff towns may have had to do with defensive considerations, although defense against what enemy we do not know.

As beautiful as many late Anasazi settlements were, they do not appear to have been the work of a highly complex society. The buildings, while superbly adapted to their environment, are quite crudely constructed. There may have been minor occupational specialization in ceramic manufacture, weaving, and turquoise carving, but most if not all the people were subsistence farmers. Nor is any evidence of differential rank expressed in domestic architecture or in grave goods. Even the irrigation system, while intricate and efficient, was probably administered through simple kinship systems.

Shortly before A.D. 1300, many once prosperous Anasazi communi-

15.8 Cliff Palace, Mesa Verde, Colorado, one of the most impressive cliff dwellings.

ties began to be abandoned, and when the Spanish arrived in the sixteenth century, they found the descendants of the Anasazi living along the Rio Grande in small villages, each of which was a largely autonomous political and economic unit.

THE MOGOLLON

The Mogollon cultures, which also developed out of the Archaic desert foraging cultures of the last several millennia B.C., were concentrated in the mountains of east central Arizona and west central New Mexico. Sedentary villages and ceramics of the Mogollon type first appear at about 300 B.C. By about A.D. 300, villages of about fifteen pit houses each were scattered along ridges, bluffs, and terraces, and nearly all the inhabitants of these settlements were subsisting on the maize-beans-squash complex, supplemented by many wild plants and game. Mogollon burials of this period were often simple inhumations in house floors accompanied by a few pottery vessels, turquoise ornaments, and stone tools.

After about A.D. 1000, the Mogollon peoples apparently were heavily influenced by Anasazi groups, and the Swarts ruins, Mimbres Valley, New Mexico, may be an example of this. River boulders set in adobe were used to construct a large complex of conjoined rectangular rooms, access to which was apparently only through the roof, since there were no exterior doors. Inside walls were plastered with mud, and doorways led from one room to another. Storage bins, shelves, fireplaces, and benches constituted the essential furnishings. Corpses were frequently interred in the floors of abandoned rooms, in occupied rooms, or within the village compound; most burials were very simple.

The Mogollon built no pyramids, ball courts, or major irrigation systems, but they did produce an extraordinarily beautiful array of ceramics, particularly the "mimbres" ceramic forms, decorated with vivid figures of frogs, insects, fish, deer, and other animal life painted against black backgrounds.

Mogollon settlement patterns show some evidence of minor emerging social ranking. Mogollon villages seem to be of two types: a small cluster of fewer than five pit houses, without any large ceremonial kivas, and larger collections of one hundred or more pit houses associated with "great kivas." The largest pit houses in these communities tend to have the greatest amount of storage space, more exotic trade items, and evidence of greater consumption of agricultural products. Lightfoot and Feinman (1982: 81) interpret this evidence and other data to mean that

a "suprahousehold" decision-making organization had developed among
the Mogollon, perhaps as a result of competition among rival political
leaders.

One of the major settlement pattern transitions in Southwestern culture history occurred during the first millennium A.D., when people
gradually, generation by generation, stopped living in relatively small
villages of semisubterranean pit houses and began building their communities in the "pueblo" style of blocks of contiguous above-ground
rooms.

For the archaeologist, of course, such a change is immediately seen
in adaptive terms: what conditions would induce this sort of long-term,
regional change? In a consideration of this question from the perspective of Mogollon settlements in western Texas, Michael Whalen notes
(1981) that the change is associated with an increase in regional population densities, the appearance of larger community size, a growing reliance on plant cultivation as the main subsistence source, and an
increasingly elaborate ceremonialism, as expressed in the design and
contents of structures. He also states that the peripheral areas that he
is concerned with went through this transition about a century later—
ca. A.D. 1100–1200—than in the central Mogollon area.

Whalen's interpretation of the reasons for the change to pueblo-style
houses involves what he cites as Romer's Rule of Organic Evolution:
"Organisms make changes of structure or behavior under stressful
conditions in order to continue their accustomed pattern of activity"
(Whalen 1981: 88). As populations grew, climates fluctuated, and settlements spread into different microenvironments, people tried to
maintain their traditional way of life by extending agriculture into
the margins of basins where water was more available. The greater
productivity of these basin margins fostered certain kinds of economic
and social changes as the domestic economy was reformed around an
agricultural specialization in which the community rather than the
family was the basic social and economic unit.

The Southwest archaeological record, like that of many other areas
of the world, has recently been intensively reexamined with the aid of
mathematical models, computer simulations, systems theory, and so
forth, and it is clear that there are many elements of trade, social organization, and subsistence that were not fully appreciated previously
(Cordell and Plog 1979; Upham, Lightfoot, and Feinman 1981). Nonetheless, these analytical techniques have produced no evidence of significant social and cultural complexity. The reason the Southwest did
not produce great states and empires seems obvious, given the technology of the Prehistoric period and the physical environment. In the

Southwest, water is scarce and sharply seasonal, with rather unpredictable fluctuations in rainfall from year to year; there are few alluvial areas where agriculture could be intensified; and transport of large amounts of food products over large areas is made difficult by the uneven topography. As Hunter-Anderson notes, to understand ancient Southwestern culture we should begin by looking

> at the payoffs for various competitive strategies such as hierarchical versus egalitarian social organization. . . . A glance at any of the several available maps of global terrestrial (and marine) primary productivity . . . reveals that the United States Southwest, in comparison with areas of the world in which hierarchically organized cultural systems have been directly observed, is extremely poorly endowed. There simply is nothing in the way of an adequate energy base on which to build a hierarchically organized social system with the internal diversity, trade monopolies, nonproductive administrators, etc., which are common characteristics of such systems. As problematic for the development of stratified social systems as an adequate energy base is the predictability of commodities that are exchanged; without this predictability, no long-range planning and effective articulation among consumers, suppliers, and nonproductive administrators can take place. Clearly the aboriginal Southwest was deficient in this respect. (1981: 197)

16

Prehistory in Perspective

What's past is prologue.

Shakespeare

Having been led from the 3-million-year-old hominid footprints of Laetolil through the European conquest of the Americas, the reader is now invited to return to the question posed in the first chapter: What does the past *mean?* Or, more precisely, how are we to understand the past? This, of course, is the question of the ages.

Although it is perhaps a bad pedagogical tactic to raise a question, review the evidence, and then conclude with "I don't know," most contemporary archaeologists find themselves in this position. Thus, rather than demonstrating the power and accuracy of any specific models of culture and history, we have simply explored the limitations and potentials of some of the more obvious theoretical approaches and have encountered more explanations and hypotheses that do not "work" than those that do.

One of the earliest casualties revealed by our archaeological review is the nineteenth-century view of mechanical cultural evolutionism, with its belief in the gradual improvement of people and their societies, generation after generation, as we "progressed" from rude, murderous savagery to the better, brighter world of industry, liberalism, and democracy. The Victorian proponents of cultural evolutionism—who number among their ranks some of the greatest intellects of all time—can be forgiven, perhaps, for this belief in progress, for they lived in an age of marvelous changes. But, as Simone Weil said, "The great mistake of the nineteenth century was to assume that by walking straight on one mounted into the air."

Even today many people, including anthropologists, tend to see the world and history in these same mechanical, evolutionist terms, with the

442

strong implication that prehistory and history describe a "progressive" trajectory, leading to ourselves. Our review of the archaeological records reveals, however, that instead of a smooth rising curve of social, technological, and moral evolution, our past has been a series of fitful cycles, where social forms and technologies have reached their limits of growth and then failed, to be replaced by new social forms and technologies, more complex in some ways than their predecessors, but neither permanent nor "better" in any evident moral or philosophical sense. Clearly, there is nothing in the archaeological record to indicate that we are on a straight path to an earthly paradise. Today, two thirds of the world's population are "involuntary vegetarians" (Harris 1977: x) whose diet, morbidity and mortality rates, and general standard of living compare poorly with those of most Pleistocene hunting and gathering bands: and even in the most industrialized countries, the vast majority labors longer for sustenance than did many of the people of prehistory. Moreover, the misery, poverty, wars, and assorted atrocities of the past several decades make the idea of mankind's moral evolution so laughable as to require no discussion.

But this lack of "progress" in the Victorian sense should not be taken as an indictment of the general cultural evolutionary model, for the archaeological record also demonstrates that despite repeated reversals and long plateaus, the past 3 million years have witnessed a gradual increase in the complexity of cultures, as measured in terms of ability to divert energy to human use and in the size, differentiation, and interdependence of social, political, and economic systems. Moreover, cultural evolution has been patterned: domestication, agriculture, cultural complexity, and many specific cultural developments appeared independently but in very similar ways in various times and places.

No general theory of culture has been able to provide a convincing framework within which these cultural parallels and transformations can be compellingly and precisely explained, and for this reason no general theory of culture has won universal acceptance. Most archaeologists employ a vaguely evolutionary perspective: they assume that cultural innovations are constantly arising in human societies, and that some of these innovations confer an adaptive advantage and are fixed within cultural systems and perpetuated until they too are outmoded and replaced. Most archaeologists also adopt a rather "vulgar" materialist determinism in that they try to understand cultural forms and dynamics as expressions of technological, environmental, and economic variables. Thus, such things as the social egalitarianism of hunters and gatherers in the Pleistocene and the rigid social stratification of emerging states are generally understood as reactions to their respective economic bases. Nonetheless, even some of the most ardent materialists (e.g., Harris 1977) stress the importance of free will, religion, and ideology in "determining" the operations of societies, and no one argues that evolutionary cultural materialism is a complete, explanatory theory of culture.

Among those archaeologists who retain the hope of making archaeology a formal, scientific, predictive discipline, there is a growing trend away from the somewhat naive, almost "pseudo-scientism" of recent decades. Most scholars are no longer searching for mechanical cause and effect relationships in which specific changes in independent variables can be shown to result uniformly in predictable changes in dependent cultural variables, à la the classical view of the laws of thermodynamics. Instead, and in concert with contemporary perspectives in the natural sciences, archaeologists interested in explaining the past in general terms are more concerned with formulating statements of probability, such that, under specified conditions, estimates can be made about the likelihood that similar variables will give rise to similar consequences. And in this context there is growing question about the productivity and appropriateness of the so-called "positivist" model of science, in which one tries to establish absolute laws by deducing and testing hypotheses from the propositions subsumed under these general laws (e.g., Dunnell 1982; Johnson 1972; Morgan 1973; Salmon 1975).

Many of the younger archaeologists of the 1960s and 1970s rejected traditional archaeology and traditional archaeologists as "stamp collectors" who had no notion of science or explanation. I have recorded in earlier chapters some of these attempts to reshape archaeology around the model of physics, by virtue of the power of mathematics. The animosities between individuals, universities, and even countries that rose out of this revolutionary period in archaeology (see, for example, Binford 1972) linger, but more and more archaeologists are in a position like that described by Mark Twain, who said: "When I was a boy of fourteen, my father was so ignorant I could hardly stand to have the old man around. But when I got to be twenty-one, I was astonished at how much the old man had learned in seven years." There is a growing sense that the archaeology of the 1970s and 1980s was not all that much more powerful and scientific than the "prerevolutionary" archaeology of the 1940s and 1950s.

Our inability to explain major cultural transformations by constructing equations involving population growth, warfare, or some other limited set of factors has led some scholars to attempt to redefine the basic terms and objectives of analyzing the past. We have considered in this context several attempts to use general systems theory, noting that despite the elegant descriptions provided for some cultural changes through systems-theory analyses, fundamental questions remain about the ultimate utility of this approach as a way of explaining culture change. Some recent systems-theory analyses of archaeological data have involved game theory, mathematical modeling, and other complex procedures, and only many more years of additional research will reveal the extent to which we can explain the past from this perspective.

There have also been renewed attempts to understand these matters from a biological perspective. The emerging discipline of sociobiology, for example, includes among its proponents those who argue that much of what we are or have been culturally is deeply embedded in the chemistry of our chromosomes, that war, greed, competition, egotism, innovation, and a long list of other human behaviors can be partially suppressed by the weight of cultural institutions, but that they persist in our physiology as potent behavioral determinates.

There is a certain attractiveness to this idea. It reduces some cultural problems to the biochemical and genetic level—a level of analysis that modern science has shown to be very productive—and it also seems to make clear why human societies have inevitably been associated with war, conflict, and social inequity: because 3 million years of evolution have shaped us that way. And thus, except for some recent Frankensteinian research with the mechanics of heredity, the sociobiological approach would seem to some extent to place fundamental changes in some human social patterns beyond the reach of human initiative.

The sociobiological perspective may well make highly significant contributions to the solution of anthropological problems, but it is unlikely that the causes and effects of the origins of culture, the evolution of agricultural economies, the rise of complex societies, or the other major problems of prehistory will be "resolved" by this approach. If there is a single major lesson of world prehistory, it would seem to be that cultures are marvelously adaptable: that, given compelling cultural reasons, people can use cultural forms to make cooperation or competition, murder or altruism, egalitarianism or privilege, or any other behaviors into vices or virtues, as the circumstances dictate.

Archaeologists, then, are still searching for a general theory and model of culture, and they disagree sharply about how this goal might best be achieved. To a large extent, however, the great majority of archaeological fieldwork has been devoted not to the larger theoretical questions about *why* cultures change, but rather to the specific ways in which particular cultural forms have appeared and changed, and in these terms archaeology has made great progress. There is no need to review in detail the archaeological information we have considered in earlier chapters about early hominid taxonomy, Paleolithic technologies, the origins of domestication and agriculture, the rise of cultural complexity, and the many other prehistoric transformations that only a century ago were not even recognized, let alone understood. True, we have identified no "prime movers" (factors whose effects are so potent that they can be used to explain much of the cultural developments of past and future societies), but we have identified many patterns and parallels. Cross-cutting cultural developments all over the world are the same essential expressions of religion, warfare, population growth, emerging social stratification, and evolving economic productivity.

We have seen, for example, that human population growth has been linked to almost every cultural transformation, from initial tool use to the appearance of industrial empires, and it is indeed true that the increasing rate of technological innovation and general cultural change is closely correlated with increasing worldwide population numbers. This relationship may even be said to be an explanatory one in the sense that the rate of technological change might be linked simply to the number of minds available to solve problems and produce innovations. But this is clearly an incomplete explanation of our past. The archaeological record time and time again discloses that the relationship between population growth and cultural change is neither consistent nor direct, and it remains for archaeologists to demonstrate the causal connections between the world's increasing population size and the specific, crucial transformations of prehistory and history.

All of the other "prime movers" have similar limitations. The recurrent nature of human interspecies violence, for example, from the casual cannibalism of early *Homo erectus* to World War II, clearly suggests that conflict is an evolutionary mechanism of considerable power; conflict must *do* something for societies, or it would be difficult to explain its depressing ubiquitousness in human affairs. But here too, the actual mechanisms whereby conflict interacted with other variables in most past societies to produce cultural change is unknown.

In sum, archaeologists have devoted many years to trying to establish simple correlations among cultural variables and/or environmental variables, but most of them now recognize that even if they are able to demonstrate a strong correlation in time and space between, say, population growth, warfare, and urbanism, they will still not have explained in a powerful way any of these factors or their relationships to each other.

Archaeology today thus bears a striking resemblance to William James's 1892 description of psychology:

a string of raw facts; a little gossip and wrangle about opinions; a little classification and generalization on the mere descriptive level, . . . not a single proposition from which any consequence can causally be deduced. We don't even know the terms between which the elementary laws would obtain if we had them. This is no science, it is only the hope of a science. (quoted in Gould 1980: 96)

LESSONS OF PREHISTORY?

It would be gratifying if we could extract from our review of world prehistory some important predictions about the future of mankind but, as we have noted, archaeology is still very far from being a formal, predictive science. This is especially true when we consider the long-range future, particularly now that mankind has instruments with which to terminate all human life on this planet. But even should we survive for millions of generations, the virtuosity of culture as an adaptive device makes extrapolations into the future an act of either ignorance or embarrassing temerity. What anthropologist, given the opportunity to stroll through Olduvai Gorge some Sunday morning 2 million years ago, could on the basis of that experience have predicted the gaudy technology and kaleidoscopic social and political forms of twentieth-century civilization?

Nonetheless, no student of world prehistory can overlook the persistent, powerful trends that tie the present, and perhaps the future, to the past. The evolution of technologies for energy capture, for example, seems to have been so basic to competitive success that we might expect that these technologies will continue to be important determinants of sociocultural and ideological forms. One obvious implication is that it might be naive to expect energy-dependent countries to refrain from using nuclear energy because of the slight attendant risk of nuclear disaster. The matter of "evolutionary potential" would also seem to have some applicability to the future, even though the world is much different now from what it was during most of the last 9,000 years, when agricultural potential was the major ingredient in evolutionary success. Throughout prehistory the evolutionary advantage frequently shifted to "marginal" groups, less complexly organized cultures located on the peripheries of the richer established cultures. In the contemporary world, where fossil fuels and raw materials are of great import, the advantage may already have shifted from the West to Russia, China, and Near Eastern and African nations.

Any number of future developments could of course change these expectations dramatically. Should a simple, inexpensive technology for using solar energy be developed, there may well be a general leveling of wealth and power among nations, particularly if what are now the world's poorer countries curb their rates of population growth.

Another apparent lesson of prehistory has to do with the uses of religion. I shall let those with more confidence in their omniscience than myself pronounce on the ultimate nature of human religiosity; it is always sobering to recollect that neither the study of world prehistory nor any other art or science has much to offer in the way of a reason why we are out here, on a small planet in an incomprehensibly infinite universe, and to all evidence very much alone. Nonetheless, taken solely on the level of its effects on other aspects of culture, religion appears to operate principally as a highly adaptable, thermodynamically efficient mechanism of social control. We have seen in the archaeological and historical record an irrefutable demonstration that there is no act so repellent, be it sacrificing thousands of one's own countrymen or incinerating hundreds of thousands of one's "enemies," that it cannot be made not only acceptable, but entirely virtuous within the context of religious systems. The exploitation of the many by the few to build massive "worthless" pyramids and public buildings, the complete catalogue of sexual "perversions," the avoidance of this or that food—all have been incorporated into state religions with no more difficulty than Christian faith, hope, or charity.

Nor should the apparent decline of formal theistic religions in the modern world be interpreted as a sign of religion's demise as an important cultural mechanism. One need only look at contemporary Communist countries, where avowedly secular, atheistic cultures have replaced traditional religions with ideologies no different in their essentials from Catholicism or Buddhism. For the future, there appears no reason to suspect that belief systems will be any less important, although clearly their contents will vary. The competitive advantage, as always, will lie with cultures that evolve belief systems that motivate people in specific, "efficient" directions, as is well illustrated in centuries past by the link between capitalism and Calvinism, and irrigation agriculture and the Sumerian pantheon.

The lessons of the archaeological record concerning the origins and significance of social and economic inequalities are not as clear as they might seem at first glance. There is the inescapable fact that there has never been an economically differentiated, complex society, especially the supposedly "classless" societies, that was not also stratified into groups having differential access to wealth, power, and prestige, but it remains to be demonstrated that cultural complexity is inextricably linked to social stratification. It would appear that in the past the complexity of managing an economy based on agriculture and, later, agriculture in combination with fossil fuels, could work effectively only through administrative and social hierarchies and class-structured societies. But if in future centuries population densities are stabilized and perhaps reduced, if control of energy and food sources is decentralized and the production of material wealth made highly automated, it would seem at least possible that human societies will someday approximate the "social justice" of the late Pleistocene.

Perhaps the archaeological record's bleakest implication concerning our future has to do with that ambiguous concept of "the quality of life." We have already noted that today most of the world's people have a diet and standard of living in many ways inferior to that of Pleistocene hunters and gatherers, and although medical technology, solar power, and contraceptives may change this by bringing the Western industrial standard of living to all parts of the world, this is by no means a certainty. Even given sufficient energy and rapid industrialization, fundamental questions remain about the short-term prospects for the quality of life on this planet. In the wealthiest countries today the abundance of luxury goods seems to convey a sense of ease and fulfillment, but modern economies work only because the vast majority of the population are coerced or are willing to spend most of their lives at hard labor, often with competitive pressures that produce unbalanced, unfulfilled lives. And it is not only the poorer, laboring class whose quality of life is questionable. It has been observed that a citizen of Athens in the fifth century B.C. would consider today's professionals—physicians, politicians, professors, and football players alike—to be in the main incomplete, undeveloped people, whose "success" has required them to devote so much of their lives to their specialty that they are grotesquely incompetent at the oratorical, conversational, athletic, philosophical, agricultural, and aesthetic skills that the Greeks would insist upon as necessary components of a "whole" person.

The past often takes on a rosy, romantic coloring from the perspective of the complexities and frustrations of the present, and we cannot ignore the illiteracy, warfare, and gross social exploitation that appear to be the very warp and woof of every ancient complex society, including ancient Athens; but many people feel that modern social and economic systems, whether they be capitalistic or socialistic, do not provide optimal environments for the balanced, liberal, personal development of the majority. Gloomy ruminations of this sort have a way of showing up in succeeding centuries as quaint quotations demonstrating the curious myopia of past generations, and I devoutly hope it will be so in this case. But despite the many advantages of modern technology, the long-term trend seems inexorably in the direction of greater specialization and compartmentalization of people, with consequent increasing alienation and frustration. How pleasant a society may be to live in has depressingly little to do with that society's evolutionary potential.

THE FUTURE OF ARCHAEOLOGY

The archaeological record is disappearing at such a rapid rate that the future of *field* archaeology on the problems of prehistory is very much in doubt. The worldwide wave of industrialism, the major destroyer of archaeological materials, seems destined to expand at ever-increasing speed.

Dismal as the loss of the archaeological record is, it may be that the major progress in archaeology in the next several generations will come not so much from the discovery of new bones and stones, but rather from a reconsideration of theoretical and methodological approaches and a reanalysis of existing data. We have recounted in this book the prospects of systems theory, simulation modeling, hypothesis testing, and other current analytical approaches, and these and more traditional perspectives are likely to increase considerably our knowledge about many specific problems, such as the origins of agriculture, the taxonomy of early humans, and the causes of urbanism. Does this mean that the general problem of the origins of cultural complexity will some day be as precisely solved as the formulae for making plastics? Probably not. These are very different kinds of questions with different criteria for solution. Yet, the history of science is replete with examples in which a seemingly impossible problem was not only solved but made routine: the general problems of prehistory we have discussed here may well fall into this category, to be solved in succeeding centuries in terms and with techniques which we now only dimly perceive. After all, people of only a few centuries ago no doubt would be astounded not only by our science and lush technology, but also by our knowledge of prehistory and the dynamics of culture.

Bibliography

Chapter 1

Adams, A. B. 1969. *Eternal Quest*. New York: Putnam's.

Binford, L. R. 1968. "Archeological Perspectives." In *New Perspectives in Archeology*, eds. Sally R. Binford and Lewis R. Binford. Chicago: Aldine.

———. 1981. *Bones: Ancient Men and Modern Myths*. New York: Academic Press.

Butzer, K. W. 1982. *Archaeology as Human Ecology*. Cambridge, Eng.: Cambridge University Press.

Cohen, G. A. 1978. *Karl Marx's Theory of History. A Defense*. Princeton: Princeton University Press.

Dunnell, R. C. 1982. "Science, Social Science, and Common Sense: The Agonizing Dilemma of Modern Archaeology." *Journal of Anthropological Research* 38: 1–25.

Eiseley, L. 1946. *The Immense Journey*. New York: Time, Inc.

———. 1979. *Darwin and the Mysterious Mr. X*. New York: Harcourt, Brace, Jovanovich.

Flannery, K. V. 1973. "Archeology with a Capital 'S.'" In *Research and Theory in Current Archeology*, ed. Charles L. Redman. New York: Wiley.

Friedman, J. and M. J. Rowlands. 1977. *The Evolution of Social Systems*. Pittsburgh: University of Pittsburgh Press.

Gould, R. A., ed. 1978. *Explorations in Ethno-Archaeology*. Albuquerque: University of New Mexico Press.

Gould, S. J. 1977. *Ever Since Darwin*. New York: Norton.

Grayson, D. K. 1983. *The Establishment of Human Antiquity*. New York: Academic Press.

Harris, M. 1968. *The Rise of Anthropological Theory*. New York: Crowell.

———. 1979. *Cultural Materialism*. New York: Random House.

Hill, J. N. 1972. "The Methodological Debate in Contemporary Archaeology: A Model." In *Models in Archaeology*, ed. David L. Clarke. London: Methuen.

Lovejoy, A. O. 1960. *The Great Chain of Being: A Study of the History of an Idea*. New York: Harper & Row.

Lumley, H. de. 1969. *Le paléolithique inférieur et moyen du Midi Méditerranéan dans son cadre géologique*: Vol. 1: *Ligurie Provence*. Paris: Éditions du Centre National de la Recherche Scientifique.

Marx, K. 1904. *The Critique of Political Economy*, trans. I. N. Stone. Chicago: International Library Publication Co.

Meehan, E. J. 1968. *Explanation in Social Sciences: A System Paradigm*. Homewood, Ill.: Dorsey.

Meek, R. L. 1953. *Marx and Engels on Malthus*. London: Lawrence and Wishart.

Orton, C. 1980. *Mathematics in Archaeology*. London: Collins.

Ross, E. B., ed. 1980. *Beyond the Myths of Culture: Essays in Cultural Materialism*. New York: Academic Press.

Sahlins, M. D. and E. R. Service, eds. 1960. *Evolution and Culture*. Ann Arbor: University of Michigan Press.

Salmon, M. H. 1982. *Philosophy and Archaeology*. New York: Academic Press.

Salmon, M. H. and W. C. Salmon. 1979. "Alternative Models of Scientific Explanation. *American Anthropologist* 81: 61–74.

Schiffer, M. B. 1981. "Some Issues in the Philosophy of Archaeology." *American Antiquity* 46: 899–908.

Spaulding, A. C. 1973. "Archeology in the Active Voice: The New Anthropology," In *Research and Theory in Current Archeology*, ed. Charles L. Redman. New York: Wiley.

Spencer, H. 1883. *Social Statics*. New York: Appleton.

Watson, P. J., S. A. LeBlanc, and C. L. Redman. 1971. *Explanation in Archeology*. New York: Columbia University Press.

Wells, P. S. 1980. *Culture Contact and Culture Change*. Cambridge: Cambridge University Press.

Wenke, R. J. 1975–1976. "Imperial Investments and Agricultural Developments in Parthian and Sasanian Khuzestan: 150 B.C. to A.D. 640." *Mesopotamia* 10–11: 31–217.

White, L. A. 1949. *The Science of Culture*. New York: Grove Press.

———. 1959. "The Concept of Culture." *American Anthropologist* 61: 227–51.

Willey, Gordon R. and Phillip Phillips. 1958. *Method and Theory in American Archaeology*. Chicago: University of Chicago Press.

Chapter 2

Badekas, J., ed. 1975. *Photogrammetric Surveys of Monuments and Sites*. New York: Elsevier.

Binford, L. R. 1964. "A Consideration of Archaeological Research Design." *American Antiquity* 29: 425–41.

Bodner, C. and R. M. Rowlett. 1980. "Separation of Bone, Charcoal, and Seeds by Chemical Flotation." *American Antiquity* 45: 110–16.

Brill, R., ed. 1971. *Science and Archaeology*. Cambridge, Mass.: MIT Press.

Browman, D. L. 1981. "Isotopic Discrimination and Correction Factors in Radiocarbon Dating." In *Advances in Archaeological Method and Theory*, vol. 4, ed. M. B. Schiffer. New York: Academic Press.

Crabtree, D. 1972. *An Introduction to Flintworking*. Occasional Papers of the Idaho State University Museum, no. 28. Pocatello.

Deetz, J. 1967. *Invitation to Archaeology*. Garden City, N.Y.: Natural History Press.

Doran, J. and F. Hodson. 1975. *Mathematics and Computers in Archaeology*. Cambridge, Mass.: Harvard University Press.

Drennan, R. D. 1976. "A Refinement of Chronological Seriation Using Nonmetric Multidimensional Scaling." *American Antiquity* 41: 290–320.

Dunnell, R. C. 1970. "Seriation Method and Its Evaluation." *American Antiquity* 35: 305–19.

———. 1971. *Systematics in Prehistory*. New York: Free Press.

Hole, F. and R. F. Heizer. 1973. *An Introduction to Prehistoric Archaeology*. 3rd ed. New York: Holt.

Joukowsky, M. 1980. *A Complete Manual of Field Archaeology*. Englewood Cliffs, N.J.: Prentice-Hall.

Keeley, L. H. 1980. *Experimental Determination of Stone Tool Use: A Microwear Analysis*. Chicago: University of Chicago Press.

Le Blanc, S. A. 1975. "Microseriation: A Method for Fine Chronological Differentiation." *American Antiquity* 40: 22–38.

Marquardt, W. H. 1979. "Advances in Archaeological Seriation." In *Advances in Archaeological Method and Theory,* vol. 1, ed. M. B. Schiffer. New York: Academic Press.

Michels, J. W. 1973. *Dating Methods in Archaeology*. New York: Seminar Press.

Mueller, J., ed. 1975. *Sampling in Archaeology*. Tucson: University of Arizona Press.

Reidhead, V. A. 1979. "Linear Programming Models in Archaeology." *Annual Review of Anthropology* 8: 543–78.

Renfrew, J. M. 1973. *Palaeoethnobotany*. New York: Columbia University Press.

Semenov, S. 1964. *Prehistoric Technology,* trans. M. W. Thompson. London: Cory, Adams & Mackay.

Strong, D. E., ed. 1973. *Archaeological Theory and Practice*. London: Seminar Press.

Thomas, D. H. 1974. *Predicting the Past: An Introduction to Anthropological Archaeology*. New York: Holt.

Tite, M. S. 1972. *Methods of Physical Examination in Archaeology*. London and New York: Seminar Press.

Wendorf, F. and R. Schild, eds. 1980. *Prehistory of the Eastern Sahara*. New York: Academic Press.

Wenke, R. J. and M. E. Lane, eds. In preparation. *Land of the Lake. 8000 Years of Human Settlement in Egypt's Fayyum Oasis*. Malibu: Undena.

Chapter 3

Adams, R. McC. 1966. *The Evolution of Urban Society*. Chicago: Aldine.

Anati, E. and N. Haas. 1967. "The Hazorea Pleistocene Site: A Preliminary Report." *Man* 2: 454–56.

Arambourg, C. 1967. "Le deuxième mission scientifique de l'Omo." *L'Anthropologie* 71: 562–66.

Ardrey, R. 1961. *African Genesis*. New York: Atheneum.

Arens, W. 1979. *The Man-Eating Myth*. New York: Oxford University Press.

Bar-Yosef, O. 1975. "Archeological Occurrences in the Middle Pleistocene of Israel." In *After the Australopithecines,* eds. K. W. Butzer and G. Isaac. The Hague: Mouton.

Binford, L. R. 1977. "A Review of *"Olorgesailie: Archaeological Studies of a Middle Pleistocene Lake Basin in Kenya,* by Glynn LI. Isaac." *Journal of Anthropological Research* 33(4): 493–502.

———. 1981. *Bones: Ancient Men and Modern Myth*. New York: Academic Press.

Birdsell, J. B. 1972. *Human Evolution*. Chicago: Rand McNally.

———. 1979. "Ecological Influences on Australian Aboriginal Social Organization." In *Primate Ecology and Human Origins: Ecological Influences and Social Organization,* eds. I. S. Bernstein and E. O. Smith. New York: Garland.

Boaz, N. T. 1979. "Hominid Evolution in Eastern Africa During the Pliocene and Early Pleistocene." *Annual Review of Anthropology* 8: 71–85.

Bowen, D. Q. 1978. *Quaternary Geology*. Oxford: Oxford University Press.

Brace, C. L. 1979. "Biological Parameters and Pleistocene Hominid Life-ways." In *Primate Ecology and Human Origins: Ecological Influences and Social Organization*, eds. I. S. Bernstein and E. O. Smith. New York: Garland.

————. 1981. "Tales of the Phylogenetic Woods: The Evolution and Significance of Evolutionary Trees." *American Journal of Physical Anthropology* 56: 411–29.

Bunn, H. T. 1981. "Archaeological Evidence for Meat-Eating by Plio-Pleistocene Hominids from Koobi Fora and Olduvai Gorge." *Nature* 291: 574–77.

Butzer, K. W. 1975. "Geological and Ecological Perspectives on the Middle Pleistocene." In *After the Australopithecines*, eds. K. W. Butzer and G. Isaac. The Hague: Mouton.

————. 1982. "The Paleo-ecology of the African Continent: The Physical Environments of Africa from the Earliest Geological to Later Stone Age Times." In *The Cambridge History of Africa*, vol. 1, ed. J. D. Clark. Cambridge, Eng.: Cambridge University Press.

Cachel, S. 1975. "A New View of Speciation." In *Australopithecus Paleoanthropology: Morphology and Paleoecology*, ed. R. H. Tuttle. The Hague: Mouton.

Cronin, J. E., N. T. Boaz, C. B. Stringer, and Y. Rak. 1981. "Tempo and Mode in Hominid Evolution." *Nature* 292: 113–22.

Crook, J. H. 1972. "Sexual Selection, Dimorphism, and Social Organization in the Primates." In *Sexual Selection and the Descent of Man 1871–1971*, ed. B. Campbell. Chicago: Aldine.

Curtis, G. H., T. Drake, T. Cerling, and X. Hampel. 1975. "Age of the KBS Tuff in Koobi Fora Formation, East Rudolf, Kenya." *Nature* 258: 395–98.

Deacon, H. J. 1975. "Demography, Subsistence, and Culture During the Acheulian in Southern Africa." In *After the Australopithecines*, eds. K. W. Butzer and G. Isaac. The Hague: Mouton.

Finkel, D. J. 1981. "An Analysis of Australopithecine Dentition." *American Journal of Physical Anthropology*. 55: 69–80.

Fisher, E. 1979. *Woman's Creation*. New York: McGraw-Hill.

Flint, R. F. 1971. *Glacial and Quaternary Geology*. New York: Wiley.

Freeman, L. G. 1975. "Acheulian Sites and Stratigraphy in Iberia and the Meghreb." In *After the Australopithecines*, eds. K. W. Butzer and G. Isaac. The Hague: Mouton.

Garn, S. and W. Block. 1970. "The Limited Nutritional Value of Cannibalism." *American Anthropologist* 72: 106.

Gould, S. J. and N. Eldredge. 1977. "Punctuated Equilibria: The Tempo and Mode of Evolution Reconsidered." *Paleobiology* 3: 115–51.

Grimaud, D. 1980. "Les Paritaux de l'*Homo erectus* comparison avec ceux des Pithecanthropes de Java." *Bulletins et Memoires de la Société XIIIe, Série n° 3*.

Hamilton, M. E. 1984. "Revising Evolutionary Narratives: A Consideration of Alternative Assumptions about Sexual Selection and Competition for Mates." *American Anthropologist* 86(3): 651–62.

Harding, R. S. and G. Teleki, eds. 1981. *Omnivorous Primates*. New York: Columbia University Press.

Hill, J. H. 1978. "Apes and Language." *Annual Review of Anthropology* 7: 89–112.

Howell, F. C. 1982. "Origins and Evolution of the African Hominidae." In *The Cambridge History of Africa*, vol. 1, ed. J. D. Clark. Cambridge, Eng.: Cambridge University Press.

Howells, W. 1973. *Evolution of the Genus Homo*. Reading, Mass.: Addison-Wesley.

Hughes, A. R. and P. V. Tobias. 1977. "A Fossil Skull Probably of the Genus *Homo* from Sterkfontein, Transvaal." *Nature* 265: 310–12.

Isaac, G. Ll. 1975. "Sorting Out the Muddle in the Middle: An Anthropologist's Post-Conference Appraisal." In *After the Australopithecines*, eds. K. W. Butzer and G. Isaac. The Hague: Mouton.

———. 1977. *Olorgesailie: Archaeological Studies of a Middle Pleistocene Lake Basin in Kenya*. Chicago: University of Chicago Press.

———. 1978. "Food-Sharing and Human Evolution: Archaeological Evidence from the Plio-Pleistocene of East Africa." *Journal of Anthropological Research* 34: 311–25.

———. 1982. "The Earliest Archaeological Traces." In *The Cambridge History of Africa*, vol. 1, ed. J. D. Clark. Cambridge, Eng.: Cambridge University Press.

Jelinek, A. J. 1977. "The Lower Paleolithic: Current Evidence and Interpretations." *Annual Review of Anthropology* 6: 11–32.

Johanson, D. C. and M. A. Edey. 1981. *Lucy: The Beginnings of Humankind*. New York: Simon and Schuster.

Johanson, D. C. and T. D. White. 1979. "A Systematic Assessment of Early African Hominids." *Science* 203: 321–29.

Klein, R. G. 1977. "The Ecology of Early Man in Southern Africa." *Science* 197: 115–26.

Kranz, G. 1975. "The Double Descent of Man." In *Australopithecus Paleoanthropology: Morphology and Paleoecology*, ed. R. H. Tuttle. The Hague: Mouton.

Lawick-Goodall, J. van. 1968. "The Behavior of Free-living Chimpanzees in the Gombe Stream Area." *Animal Behavior Monographs* 1: 161–311.

———. 1971. "Some Aspects of Aggressive Behavior in a Group of Free-living Chimpanzees." *International Social Science Journal* 23: 89–97.

———. 1973. "The Behavior of Chimpanzees in Their Natural Habitat." *American Journal of Psychiatry* 130: 1–12.

Leakey, M. G. and R. E. Leakey, eds. 1978. *Koobi Fora Research Project:* vol. 1, *The Fossil Hominids and an Introduction to Their Context, 1968–1974*. Oxford: Clarendon Press.

Lovejoy, O. 1980. "Hominid Origins: The Role of Bipedalism." *American Journal of Physical Anthropology* 52: 250.

Lumley, H. de. 1969. "A Paleolithic Camp at Nice." *Scientific American* 225: 42–59.

———. 1975. "Cultural Evolution in France in Its Paleoecological Setting During the Middle Pleistocene." In *After the Australopithecines*, eds. K. W. Butzer and G. Isaac. The Hague: Mouton.

Martin, K. and B. Voorhies. 1975. *The Female of the Species*. New York: Columbia University Press.

Morris, D. 1967. *The Naked Ape*. London: Jonathan Cape.

Napier, J. R. and P. H. Napier. 1967. *A Handbook of Living Primates*. London: Academic.

Penny, D., L. R. Foulds, and M. D. Hendy. 1982. "Testing the Theory of Evolution by Comparing Phylogenetic Trees Constructed from Five Different Protein Sequences." *Nature* 297: 197–200.

Pfeiffer, J. E. 1978. *The Emergence of Man*. 3rd ed. New York: Harper & Row.

Pianka, E. 1974. *Evolutionary Ecology*. New York: Harper & Row.

Pilbeam, D. 1975. "Middle Pleistocene Hominids." In *After the Australopithecines*, eds. K. W. Butzer and G. Isaac. The Hague: Mouton.

————. 1982. "New Hominoid Skull Material from the Miocene of Pakistan." *Nature* 295: 232–34.

Pilbeam, D. and S. J. Gould. 1974. "Size and Scaling in Human Evolution." *Science* 186: 892–901.

Poirier, F. 1973. *Fossil Man: An Evolutionary Journey*. St. Louis: Mosby.

Sagan, C. 1977. *The Dragons of Eden: Speculations on the Evolution of Human Intelligence*. New York: Ballantine Books.

Sahlins, M. 1972. *Stone Age Economics*. Chicago: Aldine.

Schaller, G. B. and G. R. Lowther. 1969. "The Relevance of Carnivore Behavior to the Study of Early Hominids." *Southwestern Journal of Anthropology* 25: 307–41.

Schwalbe, G. 1906. *Studien zur Vorgeschichte des Menschen*. Stuttgart: Scheizerbart.

Shapiro, H. L. 1974. *Peking Man*. New York: Simon and Schuster.

Simons, E. B. and D. R. Pilbeam. 1965. "Preliminary Revision of the Dryopithecinae (Pongidae, Anthropoidea)." *Folia Primatologica* 3: 81–152.

Smith, F. H. and G. C. Ranyard, 1981. "Evolution of the Supraorbital Region in Upper Pleistocene Fossil Hominids from South-central Europe. *American Journal of Physical Anthropology* 53: 589–610.

Smith, P. E. L. 1982. "The Late Paleolithic and Epi-Paleolithic of Northern Africa." In *The Cambridge History of Africa*, vol. 1, ed. J. D. Clark. Cambridge, Eng.: Cambridge University Press.

Speth, J. and D. Davis. 1976. "Seasonal Variability in Early Hominid Predation." *Science* 192: 441–45.

Swedlund, A. 1974. "The Use of Ecological Hypotheses in Australopithecine Taxonomy." *American Anthropologist* 76: 515–29.

Symons, D. 1975. "The Origins of the Family." Santa Barbara: Mimeographed.

————. 1979. *The Evolution of Human Sexuality*. New York: Oxford University Press.

Tanner, N. M. 1981. *On Becoming Human: A Model of the Transition from Ape into Human and the Reconstruction of Early Human Social Life*. Cambridge, Eng.: Cambridge University Press.

Teleki, G. 1973. "The Omnivorous Chimpanzee." *Scientific American* 228: 32–47.

————. 1981. "The Omnivorous Diet and Eclectic Feeding Habits of Chimpanzees in Gombe National Park, Tanzania." In *Omnivorous Primates*, eds. R. S. Harding and G. Teleki. New York: Columbia University Press.

Thorne, A. G. and M. Wolpoff. 1981. "Regional Continuity and Australasian Pleistocene Hominid Evolution." *American Journal of Physical Anthropology* 55: 337–349.

Townsend, P. K. 1971. "New Guinea Sago Gatherers: A Study of Demography in Relation to Subsistence." *Ecology of Food and Nutrition* 1: 19–24.

Van den Berghe, P. L. 1972. "Sex Differentiation and Infant Care: A Rejoinder to Sharlotte Neely Williams." *American Anthropologist* 74: 770–72.

Vertes, L. 1965. "Typology of the Buda Industry. A Pebble-tool Industry from the Hungarian Lower Paleolithic." *Quaternaria* 7: 185–95.

Von Koenigswald, G. H. R. 1975. "Early Man in Java: Catalogue and Problems." In *Australopithecus Paleoanthropology: Morphology and Paleoecology*, ed. R. H. Tuttle. The Hague: Mouton.

Washburn, S. L. 1968. "Discussion." In *Man the Hunter*, eds. R. Lee and I. DeVore. Chicago: Aldine.

Washburn, S. L. and R. L. Ciochon. 1974. "Canine Teeth: Notes on Controversies in the Study of Human Evolution." *American Anthropologist* 76: 765–84.

White, L. 1949. *The Science of Culture.* New York: Grove Press.

Wolpoff, M. 1971. "Vertesszöllös and the Presapiens Theory." *American Journal of Physical Anthropology* 35: 209–16.

Chapter 4

Binford, L. R. 1968. "Post-Pleistocene Adaptations." In *New Perspectives in Archeology,* eds. L. Binford and S. Binford. Chicago: Aldine.

––––––. 1982. "Comment on Rethinking the Middle/Upper Paleolithic Transition!" *Current Anthropology* 23: 177–81.

Binford, L. R. and S. Binford. 1966. "A Preliminary Analysis of Functional Variability in the Mousterian of Levallois Facies." In *Recent Studies in Paleoanthropology. American Anthropologist* special publication, pp. 238–95.

Bordes, F. 1961a. *Typologie du paléolithique ancien et moyen Bordeaux.* Publication de l'Institut de Prehistoire de l'Université de Bordeaux.

––––––. 1961b. "Mousterian Cultures in France." *Science* 134: 803–10.

––––––. 1968. *The Old Stone Age.* London: Weidenfeld & Nicholson.

––––––. 1972. *A Tale of Two Caves.* New York: Harper & Row.

––––––. 1978. "Typological Variability in the Mousterian Layers at Pech de l'Azé, II and IV." *Journal of Anthropological Research* 34: 181–93.

Bordes, F. and D. de Sonneville-Bordes. 1970. "The Significance of Variability in Paleolithic Assemblages." *World Archaeology* 2: 61–73.

Boule, M. and H. Vallois. 1932. *Fossil Men.* London: Thames and Hudson.

Brace, C. L. 1964. "The Fate of the 'Classic' Neanderthals: A Consideration of Human Catastrophism." *Current Anthropology* 5: 3.

––––––. 1967. *The Stages of Human Evolution: Human and Cultural Origins.* Englewood Cliffs, N.J.: Prentice-Hall.

––––––. 1975. "Review of *Shanidar: The First Flower People,* by R. Solecki." *Natural History* 80: 82–86.

Bricker, H. 1976. "Upper Paleolithic Archaeology." *Annual Review of Anthropology* 5: 133–48.

Brose, D. and M. Wolpoff. 1971. "Early Upper Paleolithic Man and Late Paleolithic Tools." *American Anthropologist* 73: 1156.

Brothwell, D. 1961. "Upper Pleistocene Human Skull from Niah Caves, Sarawak." *Sarawak Museum Journal* 9: 323.

Butzer, K. W. and G. Ll. Isaac, eds. 1975. *After the Australopithecines.* The Hague: Mouton.

Campbell, B., ed. 1976. *Humankind Emerging.* Boston: Little, Brown.

Carlisle, R. C. and M. I. Siegel. 1974. "Some Problems in the Interpretation of Neanderthal Speech Capabilities: A Reply to Lieberman." *American Anthropologist* 76: 319–22.

Conkey, M. 1980. "The Identification of Prehistoric Hunter-Gatherer Aggregation Sites: The Case of Altamira." *Current Anthropology* 21: 609–30.

Dubois, E. 1921. "The Proto-Australian Fossil Man of Wadjak, Java." *Proceedings: Koninklijke Nederlandse Akademie van Wetenschappen* 23: 1013.

Edey, M. A. and Editors of Time-Life, 1972. *The Missing Link.* New York: Time-Life.

Falk, D. 1975. "Comparative Anatomy of the Larynx in Man and the Chimpanzee: Implications for Language in Neanderthal." *American Journal of Physical Anthropology* 43: 123–32.

Farb, P. and G. Armelagos. 1980. *Consuming Passions*. Boston: Houghton Mifflin.

Fisher, E. 1979. *Woman's Creation*. New York: McGraw-Hill.

Frayer, D. W. 1981. "Body Size, Weapons Use, and Natural Selection in the European Upper Paleolithic and Mesolithic." *American Anthropologist* 83: 57–73.

Freeman, M. 1971. "A Social and Economic Analysis of Systematic Female Infanticide." *American Anthropologist* 73:1011–18.

Frolov, B. A. 1978–1979. "Numbers in Paleolithic Graphic Art and the Initial Stages of Development of Mathematics." *Soviet Anthropology and Archeology* 17: 41–74.

Gabow, S. L. 1977. "Population Structure and the Rate of Hominid Brain Evolution." *Journal of Human Evolution* 6: 643–65.

Garn, S. and W. Block. 1970. "The Limited Nutritional Value of Cannibalism." *American Anthropologist* 72: 106.

Gould, S. J. 1980. *The Panda's Thumb*. New York: Norton.

Howell, F. C. 1961. "Isimila: A Paleolithic Site in Africa." *Scientific American* 205: 118–31.

———. 1965. *Early Man*. New York: Time-Life.

Howells, W. W. 1975. "Neanderthal Man: Facts and Figures." In *Australopithecus Paleoanthropology: Morphology and Paleoecology*, ed. R. H. Tuttle. The Hague: Mouton.

Jelinek, A. 1982. "The Tabun Cave and Paleolithic Man in the Levant." *Science* 216: 1369–1375.

Jorgensen, G. 1977. "A Contribution of the Hypothesis of a 'Little More Fitness' of Blood Group O." *Journal of Human Evolution* 6: 741–44.

Leakey, M. D. 1975. "Cultural Patterns in the Olduvai Sequence." In *After the Australopithecines*, eds. K. W. Butzer and G. Ll. Isaac. The Hague: Mouton.

Leroi-Gourhan, A. 1968. *The Art of Prehistoric Man in Western Europe*. London: Thames and Hudson.

Lieberman, P. E. and E. S. Crelin. 1971. "On the Speech of Neanderthals." *Linguistic Inquiry*. 2: 203–22.

Lieberman, P. E., E. S. Crelin, and D. H. Klatt. 1972. "Phonetic Ability and Related Anatomy of the Newborn and Adult Human, Neanderthal Man, and the Chimpanzee." *American Anthropologist* 74: 287.

Lovejoy, O. and E. Trinkhaus. 1980. "Strength of Robusticity of the Neanderthal Tibia." *American Journal of Physical Anthropology* 53:465–70.

Luguet, G. 1930. *The Art and Religion of Fossil Man*. New Haven: Yale University Press.

Lumley, H. de. 1969. *Le Paléolithique inférieur et moyen du Midi Méditerranéen dans son cadre géologique*, vol. 1: *Ligurie Provence*. Éditions du Centre National de La Recherche Scientifique, Paris.

———. 1971. *Le Paléolithique inférieur et moyen du Midi Méditerranéan dans son cadre géologique*, vol. 2: *Bas—Languedoc, Roussillon, Catalogue*. Éditions du Centre National de La Recherche Scientifique, Paris.

Lumley, H. de and M.-A. de Lumley. 1971. "Decouverte de restes humains anteneandertaliens dates du debut du Riss à la Caune de l'Arago (Tautavel, Pyrenees-Orientales)." *Comptes Rendus de l'Academie des Sciences de Paris*. 272: 1739–42.

Lumley, M.-A. de. 1973. *Anteneandertaliens et Neandertaliens du Bassin Méditer-ranéen Occidental Européen.* Études Quaternaires, Mémoire n. 2. Université de Provence.

———. 1975. "Ante-Neanderthals of Western Europe." In *Australopithecus Paleo-anthropology: Morphology and Paleoecology,* ed. R. H. Tuttle. The Hague: Mouton.

Marshack, A. 1976. "Some Implications of the Paleolithic Symbolic Evidence for the Origins of Language." *Current Anthropology* 17: 274–82.

Pfeiffer, J. E. 1978. *The Emergence of Man.* New York: Harper & Row.

Pilbeam, D. 1975. "Middle Pleistocene Hominids." In *After the Australopithecines,* eds. K. W. Butzer and G. Ll. Isaac. The Hague: Mouton.

Poirier, F. E. 1973. *Fossil Man.* St. Louis: Mosby.

Prideaux, Tom and Editors of Time-Life. 1973. *Cro-Magnon Man.* New York: Time-Life.

Protsch, R. 1982. Public Lecture. Seattle.

Roberts, D. F. 1953. "Body Weight, Race and Climate." *American Journal of Physical Anthropology. N.S.* 11: 533–58.

Roe, D. A. 1981. *The Lower and Middle Paleolithic Periods in Britain.* London: Routledge & Kegan Paul.

Shapiro, H. 1974. *Peking Man.* New York: Simon and Schuster.

Sigmon, B. A. and J. S. Cybulski, eds. 1981. *Homo Erectus: Papers in Honor of Davidson Black.* Toronto: University of Toronto Press.

Smith, F. H. and G. C. Ranyard, 1981. "Evolution of the Supraorbital Region in Upper Pleistocene Fossil Hominids from South-central Europe." *American Journal of Physical Anthropology* 53: 589–610.

Straus, L. G. 1982. "Carnivores and Cave Sites in Cantabrian Spain." *Journal of Anthropological Research* 38: 75–96.

Straus, W. and A. Cave. 1957. "Pathology and the Posture of Neanderthal Man." *Quarterly Review of Biology* 32: 348.

Swedlund, A. 1974. "The Use of Ecological Hypotheses in Australopithecine Tax-onomy." *American Anthropologist* 76: 515–29.

Thorne, A. 1980. "The Arrival of Man in Australia." In *The Cambridge Encyclo-pedia of Archaeology,* pp. 96–100. New York: Crown Publishers/Cambridge University Press.

Tobias, P. and G. Von Koenigswald. 1964. "Comparison Between the Olduvai Hom-inines and Those of Java and Some Implications for Phylogeny." *Nature* 204: 515.

Vallois, H. 1961. "The Social Life of Early Man: The Evidence of the Skeletons." In *Social Life of Early Man,* ed. S. Washburn. Chicago: Aldine.

Vermeersch, P. M. 1979. *Elkab II: l'Elkabian épipaléolithique de la Valleé du Nil Égyptien.* Brussels: Publications du Comité des Fouilles Belges en Égypte.

White, R. 1982. "Rethinking the Middle/Upper Paleolithic Transition." *Current Anthropology* 23: 169–91.

White, J. P. and J. F. O'Connell. 1979. "Australian Prehistory: New Aspects of Antiquity." *Science* 203.

Windels, F. 1965. *The Lascaux Cave Paintings.* London: Faber and Faber.

Wobst, H. M. 1974a. "Boundary Conditions for Paleolithic Social Systems: A Simu-lation Approach," *American Antiquity.* 39: 147–78.

———. 1974b. "The Archaeology of Band Society—Some Unanswered Questions." *American Antiquity* 39: v–xiii.

Wolpoff, M. 1968. "Climatic Influence on the Skeletal Nasal Aperture." *American Journal of Physical Anthropology* 29:405–23.

———. 1970. "The Evidence for Multiple Hominid Taxa at Swartkrans." *American Anthropologist* 72: 56–57.

———. 1971. "Vertesszölös and the Presapiens Theory." *American Journal of Physical Anthropology* 35: 209.

Chapter 5

Adovasio, J. M., J. Donahue, J. D. Gunn, and R. Stuckenrath. 1981. "The Meadowcroft Papers; A Response to Dincauze." *Quarterly Review of Archaeology* 2: 14–15.

Aikens, C. M. 1978. "Archaeology of the Great Basin." *Annual Review of Anthropology* 7: 71–87.

Bada, J. L., and P. M. Helfman. 1975. "Amino Acid Racemization Dating of Fossil Bones," *World Archaeology* 7: 160–73.

Berger, R. 1975. "Advances and Results in Radiocarbon Dating: Early Man in North America." *World Archaeology* 7: 174–84.

Bettinger, R. L. 1977. "Aboriginal Human Ecology in Owens Valley: Prehistoric Change in the Great Basin." *American Antiquity* 42: 3–17.

Bonnichsen, R. 1979. *Pleistocene Bone Technology in the Beringian Refugium.* National Museum of Man, Mercury Series, No. 89.

Chard, C. S. 1956. "The Oldest Sites of Northeast Siberia." *American Antiquity* 21: 405–9.

———. 1960. "Routes to Bering Strait." *American Antiquity* 26: 283–85.

Claiborne, R. and the Editors of Time-Life. 1973. *The First Americans.* New York: Time-Life.

Cwyner, L. C. and J. C. Ritchie. 1980. "Arctic Step-Tundra: A Yukon Perspective." *Science* 208: 1375–77.

DeJarnette, D. L. 1967. "Alabama Pebbletools: The Lively Complex." *Eastern States Archaeological Federation Bulletin* 26.

deTerra, H. 1949. "Early Man in Mexico." In *Tepexpan Man,* by H. deTerra, J. Romero, and T. D. Stewart. New York: Viking Fund Publications in Anthropology 11: 11–86.

Dikov, N. N. 1977. *Monuments in Kamchatka, Chukotka, and the Upper Reaches of the Kolyma: Asia Joining America in Ancient Times.* Moscow: Nauka.

Dincauze, D. 1981. "The Meadowcroft Papers." *The Quarterly Review of Archaeology* 2: 3–4.

Dragoo, D. W. 1976. "Some Aspects of Eastern North American Prehistory: A Review 1975." *American Antiquity* 41: 3–27.

Frison, G. C., M. Wilson, and D. J. Wilson. 1976. "Fossil Bison and Artifacts from an Early Altithermal Period Arroyo Trap in Wyoming." *American Antiquity* 41: 28–57.

Grayson, D. K. 1977. "Pleistocene Avifaunas and the Overkill Hypothesis." *Science* 195: 691–3.

Greenman, E. F. 1963. "The Upper Paleolithic in the New World." *Current Anthropology* 4: 41–91.

Griffin, J. B. 1960. "Some Prehistoric Connections Between Siberia and America." *Science* 131: 801–12.

———. 1967. "Eastern North American Archaeology: A Summary." *Science* 156: 175–91.

Guthrie, R. D. 1980. "The First Americans? The Elusive Arctic Bone Culture." *The Quarterly Review of Archaeology* 1: 2.

Haag, W. G. 1962. "The Bering Strait Land Bridge." *Scientific American* 206: 112–23.

Harris, M. 1977. *Cannibals and Kings: The Origins of Culture.* New York: Random House.

Hassan, F. A. 1980. "Prehistoric settlements in Egypt." In *The Sahara and the Nile,* M. Williams and H. Fasure, eds. Rotterdam: Balkema Press.

Hayden, B. 1981. "Research and Development in the Stone Age: Technological Transitions among Hunter-Gatherers." *Current Anthropology* 22:519–48.

Haynes, C. V., Jr. 1969. "The Earliest Americans." *Science* 166: 709–15.

———. 1971. "Time, Environment, and Early Man." In *Papers from a Symposium on Early Man in North America, New Developments: 1960–1970,* ed. R. Shutler, Jr. *Arctic Anthropology* 8: 3–14.

———. 1974. "Elephant Hunting in North America." *New World Prehistory: Readings from Scientific American,* eds. E. Zubrow et al. San Francisco: Freeman.

Hopkins, D. M., ed. 1967. *The Bering Land Bridge.* Stanford: Stanford University Press.

Hopkins, D. M., J. V. Matthews, Jr., C. E. Schweger, and S. B. Young. 1982. *Paleoecology of Beringia.* New York: Academic Press.

Jairazbhoy, R. A. 1974. *Old World Origins of American Civilization.* 2 vols. London: Rauman and Littlefield.

Jennings, J. D. 1964. "The Desert West." In *Prehistoric Man in the New World.* eds. J. D. Jennings and E. Norbeck. Chicago: University of Chicago Press.

———. 1974. *The Prehistory of North America.* 2nd ed. New York: McGraw-Hill.

Jennings, J. D. and E. Norbeck, eds. 1964. *Prehistoric Man in the New World.* Chicago: University of Chicago Press.

Krieger, A. D. 1964. "Early Man in the New World." In *Prehistoric Man in the New World,* eds. J. D. Jennings and E. Norbeck. Chicago: University of Chicago Press.

Lively, M. 1965. "The Lively Complex: Announcing a Pebble Tool Industry in Alabama." *Journal of Alabama Archaeology* 11: 103–22.

Lyell, C. 1863. *Principles of Geology.* London: Murray.

MacNeish, R. S. 1971. "Early Man in the Andes." *Scientific American* 4: 36–46.

———, ed. 1973. *Early Man in America.* San Francisco: Freeman.

———. 1978. *The Science of Archaeology?* North Scituate, Mass.: Duxbury Press.

Madsen, D. B. and M. S. Berry. 1975. "A Reassessment of Northeastern Great Basin Prehistory." *American Antiquity* 40: 391–405.

Martin, P. S. 1973. "The Discovery of America." *Science* 179: 969–74.

Martin, P. S. and J. E. Guilday. 1967. "A Bestiary for Pleistocene Biologists." In *Pleistocene Extinctions: The Search for a Cause,* eds. P. S. Martin and H. E. Wright, Jr. New Haven: Yale University Press.

Martin, P. S. and H. E. Wright, Jr., eds. 1967. *Pleistocene Extinctions: The Search for a Cause.* New Haven: Yale University Press.

Mehringer, P., Jr. 1977. "Great Basin Late Quaternary Environments and Chronology." In *Models in Great Basin Prehistory: A Symposium,* ed. D. D. Fowler. Desert Research Institute Publications in the Social Sciences 12: 113–68.

Müller-Beck, H. J. 1966. "Paleo-Hunters in America: Origins and Diffusion." *Science* 152: 1191–1210.

Reeves, B. O. K. 1971. "On the Coalescence of the Laurentide and Cordilleran Ice Sheets in the Western Interior of North America." In *Aboriginal Man and Environments on the Plateau of Northwest America,* eds. A. Stryd and R. A. Smith. Calgary: University of Calgary Archaeological Association.

Stewart, T. D. 1973. *The People of America.* New York: Scribner's.

Tuohy, D. R. 1968. "Some Early Lithic Sites in Western Nevada." In *Early Man in Western North America,* ed. C. Irwin-Williams. Portales: Eastern New Mexico University Press.

Vescelius, G. S. 1981. "Early and/or Not-so-Early Man in Peru: Guitarrero Cave Revisited." *Quarterly Review of Archaeology* 2: 8–13, 19–20.

Warren, C. and A. Ranere. 1968. "Outside Danger Cave: A View of Early Men in the Great Basin." In *Early Man in Western North America,* ed. C. Irwin-Williams. Portales: Eastern New Mexico University Press.

Wheat, J. B. 1972. "The Olsen-Chubbuck Site. A Paleo-Indian Bison Kill." *Memoirs of the Society for American Archaeology,* no. 26, pt. 2.

Williams, B. J. 1974. "A Model of Band Society." *American Antiquity* 39, pt. 2, memoirs 29, pt. 2.

Chapter 6

Adams, Richard E. W. 1977. *Prehistoric Mesoamerica.* Boston: Little, Brown.

Ammerman, A. J. and L. L. Cavalli-Sforza. 1972. "A Population Model for the Diffusion of Early Farming in Europe." In *The Explanation of Culture Change: Models in Prehistory,* ed. C. Renfrew. London: Duckworth.

Athens, J. S. 1977. "Theory Building and the Study of Evolutionary Process in Complex Societies." In *For Theory Building in Archaeology,* ed. L. R. Binford. New York: Academic Press.

Beadle, G. W. 1972. "The Mystery of Maize." *Field Museum of Natural History Bulletin* 43: 2–11.

———. 1980. "The Ancestry of Corn." *Scientific American* 242: 112–19.

Belyaev, D. K. 1969. "Domestication of Animals." *Science Journal* 5: 47–52.

Binford, L. R. 1968. "Post-Pleistocene Adaptations." In *New Perspectives in Archaeology,* eds. S. R. Binford and L. R. Binford. Chicago: Aldine.

———. 1972. *An Archaeological Perspective.* New York: Seminar Press.

Boserup, E. 1965. *The Conditions of Agricultural Growth.* Chicago: Aldine.

———. 1981. *Population and Technology.* Chicago: University of Chicago Press.

Braidwood, R. J. 1960. "The Agricultural Revolution." *Scientific American* 203: 130–41.

———. 1973. "The Early Village in Southwestern Asia." *Journal of Near Eastern Studies* 32: 34–39.

Braidwood, R. J. et al. 1960. *Prehistoric Investigations in Iraqi Kurdistan.* Chicago: University of Chicago Press.

Braidwood, R. J., H. Cambel, and P. J. Watson, 1969. "Prehistoric Investigations in Southeastern Turkey." *Science* 164: 1275–76.

Brush, C. 1965. "Pox Pottery: Earliest Identified Mexican Ceramic." *Science* 149: 194–95.

Butzer, K. W. 1971. "The Significance of Agricultural Dispersal into Europe and Northern Africa." In *Prehistoric Agriculture,* ed. S. Struever. Garden City, N.Y.: Natural History Press.

Carneiro, R. 1970. "A Theory of the Origin of the State." *Science* 169: 733–38.

Carneiro, R. and D. Hilse. 1966. "On Determining the Probable Rate of Population Growth During the Neolithic." *American Anthropologist* 68: 177–81.

Caton-Thompson, G. and E. W. Gardner. 1934. *The Desert Fayum.* London: Royal Anthropological Institute.

Cauvin, J. 1972. "Nouvelles fouilles à Tell Mureybet (Syria): 1971–1972. Rapport preliminaire." *Annales Archeologiques de Syrie* 22: 105–15.

Cavalli-Sforza, L. L. and M. W. Feldman. 1981. *Cultural Transmission and Evolution: A Quantitative Approach.* Princeton: Princeton University Press.

Chang, K. C. 1976. *Early Chinese Civilization: Anthropological Perspectives.* Cambridge, Mass.: Harvard University Press.

Childe, V. Gordon. 1952. *New Light on the Most Ancient East.* 4th ed. London: Routledge and Kegan Paul.

Clark, J. G. D. 1952. *Prehistoric Europe: The Economic Basis.* London: Methuen.

———. 1980. *Mesolithic Prelude. The Paleolithic-Neolithic Transition in Old World Prehistory.* Edinburgh: Edinburgh University Press.

Coe, M. D. 1960. "Archaeological Linkages with North and South America at La Victoria, Guatemala." *American Anthropologist* 62: 363–93.

Cohen, N. M. 1977. *The Food Crisis in Prehistory.* New Haven and London: Yale University Press.

Diener, P. and E. E. Robkin. 1978. "Ecology, Evolution, and the Search for Cultural Origins: The Question of Islamic Pig Prohibition." *Current Anthropology* 19: 493–540.

Ekholm, G. F. 1964. "Transpacific Contacts." In *Prehistoric Man in the New World,* eds. J. D. Jennings and E. Norbeck. Chicago: University of Chicago Press.

Feldman, M. and E. R. Sears. 1981. "The Wild Gene Resources of Wheat." *Scientific American* 244: 102–113.

Flannery, K. V. 1965. "The Ecology of Early Food Production in Mesopotamia." *Science* 147: 1247–56.

———. 1968. "Archeological Systems Theory and Early Mesoamerica." In *Anthropological Archeology in the Americas,* ed. B. J. Meggers. Washington, D.C.: The Anthropological Society of Washington.

———. 1971. "Origins and Ecological Effects of Early Domestication in Iran and the Near East." In *Prehistoric Agriculture,* ed. S. Struever. Garden City, N.Y.: Natural History Press.

———. 1972. "The Origins of the Village as a Settlement Type in Mesoamerica and the Near East: A Comparative Study." In *Man, Settlement and Urbanism,* eds. P. J. Ucko, R. Tringham, and G. W. Dimbleby. London: Duckworth.

———. 1973. "The Origins of Agriculture." *Annual Review of Anthropology* 2: 271–310.

Flannery, K. V. and M. D. Coe. 1968. "Social and Economic Systems in Formative Mesoamerica." In *New Perspectives in Archeology,* eds., S. R. Binford and L. R. Binford. Chicago: Aldine.

Friedman, J. 1974. "Marxism, Structuralism, and Vulgar Materialism." *Man* 9: 444–69.

Frisch, R. and J. McArthur. 1974. "Menstrual Cycles: Fatness as a Determinant of Minimum Weight for Height Necessary for Their Maintenance or Onset." *Science* 185: 949–51.

Galinat, W. C. 1971. "The Origin of Maize." *Annual Review of Genetics* 5: 447–78.

Garrod, D. 1957. "The Natufian Culture: The Life and Economy of a Mesolithic People in the Near East." *Proceedings of the British Academy* 43: 211–17.

Halperin, R. 1980. "Ecology and Mode of Production: Seasonal Variation and the Division of Labor by Sex among Hunter-Gatherers." *Journal of Anthropological Research* 36: 379–99.

Harlan, J. and D. Zohary. 1966. "Distribution of Wild Wheats and Barley." *Science* 153: 1074–80.

Harlan, J., J. M. J. De Wet, and A. B. L. Stemler, eds. 1976. *Origins of African Plant Domestication*. The Hague: Mouton.

Harner, M. 1970. "Population Pressure and the Social Evolution of Agriculturalists." *Southwestern Journal of Anthropology* 26: 67–86.

Harpending, H. and H. Davis. 1976. "Some Implications for Hunter-Gatherer Ecology Derived from the Spatial Structure of Resources." *World Archaeology* 8: 275–86.

Harris, M. 1974. *Cows, Pigs, Wars, and Witches*. New York: Random House.

———. 1977. *Cannibals and Kings*. New York: Random House.

———. 1979. *Cultural Materialism*. New York: Random House.

Hassan, F. A. 1980. *Demographic Archaeology*. New York: Academic Press.

Hayden, B. 1981. "Research and Development in the Stone Age: Technological Transitions among Hunter-Gatherers." *Current Anthropology* 22: 519–48.

Helback, H. 1964. "First Impressions of the Çatal Hüyük Plant Husbandry." *Anatolian Studies* 14: 121–23.

———. 1969. "Plant Collecting, Dry-farming, and Irrigation Agriculture in Prehistoric Deh Luran." In *Prehistory and Human Ecology of the Deh Luran Plain*, eds. F. Hole, K. V. Flannery, and J. A. Neely. Memoirs of the Museum of Anthropology, University of Michigan, no. 1.

Higgs, E. S. and M. R. Jarman. 1969. "The Origins of Agriculture: A Reconsideration." *Antiquity* 43: 31–41.

Ho, P. 1969. "The Loess and the Origin of Chinese Agriculture." *American Historical Review* 75: 1–36.

Hole, F. 1962. "Archeological Survey and Excavation in Iran, 1961." *Science* 137: 524–26.

———. 1971. "Comment on 'Origins of Food Production in Southwestern Asia' by G. Wright." *Current Anthropology* 12: 472–73.

Hole, F., K. V. Flannery, and J. A. Neely. 1969. *Prehistory and Human Ecology of the Deh Luran Plain*. Memoirs of the Museum of Anthropology, University of Michigan, no. 1.

Johnson, F., ed. 1972. *The Prehistory of the Tehuacán Valley*, vol. 4. Austin: University of Texas Press.

Just, P. 1980. "Time and Leisure in the Elaboration of Culture." *Journal of Anthropological Research* 36: 105–115.

Keene, A. S. 1981. "Optimal Foraging in a Nonmarginal Environment: A Model of Prehistoric Subsistence Strategies in Michigan." In *Hunter-Gatherer Foraging Strategies*, eds. B. Winterhalder and E. A. Smith. Chicago: University of Chicago Press.

Kirkbride, D. 1968. "Beidha: Early Neolithic Village Life South of the Dead Sea." *Antiquity* 42: 263–74.

Kirkby, A. 1973. *The Use of Land and Water Resources in the Past and Present Valley of Oaxaca, Mexico.* Memoirs of the Museum of Anthropology, University of Michigan, no. 5.

Kovar, A. 1970. "The Physical and Biological Environment of the Basin of Mexico." In *The Teotihuacán Valley Project. Final Report,* vol. 1, eds. W. Sanders et al. Occasional Papers in Anthropology, Pennsylvania State University.

Lange, F. W. 1971. "Marine Resources: A Viable Subsistence Alternative for the Prehistoric Lowland Maya." *American Antiquity* 73: 619–39.

Lee, R. B. 1969. "!Kung Bushman Subsistence: An Input-Output Analysis." In *Environment and Cultural Behavior,* ed. A. P. Vayda. Garden City, N.Y.: Natural History Press.

MacNeish, R. S. 1964. "Ancient Mesoamerican Civilization." *Science* 143: 531–37.

———. 1966. "Speculations about the Beginnings of Village Agriculture in Mesoamerica." *Actas y Memorials del 35a Congreso Internacional de Americanistas* 1: 181–85.

———, gen. ed. 1972. *The Prehistory of the Tehuacán Valley: Chronology and Irrigation,* vol. 4. Austin: University of Texas Press.

Mangelsdorf, P. 1974. *Corn: Its Origin, Evolution, and Improvement.* Cambridge, Mass.: Harvard University Press.

———. 1983. "The Mystery of Corn: New Perspectives." *Proceedings of the American Philosophical Society:* 127(4): 215–47.

Martin, P. S. and P. J. Mehringer, Jr. 1965. "Pleistocene Pollen Analysis and Biography of the Southwest." In *The Quaternary of the United States, Biogeography: Phytogeography and Palynology,* part 2, eds. H. E. Wright, Jr. and D. G. Frey. Princeton: Princeton University Press.

Meggers, B. 1975. "The Transpacific Origins of Mesoamerican Civilization: A Preliminary Review of the Evidence and Its Theoretical Implications." *American Anthropologist* 77: 1–27.

Mellaart, J. 1966. *The Chalcolithic Early Bronze Ages of the Near East and Anatolia.* Beirut: Khayats.

———. 1975. *The Neolithic of the Near East.* London: Thames and Hudson.

Mortensen, P. 1972. "Seasonal Camps and Early Villages in the Zagros." In *Man, Settlement, and Urbanism,* eds. P. Ucko, R. Tringham, and G. W. Dimbleby. London: Duckworth.

Munchaev, R. M. and N. Y. Merpert. 1971. *New Studies of Early Agricultural Settlements in the Sinjar Valley.* VIII Congress International des Sciences Prehistoriques et Protohistoriques, Belgrade.

Palerm, A. and E. Wolf. 1960. "Ecological Potential and Cultural Development in Mesoamerica." *Social Science Monographs* 3: 1–38.

Perkins, D., Jr. 1973. "The Beginnings of Animal Domestication in the Near East." *American Journal of Archaeology* 77:279–82.

——— and P. Daly. 1968. "A Hunter's Village in Neolithic Turkey." *Scientific American* 210: 94–105.

Pianka, E. R. 1978. *Evolutionary Ecology.* 2nd ed. New York: Harper & Row.

Pumpelly, R. 1908. *Explorations in Turkey, the Expedition of 1904: Prehistoric Civilization of Anau,* vol. 1. Washington, D.C.: Publications of the Carnegie Institution, no. 73.

Reed, Charles A., ed. 1977. *Origins of Agriculture.* The Hague: Mouton.

Reichel-Dolmatoff, G. 1965. *Columbia.* New York: Praeger, Ancient Peoples and Places Series, no. 44.

Renfrew, C., J. E. Dixon, and J. R. Cann. 1966. "Obsidian and Early Cultural Contacts in the Near East." *Proceedings of the Prehistoric Society* 32: 30–72.

Rindos, D. 1980. "Symbiosis, Instability, and the Origins and Spread of Agriculture: A New Model." *Current Anthropology* 21: 751–72.

Sahlins, M. 1968. "Notes on the Original Affluent Society." In *Man the Hunter,* eds. R. B. Lee and I. DeVore. Chicago: Aldine.

———. 1976. *Culture and Practical Reason.* Chicago: University of Chicago Press.

———. 1978. "Comment on A. H. Berger's 'Structural and Eclectic Revisions of Marxist Strategy: A Cultural Materialist Critique.' " *Current Anthropology* 17: 298–300.

Sanders, W. T. 1965. *Cultural Ecology of the Teotihuacán Valley.* Department of Sociology and Anthropology, Pennsylvania State University.

——— and B. J. Price. 1968. *Mesoamerica: The Evolution of a Civilization.* New York: Random House.

Smith, P. E. L. 1967. "New Investigations in the Late Pleistocene Archaeology of the Kom Ombo Plain (Upper Egypt)." *Quaternaria* 9: 141–52.

———. 1972. "Ganj Dareh Tepe." *Iran* 10: 165–68.

Solecki, R. L. 1981. *An Early Village Site at Zawi Chemi Shanidar. Bibliotheca Mesopotamica* Vol. 13.

Solecki, R. S. 1964. "Shanidar Cave, a Late Pleistocene Site in Northern Iraq." VI International Congress on the Quaternary, *Reports* 4: 413–23.

Solecki, R. S. and R. L. Solecki. 1980. "Paleoecology of the Negev." *Quarterly Review of Archaeology* 1: 8, 12.

Stark, B. and B. Voorhies, eds. 1978. *Prehistoric Coastal Adaptations: The Economy and Ecology of Maritime Middle America.* New York: Academic Press.

Tauber, H. 1981. "^{13}C Evidence for Dietary Habits of Prehistoric Man in Denmark." *Nature* 292: 332–33.

Tringham, R. 1971. *Hunters, Fishers, and Farmers of Eastern Europe 6000–3000 B.C.* London: Hutchinson University Library.

Turnbull, P. F. and C. A. Reed. 1974. "The Fauna from the Terminal Pleistocene of Palegawra Cave." *Fieldiana* (Field Museum of Natural History) 63.

Van Loon, M. 1968. "The Oriental Institute Excavations at Mureybit, Syria: Preliminary Report on the 1965 Campaign." *Journal of Near Eastern Studies* 27: 265–90.

Vavilov, N. I. 1949–50: "The Origin, Variation, Immunity, and Breeding of Cultivated Plants." *Chronica Botanica* 13.

Wendorf, F. and A. E. Marks, eds. 1975. *Problems in Prehistory: North Africa and the Levant.* Dallas: SMU Press.

Western, C. 1971. "The Ecological Interpretation of Ancient Charcoals from Jericho." *Levant* 3: 31–40.

Winterhalder, B. and E. A. Smith, eds. 1981. *Hunter-Gatherer Foraging Strategies.* Chicago: University of Chicago Press.

Wright, G. 1971. "Origins of Food Production in Southwestern Asia: A Survey of Ideas." *Current Anthropology* 12: 447–77.

Wright, H. E., Jr. 1968. "Natural Environment of Early Food Production North of Mesopotamia." *Science* 161: 334–39.

————. 1976. "The Environmental Setting for Plant Domestication in the Near East." *Science* 194: 385–89.

Zeist, W. van. 1970. "The Paleobotany (Mureybit)." *Journal of Near Eastern Studies* 29: 167–76.

Zeist, W. van and W. A. Casparie. 1968. "Wild Einkorn Wheat and Barley from Tell-Mureybit in Northern Syria." *Acta Botanica Nederlandica* 17: 44–53.

Zevallos, M. C. et al. 1977. "The San Pablo Corn Kernel and Its Friends." *Science* 196: 385–89.

Chapter 7

Adams, R. N. 1981. "Natural Selection, Energetics, and 'Cultural Materialism.' " *Current Anthropology* 22: 603–24.

Alexander, R. D. 1975. "The Search for a General Theory of Behavior." *Behavioral Science* 20: 77–100.

————. 1979. "Evolution and Culture." In *Evolutionary Biology and Human Social Behavior, An Anthropological Perspective,* eds. N. Chagnon and W. Irons. North Scituate, Mass.: Duxbury Press. Pp. 59–78.

Athens, J. S. 1977. "Theory Building and the Study of Evolutionary Process in Complex Societies." In *For Theory Building in Archaeology.* New York: Academic Press.

Berlinski, D. 1976. *On Systems Analysis.* Cambridge, Mass.: MIT Press.

Berry, B. 1967. *Geography of Market Centers and Retail Distribution.* Englewood Cliffs, N.J.: Prentice-Hall.

Binford, L. R. 1971. "Mortuary Practices: Their Study and Their Potential." In *Approaches to the Social Dimensions of Mortuary Practices,* ed. J. A. Brown. Memoirs of the Society for American Archaeology 25: 6–29.

Boserup, E. 1965. *The Conditions of Agricultural Growth.* Chicago: Aldine.

Buck, R. C. 1956. "On the Logic of General Behavior Systems Theory." In *The Foundations of Science and the Concept of Psychology and Psychoanalysis,* eds. H. Feigl and M. Scriven. *Minnesota Studies in the Philosophy of Science* 1: 223–28. Minneapolis: University of Minnesota Press.

Carniero, R. 1970. "A Theory of the Origin of the State." *Science* 169: 733–38.

Cavalli–Sforza, L. L. and M. W. Feldman. 1981. *Cultural Transmission and Evolution: A Quantitative Approach.* Princeton: Princeton University Press.

Cohen, G. A. 1978. *Karl Marx's Theory of History. A Defense.* Princeton: Princeton University Press.

Cohen, R. 1981. "Evolutionary Epistemology and Human Values." *Current Anthropology* 22: 201–18.

Cowgill, G. 1975. "On the Causes and Consequences of Ancient and Modern Population Changes." *American Anthropologist* 77: 505–25.

Crumley, C. L. 1979. "Three Locational Models: An Epistemological Assessment for Anthropology and Archaeology." In *Advances in Archaeological Method and Theory,* vol. 2, ed. M. B. Schiffer. New York: Academic Press.

Darwin, C. 1871. *The Descent of Man and Selection in Relation to Sex.* New York: Appleton.

Diakonov, I., ed. 1969. *Ancient Mesopotamia.* Moscow: Nauka.

Dunnell, R. C. 1978. "Style and Function: A Fundamental Dichotomy." *American Antiquity* 43: 192–202.

————. 1980. "Evolutionary Theory and Archaeology." In *Advances in Archaeological Method and Theory*, vol. 3, ed. M. B. Schiffer. New York: Academic Press.

Dunnell, R. C. and R. J. Wenke. 1980. "An Evolutionary Model of the Development of Complex Societies." Paper Presented at the Annual Meeting of the American Association for the Advancement of Science, San Francisco.

Eisenstadt, S. N. 1963. *The Political System of Empires*. New York: Free Press of Glencoe.

Flannery, K. V. 1972. "The Cultural Evolution of Civilizations." *Annual Review of Ecology and Systematics* 3: 399–426.

————. 1973. "Archeology with a Capital S." In *Research and Theory in Current Archeology*, ed. C. L. Redman. New York: Wiley.

Fried, M. H. 1960. "On the Evolution of Social Stratification and the State." In *Culture in History*, ed. S. Diamond. New York: Columbia University Press.

————. 1967. *The Evolution of Political Society*. New York: Random House.

————. 1975. Public lecture at the University of California at Santa Barbara. Spring 1975.

Friedman, J. and M. J. Rowlands. 1977. *The Evolution of Social Systems*. Pittsburgh: University of Pittsburgh Press.

Gellner, E., ed. 1980. *Soviet and Western Anthropology*. London: Duckworth.

Harris, M. 1968. *The Rise of Anthropological Theory*. New York: Crowell.

————. 1977. *Cannibals and Kings*. New York: Random House.

————. 1980. *Cultural Materialism: The Struggle for a Science of Culture*. New York: Vintage Press.

Hill, J. N. 1977. *Explanation of Prehistoric Change*. Albuquerque: University of New Mexico Press.

Johnson, G. A. 1977. "Aspects of Regional Analysis in Archaeology." *Annual Review of Anthropology* 6: 479–508.

————. 1980. "Rank-size convexity and system integration: a view from archaeology." *Economic Geography* 56: 234–47.

————. 1982. "Organizational Structure Scalar Stress." In *Theory and Explanation in Archaeology*. New York: Academic Press.

————. In press. "Monitoring Complex System Integration and Boundary Phenomena with Settlement Size Data." In *Archaeological Approaches to the Study of Complexity*, ed. S. E. van der Leeuw.

LeBlanc, S. 1973. "Two Points of Logic Concerning Data, Hypotheses, General Laws, and Systems." In *Research and Theory in Current Archeology*, ed. C. L. Redman. New York: Wiley.

Legros, D. 1977. "Chance, Necessity, and Mode of Production: A Marxist Critique of Cultural Evolutionism." *American Anthropologist* 79: 26–41.

Lewarch, D. E. 1977. "Locational Models and the Archaeological Study of Complex Societies: A Dilemma in Data Requirements and Research Design." Paper Presented at the 76th Annual Meeting of the American Anthropological Association, Houston, Texas.

Lumsden, C. J. and E. O. Wilson. 1981. *Genes, Mind, and Culture*. Cambridge, Mass.: Harvard University Press.

Marx, K. 1973. *Grundrisse. Foundations of the Critique of Political Economy*. New York: Vintage Press. Original manuscript 1857–1858.

Marx, K. and F. Engels. 1970. *Selected Works*, in 3 vols. Moscow: Progress Publishers.

May, D. A. and D. M. Heer. 1968. "Son Survivorship, Motivation and Family Size in India: A Computer Simulation." *Population Studies* 22: 199–210.

O'Shea, J. M. 1984. *Mortuary Variability. An Archaeological Investigation.* New York: Academic Press.

Redman, C. L. 1978. *The Rise of Civilization.* San Francisco: Freeman.

Renfrew, C. 1972. *The Emergence of Civilization.* London: Methuen.

Roux, G. 1964. *Ancient Iraq.* Baltimore: Penguin.

Sahlins, M. 1968. "Notes on the Original Affluent Society." In *Man the Hunter,* eds. R. Lee and I. DeVore. Chicago: Aldine.

Salmon, M. H. and W. C. Salmon. 1979. "Alternative Models of Scientific Explanation." *American Anthropologist* 81: 61–74.

Sanders, W. T. and B. J. Price. 1968. *Mesoamerica.* New York: Random House.

Service, E. 1962. *Primitive Social Organization.* New York: Random House.

———. 1975. *Origins of the State and Civilization.* New York: Norton.

Smith, M. E. 1977. "State Systems of Settlement: Response to Crumley." *American Anthropologist* 79: 903–06.

Spooner, B., ed. 1972. *Population Growth: Anthropological Implications.* Cambridge, Mass.: MIT Press.

Steward, J. 1949. "Cultural Causality and Law: A Trial Formulation of the Development of Early Civilizations." *American Anthropologist* 51: 1–27.

Streuve, V. V. 1969. "The Problem of the Genesis, Development and Disintegration of the Slave Societies in the Ancient Orient," trans. I. Levit. In *Ancient Mesopotamia,* ed. I. M. Diakonoff. Moscow: Nauka.

Trigger, B. 1972. "Determinants of Urban Growth in Pre-Industrial Societies." In *Man, Settlement and Urbanism,* eds. P. J. Ucko, R. Tringham, and G. W. Dimbleby. London: Duckworth.

Webster, D. 1975. "Warfare and the Evolution of the State: A Reconsideration." *American Antiquity* 40: 471–75.

Weiss, K. M. 1976. "Demographic Theory and Anthropological Inference." *Annual Review of Anthropology* 5: 351–81.

Wenke, R. J. 1981. "Explaining the Evolution of Cultural Complexity: A Review." In *Advances in Archaeological Method and Theory,* vol. 4, ed. M. B. Schiffer. New York: Academic Press.

White, L. 1949. *The Science of Culture.* New York: Grove Press.

Wittfogel, K. A. 1957. *Oriental Despotism: A Comparative Study of Total Power.* New Haven: Yale University Press.

Wolf, E. R. 1966. *Peasants.* Englewood Cliffs, N.J.: Prentice-Hall.

Woodbury, R. B. 1961. "A Reappraisal of Hohokam Irrigation." *American Anthropologist* 63(3): 550–60.

Wright, H. 1977. "Recent Research on the Origin of the State." *Annual Review of Anthropology* 6: 379–97.

Chapter 8

Abu es-Soof, B. 1968. "Tell Es-Sawwan Excavations of the Fourth Season (Spring 1967). Interim Report." *Sumer* 24: 3–16.

Adams, R. McC. 1955. "Developmental Stages in Ancient Mesopotamia." In *Irrigation Civilizations: A Comparative Study,* ed. J. H. Steward. Washington, D.C.: Pan-American Union, Social Science Monographs.

———. 1965. *Land Behind Baghdad*. Chicago: University of Chicago Press.

———. 1966. *The Evolution of Urban Society: Early Mesopotamia and Prehispanic Mexico*. Chicago: Aldine.

———. 1972. "Patterns of Urbanization in Early Southern Mesopotamia." In *Man, Settlement and Urbanism*, eds. P. G. Ucko, R. Tringham, and G. Dimbleby. London: Duckworth.

———. 1975. "The Mesopotamian Social Landscape: A View from the Frontier." In *Reconstructing Complex Societies*. Supplement to the Bulletin of the American Schools of Oriental Research, no. 20.

———. 1981. *Heartland of Cities*. Chicago: Aldine.

Adams, R. McC. and H. Nissen. 1972. *The Uruk Countryside*. Chicago: University of Chicago Press.

Athens, J. S. 1977. "Theory Building and the Study of Evolutionary Process in Complex Societies." In *For Theory Building in Archaeology*, L. R. Binford, ed. New York: Academic Press.

Cowgill, G. 1975. "On Causes and Consequences of Ancient and Modern Population Changes." *American Anthropologist* 77: 505–25.

Crumley, Carole L. 1979. "Three Locational Models: An Epistemological Assessment for Anthropology and Archaeology." In *Advances in Archaeological Method and Theory, Vol. 2*, ed. M. B. Schiffer. New York: Academic Press.

Diakonoff, I. M., ed. 1969. *Ancient Mesopotamia*. Moscow: Nauka.

Diringer, D. 1962. *Writing*. New York: Praeger.

Flannery, K. V. 1972. "The Cultural Evolution of Civilizations." *Annual Review of Ecology and Systematics* 3: 399–426.

Frankfort, H. 1956. *The Birth of Civilization in the Near East*. Garden City, N.Y.: Doubleday.

Friedman, J. and M. J. Rowlands. 1977. *The Evolution of Social Systems*. Pittsburgh: University of Pittsburgh Press.

Gelb, I. J. 1952. *A Study of Writing: The Foundations of Grammatology*. Chicago: University of Chicago Press.

———. 1969. "On the Alleged Temple and State Economics in Ancient Mesopotamia." *Estratto da studi in onore di Edouard Voltera* 4: 139–54.

Gibson, M. 1972. "Population Shift and the Rise of Mesopotamian Civilization." In *The Explanation of Cultural Change: Models in Prehistory*, ed. C. Renfrew. London: Duckworth.

Hamblin, D. J. et al. 1973. *The First Cities*. New York: Time-Life.

Hole, F. 1977. "Pastoral Nomadism in Western Iran." In *Explorations in Ethnoarchaeology*, ed. R. A. Gould. Albuquerque: University of New Mexico Press.

———. 1978. "The Prehistory of Herding: Some Suggestions from Ethnography." *Colloques international du CNRS*, no. 580.

Hole, F., K. V. Flannery, and J. A. Neely. 1969. *Prehistory and Human Ecology of the Deh Luran Plain*. Memoirs of the Museum of Anthropology, University of Michigan, no. 1.

Ibrahim, M., J. A. Sauer, and K. Yassine. 1976. "The East Jordan Valley Survey, 1975." *Bulletin of the School of Oriental Research* 22: 42–64.

Jacobsen, T. and R. Adams. 1958. "Salt and Silt in Mesopotamian Agriculture." *Science* 128: 1251–58.

Jawad, A. J. 1965. *The Advent of the Era of Townships in Northern Mesopotamia*. Leiden: Brill.

Johnson, G. A. 1973. *Local Exchange and Early State Development in Southwestern Iran*. Museum of Anthropology, Anthropological Papers, University of Michigan, no. 51. Ann Arbor.

———. 1975a. "Locational Analysis and the Investigation of Uruk Local Exchange Systems." In *Ancient Civilization and Trade*, eds. J. Sabloff and C. Lamberg-Karlovsky. Albuquerque: University of New Mexico Press.

———. 1975b. "Early State Organization in Southwestern Iran: Preliminary Field Report." *Proceedings of the 4th Annual Symposium on Archaeological Research in Iran*. Teheran.

———. 1977. "Aspects of Regional Analysis in Archaeology." *Annual Review of Anthropology* 6: 479–508.

———. 1982. "Organizational Structure Scalar Stress." In *Theory and Explanation in Archaeology*. New York: Academic Press.

———. In Press. "Monitoring Complex System Integration and Boundary Phenomena with Settlement Size Data." In *Archaeological Approaches to the Study of Complexity*, ed. S. E. van der Leeuw.

Just, P. 1980. "Time and Leisure in the Elaboration of Culture." *Journal of Anthropological Research* 36: 105–15.

Kramer, S. N. 1959. *History Begins at Sumer*. Garden City, N.Y.: Doubleday.

Larsen, C. E. 1975. "The Mesopotamian Delta Region: A Reconsideration of Lees and Falcon." *Journal of the American Oriental Society* 95: 43–57.

Larsen, C. E. and G. Evans. 1978. "The Holocene History of the Tigris-Euphrates-Karun Delta." In W. C. Brice, ed., *The Environmental History of the Near and Middle East since the Last Ice Age*, pp. 227–44. London: Academic Press.

Lees, S. H. and D. G. Bates, 1974. "The Origins of Specialized Nomadic Pastoralism: A Systematic Model." *American Antiquity* 30: 187–93.

Leonard, A. Personal communication.

Loding, D. 1976. *Ur Excavations: Economic Texts from the Third Dynasty*. Philadelphia: Publication of the Joint Expedition of the British Museum and the University Museum, University of Pennsylvania.

Mallowan, Sir M. E. L. 1965. *Early Mesopotamia and Iran*. London: Thames and Hudson.

Melikishvili, G. A. 1978. "Some Aspects of the Question of the Socioeconomic Structure of Ancient Near Eastern Societies." *Soviet Anthropology and Archeology* 7:25–72.

Mellaart, J. 1965. *Earliest Civilizations of the Near East*. London: Thames and Hudson.

———. 1975. *The Neolithic of the Near East*. London: Thames and Hudson.

Mitchell, W. 1973. "The Hydraulic Hypothesis: A Reappraisal." *Current Anthropology* 4: 532–34.

Nissen, H. 1972. "The City Wall of Uruk." In *The Explanation of Cultural Change: Models in Prehistory*, ed. C. Renfrew. London: Duckworth.

Oates, J. 1980. "The Emergence of Cities in the Near East." *The Cambridge Encyclopedia of Archaeology*, pp. 112–119. New York: Crown Publishers/Cambridge University Press.

Oppenheim, A. L. 1964. *Ancient Mesopotamia: Portrait of a Dead Civilization*. Chicago: University of Chicago Press.

Pattee, H. H. 1973. *Hierarchy Theory: The Challenge of Complex Systems*. New York: Braziller.

Redman, C. L. 1978. *The Rise of Civilization.* San Francisco: W. H. Freeman.

Renfrew, C. 1975. *The Emergence of Civilization.* London: Methuen.

————, ed. 1972. *The Explanation of Cultural Change: Models in Prehistory.* London: Duckworth.

Roux, G. 1976. *Ancient Iraq.* Baltimore: Penguin.

Sabloff, J. and C. C. Lamberg-Karlovsky, eds. 1975. *Ancient Civilization and Trade.* Albuquerque: University of New Mexico Press.

Schmandt-Besserat, D. 1981. "Decipherment of the Earliest Tablets." *Science* 211: 283–84.

Service, E. R. 1962. *Primitive Social Organization.* New York: Random House.

————. 1975. *Origins of the State and Civilization.* New York: Norton.

Smith, P. E. L. and T. C. Young, Jr. 1972. "The Evolution of Early Agriculture and Culture in Greater Mesopotamia: A Trial Model." In *Population Growth: Anthropological Implications,* ed. B. Spooner. Cambridge, Mass.: MIT Press.

Spooner, B., ed. 1972. *Population Growth: Anthropological Implications.* Cambridge, Mass.: MIT Press.

Steward, J. H. 1949. "Cultural Causality and Law: A Trial Formulation of the Development of Early Civilizations." *American Anthropologist* 51: 1–27.

Taylor, R. E. and R. Berger. 1980. "The Date of Noah's Ark." *Antiquity* 54: 35–36.

Tosi, M. 1972. "The Early Urban Revolution and Settlement Pattern in the Indo-European Borderland." In *The Explanation of Cultural Change: Models in Prehistory,* ed. C. Renfrew. London: Duckworth.

Ucko, P., R. Tringham and G. Dimbleby, eds. 1972. *Man, Settlement and Urbanism.* London: Duckworth.

Webb, M. 1975. "The Flag Follows Trade: An Essay on the Necessary Integration of Military and Commercial Factors in State Formation." In *Ancient Civilization and Trade,* eds. J. Sabloff and C. C. Lamberg-Karlovsky. Albuquerque: University of New Mexico Press.

Weiss, H. 1977. "Periodization, Population, and Early State Formation in Khuzestan." In *Mountains and Lowlands: Essays in the Archaeology of Greater Mesopotamia,* eds. L. D. Levine and T. C. Young, Jr. Malibu: Undena.

Wenke, R. J. 1975–76. "Imperial Investments and Agricutural Developments in Parthian and Sasanian Khuzestan: 150 B.C. to A.D. 640." *Mesopotamia* 10–11: 31–217.

————. 1981. "Explaining the Evolution of Cultural Complexity: A Review." In *Advances in Archaeological Method and Theory,* vol. 4, ed. M. B. Schiffer. New York: Academic Press.

White, L. 1949. *The Science of Culture.* New York: Grove Press.

Wittfogel, K. A. 1957. *Oriental Despotism: A Comparative Study of Total Power.* New Haven: Yale University Press.

Wolkstein, D and S. N. Kramer. 1983. *Inanna. Queen of Heaven and Earth.* New York: Harper & Row.

Woolley, Sir L. 1965. *Excavations at Ur.* New York: Crowell.

Wright, H. T. 1969. *The Administration of Rural Production in an Early Mesopotamian Town.* Museum of Anthropology, Anthropological Papers, University of Michigan, no. 38. Ann Arbor.

————. 1977. "Recent Research on the Origin of the State." *Annual Review of Anthropology* 6: 379–97.

Wright, H. T. and G. A. Johnson. 1975. "Population, Exchange, and Early State Formation in Southwestern Iran." *American Anthropologist* 77: 267–89.

Yasin, W. 1970. "Excavation at Tell Es-Sawwan, 1969 (6th season)." *Sumer* 26: 4–11.

Young, T. C., Jr., 1972 "Population Densities and Early Mesopotamian Origins." In *Man, Settlement and Urbanism,* eds. P. J. Ucko, R. Tringham, and G. W. Dimbleby. London: Duckworth.

Chapter 9

Aldred, C. 1961. *The Egyptians.* New York: Praeger.

Arkell, A. J. and P. J. Ucko. 1965. "Review of Predynastic Development in the Nile Valley." *Current Anthropology* 6: 145–66.

Baumgartel, E. J. 1970. "Predynastic Egypt." In *Cambridge Ancient History,* rev. ed. 1: 463–97.

Bietak, M. 1979. "The Present State of Egyptian Archaeology." *Journal of Egyptian Archaeology* 65: 156–60.

Brothwell, D. R. and B. A. Chiarelli, eds. 1973. *Population Biology of the Ancient Egyptians.* London: Academic Press.

Butzer, K. W. 1960. "Archaeology and Geology in Ancient Egypt." *Science* 132: 1617–24.

———. 1976. *Early Hydraulic Civilization in Egypt.* Chicago: University of Chicago Press.

Butzer, K. W., G. Isaac, J. L. Richardson, and C. K. Washbourn-Kamau. 1972. "Radiocarbon Dating of East African Lake Levels." *Science* 175: 1069–76.

Clark, J. D. 1971. "A Re-Examination of the Evidence for Agricultural Origins in the Nile Valley." *Proceedings of the Prehistoric Society* 37(2).

———. 1976. "Prehistoric Populations and Resources Favoring Plant Domestication in Africa." In *Origins of African Plant Domestication,* eds. J. R. Harlan et al. The Hague: Mouton.

Edwards, I. E. S. 1961. *The Pyramids of Egypt.* London: Parrish.

Farooq, M. 1973. "Historical Development." In *Epidemiology and Control of Schistosomiasis (Bilharziasis),* ed. N. Ansari. Baltimore: University Park Press.

Frankfort, H. 1956. *The Birth of Civilization in the Near East.* Garden City, N.Y.: Doubleday.

Frankfort, H., J. Wilson, and T. Jacobsen. 1949. *Before Philosophy.* Baltimore: Penguin.

Friedman, J. and M. J. Rowlands. 1977. *The Evolution of Social Systems.* Pittsburgh: University of Pittsburgh Press.

Hamilton, E. 1930. *The Greek Way.* New York: Norton.

Harlan, J. R. 1982. "The Origins of Indigenous African Agriculture." In *The Cambridge History of Africa,* vol. 1, ed. J. D. Clark. Cambridge, Eng.: Cambridge University Press.

Harlan, J. R., J. M. de Wet, and A. B. Stemler, eds. 1976. *Origins of African Plant Domestication.* The Hague: Mouton.

Harris, J. E. and Kent R. Weeks. 1973. *X-Raying the Pharaohs.* New York: Scribner's.

Hoffman, M. 1970. "Culture History and Cultural Ecology at Hierakonpolis from Paleolithic Times to the Old Kingdom." Unpublished doctoral dissertation, University of Wisconsin.

————. 1980. *Egypt Before the Pharaohs: The Prehistoric Foundations of Egyptian Civilization*. New York: Knopf.

————. 1982. *The Predynastic of Hierakonpolis—An Interim Report*. Egyptian Studies Association Publication no. 1. Cairo: Cairo University Herbarium and the authors.

Kaster, J., trans. and ed. 1968. *Wings of the Falcon*. New York: Holt.

Kemp, B. J. 1977. "The Early Development of Towns in Egypt." *Antiquity* 51: 185–200.

————. 1982. "Old Kingdom, Middle Kingdom and Second Intermediate Period in Egypt." In *The Cambridge History of Africa*, vol. 1, ed. J. D. Clark. Cambridge, Eng.: Cambridge University Press.

Kitto, H. D. F. 1951. *The Greeks*. Harmondsworth: Pelican.

Lehner, M. in press. "A Contextual Approach to the Giza Pyramids." *Archiv für Orientforschung*.

O'Connor, D. 1982. "Egypt, 1552–664 B.C." In *The Cambridge History of Africa*, vol. 1, ed. J. D. Clark. Cambridge, Eng.: Cambridge University Press.

O'Connor, P. 1972. "A Regional Population in Egypt to Circa 600 B.C." In *Population Growth: Anthropological Implications*, ed. B. Spooner. Cambridge, Mass.: MIT Press.

Posnansky, M. and R. McIntosh. 1976. "New Radiocarbon Dates for Northern and Western Africa." *Journal of African History* 17: 161–95.

Service, E. 1975. *Origins of the State and Civilization*. New York: Norton.

Trigger, B. G. 1982. The Rise of Civilization in Egypt." In *The Cambridge History of Africa*, vol. 1, ed. J. D. Clark. Cambridge, Eng.: Cambridge University Press.

Wendorf, F. 1968. *The Prehistory of Nubia*. 2 vols. and atlas. Dallas: Fort Bergwin Research Center and Southern Methodist University Press.

————. 1976. "The Use of Ground Grain during the Late Paleolithic of the Lower Nile Valley, Egypt." In *Origins of African Plant Domestication*, eds. J. R. Harlan et al. The Hague: Mouton.

Wendorf, F., R. Said, and R. Schild. 1970. "Egyptian Prehistory: Some New Concepts." *Science* 169: 1161.

Wendorf, F. and R. Schild. 1975. "The Paleolithic of the Lower Nile Valley." In *Problems in Prehistory: North Africa and the Levant*, eds. F. Wendorf and A. Marks. Dallas: SMU Press.

————. 1980. *Prehistory of the Eastern Sahara*. New York: Academic Press.

————, ed. A. E. Close. 1980. *Loaves and Fishes: The Prehistory of Wadi Kubbaniya*. New Delhi: Pauls Press.

White, L. 1949. *The Science of Culture*. New York: Grove Press.

Wilson, J. A. 1946. "Egypt: The Nature of the Universe." In *Before Philosophy*, eds. H. A. Frankfort et al. Baltimore: Penguin.

————. 1951. *The Culture of Ancient Egypt*. Chicago: University of Chicago Press.

————. 1960. "Civilizations Without Cities." In *City Invincible*, eds. C. H. Kraeling and R. McC. Adams. Chicago: University of Chicago Press.

Wittfogel, K. A. 1957. *Oriental Despotism: A Comparative Study of Total Power*. New Haven: Yale University Press.

Chapter 10

Agrawal, D. P. 1971. *The Copper Bronze Age in India.* New Delhi: Manoharlal.

Agrawal, D. P. and S. D. Kusumgar. 1974. *Prehistoric Chronology and Radiocarbon Dating in India.* New Delhi: Manoharlal.

Allchin, B. and F. R. Allchin. 1968. *The Birth of Indian Civilization.* Baltimore: Penguin.

Allchin, F. R. 1960. *Piklihal Excavations.* Hyderabad: Government of Andhra Pradesh.

————. 1961. *Utnur Excavations.* Hyderabad: Government of Andhra Pradesh.

————. 1963. *Neolithic Cattle-keepers of South India.* Cambridge, Eng.: Cambridge University Press.

————. 1968. "Early Domestic Animals in India and Pakistan." In *Man, Settlement and Urbanism,* eds. P. J. Ucko, R. Tringham, and G. W. Dimbleby. London: Duckworth.

————. 1974. "India from the Late Stone Age to the Decline of Indus Civilization." *Encyclopaedia Britannica.* 9: 336–48.

Allchin, F. R. and D. K. Chakrabarti, eds. 1979. *A Source Book of Indian Archaeology,* vol. 1. New Delhi: Munshirman Maroharlal.

Clauson, G. and J. Chadwick. 1969. "The Indus Script Deciphered?" *Antiquity* 43: 200–07.

Dales, G. F. 1966. "Recent Trends in the Pre- and Protohistoric Archaeology of South Asia." *Proceedings of the American Philosophical Society* 110: 130–39.

Fairservis, W. A., Jr. 1956. "Excavations in the Quetta Valley, West Pakistan." Anthropological Papers of the American Museum of Natural History 45(2). New York.

————. 1975. *The Roots of Ancient India.* 2nd ed. rev. Chicago: University of Chicago Press.

Gupta, S. P. 1978. *Archaeology of Soviet Central Asia and the Indian Borderlands,* vol. 1. New Delhi: B. R. Publishing Co.

Ikawa-Smith, F., ed. 1978. *Early Paleolithic in South and East Asia.* The Hague: Mouton.

Jacobson, J. 1979. "Recent Developments in South Asian Prehistory and Protohistory." *Annual Review of Anthropology* 8: 467–502.

Johnson, G. A. 1973. *Local Exchange and Early State Development in Southwestern Iran.* Museum of Anthropology, Anthropological Papers, University of Michigan, no. 51, Ann Arbor.

Kennedy, K. and G. L. Possehl, eds. 1976. *Ecological Backgrounds of South Asian Prehistory. South Asia Occasional Papers and Theses,* no. 4.

Lamberg-Karlovsky, C. C. 1967. "Archaeology and Metallurgical Technology in Prehistoric Afghanistan, India and Pakistan." *American Anthropologist* 69: 145–62.

Leshnik, L. S. 1968. "The Harappan 'Port' at Lothal: Another View." *American Anthropologist* 70: 911–22.

McEvedy, C. 1967. *The Penguin Atlas of Ancient History.* Harmondsworth: Penguin.

Mughal, M. R. 1970. "The Early Harappan Period in the Greater Indus Valley and Northern Baluchistan." Unpublished doctoral dissertation, University of Pennsylvania.

———. 1974. "New Evidence of the Early Harappan Culture from Jalilpur, Pakistan." *Archaeology* 27: 106–13.

Perrtula, T. 1977. "Between the Indus and Euphrates: The Comparison of the Evolution of Complex Societies." Seattle. Mimeographed.

Pfeiffer, J. E. 1977. *The Emergence of Society.* New York: McGraw-Hill.

Piggott, S. 1950. *Prehistoric India.* London: Pelican.

Possehl, G. L. 1974. "Variation and Change in the Indus Civilization." Unpublished doctoral dissertation, University of Chicago.

———. 1976. "Lothal: A Gateway Settlement of the Harappan Civilization." In *Ecological Backgrounds of South Asian Prehistory,* eds. A. P. Kennedy and G. L. Possehl. *South Asia Occasional Papers and Theses* 4: 118–31. Ithaca.

———. 1980. "African Millets in South Asian Prehistory." Mimeographed.

———. n.d. "The End of a State and the Continuity of a Tradition in Proto-Historic India." In *Realm and Region in India,* ed., R. Fox. Durham: Duke University.

Raikes, R. 1965. "The Mohenjo-Daro Floods." *Antiquity* 39: 196–203.

Rao, S. R. 1973. *Lothal and the Indus Civilization.* Bombay: Asia House.

Service, E. 1975. *Origins of the State and Civilization.* New York: Norton.

Shaffer, J. 1982. "Harappan Culture: A Reconsideration." In *Harappan Civilization,* ed. G. L. Possehl. New Delhi: Oxford and Ibh.

Van Lohnizen-de Leeuw, J. E. and J. M. M. Ubagns, eds. 1974. *South Asian Archaeology.* Leiden: Brill.

Vishnu-Mittre. 1977. "Discussion on Local and Introduced Crops." in *The Early History of Agriculture: A Joint Symposium of The Royal Society and the British Academy,* organized by J. Hutchinson. London: Oxford University Press.

Wheeler, Sir M. 1966. *Civilizations of the Indus Valley and Beyond.* New York: McGraw-Hill.

———. 1968. *The Indus Civilization.* 3rd ed. Supplementary volume to the *Cambridge History of India.* Cambridge, Eng.: Cambridge University Press.

Wheeler, R. E. M. 1950. *Five Thousand Years of Pakistan.* London: Royal India and Pakistan Society.

Chapter 11

Anonymous. 1982. (trans. Du YouIiang [*sic*.]), *Neolithic Site at Banpo Near Xian.* [Guide to the Banpo Museum, printing data written in Chinese].

Barnard, N. 1972. "The First Radiocarbon Dates from China." *Monograph on Far Eastern History* 8. School of Pacific Studies, A.N.U. Canberra.

Bayard, D. 1979. "The Chronology of Prehistoric Metallurgy in North-East Thailand: Silabhumi or Samrddhabhumi?" in *Early South-East Asia,* eds. R. B. Smith and W. Watson. London: Oxford University Press.

Chang, K. C. 1963. *The Archaeology of Ancient China.* New Haven: Yale University Press.

———. 1970. "The Beginning of Agriculture in the Far East." *Antiquity* 44: 175–85.

———. 1976. *Early Chinese Civilization: Anthropological Perspectives.* Cambridge, Mass.: Harvard University Press.

———. 1977. *The Archaeology of Ancient China.* 3rd ed. New Haven: Yale University Press.

————. 1981. "In Search of China's Beginnings: New Light on an Old Civilization." *American Scientist* 69: 148–58.

Chang, S. 1963. "The Historical Trend of Chinese Urbanization." *Annals of the Association of American Geographers* 53: 109–43.

Chêng, T. 1957. *Archaeological Studies in Szechwan.* Cambridge, Eng.: Cambridge University Press.

————. 1963. *Archaeology in China,* vol. 3: *Chou China,* Cambridge: Heffer.

Lattimore, O. 1951. *Inner Asian Frontiers of China.* Boston: Beacon Press.

Li, C. 1957. *The Beginnings of Chinese Civilization.* Seattle: University of Washington Press.

Meacham, W. 1977. "Continuity and Local Evolution in the Neolithic of South China: A Non-Nuclear Approach." *Current Anthropology* 18: 419–40.

Nai, H. 1957. "Our Neolithic Ancestors." *Archaeology* 10: 181–87.

Service, E. 1975. *Origins of the State and Civilization.* New York: Norton.

Skinner, G. W. 1964. "Marketing and Social Structure in Rural China." *Journal of Asian Studies* 24: 3–43.

Stover, L. E. 1974. *The Cultural Ecology of Chinese Civilization.* New York: Pica Press.

Toynbee, A., ed. 1973. *Half the World.* New York: Holt.

Triestman, J. 1972. *The Prehistory of China.* Garden City, N.Y.: Natural History Press.

Watson, W. 1960. *Archaeology in China.* London: Parrish.

————. 1971. *Cultural Frontiers in Ancient East Asia.* Edinburgh: Edinburgh University Press.

————. 1974. *Ancient China.* Greenwich, Conn.: New York Graphic Society.

Wheatley, P. 1971. *The Pivot of the Four Quarters.* Chicago: Aldine.

Wittfogel, K. A. 1957. *Oriental Despotism. A Comparative Study of Total Power.* New Haven: Yale University Press.

Chapter 12

No attempt is made here to provide a bibliography for the many secondary states and empires of the ancient world. The interested reader may wish to consult a good encyclopedia of archaeology, such as the *Cambridge Encyclopedia of Archaeology* (1981), ed. A. Sheratt (Cambridge, Eng.: Cambridge University Press). The titles listed below may also be of interest.

Bellwood, P. S. "The Peopling of the Pacific." *Scientific American* 243: 174–85.

Bronson, B. 1980. "South-east Asia: Civilizations of the Tropical Forest." *Cambridge Encyclopedia of Archaeology,* pp. 262–66. New York: Crown Publishers/Cambridge University Press.

Fitzhugh, W. 1975. *Prehistoric Maritime Adaptations of the Circumpolar Zone.* The Hague: Mouton.

Milisauskas, S. 1978. *European Prehistory.* New York: Academic Press.

Weissleder, W. 1978. *The Nomadic Alternative: Models and Models of Interaction in the African-Asian Deserts and Steppes.* The Hague: Mouton.

Wemick, R., and the editors of Time-Life. 1973. *The Monument Builders.* Alexandria, Va.: Time-Life.

Chapter 13

Adams, R. E. W. 1977. *Prehistoric Mesoamerica*. Boston: Little, Brown.

Alden, J. R. 1979. "A Reconstruction of the Toltec Period Political Units in the Valley of Mexico." In *Transformations: Mathematical Approaches to Culture Change*, eds. C. Renfrew and K. L. Cooke. New York: Academic Press.

Armillas, P. 1971. "Gardens on Swamps." *Science* 174: 653–61.

Arnold, J. E. and A. Ford. 1980. "A Statistical Examination of Settlement Patterns at Tikal, Guatemala." *American Antiquity* 45: 713–26.

Ashmore, W., ed. 1981. *Lowland Maya Settlement Patterns*. Albuquerque: University of New Mexico Press.

Blanton, R. E. 1972. "Prehistoric Adaptation in the Ixtapalapa Region, Mexico." *Science* 175: 1317–26.

———. 1976. "The Origins of Monte Albán." In *Cultural Change and Continuity*, ed. C. E. Cleland. New York: Academic Press.

———. 1978. *Monte Albán: Settlement Patterns at the Ancient Zapotec Capital*. New York: Academic Press.

———. 1980. "Cultural ecology reconsidered." *American Antiquity* 45: 145–51.

Blanton, R. E., S. A. Kowalewski, G. Feinman, and J. Appel. 1981. *Ancient Mesoamerica, A Comparison of Change in Three Regions*. Cambridge, Eng.: Cambridge University Press.

Bove, F. J. 1981. "Trend Surface Analysis and the Lowland Classic Maya Collapse." *American Antiquity* 46: 93–112.

Brumfiel, E. 1976. "Regional Growth in the Eastern Valley of Mexico: A Test of the 'Population Pressure' Hypothesis." In *The Early Mesoamerican Village*, ed. K. V. Flannery. New York: Academic Press.

Brush, C. F. 1969. "A Contribution to the Archaeology of Coastal Guerrero, Mexico." Unpublished doctoral dissertation. Columbia University, New York.

Coe, M. D. 1962. *Mexico*. New York: Praeger.

———. 1965a. *The Jaguar's Children: Pre-Classic Central Mexico*. New York: Museum of Primitive Art.

———. 1965b. "The Olmec Style and Its Distribution." *Handbook of Middle American Indians* 3: 739–75.

———. 1966. *The Maya*. New York: Praeger.

———. 1968. "San Lorenzo and the Olmec Civilization." In *Dumbarton Oaks Conference on the Olmec*, ed. E. P. Benson. Dumbarton Oaks, Washington, D.C.

———. 1970. "The Archaeological Sequence at San Lorenzo Tenochtitlán, Veracruz, Mexico." *Contributions of the University of California Archaeological Research Facility*, no. 8, pp. 21–34.

———. 1984. *Mexico*. New York: Thames and Hudson.

Coe, M. and R. Diehl. 1980. *In the Land of the Olmec*, 2 vols. Austin: University of Texas Press.

Cook, S. 1946. "Human Sacrifice and Warfare as Factors in the Demography of Precolonial Mexico." *Human Biology* 18: 81–102.

Cowgill, G. 1974. "Quantitative Studies of Urbanization at Teotihuacán." In *Mesoamerican Archaeology: New Approaches*, ed. N. Hammond, pp. 363–96. Austin: University of Texas Press.

———. 1976. Public Lecture, Seattle.

Cowgill, U. 1962. "An Agricultural Study of the Southern Maya Lowlands." *American Anthropologist* 64: 273–86.

Culbert, T. P. 1973. *The Classic Maya Collapse*. Albuquerque: University of New Mexico Press.

Dickson, D. Bruce. 1981. "Further Simulations of Ancient Agriculture and Population at Tikal, Guatemala." *American Antiquity* 46: 922–26.

Doty, D. C. 1979. "A New Mayan Long Count–Gregorian Conversion Computer Program." *American Antiquity* 44: 780–83.

Drennan, R. D. 1976. "Religion and Social Evolution in Formative Mesoamerica." In *The Early Mesoamerican Village*, ed. K. V. Flannery. New York: Academic Press.

Earle, T. 1976. "A Nearest-Neighbor Analysis of Two Formative Settlement Systems." In *The Early Mesoamerican Village*, ed. K. V. Flannery. New York: Academic Press.

Ferdon, E. M. 1959. "Agricultural Potential and the Development of Cultures." *Southwestern Journal of Anthropology* 15: 1–19.

Flannery, K. V. 1968. "The Olmec and the Valley of Oaxaca: A Model for Inter-Regional Interaction in Formative Times." In *Dumbarton Oaks Conference on the Olmec,* ed. E. P. Benson. Dumbarton Oaks, Washington, D.C.

———. 1976a. "The Early Mesoamerican House." In *The Early Mesoamerican Village,* ed. K. V. Flannery. New York: Academic Press.

———. 1976b. "Evolution of Complex Settlement Systems." In *The Early Mesoamerican Village,* ed. K. V. Flannery. New York: Academic Press.

———. 1976c. "Linear Stream Patterns and Riverside Settlement Rules." In *The Early Mesoamerican Village,* ed. K. V. Flannery. New York: Academic Press.

———. 1976d. "Contextual Analysis of Ritual Paraphernalia from Formative Oaxaca." In *The Early Mesoamerican Village,* ed. K. V. Flannery. New York: Academic Press.

Flannery, K. V. ed., 1982. *Maya Subsistence. Studies in Memory of Dennis E. Puleston.* New York: Academic Press.

Flannery, K. V., J. Marcus, and S. A. Kowalewski, 1981. "The Preceramic and Formative of the Valley of Oaxaca," *Supplement to the Handbook of Middle American Indians,* pp. 48–93, Austin: University of Texas Press.

Flannery, K. V. and M. C. Winter. 1976. "Analyzing Household Activities." In *The Early Mesoamerican Village,* ed. K. V. Flannery. New York: Academic Press.

Fry, R., ed. 1980. *Models and Methods in Regional Exchange.* SAA Papers No. 1. Washington.

Fry, R. and S. Cox. 1974. "The Structure of Ceramic Exchange at Tikal, Guatemala." *World Archaeology* 6: 209–25.

Grennes-Ravits, R. and G. Coleman. 1976. "The Quintessential Role of Olmec in the Central Highlands of Mexico." *American Antiquity* 41: 196–205.

Grove, D. C. 1968. "The Pre-Classic Olmec in Central Mexico: Site Distribution and Inferences." In *Dumbarton Oaks Conference on the Olmec,* ed. E. P. Benson. Dumbarton Oaks, Washington, D.C.

Harner, M. 1977. "The Ecological Basis for Aztec Sacrifice." *American Ethnologist* 4: 117–35.

Harris, M. 1977. *Cannibals and Kings: The Origins of Cultures.* New York: Random House.

Hunt, R. C. and E. Hunt. 1976. "Canal Irrigation and Local Social Organization." *Current Anthropology* 17: 389–411.

Kelley, D. H. 1981. *Mayan Culture History as Process*. Ithaca: Cornell University Press.

Lees, S. H. 1973. *Sociopolitical Aspects of Canal Irrigation in the Valley of Oaxaca*. Ann Arbor: Memoir of the Museum of Anthropology, University of Michigan, no. 6.

Lowe, J. W. G. 1982. "On Mathematical Models of the Classic Maya Collapse: The Class Conflict Hypothesis Reexamined." *American Antiquity* 47: 643–52.

MacNeish, R. S. 1962. *Second Annual Report of the Tehuacán Archaeological-Botanical Project*. Andover, Mass.: R. S. Peabody Foundation for Archaeology.

———. 1964. "Ancient Mesoamerican Civilization." *Science* 143: 531–37.

Marcus, J. 1973. "Territorial Organization of the Lowland Classic Maya." *Science* 180: 911–16.

———. 1974. "The Iconography of Power Among the Classic Maya." *World Archaeology* 6: 83–94.

———. 1976a. "The Size of the Early Mesoamerican Village." In *The Early Mesoamerican Village*, ed. K. V. Flannery. New York: Academic Press.

———. 1976b. "The Origins of Mesoamerican Writing." *Annual Review of Anthropology* 5: 35–68.

———. 1976c. "The Iconography of Militarism at Monte Albán and Neighboring Sites in the Valley of Oaxaca." In *The Origins of Religious Art and Iconography in Preclassic Mesoamerica*, ed. H. B. Nicholson. Latin American Center, U.C.L.A.

Matheny, R. T. 1976. "Maya Lowland Hydraulic Systems." *Science* 193: 639–46.

Meggers, B. J. 1954. "Environmental Limitation in the Development of Culture." *American Anthropologist* 56.

Millon, R. 1974. "The Study of Urbanism at Teotihuacán, Mexico." In *Mesoamerican Archaeology: New Approaches*, ed. N. Hammond. Austin: University of Texas Press.

Millon, R., R. B. Drewitt, and G. L. Cowgill. 1973. *Urbanization at Teotihuacán, Mexico*, vol. 1, Parts 1 and 2. Austin: University of Texas Press.

Murdy, C. N. 1981. "Congenital Deformities and the Olmec Were-Jaguar Motif." *American Antiquity* 46: 861–69.

Nations, J. D. 1980. "The Evolutionary Potential of Lacondon Maya Sustained-Yield Tropical Forest Agriculture." *Journal of Anthropological Research* 36: 1–30.

Nichols, D. L. 1982. "A Middle Formative Irrigation System Near Santa Clara Coatitlan in the Basin of Mexico." *American Antiquity* 47: 133–44.

Offner, J. A. 1981. "On the Inapplicability of 'Oriental Despotism' and the 'Asiatic Mode of Production' to the Aztecs of Texcoco." *American Antiquity* 46: 43–61.

Palerm, A. and E. Wolf. 1957. "Ecological Potential and Cultural Development in Mesoamerica." In *Studies in Human Ecology. Social Science Monographs* 3: 1–38.

Parsons, J. R. 1968. "Teotihuacán, Mexico, and Its Impact on Regional Demography." *Science* 162: 872–77.

———. 1971. *Prehistoric Settlement Patterns in the Texcoco Region, Mexico*. Ann Arbor: Memoir of the Museum of Anthropology, University of Michigan, no. 3.

————. 1974. "The Development of a Prehistoric Complex Society: A Regional Perspective from the Valley of Mexico." *Journal of Field Archaeology* 1: 81–108.

Pelzer, K. J. 1945. *Pioneer Settlement in the Asiatic Tropics.* New York: American Geographical Society, Special Publications, no. 29.

Pires-Ferreira, J. W. 1975. *Formative Mesoamerican Exchange Networks with Special Reference to the Valley of Oaxaca.* Ann Arbor: Memoirs of the Museum of Anthropology, University of Michigan, no. 7.

Pollard, H. P. 1980. "Central Places and Cities: A Consideration of the Protohistoric Tarascan State." *American Antiquity* 45: 677–97.

Porter, M. N. 1953. *Tlatilco and the Pre-Classic Cultures of the New World.* New York: Viking Fund Publications in Anthropology, no. 19.

Puleston, D. E. and O. S. Puleston. 1971. "An Ecological Approach to the Origins of Maya Civilization." *Archaeology* 24: 330–36.

Pyne, N. M. 1976. "The Fire-Serpent and Were-Jaguar in Formative Oaxaca: A Contingency Table Analysis." In *The Early Mesoamerican Village,* ed. K. V. Flannery. New York: Academic Press.

Rathje, W. L. 1971. "The Origin and Development of Lowland Classic Maya Civilization." *American Antiquity* 36: 275–85.

————. 1973. "Classic Maya Development and Denouement: A Research Design." In *The Classic Maya Collapse,* ed. T. P. Culbert. Albuquerque: University of New Mexico Press.

Sahagún, F. B. de. 1976. *A History of Ancient Mexico,* trans. F. R. Bandelier from the Spanish version of Carlos Maria de Bustamante. Glorieta, New Mexico: Rio Grande Press.

Sahlins, M. 1968. "Notes on the Original Affluent Society." In *Man the Hunter,* eds. R. B. Lee and I. DeVore. Chicago: Aldine.

Sanders, W. T. 1973. "The Cultural Ecology of the Lowland Maya: A Re-Evaluation." In *The Classic Maya Collapse,* ed. T. P. Culbert. Albuquerque: University of New Mexico Press.

Sanders, W. T., J. R. Parsons, and M. H. Logan. 1976. "Summary and Conclusions." In *The Valley of Mexico,* ed. E. Wolf. Albuquerque: University of New Mexico Press.

Sanders, W. T., J. R. Parsons, and R. S. Santley. 1979. *The Basin of Mexico: Ecological Processes in the Evolution of a Civilization.* New York: Academic Press.

Sanders, W. T. and B. Price. 1968. *Mesoamerica: The Evolution of a Civilization.* New York: Random House.

Siemens, A. H. and D. E. Puleston. 1972. "Ridged Fields and Associated Features in Southern Campeche: New Perspectives on the Lowland Maya." *American Antiquity* 37: 228–39.

Sisson, E. B. 1970. "Settlement Patterns and Land Use in the Northwestern Chontalpa, Tabasco, Mexico: A Progress Report." *Ceramica de Cultura Maya* 6: 41–54.

Sjoberg, G. 1965. "The Origin and Evolution of Cities." *Scientific American* 213(3): 54–63.

Smith, M. 1979. "The Aztec Marketing System and Settlement Pattern in the Valley of Mexico: A Central Place Analysis." *American Antiquity* 44: 110–24.

Soustelle, J. 1961. *Daily Life of the Aztecs,* trans. P. O'Brian. Stanford: Stanford University Press.

Steponaitis, V. P. 1981. "Settlement Hierarchies and Political Complexity in Non-market Societies: The Formative Period in the Valley of Mexico." *American Anthropologist* 83: 320–63.

Thomas, P. M. 1981. *Prehistoric Maya Settlement Patterns at Becan, Campeche, Mexico.* Publication 45, Middle American Research Institute, Tulane University, New Orleans.

Tolstoy, P. 1981. "Advances in the Basin of Mexico," pt. 1. *The Quarterly Review of Archaeology* 2: 33–4,6.

Tolstoy, P. and A. Guínette. 1965. "Le Placement de Tlatilco dans de Cadre du Pré-Classique du Basin de Mexico." *Journal de la Société des Americanistes* (Paris) 54: 47–91.

Tolstoy, P. and L. Paradis. 1970. "Early and Middle Preclassic Culture in the Basin of Mexico." *Science* 167: 344–51.

Turner, B. L. II. 1974. "Prehistoric Intensive Agriculture in the Maya Lowlands." *Science* 185: 118–24.

Weaver, M. P. 1972. *The Aztecs, Maya, and Their Predecessors.* New York: Seminar Press.

Whalen, M. E. 1974. "Community Development and Integration During the Formative Period in the Valley of Oaxaca, Mexico." Paper read at the Annual Meeting of the American Anthropological Association, Mexico City.

———. 1976. "Zoning Within an Early Formative Community in the Valley of Oaxaca." In *The Early Mesoamerican Village,* ed. K. V. Flannery. New York: Academic Press.

———. 1981. *Excavations at Santo Domingo Tomaltepec: Evolution of a Formative Community in the Valley of Oaxaca, Mexico.* Memoir 12, Museum of Anthropology, University of Michigan.

Winter, M. 1972. "Tierras Largas: A Formative Community in the Valley of Oaxaca, Mexico." Unpublished doctoral thesis, University of Arizona.

———. 1976. "The Archaeological Household Cluster in the Valley of Oaxaca." In *The Early Mesoamerican Village,* ed. K. V. Flannery. New York: Academic Press.

Wolf, E. 1959. *Sons of the Shaking Earth.* Chicago: University of Chicago Press.

Wolf, E., ed. 1976. *The Valley of Mexico.* Albuquerque: University of New Mexico Press.

Chapter 14

Ascher, M. and R. Ascher. 1982. *Code of the Quipu: A Study in Media, Mathematics, and Culture.* Ann Arbor: University of Michigan Press.

Benson, E. P., ed. 1971. *Dumbarton Oaks Conference on Chavin.* Washington, D.C.: Dumbarton Oaks Research Library and Collection.

Browman, D. L. 1974. "Pastoral Nomadism in the Andes." *Current Anthropology* 15: 188–96.

———. 1975. "Trade Patterns in the Central Highlands of Peru in the First Millennium B.C." *World Archaeology* 6: 322–30.

Bushnell, G. H. S. 1963. *Peru.* Rev. ed. New York: Praeger.

Carneiro, R. 1970. "A Theory of the Origin of the State." *Science* 169: 733–38.

Collier, G. A., R. I. Roslado, and J. D. Wirth, eds. 1982. *The Inca and Aztec States, 1400–1800.* New York: Academic Press.

Conrad, G. W. 1981. "Cultural Materialism, Split Inheritance, and the Expansion of Ancient Peruvian Empires." *American Antiquity* 46: 3–26.

Donnan, C. B. 1973. *Moche Occupation of the Santa Valley, Peru.* Berkeley: University of California Publication in Anthropology, no. 8.

————. 1976. *Moche Art and Iconography.* Los Angeles: U.C.L.A. Latin American Center Publications.

Engel, F. 1957. "Early Sites on the Peruvian Coast." *Southwestern Journal of Anthropology* 13: 54–68.

Engl, L. and T. Engl. 1969. *Twilight of Ancient Peru,* trans. A. Jaffe. New York: McGraw-Hill.

Flannery, K. V. 1973. "The Origins of Agriculture." *Annual Review of Anthropology* 2: 271–310.

Greider, T. 1978. *The Art and Archaeology of Pashash.* Austin: University of Texas Press.

Gross, D. R. 1975. "Protein Capture and Cultural Development in the Amazon Basin." *American Anthropologist* 77: 526–49.

Idyll, C. P. 1973. "The Anchovy Crisis." *Scientific American* 228: 22–29.

Japanese Scientific Expedition to Nuclear America. 1979. *Excavations at La Pampa in the North Highlands of Peru, 1975.* Tokyo: University of Tokyo Press.

Jones, G. D. and R. R. Kautz, eds. 1981. *The Transition to Statehood in the New World.* Cambridge, Eng.: Cambridge University Press.

Kaplan, L., T. Lynch, and E. E. Smith, Jr. 1973. "Early Cultivated Beans (*Phaseolus vulgaris*) from an Intermontane Peruvian Valley." *Science* 179: 76–77.

Keatinge, R. W. 1974. "Chimú Rural Administration Centers in the Moche Valley, Peru." *World Archaeology* 6: 66–82.

Lanning, E. P. 1967. *Peru Before the Incas.* Englewood Cliffs, N.J.: Prentice-Hall.

Lathrap, D. W. 1968. "Relationships Between Mesoamerica and the Andean Areas." In *Handbook of Middle American Indians,* vol. 4. Austin: University of Texas Press.

Lumbreras, L. G. 1974. *The Peoples and Cultures of Ancient Peru,* trans. B. J. Meggers. Washington, D.C.: Smithsonian Institution Press.

Lynch, T., ed. 1980. *Guitarrero Cave: Early Man in the Andes.* New York: Academic Press.

Moseley, M. E. 1972. "Subsistence and Demography: An Example of Interaction from Prehistoric Peru." *Southwestern Journal of Anthropology* 28: 25–49.

————. 1975. *The Maritime Foundations of Andean Civilization.* Menlo Park, Calif.: Cummings.

Moseley, M. E. and K. C. Day, eds. 1982. *Chan Chan: Andean Desert City.* Albuquerque: University of New Mexico Press.

Murra, J. 1958. "On Inca Political Structure." In *Systems of Political Control and Bureaucracy in Human Society,* ed. V. F. Ray. Seattle: University of Washington Press.

————. 1965. "Herds and Herders in the Inca State." In *Man, Culture and Animals.* Washington, D.C.: American Association for the Advancement of Science.

Murra, J. and C. Morris. 1976. "Dynastic Oral Tradition, Administrative Records, and Archaeology in the Andes." *World Archaeology* 7: 269–79.

Ortloff, C. R., M. E. Moseley, and R. A. Feldman. "Hydraulic Engineering Aspects of the Chimú Chicama-Moche Intervalley Canal." *American Antiquity* 47: 572–95.

Parsons, J. 1968. "An Estimate of Size and Population for Middle Horizon Tia-huanaco, Bolivia." *American Antiquity* 33: 243–45.

———. 1977. Personal communication with author.

Parsons, J. and N. Psuty. 1975. "Sunken Fields and Prehispanic Subsistence on the Peruvian Coast." *American Antiquity* 40: 259–82.

Parsons, M. 1970. "Preceramic Subsistence on the Peruvian Coast." *American Antiquity* 35: 292–303.

Patterson, T. C. 1966. "Early Cultural Remains on the Central Coast of Peru." *Nawpa Pacha* 4: 145–55.

———. 1971a. "Chavín: An Interpretation of Its Spread and Influence." In *Dumbarton Oaks Conference on Chavín,* ed. E. Benson. Dumbarton Oaks, Washington, D.C.

———. 1971b. "Central Peru: Its Population and Economy." *Archaeology* 24: 316–21.

Patterson, T. C. and E. P. Lanning. 1964. "Changing Settlement Patterns on the Central Peruvian Coast." *Nawpa Pacha* 2: 113–23.

Patterson, T. C. and M. E. Moseley. 1968. "Late Preceramic and Early Ceramic Cultures of the Central Coast of Peru." *Nawpa Pacha* 6: 115–33.

Pickersgill, B. 1969. "The Archaeological Record of Chile Peppers (*Capsicum spp.*) and the Sequence of Plant Domestication in Peru." *American Antiquity* 34: 54–61.

Pickersgill, B. and A. Bunting. 1969. "Cultivated Plants and the Kon-Tiki Theory." *Nature* 222: 225–27.

Prescott, W. H. 1908. *History of the Conquest of Peru.* London and New York: Everyman's Library.

Rick, J. W. 1980. *Prehistoric Hunters of the High Andes.* New York: Academic Press.

Rowe, J. H. 1946. "Inca Culture at the Time of the Spanish Conquest." *Bureau of American Ethnology Bulletin,* no. 143: 183–331. Smithsonian Institution, Washington, D.C.

———. 1967. "Form and Meaning in Chavín Art." In *Peruvian Archaeology: Selected Readings.* Palo Alto: Peek Publishers.

Scott, R. J. 1981. "The Maritime Foundations of Andean Civilization: A Reconsideration." *American Antiquity* 46: 806–21.

Shady, R. and A. Ruiz. 1979. "Evidence for Interregional Relationships During the Middle Horizon on the North-Central Coast of Peru." *American Antiquity* 44: 670–84.

Vescelius, G. 1981. "Early and/or Not-so-Early Man in Peru: Guitarrero Cave Revisited." *The Quarterly Review of Archaeology* 2: 8–13.

Von Hagen, V. W. 1952. "America's Oldest Roads." *Scientific American* 187: 17–21.

———. 1965. *The Desert Kingdoms of Peru.* London: Weidenfeld and Nicolson.

Willey, G. R. 1962. "The Early Great Art Styles and the Rise of Pre-Columbian Civilizations." *American Anthropologist* 64: 1–14.

Wilson, D. J. 1981. "Of Maize and Men: A Critique of the Maritime Hypothesis of State Origins on the Coast of Peru." *American Anthropologist* 83: 93–114.

Wing, E. S. 1973. "Utilization of Animal Resources in the Andes." Report NSF GS 3021. Florida State Museum, Gainesville, Florida.

———. 1973. "Animal Domestication in the Andes." Paper presented at the Twelfth International Congress of Prehistoric and Protohistoric Sciences, Chicago.

Chapter 15

Braun, D. P. and S. Plog. 1982. "Evolution of 'Tribal' Social Networks: Theory and Prehistoric North American Evidence." *American Antiquity* 47: 504–25.

Brose, D. S. and N. Greber, eds. 1979. *Hopewell Archaeology: The Chillicothe Conference.* Kent: The Kent State University Press.

Brown, J. A. 1977. "Current Directions in Midwestern Archaeology." *Annual Review of Anthropology* 6: 161–79.

Broyles, B. J. 1971. "Second Preliminary Report: The St. Albans Site, Kanawha County, West Virginia." West Virginia Geological and Economic Survey Report, Archaeological Investigation 3.

Bullen, R. P. 1971. "The Beginnings of Pottery in Eastern United States as Seen from Florida." *Eastern States Archaeological Federation Bulletin,* no. 30: 10–11.

Caldwell, J. 1971. "Eastern North America." In *Prehistoric Agriculture,* ed. S. Struever. Garden City, N.Y.: Natural History Press.

Cleland, C. E. 1966. *The Prehistoric Animal Ecology and Ethnozoology of the Upper Great Lakes Region.* Ann Arbor: Museum of Anthropology, Anthropological Papers, University of Michigan, no. 29.

Cordell, L. S. and F. Plog. 1979. "Escaping the Confines of Normative Thought: A Reevaluation of Puebloan Prehistory." *American Antiquity* 44: 405–429.

Cressman, L. S. 1977. *Prehistory of the Far West.* Salt Lake City: University of Utah Press.

DeJarnette, D. L. 1967. "Alabama Pebble Tools: The Lively Complex." *Eastern States Archaeological Federation Bulletin,* no. 26.

Dickson, D. B. 1975. "Settlement Pattern Stability and Change in the Middle Northern Rio Grande Region, New Mexico: A Test of Some Hypotheses." *American Antiquity* 40: 159–71.

———. 1981. "The Yanomamo of the Mississippi Valley? Some Reflections on Larson . . . Gibson . . . and Mississippi Period Warfare in the Southeastern United States." *American Antiquity* 46: 909–16.

Dragoo, D. W. 1963. "Mounds for the Dead." *Annals of Carnegie Museum* 37: 1–315.

———. 1976. "Some Aspects of Eastern North American Prehistory: A Review." *American Antiquity* 41: 3–27.

Dunnell, R. C. 1967. "The Prehistory of Fishtrap, Kentucky: Archaeological/ Interpretation in Marginal Areas." Unpublished doctoral dissertation, Yale University.

Farnsworth, K. B. 1973. "An Archaeological Survey of the Macoupin Valley." Springfield: Illinois State Museum, Reports of Investigations, no. 26.

Ford, R. I. 1974. "Northeastern Archeology: Past and Future Directions." *Annual Review of Anthropology* 3: 385–414.

Fowler, M. L. 1969. "Explorations into Cahokia Archaeology." *Illinois Archaeological Survey Bulletin* 7.

———. 1971. "Agriculture and Village Settlement in the North American East: The Central Mississippi Valley Area, a Case History." In *Prehistoric Agriculture,* ed. S. Struever. Garden City, N.Y.: Natural History Press.

———. 1975. "A Pre-Columbian Urban Center on the Mississippi." *Scientific American* (August).

Glassow, M. A. 1980. *Prehistoric Agricultural Development in the Northern South-west: A Study in Changing Patterns of Land Use.* Socorro (New Mexico): Ballena Press.

Griffin, J. B. 1967. "Eastern North American Archaeology: A Summary." *Science* 156: 175–91.

Haury, E. W. 1976. *The Hohokam: Desert Farmers and Craftsmen.* Tucson: University of Arizona Press.

Hill, J. N. 1966. "A Prehistoric Community in Eastern Arizona." *Southwestern Journal of Anthropology* 22: 9–30.

———. 1970. *Broken K Pueblo: Prehistoric Social Organization in the American Southwest.* Tucson: University of Arizona Press.

Hines, P. 1977. "On Social Organization in the Middle Mississippian: States or Chiefdoms?" *Current Anthropology* 18: 337–38.

Houart, G. L. 1971. "Koster: A Stratified Archaic Site in the Illinois Valley." Springfield: Illinois State Museum. Reports of Investigations, no. 22.

Hunter-Anderson, R. L. 1981. "Comments on Cordell and Plog's 'Escaping the Confines of Normative Thought.'" *American Antiquity* 46: 194–97.

Irwin-Williams, C. 1968. "The Reconstruction of Archaic Culture History in the Southwestern United States." In *Archaic Prehistory in the Western United States,* ed. C. Irwin-Williams. Portales: Eastern New Mexico University Contributions in Anthropology.

Jennings, J. D. 1974. *Prehistory of North America.* 2nd ed. New York: McGraw-Hill.

Lightfoot, K. G. and G. M. Feinman. 1982. "Social Differentiation and Leadership Development in Early Pithouse Villages in the Mogollon Region of the American Southwest." *American Antiquity* 47: 64–81.

Longacre, W. A. 1975. "Population Dynamics at the Grasshopper Pueblo, Arizona." In *Population Studies in Archaeology and Biological Anthropology: A Symposium,* ed. A. C. Swedlund. *American Antiquity* 40: 71–74, memoir 30.

Madsen, D. B. 1979. "The Fremont and the Sevier: Defining Prehistoric Agriculturalists North of the Anasazi." *American Antiquity* 44: 711–22.

Ortiz, A. 1979. "Southwest." *Handbook of North American Indians,* vol. 9. Washington, D.C.: Smithsonian Institution.

Pfeiffer, J. E. 1977. *The Emergence of Society.* New York: McGraw-Hill.

Porter, J. W. 1969. "The Mitchell Site and Prehistoric Exchange Systems at Cahokia: A.D. 1000± 300." *Illinois Archaeological Survey Bulletin,* no. 7.

Prufer, O. H. 1964. "The Hopewell Cult." *Scientific American* 211: 90–102.

———. 1965. "The McGraw Site: A Study in Hopewellian Dynamics." Cleveland Museum of Natural History Scientific Publications, n.s. 4(1).

Rice, G. E. 1975. "A Systemic Explanation of a Change in Mogollon Settlement Patterns." Unpublished doctoral dissertation, University of Washington.

Ritchie, W. A. 1969. *The Archaeology of New York State.* 2nd ed. Garden City, N.Y.: Natural History Press.

Rothschild, N. A. 1979. "Mortuary Behavior and Social Organization at Indian Knoll and Dickson Mounds." *American Antiquity* 44: 658–75.

Schoenwetter, J. 1962. "Pollen Analysis of Eighteen Archaeological Sites in Arizona and New Mexico." In *Prehistory of Eastern Arizona,* eds. P. S. Martin et al. *Fieldiana: Anthropology* 53: 168–209.

Smith, B. 1974. "Middle Mississippi Exploitation of Animal Populations: A Predictive Model." *American Antiquity* 39: 274–91.

Stewart, T. D. 1973. *The People of America*. New York: Scribner's.

Struever, S. and G. L. Houart. 1972. "Analysis of the Hopewell Interaction Sphere." In *Social Exchange and Interaction*. Ann Arbor: Museum of Anthropology, Anthropological Papers, no. 46. University of Michigan.

Struever, S. and K. D. Vickery. 1973. "The Beginnings of Cultivation in the Midwest-Riverine Area of the United States." *American Anthropologist* 75: 1197–1220.

Tainter, J. 1975. "Social Inference and Mortuary Practices: An Experiment in Numerical Classification." *World Archaeology* 7: 1–15.

Tuck, J. A. 1971. "An Archaic Cemetery at Port au Choix, Newfoundland." *American Antiquity* 36: 343–58.

Upham, S., K. G. Lightfoot, and G. M. Feinman. 1981. "Explaining Socially Determined Ceramic Distributions in the Prehistoric Southwest." *American Antiquity* 46: 822–36.

Vogel, J. C. and N. J. Van Der Merwe. 1977. "Isotopic Evidence for Early Maize Cultivation in New York State." *American Antiquity* 42: 238–42.

Washburn, D. K. 1975. "The American Southwest." In S. Gorenstein et al., eds. *North America*. New York: St. Martin's Press.

Watson, P. J. 1974. *Archeology of the Mammoth Cave Area*. New York: Academic Press.

Whalen, M. 1981. "Cultural-Ecological Aspects of the Pithouse-to-Pueblo Transition in a Portion of the Southwest." *American Antiquity* 46: 75–91.

Willey, G. R. 1966. *An Introduction to American Archaeology*, vol. 1: *North and Middle America*. Englewood Cliffs, N.J.: Prentice-Hall.

Yarnell, R. A. 1965. "Early Woodland Plant Remains and the Question of Cultivation." *The Florida Archaeologist* 18: 78–81.

Chapter 16

Alexander, R. D. 1977. "Review of *The Use and Abuse of Biology: An Anthropological Critique of Sociobiology* by M. D. Sahlins." *American Anthropologist* 79: 917–20.

Binford, L. R., ed. 1972. *An Archaeological Perspective*. New York: Academic Press.

Dunnell, R. C. 1982. "Science, Social Science, and Common Sense: The Agonizing Dilemma of Modern Archaeology." *Journal of Anthropological Research* 38: 1–25.

Gould, S. J. 1980. "The Promise of Paleobiology as a Nomothetic, Evolutionary Discipline." *Paleobiology* 6: 96–118.

Harris, M. 1977. *Cannibals and Kings*. New York: Random House.

Johnson, L. 1972. "Problems in 'Avant-Garde' Archaeology." *American Anthropologist* 74: 366–77.

Kitto, H. D. F. 1951. *The Greeks*. Baltimore: Penguin.

Morgan, C. G. 1973. "Archaeology and Explanation." *World Archaeology* 4: 259–76.

Salmon, M. H. 1975. "Confirmation and Explanation in Archaeology." *American Antiquity* 4: 459–64.

Credits

Chapter 1

1.1 The Bancroft Library, Univ. of California.

1.2 Hirmer Fotoarchiv, Munich.

1.3 Sir William Hamilton, *Campi Phlgraei* (1765), Illus. by Peter Fabris from Vol. 1, American Museum of Natural History; photo courtesy of Kay Zakariasen and David Hanson.

1.4 American Museum of Natural History.

1.6 Radio Times Hulton Picture Library.

Chapter 2

2.1 Victor R. Boswell, Jr., © National Geographic Society. From *Ancient Egypt: Discovering its Splendors*, 1978.

2.2 Danish National Museum.

2.3 From F. Hole, K. V. Flannery, and J. Neely, *Prehistory and Human Ecology of the Deh Luran Plain*, Mem. of the Museum of Anthropology, No. 1 (Univ. of Michigan, 1969), Fig. 15. Reproduced by permission of Museum of Anthropology–Publications.

2.4 From W. J. Judge, J. I. Ebert, and R. K. Hitchcock, "Sampling in Regional Archaeological Survey," in J. W. Mueller, ed., *Sampling in Archaeology* (Univ. of Arizona Press, copyright 1975), Fig. 6.4. Reproduced by permission of the Univ. of Arizona Press.

2.5 From J. D. Jennings, *Prehistory of North America* (McGraw-Hill, 1974), Fig. 1.4. © 1968, 1974 by McGraw-Hill, Inc., all rights reserved. Reproduced by permission of McGraw-Hill Book Co.

2.6 From J. W. Michaels, *Dating Methods in Archaeology* (Seminar Press, 1973), Fig. 1. © Academic Press, Inc. Reproduced by permission of J. W. Michaels and Academic Press, Inc.

2.7 From J. Deetz, *Invitation to Archaeology* (Doubleday, 1967), Fig. 4. © 1967 by James Deetz. Reproduced by permission of Doubleday & Co., Inc.

Chapter 3

3.1 American Museum of Natural History.

3.2 After Jerison, 1976.

3.3 San Diego Zoological Society.

3.4 Reproduced from *The Cambridge Encyclopedia of Archaeology*, © Sceptre Books Limited, London.

3.5 After Simons, 1977.

3.6 From J. B. Birdsell, *Human Evolution: An Introduction to the New Physical Anthropology*, 2nd ed. (Rand McNally, 1975), Fig. 6.7. Reproduced by permission of J. B. Birdsell.

3.7 After Howells, 1973.

3.8 From *The Annual Review of Anthropology*, Vol. 1, © 1972 by Annual Reviews, Inc. Reproduced by permission of B. G. Campbell and *The Annual Review of Anthropology*.

3.9 From J. E. Cronin et al., "Tempo and mode in hominid evolution." Reprinted by permission from *Nature*, Vol. 292 (1981), p. 118. © Macmillan Journals Limited.

3.10 From W. Howells, *Evolution of Genus Homo* (Benjamin/Cummings Pub. Co., copyright © 1973), p. 47. Reproduced by permission of Benjamin/Cummings Pub. Co.

3.11 Reprinted by permission from *Nature,* Vol. 297 (1982), p. 199. © Macmillan Journals Limited.

3.12 Irven DeVore, Anthro Photo.

3.13 Geza Teleki.

3.14 From M. D. Leakey, *Olduvai Gorge Vol. 3* (Cambridge Univ. Press, 1971), Fig. 47. Reproduced by permission of Cambridge Univ. Press.

3.15 From B. Fagan, *People of the Earth,* 2nd ed. (Little, Brown, 1977), drawing p. 60. Reproduced by permission of Little, Brown & Co., Inc.

3.17 American Museum of Natural History.

Chapter 4

4.1 Henry de Lumley, Centre national de la recherche scientifique, Marseille.

4.2 Zdenek Burian.

4.3 From F. Bordes, *The Old Stone Age* (Weidenfeld & Nicolson, 1968). Reproduced by permission of Weidenfeld & Nicolson.

4.4 From A. J. Jelinek, "The Tabun Cave and Paleolithic Man in the Levant," *Science,* Vol. 216 (1982), pp. 1369–1375. © 1982 American Association for the Advancement of Science.

4.5 From W. A. Fairservis, *The Threshold of Civilization,* drawings by Jan Fairservis (Chas. Scribner's Sons, 1975), pp. 82–83. Reproduced by permission of Jan Fairservis.

4.6 French Cultural Service, New York.

4.7 From A. Leroi-Gourhan, "The Evolution of Paleolithic Cave Art," *Scientific American,* Feb. 1968, p. 66. Copyright © 1968 by Scientific American, Inc. All rights reserved.

4.8 Austrian Institute, New York.

Chapter 5

5.1 Philadelphia Museum of Art.

5.2 After Jennings, 1974.

5.3 From C. Dunbar and K. Waage, *Historical Geology,* 3rd ed. (Wiley, 1969). Reproduced by permission of John Wiley & Sons, Inc.

5.4 From R. F. Flint, *Glacial and Quaternary Geology* (Wiley, 1971), Fig. 29.7 modified from Martin and Guilday in P. S. Martin and H. E. Wright, Jr., eds., *Pleistocene Extinctions: The Search for a Cause* (Yale Univ. Press, 1967, p. 1). Reproduced by permission of John

Wiley & Sons, Inc., and Yale Univ. Press.

5.5 From J. J. Hester, *Introduction to Archaeology* (Holt, Rinehart and Winston, 1976). Compiled from A. Krieger, "Early Man in the New World," in J. D. Jennings and E. Norbeck, eds., *Prehistoric Man in the New World* (University of Chicago Press, 1964). Reproduced by permission of the Univ. of Chicago Press.

5.7 From Don W. Dragoo, "Some Aspects of Eastern North American Prehistory," *American Antiquity,* 41:6, 1976, Fig. 1. Reproduced by permission of the Society for Amer. Archaeology.

5.8 From J. D. Jennings, *Prehistory of North America* (McGraw-Hill, 1974), Figs. 4.19, 20, 21. Reproduced by permission of McGraw-Hill Book Co. and J. D. Jennings.

Chapter 6

6.1 From K. P. Oakley, *Man the Tool-Maker* (Univ. of Chicago Press, © 1949, 1961 by the Trustees of the British Museum. All rights reserved), Fig. 39. Reproduced by permission of the Univ. of Chicago Press and the Trustees of the British Museum (Natural History).

6.5 From F. Hole et al., *Prehistory and Human Ecology of the Deh Luran Plain,* Mem. of the Mus. of Anthropology, No. 1 (Univ. of Michigan, 1969), Fig. 115. Reproduced by permission of Mus. of Anthropology Publications.

6.6 British School of Archaeology in Jerusalem.

6.8 State Antiquities Organization, Baghdad.

6.9 From G. Clark and S. Piggott, *Prehistoric Societies* (Knopf, 1965). Reproduced by permission of Alfred A. Knopf, Inc.

6.10 After Fagan, 1977.

6.11 R. S. Peabody Foundation for Archaeology.

6.12 From B. Winterhalder and E. A. Smith, *Hunter-Gatherer Foraging Strategies,* Fig. 2.1, 1981, University of Chicago Press.

Chapter 7

7.1 From K. V. Flannery, ed., *The Early Mesoamerican Village,* Fig. 6.5, 1976, Academic Press. Reproduced by permission of Academic Press, Inc.

7.2 After Wright, 1977.

7.3 From J. Friedman and M. J. Rowlands, eds., *The Evolution of Social Systems,* Duckworth.
7.4 Compiled and drawn by M. Lehner.

Chapter 8

8.3 Frank Hole.
8.4 British School of Archaeology in Jerusalem.
8.6 From J. Mellaart, *Çatal Hüyük* (McGraw-Hill, 1967), pp. 118, 120, 125. © 1967 Thames and Hudson Ltd. Reproduced by permission of J. Mellaart.
8.7 From J. Mellaart, *The Neolithic of the Near East* (Charles Scribner's Sons, 1975), Figs. 97, 91, 93, 94. © 1975 Thames and Hudson Ltd., London. Reproduced by permission of Charles Scribner's Sons and Thames and Hudson Ltd.
8.8 Hirmer Fotoarchiv, Munich.
8.10 From G. A. Johnson, "Locational Analysis and the Investigation of Uruk Local Exchange Systems," in G. A. Sabloff, ed., *Ancient Civilization and Trade* (Univ. of New Mexico Press, 1975), Fig. 31. Reproduced by permission of the School of American Research, Santa Fe.
8.11 State Antiquities Organization, Baghdad.
8.12 From S. N. Kramer, "The Sumerians," *Scientific American,* Oct. 1957, p. 76. Copyright © 1957 by Scientific American, Inc. All rights reserved.
8.13 Hirmer Fotoarchiv, Munich.
8.14 (top) Hirmer Fotoarchiv, Munich. (bottom) University Museum, Philadelphia.
8.15 The Oriental Institute, Univ. of Chicago.
8.17 From Robert McC. Adams, *Heartland of Cities,* Fig. 17, 1981, University of Chicago Press.
8.18 From Charles Redman, *The Rise of Civilization,* Fig. 7.7, W. H. Freeman and Company.

Chapter 9

9.3 Hirmer Fotoarchiv, Munich.
9.4 TWA.
9.5 From James E. Harris and Edward F. Wente, eds., *An X Ray Atlas of the Royal Mummies,* University of Chicago Press.
9.6 From the collection of Peter B. Rathbone.
9.7 From A. Wolinski and C. M. Sheikholeslami, *The Culture of Ancient Egypt*

(Univ. of Washington Continuing Education, 1978), Study Guide, p. 18.
9.8 and 9.9 Victor R. Boswell, Jr., © National Geographic Society. From *Ancient Egypt: Discovering its Splendors,* 1978.

Chapter 10

10.2 After Dales, 1966.
10.3 Josephine Powell.
10.4 Jan Fairservis.
10.5 National Museum, New Delhi.
10.6 University Museum, Philadelphia.

Chapter 11

11.1 and 11.2 From K. C. Chang, "In search of China's beginnings: New light on an old civilization," *American Scientist,* Vol. 69, pp. 151, 153.
11.3 From W. Watson, *Ancient China* (New York Graphic Society, 1974), Fig. 12.
11.4 Judith M. Triestman, courtesy Doubleday & Co.
11.6 Institute of Archaeology, Academia Sinica, Peking.

Chapter 12

12.1 and 12.2 Reproduced from *The Cambridge Encyclopedia of Archaeology,* © Sceptre Books Limited, London.
12.3 From M. Shinnie, *Ancient African Kingdoms,* 1965, St. Martin's Press. Reproduced by permission of St. Martin's Press, Inc.

Chapter 13

13.3 American Museum of Natural History.
13.5 Library of Congress.
13.6 The Metropolitan Museum of Art, New York, Michael C. Rockefeller Mem. Coll. of Primitive Art.
13.7 Robert Drennan.
13.8 Jeffrey House.
13.9 Mexican National Tourist Council.
13.10 Jeffrey House.
13.11, 13.12 From M. D. Coe, *The Maya* (Praeger, 1966), Figs. 48 and 8. Reproduced by permission of M. D. Coe.
13.13 From J. R. Parsons, "The Development of a Prehistoric Complex Society: A Regional Perspective from the Valley of Mexico," *Jour. of Field Archaeology,* 1, 1974. Reproduced by permission of Jour.

Index